Collins
Primary
Spanish
Dictionary

Published by Collins

An imprint of HarperCollins Publishers
Westerhill Road, Bishopbriggs, Glasgow G64 2QT

HarperCollins Publishers
Macken House, 39/40 Mayor Street Upper,
Dublin 1, D01 C9W8, Ireland

First Edition 2019

10 9 8 7 6

Text © HarperCollins Publishers 2019
Illustrations © Maria Herbert-Liew 2019

ISBN 978-0-00-831269-5

Collins® is a registered trademark of
HarperCollins Publishers Limited

www.collins.co.uk/dictionaries

Typeset by Davidson Publishing Solutions,
Glasgow

Printed by Replika Press Pvt. Ltd.

A catalogue record for this book is available
from the British Library.

If you would like to comment on any
aspect of this book, please contact us
at the given address or e-mail
dictionaries@harpercollins.co.uk.

Acknowledgements

We would like to thank those authors and
publishers who kindly gave permission for
copyright material to be used in the Collins
Corpus. We would also like to thank Times
Newspapers Ltd for providing valuable data.

Managing Editors:

Maree Airlie
Teresa Alvarez

Artwork and Design:

Maria Herbert-Liew

For the Publisher:

Kerry Ferguson
Laura Waddell

Free online activities
and resources at
collins.co.uk/homeworkhelp.

MIX
Paper | Supporting
responsible forestry
FSC C007454
www.fsc.org

This book contains FSC™ certified paper and other controlled
sources to ensure responsible forest management.

For more information visit: www.harpercollins.co.uk/green

Contents

Introduction   5
How to use this dictionary   6
Word classes   8

Spanish-English A-Z   11

Language Plus   267

English-Spanish A-Z   317

Introduction

The **Collins Primary Spanish Dictionary** is a bilingual dictionary aimed at primary school pupils who are starting to learn Spanish.

The dictionary is presented in an easy-to-use format which is intended to be easily accessible to young people of primary school age. The colourful illustrations have been designed to appeal to young learners, encouraging them to engage with the language. The dictionary also provides lots of simple, relevant examples and tips on how to remember words, as well as how to avoid some of the pitfalls of translation. Finally, it features key phrases and information about life in Spain, making it an invaluable and exciting resource.

Access to a dictionary which is pitched at an appropriate level is a vital part of the language-learning process. The content of this dictionary has been carefully selected to reflect current trends in primary education and help young people with acquiring basic language-learning skills.

The key aims of the **Collins Primary Spanish Dictionary** are:

- to develop both language skills in Spanish and language-learning skills in general
- to cover the four key areas of language attainment: listening, speaking, reading and writing
- to reinforce key aspects of the language by the use of notes and feature boxes throughout the entries
- to extend cultural awareness by providing information about Spain, especially where traditions differ from those in Britain

The **Collins Primary Spanish Dictionary** supports language learning in a number of specific ways:

- it develops learners' knowledge of how language works by encouraging them to understand, analyse and use simple aspects of grammar
- it develops young people's individual learning skills by using a wide range of notes that explain things in a simple but interesting way
- it enables learners to make comparisons between Spanish and English by encouraging them to explore the similarities and differences between the two languages and cultures
- it introduces young learners to all the basic elements of a bilingual dictionary and provides detailed instructions on how to get the most out of using the dictionary

How to use this dictionary

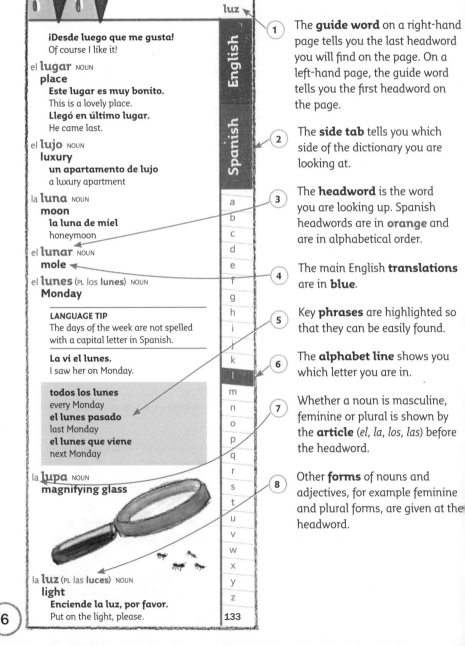

luz

English
Spanish

¡Desde luego que me gusta!
Of course I like it!

el **lugar** NOUN
place
Este lugar es muy bonito.
This is a lovely place.
Llegó en último lugar.
He came last.

el **lujo** NOUN
luxury
un apartamento de lujo
a luxury apartment

la **luna** NOUN
moon
la luna de miel
honeymoon

el **lunar** NOUN
mole

el **lunes** (PL los **lunes**) NOUN
Monday

LANGUAGE TIP
The days of the week are not spelled
with a capital letter in Spanish.

La vi el lunes.
I saw her on Monday.

todos los lunes
every Monday
el lunes pasado
last Monday
el lunes que viene
next Monday

la **lupa** NOUN
magnifying glass

la **luz** (PL las **luces**) NOUN
light
Enciende la luz, por favor.
Put on the light, please.

a b c d e f g h i j k l m n o p q r s t u v w x y z

133

1. The **guide word** on a right-hand page tells you the last headword you will find on the page. On a left-hand page, the guide word tells you the first headword on the page.

2. The **side tab** tells you which side of the dictionary you are looking at.

3. The **headword** is the word you are looking up. Spanish headwords are in **orange** and are in alphabetical order.

4. The main English **translations** are in **blue**.

5. Key **phrases** are highlighted so that they can be easily found.

6. The **alphabet line** shows you which letter you are in.

7. Whether a noun is masculine, feminine or plural is shown by the **article** (*el, la, los, las*) before the headword.

8. Other **forms** of nouns and adjectives, for example feminine and plural forms, are given at the headword.

9 The **headword** is the word you are looking up. English headwords are in **blue** and are in alphabetical order.

10 The main Spanish **translations** are in *orange*.

11 Where a word has more than one meaning, look at each **number** to make sure you find the meaning you need.

12 **Did you know...?** notes give you extra information about culture and traditions in Spanish-speaking countries.

13 **Phrases** and **examples** show you how the headword is used in a sentence.

14 Colourful **illustrations** make the book fun to use.

15 **Language Tips** give you extra information about spelling and grammar in Spanish.

16 The **word class** tells you if the headword is, for example, a noun, a verb, an adjective, an adverb or a pronoun.

17 Noun and adjective translations are followed by information on whether they are masculine or feminine.

---

chef NOUN
el **chef** *masc*

chemist NOUN
1 la **farmacia** *fem* (shop)
You get it from the chemist.
Lo compras en la farmacia.
the chemist's
la farmacia

DID YOU KNOW...?
Spanish chemists are identifiable by a red or green cross outside the shop. Go to a **perfumería** instead if you want to buy cosmetics or toiletries.

---
2 el **farmacéutico** *masc*
la **farmacéutica** *fem* (pharmacist)

chemistry NOUN
la **química** *fem*
the chemistry teacher
el profesor de química

cherry NOUN
la **cereza** *fem*
I love cherries.
Me encantan las cerezas.

chess NOUN
el **ajedrez** *masc*
I can play chess.
Sé jugar al ajedrez.

LANGUAGE TIP
In Spanish, you need to include **al** or **a la** before the names of sports or games when talking about playing them.

---
chest NOUN
el **pecho** *masc*

chest of drawers NOUN
la **cómoda** *fem*

chewing gum NOUN
el **chicle** *masc*
Put your chewing gum in the bin!
¡Tira el chicle a la papelera!

Word classes

Each word in this dictionary belongs to a particular word class, for example, nouns, verbs or adjectives.

In this dictionary, abbreviations have been used in some places. These are:

pl	plural
masc	masculine
fem	feminine

Nouns

A **noun** is a word that is used for talking about a person or thing. **Nouns** are sometimes called "naming words" because they are often the names of people, places, things and ideas. Examples of nouns are **book**, **child** and **smile** in English, and **manzana**, **caballo** and **hermano** in Spanish. Nouns in English and in Spanish can be *singular* (only one) or *plural* (more than one). In Spanish, they can also be *masculine* or *feminine*.

> **It's a very good <u>film</u>.**
> Es una <u>película</u> muy buena.
> **I'm wearing stripy <u>socks</u>.**
> Llevo <u>calcetines</u> de rayas.

Adjectives

An **adjective** is a word that tells you more about a person or thing. **Adjectives** are often called "describing words" because they describe what something looks, feels or smells like. Examples of adjectives are **happy**, **green** and **cloudy** in English, and **grande**, **negro** and **frecuente** in Spanish.

> **I've got <u>blue</u> eyes.**
> Tengo los ojos <u>azules</u>.
> **She's very <u>smart</u>.**
> Es muy <u>inteligente</u>.

Verbs

A **verb** is a word that you use for saying what someone or something does. **Verbs** are often called "doing words" because they talk about an action that someone or something is doing. Examples of verbs are **walk**, **speak** and **look** in English, and **nadar**, **leer** and **escribir** in Spanish.

> **I <u>play</u> the flute.**
> <u>Toco</u> la flauta.
> **I don't <u>understand</u>.**
> No <u>entiendo</u>.

Adverbs

An **adverb** is a word that tells you more about how someone does something. Examples of adverbs are **slowly**, **loudly** and **hungrily** in English, and **pronto** and **realmente** in Spanish.

> **The bus is <u>always</u> late.**
> El autobús <u>siempre</u> llega tarde.
> **They live <u>opposite</u>.**
> Viven <u>enfrente</u>.

Pronouns

A **pronoun** is a word you use instead of a noun to refer to someone or something. Examples of pronouns are **he**, **it** and **theirs** in English, and **ella** and **te** in Spanish.

> **<u>They</u> are not going but <u>we</u> are.**
> <u>Ellos</u> no van pero <u>nosotros</u> sí.
> **This book is for <u>you</u>.**
> Este libro es para <u>ti</u>.

Prepositions

A **preposition** is a word that links a noun, pronoun or noun phrase to some other word in the sentence. Examples of prepositions are **under**, **in** and **with** in English, and **con** and **de** in Spanish.

> **We're going <u>to</u> a restaurant.**
> Vamos <u>a</u> un restaurante.
> **Have you got any plans <u>for</u> the holidays?**
> ¿Tienes planes <u>para</u> las vacaciones?

Conjunctions

A **conjunction** is a word that links two words or phrases or two parts of a sentence. Examples of conjunctions are **and**, **but** and **because** in English, and **y** and **aunque** in Spanish.

> **Thanks, <u>but</u> I'm not hungry.**
> Gracias, <u>pero</u> no tengo hambre.
> **You can go <u>if</u> you like.**
> Puedes ir <u>si</u> quieres.

Articles

An **article** is a specific word you use before a noun and/or an adjective. Examples of articles are **the**, **a** and **an** in English, and **un**, **una**, **el**, **la**, **los** and **las** in Spanish.

Spanish-English

a PREPOSITION

LANGUAGE TIP
When **a** is followed by a masculine noun, **a** and the article **el** turn into **al**.

1 **to** (*with places*)
Fueron a Madrid.
They went to Madrid.
2 (*with movement*)
Me caí al río.
I fell into the river.
Se subieron al tejado.
They climbed onto the roof.
Marta llegó tarde a la estación.
Marta arrived at the station late.
3 (*with distances*)
Está a quince kilómetros de aquí.
It's fifteen kilometres from here.
4 **at** (*with time, ages, speed*)
a las diez
at ten o'clock
a medianoche
at midnight
a los veinticuatro años
at the age of twenty-four
Íbamos a más de noventa kilómetros por hora.
We were going at over ninety kilometres an hour.
5 (*with dates*)
Estamos a nueve de julio.
It's the ninth of July.
6 (*with prices*)
Los cómics están a un euro con cincuenta.
Comics are one euro fifty.
7 (*before an infinitive or a direct object*)
Voy a verla.
I'm going to see her.

Vine a hablar con Lara.
I came to talk to Lara.
Me obligaban a comer.
They forced me to eat.
Nos cruzamos al salir.
We bumped into each other as we were going out.
Se lo di a Ana.
I gave it to Ana.
Le enseñé a Mauro el libro que me dejaste.
I showed Mauro the book you lent me.
Se lo compré a él.
I bought it from him.
Vi a Juan.
I saw Juan.
Llamé al médico.
I called the doctor.

abajo ADVERB
1 **below**
Los platos y las tazas están abajo.
The plates and cups are below.
La montaña no parece tan alta desde abajo.
The mountain doesn't seem so high from below.
Mete las botellas abajo del todo.
Put the bottles right at the bottom.
el estante de abajo
the bottom shelf
2 **downstairs**
Abajo están la cocina y el salón.
The kitchen and lounge are downstairs.
Hay una fiesta en el piso de abajo.
There's a party in the flat downstairs.

la **abeja** NOUN
bee

el **abeto** NOUN
fir tree

abierto

---
abierto can be an adjective or part of the verb **abrir**.

A ADJECTIVE (FEM **abierta**)
1 **open**
¿Están abiertas las tiendas?
Are the shops open?

English · **Spanish**

A
B
C
D
E
F
G
H
I
J
K
L
M
N
O
P
Q
R
S
T
U
V
W
X
Y
Z

2 on
No dejes el gas abierto.
Don't leave the gas on.
B VERB ▷ *see* **abrir**
He abierto la puerta.
I've opened the door.

abrazar VERB
to hug
Al verme me abrazó.
He hugged me when he saw me.
¡Abrázame fuerte!
Give me a big hug!
■ **abrazarse**
to hug
Se abrazaron y se besaron.
They hugged and kissed.

el abrazo NOUN
hug
¡Dame un abrazo!
Give me a hug!

un abrazo
love

DID YOU KNOW...?
Did you know that Spanish speakers
sometimes end emails, postcards and
letters to friends with **un abrazo**?

abrigar VERB
Esta chaqueta abriga mucho.
This jacket's really warm.
■ **abrigarse**
to wrap
up well

el abrigo
NOUN
coat
un abrigo
de pieles
a fur coat
ropa de
abrigo
warm clothing

abril MASC NOUN
April

LANGUAGE TIP
Months are not spelled with a capital
letter in Spanish.

Nació el veinte de abril.
He was born on the twentieth of April.

en abril
in April

abrir VERB
1 to open
Las tiendas abren a las diez.
The shops open at ten o'clock.
Abre la ventana.
Open the window.
¡Abre, soy yo!
Open the door, it's me!
2 to turn on
Abre el gas.
Turn the gas on.
■ **abrirse**
to open
De repente se abrió la puerta.
Suddenly the door opened.

abrocharse VERB
to do up
Abróchate la camisa.
Do your shirt up.
Abróchense los cinturones.
Please fasten your seatbelts.

la abuela NOUN
grandmother
mi abuela
my grandmother
¿Dónde está
la abuela?
Where's Gran?

el **abuelo** NOUN
grandfather
mi abuelo
my grandfather
¿Dónde está
el abuelo?
Where's Granddad?
mis abuelos
my grandparents

aburrido (FEM **aburrida**) ADJECTIVE
1 **bored**
Estaba aburrida y me marché.
I was bored so I left.
2 **boring**
No seas aburrida y vente al cine.
Don't be boring and come to the cinema.
una película muy aburrida
a very boring film

aburrirse VERB
to get bored
Me aburro viendo la tele.
I get bored watching television.

acabar VERB
to finish
¿Has acabado los deberes?
Have you finished your homework?
Acabo de ver a tu padre.
I've just seen your father.
■ **acabarse**
to run out
La impresora te avisa cuando se acaba el papel.
The printer tells you when the paper runs out.

acaso ADVERB
por si acaso
just in case

el **accidente** NOUN
accident
los accidentes de carretera
road accidents
Han tenido un accidente.
They've had a car accident.

la **acción** (PL las **acciones**) NOUN
action
una película llena de acción
an action-packed film

el **aceite** NOUN
oil
el aceite de oliva
olive oil

la **aceituna** NOUN
olive
aceitunas rellenas
stuffed olives

el **acento** NOUN
accent
"Té" lleva acento cuando significa "tea".
'Té' has an accent when it means 'tea'.
Tiene un acento cerrado del sur.
He has a strong southern accent.

aceptar VERB
to accept
Acepté su invitación.
I accepted his invitation.
Acepté ayudarles.
I agreed to help them.

la **acera** NOUN
pavement

acerca ADVERB
acerca de
about
un documental acerca de la fauna africana
a documentary about African wildlife

acercar VERB
1 **to pass**
¿Me acercas la sal?
Could you pass me the salt?

15

Spanish | **English**

2 to bring over
Acerca la silla.
Bring your chair over here.
¿Acerco más la cama a la ventana?
Shall I put the bed nearer the window?
Nos acercaron al aeropuerto.
They gave us a lift to the airport.
■ **acercarse**
1 to come closer
Acércate, que te vea.
Come closer so that I can see you.
2 to go over
Me acerqué a la ventana.
I went over to the window.
Acércate a la tienda y trae una botella de agua.
Go over to the shop and get a bottle of water.

acertar VERB
1 to get ... right
He acertado todas las respuestas.
I got all the answers right.
No acerté.
I got it wrong.
2 to guess
Si aciertas cuántos caramelos hay, te los regalo todos.
If you guess how many sweets there are, I'll give you all of them.

el **acierto**

> **acierto** can be a noun or part of the verb **acertar**.

A NOUN
right answer
Tuve más aciertos que fallos en el examen.
I got more right answers than wrong ones in the exam.
B VERB ▷ *see* **acertar**
Si lo acierto gano un premio.
If I get it right, I win a prize.

aclarar VERB
to clear up

Necesito que me aclares unas dudas.
I need you to clear up some doubts for me.
Con tantos números no me aclaro.
There are so many numbers that I can't make head nor tail of it.

acompañar VERB
acompañar a alguien
to come with somebody/to go with somebody

LANGUAGE TIP
acompañar a alguien has two meanings. Look at the examples.

Si quieres te acompaño.
I'll come with you if you like.
Me pidió que la acompañara a la tienda.
She asked me to go to the shop with her.

aconsejar VERB
to advise
Te aconsejo que lo hagas.
I'd advise you to do it.

acordarse VERB
to remember
Ahora mismo no me acuerdo.
Right now I can't remember.
acordarse de
to remember
¿Te acuerdas de mí?
Do you remember me?
Acuérdate de cerrar la puerta con llave.
Remember to lock the door.

acostado (FEM **acostada**) ADJECTIVE
estar acostado
to be in bed

acostarse VERB
1 **to lie down**
2 **to go to bed**

acostumbrarse VERB
acostumbrarse a
to get used to
No me acostumbro a la comida del colegio.
I can't get used to the food at school.
Ya me he acostumbrado a usar las gafas.
I've got used to wearing glasses.

el **acto** NOUN
ceremony

en el acto
instantly

el **actor** NOUN
actor

la **actriz** (PL las **actrices**) NOUN
actress

la **actuación** (PL las **actuaciones**) NOUN
performance
Fue una actuación muy buena.
It was a very good performance.

actual (FEM **actual**) ADJECTIVE
present
el actual portero del equipo
the team's current goalkeeper
uno de los mejores grupos de la música actual
one of the greatest bands of the moment

___

LANGUAGE TIP
Be careful! **actual** does not mean **actual**.

___

actualizar VERB
to update
Tenemos que actualizar el programa.
We have to update the program.

actualmente ADVERB
1 **nowadays**
Actualmente no se utilizan las máquinas de escribir.
Typewriters are not used nowadays.
2 **currently**
Actualmente juega de delantero.
He currently plays as a striker.

___

LANGUAGE TIP
Be careful! **actualmente** does not mean **actually**.

___

actuar VERB
1 **to act**
Es difícil actuar con naturalidad delante de las cámaras.
It's hard to act naturally in front of the cameras.
No comprendo tu forma de actuar.
I can't understand your behaviour.
No actuó en esa película.
He wasn't in that film.
2 **to perform**
Hoy actúan en el Café del Jazz.
Today they'll be performing at the Café del Jazz.

el **acuario** NOUN
1 **aquarium**
2 **fish tank**

el **acuerdo**

acuerdo can be a noun or part of the verb **acordarse**.

A NOUN
agreement

llegar a un acuerdo
to reach an agreement
¡De acuerdo!
All right!

B VERB ▷ see **acordarse**
Ahora no me acuerdo.
I can't remember it now.

English
Spanish

a
b
c
d
e
f
g
h
i
j
k
l
m
n
o
p
q
r
s
t
u
v
w
x
y
z

acusar VERB
to accuse
> **Su novia lo acusaba de mentiroso.**
> His girlfriend accused him of being a liar.

adelantado (FEM **adelantada**)
ADJECTIVE
1 advanced
> **Suecia es un país muy adelantado.**
> Sweden is a very advanced country.
> **los niños más adelantados de la clase**
> the children who are doing best in the class
2 fast
> **Este reloj va adelantado.**
> This watch is fast.

adelantar VERB
1 to bring ... forward
> **Tuvimos que adelantar las vacaciones.**
> We had to bring the holiday forward.
2 to overtake
> **Adelanta a ese camión cuando puedas.**
> Overtake that lorry when you can.
3 to put ... forward
> **El domingo hay que adelantar los relojes una hora.**
> On Sunday we'll have to put the clocks forward an hour.
■ **adelantarse**
to go on ahead
> **Me adelanté para coger asiento.**
> I went on ahead to get a seat.

adelante

> **adelante** can be an adverb or an exclamation.

A ADVERB
> **Se inclinó hacia adelante.**
> He leant forward.
> **más adelante**
> further on/later

LANGUAGE TIP
más adelante has two meanings. Look at the examples.

> **El pueblo está más adelante.**
> The village is further on.
> **Más adelante hablaremos de los resultados.**
> We'll discuss the results later.

B EXCLAMATION
1 come on!
2 come in!

adelgazar VERB
to lose weight
> **¡Cómo has adelgazado!**
> You've really lost weight!
> **He adelgazado cinco kilos.**
> I've lost five kilos.

además ADVERB
1 as well
> **Es profesor y además carpintero.**
> He's a teacher and a carpenter as well.
2 what's more
> **La bici es demasiado pequeña y, además, los frenos no funcionan.**
> The bike is too small and, what's more, the brakes don't work.
3 besides
> **Además, no tienes nada que perder.**
> Besides, you've got nothing to lose.

adentro ADVERB
inside
> **Empezó a llover y se metieron adentro.**
> It began to rain so they went inside.

adhesivo (FEM **adhesiva**) ADJECTIVE
sticky
> **cinta adhesiva**
> sticky tape

adiós EXCLAMATION
goodbye!

> **decir adiós a alguien**
> to say goodbye to somebody

adivinar VERB
to guess
Adivina quién viene.
Guess who's coming.
adivinar el pensamiento a
alguien
to read somebody's mind

el **adjetivo** NOUN
adjective

admirar VERB
to admire
Todos la admiran.
Everyone admires her.
Me admira lo rápido que lees.
I'm amazed at how fast you read

admitir VERB
1 to admit
Admite que estabas equivocado.
Admit you were wrong.
2 to accept
La máquina no admite monedas
de dos euros.
The machine doesn't accept two-euro
coins.
Espero que me admitan en el
equipo.
I hope I'll get a place on the team.

el/la **adolescente** NOUN
teenager

adónde ADVERB
where
¿Adónde ibas?
Where were you going?

adornar VERB
to decorate

el **adulto**
la **adulta** NOUN
adult

el **adverbio** NOUN
adverb

advertir VERB
to warn
Ya te advertí que sería difícil.
I warned you it would be difficult.

Te advierto que no va a ser nada
fácil.
I must warn you that it won't be at all
easy.

aéreo (FEM **aérea**) ADJECTIVE
air
un ataque aéreo
an air raid

el **aeropuerto** NOUN
airport

afectar VERB
to affect
Esto a ti no te afecta.
This doesn't affect you.

afeitarse VERB
to shave
Voy a afeitarme.
I'm going to shave.

la **afición** (PL las **aficiones**) NOUN
hobby
Su afición es el monopatín.
Her hobby is skateboarding.

Tengo mucha afición por el
ciclismo.
I'm very keen on cycling.

aficionado (FEM **aficionada**)

aficionado can be a noun or an
adjective.

A MASC/FEM NOUN
1 enthusiast
un libro para los aficionados al
ciclismo
a book for cycling enthusiasts

2 amateur
un partido para aficionados
a game for amateurs
B ADJECTIVE
1 keen
Es muy aficionada a la pintura.
She's very keen on painting.
2 amateur
un equipo de fútbol aficionado
an amateur football team

aficionarse VERB
aficionarse a algo
to take up something/to become interested in something

LANGUAGE TIP
aficionarse a algo has two meanings. Look at the examples.

Raúl se aficionó al tenis.
Raúl took up tennis.
Me he aficionado al teatro.
I've become interested in theatre.

afirmar VERB
afirmar que ...
to say that ...
Afirmaba que no la conocía.
He said that he didn't know her.

aflojar VERB
to loosen
■ aflojarse
to come loose
Se ha aflojado un tornillo.
A screw has come loose.

afónico (FEM **afónica**) ADJECTIVE
Estoy afónico.
I've lost my voice.

afortunado (FEM **afortunada**)
ADJECTIVE
lucky
Es un tipo afortunado.
He's a lucky guy.

afuera ADVERB
outside
Vámonos afuera.
Let's go outside.

las **afueras** NOUN
outskirts
en las afueras de Barcelona
on the outskirts of Barcelona

agacharse VERB
to crouch down

agarrar VERB
1 to grab
Agarró a su hermano por el hombro.
He grabbed his brother by the shoulder.
2 to hold
Agarra bien el manillar.
Hold the handlebars firmly.
■ agarrarse
to hold on
Agárrate a la barandilla.
Hold on to the rail.

la **agenda** NOUN
1 diary
2 address book

LANGUAGE TIP
Be careful! The Spanish word **agenda** does not mean **agenda**.

agitar VERB
to shake
Agitar antes de usar.
Shake before use.

agosto MASC NOUN
August

LANGUAGE TIP
Months are not spelled with a capital letter in Spanish.

en agosto
in August
el ocho de agosto
the eighth of August
Nació el ocho de agosto.
He was born on the eighth of August.

agotado (FEM **agotada**) ADJECTIVE
1 exhausted
Estoy agotado.
I'm exhausted.

2 sold out
Ese modelo en concreto está agotado.
That particular model is sold out.

agotar VERB
1 to use up
Agotamos todas nuestras reservas.
We used up all our supplies.
2 to tire out
Me agota tanto ejercicio.
All this exercise is tiring me out.
■ **agotarse**
to run out
Se está agotando la batería.
The battery's running out.
Se agotaron todas las entradas.
The tickets all sold out.

agradable (FEM **agradable**) ADJECTIVE
nice

agradecer VERB
agradecer algo a alguien
to thank somebody for something
Te agradezco tu interés.
Thank you for your interest.

la **agresión** (PL las **agresiones**) NOUN
attack

el **agricultor**
la **agricultora** NOUN
farmer

la **agricultura** NOUN
farming

el **agua** FEM NOUN
water
agua corriente
running water
agua potable
drinking water

aguantar VERB
1 to stand
No aguanto la ópera.
I can't stand opera.
Su vecina no la aguanta.
Her neighbour can't stand her.
Últimamente estás que no hay quien te aguante.
You've been unbearable lately.

2 to take
La estantería no va a aguantar el peso.
The shelf won't take the weight.
3 to hold
Aguántame el martillo un momento.
Can you hold the hammer for me for a moment?
Aguanta la respiración.
Hold your breath.
No pude aguantar la risa.
I couldn't help laughing.
Si no puede venir, que se aguante.
If he can't come, he'll just have to lump it.

agudo (FEM **aguda**) ADJECTIVE
1 sharp
2 high-pitched
3 witty

la **aguja** NOUN
1 needle
2 hand

el **agujero** NOUN
hole
hacer un agujero
to make a hole

ahí ADVERB
there
¡Ahí están!
There they are!
Lo tienes ahí mismo.
You've got it right there.

LANGUAGE TIP
por ahí has several meanings. It can be translated as **over there**, **somewhere** and **thereabouts**. Look at the examples.

Tú busca por ahí.
You look over there.
¿Has visto las tijeras? — Andarán por ahí.
Have you seen the scissors? — They must be somewhere around.

21

doscientos o por ahí
two hundred or thereabouts

ahogarse VERB
to drown
Se ahogó en el río.
He drowned in the river.

ahora ADVERB
now
¿Dónde vamos ahora?
Where are we going now?
Ahora te lo digo.
I'll tell you in a moment.
Ahora mismo voy.
I'm just coming.
Ahora mismo está de viaje.
He's away on a trip right now.
Por ahora no cambies nada.
Don't change anything for the moment.

de ahora en adelante
from now on
¡Hasta ahora!
See you shortly!

ahorrar VERB
to save

el **aire** NOUN
1 air
Necesitamos aire para respirar.
We need air to breathe.
aire acondicionado
air conditioning
2 wind
El aire le voló la gorra.
The wind blew his cap off.
al aire libre
outdoors/outdoor

LANGUAGE TIP
al aire libre has two meanings. Look at the examples.

Comimos al aire libre.
We had lunch outdoors.
una fiesta al aire libre
an outdoor party

el **ajo** NOUN
garlic

al PREPOSITION
(= a + el) ▷ see **a**
Fui al cine.
I went to the cinema.

el **ala** FEM NOUN
wing

alargar VERB
1 to make … longer
Hay que alargar un poco las mangas.
We'll need to make the sleeves a bit longer.
2 to extend
Decidieron alargar las vacaciones.
They decided to extend their holidays.
■ **alargarse**
to get longer
Ya van alargándose los días.
The days are getting longer.

la **alarma** NOUN
alarm
Saltó la alarma.
The alarm went off.
dar la voz de alarma
to raise the alarm
alarma de incendios
fire alarm

el **alboroto** NOUN
racket
¡Vaya alboroto!
What a racket!

alcanzar VERB
1 to catch up with
La alcancé cuando salía por la puerta.
I caught up with her just as she was going out of the door.
2 to reach
alcanzar la cima de la montaña
to reach the top of the mountain
3 to pass
¿Me alcanzas las tijeras?
Could you pass me the scissors?

alegrar VERB
to cheer up
Intenté alegrarlos con unos chistes.
I tried to cheer them up with a few jokes.
Me alegra que hayas venido.
I'm glad you've come.
- **alegrarse**
to be glad
¿Te gusta? Me alegro.
You like it? I'm glad.
Me alegro de su éxito.
I'm glad about his success.
alegrarse por alguien
to be happy for somebody
Me alegro por ti.
I'm happy for you.

alegre (FEM **alegre**) ADJECTIVE
cheerful

la alegría NOUN
Sentí una gran alegría.
I was really happy.

¡Qué alegría!
How lovely!

alejarse VERB
to move away
Aléjate un poco del fuego.
Move a bit further away from the fire.

la alergia NOUN
allergy
¿Tienes alguna alergia?
Have you got any allergies?
alergia al polen
hay fever

las aletas PLURAL NOUN
flippers

la alfombra NOUN
1 **rug**
2 **carpet**

algo

algo can be a pronoun or an adverb.

A PRONOUN
1 **something**

Algo se está quemando.
Something is burning.
¿Quieres algo de comer?
Would you like something to eat?
¿Te pasa algo?
Is something the matter?
Aún queda algo de zumo.
There's still some juice left.
2 **anything**
¿Algo más?
Anything else?
B ADVERB
rather
La falda te está algo corta.
The skirt's rather short on you.

el algodón (PL los **algodones**) NOUN
cotton
Me puse algodones en los oídos.
I put cotton wool in my ears.
el algodón de azúcar
candyfloss

alguien PRONOUN
1 **somebody**
Alguien llama a la puerta.
There's somebody knocking at the door.
¿Necesitas que te ayude alguien?
Do you need somebody to help you?
2 **anybody**
¿Conoces a alguien aquí?
Do you know anybody here?

algún ADJECTIVE (FEM **alguna**, MASC PL **algunos**)
1 **some**
Algún día iré.
I'll go there some day.
2 **any**
¿Compraste algún cuadro?
Did you buy any pictures?
¿Quieres alguna cosa más?
Was there anything else?

algún que otro ...
the odd ...

English / **Spanish**

alguno PRONOUN (FEM **alguna**)

1 somebody
Siempre hay alguno que se queja.
There's always somebody who complains.
Algunos no están de acuerdo
Some people disagree.

2 some
Solo conozco a algunos de los vecinos.
I only know some of the neighbours.
Tiene que estar en alguna de estas cajas.
It must be in one of these boxes.

3 any
Necesito una aspirina. ¿Te queda alguna?
I need an aspirin. Have you got any left?
Si alguno quiere irse que se vaya.
If any of them want to leave, fine.
¿Lo sabe alguno de vosotros?
Do any of you know?

el **alimento** NOUN
food
alimentos congelados
frozen food

allá ADVERB
over there
Tu libro está allá.
Your book is over there.
Échate un poco más allá.
Move over that way a bit.

allí ADVERB
there
Allí está.
There it is.
Allí viene tu hermana.
Here comes your sister.

el **alma** FEM NOUN
soul
Lo siento en el alma.
I'm really sorry.

la **almohada** NOUN
pillow

almorzar VERB
to have lunch
No he almorzado todavía.
I haven't had lunch yet.
¿Qué has almorzado?
What did you have for lunch?

el **almuerzo** NOUN
lunch

alrededor ADVERB
alrededor de
around/about

LANGUAGE TIP
alrededor de has two meanings. Look at the examples.

El satélite gira alrededor de la Tierra.
The satellite goes around the Earth.
Deben de ser alrededor de las dos.
It must be about two o'clock.

los **alrededores** PLURAL NOUN
Ocurrió en los alrededores de Madrid.
It happened near Madrid.
Hay muchas tiendas en los alrededores del museo.
There are a lot of shops in the area around the museum.

alto (FEM **alta**)

alto can be an adjective, a pronoun or an exclamation.

A ADJECTIVE
1 tall
Es un chico muy alto.
He's a very tall boy.
un edificio muy alto
a very tall building

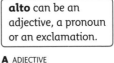

2 high
El Everest es la montaña más alta del mundo.
Everest is the highest mountain in the world.
Sacó notas altas en todos los exámenes.
He got high marks in all his exams.
3 loud
La música está demasiado alta.
The music's too loud.

B ADVERB
high
subir muy alto
to go up very high
Pepe habla muy alto.
Pepe has got a very loud voice.
¡Más alto, por favor!
Speak up, please!
Pon el volumen más alto.
Turn the volume up.

C EXCLAMATION
stop!

la **altura** NOUN
height
Volamos a una altura de quince mil pies.
We're flying at a height of fifteen thousand feet.
La pared tiene dos metros de altura.
The wall's two metres high.

el **alumno**
la **alumna** NOUN
pupil

amable (FEM **amable**) ADJECTIVE
kind

amanecer

amanecer can be a verb or a noun.

A VERB
to get light
Amanece a las siete.
It gets light at seven.

B MASC NOUN
dawn

al amanecer
at dawn

amar VERB
to love

amargo (FEM **amarga**) ADJECTIVE
bitter

amarillo
A ADJECTIVE
(FEM **amarilla**)
yellow
B MASC NOUN
yellow

el **ambiente** NOUN
atmosphere
En el grupo hay un ambiente tenso.
There's a tense atmosphere in the group.
el medio ambiente
the environment

amenace VERB ▷ see **amenazar**
No voy a hacerlo aunque me amenace.
I'm not going to do it even if he threatens me.

la **amenaza** NOUN
threat

amenazar VERB
to threaten
Amenazó con decírselo al profesor.
He threatened to tell the teacher.

el **amigo**
la **amiga** NOUN
friend

hacerse amigos
to become friends

a
b
c
d
e
f
g
h
i
j
k
l
m
n
o
p
q
r
s
t
u
v
w
x
y
z

English
Spanish

A
B
C
D
E
F
G
H
I
J
K
L
M
N
O
P
Q
R
S
T
U
V
W
X
Y
Z

el **amor** NOUN
love

ancho (FEM **ancha**) ADJECTIVE
1 wide
una calle ancha
a wide street
2 loose
Le gusta llevar ropa ancha.
He likes to wear loose clothing.
Me está ancho el vestido.
The dress is too big for me.

anda EXCLAMATION
1 well I never!
¡Anda, un billete de cincuenta euros!
Well I never, a fifty-euro note!
2 come on
¡Anda, ponte el abrigo y vámonos!
Come on, put your coat on and let's go!

¡Anda ya!
You're not serious!

andar VERB
1 to walk
Anduvimos varios kilómetros.
We walked several kilometres.
Iremos andando a la estación.
We'll walk to the station.

2 to be
Últimamente ando muy liado.
I've been very busy lately.
No sé por dónde anda.
I don't know where he is.
¿Qué tal andas?
How are you?
andar mal de dinero
to be short of money

anduve VERB ▷ *see* **andar**
Anduve dos horas.
I walked for two hours

el **ángel** NOUN
angel

el **ángulo** NOUN
angle
en ángulo recto
at right angles

el **anillo** NOUN
ring
un anillo de boda
a wedding ring

animado
(FEM **animada**) ADJECTIVE
1 cheerful
Últimamente parece que está más animada.
She has seemed more cheerful lately.
2 lively
Fue una fiesta muy animada.
It was a very lively party.
dibujos animados
cartoons

el **animal** NOUN
animal
los animales domésticos
pets

animar VERB
1 to cheer up
Lo ha pasado muy mal y necesita que la animen.
She has had a rough time and needs cheering up.

2 to cheer on
Estuvimos animando al equipo.
We were cheering the team on.

3 to encourage
animar a alguien a que haga algo
to encourage somebody to do
something
**Nos animaron a que fuésemos a
la fiesta.**
They encouraged us to go to the party.

■ **animarse**
to cheer up
¡Vamos, anímate hombre!
Come on, cheer up mate!
animarse a hacer algo
to make up one's mind to do
something

ánimo EXCLAMATION
cheer up!
**¡Ánimo, chaval, que no es el fin
del mundo!**
Cheer up mate, it's not the end of the
world!

anoche ADVERB
last night
antes de anoche
the night before last

anochecer VERB
to get dark
**En invierno anochece muy
temprano.**
It gets dark very early in winter.

anteayer ADVERB
the day before yesterday

la **antena** NOUN
aerial
una antena parabólica
a satellite dish

anterior (FEM **anterior**) ADJECTIVE
before
La semana anterior llovió mucho.
It rained a lot the week before.
**Su examen fue anterior al
nuestro.**
Their exam was before ours.

antes ADVERB
1 before
Esta película ya la he visto antes.
I've seen this film before.
antes de la cena
before dinner
antes de que te vayas
before you go
Él estaba aquí antes que yo.
He was here before me.
Antes no había tantos juguetes.
People didn't use to have so many toys.
2 first
Nosotros llegamos antes.
We arrived first.

lo antes posible
as soon as possible

antiguo (FEM **antigua**) ADJECTIVE
old
Este reloj es muy antiguo.
This clock is very old.

antipático (FEM **antipática**) ADJECTIVE
unfriendly

anual (FEM **anual**) ADJECTIVE
annual

anunciar VERB
to announce
anunciar una decisión
to announce a decision

el **anuncio** NOUN
1 advertisement
**Ponen demasiados anuncios en
la tele.**
They put too many advertisements on
the TV.
2 announcement
**Tengo que hacer un anuncio
importante.**
I have an important announcement to
make.

añadir VERB
to add

el **año** NOUN
year

Estuve allí el año pasado.
I was there last year.
¿Cuántos años tiene?
How old is he?
Tiene quince años.
He's fifteen.

¡Feliz Año Nuevo!
Happy New Year!
el año que viene
next year
el año pasado
last year
los años ochenta
the eighties

apagar VERB
to switch off
Apaga la tele.
Switch the TV off.

aparecer VERB
1 to appear
De repente apareció la policía.
The police suddenly appeared.
2 to turn up
¿Han aparecido ya las tijeras?
Have the scissors turned up yet?

el **apartamento** NOUN
flat

apartar VERB
to move out of the way
Aparta todas las sillas.
Move all the chairs out of the way.
¡Aparta!
Stand back!
■ **apartarse**
to stand back
Apártense de la puerta.
Stand back from the door.

el **apellido** NOUN
surname

apenas ADVERB, CONJUNCTION
1 hardly
No tenemos apenas nada de comer.
We've got hardly anything to eat.

Apenas podía levantarse.
He could hardly stand up.
2 hardly ever
Apenas voy al cine.
I hardly ever go to the cinema.
3 barely
Hace apenas diez minutos que hablé con ella.
I spoke to her barely ten minutes ago.
Terminé en apenas dos horas.
It only took me two hours to finish.

el **aperitivo** NOUN
snack

apestar VERB
to stink
Te apestan los pies.
Your feet stink.
apestar a
to stink of

apetecer VERB
¿Te apetece una tortilla?
Do you fancy an omelette?
No, gracias, ahora no me apetece.
No, thanks, I don't feel like it just now.

el **apetito** NOUN
appetite
Eso te va a quitar el apetito.
You won't have any appetite left.
No tengo apetito.
I'm not hungry.

aplastar VERB
to squash
Me senté encima del regalo y lo aplasté.
I sat on the present and squashed it.

aplaudir VERB
to clap
Todos aplaudían.
Everyone clapped.

el **aplauso** NOUN
applause
Los aplausos duraron varios minutos.
The applause lasted for several minutes.

aplazar VERB
  to postpone

apostar VERB
  to bet
    apostar por algo
    to bet on something
    ¿Qué te apuestas a que ... ?
    How much do you bet that...?

apoyar VERB
  1 **to lean**
    Apoya el espejo contra la pared.
    Lean the mirror against the wall.
  2 **to rest**
    Apoya la espalda en este cojín.
    Rest your back against this cushion.
  3 **to support**
    Todos mis compañeros me apoyan.
    All my colleagues support me.
  ■ **apoyarse**
    to lean
    No te apoyes en la mesa.
    Don't lean on the table.

aprender VERB
  to learn
    Ya me he aprendido los verbos irregulares.
    I've already learnt the irregular verbs.
    aprender a hacer algo
    to learn to do something
    Estoy aprendiendo a tocar la guitarra.
    I'm learning to play the guitar.

aprender algo de memoria
to learn something off by heart

apretado (FEM **apretada**) ADJECTIVE
  1 **tight**
    Estos pantalones me están muy apretados.
    These trousers are very tight on me.
  2 **cramped**
    Íbamos muy apretados en el autobús.
    We were very cramped on the bus.

apretar VERB
  1 **to tighten**
    Aprieta bien los tornillos.
    Tighten up the screws.
  2 **to press**
    Aprieta este botón.
    Press this button.
    Me aprietan los zapatos.
    My shoes are too tight.

aprobar VERB
  to pass
    aprobar un examen
    to pass an exam
    aprobar por los pelos
    to scrape through

aprovechar VERB
  1 **to make good use of**
    No aprovecha el tiempo.
    He doesn't make good use of his time.
  2 **to use**
    Aprovecharé los ratos libres para estudiar.
    I'll use my spare time to study.
    aprovecharse de
    to take advantage of
    Me aproveché de la situación.
    I took advantage of the situation.
    Todos se aprovechan del pobre chico.
    Everyone takes advantage of the poor boy.

¡Que aproveche!
Enjoy your meal!

apruebo VERB ▷ see **aprobar**
    Si no apruebo, mis padres se enfadarán.
    If I fail, my parents will be angry.

apuesto VERB ▷ *see* **apostar**
Te apuesto a que no le va a gustar.
I bet you she won't like it.

apuntar VERB
1 to write down
Apúntalo o se te olvidará.
Write it down or you'll forget.
Apunta mi teléfono.
Can you take a note of my phone number?
2 to point
Me apuntó con el dedo.
He pointed at me.
▪ **apuntarse**
to put one's name down
Nos hemos apuntado para el viaje a Marruecos.
We've put our names down for the trip to Morocco.
apuntarse a un curso
to enrol on a course

¡Yo me apunto!
Count me in!

los **apuntes** NOUN
notes

tomar apuntes
to take notes

aquel (FEM **aquella**, MASC PL **aquellos**, FEM PL **aquellas**)

aquel can be an adjective or a pronoun.

A ADJECTIVE
that
Me gusta más aquella mesa.
I prefer that table.
B PRONOUN
that one
Aquel no es el mío.
That one isn't mine.
Dame aquellas de allí.
Give me those ones over there.

aquello PRONOUN
aquello que hay allí
that thing over there

aquí ADVERB
1 here
Aquí está el videojuego que me pediste.
Here's the video game you asked me for.
2 now
de aquí en adelante
from now on
por aquí
around here/this way

LANGUAGE TIP
por aquí has two meanings. Look at the examples.

Lo tenía por aquí en alguna parte.
I had it around here somewhere.
Pasa por aquí, por favor.
Please come this way.

la **araña** NOUN
spider
¡Hay una araña en la bañera!
There's a spider in the bath!

arañar VERB
to scratch
El gato me arañó.
The cat scratched me.

el **árbitro**
la **árbitra**
NOUN
referee

el **árbol** NOUN
tree
un árbol frutal
a fruit tree
el árbol de Navidad
the Christmas tree

el **arco** NOUN
1 bow
2 arch
el arco iris
the rainbow

arder VERB
to burn
> **Ese tronco no va a arder.**
> That log won't burn.
> **¡La sopa está ardiendo!**
> The soup's boiling hot!

la **ardilla** NOUN
squirrel

el **área** FEM NOUN
area

la **arena** NOUN
sand

arenas movedizas
quicksand

armar VERB
1 to assemble
> **El juguete viene desmontado y luego tú lo armas.**
> The toy comes in pieces and you assemble it.

2 to make
> **Los vecinos de arriba arman mucho jaleo.**
> Our upstairs neighbours make a lot of noise.
> **armarse un lío**
> to get in a muddle
> **Me voy a armar un lío con tantos números.**
> I'm going to get into a muddle with all these numbers.

el **armario** NOUN
1 cupboard
> **un armario de cocina**
> a kitchen cupboard

2 wardrobe

arrancar VERB
1 to pull up
> **Estaba arrancando malas hierbas.**
> I was pulling up weeds.

2 to pull out
> **Le arranqué una espina del dedo.**
> I pulled a thorn out of his finger.

arrastrar VERB
to drag
> **Arrastraba una maleta enorme.**
> He was dragging an enormous suitcase.

■ **arrastrarse**
to crawl
> **Llegaron hasta la valla arrastrándose.**
> They crawled up to the fence.

arreglar VERB
to fix
> **¿Puedes arreglar el juguete?**
> Can you fix the toy?

■ **arreglarse**
1 to get ready
> **Se arregló para salir.**
> She got ready to go out.

2 to work out
> **Ya verás como todo se arregla.**
> It'll all work out, you'll see.

el **arreglo** NOUN
repair
> **El patinete solo necesita un pequeño arreglo.**
> The scooter only needs a minor repair.
> **Esta tele no tiene arreglo.**
> This TV is unrepairable.
> **Este problema no tiene arreglo.**
> There's no solution to this problem.

arriba ADVERB
1 above
> **Los platos y las tazas están arriba.**
> The plates and mugs are above.
> **Visto desde arriba parece más pequeño.**
> Seen from above it looks smaller.

Spanish · English

A
B
C
D
E
F
G
H
I
J
K
L
M
N
O
P
Q
R
S
T
U
V
W
X
Y
Z

Pon esos libros arriba del todo.
Put those books on top.

2 upstairs
los vecinos de arriba
our upstairs neighbours

Arriba están los dormitorios.
The bedrooms are upstairs.

más arriba
further up

arriesgado (FEM **arriesgada**) ADJECTIVE
risky

la **arroba** NOUN
at
Mi e-mail es loveday arroba collins punto E-S (loveday@collins.es).
My email address is loveday at collins dot E-S (loveday@collins.es).

arrojar VERB
to throw
Arrojaban piedras y palos.
They were throwing sticks and stones.

el **arroyo** NOUN
stream

el **arroz** NOUN
rice
arroz blanco
white rice
arroz con leche
rice pudding

la **arruga** NOUN
1 wrinkle
2 crease

el **arte** (PL las **artes**) NOUN
art
el arte abstracto
abstract art

el **artículo** NOUN
article
el artículo determinado
the definite article
el artículo indeterminado
the indefinite article

artificial (FEM **artificial**) ADJECTIVE
artificial

el/la **artista** NOUN
1 artist
2 un artista
an actor
una artista
an actress

asar VERB
to roast
asar algo a la parrilla
to grill something

Me aso de calor.
I'm boiling.

el **ascensor** NOUN
lift

el **asco** NOUN
El ajo me da asco.
I think garlic's revolting.
La casa está hecha un asco.
The house is filthy.

¡Qué asco!
How revolting!

el **aseo** NOUN
el aseo personal
personal hygiene
los aseos
the toilets

así ADVERB
1 like this
Se hace así.
You do it like this.

2 like that
Es así: como lo hace Jorge.
It's like that: the way Jorge is doing it.
¿Ves aquel abrigo? Quiero algo así.
Do you see that coat? I'd like
something like that.
un tomate así de grande
a tomato this big

el **asiento** NOUN
seat
el asiento delantero
the front seat
el asiento trasero
the back seat

la **asignatura** NOUN
subject
Tiene dos asignaturas
pendientes.
He's got two subjects to retake.

asomar VERB
No asomes la cabeza por la
ventanilla.
Don't lean out of the window.
Asómate a la ventana.
Look out of the window.

asombrar VERB
to amaze
Me asombra que no lo sepas.
I'm amazed you don't know.
■ **asombrarse**
to be amazed
Se asombró de lo tarde que era.
He was amazed at how late it was.

el **aspecto** NOUN
appearance
A ver si cuidas más tu aspecto.
You need to take a bit more care with
your appearance.

la **aspiradora** NOUN
vacuum cleaner

asqueroso (FEM **asquerosa**) ADJECTIVE
1 disgusting
2 filthy
Esta cocina está asquerosa.
This kitchen is filthy.

el **asunto** NOUN
matter
Es un asunto muy complicado.
It's a very complicated matter.
No me gusta que se metan en mis
asuntos.
I don't like anyone meddling in my affairs.
¡Eso no es asunto tuyo!
That's none of your business!

asustar VERB
1 to frighten
No me asustan los fantasmas.
I'm not frightened of ghosts.
2 to startle
¡Huy! Me has asustado.
Goodness! You startled me.
■ **asustarse**
to get frightened
Se asusta por nada.
He gets frightened over nothing.

atacar VERB
to attack

el **atajo** NOUN
short cut
Cogeremos un atajo.
We'll take a short cut.

el **ataque** NOUN
attack
un ataque contra alguien
an attack on somebody
Le dio un ataque de risa.
He burst out laughing.

atar VERB
to tie
Ata al perro a la farola.
Tie the dog to the lamppost.
Átate los cordones.
Tie your shoelaces up.

atardecer

atardecer can be a verb or a noun.

A VERB
to get dark
Está atardeciendo.
It's getting dark.

B MASC NOUN
dusk

al atardecer
at dusk

el **atasco** NOUN
traffic jam

atención

atención can be a noun or an exclamation.

A FEM NOUN
Hay que poner más atención.
You should pay more attention.
Escucha con atención.
Listen carefully.
El director del colegio le llamó la atención.
The headmaster gave him a talking-to.
Estás llamando la atención con esa ropa.
You're attracting attention to yourself in those clothes.

B EXCLAMATION
¡Atención, por favor!
May I have your attention please?
"¡Atención!"
'Danger!'

atender VERB
1 to pay attention to
Todos en clase atendían al profesor.
Everyone in the class was paying attention to the teacher.
2 to serve (*in a shop*)

el **atentado** NOUN
attack

un atentado terrorista
a terrorist attack

atento (FEM **atenta**) ADJECTIVE
thoughtful
Es un chico muy atento.
He's a very thoughtful boy.
Estaban atentos a las explicaciones del profesor.
They were paying attention to the teacher's explanations.

el **aterrizaje** NOUN
landing
un aterrizaje forzoso
an emergency landing

aterrizar VERB
to land

atiendo VERB ▷ *see* **atender**
Ahora mismo la atiendo.
I will be with you right away.

la **atracción** (PL las **atracciones**) NOUN
attraction
una atracción turística
a tourist attraction
sentir atracción por algo
to be attracted to something
Sentía atracción por él.
I was attracted to him.

atractivo (FEM **atractiva**) ADJECTIVE
attractive
un hombre muy atractivo
a very attractive man

atrapar VERB
to catch
Mi gato atrapa pájaros.
My cat catches birds.

atrás ADVERB
Los niños viajan siempre atrás.
The children always travel in the back.
la parte de atrás
the back
el asiento de atrás
the back seat
Mirar hacia atrás.
To look back.

Está más atrás.
It's further back.
ir para atrás
to go backwards
El coche de atrás va a adelantarnos.
The car behind is going to overtake us.
Yo me quedé atrás porque iba muy cansado.
I stayed behind because I was very tired.

atrasado (FEM **atrasada**) ADJECTIVE
1 **backward**
Es un país muy atrasado.
It's a very backward country.
2 **behind**
Va bastante atrasado en la escuela.
He's rather behind at school.
Tengo mucho trabajo atrasado.
I'm very behind with my work.
3 **El reloj está atrasado.**
The clock's slow.

atravesar VERB
to cross
Atravesamos el río.
We crossed the river.

atreverse VERB
to dare
No me atreví a decírselo.
I didn't dare tell him.
No me atrevo.
I daren't.

atropellar VERB
to run over
Un coche atropelló al perro.
The dog was run over by a car.

el **aula** FEM NOUN
classroom

el **aumento** NOUN
increase
Ha habido un aumento de los precios.
There's been an increase in prices.

aun ADVERB
even
Aun sentado me duele la pierna.
Even when I'm sitting down, my leg hurts.

aun así
even so

aún ADVERB
1 **still**
Aún me queda un poco para terminar.
I've still got a little bit left to finish.
¿Aún te duele?
Is it still hurting?
2 **yet**
Aún no ha llegado mi madre.
My mum hasn't arrived yet.
Y aún no me has devuelto el libro.
You still haven't given me the book back.
3 **even**
La película es aún más aburrida de lo que creía.
The film's even more boring than I thought it would be.

aunque CONJUNCTION
1 **although**
Me gusta el francés, aunque prefiero el alemán.
I like French, although I prefer German.
Estoy pensando en ir, aunque no sé cuándo.
I'm thinking of going, though I don't know when.
Seguí andando, aunque me dolía mucho la pierna.
I went on walking, even though my leg was hurting a lot.
No te lo daré, aunque protestes.
You can complain all you like but you're not getting it.
2 **even if**
Pienso irme, aunque tenga que salir por la ventana.
I shall leave, even if I have to climb out of the window.

ausente (FEM **ausente**) ADJECTIVE
absent

auténtico (FEM **auténtica**) ADJECTIVE
1 **real**
 Es un auténtico campeón.
 He's a real champion.
2 **genuine**
 El cuadro era auténtico.
 The painting was genuine.

el **autobús** (PL los **autobuses**) NOUN
bus

 en autobús
 by bus

automático (FEM **automática**)
ADJECTIVE
automatic

la **autopista** NOUN
motorway
 autopista de peaje
 toll motorway

el **autor**
 la **autora** NOUN
author

la **autoridad** NOUN
authority

autorizar VERB
to authorize
 No le han autorizado salir del colegio.
 They have not authorized him to leave school.

auxilio EXCLAMATION
help!

avanzar VERB
to make progress
 Isabel avanzó mucho el pasado trimestre.
 Isabel made a lot of progress last term.

el **ave** FEM NOUN
bird
 un ave de rapiña
 a bird of prey

la **aventura** NOUN
adventure
 Te contaré nuestras aventuras en la playa.
 I'll tell you about our adventures at the beach.

avergonzar VERB
to embarrass
 Me avergonzaste delante de todos.
 You embarrassed me in front of everyone.
 Me avergüenza hablar delante de la gente.
 I find it embarrassing to talk in from of people.
 avergonzarse de algo
 to be ashamed of something
 No hay de qué avergonzarse.
 There's nothing to be ashamed of.

la **avería** NOUN
 El coche tiene una avería.
 The car has broken down.

averiarse VERB
to break down

el **avión** (PL los **aviones**) NOUN
plane

 ir en avión
 to fly

avisar VERB
1 **to warn**
 Ya nos avisaron de que haría mucho frío.
 They warned us that it would be very cold.

2 to let ... know
Avísanos si hay alguna novedad.
Let us know if there's any news.

el **aviso** NOUN
notice
Había un aviso en la puerta.
There was a notice on the door.

la **avispa** NOUN
wasp

ay EXCLAMATION
1 ow!
¡Ay! ¡Me has pisado!
Ow! You've trodden on my toe!
2 oh no!
¡Ay! ¡Creo que nos han engañado!
Oh no! I think they've cheated us!

ayer ADVERB
yesterday
ayer por la mañana
yesterday morning
ayer por la tarde
yesterday afternoon/yesterday evening

LANGUAGE TIP
ayer por la tarde has two meanings.
It can be translated as **yesterday afternoon** and **yesterday evening**.

---

ayer por la noche
last night

antes de ayer
the day before yesterday

la **ayuda** NOUN
help
Gracias por tu ayuda.
Thanks for your help.

el/la **ayudante** NOUN
assistant

ayudar VERB
to help
¿Me ayudas con los ejercicios?
Could you help me with these
exercises?
**Me está ayudando a hacer los
deberes.**
He's helping me do my homework.

el **ayuntamiento** NOUN
1 town hall
2 city hall

la **azafata** NOUN
flight attendant

el **azúcar** NOUN
sugar

azul ADJECTIVE, MASC NOUN
blue
una puerta azul
a blue door
azul celeste
sky blue
azul marino
navy blue
Yo iba de azul.
I was wearing blue.

English
Spanish

a
b
c
d
e
f
g
h
i
j
k
l
m
n
o
p
q
r
s
t
u
v
w
x
y
z

37

el **bache** NOUN
1 **pothole**
2 **bump**

el **Bachillerato** NOUN

DID YOU KNOW...?
The **Bachillerato** is a two-year secondary school course leading to university.

---

la **bacteria** NOUN
bacterium

la **bahía** NOUN
bay

bailar VERB
to dance
sacar a bailar a alguien
to ask somebody to dance

el **bailarín**
la **bailarina** NOUN (MASC PL los bailarines)
dancer

el **baile** NOUN
dance
El colegio ha organizado un baile.
The school has organized a dance.

bajar VERB
1 **to go down**
Bajó la escalera muy despacio.
He went down the stairs very slowly.
2 **to come down**
Baja y ayúdame.
Come down and help me.
3 **to take down**
¿Has bajado la basura?
Have you taken the rubbish down?
4 **to bring down**
¿Me bajas el abrigo?
Could you bring my coat down?
5 **to fall**
Han bajado los precios.
Prices have fallen.
6 **to turn down**
Baja la radio.
Turn the radio down.
7 **to download**
■ **bajarse de**
to get off/to get out of/to get down from

LANGUAGE TIP
bajarse de has three meanings. Look at the examples.

Se bajó del autobús antes que yo.
He got off the bus before me.
¡Bájate del coche!
Get out of the car!
¡Bájate del árbol!
Get down from the tree!

bajo

bajo can be an adjective, a preposition or an adverb.

A ADJECTIVE (FEM **baja**)
1 **low**
una silla muy baja
a very low chair
la temporada baja
the low season
Hablaban en voz baja.
They were speaking quietly.
2 **short**
Mi hermano es muy bajo.
My brother is very short.
3 **ground**
Viven en la planta baja.
They live on the ground floor.
B PREPOSITION
under
Dani llevaba un libro bajo el brazo.
Dani was carrying a book under his arm.

C ADVERB

1 low
El avión volaba muy bajo.
The plane was flying very low.

2 quietly
¡Habla bajo!
Speak quietly!

la **bala** NOUN
bullet

el **balcón** (PL los **balcones**) NOUN
balcony

la **baldosa** NOUN
tile

la **ballena** NOUN
whale

el **ballet** (PL los **ballets**) NOUN
ballet

el **balón** (PL los **balones**) NOUN
ball
balón de fútbol
football

el **baloncesto** NOUN
basketball
jugar al baloncesto
to play basketball

el **balonvolea** NOUN
volleyball
jugar al balonvolea
to play volleyball

el **banco** NOUN
1 bank
2 bench

la **banda** NOUN
1 band
Toca la trompeta en una banda.
He plays the trumpet with a band.

2 gang
La policía ha cogido a toda la banda.
The police have caught the whole gang.

3 la banda ancha
broadband
la banda sonora
the soundtrack

la **bandeja** NOUN
tray

la **bandera** NOUN
flag

la **banqueta** NOUN
stool

el **banquillo** NOUN
bench
El entrenador está en el banquillo.
The trainer is sitting on the bench.

el **bañador** NOUN
1 swimming trunks
2 swimming costume

Spanish | **English**

A
B
C
D
E
F
G
H
I
J
K
L
M
N
O
P
Q
R
S
T
U
V
W
X
Y
Z

bañarse VERB
1 **to have a bath**
Me gusta más bañarme que ducharme.
I prefer having a bath to having a shower.
2 **to go for a swim**
Estuve en la playa pero no me bañé.
I went to the beach but I didn't go for a swim.

la **bañera** NOUN
bath

el **baño** NOUN
1 **bathroom**
La casa tiene dos baños.
The house has two bathrooms.
darse un baño
to have a bath/to go for a swim

LANGUAGE TIP
darse un baño has two meanings. It can be translated by **to have a bath** or **to go for a swim**.

---

2 **toilet**
¿Puedo usar el baño, por favor?
Can I use the toilet, please?

el **bar** NOUN
bar

la **baraja** NOUN
pack of cards

barato

---
barato can be an adjective or an adverb.

A ADJECTIVE (FEM **barata**)
cheap

Esta marca es más barata que aquélla.
This brand is cheaper than that one.
B ADVERB
cheaply
Aquí se come muy barato.
You can eat really cheaply here.

la **barba** NOUN
beard
dejarse barba
to grow a beard

la **barbaridad** NOUN
1 **atrocity**
Hicieron barbaridades en la guerra.
They committed atrocities during the war.
2 **Pablo come una barbaridad.**
Pablo eats an awful lot.

la **barbilla** NOUN
chin

la **barca** NOUN
boat

el **barco** NOUN
1 **ship**

2 **boat**
un barco de vela
a sailing boat

la **barra** NOUN
bar
una barra metálica
a metal bar
Tomamos un batido en la barra.
We had a smoothie at the bar.
una barra de pan
a French stick
una barra de labios
a lipstick

barrer VERB
to sweep

la **barrera** NOUN
barrier

la **barriga** NOUN
belly
Estás echando barriga.
You're getting a bit of a belly.
Me duele la barriga.
I've got a stomachache.

el **barrio** NOUN
area
Ese chico no es del barrio.
That boy's not from this area.

el **barro** NOUN
mud
Me llené los zapatos de barro.
My shoes got covered in mud.

el **barullo** NOUN
racket
armar barullo
to make a racket

la **báscula** NOUN
scales

la **base** NOUN
base
la base de la columna
the base of the column

básico (FEM **básica**) ADJECTIVE
basic

bastante

> **bastante** can be an adjective or an adverb.

A ADJECTIVE (FEM **bastante**)
1 enough
No tengo bastante dinero.
I haven't got enough money.
Ya hay bastantes libros en casa.
There are enough books in the house.
2 quite a lot of
Vino bastante gente.
Quite a lot of people came.

Se tarda bastante tiempo en llegar.
It takes quite a while to get there.
B ADVERB
quite
Son bastante ricos.
They are quite rich.

bastar VERB
to be enough
Con esto basta.
That's enough.
¡Basta ya de tonterías!
That's enough of your nonsense!

> **¡Basta!**
> That's enough!

la **basura** NOUN
1 rubbish
Eso es basura.
That's rubbish.
tirar algo a la basura
to put something in the bin
2 litter

el **basurero** NOUN
dustman

la **bata** NOUN
overall

la **batalla** NOUN
battle

batería

> **batería** can be a feminine or masculine noun.

A FEM NOUN
1 battery
Se ha agotado la batería.
The battery is flat.
2 drums
¿Tocas la batería?
Do you play the drums?
B MASC/FEM NOUN
drummer

el **batido** NOUN
1 milkshake

English / **Spanish**

un batido de fresa
a strawberry milkshake
2 smoothie

batir VERB
1 **to break**
2 **to beat**

el **baúl** NOUN
1 **chest**
2 **trunk**

el **bautizo** NOUN
christening

beber VERB
to drink
> **Hay que beber mucha agua en verano.**
> You need to drink a lot of water in the summer.

la **bebida** NOUN
drink
> **bebidas alcohólicas**
> alcoholic drinks

la **beca** NOUN
1 **grant**
2 **scholarship**

el **beicon** NOUN
bacon

la **belleza** NOUN
beauty

bello (FEM **bella**) ADJECTIVE
beautiful

bendecir VERB
to bless

la **bendición** (PL las **bendiciones**) NOUN
blessing

las **bermudas** NOUN
Bermuda shorts
> **Le compré unas bermudas.**
> I bought him a pair of Bermuda shorts.

besar VERB
to kiss
> **Ana y Pepe se besaron.**
> Ana and Pepe kissed each other.

el **beso** NOUN
kiss
> **Dame un beso.**
> Give me a kiss.

> **besos**
> love

DID YOU KNOW...?
Did you know that Spanish speakers sometimes end emails, postcards and letters to friends with **un beso** (a kiss) or **besos** (kisses)?

la **bestia** NOUN
beast

la **Biblia** NOUN
Bible

la **biblioteca** NOUN
library

el **bicho** NOUN
insect
> **Me ha picado un bicho.**
> I've been bitten by an insect.
> **David es un bicho raro.**
> (*informal*) David's weird.

la **bici** NOUN
(*informal*)
bike

la **bicicleta** NOUN
bicycle
> **una bicicleta de montaña**
> a mountain bike

bien

> **bien** can be an adverb or a noun.

A ADVERB

1 well
Habla bien el español.
He speaks Spanish well.

2 good
Huele bien.
It smells good.
Lo pasamos muy bien.
We had a very good time.
Ese libro está muy bien.
That's a very good book.
¡Está bien! Lo haré.
OK! I'll do it.

3 very
un café bien caliente
a very hot coffee
Has contestado bien.
You gave the right answer.
Hiciste bien en decírselo.
You were right to tell him.

¡Qué bien!
Excellent!

B MASC NOUN
good
Lo digo por tu bien.
I'm telling you for your own good.
los bienes
possessions
todos los bienes de la familia
all the family's possessions

la **bienvenida** NOUN
dar la bienvenida a alguien
to welcome somebody
una fiesta de bienvenida
a welcome party

bienvenido (FEM **bienvenida**)

bienvenido can be an adjective or an exclamation.

A ADJECTIVE
welcome
Siempre serás bienvenido aquí.
You will always be welcome here.

B EXCLAMATION
welcome!

el **bigote** NOUN
moustache

el **bikini** NOUN
bikini

bilingüe (FEM **bilingüe**) ADJECTIVE
bilingual

el **billar** NOUN
billiards
el billar americano
pool

el **billete** NOUN

1 ticket
un billete de metro
an underground ticket
un billete de ida y vuelta
a return ticket

2 note
un billete de veinte euros
a twenty-euro note

el **billón** (PL los **billones**) NOUN
un billón
a million millions

LANGUAGE TIP
Be careful! **billón** does not mean **billion**.

biodegradable (FEM **biodegradable**)
ADJECTIVE
biodegradable

la **biografía** NOUN
biography

la **biología** NOUN
biology

biológico (FEM **biológica**) ADJECTIVE
1 organic
2 biological

el **biquini** NOUN
bikini

la **bisabuela** NOUN
great-grandmother

el **bisabuelo** NOUN
great-grandfather
mis bisabuelos
my great-grandparents

English

Spanish

a
b
c
d
e
f
g
h
i
j
k
l
m
n
o
p
q
r
s
t
u
v
w
x
y
z

el **bistec** (PL los **bistecs**) NOUN
steak

bizco (FEM **bizca**) ADJECTIVE
cross-eyed

el **bizcocho** NOUN
sponge cake

blanco

> **blanco** can be an adjective or a noun.

A ADJECTIVE (FEM **blanca**)
white
un vestido blanco
a white dress

B MASC NOUN
white
Me gusta el blanco.
I like white.
Me quedé en blanco.
My mind went blank.

blando (FEM **blanda**) ADJECTIVE
soft
Este colchón es muy blando.
This mattress is very soft.

el **bloc** (PL los **blocs**) NOUN
writing pad
un bloc de dibujo
a drawing pad

el **blog** NOUN
blog

el **bloguero**
la **bloguera** NOUN
blogger
Es una joven bloguera con muchos seguidores.
She is a young blogger who has a lot of followers.

el **bloque** NOUN
block
un bloque de pisos
a block of flats

bloquear VERB
to block
La nieve bloqueó las carreteras.
The snow blocked the roads.

la **blusa** NOUN
blouse

la **bobada** NOUN
Este programa es una bobada.
This programme is stupid.

decir bobadas
to talk nonsense

bobo (FEM **boba**) ADJECTIVE
silly

la **boca** NOUN
mouth
No debes hablar con la boca llena.
You shouldn't talk with your mouth full.
No abrió la boca en toda la tarde.
He didn't open his mouth all afternoon.
Me quedé con la boca abierta.
I was speechless.

boca abajo
face down
boca arriba
face up

el **bocadillo** NOUN
baguette sandwich

DID YOU KNOW...?
In Spain, a **bocadillo** is usually made with a baguette.

el **bocado** NOUN
bite
Dame un bocado de tu pizza.
Let me have a bite of your pizza.
No he probado bocado desde ayer.
I haven't had a bite to eat since yesterday.

el **bocata** NOUN (*informal*)
baguette sandwich
un bocata de queso
a cheese sandwich

DID YOU KNOW...?
In Spain, a **bocata** is usually made with a baguette.

la **boda** NOUN
wedding

la **bofetada** NOUN
slap
> **Le dio una bofetada.**
> She slapped him.

la **bola** NOUN
1 ball
> **una bola de nieve**
> a snowball
2 scoop

el **boli** NOUN (*informal*)
pen

el **bolígrafo** NOUN
pen

el **bollo** NOUN
bun
> **Me he comido un bollo para desayunar.**
> I had a bun for breakfast.

los **bolos** NOUN
tenpin bowling

la **bolsa** NOUN
bag
> **una bolsa de plástico**
> a plastic bag

el **bolsillo** NOUN
pocket
> **Sacó las llaves del bolsillo.**
> He took the keys out of his pocket.
> **un libro de bolsillo**
> a paperback

el **bolso** NOUN
bag

la **bomba** NOUN
bomb

la **bombera** NOUN
firefighter

el **bombero** NOUN
firefighter

la **bombilla** NOUN
lightbulb

el **bombón** (PL los **bombones**) NOUN
chocolate

la **bombona** NOUN
gas cylinder

bonito (FEM **bonita**) ADJECTIVE
pretty
> **una casa muy bonita**
> a very pretty house

el **borde** NOUN
edge
> **al borde de la mesa**
> at the edge of the table

borracho (FEM **borracha**) ADJECTIVE
drunk
> **Estaba borracho.**
> He was drunk.

el **borrador** NOUN
1 duster
> **Usó un trapo como borrador.**
> He used a rag as a duster.
2 rough draft
> **Escribe primero un borrador.**
> First write a rough draft.

borrar VERB
1 to rub out
> **Borra toda la palabra.**
> Rub out the whole word.
2 to clean
> **Borra la pizarra.**
> Clean the board.
▪ **borrarse de**

LANGUAGE TIP
borrarse de has two meanings.
Look at the examples.

Voy a borrarme de la lista.
I'm going to take my name off the list.
Se borró del club.
He left the club.

el **bosque** NOUN
1 wood
2 forest

A B C D E F G H I J K L M N O P Q R S T U V W X Y Z

bostezar VERB
to yawn

la **bota** NOUN
boot

botar VERB
to bounce
   Esta pelota no bota.
   This ball doesn't bounce.

el **bote** NOUN
   1 **boat**
   un bote salvavidas
   a lifeboat
   2 **jar**

   pegar un bote
   to jump

la **botella** NOUN
bottle

el **botón** (PL los **botones**) NOUN
button
   He perdido un botón de la camisa.
   I've lost a button off my shirt.
   pulsar un botón
   to press a button

boxear VERB
to box

el **boxeo** NOUN
boxing

las **bragas** NOUN
knickers
   unas bragas
   a pair of knickers

la **bragueta** NOUN
fly (*of trousers*)

bravo EXCLAMATION
well done!

la **braza** NOUN
breaststroke
   nadar a braza
   to do the breaststroke

el **brazo** NOUN
arm
   Me duele el brazo.
   My arm hurts.
   Estaba sentada con los brazos cruzados.
   She was sitting with her arms folded.

breve (FEM **breve**) ADJECTIVE
short
   un relato breve
   a short story

brillante

   brillante can be an adjective or a noun.

   A ADJECTIVE (FEM **brillante**)
   shiny
   Tenía el pelo brillante.
   Her hair was shiny.
   B MASC NOUN
   diamond

brillar VERB
   1 **to shine**
   Hoy brilla el sol.
   The sun is shining today.
   2 **to sparkle**

el **brillo** NOUN
   1 **shine**
   2 **sparkle**

británico (FEM **británica**)

   británico can be an adjective or a noun.

   A ADJECTIVE
   British
   B MASC/FEM NOUN
   British person
   los británicos
   the British

la **brocha** NOUN
paintbrush

el **broche** NOUN
1 **clasp**
2 **brooch**

la **broma** NOUN
joke
Le gastamos una broma al profesor.
We played a joke on the teacher.
decir algo en broma
to say something as a joke
una broma pesada
a practical joke

bromear VERB
to joke

el/la **bromista** NOUN
joker

la **bronca** NOUN
1 **row**
Tuvieron una bronca muy gorda.
They had a huge row.
2 **fuss**

echar una bronca a alguien
to tell somebody off

el **bronce** NOUN
bronze

el **bronceado** NOUN
suntan

el **bronceador** NOUN
suntan lotion

la **bruja** NOUN
witch

el **brujo** NOUN
wizard

la **brújula** NOUN
compass

bruto (FEM **bruta**) ADJECTIVE
rough
¡No seas bruto!
Don't be so rough!

bucear VERB
to dive

buen ADJECTIVE ▷ *see* bueno

LANGUAGE TIP
When **bueno** goes in front of a masculine singular noun it is shortened to **buen**.

Es un buen hombre.
He's a good man.

bueno (FEM **buena**) ADJECTIVE
good
Es un buen libro.
It's a good book.
Hace buen tiempo.
The weather's good.
Es buena persona.
He's a good person.
un buen trozo
a good slice
ser bueno para
to be good for
Está muy bueno este bizcocho.
This sponge cake is lovely.
¡Buenos días!
Good morning!
¡Buenas tardes!
Good afternoon!/Good evening!
¡Buenas noches!
Good evening!/Good night!

LANGUAGE TIP
Did you know that the Spanish use **¡buenas tardes!** in the afternoon and early evening and **¡buenas noches!** when it starts to get dark as well as when they say good night?

¡Bueno!
OK!

la **bufanda** NOUN
scarf

el **búho** NOUN
owl

el **bulto** NOUN
lump
**Tengo un
bulto en
la frente.**
I have a lump
on my forehead.

la **burbuja** NOUN
bubble
un refresco sin burbujas
a still drink
un refresco con burbujas
a fizzy drink

la **burla** NOUN
Me hizo burla.
He made fun of me.

burlarse VERB
Siempre se burlan de mí.
They are always making fun of me.

la **burrada** NOUN (*informal*)
**Siempre andan haciendo
burradas.**
They're always messing around.

burro

> **burro** can be a noun or an adjective.

A MASC NOUN
1 donkey
2 idiot
Eres un burro.
You're an idiot.
B ADJECTIVE (FEM **burra**)
1 thick
2 rough

el **buscador** NOUN
search engine

buscar VERB
1 to look for
Estoy buscando las gafas.
I'm looking for my glasses.
2 to pick up
**Mi madre siempre me viene a
buscar al colegio en coche.**
My mother always picks me up from
school in the car.
3 to look up
**Busca la palabra en el
diccionario.**
Look the word up in the dictionary.
Él se lo ha buscado.
He was asking for it.

la **búsqueda** NOUN
search

la **butaca** NOUN
armchair

el **buzo** NOUN
diver

el **buzón** (PL los **buzones**) NOUN
1 letterbox

DID YOU KNOW...?
Spanish **letterboxes** tend to be
individual boxes in which the postman
leaves any mail rather than the hole in
the door that is common in the UK.

---

2 postbox
echar una carta al buzón
to post a letter
buzón de voz
voice mail

A B C D E F G H I J K L M N O P Q R S T U V W X Y Z

C c

el **caballo** NOUN
horse
¿Te gusta montar a caballo?
Do you like horseriding?

el **cabello** NOUN
hair

caber VERB
to fit
No cabe en mi armario.
It won't fit in my cupboard.
No cabe nadie más.
There's no room for anyone else.

la **cabeza** NOUN
head
Se rascó la cabeza.
He scratched his head.

la **cabina** NOUN
phone box

el **cable** NOUN
cable

la **cabra** NOUN
goat

cabrá VERB
▷ see **caber**
No sé si cabrá.
I don't know
whether it will fit.

el **cachorro**
la **cachorra** NOUN
1 puppy

2 cub

---

cada (FEM **cada**) ADJECTIVE
1 each
Cada libro es de un color distinto.
Each book is a different colour.
cada uno
each one
2 every
cada año
every year
cada vez que la veo
every time I see her
Viene cada vez más gente.
More and more people are coming.
Viene cada vez menos.
He comes less and less often.
Cada vez hace más frío.
It's getting colder and colder.

la **cadena** NOUN
1 chain
una cadena de oro
a gold chain
2 channel
Por la cadena tres ponen una película.
There's a film on channel three.

tirar de la cadena
to flush the toilet

caer VERB
1 to fall
¡Cuidado que vas a caer!
Careful or you'll fall!
2 Su hermano me cae muy bien.
I really like his brother.
Nadia me cae muy mal.
I can't stand Nadia.
■ **caerse**
1 to fall
Tropecé y me caí.
I tripped and fell.
2 Se me cayeron las monedas.
I dropped the coins.

el **café** (PL los **cafés**) NOUN
1 coffee
un café con leche
a white coffee
2 café

caigo VERB ▷ *see* **caer**
¡Ahora caigo!
Now I remember!

la **caja** NOUN
1 **box**
una caja de zapatos
a shoe box
2 **checkout**

el **cajón** (PL los **cajones**) NOUN
drawer

el **calcetín** (PL los **calcetines**)
NOUN
sock

la **calculadora** NOUN
calculator

la **calefacción** NOUN
heating
calefacción central
central heating

el **calendario** NOUN
calendar

el **calentamiento** NOUN
el calentamiento global
global warming
ejercicios de calentamiento
warm-up exercises

calentar VERB
1 **to heat up**
¿Quieres que te caliente la leche?
Do you want me to heat up the milk for you?
2 **to warm up**
■ **calentarse**
1 **to heat up**
Espera a que se caliente el agua.
Wait for the water to heat up.
2 **to warm up**
Deja que se caliente el motor.
Let the engine warm up.

caliente (FEM **caliente**) ADJECTIVE
hot
Esta sopa está muy caliente.
This soup is very hot.

la **calificación** (PL las **calificaciones**)
NOUN
mark
Obtuvo buenas calificaciones.
He got good marks.
boletín de calificaciones
school report

callado (FEM **callada**) ADJECTIVE
quiet
una persona muy callada
a very quiet person

callar VERB
to be quiet
Calla, que no me dejas concentrarme.
Be quiet, I can't concentrate.
■ **callarse**
1 **to stop talking**
Al entrar el profesor, todos se callaron.
When the teacher came in, everyone stopped talking.
2 **to keep quiet**
Prefirió callarse.
He preferred to keep quiet.

la **calle** NOUN
street
Viven en la calle Peñalver, 13.
They live at number 13, Peñalver Street.
Hoy no he salido a la calle.
I haven't been out today.

calmar VERB
to calm down
Intenté calmarla un poco.
I tried to calm her down a little.
■ **calmarse**
to calm down
¡Cálmate!
Calm down!

el **calor** NOUN
heat
No se puede trabajar con este calor.
It's impossible to work in this heat.

Hace calor.
It's hot.

Tengo calor.
I'm hot.

los **calzoncillos** NOUN
underpants
unos calzoncillos
a pair of underpants

la **cama** NOUN
bed
Está en la cama.
He's in bed.

hacer la cama
to make the bed
irse a la cama
to go to bed

la **cámara** NOUN
camera
la cámara del móvil
the phone camera

la **camarera** NOUN
waitress

el **camarero** NOUN
waiter

cambiar VERB
1 to change
No has cambiado nada.
You haven't changed a bit.
2 to swap
Me gusta el tuyo, te lo cambio.
I like yours, let's swap.
■ **cambiarse**
to get changed
Voy a cambiarme.
I'm going to get changed.

cambiar de idea
to change one's mind

el **cambio** NOUN
change
un cambio brusco de temperatura
a sudden change in temperature
¿Tiene cambio de veinte euros?
Have you got change of twenty euros?

caminar VERB
to walk

el **camino** NOUN
1 path
2 way
¿Sabes el camino a su casa?
Do you know the way to his house?
El parque nos pilla de camino.
The park is on our way.

el **camión** (PL los **camiones**) NOUN
lorry

la **camisa** NOUN
shirt

la **camiseta** NOUN
1 T-shirt
2 vest
3 shirt

el **campamento** NOUN
camp
un campamento de verano
a summer camp

la **campana** NOUN
bell

English

Spanish

A
B
C
D
E
F
G
H
I
J
K
L
M
N
O
P
Q
R
S
T
U
V
W
X
Y
Z

el **campeón**
la **campeona** NOUN
champion

el **camping** (PL los **campings**) NOUN
1 **camping**
Fuimos de camping este verano.
We went camping this summer.
2 **campsite**
Estamos en un camping.
We're at a campsite.

el **campo** NOUN
1 **country**
Prefiero vivir en el campo.
I prefer living in the country.
2 **pitch**
un campo de fútbol
a football pitch

el **canal** NOUN
1 **channel**
Por el canal dos ponen una película.
They're showing a film on channel two.
2 **channel**
el Canal de la Mancha
the English Channel

la **canción**
(PL las **canciones**)
NOUN
song

el **cangrejo** NOUN
crab

cansado
(FEM **cansada**)
ADJECTIVE
tired
Estoy muy cansado.
I'm very tired.
Estoy cansado de hacer lo mismo todos los días.
I'm tired of doing the same thing every day.

cansarse VERB
to get tired
Está muy débil y enseguida se cansa.
He is very weak and gets tired quickly.
Me cansé de esperarlo y me marché.
I got tired of waiting for him and I left.

el/la **cantante** NOUN
singer

cantar VERB
to sing

la **cantidad** NOUN
1 **quantity**
La calidad es más importante que la cantidad.
Quality is more important than quantity.
¡Qué cantidad de gente!
What a lot of people!
2 **amount**
una cierta cantidad de dinero
a certain amount of money

la **capa** NOUN
layer
la capa de ozono
the ozone layer

el **capitán**
la **capitana** NOUN
captain

el **capítulo** NOUN
chapter

la **capucha** NOUN
hood

la **cara** NOUN
1 face
Tiene la cara alargada.
He has a long face.
Tienes mala cara.
You don't look well.
No pongas esa cara.
Don't look like that.
2 cheek
¡Qué cara!
What a cheek!
3 side
un folio escrito por las dos caras
a sheet written on both sides

¿Cara o cruz?
Heads or tails?

el **caramelo** NOUN
sweet

la **carga** NOUN
refill

cargar VERB
1 to load
Cargaron el coche de maletas.
They loaded the car with suitcases.
2 to charge

las **caries** (PL las **caries**) NOUN
1 tooth decay
2 cavity

cariñoso (FEM **cariñosa**) ADJECTIVE
affectionate
Es muy cariñosa con los niños.
She is very affectionate towards the
children.

la **carne** NOUN
meat
No como carne.
I don't eat meat.
carne de cerdo
pork

carne picada
mince
carne de ternera
veal
carne de vaca
beef

el **carnet** (PL los **carnets**) NOUN
card
el carnet de identidad
identity card
un carnet de conducir
a driving licence

caro
A ADJECTIVE (FEM **cara**)
expensive
B ADVERB
expensive
Aquí cuesta todo muy caro.
Everything is very expensive here.

la **carpeta** NOUN
folder

la **carrera** NOUN
race

una carrera de caballos
a horse race

la **carretera** NOUN
road

el **carrito** NOUN
trolley

el **carro** NOUN
1 cart
2 trolley

English

Spanish

A
B
C
D
E
F
G
H
I
J
K
L
M
N
O
P
Q
R
S
T
U
V
W
X
Y
Z

54

la **carta** NOUN
  1 letter
    Le he escrito una carta a Juan.
    I've written Juan a letter.

  2 card
    jugar a las cartas
    to play cards

el **cartel** NOUN
  1 poster
  2 sign

la **cartera** NOUN
  1 satchel
  2 wallet
  3 postwoman

el **cartero** NOUN
  postman

el **cartón** (PL los **cartones**) NOUN
  cardboard
    una caja de cartón
    a cardboard box

el **cartucho** NOUN
  cartridge

la **cartulina** NOUN
  card

la **casa** NOUN
  1 house
  2 home
    Estábamos en casa.
    We were at home.
    Nos vamos a casa.
    We're going home.

Estábamos en casa de Juan.
We were at Juan's.

casado (FEM **casada**) ADJECTIVE
  married
    una mujer casada
    a married woman
    Está casado con una francesa.
    He's married to a French woman.

casarse VERB
  to get married
    Quieren casarse.
    They want to get married.

la **cascada** NOUN
  waterfall

la **cáscara** NOUN
  1 shell
  2 skin

casi ADVERB
  almost
    Casi me ahogo.
    I almost drowned.
    Son casi las cinco.
    It's nearly five o'clock.
    Casi no comí.
    I hardly ate.

la **casilla** NOUN
  box

el **caso** NOUN
  case
    En casos así es mejor callarse.
    In such cases it's better to keep quiet.
    El caso es que no me queda dinero.
    The thing is, I haven't got any money left.
    No le hagas caso.
    Don't take any notice of him.

la **caspa** NOUN
  dandruff

la **castaña** NOUN
  chestnut

castaño (FEM **castaña**) ADJECTIVE
  brown
    Mi hermana tiene el pelo castaño.
    My sister has brown hair.

castigar VERB
to punish
Mi padre me castigó por contestarle.
My father punished me for answering him back.

el **castigo** NOUN
punishment
Tuve que escribirlo diez veces, como castigo.
I had to write it out ten times, as punishment.

el **castillo** NOUN
castle

un castillo de arena
a sandcastle

la **casualidad** NOUN
coincidence
¡Qué casualidad!
What a coincidence!
Nos encontramos por casualidad.
We met by chance.

el **catarro** NOUN
cold
Vas a pillar un catarro.
You're going to catch a cold.

la **catástrofe** NOUN
catastrophe

catorce (FEM **catorce**) ADJECTIVE, PRONOUN
fourteen

el catorce de enero
the fourteenth of January
Nació el catorce de enero.
He was born on the fourteenth of January.

la **causa** NOUN
cause
No se sabe la causa del accidente.
The cause of the accident is unknown.

a causa de
because of

causar VERB
to cause
La lluvia causó muchos daños.
The rain caused a lot of damage.

cayendo VERB ▷ see **caer**
Está cayendo nieve.
It's snowing.

la **cazadora** NOUN
jacket

la **cebolla** NOUN
onion

la **ceja** NOUN
eyebrow

celebrar VERB
to celebrate

el **celo** NOUN
Sellotape®

los **celos** NOUN
jealousy
Lo hizo por celos.
He did it out of jealousy.
Tiene celos de su mejor amiga.
She's jealous of her best friend.

celoso (FEM **celosa**) ADJECTIVE
jealous
Está celoso de su hermano.
He's jealous of his brother.

el **cemento** NOUN
cement

la **cena** NOUN
dinner
La cena es a las ocho.
Dinner is at eight o'clock.

cenar VERB
to have dinner
No he cenado.
I haven't had dinner.
¿Qué quieres cenar?
What do you want for dinner?

DID YOU KNOW...?
In Spain, people generally eat later than in the UK. Lunch is usually around two and people tend to have dinner around nine or ten.

---

el **cenicero** NOUN
ashtray

la **ceniza** NOUN
ash

centígrado (FEM **centígrada**)
ADJECTIVE
centigrade
veinte grados centígrados
twenty degrees centigrade

el **centímetro** NOUN
centimetre

el **céntimo** NOUN
cent

central (FEM **central**) ADJECTIVE
central

el **centro** NOUN
centre
un centro comercial
a shopping centre
Fui al centro a hacer unas compras.
I went into town to do some shopping.

cepillar VERB
to brush
Se está cepillando los dientes.
He's brushing his teeth.

el **cepillo** NOUN
brush
un cepillo de dientes
a toothbrush

la **cera** NOUN
wax

cerca ADVERB
near
El colegio está muy cerca.
The school is very near.
cerca de la iglesia
near the church
cerca de dos horas
nearly two hours
Quería verlo de cerca.
I wanted to see it close up.

el **cerdo** NOUN
1 pig
2 pork
No comemos cerdo.
We don't eat pork.

el **cereal** NOUN
cereal
Los niños desayunan cereales.
The children have cereal for breakfast.

el **cerebro** NOUN
brain

la **cerilla** NOUN
match
una caja de cerillas
a box of matches

el **cero** NOUN
zero
Estamos a cinco grados bajo cero.
It's five degrees below zero.
Van dos a cero.
The score is two-nil.
Tuve que empezar desde cero.
I had to start from scratch.

cerrado (FEM **cerrada**) ADJECTIVE
closed
Las tiendas están cerradas.
The shops are closed.

la **cerradura** NOUN
lock

cerrar VERB
1 **to close**
**No cierran
al mediodía.**
They don't close at lunchtime.
Cerró el libro.
He closed the book.
Cerré la puerta con llave.
I locked the door.
Se me cierran los ojos.
I can't keep my eyes open.
No puedo cerrar la maleta.
I can't shut this suitcase.
2 **to turn off**
Cierra el grifo.
Turn off the tap.

la **cerveza** NOUN
beer

el **césped** NOUN
grass
"no pisar el césped"
'keep off the grass'

el **chaleco** NOUN
waistcoat
un chaleco salvavidas
a life-jacket

el **chalet** (PL los **chalets**) NOUN
1 **house**
2 **cottage**

el **champú** (PL los **champús**) NOUN
shampoo

el **chándal** (PL los **chándals**) NOUN
tracksuit

la **chaqueta** NOUN
1 **cardigan**
2 **jacket**

charlar VERB
to chat

el **chat** NOUN
chatroom

la **chatarra** NOUN
scrap metal

la **chica** NOUN
1 **girl**
2 **girlfriend**
Fui al cine con mi chica.
I went to the cinema with my girlfriend.

el **chichón** (PL los **chichones**) NOUN
bump
**Me ha salido un chichón en la
frente.**
I've got a bump on my forehead.

el **chicle** NOUN
chewing gum

el **chico** NOUN
1 **boy**
**Fueron todos los chicos de la
clase.**
All the boys in the class went.
2 **boyfriend**
Iré con mi chico.
I'll go with my boyfriend.

chillar VERB
to scream

la **chimenea** NOUN
1 **chimney**
2 **fireplace**

la **chincheta** NOUN
drawing pin

el **chiste** NOUN
joke
El maestro nos contó un chiste.
The teacher told us a joke.

chocar VERB
1 **to bump**
Choqué contra una farola.
I bumped into a lamppost.
El coche chocó contra un árbol.
The car hit a tree.
2 **to crash**
Chocó contra un muro.
He crashed into a wall.

el **chocolate** NOUN
chocolate

el **chorizo** NOUN
chorizo

el chubasquero NOUN
cagoule

chulo (FEM **chula**) ADJECTIVE
1 **cocky** (*informal*)
2 **cool** (*informal*)
¡Qué mochila más chula!
What a cool rucksack!

chupar VERB
to suck
Se chupaba el dedo.
He was sucking his thumb.

los churros
PLURAL NOUN
long sweet fritters

DID YOU KNOW...?
churros are a kind of fritter that people often eat on the streets in a paper bag or order in a café typically with a cup of thick, hot chocolate: **chocolate con churros**.

---

el cíber NOUN
internet café

el cibercafé NOUN
internet café

el/la ciclista NOUN
cyclist

ciego (FEM **ciega**)

ciego can be an adjective or a noun.

A ADJECTIVE
blind
Mi abuelo es ciego.
My grandfather is blind.

quedarse ciego
to go blind

B MASC/FEM NOUN
un ciego
a blind man

una ciega
a blind woman

el cielo NOUN
sky
No había ni una nube en el cielo.
There wasn't a single cloud in the sky.

cien (FEM **cien**) ADJECTIVE, PRONOUN
a hundred
Había unos cien invitados en la boda.
There were about a hundred guests at the wedding.

cien mil
a hundred thousand
cien por cien
a hundred percent

la ciencia NOUN
science
Me gustan mucho las ciencias.
I really enjoy science.

ciento (FEM **ciento**) ADJECTIVE, PRONOUN
a hundred
ciento cuarenta y dos libras
a hundred and forty two pounds
Recibimos cientos de mensajes.
We received hundreds of messages.
el diez por ciento de la población
ten percent of the population

cierro VERB ▷ *see* **cerrar**
Cuando cierro al puerta hace un ruido extraño.
When I close the door it makes a funny noise.

cierto (FEM **cierta**) ADJECTIVE
true
No, eso no es cierto.
No, that's not true.

por cierto
by the way

Spanish ~ English (sidebar)

el **ciervo** NOUN
deer

la **cifra** NOUN
figure
    un número de cuatro cifras
    a four-figure number

el **cigarrillo** NOUN
cigarette

cinco (FEM **cinco**) ADJECTIVE, PRONOUN
five
    Tiene cinco años.
    He's five.

> **el cinco de enero**
> the fifth of January
> **Nació el cinco de enero.**
> He was born on the fifth of January.
> **Son las cinco.**
> It's five o'clock.

cincuenta (FEM **cincuenta**) ADJECTIVE, PRONOUN
fifty
    Tiene cincuenta años.
    He's fifty.

el **cine** NOUN
cinema
    Mañana voy al cine.
    I'm going to the cinema tomorrow.

la **cintura** NOUN
waist
    Dóblate por la cintura.
    Bend at the waist.

el **cinturón** (PL los **cinturones**) NOUN
belt
    el cinturón de seguridad
    the safety belt

el **circo** NOUN
circus

el **círculo** NOUN
circle
    Dibuja un círculo.
    Draw a circle.

el **cisne** NOUN
swan

la **cita** NOUN
  1 date
    No llegues tarde a la cita.
    Don't be late for your date.
  2 appointment
    Tengo cita con el médico.
    I've got a doctor's appointment.

la **ciudad** NOUN
  1 city
  2 town

la **clara** NOUN
white

claro

> **claro** can be an adjective or an
> adverb.

A ADJECTIVE (FEM **clara**)
  1 clear
    Lo quiero mañana. ¿Está claro?
    I want it tomorrow. Is that clear?
    Está claro que esconden algo.
    It's obvious that they are hiding
    something.
  2 light
    una camisa azul claro
    a light blue shirt
B ADVERB
  clearly
    Lo oí muy claro.
    I heard it very clearly.
    ¡Claro!
    Of course!
    ¿Te oyó? — ¡Claro que me oyó!
    Did he hear you? — Of course he
    heard me!

la **clase** NOUN
  1 class
    A las diez tengo clase de física.
    I have a physics class at ten.
    **Mi hermana da clases de
    inglés.**
    My sister teaches English.

English

Spanish

a
b
c
d
e
f
g
h
i
j
k
l
m
n
o
p
q
r
s
t
u
v
w
x
y
z

Hoy no hay clase.
There's no school today.
clases particulares
private lessons
2 **classroom**
3 **kind**
Había juguetes de todas clases.
There were all kinds of toys.

clásico (FEM **clásica**) ADJECTIVE
classical
Me gusta la música clásica.
I like classical music.

clasificar VERB
to classify
■ **clasificarse**
to qualify
Esperan clasificarse para la final.
They hope to qualify for the final.
Se clasificaron en tercer lugar.
They came third.

la **clave** NOUN
code
un mensaje en clave
a coded message

el **clic** NOUN
click
hacer clic en algo
to click on something

el **clima** NOUN
climate
Es un país de clima tropical.
It's a country with a tropical climate.

la **clínica** NOUN
hospital

el **clip** (PL los **clips**) NOUN
paper clip

cobarde (FEM **cobarde**) ADJECTIVE
cowardly
¡No seas cobarde!
Don't be such a coward!

el **coche** NOUN
car

Fuimos a Sevilla en coche.
We went to Seville by car.
un coche de carreras
a racing car
los coches de choque
the bumper cars
un coche de bomberos
a fire engine

la **cocina** NOUN
1 **kitchen**
Comemos en la cocina.
We eat in the kitchen.
2 **cooker**
una cocina de gas
a gas cooker
3 **cookery**
un libro de cocina
a cookery book
la cocina vasca
Basque cuisine

cocinar VERB
to cook
No sabe cocinar.
He can't cook.
Cocinas muy bien.
You're a very good cook.

el **codo** NOUN
elbow

coger VERB
1 **to take**
Coge el que más te guste.
Take the one you like best.
Voy a coger el autobús.
I'm going to get the bus.

2 to catch
¡Coge la pelota!
Catch the ball!
La cogieron robando.
They caught her stealing.
He cogido un resfriado.
I've caught a cold.

el **cohete** NOUN
rocket

el **cojín**
(PL los **cojines**)
NOUN
cushion

cojo

> **cojo** can be an adjective or part of the verb **coger**.

A ADJECTIVE (FEM **coja**)
Es algo cojo.
He has a bit of a limp.
B VERB ▷ *see* **coger**
¡Si te cojo!
If I catch you!

la **cola** NOUN
1 tail
2 queue
Había mucha cola para el baño.
There was a long queue for the toilets.
3 glue

hacer cola
to queue

colarse VERB
to push in
No te cueles.
Don't push in.
Nos colamos en el cine.
We sneaked into the cinema without paying.

el/la **colega** NOUN
1 mate
2 colleague

el **colegio** NOUN
school
¿Todavía vas al colegio?
Are you still at school?
un colegio público
a state school

colgar VERB
1 to hang
Colguemos el cuadro en esta pared.
Let's hang the picture on this wall.
¡No dejes la chaqueta en la silla, cuélgala!
Don't leave your jacket on the chair, hang it up!
2 to hang up
¡No cuelgues!
Don't hang up!
Me colgó el teléfono.
He hung up on me.

el **collar** NOUN
1 necklace
2 collar

el **colmo** NOUN
¡Esto ya es el colmo!
This really is the last straw!

colocar VERB
to put
Colocamos la mesa en medio del comedor.
We put the table in the middle of the dining room.

la **colonia** NOUN
perfume
¿Qué colonia llevas?
What perfume are you wearing?

una colonia de verano
a summer camp

el **color** NOUN
colour

a
b
c
d
e
f
g
h
i
j
k
l
m
n
o
p
q
r
s
t
u
v
w
x
y
z

A
B
C
D
E
F
G
H
I
J
K
L
M
N
O
P
Q
R
S
T
U
V
W
X
Y
Z

¿De qué color son?
What colour are they?
un vestido de color azul
a blue dress

la **columna** NOUN
column

el **columpio** NOUN
swing

la **coma** NOUN
comma
Separa las palabras con una coma.
Separate the words with a comma.
cero coma ocho
zero point eight

DID YOU KNOW...?
In Spanish you use a comma instead of a point in decimal numbers.

---

la **comba** NOUN
skipping rope

> **saltar a la comba**
> to skip

el **comedor** NOUN
1 **dining room**
2 **canteen**

comenzar VERB
to begin
Comenzó a llover.
It began to rain.

comer VERB
1 **to eat**
¿Quieres comer algo?
Do you want something to eat?
Le estaba dando de comer a su hijo.
She was feeding her son.
2 **to have lunch**
Comimos en el hotel.
We had lunch in the hotel.
Hemos comido paella.
We had paella for lunch.
¿Qué hay para comer?
What's for lunch?

DID YOU KNOW...?
In Spain, people generally eat later than in the UK. Lunch is usually around two and people tend to have dinner around nine or ten.

cometa

> **cometa** can be a masculine or a feminine noun.

A MASC NOUN
comet
B FEM NOUN
kite

el **cómic** NOUN
comic

la **comida** NOUN
1 **food**
La comida del hotel es muy buena.
The food in the hotel is very good.
2 **lunch**
La comida es a la una y media.
Lunch is at half past one.

DID YOU KNOW...?
In Spain, people generally eat later than in the UK. Lunch is usually around two and people tend to have dinner around nine or ten.

---

3 **meal**
Es la comida más importante del día.
It's the most important meal of the day.

comienzo VERB ▷ see **comenzar**
Yo comienzo y después tú me sigues.
I go first and then you follow me.

como ADVERB, CONJUNCTION
1 **like**
Tienen un perro como el nuestro.
They've got a dog like ours.
blanco como la nieve
as white as snow
Es tan alto como tú.
He is as tall as you.
2 **as**
Como ella no llegaba, me fui.
As she didn't arrive, I left.
Lo usé como cuchara.
I used it as a spoon.
3 **if**
Como lo vuelvas a hacer se lo digo a tu madre.
If you do it again, I'll tell your mother.
4 **about**
Vinieron como unas diez personas.
About ten people came.
como si
as if
Siguió leyendo, como si no hubiera oído nada.
He kept on reading, as if he had heard nothing.

cómo ADVERB
how
¿Cómo se dice en inglés?
How do you say it in English?
¿Cómo están tus padres?
How are your parents?
¿Cómo es de grande?
How big is it?
¿Cómo es el clima?
What's the weather like?
Perdón, ¿cómo has dicho?
Sorry, what did you say?
¡Cómo! ¿Mañana?
What? Tomorrow?

cómodo (FEM **cómoda**) ADJECTIVE
comfortable
un sillón cómodo
a comfortable chair

el **compañero**
la **compañera** NOUN
1 **classmate**
2 **workmate**
3 **partner**

la **compañía** NOUN
company
Amanda vino a hacerme compañía.
Amanda came to keep me company.

comparar VERB
to compare
Siempre me comparan con mi hermana.
I'm always being compared to my sister.

compartir VERB
to share

el **compás** (PL los **compases**) NOUN
compass

la **competición** (PL las **competiciones**) NOUN
competition

el **complejo** NOUN
complex
Tiene complejo porque está gordo.
He's got a complex about being fat.
un complejo deportivo
a sports complex

completo (FEM **completa**) ADJECTIVE
full
Los hoteles estaban completos.
The hotels were full.
Me olvidé por completo.
I completely forgot.

complicado (FEM **complicada**) ADJECTIVE
complicated

la **compra** NOUN
shopping

> **ir de compras**
> to go shopping

comprar VERB
to buy
  Quiero comprarme unos zapatos.
  I want to buy a pair of shoes.

comprender VERB
to understand
  ¡No lo comprendo!
  I don't understand it!

común (FEM **común**) ADJECTIVE
common
  un apellido muy común
  a very common surname
  No tenemos nada en común.
  We have nothing in common.
  Hicimos el trabajo en común.
  We did the work between us.

la **comunidad** NOUN
community

con PREPOSITION
with
  Vivo con mis padres.
  I live with my parents.
  ¿Con quién vas a ir?
  Who are you going with?
  Lo he escrito con bolígrafo.
  I wrote it in pen.
  Voy a hablar con Hasim.
  I'll talk to Hasim.
  con tal de que no llegues tarde
  as long as you don't arrive late

la **concha** NOUN
shell

el **concurso** NOUN
competition

la **condición** (PL las **condiciones**)
NOUN
condition
  a condición de que apruebes
  on condition that you pass

**El piso está en muy malas
condiciones.**
The flat is in a very bad state.
No está en condiciones de viajar.
He's not fit to travel.

conducir VERB
to drive

  Mi hermano no sabe conducir.
  My brother can't drive.

el **conductor**
la **conductora** NOUN
driver

conduzco VERB ▷ *see* conducir
  **Siempre tengo mucho cuidado
  cuando conduzco.**
  I'm always very careful when I'm
  driving.

el **conejo** NOUN
rabbit

la **conferencia**
NOUN
lecture

confesar VERB
to admit
  Confesó que había sido él.
  He admitted that it had been him.

la **confianza** NOUN
trust
  Tengo confianza en ti.
  I trust you.
  No tiene confianza en sí mismo.
  He has no self-confidence.

confiar VERB
to trust
  No confío en ella.
  I don't trust her.

confieso VERB ▷ *see* **confesar**
 Confieso que estaba equivocado.
 I admit I was wrong.

la **configuración** NOUN
 settings
 He cambiado la configuración de mi móvil.
 I have changed my phone settings.

conformarse VERB
 conformarse con
 to make do with
 Tendrás que conformarte con uno más barato.
 You'll have to make do with a cheaper one.

confundir VERB
 1 **to mistake**
 La gente me confunde con mi hermana.
 People mistake me for my sister.
 2 **to confuse**
 Su explicación me confundió todavía más.
 His explanation confused me even more.
 Confundí las fechas.
 I got the dates mixed up.

congelado (FEM **congelada**) ADJECTIVE
 frozen

el **congelador** NOUN
 freezer

congelar VERB
 to freeze
 Me estoy congelando.
 I'm freezing.

el **conjunto** NOUN
 group
 un conjunto de música pop
 a pop group

conmigo PRONOUN
 with me
 ¿Por qué no vienes conmigo?
 Why don't you come with me?
 Lidia quiere hablar conmigo.
 Lidia wants to talk to me.

No estoy satisfecho conmigo mismo.
 I'm not proud of myself.

conocer VERB
 1 **to know**
 Conozco a todos sus hermanos.
 I know all his brothers.
 Nos conocemos desde el colegio.
 We know each other from school.
 2 **to meet**
 La conocí en una fiesta.
 I met her at a party.

conocido (FEM **conocida**) ADJECTIVE
 well-known
 un actor muy conocido
 a well-known actor

el **conocimiento** NOUN
 consciousness
 perder el conocimiento
 to lose consciousness

conozco VERB ▷ *see* **conocer**
 No la conozco.
 I don't know her.

conseguir VERB
 to get
 Él me consiguió la entrada.
 He got me the ticket.

el **consejo** NOUN
 advice
 ¿Quieres que te dé un consejo?
 Would you like me to give you some advice?

consigo

 consigo can be a pronoun or part of the verb **conseguir**.

A PRONOUN
 1 **with him**
 Se llevó a Laura consigo.
 He took Laura with him.
 2 **with her**
 3 **with you**
B VERB ▷ *see* **conseguir**
 No consigo olvidarme de lo que pasó.
 I can't forget what happened.

constipado

> **constipado** can be and adjective or a noun.

A ADJECTIVE (FEM **constipada**)
estar constipado
to have a cold

B MASC NOUN
cold
coger un constipado
to catch a cold

LANGUAGE TIP
Be careful! **constipado** does not mean **constipated**.

---

construir VERB
to build

la **consulta** NOUN
surgery
horas de consulta
surgery hours

consultar VERB
to consult
Deberías consultar a un médico.
You should consult a doctor.
Tengo que consultarlo con mi familia.
I need to discuss it with my family.

contagioso (FEM **contagiosa**) ADJECTIVE
infectious

la **contaminación** NOUN
pollution
la contaminación del aire
air pollution

contar VERB
1 to count
Sabe contar hasta diez.
He can count to ten.

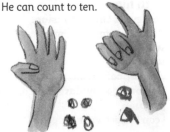

2 to tell
Les conté un cuento a los niños.
I told the children a story.
Cuéntame lo que pasó.
Tell me what happened.
Cuento contigo.
I'm counting on you.

el **contenido** NOUN
contents
el contenido de la maleta
the contents of the suitcase

contento (FEM **contenta**) ADJECTIVE
happy

Estaba contento porque era su cumpleaños.
He was happy because it was his birthday.
Estoy contento con la bici nueva.
I'm pleased with my new bike.

contestar VERB
to answer
Contesté a todas las preguntas.
I answered all the questions.
Me escribieron y tengo que contestarles.
They wrote to me and I have to reply to them.

contigo PRONOUN
with you
Quiero ir contigo.
I want to go with you.
Necesito hablar contigo.
I need to talk to you.

el **continente** NOUN
continent

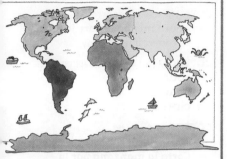

contra PREPOSITION
against
>**Eran dos contra uno.**
>They were two against one.
>**El domingo jugamos contra el Málaga.**
>We play against Málaga on Sunday.

contrario (FEM **contraria**) ADJECTIVE
1 **opposing**
2 **opposite**
>**Los dos coches iban en dirección contraria.**
>The two cars were travelling in opposite directions.
>**Ella opina lo contrario.**
>She thinks the opposite.
>**Al contrario, me gusta mucho.**
>On the contrary, I like it a lot.
>**De lo contrario, tendré que castigarte.**
>Otherwise, I will have to punish you.

la **contraseña** NOUN
password

el **control** NOUN
control
>**Nunca pierde el control.**
>He never loses control.

la **conversación** (PL las conversaciones) NOUN
conversation
>**Necesito clases de conversación.**
>I need conversation classes.

convertir VERB
to turn
>**Convirtieron la casa en colegio.**
>They turned the house into a school.
- **convertirse en**
to become/to turn into

___
LANGUAGE TIP
convertirse en has two meanings. Look at the examples.
___

>**Se convirtió en un hombre rico.**
>He became a rich man.
>**Se convirtió en una pesadilla.**
>It turned into a nightmare.

la **copa** NOUN
glass

la **copia** NOUN
copy
>**hacer una copia**
>to make a copy

copiar VERB
to copy
>**copiar y pegar**
>to copy and paste

el **corazón** (PL los **corazones**) NOUN
heart

el **cordón** (PL los **cordones**) NOUN
shoelace

la **corona** NOUN
crown

la **correa** NOUN
1 **lead**
2 **strap**

correcto (FEM **correcta**) ADJECTIVE
correct
>**Las respuestas eran correctas.**
>The answers were correct.

el **corredor**
la **corredora** NOUN
runner

corregir VERB
1 **to correct**
>**Corrígeme si me equivoco.**
>Correct me if I'm wrong.

2 to mark
El profesor corrigió los exámenes.
The teacher marked the exams.

el **correo** NOUN
post

Me lo mandó por correo.
He sent it to me by post.
Correos
the post office
correo electrónico
email

correr VERB
1 to run
Tuve que correr para coger el autobús.
I had to run to catch the bus.
2 to hurry
Corre que llegamos tarde.
Hurry or we'll be late.
3 to go fast
No corras tanto, que hay hielo en la carretera.
Don't go so fast, the road's icy.
4 to move
Córrete un poco hacia la izquierda.
Move a bit to the left.

corriente

> **corriente** can be an adjective or a noun.

A ADJECTIVE (FEM **corriente**)
common
Pérez es un apellido muy corriente.
Pérez is a very common surname.

B FEM NOUN
1 current
2 draught

corrijo VERB ▷ see **corregir**
Ahora mismo lo corrijo.
I'll correct it right away.

cortado (FEM **cortada**) ADJECTIVE
1 sour
2 chapped
3 closed

cortar VERB
to cut
Corta la manzana por la mitad.
Cut the apple in half.
Me corté el dedo.
I cut my finger.
Te vas a cortar.
You're going to cut yourself.
Estas tijeras no cortan.
These scissors are blunt.
Fui a cortarme el pelo.
I went to get my hair cut.

el **corte** NOUN
1 cut
Tenía un corte en la frente.
He had a cut on his forehead.
un corte de pelo
a haircut
2 Me da corte pedírselo.
I'm embarrassed to ask him.

la **corteza** NOUN
crust

la **cortina** NOUN
curtain

corto (FEM **corta**) ADJECTIVE
short
Lucía tiene el pelo corto.
Lucía has short hair.

la **cosa** NOUN
thing
¿Qué es esa cosa redonda?
What's that round thing?
Cogí mis cosas y me fui.
I picked up my things and left.

¿Me puedes decir una cosa?
Can you tell me something?
¡Qué cosa más rara!
How strange!

cualquier cosa
anything

coser VERB
to sew

las cosquillas NOUN
hacer cosquillas a alguien
to tickle somebody
Tiene muchas cosquillas.
He's very ticklish.

la costa NOUN
coast
Pasamos el verano en la costa.
We spent the summer on the coast.

costar VERB
to cost
Cuesta mucho dinero.
It costs a lot of money.
Me costó diez euros.
It cost me ten euros.
Las matemáticas le cuestan mucho.
He finds maths very difficult.

¿Cuánto cuesta?
How much is it?

la costilla NOUN
rib

la costumbre NOUN
1 **habit**
Tiene la mala costumbre de mentir.
He has the bad habit of lying.
Se le olvidó, como de costumbre.
He forgot, as usual.
2 **custom**
una costumbre británica
a British custom

cotillear VERB
to gossip

crecer VERB
to grow
Me crece mucho el pelo.
My hair grows very fast.
¡Cómo has crecido!
Haven't you grown!

creer VERB
1 **to believe**
Nadie me cree.
Nobody believes me.
¿Crees en los fantasmas?
Do you believe in ghosts?
2 **to think**
No creo que pueda ir.
I don't think I'll be able to go.

Creo que sí.
I think so.
Creo que no.
I don't think so.

la crema NOUN
cream
Me pongo crema en las manos.
I put cream on my hands.
la crema solar
suncream

la cremallera NOUN
zip
Súbete la cremallera.
Do your zip up.

el cristal NOUN
1 **glass**
una botella de cristal
a glass bottle
En el suelo había cristales rotos.
There was some broken glass on the floor.
2 **window pane**
Los niños rompieron el cristal.
The children broke the window pane.
limpiar los cristales
to clean the windows

English · **Spanish**

el **cromo** NOUN
picture card

la **croqueta** NOUN
croquette
croquetas de pollo
chicken croquettes

el **cruce** NOUN
crossroads
En el cruce hay un semáforo.
There are traffic lights at the
crossroads.
un cruce de peatones
a pedestrian crossing

crudo (FEM **cruda**) ADJECTIVE
raw
las zanahorias crudas
raw carrots

crujiente (FEM **crujiente**) ADJECTIVE
crunchy

la **cruz** (PL las **cruces**) NOUN
cross

cruzar VERB
1 **to cross**
2 **to fold**
**Nos cruzamos en
la calle.**
We passed each
other in the
street.

el **cuaderno**
NOUN
notebook
**un cuaderno
de ejercicios**
an exercise book

la **cuadra** NOUN
stable

cuadrado

cuadrado can be an adjective or
noun.

A ADJECTIVE (FEM **cuadrada**)
square

B MASC NOUN
square

el **cuadro** NOUN
painting

cual PRONOUN (PL **cuales**)
1 **who**
**el primo del cual te estuve
hablando**
the cousin who I was telling you about
2 **which**
**la ventana desde la cual nos
observaban**
the window from which they were
watching us

cuál PRONOUN (PL **cuáles**)
1 **what**
No sé cuál es la solución.
I don't know what the solution is.
2 **which one**
¿Cuál te gusta más?
Which one do you like best?
¿Cuáles quieres?
Which ones do you want?

cualquier ADJECTIVE ▷ see **cualquiera**

cualquiera (FEM **cualquiera**)

cualquiera can be an adjective or a
pronoun.

A ADJECTIVE
any
**Puedes usar un bolígrafo
cualquiera.**
You can use any pen.
No es un equipo cualquiera.
It's not just any team.

LANGUAGE TIP
When **cualquiera** goes in front of a
noun it is shortened to **cualquier**.

cualquier cosa
anything
en cualquier sitio
anywhere

B PRONOUN
1 anyone
Cualquiera puede hacer eso.
Anyone can do that.
cualquiera que le conozca
anyone who knows him
2 any one
Me da igual, cualquiera.
It doesn't matter, any one.
en cualquiera de las habitaciones
in any one of the rooms
cualquiera que elijas
whichever one you choose
3 either
¿Cuál de los dos prefieres?
— Cualquiera.
Which of the two do you prefer?
— Either.

cuando CONJUNCTION
when
Lo haré cuando tenga tiempo.
I'll do it when I have time.
Puedes venir cuando quieras.
You can come whenever you like.

cuándo ADVERB
when
¿Cuándo te va mejor?
When suits you?
No sabe cuándo ocurrió.
He doesn't know when it happened.

cuanto (FEM **cuanta**) ADJECTIVE, PRONOUN
Termínalo cuanto antes.
Finish it as soon as possible.
Cuanto más lo pienso menos lo entiendo.
The more I think about it, the less I understand it.
Cuantas menos personas haya mejor.
The fewer people the better.
En cuanto oí su voz me eché a llorar.
As soon as I heard his voice I began to cry.

Había solo unos cuantos alumnos.
There were only a few pupils.

en cuanto a
as for

cuánto (FEM **cuánta**) ADJECTIVE, PRONOUN
1 how much
¿Cuánto dinero tienes?
How much money do you have?
Me dijo cuánto costaba.
He told me how much it was.
¡Cuánta gente!
What a lot of people!
¿Cuánto tiempo llevas estudiando inglés?
How long have you been studying English?
¿Cuánto hay de aquí a Bilbao?
How far is it from here to Bilbao?
2 how many
¿Cuántas sillas?
How many chairs?
No sé cuántos necesito.
I don't know how many I need.
¿A cuántos estamos?
What's the date?

cuarenta (FEM **cuarenta**) ADJECTIVE, PRONOUN
forty
Tiene cuarenta años.
He's forty.

cuarto

cuarto can be an adjective, a pronoun or a noun.

A ADJECTIVE, PRONOUN (FEM **cuarta**)
fourth
Vivo en el cuarto piso.
I live on the fourth floor.
B MASC NOUN
1 room
Los niños jugaban en su cuarto.
The children were playing in their room.

el cuarto de estar
the living room
el cuarto de baño
the bathroom
2 **quarter**
un cuarto de hora
a quarter of an hour

> **Son las once y cuarto.**
> It's a quarter past eleven.
> **A las diez menos cuarto.**
> At a quarter to ten.

cuatro (FEM **cuatro**) ADJECTIVE, PRONOUN
four

> **Son las cuatro.**
> It's four o'clock.
> **el cuatro de julio**
> the fourth of July
> **Nació el cuatro de julio.**
> He was born on the fourth of July.

cuatrocientos (FEM **cuatrocientas**)
ADJECTIVE, PRONOUN
four hundred

cubierto

> **cubierto** can be an adjective or part
> of the verb **cubrir**.

A ADJECTIVE (FEM **cubierta**)
covered
Estaba todo cubierto de nieve.
Everything was covered in snow.
B VERB ▷ see **cubrir**
Cubrimos la mesa con papel de periódico.
We covered the table with newspaper.

los **cubiertos** NOUN
cutlery

el **cubito de hielo** NOUN
ice cube

el **cubo** NOUN
bucket
el cubo y la pala
the bucket and spade

el cubo de la basura
the dustbin

cubrir VERB
to cover
Tenemos que cubrir los cuadernos.
We have to cover our exercise books.
El agua casi me cubría.
I was almost out of my depth.

la **cuchara** NOUN
spoon

la **cucharada** NOUN
spoonful
una cucharada de jarabe
a spoonful of syrup

la **cucharilla** NOUN
teaspoon

cuchichear VERB
to whisper

el **cuchillo** NOUN
knife

el **cucurucho** NOUN
cone

cuelgo VERB ▷ see **colgar**
¿Dónde cuelgo el abrigo?
Where can I hang the coat?

el **cuello** NOUN
neck

la **cuenta** NOUN
1 **bill**
El camarero nos trajo la cuenta.
The waiter brought us the bill.
2 **account**
una cuenta de correo
an email account
3 **darse cuenta**
to realize/to notice

LANGUAGE TIP
darse cuenta has two meanings.
Look at the examples.

Perdona, no me di cuenta de que eras vegetariano.
Sorry, I didn't realize you were a vegetarian.

¿Te has dado cuenta de que han cortado el árbol?
Did you notice they've cut down that tree?

cuento

> **cuento** can be a noun or part of the verb **contar**.

A MASC NOUN
story
La abuela nos contaba cuentos.
Grandma used to tell us stories.
un cuento de hadas
a fairy-tale

B VERB ▷ *see* **contar**
Si quieres te cuento lo que pasó.
If you want, I'll tell you what happened.

la **cuerda** NOUN

1 rope
Construyeron un columpio con una tabla y una cuerda.
They built a swing with a board and some rope.

2 string
Necesito una cuerda para atar este paquete.
I need some string to tie up this parcel.

el **cuero** NOUN
leather
una chaqueta de cuero
a leather jacket

el **cuerpo** NOUN
body
el cuerpo humano
the human body
el cuerpo de bomberos
the fire brigade

cuesta

> **cuesta** can be a noun or part of the verb **costar**.

A FEM NOUN
slope
una cuesta muy empinada
a very steep slope

ir cuesta abajo
to go downhill
ir cuesta arriba
to go uphill

B VERB ▷ *see* **costar**
¿Cuánto cuesta esa bicicleta?
How much does that bicycle cost?

la **cueva** NOUN
cave

el **cuidado** NOUN
care
Conducía con cuidado.
He was driving carefully.

¡Cuidado!
Careful!

cuidar VERB
to look after
Ella cuida de los niños.
She looks after the children.
■ **cuidarse**
to look after oneself
Tienes que cuidarte.
You need to look after yourself.

¡Cuídate!
Take care!

la **culpa** NOUN
fault
La culpa es mía.
It's my fault.
Siempre me echan la culpa a mí.
They're always blaming me.

culpable (FEM culpable)

> **culpable** can be an adjective or a noun.

A
B
C
D
E
F
G
H
I
J
K
L
M
N
O
P
Q
R
S
T
U
V
W
X
Y
Z

A ADJECTIVE
guilty
Yo no soy culpable.
I'm not guilty.
B MASC/FEM NOUN
culprit
Ella es la culpable de todo.
She is to blame for everything.

la **cultura** NOUN
culture

la **cumbre** NOUN
summit

el **cumpleaños** (PL los **cumpleaños**)
NOUN
birthday

> **¡Feliz cumpleaños!**
> Happy birthday!

cumplir VERB
1 **to carry out**
2 **to keep**
3 **Mañana cumplo diez años.**
I'll be ten tomorrow.

la **cuna** NOUN
cradle

la **cuñada** NOUN
sister-in-law

el **cuñado** NOUN
brother-in-law

cupo VERB ▷ see **caber**
No cupo por la puerta.
It wouldn't go through the door.

el **cura** NOUN
priest

curar VERB
1 **to cure**
un remedio para curar una pulmonía
a treatment to cure pneumonia
Espero que te cures pronto.
I hope that you get better soon.
2 **to heal**
Ya se le ha curado la herida.
His wound has already healed.

cursi (FEM **cursi**) ADJECTIVE
1 **affected**
2 **twee**

el **cursillo** NOUN
course
un cursillo de informática
a computer course
hacer un cursillo de natación
to have swimming lessons

el **curso** NOUN
1 **year**
un chico de mi curso
a boy in my year
Hago segundo curso.
I'm in Year two.
2 **course**
Hice un curso de alemán.
I did a German course.

la **curva** NOUN
bend
Hay algunas curvas muy cerradas.
There are some very sharp bends.

Dd

la **dama** NOUN
lady
damas y caballeros
ladies and gentlemen
las damas
draughts
jugar a las damas
to play draughts

el **daño** NOUN
damage
El daño no es muy grave.
The damage isn't very serious.
¡Me estás haciendo daño!
You're hurting me!

hacerse daño
to hurt oneself

dar VERB
to give
Se lo di a Teresa.
I gave it to Teresa.
Se me dan bien las ciencias.
I'm good at science.

los **datos** PLURAL NOUN
data
Se me han acabado los datos.
I've run out of data.

de PREPOSITION

LANGUAGE TIP
de + **el** = **del**.

1 **of**
un paquete de caramelos
a packet of sweets
un vaso de agua
a glass of water
las clases de inglés
English lessons
un anillo de oro
a gold ring
la casa de Isabel
Isabel's house
2 **from**
Soy de Madrid.
I'm from Madrid.
un regalo de mi tía
a present from my aunt
Son del año pasado.
They're from last year.
3 **than**
Es más difícil de lo que creía.
It's more difficult than I thought.

dé VERB ▷ *see* **dar**
Quiero que me dé la pelota.
I want him to give me the ball.

debajo ADVERB
underneath
Levanta la maceta, la llave está debajo.
Lift up the flowerpot, the key's underneath.
debajo de
under
debajo de la cama
under the bed

deber

deber can be a noun or a verb.

A MASC NOUN
duty
Solo cumplí con mi deber.
I simply did my duty.
los deberes
homework
B VERB
1 **must**
Debo intentarlo.
I must try it.

No debes preocuparte.
You mustn't worry.
No deberías dejarla sola.
You shouldn't leave her alone.
deber de
must
Debe de ser canadiense.
He must be Canadian.
2 to owe
¿Cuánto le debo?
How much do I owe you?

hacer los deberes
to do one's homework

débil (FEM **débil**) ADJECTIVE
weak

decidir VERB
to decide
Tú decides.
You decide.
He decidido aprender inglés.
I've decided to learn English.
¡Decídete!
Make up your mind!

décimo (FEM **décima**) ADJECTIVE, PRONOUN
tenth
Vivo en el décimo.
I live on the tenth floor.

decir VERB
1 to say
¿Qué dijo?
What did he say?
¿Cómo se dice "casa" en inglés?
How do you say 'casa' in English?
No sé lo que quiere decir.
I don't know what it means.
2 to tell
Nunca me dice la verdad.
He never tells me the truth.
Me dijo que esperara fuera.
He told me to wait outside.

es decir
that's to say
¡No me digas!
Really?

el **dedo** NOUN
1 finger
2 toe
el dedo gordo
the thumb/
the big toe

LANGUAGE TIP
el dedo gordo has two meanings. It can be translated as **the thumb** or **the big toe**.

dejar VERB
1 to leave
He dejado las llaves en la mesa.
I've left the keys on the table.
No me dejes sola.
Don't leave me on my own.
2 to let
Mis padres no me dejan ir al parque.
My parents won't let me go to the park.
dejar caer
to drop
Dejó caer la bandeja.
She dropped the tray.
3 to lend
Le dejé mi libro de matemáticas.
I lent him my maths book.
4 dejar de
to stop
He dejado de morderme las uñas.
I've stopped biting my nails.

del PREPOSITION ▷ *see* **de**
Vengo del colegio.
I'm coming from school.

delante ADVERB
in front
Siéntate delante.
You sit in front.
la parte de delante
the front
de delante
front
la rueda de delante
the front wheel

Se inclinó hacia delante.
He leaned forward.
delante de
in front of/opposite

LANGUAGE TIP
delante de has two meanings. Look at the examples.

No digas nada delante de Lara.
Don't say anything in front of Lara.
Mi casa está delante de la escuela.
My house is opposite the school.

delgado (FEM **delgada**) ADJECTIVE
thin
  Estás muy delgado.
  You're too thin.

demás

> **demás** can be an adjective or a pronoun.

A ADJECTIVE (FEM **demás**)
other
los demás niños
the other children
B PRONOUN
los demás
the others
lo demás
the rest
Yo limpio las ventanas y lo demás lo limpias tú.
I'll clean the windows and you clean the rest.

demasiado

> **demasiado** can be an adjective or an adverb.

A ADJECTIVE (FEM **demasiada**)
too much
demasiado tiempo
too much time
demasiados libros
too many books
B ADVERB
too much

Hablas demasiado.
You talk too much.
Es demasiado pesado para levantarlo.
It's too heavy to lift.
Caminas demasiado deprisa.
You walk too quickly.

el **dentífrico** NOUN
toothpaste

el/la **dentista** NOUN
dentist
  Mi madre es dentista.
  My mum is a dentist.

dentro ADVERB
inside
  ¿Qué hay dentro?
  What's inside?
  dentro de
  in
  Mételo dentro del sobre.
  Put it in the envelope.
  dentro de tres meses
  in three months
  por dentro
  inside
  Mira bien por dentro.
  Have a good look inside.
  Está aquí dentro.
  It's in here.

dentro de poco
soon

depender VERB
  depender de
  to depend on
  El precio depende del tamaño.
  The price depends on the size.

Depende.
It depends.

el **deporte** NOUN
sport
  No hago mucho deporte.
  I don't do much sport.

English | **Spanish**

A
B
C
D
E
F
G
H
I
J
K
L
M
N
O
P
Q
R
S
T
U
V
W
X
Y
Z

deportista (FEM **deportista**)

> **deportista** can be an adjective or a noun.

A ADJECTIVE
sporty
Alicia es poco deportista.
Alicia is not very sporty.

B MASC NOUN
sportsman

C FEM NOUN
sportswoman

deprisa ADVERB
quickly
Acabaron muy deprisa.
They finished very quickly.
Lo hacen todo deprisa y corriendo.
They do everything in a rush.

> **¡Deprisa!**
> Hurry up!

la **derecha** NOUN
1 right hand
Escribo con la derecha.
I write with my right hand.
2 right
doblar a la derecha
to turn right
a la derecha
on the right
Coge la segunda calle a la derecha.
Take the second turning on the right.

derecho

> **derecho** can be an adjective, an adverb or a noun.

A ADJECTIVE (FEM **derecha**)
1 right
Escribo con la mano derecha.
I write with my right hand.
2 straight
¡Ponte derecho!
Stand up straight!

B ADVERB
straight
Sigue todo derecho.
Carry straight on.

C MASC NOUN
right
los derechos humanos
human rights

> **¡No hay derecho!**
> It's not fair!

desagradable (FEM **desagradable**)
ADJECTIVE
unpleasant
un olor muy desagradable
a very unpleasant smell
Fuiste muy desagradable con tu prima.
You were really nasty to your cousin.

desaparecer VERB
to disappear
La mancha ha desaparecido.
The stain has disappeared.

el **desastre** NOUN
disaster
La función fue un desastre.
The show was a disaster.
Soy un desastre para la gimnasia.
I'm hopeless at gymnastics.

desayunar VERB
1 to have breakfast
Desayuno a las ocho.
I have breakfast at eight.
2 to have … for breakfast
Desayuné café con leche y un bollo.
I had coffee and a roll for breakfast.

el **desayuno** NOUN
breakfast

descalzarse VERB
to take one's shoes off
  Descálzate.
  Take your shoes off.

descalzo (FEM **descalza**) ADJECTIVE
barefoot
  Paseaban descalzos por la playa.
  They walked barefoot along the beach.
  No entres en la cocina descalzo.
  Don't come into the kitchen in bare feet.

descansar VERB
to rest
  Tienes que descansar.
  You must rest.

el **descanso** NOUN
1 rest
  He caminado mucho, necesito un descanso.
  I've done a lot of walking, I need a rest.
2 break
  Después de estudiar dos horas nos tomamos un descanso.
  After studying for two hours we had a break.

descarado (FEM **descarada**) ADJECTIVE
cheeky
  ¡No seas descarado!
  Don't be cheeky!

descargar VERB
to download
  ■ **descargarse**
  to go flat

desconectar VERB
to unplug

el **descubrimiento** NOUN
discovery

desde PREPOSITION
1 from
  Desde aquí hasta la puerta hay diez metros.
  It's ten metres from here to the door.
2 since
  La conozco desde niño.
  I've known her since I was a child.
  ¿Desde cuándo vives aquí?
  How long have you been living here?

  desde entonces
  since then
  desde luego
  of course

desear VERB
to wish
  Te deseo mucha suerte.
  I wish you lots of luck.

desenchufar VERB
to unplug

el **deseo** NOUN
wish

el **desfile** NOUN
parade

la **desgracia** NOUN
tragedy
  Su muerte fue una auténtica desgracia.
  His death was an absolute tragedy.
  por desgracia
  unfortunately
  Por desgracia he vuelto a suspender.
  Unfortunately I've failed again.

deshacer VERB
to untie

el **desierto** NOUN
desert

English / **Spanish**

A
B
C
D
E
F
G
H
I
J
K
L
M
N
O
P
Q
R
S
T
U
V
W
X
Y
Z

desnatado (FEM **desnatada**) ADJECTIVE
skimmed

desnudarse VERB
to get undressed

desnudo (FEM **desnuda**) ADJECTIVE
naked

desobedecer VERB
to disobey

desobediente (FEM **desobediente**)
ADJECTIVE
disobedient

el **desodorante** NOUN
deodorant

desordenado (FEM **desordenada**)
ADJECTIVE
untidy
Tengo la habitación muy desordenada.
My room's really untidy.

despacio ADVERB
slowly
Baja despacio.
Come down slowly.

¡Despacio!
Take it easy!

despedir VERB
to say goodbye to
Se despidieron en la estación.
They said goodbye at the station.

el **despertador** NOUN
alarm clock

despertar VERB
to wake up
No me despiertes hasta las once.
Don't wake me up until eleven o'clock.

despierto (FEM **despierta**) ADJECTIVE
awake
A las siete ya estaba despierto.
He was already awake by seven o'clock.

después ADVERB
1 **later**
Ellos llegaron después.
They arrived later.
un año después
a year later
2 **next**
¿Qué viene después?
What comes next?
después de
after
Tu nombre está después del mío.
Your name comes after mine.
Después de comer fuimos de paseo.
After lunch we went for a walk.

el **destornillador** NOUN
screwdriver

destrozar VERB
to wreck
Tu perro ha destrozado la silla.
Your dog has wrecked the chair.

destruir VERB
to destroy
Los huracanes destruyen edificios enteros.
Hurricanes can destroy whole buildings.

la **desventaja** NOUN
disadvantage

el **detalle** NOUN
detail
No recuerdo todos los detalles.
I don't remember all the details.

detener VERB
1 **to stop**
¡Detenlos!
Stop them!

2 to arrest
Han detenido a los ladrones.
They've arrested the thieves.
■ **detenerse**
to stop
Nos detuvimos en el semáforo.
We stopped at the lights.

el **detergente** NOUN
detergent

detrás ADVERB
behind
El resto de los niños vienen detrás.
The rest of the children are coming on behind.
detrás de
behind
Se escondió detrás de un árbol.
He hid behind a tree.

devolver VERB
1 to give back
¿Me puedes devolver el libro que te presté?
Could you give me back the book I lent you?
2 to take back
Devolví la falda porque me iba pequeña.
I took the skirt back as it was too small for me.
3 to throw up (*informal*)

di VERB
1 ▷ *see* **decir**
Di, ¿qué te parece?
Tell me, what do you think?
2 ▷ *see* **dar**
Se lo di a ella.
I gave it to her.

el **día** NOUN
day
Pasaré dos días en la playa.
I'll spend a couple of days at the beach.

Es de día.
It's daylight.
¿Qué día es hoy?
What day is it today?/What's the date today?

LANGUAGE TIP
¿qué día es hoy? has two meanings. It can be translated as **what day is it today?** and **what's the date today?**

un día de fiesta
a public holiday
el día de los enamorados
Saint Valentine's Day
el día de los Santos Inocentes
the Feast of the Holy Innocents

DID YOU KNOW...?
In Spanish-speaking countries the day people play April-Fool-type practical jokes on each other is 28 December, **el día de los Santos Inocentes**.

al día siguiente
the following day
¡Buenos días!
Good morning!
todos los días
every day

el **diablo** NOUN
devil

diagonal ADJECTIVE, FEM NOUN
diagonal
en diagonal
diagonally

el **diamante** NOUN
diamond

el **diámetro** NOUN
diameter

diario

diario can be an adjective or a noun.

A ADJECTIVE (FEM **diaria**)
daily

A
B
C
D
E
F
G
H
I
J
K
L
M
N
O
P
Q
R
S
T
U
V
W
X
Y
Z

la rutina diaria
the daily routine
la ropa de diario
everyday clothes
a diario
every day
Toca el piano a diario.
He plays the piano every day.
B MASC NOUN
diary

la **diarrea** NOUN
diarrhoea

dibujar VERB
to draw
No sé dibujar.
I can't draw.

el **dibujo** NOUN
drawing
Me hizo un dibujo.
She did me a drawing.
los dibujos animados
cartoons

el **diccionario** NOUN
dictionary

dicho VERB ▷ *see* **decir**
Ya te he dicho que no lo quiero.
I've already told you that I don't want it.

diciembre MASC NOUN
December

LANGUAGE TIP
Months are not written with a capital
letter in Spanish.

---

en diciembre
in December
Nació el seis de diciembre.
He was born on the sixth of December.

diciendo VERB ▷ *see* **decir**
Como iba diciendo ...
As I was saying ...

diecinueve (FEM **diecinueve**) ADJECTIVE,
PRONOUN
nineteen

Tengo diecinueve años.
I'm nineteen.

el diecinueve de julio
the nineteenth of July
Nació el diecinueve de julio.
He was born on the nineteenth of July.

dieciocho (FEM **dieciocho**) ADJECTIVE,
PRONOUN
eighteen
Tengo dieciocho años.
I'm eighteen.

el dieciocho de abril
the eighteenth of April
Nació el dieciocho de abril.
He was born on the eighteenth
of April.

dieciséis (FEM **dieciséis**) ADJECTIVE,
PRONOUN
sixteen
Tengo dieciséis años.
I'm sixteen.

el dieciséis de febrero
the sixteenth of February
Nació el dieciséis de febrero.
He was born on the sixteenth of
February.

diecisiete (FEM **diecisiete**) ADJECTIVE,
PRONOUN
seventeen
Tengo diecisiete años.
I'm seventeen.

el diecisiete de enero
the seventeenth of January
Nació el diecisiete de enero.
He was born on the seventeenth
of January.

el **diente** NOUN
tooth
**Me lavo los dientes tres veces al
día.**
I brush my teeth three times a day.

un diente de leche
a milk tooth
un diente de ajo
a clove of garlic

la **dieta** NOUN
diet
una dieta vegetariana
a vegetarian diet

estar a dieta
to be on a diet

diez (FEM **diez**) ADJECTIVE, PRONOUN
ten
Tengo diez años.
I'm ten.

Son las diez.
It's ten o'clock.
el diez de agosto
the tenth of August
Nació el diez de agosto.
He was born on the tenth of August.

la **diferencia** NOUN
difference
¿Qué diferencia hay entre los dos?
What's the difference between the two?

diferenciar VERB
¿En qué se diferencian?
What's the difference between them?
Solo se diferencian en el tamaño.
The only difference between them is their size.

diferente (FEM **diferente**) ADJECTIVE
different

difícil (FEM **difícil**) ADJECTIVE
difficult
Es un problema difícil de entender.
It's a difficult problem to understand.

la **digestión** NOUN
digestion

hacer la digestión
to digest

digital (FEM **digital**) ADJECTIVE
digital
una cámara digital
a digital camera

una huella digital
a fingerprint

digo VERB ▷ see **decir**
Porque lo digo yo.
Because I say so.

dije VERB ▷ see **decir**
¡Yo no dije eso!
I didn't say that!

el **dinero** NOUN
money
No tengo más dinero.
I haven't got any more money.
dinero suelto
loose change

dio VERB ▷ see **dar**
Me dio un libro.
He gave me a book.

Dios MASC NOUN
God

el **dios** (PL los **dioses**) NOUN
god

dirá VERB ▷ see **decir**
¿Qué dirá mi madre cuando se entere?
¿What will my mother say when she finds out?

la **dirección** (PL las **direcciones**) NOUN
1 direction
Íbamos en dirección equivocada.
We were going in the wrong direction.
una calle de dirección única
a one-way street

English

Spanish

A
B
C
D
E
F
G
H
I
J
K
L
M
N
O
P
Q
R
S
T
U
V
W
X
Y
Z

84

2 address
¿Me apuntas tu dirección aquí?
Can you write your address down here for me?
dirección de correo electrónico
email address

directo (FEM **directa**) ADJECTIVE
direct
Hay un tren directo a Valencia.
There's a direct train to Valencia.
una pregunta directa
a direct question

el **director**
la **directora** NOUN
1 headteacher
2 manager
3 director

discapacidad FEM NOUN
disability
personas con discapacidades
people with disabilities

discapacitado
discapacitada ADJECTIVE
disabled

el **disco** NOUN
record
un disco compacto
a compact disc
el disco duro
the hard disk

la **discusión** (PL las **discusiones**) NOUN
argument
Tuve una discusión con mi madre.
I had an argument with my mother.

discutir VERB
to argue
Siempre discuten por la videoconsola.
They're always arguing about the games console.
Discutió con su madre.
He had an argument with his mother.

el **disfraz** (PL los **disfraces**) NOUN
costume

un disfraz de vaquero
a cowboy costume
una fiesta de disfraces
a fancy-dress party

disfrazarse VERB
disfrazarse de
to dress up as
Se disfrazó con la ropa de su madre.
She dressed up in her mum's clothes.

disfrutar VERB
to enjoy oneself
Disfruté mucho en la fiesta.
I really enjoyed myself at the party.
Disfruto leyendo.
I enjoy reading.

disgustado (FEM **disgustada**) ADJECTIVE
upset

LANGUAGE TIP
Be careful! **disgustado** does not mean **disgusted**.

---

disimular VERB
to hide
Intentó disimular su enfado.
He tried to hide his annoyance.
No disimules, sé que has sido tú.
Don't bother pretending, I know it was you.

el **disparate** NOUN
silly thing
Siempre hace disparates.
He always does silly things.

No digas disparates.
Don't talk rubbish.

el **disparo** NOUN
shot

la **distancia** NOUN
distance
la distancia entre dos coches
the distance between two cars
¿Qué distancia hay entre Madrid y Barcelona?
How far is Madrid from Barcelona?
¿A qué distancia está la estación?
How far's the station?
a veinte kilómetros de distancia
twenty kilometres away

distinguir VERB
to distinguish
Resulta difícil distinguir el macho de la hembra.
It's difficult to distinguish the male from the female.
No distingue entre el rojo y el verde.
He can't tell the difference between red and green.
Se parecen tanto que no los distingo.
They're so alike that I can't tell them apart.

distinto (FEM **distinta**) ADJECTIVE
1 **different**
Carlos es distinto a los demás.
Carlos is different to everyone else.
2 **distintos**
several
Tenemos distintas clases de coches
We have several types of car.

la **distracción** (PL las **distracciones**) NOUN
pastime
Pintar es mi distracción favorita.
My favourite pastime is painting.

distraer VERB
1 **to keep ... entertained**
Les pondré un vídeo para distraerlos.
I'll put a video on to keep them entertained.
Me distrae mucho escuchar música.
I really enjoy listening to music.
2 **to distract**
No me distraigas, que tengo trabajo.
Don't distract me. I've got work to do.

distraído (FEM **distraída**) ADJECTIVE
absent-minded
Mi padre es muy distraído.
My father is very absent-minded.
Perdona, estaba distraído.
Sorry, I wasn't paying attention.

la **diversión** (PL las **diversiones**) NOUN
entertainment

LANGUAGE TIP
Be careful! **diversión** does not mean **diversion**.

---

divertido (FEM **divertida**) ADJECTIVE
funny
Fue muy divertido.
It was great fun.

divertir VERB
to entertain
Nos divirtió con sus cuentos.
He entertained us with his stories.
▪ **divertirse**
to have a good time

dividir VERB
to divide
El libro está dividido en dos partes.
The book is divided into two parts.

Divide cuatro entre dos.
Divide four by two.
■ **dividirse**
to divide/to share

LANGUAGE TIP
dividirse has two meanings. Look at the examples.

Nos dividimos el trabajo entre los tres.
We divided the work between the three of us.
Se dividieron los caramelos.
They shared the sweets between them.

divierto VERB ▷ *see* **divertir**
Me divierto mucho con ellos.
I have a good time when I'm with them.

la **división** (PL las **divisiones**) NOUN
division
en primera división
in the first division
Ya sabe hacer divisiones.
He already knows how to do division.

el **DNI** ABBREVIATION
(= **Documento Nacional de Identidad**)
ID card

doble

doble can be an adjective or a noun.

A (FEM **doble**)
double
una ración doble
a double helping
B MASC NOUN
twice as much
Comes el doble que yo.
You eat twice as much as I do.

doce (FEM **doce**) ADJECTIVE, PRONOUN
twelve
Tengo doce años.
I'm twelve.

Son las doce.
It's twelve o'clock.

el doce de diciembre
the twelfth of December
Nació el doce de diciembre.
He was born on the twelfth of December.

la **docena** NOUN
dozen

el **doctor**
la **doctora** NOUN
doctor
Cuando crezca me gustaría ser doctor.
I want to be a doctor when I grow up.

el **documental** NOUN
documentary

el **documento** NOUN
document
un documento oficial
an official document
el documento nacional de identidad
the identity card

doler VERB
to hurt
Me duele el brazo.
My arm hurts.

Me duele la cabeza.
I've got a headache.
Me duele la garganta.
I've got a sore throat.

el **dolor** NOUN
pain
Gritó de dolor.
He cried out in pain.

Tengo dolor de cabeza.
I've got a headache.
Tengo dolor de garganta.
I've got a sore throat.
Tengo dolor de estómago.
I've got a stomachache.

doméstico (FEM **doméstica**) ADJECTIVE
domestic

para uso doméstico
for domestic use
las tareas domésticas
the housework
un animal doméstico
a pet

el **domingo** NOUN
Sunday

LANGUAGE TIP
The days of the week are not spelled
with a capital letter in Spanish.

La vi el domingo.
I saw her on Sunday.

todos los domingos
every Sunday
el domingo pasado
last Sunday
el domingo que viene
next Sunday

don MASC NOUN
don Juan Gómez
Mr Juan Gómez

donde ADVERB
where
La nota está donde la dejaste.
The note's where you left it.

dónde ADVERB
where
¿Dónde vives?
Where do you live?
**Le pregunté dónde estaban los
aseos.**
I asked him where the toilets were.
¿Sabes dónde está?
Do you know where he is?
¿De dónde eres?
Where are you from?

¿Por dónde se va al cine?
How do you get to the cinema?

doña FEM NOUN
doña Marta García
Mrs Marta García

dorado (FEM **dorada**) ADJECTIVE
golden

dormir VERB
to sleep
Toni durmió diez horas.
Toni slept for ten hours.
dormir la siesta
to have a nap
estar medio dormido
to be half asleep
■ **dormirse**
to fall asleep
Me dormí en el tren.
I fell asleep on the train.
Se me ha dormido el brazo.
My arm has gone to sleep.

el **dormitorio** NOUN
bedroom

dos (FEM **dos**) ADJECTIVE, PRONOUN
1 **two**
Tenemos dos gatos.
We have two cats.
2 **both**
Al final vinieron los dos.
In the end they both came.
Los hemos invitado a los dos.
We've invited both of them.

Tiene dos años.
He's two.
Son las dos.
It's two o'clock.
el dos de enero
the second of January
Nació el dos de enero.
He was born on the second of
January.

doscientos (FEM **doscientas**) ADJECTIVE,
PRONOUN
two hundred

87

doscientos cincuenta
two hundred and fifty

doy VERB ▷ *see* **dar**
Si quieres, te doy uno.
If you want, I'll give you one.

el **drogadicto**
la **drogadicta** NOUN
drug addict

el **dron** NOUN
drone

la **ducha** NOUN
shower

> **darse una ducha**
> to have a shower

ducharse VERB
to have a shower

la **duda** NOUN
doubt
Tengo mis dudas.
I have my doubts.
Tengo una duda.
I have a query.
¿Alguna duda?
Any questions?

dudar VERB
to doubt
Lo dudo.
I doubt it.
Dudo que sea cierto.
I doubt if it's true.
Dudaba si comprarlo o no.
He wasn't sure whether to buy it or
not.

el **dueño**
la **dueña** NOUN
owner

duermo VERB ▷ *see* **dormir**
**Duermo ocho horas todos los
días.**
I sleep eight hours every day.

dulce

> **dulce** can be an adjective or a noun.

A ADJECTIVE (FEM **dulce**)
sweet
B MASC NOUN
sweet

durante ADVERB
1 during
**Tuvo que estudiar durante las
vacaciones.**
He had to study during the holidays.
2 for
Habló durante una hora.
He spoke for an hour.
durante toda la noche
all night long

durar VERB
to last
La película dura dos horas.
The film lasts two hours.

durmiendo VERB ▷ *see* **dormir**
Me estoy durmiendo.
I'm falling asleep.

duro

> **duro** can be an adjective or an
> adverb.

A ADJECTIVE (FEM **dura**)
1 hard
**Los diamantes son muy
duros.**
Diamonds are very hard.
2 tough
Esta carne está dura.
This meat's tough.
B ADVERB
hard
trabajar duro
to work hard

Ee

e CONJUNCTION

LANGUAGE TIP
e is used instead of **y** in front of words beginning with 'i' and 'hi', but not 'hie'.
and

Pablo e Inés.
Pablo and Inés.

echar VERB
1 **to throw**
Échame la goma.
Throw me the rubber.
2 **to throw out**
Me echó de su casa.
He threw me out of the house.
3 **to expel**
Lo han echado del colegio.
He's been expelled from school.
4 **Echo de menos a mi familia.**
I miss my family.

ecológico (FEM **ecológica**) ADJECTIVE
ecological
un desastre ecológico
an ecological disaster
un producto ecológico
an environmentally friendly product

ecologista (FEM **ecologista**)

ecologista can be an adjective or a noun.

A ADJECTIVE
environmental
un grupo ecologista
an environmental group
B MASC/FEM NOUN
environmentalist

la **edad** NOUN
age
Tenemos la misma edad.
We're the same age.

¿Qué edad tiene?
How old is he?

el **edificio** NOUN
building

la **educación** NOUN
1 **education**
educación física
PE
2 **upbringing**
Rosa recibió una educación muy estricta.
Rosa had a very strict upbringing.
Señalar es de mala educación.
It's rude to point.
Es una falta de educación hablar con la boca llena.
It's bad manners to speak with your mouth full.

educado (FEM **educada**) ADJECTIVE
polite
Es un chico bien educado.
He's a polite boy.

egoísta (FEM **egoísta**) ADJECTIVE
selfish

el **ejemplo** NOUN
example
¿Puedes ponerme un ejemplo?
Can you give me an example?

por ejemplo
for example

el **ejercicio** NOUN
exercise
La maestra nos puso varios ejercicios.
The teacher gave us several exercises to do.

hacer ejercicio
to do exercise

el (FEM SING **la**, MASC PL **los**, FEM PL **las**) ARTICLE
the
>**Perdí el autobús.**
>I missed the bus.
>**Yo fui el que lo encontró.**
>I was the one who found it.
>**Ayer me lavé la cabeza.**
>I washed my hair yesterday.
>**Me puse el abrigo.**
>I put my coat on.
>**Tiene unos zapatos bonitos, pero prefiero los míos.**
>Her shoes are nice but I prefer mine.
>**No me gusta el pescado.**
>I don't like fish.

él PRONOUN
1 **he**
>**Me lo dijo él.**
>He told me.
2 **him**
>**Se lo di a él.**
>I gave it to him.
>**Su mujer es más alta que él.**
>His wife is taller than him.
>**él mismo**
>himself
>**No lo sabe ni él mismo.**
>He doesn't even know himself.
>**de él**
>his
>**El patinete es de él.**
>The scooter is his.

la **electricidad** NOUN
electricity

eléctrico (FEM **eléctrica**) ADJECTIVE
electric
>**una guitarra eléctrica**
>an electric guitar

el **elefante** NOUN
elephant

elegir VERB
to choose
>**No sabía qué libro elegir.**
>I didn't know what book to choose.

elijo VERB ▷ see **elegir**
>**Yo elijo el blanco.**
>I choose the white one.

ella PRONOUN
1 **she**
>**Ella no estaba en casa.**
>She was not at home.
2 **her**
>**El regalo es para ella.**
>The present's for her.
>**Él estaba más nervioso que ella.**
>He was more nervous than her.
>**ella misma**
>herself
>**Me lo dijo ella misma.**
>She told me herself.
>**de ella**
>hers
>**Este abrigo es de ella.**
>This coat's hers.

e-mail NOUN
1 **email**
2 **email address**

embarazada ADJECTIVE
pregnant
>**Estaba embarazada de cuatro meses.**
>She was four months pregnant.

LANGUAGE TIP
Be careful! **embarazada** does not mean **embarrassed**.

embarazoso (FEM **embarazosa**)
ADJECTIVE
embarrassing

la **emergencia** NOUN
emergency
   la salida de emergencia
   the emergency exit

emocionante (FEM **emocionante**)
ADJECTIVE
exciting
   El partido fue muy emocionante.
   The match was very exciting.

el **empaste** NOUN
filling

empatar VERB
to draw
   Empatamos a uno.
   We drew one-all.

el **empate** NOUN
draw
   un empate a cero
   a goalless draw

empezar VERB
to start
   Las vacaciones empiezan el día uno.
   The holidays start on the first.
   Ha empezado a nevar.
   It's started snowing.
   volver a empezar
   to start again

el **empleo** NOUN
job
   Ha encontrado empleo en un restaurante.
   He has found a job in a restaurant.
   estar sin empleo
   to be unemployed

empollar VERB
to swot
   Me pasé la noche empollando.
   I spent the whole night swotting.

el **empollón**
la **empollona**, MASC PL los **empollones**
NOUN
swot

la **empresa** NOUN
company
   Mi padre trabaja en una empresa de informática.
   My dad works for a computer company.

empujar VERB
to push
   Empuja la puerta.
   Push the door.

en PREPOSITION
1 **in**
   en el armario
   in the wardrobe
   Viven en Granada.
   They live in Granada.
   Nació en invierno.
   He was born in winter.
   Lo hice en dos días.
   I did it in two days.
   Está en el hospital.
   She's in hospital.
2 **into**
   Entré en la cocina.
   I went into the kitchen.
3 **on**
   Las llaves están en la mesa.
   The keys are on the table.
   La librería está en la calle Pelayo.
   The bookshop is on Pelayo Street.
   Mi clase está en la segunda planta.
   My classroom is on the second floor.
4 **at**
   Yo estaba en casa.
   I was at home.
   Te veo en el cine.
   See you at the cinema.
5 **by**
   Vinimos en avión.
   We came by plane.

enamorado (FEM **enamorada**) ADJECTIVE
estar enamorado de alguien
to be in love with somebody

enamorarse VERB
to fall in love
Se ha enamorado de Claudia.
He's fallen in love with Claudia.

encantado (FEM **encantada**) ADJECTIVE
1 **delighted**
Está encantada con su abrigo nuevo.
She loves her new coat.

Encantado de conocerle.
Pleased to meet you.

2 **enchanted**
un castillo encantado
an enchanted castle

encantar VERB
to love
Me encantan los animales.
I love animals.
Les encanta esquiar.
They love skiing.

encargar VERB
to order
Encargamos dos pizzas.
We ordered two pizzas.

encender VERB
1 **to light**
2 **to switch on**

encendido (FEM **encendida**) ADJECTIVE
on
La tele estaba encendida.
The telly was on.

el **enchufado**
la **enchufada** NOUN
Amelia es la enchufada del profesor.
(*informal*) Amelia's the teacher's pet.

enchufar VERB
to plug in
Enchufa la tele.
Plug the TV in.

el **enchufe** NOUN
1 **plug**
2 **socket**

enciendo VERB ▷ *see* encender
¿Cómo enciendo el ordenador?
How do I switch the computer on?

encima ADVERB
on
Pon la taza aquí encima.
Put the cup on here.
encima de
on/on top of

LANGUAGE TIP
encima de has two meanings. Look at the examples.

Ponlo encima de la mesa.
Put it on the table.
Mi maleta está encima del armario.
My case is on top of the wardrobe.

encontrar VERB
to find
No encuentro mi estuche.
I can't find my pencil case.
■ **encontrarse**
1 **to feel**
Ahora se encuentra mejor.
Now she's feeling better.
2 **to meet**
Nos encontramos en el cine.
We met at the cinema.
Me encontré con Mario en la calle.
I bumped into Mario in the street.

enemigo (FEM **enemiga**) ADJECTIVE, NOUN
enemy

la **energía** NOUN
energy

enero MASC NOUN
January

LANGUAGE TIP
Months are not written with a capital letter in Spanish.

en enero
in January
Nació el seis de enero.
He was born on the sixth of January.

enfadado (FEM **enfadada**) ADJECTIVE
angry
Mi padre estaba muy enfadado conmigo.
My father was very angry with me.

enfadarse VERB
to be angry
Papá se va a enfadar mucho contigo.
Dad will be very angry with you.

la **enfermedad** NOUN
illness
No pudo venir al colegio durante su enfermedad.
He couldn't come to school during his illness.

el **enfermero**
la **enfermera** NOUN
nurse
Mi madre es enfermera.
My mother's a nurse.

enfermo (FEM **enferma**)

> **enfermo** can be an adjective or a noun.

A ADJECTIVE
ill
He estado enferma toda la semana.
I've been ill all week.
B MASC/FEM NOUN
patient
un enfermo del Dr. Rojas
one of Dr Rojas' patients
Los enfermos deben tener especial cuidado.
Sick people need to be especially careful.

enfrente ADVERB
opposite

Luisa estaba sentada enfrente.
Luisa was sitting opposite.
La panadería está enfrente.
The baker's is across the street.
de enfrente
opposite
la casa de enfrente
the house opposite

enfriarse VERB
1 **to get cold**
La sopa se ha enfriado.
The soup has got cold.
2 **to cool down**
Deja que la sopa se enfríe un poco.
Let the soup cool down a bit.
3 **to catch cold**
Ponte el abrigo que te vas a enfriar.
Put your coat on or you'll catch cold.

engordar VERB
1 **to put on weight**
No quiero engordar.
I don't want to put on weight.
He engordado dos kilos.
I've put on two kilos.
2 **to be fattening**
Los caramelos engordan mucho.
Sweets are very fattening.

la **enhorabuena** NOUN
¡Enhorabuena!
Congratulations!

enorme (FEM **enorme**) ADJECTIVE
enormous
Tienen una casa enorme.
They have an enormous house.

la **ensalada** NOUN
salad

A
B
C
D
E
F
G
H
I
J
K
L
M
N
O
P
Q
R
S
T
U
V
W
X
Y
Z

enseguida ADVERB
straight away
La ambulancia llegó enseguida.
The ambulance arrived straight
away.

la **enseñanza** NOUN
1 **teaching**
2 **education**
la enseñanza primaria
primary education

enseñar VERB
1 **to teach**
Ricardo enseña inglés en un
colegio.
Ricardo teaches English in a school.
Mi padre me enseñó a nadar.
My father taught me to swim.
2 **to show**
Ana me enseñó todos sus
videojuegos.
Ana showed me all her video games.

ensuciar VERB
to get ... dirty
Vas a ensuciar el sofá.
You'll get the sofa dirty.

entender VERB
to understand
No entiendo francés.
I don't understand French.
¿Lo entiendes?
Do you understand?

enterarse VERB
1 **to find out**
Me enteré por Hugo.
I found out from Hugo.
Se enteraron del accidente por
la tele.
They heard about the accident on the
TV.
2 **to notice**
Me sacaron una muela y ni me
enteré.
They took out a tooth and I didn't
notice a thing.

entero (FEM **entera**) ADJECTIVE
whole
Se comió el paquete entero de
galletas.
He ate the whole packet of biscuits.
Se pasó la tarde entera
estudiando.
He spent the whole afternoon
studying.

entiendo VERB ▷ see **entender**
No lo entiendo.
I can't understand it.

el **entierro** NOUN
funeral

entonces ADVERB
then
Me recogió y entonces fuimos
al cine.
He picked me up and then we went
to the cinema.

la **entrada** NOUN
1 **entrance**
Nos vemos en la entrada.
I'll see you at the entrance.
2 **ticket**
Tengo entradas para el teatro.
I've got tickets for the theatre.
"prohibida la entrada"
'no entry'

entrar VERB
1 **to go in**
Abrí la puerta y entré.
I opened the door and went in.
2 **to come in**
¿Se puede? — Sí, entra.
May I? — Yes, come in.
3 Le entraron ganas de reír.
She wanted to laugh.
De repente le entró sueño.
He suddenly felt sleepy.
Me ha entrado hambre al verte
comer.
Watching you eat has made me
hungry.

entre PREPOSITION
 1 between
  Lo terminamos entre los dos.
  Between the two of us we finished it.
  Vendrá entre las diez y las once.
  He'll be coming between ten and eleven.
  Le compraremos un regalo entre todos.
  We'll buy her a present between all of us.
 2 among
  Las mujeres hablaban entre sí.
  The women were talking among themselves.

entregar VERB
 to hand in
  Olivia entregó el examen.
  Olivia handed her exam paper in.

el **entrenamiento** NOUN
 training

entrenarse VERB
 to train

entretenerse VERB
 1 to amuse oneself
  Se entretienen viendo los dibujos animados.
  They amuse themselves watching cartoons.
 2 to hang about
  No os entretengáis jugando.
  Don't hang about playing.

la **entrevista** NOUN
 interview

entrevistar VERB
 to interview

entusiasmado (FEM **entusiasmada**)
 ADJECTIVE
 excited
  Estaba entusiasmado con su fiesta de cumpleaños.
  He was excited about his birthday party.

entusiasmarse VERB
 to get excited
  Se entusiasmó con la idea de ir a la playa.
  He got very excited about the idea of going to the beach.

enviar VERB
 to send
  Envíame las fotos.
  Send me the photos.

la **envidia** NOUN
 envy
  ¡Qué envidia!
  I'm so jealous!
  Le tiene envidia a Ana.
  He's jealous of Ana.

envidiar VERB
 to envy
  ¡No te envidio!
  I don't envy you!

envolver VERB
 to wrap up
  ¿Quiere que se lo envuelva?
  Would you like me to wrap it up for you?

envuelto VERB ▷ *see* **envolver**
  Estaba envuelto con papel de embalar.
  It was wrapped in brown paper.

el **equipaje** NOUN
 luggage
  equipaje de mano
  hand luggage

el **equipo** NOUN
 1 team
  un equipo de baloncesto
  a basketball team

2 kit
Que no se te olvide el equipo de gimnasia.
Don't forget your gym kit.

equivocado (FEM **equivocada**)
ADJECTIVE
wrong
Estás equivocada.
You're wrong.
Elena me dio el número equivocado.
Elena gave me the wrong number.

equivocarse VERB
1 to make a mistake
Perdona, me equivoqué.
Sorry, I made a mistake.
2 to be wrong
Si crees que voy a dejarte ir, te equivocas.
If you think I'm going to let you go, you're wrong.
Perdone, me he equivocado de número.
Sorry, wrong number.

era VERB ▷ see **ser**
Era yo.
It was me.

eres VERB ▷ see **ser**
Eres muy amable.
You're very kind.

el erizo NOUN
hedgehog

el error NOUN
mistake
Fue un error contárselo a Lola.
Telling Lola about it was a mistake.
Cometí muchos errores en el examen.
I made a lot of mistakes in the exam.

es VERB ▷ see **ser**
Es un árbol.
It's a tree.

esa ▷ see **ese**

la **escalera** NOUN
stairs
bajar las escaleras
to go down the stairs
una escalera de mano
a ladder
una escalera mecánica
an escalator

el **escándalo** NOUN
scandal
La pelea causó un gran escándalo.
The fight caused a huge scandal.

escaparse VERB
to escape
El ladrón se escapó de la cárcel.
The thief escaped from prison.

la **escayola** NOUN
plaster
Mañana me quitan la escayola.
I'm getting my plaster taken off tomorrow.

la **escoba** NOUN
broom

escocés (FEM **escocesa**, MASC PL **escoceses**)

escocés can be an adjective or a noun.

A ADJECTIVE
Scottish
B MASC/FEM NOUN
un escocés
a Scotsman
una escocesa
a Scotswoman
los escoceses
Scottish people

Escocia FEM NOUN
Scotland

escoger VERB
to choose
>Yo escogí el azul.
>I chose the blue one.

escolar (FEM **escolar**) ADJECTIVE
school
>el uniforme escolar
>the school uniform

esconder VERB
to hide
>Lo escondí en el cajón.
>I hid it in the drawer.
>Me escondí debajo de la cama.
>I hid under the bed.

escondidas FEM NOUN
>a escondidas
>in secret
>Me pasó el papel a escondidas.
>She passed the paper to me in secret.

el **escondite**
NOUN
>jugar al escondite
>to play hide-and-seek

la **escopeta**
NOUN
shotgun

escribir VERB
to write
>Les escribí una carta.
>I wrote them a letter.
>Escribe pronto.
>Write soon.

>Nos escribimos de vez en cuando.
>We write to each other from time to time.
>¿Cómo se escribe tu nombre?
>How do you spell your name?

escrito
(FEM **escrita**)
ADJECTIVE
written
>un examen escrito
>a written exam

el **escritor**
la **escritora** NOUN
writer
>Su padre es escritor.
>His father is a writer.

escuchar VERB
to listen
>Dani escuchaba con atención.
>Dani was listening attentively.
>Me gusta escuchar música.
>I like listening to music.

la **escuela** NOUN
school
>Hoy no tengo que ir a la escuela.
>I don't have to go to school today.
>la escuela primaria
>primary school

escupir VERB
to spit

ese (FEM **esa**, MASC PL **esos**, FEM PL **esas**)

> **ese** can be an adjective or a pronoun.

A ADJECTIVE
that
>Dame ese libro.
>Give me that book.
>Trae esas sillas aquí.
>Bring those chairs over here.
B PRONOUN
that one
>Ese es mío.
>That one is mine.

Esos de ahí son mejores.
Those ones over there are better.
¿Cuánto valen esas?
How much are those?

LANGUAGE TIP
Traditionally, the pronouns **ése**, **ésa**, **ésos** and **ésas** were written with an accent to distinguish them from the unaccented adjective forms.
Nowadays, you don't have to give the accents unless the sentence would be confusing otherwise.

---

esforzarse VERB
to make an effort
Tienes que esforzarte si quieres ganar.
You have to make an effort if you want to win.

el **esfuerzo** NOUN
effort
Tuve que hacer un esfuerzo para aprobar el examen.
I had to make an effort to pass the exam.

el **esguince** NOUN
sprain
Me hice un esguince en el tobillo.
I sprained my ankle.

la **ESO** ABBREVIATION
(= Enseñanza Secundaria obligatoria)

DID YOU KNOW...?
ESO is the compulsory secondary education course done by 12 to 16 year-olds.

---

eso PRONOUN
that
Eso es mentira.
That's a lie.
Por eso te lo dije.
That's why I told you.
¡Y eso que estaba lloviendo!
And it was raining and everything!

¡Eso es!
That's it!

esos
A ADJECTIVE ▷ *see* **ese**
Dame esos lápices.
Give me those pencils.
B PRONOUN ▷ *see* **ese**
Esos son míos.
Those ones are mine.

el **espacio** NOUN
1 space
Deja más espacio entre las líneas.
Leave more space between the lines.
viajar por el espacio
to travel in space

2 room
El piano ocupa mucho espacio.
The piano takes up a lot of room.

la **espada** NOUN
sword

LANGUAGE TIP
Be careful! **espada** does not mean **spade**.

---

la **espalda** NOUN
back
Estaba tumbada de espaldas.
She was lying on her back.

España FEM NOUN
Spain

español (FEM **española**)

español can be an adjective or a noun.

English Spanish
A B C D E F G H I J K L M N O P Q R S T U V W X Y Z

A ADJECTIVE
Spanish
B MASC/FEM NOUN
español/española
Spaniard
los españoles
the Spanish
C MASC NOUN
Spanish
¿Hablas español?
Do you speak Spanish?

especial (FEM **especial**) ADJECTIVE
special
Fue un día muy especial.
It was a very special day.

especialmente ADVERB
1 **especially**
Me gusta mucho el pan, especialmente el integral.
I love bread, especially wholemeal bread.
2 **specially**
un vestido diseñado especialmente para ella
a dress designed specially for her

la **especie** NOUN
species

el **espectador**
la **espectadora** NOUN
spectator
los espectadores
the audience

el **espejo** NOUN
mirror
Me miré en el espejo.
I looked at myself in the mirror.

esperar VERB
1 **to wait**
Espera en la puerta, ahora mismo voy.
Wait at the door. I'm just coming.
2 **to wait for**
No me esperéis.
Don't wait for me.
Me hizo esperar una hora.
He kept me waiting for an hour.
3 **to meet**
Fuimos a esperarla a la estación.
We went to the station to meet her.
4 **to expect**
Llegaron antes de lo que yo esperaba.
They arrived sooner than I expected.
5 **to hope**
Espero que no sea nada grave.
I hope it isn't anything serious.
¿Vendrás a la fiesta? — Espero que sí.
Are you coming to the party?
— I hope so.
¿Crees que Carmen se enfadará? — Espero que no.
Do you think Carmen will be angry?
— I hope not.

la **espina** NOUN
1 **thorn**
2 **bone**

la **esponja** NOUN
sponge

la **esposa** NOUN
1 **wife**
2 **las esposas**
handcuffs

el **esposo** NOUN
husband

la **espuma** NOUN
foam

el **esqueleto** NOUN
skeleton

el **esquiador**
la **esquiadora** NOUN
skier

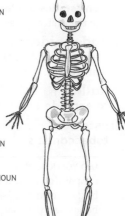

esquiar VERB
to ski
¿Sabes esquiar?
Can you ski?

la **esquina** NOUN
corner

esta
A ADJECTIVE ▷ *see* **este**
Esta pelota es mía.
This ball is mine.
B PRONOUN ▷ *see* **este**
Escogí esta.
I chose this one.

está VERB ▷ *see* **estar**
Está frío.
It's cold.

la **estación** (PL las **estaciones**) NOUN
1 station
la estación de autobuses
the bus station
la estación de ferrocarril
the railway station
2 season
las cuatro estaciones del año
the four seasons of the year

el **estadio** NOUN
stadium

los **Estados Unidos** NOUN
the United States
en Estados Unidos
in the United States

estadounidense
(FEM **estadounidense**) ADJECTIVE, NOUN
American

estallar VERB
to explode

el **estanco** NOUN
tobacconist's

DID YOU KNOW...?
In Spain, an **estanco** is recognizable by the brown and yellow 'T' sign that hangs over the door. As well as tobacco, they sell stamps and coupons for the football pools.

el **estanque** NOUN
pond

la **estantería** NOUN
1 shelves
2 bookshelves

estar VERB
1 to be
Madrid está en el centro de España.
Madrid is in the centre of Spain.
Papá está en la cocina.
Dad's in the kitchen.
¿Dónde estabas?
Where were you?
¿Está Amina?
Is Amina there?
¿Cómo estás?
How are you?
Estoy muy cansada.
I'm very tired.
Estamos de vacaciones.
We're on holiday.
Estamos a treinta de enero.
It's the thirtieth of January.
Estábamos a 30°C.
The temperature was 30°C.
Estamos esperando a Manolo.
We're waiting for Manolo.
María estaba sentada en la arena.
María was sitting on the sand.
2 to look
Ese vestido te está muy bien.
That dress looks very good on you.

la **estatua** NOUN
statue

este
(FEM **esta**, MASC PL **estos**, FEM PL **estas**)

este can be an adjective, a pronoun or a noun.

A ADJECTIVE
this
este libro
this book
estas revistas
these magazines

B PRONOUN
this one
Me gusta más este.
I prefer this one.
Estos son muy caros.
These ones are very expensive.
¿Cuánto valen estos?
How much are these?

LANGUAGE TIP
Traditionally, the pronouns **éste**, **ésta**, **éstos** and **éstas** were written with an accent to distinguish them from the unaccented adjective forms. Nowadays, you don't have to give the accents unless the sentence would be confusing otherwise.

C MASC NOUN, ADJECTIVE
east
el este del país
the east of the country

LANGUAGE TIP
When it means 'east', the adjective **este** never changes its ending, no matter what it describes.

en la costa este
on the east coast

esté VERB ▷ see **estar**
Espero que no esté muy lejos.
I hope it won't be too far.

estimado (FEM **estimada**) ADJECTIVE
Estimado Sr. Pérez:
Dear Mr Pérez,

LANGUAGE TIP
Did you notice that there's a colon (:) at the end of the opening line of a letter in Spanish, not a comma?

estirar VERB
to stretch
No quiero estirar el jersey.
I don't want to stretch my jumper.

esto PRONOUN
this
¿Para qué es esto?
What's this for?

el **estómago** NOUN
stomach
Me dolía el estómago.
I had a stomachache.

estorbar VERB
to be in the way
Las maletas estorban aquí.
The cases are in the way here.

estornudar VERB
to sneeze

estos
A PLURAL ADJECTIVE ▷ see **este**
Estos libros son bastante baratos.
These books are quite cheap.
B PLURAL PRONOUN ▷ see **este**
Estos son míos.
These ones are mine.

estoy VERB ▷ see **estar**
Estoy cansado.
I'm tired.

estrecho (FEM **estrecha**) ADJECTIVE
1 narrow
2 tight
La falda me queda muy estrecha.
The skirt is very tight on me.

la **estrella** NOUN
star
una estrella de cine
a film star
una estrella de mar
a starfish

estreñido (FEM **estreñida**) ADJECTIVE
constipated

estropeado (FEM **estropeada**) ADJECTIVE
1 broken
2 broken down

English
Spanish
a b c d e f g h i j k l m n o p q r s t u v w x y z

101

estropear VERB
1 **to break**
2 **to ruin**
   La lluvia nos estropeó las vacaciones.
   The rain ruined our holidays.
   ■ **estropearse**
   to break
   Se nos ha estropeado la tele.
   The TV's broken.

el **estuche** NOUN
pencil case

el/la **estudiante** NOUN
student

estudiar VERB
1 **to study**
   Quiere estudiar medicina.
   She wants to study medicine.
2 **to learn**
   Tengo que estudiar cuatro lecciones para el examen.
   I have to learn four lessons for the exam.

el **estudio** NOUN
   Ha dejado los estudios.
   He's given up his studies.

la **estufa** NOUN
heater
   una estufa eléctrica
   an electric heater

estupendo (FEM **estupenda**) ADJECTIVE
great
   Pasamos unas Navidades estupendas.
   We had a great Christmas.
   ¡Estupendo!
   Great!

la **estupidez** (PL las **estupideces**) NOUN
   No dice más que estupideces.
   He just talks rubbish.
   Lo que hizo fue una estupidez.
   What he did was stupid.

estúpido (FEM **estúpida**)

> **estúpido** can be an adjective or a noun.

A ADJECTIVE
stupid
B MASC/FEM NOUN
idiot
   Ese tío es un estúpido.
   That guy's an idiot.

estuve VERB ▷ *see* **estar**
   Estuve una semana de vacaciones.
   I was on holiday for a week.

la **etiqueta** NOUN
label

el **euro** NOUN
euro

Europa FEM NOUN
Europe

europeo (FEM **europea**) ADJECTIVE, NOUN
European

evitar VERB
1 **to avoid**
   Quiero evitar ese riesgo.
   I want to avoid that risk.
   Intento evitar a Carmen.
   I'm trying to avoid Carmen.
   No pude evitarlo.
   I couldn't help it.
2 **to save**
   Esto nos evitará muchos problemas.
   This will save us a lot of problems.

exacto (FEM **exacta**) ADJECTIVE
exact
   el precio exacto
   the exact price

exagerado (FEM **exagerada**) ADJECTIVE
exaggerated
   una descripción exagerada
   an exaggerated description
   ¡No seas exagerado, el pez no era tan grande!
   Don't exaggerate! The fish wasn't that big.
   El precio me parece exagerado.
   The price seems far too high.

A B C D E F G H I J K L M N O P Q R S T U V W X Y Z

English Spanish

el **examen** (PL los **exámenes**) NOUN
exam

examinar VERB
to examine
El médico la examinó.
The doctor examined her.
Mañana me examino de inglés.
Tomorrow I've got an English exam.

excelente (FEM **excelente**) ADJECTIVE
excellent

excepto PREPOSITION
except for
todos, excepto Juan
everyone, except for Juan

excluyendo VERB ▷ see **excluir**
Excluyendo a mis padres,
somos tres.
Not counting my parents, there are
three of us.

la **excursión** (PL las **excursiones**) NOUN
trip
Mañana vamos de excursión con
el colegio.
Tomorrow we're going on a school
trip.

la **excusa** NOUN
excuse

existir VERB
to exist
¿Existen los fantasmas?
Do ghosts exist?

el **éxito** NOUN
success
Esa novela será un gran éxito.
That novel will be a great success.
Su película tuvo mucho éxito.
His film was very successful.
Acabaron con éxito el proyecto.
They completed the project
successfully.

LANGUAGE TIP
Be careful! **éxito** does not mean **exit**.

---

la **experiencia** NOUN
experience

el **experimento** NOUN
experiment

el **experto**
la **experta** NOUN
expert
Es una experta
en informática.
She's a computer expert.

la **explicación** (PL las **explicaciones**)
NOUN
explanation

explicar VERB
to explain
¿Quieres que te explique cómo
hacerlo?
Do you want me to explain to you
how to do it?

la **explosión** (PL las **explosiones**) NOUN
explosion

la **exposición** (PL las **exposiciones**)
NOUN
exhibition
montar una exposición
to put on an exhibition

expresar VERB
to express
No sabe expresarse.
He doesn't know how to express
himself.

la **expresión** (PL las **expresiones**) NOUN
expression

extender VERB
to spread
Extendí la toalla sobre la arena.
I spread the towel out on the sand.
El fuego se extendió
rápidamente.
The fire spread quickly.

exterior (FEM **exterior**) ADJECTIVE
outside

extinto (FEM **extinta**) ADJECTIVE
extinct

extra (FEM **extra**) ADJECTIVE
extra
   una manta extra
   an extra blanket

extraescolar (FEM **extraescolar**)
ADJECTIVE
   actividades extraescolares
   extracurricular activities

extranjero (FEM **extranjera**)

> **extranjero** can be an adjective or a noun.

A ADJECTIVE
   foreign
B MASC/FEM NOUN
   foreigner

   viajar al extranjero
   to travel abroad

extrañar VERB
to miss
   Extraña mucho a sus padres.
   He misses his parents a lot.
   Me extraña que no haya llegado.
   I'm surprised he hasn't arrived.
   ¡Ya me extrañaba a mí!
   I thought it was strange!

extraño (FEM **extraña**) ADJECTIVE
strange
   ¡Qué extraño!
   How strange!

extraordinario (FEM **extraordinaria**)
ADJECTIVE
extraordinary

el **extremo** NOUN
end
   Cogí la cuerda por un extremo.
   I took hold of one end of the rope.
   pasar de un extremo a otro
   to go from one extreme to the other

la **fábrica** NOUN
factory

> **LANGUAGE TIP**
> Be careful! **fábrica** does not mean
> **fabric**.

fácil (FEM **fácil**) ADJECTIVE
easy
un ejercicio fácil
an easy exercise

la **falda** NOUN
skirt

el **fallo** NOUN
1 **fault**
2 **mistake**
¡Qué fallo!
What a stupid mistake!

falso (FEM **falsa**) ADJECTIVE
1 **false**
2 **forged**

la **falta** NOUN
1 **lack**
la falta de dinero
lack of money
2 **mistake**
una falta de ortografía
a spelling mistake

> **Me hace falta un ordenador.**
> I need a computer.
> **No hace falta que vengáis.**
> You don't need to come.

faltar VERB
1 **to be missing**

Me falta un bolígrafo.
One of my pens is missing.
No podemos irnos. Falta Guille.
We can't go. Guille isn't here yet.
A la sopa le falta sal.
There isn't enough salt in the soup.
faltar al colegio
to miss school
No debes faltar al colegio.
You mustn't miss school.
2 **Falta media hora para comer.**
There's half an hour to go before
lunch.
¿Te falta mucho?
Will you be long?

la **fama** NOUN
1 **fame**
2 **reputation**
tener fama de
to have a reputation for
Tiene fama de mandona.
She has a reputation for being bossy.

la **familia** NOUN
family

familiar (FEM **familiar**) ADJECTIVE
1 **family**
la vida familiar
family life
2 **familiar**
Su cara me resulta familiar.
His face is familiar.

famoso (FEM **famosa**) ADJECTIVE
famous

el **fantasma** NOUN
ghost

la **farmacia** NOUN
chemist's
Lo compré en la farmacia.
I bought it at the chemist's.

> **DID YOU KNOW...?**
> Spanish chemists are identifiable by
> a red or green cross outside the shop.
> Go to a **perfumería** instead if you
> want to buy cosmetics or toiletries.

English

Spanish

A
B
C
D
E
F
G
H
I
J
K
L
M
N
O
P
Q
R
S
T
U
V
W
X
Y
Z

el **faro** NOUN
1 **headlight**
2 **lighthouse**

fastidiar VERB
to annoy
Lo que más me fastidia es tener que decírselo.
What annoys me most is having to tell him.

fatal

> **fatal** can be an adjective or an adverb.

A ADJECTIVE (FEM **fatal**)
awful
Me siento fatal.
I feel awful.
B ADVERB
Lo pasé fatal.
I had an awful time.
Lo hice fatal.
I made a mess of it.

el **favor** NOUN
favour
¿Puedes hacerme un favor?
Can you do me a favour?

por favor
please

favorito (FEM **favorita**) ADJECTIVE
favourite
¿Cuál es tu color favorito?
What's your favourite colour?

febrero MASC NOUN
February

LANGUAGE TIP
Months are not spelled with a capital letter in Spanish.

en febrero
in February
Nació el quince de febrero.
He was born on the fifteenth of February.

la **fecha** NOUN
date
¿A qué fecha estamos?
What's the date today?
su fecha de nacimiento
his date of birth

la **felicidad** NOUN
happiness
¡Felicidades!
Happy birthday!/Congratulations!

LANGUAGE TIP
¡Felicidades! has two meanings.

felicitar VERB
to congratulate
La felicité por sus notas.
I congratulated her on her exam results.
Felicítalo por su cumpleaños.
Wish him a happy birthday.

feliz
(FEM **feliz**,
PL **felices**)
ADJECTIVE
happy
Se la ve muy feliz.
She looks very happy.

¡Feliz cumpleaños!
Happy birthday!
¡Feliz Año Nuevo!
Happy New Year!
¡Feliz Navidad!
Happy Christmas!

femenino (FEM **femenina**) ADJECTIVE
1 **feminine**
2 **female**
el sexo femenino
the female sex

feo (FEM **fea**) ADJECTIVE
ugly

festivo (FEM **festiva**) ADJECTIVE
un día festivo
a holiday

fiarse VERB
fiarse de alguien
to trust somebody
No me fío de él.
I don't trust him.

la **ficha** NOUN
counter

los **fideos** NOUN
noodles

la **fiebre** NOUN
temperature
Tiene fiebre.
She has a temperature.

la **fiesta** NOUN
1 party
Voy a dar una fiesta para celebrarlo.
I'm going to have a party to celebrate.
El pueblo está en fiestas.
There's a fiesta on in the town.
una fiesta de cumpleaños
a birthday party
2 holiday
El lunes es fiesta.
Monday is a holiday.

la **fila** NOUN
1 row
Nos sentamos en la segunda fila.
We sit in the second row.
2 line
Los niños se pusieron en fila.
The children got into line.

el **filete** NOUN
1 steak
un filete con patatas fritas
steak and chips
2 fillet
un filete de merluza
a hake fillet

el **fin** NOUN
end
En fin, ¿qué le vamos a hacer?
Oh well, what can we do about it?
por fin
at last
¡Por fin hemos llegado!
We've got here at last!

el fin de año
New Year's Eve
el fin de semana
the weekend

final

> **final** can be an adjective or a noun.

A ADJECTIVE (FEM **final**)
final
el resultado final
the final result
B MASC NOUN
end
Al final de la calle hay un colegio.
At the end of the street there's a school.
a finales de mayo
at the end of May
al final
in the end
Al final tuve que darle la razón.
In the end I had to admit that he was right.
un final feliz
a happy ending
C FEM NOUN
final
la final de la copa
the cup final

fingir VERB
to pretend
Fingió no haberme oído.
He pretended not to have heard me.
Finge dormir.
He's pretending to be asleep.

fino (FEM **fina**) ADJECTIVE
1 thin
2 fine

la **firma** NOUN
signature

firmar VERB
to sign

firme (FEM **firme**) ADJECTIVE
steady
Mantén la escalera firme.
Can you hold the ladder steady?

la **flauta** NOUN
1 recorder
2 flute

la **flecha** NOUN
arrow

el **flequillo** NOUN
fringe

flojo (FEM **floja**) ADJECTIVE
1 loose
2 weak
Todavía tengo las piernas muy flojas.
My legs are still very weak.
Está flojo en matemáticas.
He's weak at maths.

la **flor** NOUN
flower

el **flotador** NOUN
rubber ring

el **folio** NOUN
1 sheet of paper
2 page

el **folleto** NOUN
1 brochure
2 leaflet

el **fondo** NOUN
1 bottom
en el fondo del mar
at the bottom of the sea
2 end
Mi habitación está al fondo del pasillo.
My room's at the end of the corridor.

el **fontanero**
la **fontanera** NOUN
plumber

la **forma** NOUN
way
Andaba de una forma extraña.
She was walking in a strange way.
de todas formas
anyway

De todas formas, debes ir a verlo.
You should go to see him anyway.

formal (FEM **formal**) ADJECTIVE
responsible
un chico muy formal
a very responsible boy

forrar VERB
to cover

la **foto** NOUN
photo
Les hice una foto a los niños.
I took a photo of the children.

la **fotocopia** NOUN
photocopy

fotocopiar VERB
to photocopy

la **fotografía** NOUN
photograph
una fotografía de mis padres
a photograph of my parents

la **frambuesa** NOUN
raspberry

la **frase** NOUN
sentence

la **frecuencia** NOUN
frequency
Nos vemos con frecuencia.
We often see each other.

frecuente (FEM **frecuente**) ADJECTIVE
common
un error bastante frecuente
a fairly common mistake

el **fregadero** NOUN
sink

fregar VERB
to wash
Tengo que fregar la cazuela.
I've got to wash the pan.
Yo estaba en la cocina fregando.
I was in the kitchen washing the dishes.
Deberías fregar el suelo.
You should mop the floor.

freír VERB
to fry

el **freno** NOUN
brake
el freno de mano
the handbrake

la **frente** NOUN
forehead
Tiene una cicatriz en la frente.
He has a scar on his forehead.

el **frente** NOUN
front
frente a
opposite
Frente al hotel hay un banco.
There's a bank opposite the hotel.

la **fresa** NOUN
strawberry

fresco

> **fresco** can be an adjective or a noun.

A ADJECTIVE (FEM **fresca**)
1 cool
2 fresh
B MASC NOUN
fresh air
Salimos fuera a tomar el fresco.
We went outside to get some fresh air.
Hace fresco.
It's chilly./It's cool.

LANGUAGE TIP
hace fresco has two meanings. Look at the examples.

No quiero salir porque hace fresco.
I don't want to go out because it's a bit chilly.
En esta casa hace fresco en verano.
This house is cool in summer.
Hace más fresco dentro.
It's cooler inside.

friego VERB ▷ see **fregar**
Yo friego y tu seca.
I'll wash and you dry.

frío

> **frío** can be an adjective, noun or part of the verb **freír**.

A ADJECTIVE (FEM **fría**)
cold
Tengo las manos frías.
My hands are cold.
B MASC NOUN
cold
Hace frío.
It's cold.
Tengo mucho frío.
I'm very cold.
C VERB ▷ see **freír**
¿Te frío un huevo?
Shall I fry you an egg?

frito

> **frito** can be an adjective or part of the verb **freír**.

A ADJECTIVE (FEM **frita**)
fried
huevos fritos
fried eggs
B VERB ▷ see **freír**
He frito un huevo.
I've fried an egg.

la **frontera** NOUN
border
Nos pararon en la frontera.
We were stopped at the border.

la **fruta** NOUN
fruit
La fruta está muy cara.
Fruit is very expensive.

fue VERB ▷ see **ir**, **ser**
Fue a la escuela en Barcelona.
He went to school in Barcelona.
Fue él.
It was him.

el **fuego** NOUN
fire
Enciende el fuego.
Light the fire.

Puse la cazuela al fuego.
I put the pot on to heat.
**¿Tiene fuego,
por favor?**
Have you got a light,
please?
fuegos artificiales
fireworks

la **fuente** NOUN
fountain

fuera

> **fuera** can be an adverb or part of the
> verbs **ir** and **ser**.

A ADVERB
outside
Los niños estaban jugando fuera.
The children were playing outside.
Por fuera es blanco.
It's white on the outside.
¡Estamos aquí fuera!
We are out here!
Hoy vamos a cenar fuera.
We're going out for dinner tonight.
B VERB ▷ *see* **ir**, **ser**
Quería que fuera con ella.
She wanted me to go with her.
Si fuera yo, no se lo diría.
If I were you, I wouldn't tell him.

fuerte

> **fuerte** can be an adjective or an
> adverb.

A ADJECTIVE (FEM **fuerte**)
1 **strong**
2 **loud**
3 **hard**
B ADVERB
1 **hard**
**No le des
tan fuerte.**
Don't hit it so hard.
2 **loudly**
Siempre habla fuerte.
He always talks loudly.
3 **Agárrate fuerte.**
Hold on tight.

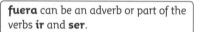

la **fuerza** NOUN
strength
No le quedaban fuerzas.
He had no strength left.
No te lo comas a la fuerza.
Don't force yourself to eat it.
la fuerza de la gravedad
the force of gravity
la fuerza de voluntad
willpower

fui VERB ▷ *see* **ir**, **ser**
Ayer fui al cine.
I went to the cinema yesterday.
Fui yo.
It was me.

el **fumador**
la **fumadora** NOUN
smoker

fumar VERB
to smoke
Mi padre quiere dejar de fumar.
My dad wants to give up smoking.

funcionar VERB
to work
El ascensor no funciona.
The lift isn't working.
Funciona con pilas.
It runs on batteries.

el **funeral** NOUN
funeral

la **furgoneta** NOUN
van

furioso (FEM **furiosa**) ADJECTIVE
furious

el **fútbol** NOUN
football
jugar al fútbol
to play football

el **futbolín** (PL los **futbolines**) NOUN
table football

el/la **futbolista** NOUN
footballer
Quiere ser futbolista.
He wants to be a footballer.

Gg

las **gafas** NOUN
1 **glasses**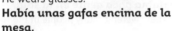
Lleva gafas.
He wears glasses.
Había unas gafas encima de la mesa.
There was a pair of glasses on the table.
gafas de sol
sunglasses
2 **goggles**

Gales MASC NOUN
Wales
el País de Gales
Wales

la **galleta** NOUN
biscuit
una galleta salada
a cracker

gallina
FEM NOUN
hen

el **gallo** NOUN
cock

el **gamberro**
la **gamberra** NOUN
hooligan

la **gana** NOUN
Hazlo como te dé la gana.
Do it however you like.
Lo hizo de mala gana.
She did it reluctantly.
Tengo ganas de que llegue el sábado.
I'm looking forward to Saturday.

¡No me da la gana!
I don't want to!

el **ganador**
la **ganadora** NOUN
winner

ganar VERB
1 **to win**
Lo importante no es ganar.
Winning isn't the most important thing.
Con eso no ganas nada.
You won't achieve anything by doing that.
2 **to beat**
Ganamos al Olimpic tres a cero.
We beat Olimpic three-nil.
3 **to earn**
Gana un buen sueldo.
He earns a good wage.

el **garaje** NOUN
garage

la **garganta** NOUN
throat
Me duele la garganta.
I've got a sore throat.

el **gas** (PL los **gases**) NOUN
gas
¿Te huele a gas?
Can you smell gas?
agua mineral sin gas
still mineral water
agua mineral con gas
sparkling mineral water

la **gaseosa** NOUN

DID YOU KNOW...?
Gaseosa is a sweet fizzy drink a bit like lemonade or soda.

---

la **gasolina** NOUN
petrol

la **gasolinera** NOUN
petrol station

A
B
C
D
E
F
G
H
I
J
K
L
M
N
O
P
Q
R
S
T
U
V
W
X
Y
Z

gastado (FEM **gastada**) ADJECTIVE
worn

gastar VERB
1 **to spend**
2 **to use**
Gastamos mucha electricidad.
We use a lot of electricity.
3 **Le gastamos una broma a Juan.**
We played a joke on Juan.
■ **gastarse**
to run out
Se han gastado las pilas.
The batteries have run out.

la **gata** NOUN
cat

andar a gatas
to crawl
El niño todavía anda a gatas.
The baby is still crawling.

el **gato** NOUN
cat

la **gaviota** NOUN
gull

el **gemelo**
la **gemela** NOUN
identical twin

los **gemelos** NOUN
binoculars

general (FEM **general**) ADJECTIVE
general

por lo general
generally

genial (FEM **genial**) ADJECTIVE
brilliant

el **genio** NOUN
1 **temper**
¡Menudo genio tiene tu padre!
Your father has got such a temper!
Tiene mal genio.
He has a bad temper
2 **genius**
¡Eres un genio!
You're a genius!

la **gente** NOUN
people
Había poca gente en la sala.
There weren't many people in the room.

la **geografía** NOUN
geography

el **gesto** NOUN
Hizo un gesto de alivio.
He looked relieved.
Me hizo un gesto para que me sentara.
He signalled for me to sit down.

la **gimnasia** NOUN
gymnastics
Mi madre hace gimnasia todas las mañanas.
My mother does some exercise every morning.

el **gimnasio** NOUN
gym

girar VERB
to turn
Giré la cabeza para ver quién era.
I turned my head to see who it was.

global (FEM **global**) ADJECTIVE
global

el **globo** NOUN
balloon

el **gobierno** NOUN
government

el **gol** NOUN
goal

Metió un gol.
He scored a goal.

la **golosina** NOUN
sweet

goloso (FEM **golosa**) ADJECTIVE
Soy muy golosa.
I've got a very sweet tooth.

el **golpe** NOUN
1 **Se dio un golpe contra la pared.**
He hit the wall.
Me he dado un golpe en el codo.
I've banged my elbow.
2 **knock**
Oímos un golpe en la puerta.
We heard a knock at the door.
3 **de golpe**
suddenly
De golpe decidió marcharse.
He suddenly decided to leave.

golpear VERB
1 **to hit**
Me golpeó en la cara con su raqueta.
He hit me in the face with his racquet.
2 **to bang**
El maestro golpeó el pupitre con la mano.
The teacher banged the desk with his hand.

la **goma** NOUN
1 **rubber**
¿Me prestas la goma?
Can you lend me your rubber?
2 **elastic band**
Necesito una goma para el pelo.
I need an elastic band for my hair.

gordo (FEM **gorda**) ADJECTIVE
fat
No es tan gordo.
He's not so fat.

la **gorra** NOUN
1 **cap**
2 **de gorra**
for free
Entramos de gorra.
We got in for free.

el **gorro** NOUN
hat
Llevaba un gorro de lana.
He wore a woolly hat.
un gorro de baño
a swimming cap

la **gota** NOUN
drop
Solo bebí una gota de zumo.
I only had a drop of juice.
Están cayendo cuatro gotas.
It's spitting.

grabar VERB
1 **to record**
Lo grabaron en directo.
It was recorded live.
2 **to engrave**

la **gracia** NOUN
Sus chistes tienen mucha gracia.
His jokes are very funny.
Yo no le veo la gracia.
I don't see what's so funny.
Me hizo mucha gracia.
It was so funny.
No me hace gracia tener que salir con este tiempo.
I'm not too pleased about having to go out in this weather.

gracias a
thanks to
¡Gracias!
Thank you!
¡Muchas gracias!
Thanks very much!
dar las gracias a alguien
to thank somebody

gracioso (FEM **graciosa**) ADJECTIVE
funny
¡Qué gracioso!
How funny!

el **grado** NOUN
degree
Estaban a diez grados bajo cero.
It was ten degrees below zero.

la **gramática** NOUN
grammar

el **gramo** NOUN
gram

gran ADJECTIVE ▷ see grande
un gran artista
a great artist
un gran número de gente
a large number of people

Gran Bretaña FEM NOUN
Great Britain

grande (FEM **grande**) ADJECTIVE

LANGUAGE TIP
grande becomes **gran** before a
singular noun.

---

1 **big**
¿Cómo es de grande?
How big is it?
La camisa me está grande.
The shirt is too big for me.
unos grandes almacenes
a department store
2 **large**
un gran número de visitantes
a large number of visitors

el **granizo** NOUN
hail

la **granja** NOUN
farm

el **grano** NOUN
1 **spot**
**Me ha salido un grano en la
frente.**
I've got a spot on my forehead.
2 **grain**

gratis

gratis can be an adjective or an
adverb.

A ADJECTIVE (FEM+PL **gratis**)
free
La entrada es gratis.
Entry is free.

B ADVERB
for free
Te lo arreglan gratis.
They'll fix it for free.

grave (FEM **grave**) ADJECTIVE
serious
Tenemos un problema grave.
We've got a serious problem.

el **grifo** NOUN
tap
Abre el grifo.
Turn on the tap.
Cierra el grifo.
Turn off the tap.

la **gripe** NOUN
flu
Tengo la gripe
I've got flu.

gris ADJECTIVE, MASC NOUN
grey

gritar VERB
1 **to shout**
Niños, no gritéis tanto.
Children, stop shouting so much.
2 **to scream**
**El enfermo no podía dejar de
gritar.**
The patient couldn't stop screaming.

el **grito** NOUN
1 **shout**
¡No des esos gritos!
Stop shouting like that!
2 **scream**
Oímos un grito en la calle.
We heard a scream outside.

grosero (FEM **grosera**) ADJECTIVE
rude

la **grúa** NOUN
crane

el **grupo** NOUN
1 **group**
**Los alumnos trabajan en
grupo.**
The students work in groups.

2 band
un grupo de rock
a rock band

el **guante** NOUN
glove
unos guantes
a pair of gloves

guapo (FEM **guapa**) ADJECTIVE
1 **handsome**
2 **pretty**

guardar VERB
1 **to put away**
Los niños guardaron los juguetes.
The children put away their toys.
2 **to keep**
No sabe guardar un secreto.
He can't keep a secret.
3 **to save**
Debes guardar el fichero.
You must save the file.

la **guardería** NOUN
nursery

el/la **guardia** NOUN
police officer

el **guarro**
la **guarra** NOUN (*informal*)
¡Eres un guarro!
You're disgusting!

guay (FEM **guay**) ADJECTIVE
cool (*informal*)
¡Qué moto más guay!
What a cool bike!

la **guerra** NOUN
war

guía
A MASC/FEM NOUN
guide

B FEM NOUN
guidebook
Compré una guía turística de
Londres.
I bought a tourist guidebook to
London.

guiñar VERB
to wink
Me guiñó el ojo.
He winked at me.

la **guitarra** NOUN
guitar

el **gusano** NOUN
worm

gustar VERB
1 Me gustan las uvas.
I like grapes.
¿Te gusta viajar?
Do you like travelling?
Le gusta más llevar
pantalones.
She prefers to wear trousers.
2 Me gusta su hermana.
I fancy his sister.

Hh

ha VERB ▷ *see* **haber**
Me ha comprado un libro.
He has bought me a book.

haber VERB

1 to have

LANGUAGE TIP
haber is used to make the past tense of verbs.

He comido.
I have eaten.
¿Habéis comido?
Have you eaten?
Había comido.
I had eaten.
Se ha sentado.
She's sat down.

2 hay
there is/there are

LANGUAGE TIP
hay has two meanings: **there is** and **there are**. Look at the examples.

Hay una iglesia en la esquina.
There's a church on the corner.
Hay treinta alumnos en mi clase.
There are thirty pupils in my class.
¿Hay entradas?
Are there any tickets?

3 hay que
you must
Hay que ser respetuoso.
You must be respectful.

la habitación (PL las **habitaciones**)
NOUN

1 bedroom

Esta es la habitación de mi hermana.
This is my sister's bedroom.

2 room
una habitación doble
a double room
una habitación individual
a single room

el/la **habitante** NOUN
inhabitant
los habitantes de la zona
people living in the area

hablar VERB

1 to speak
¿Hablas español?
Do you speak Spanish?
¿Has hablado con el profesor?
Have you spoken to the teacher?

2 to talk
Estuvimos hablando toda la tarde.
We were talking all afternoon.
Solo hablan de fútbol.
They only talk about football.
¡Ni hablar!
No way!

habré VERB ▷ *see* **haber**
¿Dónde habré puesto las llaves?
Where did I put my keys?

hacer VERB

1 to make
Tengo que hacer la cama.
I've got to make the bed.
Estáis haciendo mucho ruido.
You're making a lot of noise.

2 to do
¿Qué haces?
What are you doing?
Tengo que hacer los deberes.
I have to do my homework.
Hace mucho deporte.
She does a lot of sport.

hacer clic en algo
to click on something
3 to be
Hace calor.
It's hot.
4 hace ...
... ago/for ...

LANGUAGE TIP
When talking about time, **hace** can mean **ago** or **for**. Look at the examples.

Terminé hace una hora.
I finished an hour ago.
Hace un mes que voy.
I've been going for a month.
¿Hace mucho que esperas?
Have you been waiting long?
■ **hacerse**
to become
Quiere hacerse famoso.
He wants to become famous.

hacia PREPOSITION
1 towards
Venía hacia mí.
He was coming towards me.
2 hacia adelante
forwards
hacia atrás
backwards
hacia dentro
inside
hacia fuera
outside
hacia abajo
down
hacia arriba
up

hago VERB ▷ *see* **hacer**
Y ahora, ¿qué hago?
And now, what do I do?

el **hambre** NOUN
hunger
tener hambre
to be hungry
No tengo mucha hambre.
I'm not very hungry.

la **hamburguesa** NOUN
hamburger

haré VERB ▷ *see* **hacer**
Lo haré mañana.
I'll do it tomorrow.

hartarse VERB
hartarse de algo
to get fed up with something/to stuff oneself with something

LANGUAGE TIP
hartarse de has two meanings. Look at the examples.

Me harté de estudiar.
I got fed up with studying.
Me harté de pasteles.
I stuffed myself with cakes.

harto (FEM **harta**) ADJECTIVE
fed up
Estoy harto de repetirlo.
I'm fed up with repeating it.
¡Me tienes harto!
I'm fed up with you!

hasta

hasta can be a preposition, conjunction or adverb.

A PREPOSITION, CONJUNCTION
till
Está abierto hasta las cuatro.
It's open till four o'clock.
¿Hasta cuándo?
How long?
¿Hasta cuándo te quedas?
— Hasta la semana que viene.
How long are you staying? — Till next week.
hasta que
until
Espera aquí hasta que te llamen.
Wait here until you're called.

¡Hasta luego!
See you!
¡Hasta mañana!
See you tomorrow!

¡Hasta el sábado!
See you on Saturday!

B ADVERB
even
Estudia hasta cuando está de vacaciones.
He even studies when he's on holiday.

hay VERB ▷ *see* **haber**
Hay tres casas.
There are three houses.

haz VERB ▷ *see* **hacer**
Haz lo que quieras.
Do whatever you like.

he VERB ▷ *see* **haber**
No he estado nunca en Londres.
I've never been to London.

hecho

> **hecho** can be an adjective or part of the verb **hacer**.

A ADJECTIVE (FEM **hecha**)
made
¿De qué está hecho?
What's it made of?
hecho a mano
handmade
¡Bien hecho!
Well done!
B VERB ▷ *see* **hacer**
Ya lo he hecho.
I've done it already.

helado

> **helado** can be a noun or an adjective.

A MASC NOUN
ice cream

un helado de chocolate
a chocolate ice cream

B ADJECTIVE (FEM **helada**)
1 frozen
El lago está helado.
The lake's frozen over.
2 freezing
¡Estoy helado!
I'm freezing!

el **helicóptero** NOUN
helicopter

hemos VERB ▷ *see* **haber**
Ya hemos llegado.
We've arrived.

la **herida** NOUN
wound

herido (FEM **herida**) ADJECTIVE
1 wounded
2 injured

herir VERB
to wound
Lo hirieron en el pecho.
He was wounded in the chest.

la **hermana** NOUN
sister
mi media hermana
my half sister

la **hermanastra** NOUN
stepsister

el **hermanastro** NOUN
stepbrother
mis hermanastros
my stepbrothers/my stepbrothers and sisters

LANGUAGE TIP
mis hermanastros has two meanings. It can be translated as **my stepbrothers** or **my stepbrothers and sisters**.

el **hermano** NOUN
brother
> **mi medio hermano**
> my half brother

mis hermanos
my brothers/my brothers and sisters

LANGUAGE TIP
mis hermanos has more than one meaning. It can be translated as **my brothers** or **my brothers and sisters**.

el **héroe** NOUN
hero

la **herramienta** NOUN
tool

hervir VERB
to boil
> **El agua está hirviendo.**
> The water's boiling.

hice VERB ▷ *see* **hacer**
> **Lo hice yo solo.**
> I did it on my own.

el **hielo** NOUN
ice

la **hierba** NOUN
grass

el **hierro** NOUN
iron

la **higiene** NOUN
hygiene

higiénico (FEM **higiénica**) ADJECTIVE
hygienic
> **poco higiénico**
> unhygienic

la **hija** NOUN
daughter
> **Soy hija única.**
> I'm an only child.

la **hijastra** NOUN
stepdaughter

el **hijastro** NOUN
stepson
> **mis hijastros**
> my stepsons/my stepchildren

LANGUAGE TIP
mis hijastros has two meanings. It can be translated as **my stepsons** or **my stepchildren**.

el **hijo** NOUN
son
> **su hijo mayor**
> his oldest son
> **Soy hijo único.**
> I'm an only child.
> **mis hijos**
> my sons/my children

LANGUAGE TIP
mis hijos has two meanings. It can be translated as **my sons** or **my children**.

hinchado (FEM **hinchada**) ADJECTIVE
swollen

el **hipo** NOUN
hiccups
> **Tengo hipo.**
> I've got hiccups.

hirviendo VERB ▷ *see* **hervir**
> **La leche está hirviendo.**
> The milk is boiling.

la **historia** NOUN
history
> **mi profesor de historia**
> my history teacher

hizo VERB ▷ *see* **hacer**
> **Lo hizo mi hermana.**
> My sister did it.

el hobby NOUN
hobby
> Lo hago por hobby.
> I do it as a hobby.

el hogar NOUN
home

la hoja NOUN
> **1** leaf
> **2** sheet
> **una hoja de papel**
> a sheet of paper
> **3** page
> **las hojas de un libro**
> the pages of a book

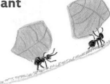

hola EXCLAMATION
hello!

holgazán (FEM **holgazana**, MASC PL **holgazanes**) ADJECTIVE
lazy

el hombre NOUN
man
> **un hombre de negocios**
> a businessman

el hombro NOUN
shoulder

hondo (FEM **honda**) ADJECTIVE
deep
> **la parte honda de la piscina**
> the deep end of the pool

la hora NOUN
> **1** hour
> **El viaje dura una hora.**
> The journey lasts an hour.
> **2** time
> **¿A qué hora te levantas?**
> What time do you get up?
> **¿Tienes hora?**
> Have you got the time?
> **la hora de cenar**
> dinner time
> **a última hora**
> at the last minute

> **¿Qué hora es?**
> What's the time?

el horario NOUN
timetable

horizontal (FEM **horizontal**) ADJECTIVE
horizontal

el horizonte NOUN
horizon

la hormiga NOUN
ant

el horno NOUN
oven
> **pollo al horno**
> roast chicken

el horóscopo NOUN
horoscope

la horquilla NOUN
hairgrip

horrible (FEM **horrible**) ADJECTIVE
awful
> **Ha hecho un tiempo horrible.**
> The weather has been awful.

el hospital NOUN
hospital
> **La llevaron al hospital.**
> She was taken to hospital.

el **hotel** NOUN
hotel

hoy ADVERB
today
¿Qué día es hoy?
What's the date today?
de hoy en adelante
from now on
hoy por la mañana
this morning

la **hucha** NOUN
moneybox

hueco

> **hueco** can be an adjective or a noun.

A ADJECTIVE (FEM **hueca**)
hollow
B MASC NOUN
space
Deja un hueco para la respuesta.
Leave a space for the answer.

la **huella** NOUN
footprint
las huellas del ladrón
the thief's footprints
huella digital
fingerprint

huelo VERB ▷ see **oler**
Lo huelo desde aquí.
I can smell it from here.

el **hueso** NOUN
1 **bone**
2 **stone**

el **huevo** NOUN
egg
un huevo duro
a hard-boiled egg

un huevo frito
a fried egg
huevos revueltos
scrambled eggs
un huevo pasado por agua
a soft-boiled egg

humano (FEM **humana**) ADJECTIVE
human
el cuerpo humano
the human body
los seres humanos
human beings

húmedo (FEM **húmeda**) ADJECTIVE
1 **damp**
Mi camiseta está húmeda todavía.
My t-shirt is still damp.
2 **humid**

el **humo** NOUN
smoke
Salía humo de la chimenea.
Smoke was coming out of the chimney.

el **humor** NOUN
mood
No está de humor para bromas.
He's not in the mood for jokes.
estar de buen humor
to be in a good mood
estar de mal humor
to be in a bad mood

hundirse VERB
to sink
El barco se hundió durante la tormenta.
The boat sank during the storm.

huyendo VERB ▷ see **huir**
Estaban huyendo de un perro.
They were running away from a dog.

English

Spanish

a
b
c
d
e
f
g
h
i
j
k
l
m
n
o
p
q
r
s
t
u
v
w
x
y
z

121

I i

iba VERB ▷ see **ir**
Iba por la calle.
He was walking down the street.

la **ida** NOUN
single
¿Cuánto cuesta la ida?
How much does a single cost?
El viaje de ida duró dos horas.
The journey there took two hours.
un billete de ida y vuelta
a return ticket

la **idea** NOUN
idea
¡Qué buena idea!
What a good idea!
Ya me voy haciendo a la idea.
I'm beginning to get used to the idea.
cambiar de idea
to change one's mind
He cambiado de idea.
I've changed my mind.

No tengo ni idea.
I have no idea.

ideal (FEM **ideal**) ADJECTIVE
ideal
Es el lugar ideal para las vacaciones.
It's the ideal place for a holiday.

idéntico (FEM **idéntica**) ADJECTIVE
identical
Tiene una falda idéntica a la mía.
She has an identical skirt to mine.
Es idéntica a su padre.
She's the spitting image of her father.

el **idioma** NOUN
language
Habla tres idiomas.
He speaks three languages.

idiota (FEM **idiota**)

idiota can be an adjective or a noun.

A ADJECTIVE
stupid
¡No seas tan idiota!
Don't be so stupid!
B MASC/FEM NOUN
idiot

la **iglesia** NOUN
church
Voy a la iglesia todos los domingos.
I go to church every Sunday.
la Iglesia católica
the Catholic Church

ignorante (FEM **ignorante**) ADJECTIVE
ignorant

igual

igual can be an adjective or an adverb.

A ADJECTIVE (FEM **igual**)
1 equal
Dividieron el pastel en partes iguales.
They divided the cake into equal portions.
X es igual a Y.
X is equal to Y.
2 the same
Todas las casas son iguales.
All the houses are the same.
Es igual a su madre.
She looks just like her mother./
She's just like her mother.

LANGUAGE TIP
ser igual a has two meanings. It can be translated as **to look just like** and **to be just like**.

Tengo una falda igual que la
tuya.
I've got a skirt just like yours.

Me da igual.
I don't mind.

B ADVERB

1 **the same**
Se visten igual.
They dress the same.

2 **maybe**
Igual no lo saben todavía.
Maybe they don't know yet.

3 **anyway**
No hizo nada pero la castigaron
igual.
She didn't do anything but they
punished her anyway.

igualmente ADVERB
the same to you
¡Feliz Navidad! — Gracias,
igualmente.
Happy Christmas! — Thanks, the same
to you.

ilegal (FEM **ilegal**) ADJECTIVE
illegal

la **ilusión** (PL las **ilusiones**) NOUN

1 **hope**
No te hagas muchas
ilusiones.
Don't build
your hopes up.

2 **dream**

Mi mayor ilusión es llegar a ser
médico.
My dream is to become a doctor.

LANGUAGE TIP
hacer ilusión has several meanings.
Look at the examples.

Le hace mucha ilusión que
vengas.
He's really looking forward to you
coming.
Tu regalo me hizo mucha ilusión.
I was really pleased with your present.

la **imagen** (PL las **imágenes**) NOUN
image
Han decidido cambiar de imagen.
They've decided to change their image.
Es la viva imagen de su madre.
She's the spitting image of her mother.

la **imaginación** (PL las
imaginaciones) NOUN
imagination
Tiene mucha imaginación.
He has a vivid imagination.
Ni se me pasó por la imaginación.
It never even occurred to me.

imaginarse VERB
to imagine
Me imagino que seguirá en
Madrid.
I imagine that he's still in Madrid.
¿Se enfadó mucho? — ¡imagínate!
Was he very angry? — What do you
think!

imbécil (FEM **imbécil**)

imbécil can be an adjective or a
noun.

A ADJECTIVE
stupid
¡No seas imbécil!
Don't be stupid!

B MASC/FEM NOUN
idiot

imitar VERB

1 **to copy**
Imita todo lo que hace su
hermano.
He copies everything his brother does.

2 **to do an impression of**
Imita muy bien a la directora.
She does a very good impression of the
headmistress.

English

Spanish

A
B
C
D
E
F
G
H
I
J
K
L
M
N
O
P
Q
R
S
T
U
V
W
X
Y
Z

impar

> **impar** can be an adjective or a noun.

A ADJECTIVE (FEM **impar**)
odd
un número impar
an odd number

B MASC NOUN
odd number

el **imperdible** NOUN
safety pin

la **importancia** NOUN
importance
tener importancia
to be important
La educación tiene mucha importancia.
Education is very important.

importante (FEM **importante**) ADJECTIVE
important
lo importante
the important thing
Lo importante es que vengas.
The important thing is that you come.

importar VERB
1 to matter
¿Y eso qué importa?
And what does that matter?
No me importa levantarme temprano.
I don't mind getting up early.

2 no importa
it doesn't matter/never mind

LANGUAGE TIP
no importa has two meanings. Look at the examples.

No importa lo que piensen los demás.
It doesn't matter what other people think.
No importa, podemos hacerlo mañana.
Never mind, we can do it tomorrow.

imposible (FEM **imposible**) ADJECTIVE
impossible
Es imposible saber quién ganará.
It's impossible to know who will win.
Es imposible que lo sepan.
They can't possibly know.

imprescindible (FEM **imprescindible**)
ADJECTIVE
essential

la **impresión** (PL las **impresiones**) NOUN
impression
Le causó muy buena impresión a mis padres.
He made a very good impression on my parents.
Tengo la impresión de que no va a venir.
I have a feeling that he won't come.

impresionante (FEM **impresionante**)
ADJECTIVE
1 impressive
un espectáculo impresionante
an impressive show

2 amazing
una cantidad impresionante de videojuegos
an amazing number of video games

imprimir VERB
to print

inaceptable (FEM **inaceptable**)
ADJECTIVE
unacceptable

incapaz (FEM **incapaz**, PL **incapaces**)
ADJECTIVE
incapable
Es incapaz de estarse callado.
He is incapable of keeping quiet.
Hoy soy incapaz de concentrarme.
I can't concentrate today.

el **incendio** NOUN
fire
Se declaró un incendio en el hotel.
A fire broke out in the hotel.

el **incidente** NOUN
incident

inclinarse VERB
to lean
inclinarse hacia delante
to lean forward
inclinarse hacia atrás
to lean back

incluido (FEM **incluida**) ADJECTIVE
included
Todos los miembros del equipo, incluido yo.
All the team members, myself included.

incluir VERB
to include
El precio incluye un refresco.
The price includes a soft drink.

incluso ADVERB
even
He tenido que estudiar incluso los domingos.
I've even had to study on Sundays.

incluyendo VERB ▷ *see* **incluir**
Somos cinco, incluyendo a mi abuela.
It's five of us, including my grandmother.

incómodo (FEM **incómoda**) ADJECTIVE
uncomfortable
Este asiento es muy incómodo.
This seat is very uncomfortable.

inconsciente (FEM **inconsciente**)
ADJECTIVE
unconscious
Quedó inconsciente con el golpe.
The force of the blow left him unconscious.

inconveniente

> **inconveniente** can be an adjective or a noun.

A ADJECTIVE (FEM **inconveniente**)
inconvenient
a una hora inconveniente
at an inconvenient time

B MASC NOUN
problem
Ha surgido un inconveniente.
A problem has come up.

incorrecto (FEM **incorrecta**) ADJECTIVE
incorrect
una respuesta incorrecta
an incorrect answer

increíble (FEM **increíble**) ADJECTIVE
incredible

indicar VERB
to indicate
El termómetro indicaba treinta grados.
The thermometer indicated thirty degrees.

el **índice** NOUN
1 index
un índice alfabético
an alphabetical index
el índice de materias
the table of contents
2 index finger

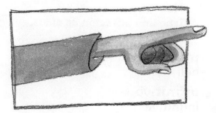

la **indirecta** NOUN
hint

individual (FEM **individual**) ADJECTIVE
1 individual
Los venden en paquetes individuales.
They're sold in individual packets.
2 single
Quisiera una habitación individual.
I'd like a single room.

la **industria** NOUN
industry

English

Spanish

A
B
C
D
E
F
G
H
I
J
K
L
M
N
O
P
Q
R
S
T
U
V
W
X
Y
Z

inesperado (FEM **inesperada**) ADJECTIVE

unexpected
una visita inesperada
an unexpected visit

infantil (FEM **infantil**) ADJECTIVE

1 **children's**
un programa infantil
a children's programme

LANGUAGE TIP
children's en este caso va siempre delante del nombre.

---

2 **childish**
¡No seas tan infantil!
Don't be so childish!

el **infarto** NOUN

heart attack
Le dio un infarto.
He had a heart attack.

la **infección** (PL las **infecciones**) NOUN

infection
tener una infección
to have an infection
Tiene una infección de oídos.
He has got an ear infection.

el **infierno** NOUN

hell

el **infinitivo** NOUN

infinitive

inflar VERB

1 **to blow up**
2 **to inflate**

la **información** (PL las **informaciones**) NOUN

information
Quisiera información sobre cursos de inglés.
I'd like some information on English courses.
una información muy importante
a very important piece of information

informal (FEM **informal**) ADJECTIVE

1 **informal**
un ambiente muy informal
a very informal atmosphere
Prefiero la ropa informal.
I prefer casual clothes.
2 **unreliable**
Es una persona muy informal.
He's a very unreliable person.

informar VERB

to inform
Nadie me informó del cambio de planes.
Nobody informed me of the change of plan.
¿Me podría informar sobre los cursos de inglés?
Could you give me some information about English courses?

la **informática** NOUN

1 **computing**
los avances de la informática
advances in computing
Quiere estudiar informática.
He wants to study computer science.
2 **computer expert**

informático

---

informático can be an adjective or a noun.

A ADJECTIVE (FEM **informática**)
computer
un programa informático
a computer program
B MASC NOUN
computer expert

el **informe** NOUN

report
Hay que escribir un informe sobre lo que hemos hecho.
We have to write a report about what we have done.

Inglaterra FEM NOUN

England

inglés (FEM **inglesa**, MASC PL **ingleses**)

> **inglés** can be an adjective or a noun.

A ADJECTIVE
English
la comida inglesa
English food

B MASC/FEM NOUN
un inglés
an Englishman
una inglesa
an Englishwoman
los ingleses
English people

C MASC NOUN
English
Estudio inglés.
I'm studying English.

el **ingrediente** NOUN
ingredient

ingresar VERB
ingresar en el hospital
to go into hospital
ingresar en un club
to join a club

el **inhalador** NOUN
inhaler

la **inicial** NOUN
initial

injusto (FEM **injusta**) ADJECTIVE
unfair

inmediato (FEM **inmediata**) ADJECTIVE
immediate

> **de inmediato**
> immediately

el/la **inmigrante** NOUN
immigrant

inocente (FEM **inocente**) ADJECTIVE
innocent
> **Soy inocente.**
> I'm innocent.

inolvidable (FEM **inolvidable**) ADJECTIVE
unforgettable

inquietante (FEM **inquietante**)
ADJECTIVE
worrying

inquieto (FEM **inquieta**) ADJECTIVE
worried
> **Estaba inquieta porque su hijo
> no había llegado a casa.**
> She was worried because her son
> hadn't come home.

insatisfecho (FEM **insatisfecha**)
ADJECTIVE
dissatisfied

inscribirse VERB
to enrol
> **Se inscribió en un curso de
> idiomas.**
> He enrolled on a language course.

inscrito VERB ▷ *see* **inscribirse**
> **Estoy inscrito en un curso de
> informática.**
> I've enrolled on a computing
> course.

el **insecto**
NOUN
insect

inseguro
(FEM **insegura**) ADJECTIVE
1 insecure
2 unsafe

insistir VERB
to insist
> **Insistió en hablar conmigo.**
> He insisted on talking to me.

insolente (FEM **insolente**) ADJECTIVE
insolent

insoportable (FEM insoportable)
ADJECTIVE
unbearable

el **inspector**
la **inspectora** NOUN
inspector

el **instante** NOUN
moment
> **A cada instante suena el teléfono.**
> The phone rings all the time.

el **insti** NOUN
secondary school
> **mis amigos del insti**
> my secondary school friends

el **instinto** NOUN
instinct

el **instituto** NOUN
institute
> **un instituto de enseñanza secundaria**
> a secondary school
> **un instituto de bachillerato**
> a secondary school

DID YOU KNOW...?
In Spain the **institutos de bachillerato** are state secondary schools for 12- to 18-year-olds.

---

las **instrucciones** NOUN
instructions

el **instructor**
la **instructora** NOUN
instructor
> **un instructor de esquí**
> a ski instructor
> **un instructor de autoescuela**
> a driving instructor

el **instrumento** NOUN
instrument

insuficiente

> **insuficiente** can be an adjective or a noun.

A ADJECTIVE (FEM insuficiente)
insufficient
> **una cantidad insuficiente de dinero**
> an insufficient amount of money

B MASC NOUN
> **Sacó un insuficiente en francés.**
> He failed in French.

insultar VERB
to insult

el **insulto** NOUN
insult

la **inteligencia** NOUN
intelligence

inteligente (FEM inteligente) ADJECTIVE
intelligent

la **intención** (PL las intenciones) NOUN
intention
> **No tengo la más mínima intención de hacerlo.**
> I haven't got the slightest intention of doing it.
> **tener intención de hacer algo**
> to intend to do something
> **Tenía intención de descansar un rato.**
> He intended to rest for a while.

intensivo (FEM intensiva) ADJECTIVE
intensive
> **un curso intensivo de inglés**
> an intensive English course

intenso (FEM intensa) ADJECTIVE
intense

intentar VERB
to try
> **¿Por qué no lo intentas otra vez?**
> Why don't you try again?
> **intentar hacer algo**
> to try to do something

Voy a intentar llamarle esta noche.
I'm going to try to call him tonight.

el **intento** NOUN
attempt
Aprobó al primer intento.
He passed at the first attempt.

el **intercambio** NOUN
exchange

el **interés** (PL los **intereses**) NOUN
interest
Tienes que poner más interés en tus estudios.
You must take more of an interest in your studies.

interesante (FEM **interesante**) ADJECTIVE
interesting

interesar VERB
to interest
Eso es algo que siempre me ha interesado.
That's something that has always interested me.
Me interesa mucho la física.
I'm very interested in physics.

interior

> **interior** can be an adjective or a noun.

A ADJECTIVE (FEM **interior**)
inside
B MASC NOUN
inside
el interior del túnel
the inside of the tunnel

intermedio

> **intermedio** can be an adjective or a noun.

A ADJECTIVE (FEM **intermedia**)
intermediate
B MASC NOUN
1 interval
2 break

el **intermitente** NOUN
indicator

internacional (FEM **internacional**)
ADJECTIVE
international

el/la **internauta** NOUN
internet user

el/la **internet** NOUN
the internet
en internet
on the internet

interno (FEM **interna**)

> **interno** can be an adjective or a noun.

A ADJECTIVE
estar interno en un colegio
to be at boarding school
B MASC/FEM NOUN
boarder

interpretar VERB
to play
Interpreta el papel de Victoria.
She plays the part of Victoria.

el/la **intérprete** NOUN
interpreter
Quiere ser intérprete.
She wants to be an interpreter.

interrogar VERB
to question
Fue interrogado por la policía.
He was questioned by the police.

interrumpir VERB
to interrupt

la **interrupción** (PL las interrupciones) NOUN
interruption

el **interruptor** NOUN
switch

intervenir VERB
1 **to take part**
   No intervino en el debate.
   He did not take part in the debate.
2 **to intervene**
   La maestra intervino para separarlos.
   The teacher intervened to separate them.

intimidar VERB
to intimidate

íntimo (FEM íntima) ADJECTIVE
intimate
   mis secretos íntimos
   my intimate secrets
   Es un amigo íntimo.
   He's a close friend.

la **introducción** (PL las introducciones) NOUN
introduction

introducir VERB
1 **to introduce**
2 **to insert**
   Introdujo la moneda en la ranura.
   He inserted the coin in the slot.

la **inundación** (PL las **inundaciones**) NOUN
flood

inundar VERB
to flood
   El río inundó el pueblo.
   The river flooded the village.
■ **inundarse**
   to be flooded
   Se nos inundó el baño.
   Our bathroom was flooded.

inútil (FEM inútil)

> **inútil** can be an adjective or a noun.

A ADJECTIVE
   useless
   El sótano está llena de trastos inútiles.
   The cellar is full of useless rubbish.
   Es inútil tratar de hacerle entender.
   It's useless trying to make him understand.
B MASC/FEM NOUN
   ¡Es un inútil!
   He's useless!

invadir VERB
to invade

inventar VERB
1 **to invent**
   Inventaron un nuevo sistema.
   They invented a new system.
2 **to make up**
   Inventó toda la historia.
   He made up the whole story.

el **invento** NOUN
invention

el **inventor**
la **inventora** NOUN
inventor

el **invernadero** NOUN
greenhouse
   el efecto invernadero
   the greenhouse effect

invernar VERB
to hibernate

invertir VERB
to invest
 Hemos invertido muchas horas en el proyecto.
 We've invested a lot of time in the project.

el **invierno** NOUN
winter

 en invierno
 in winter

invisible (FEM **invisible**) ADJECTIVE
invisible

la **invitación** (PL las **invitaciones**) NOUN
invitation

el **invitado**
la **invitada** NOUN
guest
 Es el invitado de honor.
 He's the guest of honour.

invitar VERB
to invite
 Me invitó a una fiesta.
 He invited me to a party.
 Me gustaría invitarla a cenar.
 I'd like to invite her to dinner.
 Te invito a una Coca-Cola.
 I'll buy you a Coke.
 Esta vez invito yo.
 This time it's on me.

el **iPod**® NOUN
iPod®

ir VERB
1 to go
 ¿A qué colegio vas?
 What school do you go to?

 Anoche fuimos al cine.
 We went to the cinema last night.
 ir a por
 to go and get
 Voy a por el paraguas.
 I'll go and get the umbrella.
 Voy a hacerlo mañana.
 I'm going to do it tomorrow.
 Va a ser difícil.
 It's going to be difficult.
 vamos
 let's go
 Vamos a casa.
 Let's go home.
 ¡Vamos!
 Come on!
 ¡Vamos! ¡Di algo!
 Come on! Say something!
2 to come
 ¡Ahora voy!
 I'm just coming!
 ¿Puedo ir contigo?
 Can I come with you?
3 to be
 Va muy bien vestido.
 He's very well dressed.
 Iba con su madre.
 He was with his mother.

 ir a pie
 to walk
 ir en avión
 to fly
 ir de vacaciones
 to go on holiday
 ¡Qué va!
 No way!

■ **irse** VERB
to leave
 Acaba de irse.
 He has just left.
 Vete a hacer los deberes.
 Go and do your homework.

 ¡Vámonos!
 Let's go!
 ¡Vete!
 Go away!

Irlanda FEM NOUN
Ireland

irlandés (FEM **irlandesa**, MASC PL **irlandeses**)

> **irlandés** can be an adjective or a noun.

A ADJECTIVE
Irish
un café irlandés
an Irish coffee

B MASC/FEM NOUN
un irlandés
an Irishman
una irlandesa
an Irishwoman
los irlandeses
Irish people

irónico (FEM **irónica**) ADJECTIVE
ironic

irresistible (FEM **irresistible**) ADJECTIVE
irresistible

irresponsable (FEM **irresponsable**) ADJECTIVE
irresponsible

irritar VERB
to irritate

la **isla** NOUN
island

una isla desierta
a desert island

el **Islam** NOUN
Islam

la **izquierda** NOUN
1 left hand
Escribo con la izquierda.
I write with my left hand.
2 left
doblar a la izquierda
to turn left
a la izquierda
on the left
la segunda calle a la izquierda
the second turning on the left
a la izquierda del edificio
to the left of the building

izquierdo (FEM **izquierda**) ADJECTIVE
left
Levanta la mano izquierda.
Raise your left hand.
Escribo con la mano izquierda.
I write with my left hand.
el lado izquierdo
the left side
a mano izquierda
on the left-hand side

J j

el jabón (PL los **jabones**) NOUN
soap

jamás ADVERB
never
Jamás he visto nada parecido.
I've never seen anything like it.

el jamón (PL los **jamones**) NOUN
ham
un bocadillo de jamón
a ham sandwich
jamón serrano
Serrano ham
jamón de York
cooked ham

el jarabe NOUN
syrup
un jarabe para la tos
a cough syrup

el jardín (PL los **jardines**) NOUN
garden
Tienen una piscina en el jardín.
They have a swimming pool in the garden.

la jarra NOUN
jug
una jarra de agua
a jug of water

el jarrón (PL los **jarrones**) NOUN
vase

el jefe
la jefa NOUN
boss
Carmen es la jefa.
Carmen is the boss.

el jersey
(PL los **jerséis**)
NOUN
jumper

Jesús EXCLAMATION
Bless you!

joven
(FEM **joven**, PL **jóvenes**)

> **joven** can be an adjective or a noun.

A ADJECTIVE
young
una chica joven
a young girl
B MASC/FEM NOUN
un joven
a young man
una joven
a young woman
los jóvenes
young people

la joya NOUN
jewel
Me han robado las joyas.
My jewellery has been stolen.

jubilado (FEM **jubilada**)

> **jubilado** can be an adjective or a noun.

A ADJECTIVE
retired
estar jubilado
to be retired
B MASC/FEM NOUN
pensioner

jubilarse VERB
to retire

la judía NOUN
1 **Jew**
2 **bean**
judía verde
green bean

el judío NOUN
Jew

English

Spanish

a
b
c
d
e
f
g
h
i
j
k
l
m
n
o
p
q
r
s
t
u
v
w
x
y
z

English · **Spanish**

el **judo** NOUN
judo

juego

> **juego** can be a noun or part of the verb **jugar**.

A MASC NOUN

1 **game**
un juego de ordenador
a computer game
juegos de cartas
card games

2 **set**
un juego de café
a coffee set
No hace juego con la falda.
It doesn't go with the skirt.

B VERB ▷ *see* **jugar**
Juego al tenis todos los días.
I play tennis every day.

la **juerga** NOUN
En vez de estudiar están de juerga en la clase.
Instead of studying, they are having fun in class.

el **jueves** (PL los **jueves**) NOUN
Thursday

> **LANGUAGE TIP**
> Days of the week are not spelled with a capital letter in Spanish.

La vi el jueves.
I saw her on Thursday.

el jueves que viene
next Thursday
el jueves pasado
last Thursday
todos los jueves
every Thursday

el **jugador**
la **jugadora** NOUN
player

jugar VERB
to play
Los domingos jugamos al fútbol.
We play football on Sundays.
jugar una partida de dominó
to have a game of dominoes

el **juguete** NOUN
toy
un avión de juguete
a toy plane

julio MASC NOUN
July

> **LANGUAGE TIP**
> Months are not spelled with a capital letter in Spanish.

en julio
in July
Nació el cuatro de julio.
He was born on the fourth of July.

junio MASC NOUN
June

> **LANGUAGE TIP**
> Months are not written with a capital letter in Spanish.

en junio
in June
Nació el veinte de junio.
He was born on the twentieth of June.

juntar VERB
to put together
> **Vamos a juntar los pupitres.**
> Let's put the desks together.

- **juntarse**
to move closer together/to get together

LANGUAGE TIP
juntarse has two meanings. Look at the examples.

> **Si os juntáis más, cabremos todos.**
> If you move closer together, we'll all fit in.
> **Nos juntamos para ver el partido.**
> We got together to watch the match.

junto

> **junto** can be an adjective or an adverb.

A ADJECTIVE (FEM **junta**)
together
> **Cuando estamos juntos lo pasamos muy bien.**
> We have a good time when we're together.
> **todo junto**
> all together
> **Ponlo todo junto en una bolsa.**
> Put it all together in one bag.
> **Los muebles están muy juntos.**
> The furniture is too close together.

B ADVERB
junto a
by
> **Hay una mesa junto a la ventana.**
> There's a table by the window.
> **Mi apellido se escribe todo junto.**
> My surname is all one word.

jurar VERB
to swear

la justicia NOUN
justice

justo

> **justo** can be an adjective or an adverb.

A ADJECTIVE (FEM **justa**)
1 fair
> **No es justo.**
> It's not fair.
2 tight
> **Me están muy justos estos pantalones.**
> These trousers are tight on me.
3 just enough
> **Tengo el dinero justo para un bocadillo.**
> I have just enough money for a sandwich.
4 right
> **en el momento justo**
> at the right time

B ADVERB
just
> **Está justo al doblar la esquina.**
> It's just round the corner.
> **Me dio un golpe justo en la nariz.**
> He hit me right on the nose.

juvenil (FEM **juvenil**) ADJECTIVE
young
> **la moda juvenil**
> young people's fashion
> **el equipo juvenil**
> the youth team

la juventud NOUN
youth
> **Fue soldado en su juventud.**
> He was a soldier in his youth.

Kk

Spanish | **English**

el **kárate** NOUN
karate

el **kilo** NOUN
kilo
un kilo de tomates
a kilo of tomatoes

el **kilogramo** NOUN
kilogramme

el **kilómetro** NOUN
kilometre
Está a tres kilómetros de aquí.
It's three kilometres from here.
a noventa kilómetros por hora
at ninety kilometres an hour

el **kiosco** NOUN
news stand

DID YOU KNOW...?
In Spain you'll come across **kioscos**,
newsstands on the street which sell
newspapers, magazines and other items.

A B C D E F G H I J K L M N O P Q R S T U V W X Y Z

la

> **la** can be an article or a pronoun.

A ARTICLE
the
la pared
the wall
la del sombrero rojo
the girl in the red hat
Yo fui la que te desperté.
I was the one who woke you up.
Ayer me lavé la cabeza.
I washed my hair yesterday.
Abróchate la camisa.
Do your shirt up.
No me gusta la fruta.
I don't like fruit.
Vendrá la semana que viene.
He'll come next week.
Me he encontrado a la Sra. Sendra.
I bumped into Mrs Sendra.

B PRONOUN
1 her
La quiero.
I love her.
La han despedido.
She has been sacked.
2 you
La acompaño hasta la puerta.
I'll see you out.
3 it
No la toques.
Don't touch it.

el **labio** NOUN
lip

el **lado** NOUN
side
a los dos lados de la carretera
on both sides of the road
Hay gente por todos lados.
There are people everywhere.
Tiene que estar en otro lado.
It must be somewhere else.
Mi casa está aquí al lado.
My house is right nearby.
al lado de
beside
la silla que está al lado del armario
the chair beside the wardrobe
Oscar se sentó a mi lado.
Oscar sat beside me.

ladrar VERB
to bark
El perro les ladró.
The dog barked at them.

el **ladrillo** NOUN
brick

el **ladrón**
la **ladrona** NOUN
1 thief

Un ladrón me quitó el bolso.
A thief took my bag.
2 burglar
Los ladrones entraron en la casa.
The burglars broke into the house.
3 robber
Tres ladrones atracaron el banco.
Three robbers raided the bank.

English

Spanish

A
B
C
D
E
F
G
H
I
J
K
L
M
N
O
P
Q
R
S
T
U
V
W
X
Y
Z

el **lago** NOUN
lake

la **lágrima** NOUN
tear

lamentar VERB
Lamento lo ocurrido.
I am sorry about what happened.
- **lamentarse**
to complain
De nada vale lamentarse.
There's no use complaining.

la **lámpara** NOUN
lamp

la **lancha** NOUN
motorboat

una lancha de salvamento
a lifeboat

lanzar VERB
to throw
Lanzó una piedra al río.
He threw a stone into the river.
- **lanzarse**
to dive
Los niños se lanzaron a la piscina.
The children dived into the swimming pool.

el **lápiz** (PL los **lápices**) NOUN
pencil
Escríbelo a lápiz.
Write it in pencil.
los lápices de colores
crayons

largo

> **largo** can be an adjective or a noun.

A ADJECTIVE (FEM **larga**)
long
Esta cuerda es demasiado larga.
This piece of string is too long.
B MASC NOUN
length
Nadé cuatro largos de la piscina.
I swam four lengths of the pool.
¿Cuánto mide de largo?
How long is it?
Tiene nueve metros de largo.
It's nine metres long.
a lo largo del río
along the river
a lo largo de la semana
throughout the week
Pasó de largo sin saludar.
He passed by without saying hello.

LANGUAGE TIP
Be careful! **largo** does not mean **large**.

las

> **las** can be an article or a pronoun.

A ARTICLE
the
las paredes
the walls
las del estante de arriba
the ones on the top shelf
Me duelen las piernas.
My legs hurt.
Poneos las bufandas.
Put on your scarves.
No me gustan las arañas.
I don't like spiders.
Vino a las seis de la tarde.
He came at six in the evening.
B PRONOUN
1 them
Las vi por la calle.
I saw them in the street.
Las han despedido.
They've been sacked.

2 you
**Las acompañaré hasta la puerta,
señoras.**
I'll see you out, ladies.

la **lata** NOUN
1 tin
2 can
3 Deja de dar la lata.
Stop being a pain.

el **latido** NOUN
beat

el **lavabo** NOUN
1 sink
Llené el lavabo de agua.
I filled the sink with water.
2 toilet
Voy al lavabo.
I'm going to the toilet.

la **lavadora** NOUN
washing machine

lavar VERB
to wash
Lava estos vasos.
Wash these glasses.
lavar la ropa
to do the washing
■ **lavarse**
to wash
Me lavo todos los días.
I wash every day.
Ayer me lavé la cabeza.
I washed my hair yesterday.
Lávate los dientes.
Brush your teeth.

el **lazo** NOUN
1 bow
2 ribbon

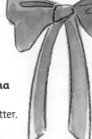

le PRONOUN
1 him
**Le mandé una
carta.**
I sent him a letter.
**Le miré con
atención.**
I watched him carefully.

Le abrí la puerta.
I opened the door for him.
Le huelen los pies.
His feet smell.
2 her
Le mandé una carta.
I sent her a letter.
No le hablé de ti.
I didn't speak to her about you.
Le busqué el libro.
I looked for the book for her.
3 you
Le presento a la Sra. Díaz.
Let me introduce you to Mrs Díaz.
Le he arreglado el ordenador.
I've fixed the computer for you.

la **lección** (PL las **lecciones**) NOUN
lesson

la **leche** NOUN
milk
**la leche
desnatada**
skimmed milk

leer VERB
to read

lejos ADVERB
far
¿Está lejos?
Is it far?
**No está
lejos de aquí.**
It's not far from here.
De lejos parecía un avión.
From a distance it looked like a plane.

la **lengua** NOUN
1 tongue
Me he mordido la lengua.
I've bitten my tongue.
2 mi lengua materna
my mother tongue

el **lenguaje** NOUN
language

la **lente** NOUN
lense
las lentes de contacto
contact lenses

English · **Spanish**

A
B
C
D
E
F
G
H
I
J
K
L
M
N
O
P
Q
R
S
T
U
V
W
X
Y
Z

la **lentilla** NOUN
contact lens

lento

> **lento** can be an adjective or an adverb.

A ADJECTIVE (FEM **lenta**)
slow
un tren lento
a slow train
B ADVERB
slowly
Vas un poco lento.
You're going a bit slowly.

el **león**
(PL los **leones**)
NOUN
lion

la **leona** NOUN
lioness

les PRONOUN
1 them
Les mandé una carta.
I sent them a letter.
Les miré con atención.
I watched them carefully.
Les abrí la puerta.
I opened the door for them.
Les eché de comer a los gatos.
I gave the cats something to eat.
2 you
Les presento a la Sra. Gutiérrez.
Let me introduce you to Mrs Gutiérrez.
Les he arreglado el ordenador.
I've fixed the computer for you.

la **lesión** (PL las **lesiones**) NOUN
injury

la **letra** NOUN
1 letter
la letra "a"
the letter 'a'

2 handwriting
Tengo muy mala letra.
My handwriting's very poor.

el **letrero** NOUN
sign

levantar VERB
to lift
Levanta la tapa.
Lift the lid.
Levantad la mano si tenéis alguna duda.
Raise your hand if you are unclear.
▪ **levantarse**
to get up
Hoy me he levantado temprano.
I got up early this morning.
Me levanté y seguí caminando.
I got up and carried on walking.

la **ley** (PL las **leyes**) NOUN
law
la ley de la gravedad
the law of gravity

leyendo VERB ▷ see **leer**
Estaba leyendo un cuento.
I was reading a story.

liar VERB
to confuse
Me liaron con tantas explicaciones.
They confused me with all their explanations.
A mí no me líes en esto.
Don't get me mixed up in this.
▪ **liarse**
to get muddled up
Me estoy liando, empezaré otra vez.
I'm getting muddled up, I'll start again.

la **libra** NOUN
pound
libra esterlina
pound sterling

librarse VERB
librarse de
to get out of/to get rid of

librarse de has two meanings. Look at the examples.

¡No te librarás de fregar los platos!
You're not going to get out of doing the washing-up!
Logré librarme de mi hermana.
I managed to get rid of my sister.

libre (FEM **libre**) ADJECTIVE
free
¿Está libre este asiento?
Is this seat free?
El martes estoy libre.
I'm free on Tuesday.

la **librería** NOUN
bookshop

Be careful! **librería** does not mean **library**.

la **libreta** NOUN
notebook

el **libro** NOUN
book
un libro de texto
a text book
un libro electrónico
an e-book

ligero (FEM **ligera**) ADJECTIVE
1 **light**
Me gusta llevar ropa ligera.
I like to wear light clothing.
Comimos algo ligero.
We ate something light.
2 **slight**
Tengo un ligero dolor de cabeza.
I have a slight headache.
Andaba a paso ligero.
He walked quickly.

el **límite** NOUN
limit
el límite de velocidad
the speed limit
fecha límite
deadline

el **limón** (PL los **limones**) NOUN
lemon

limpiar VERB
1 **to clean**
El sábado voy a limpiar mi habitación.
I'm going to clean my room on Saturday.
2 **to wipe**
¿Has limpiado la mesa?
Have you wiped the table?
Límpiate la nariz.
Wipe your nose.

la **limpieza** NOUN
cleaning
Hacen la limpieza los sábados.
They do the cleaning on Saturdays.

limpio (FEM **limpia**) ADJECTIVE
clean
El baño está muy limpio.
The bathroom's very clean.
Voy a pasar esto a limpio.
I'm going to write this out in neat.

la **línea** NOUN
line
Dibujó una línea recta.
He drew a straight line.
una línea aérea
an airline
juegos en línea
online games

el **lío** NOUN
muddle
hacerse un lío
to get muddled up
Se hizo un lío con tantos nombres.
He got muddled up with all the names.

el **líquido** NOUN
liquid

liso (FEM **lisa**) ADJECTIVE
1 **smooth**
2 **straight**

la **lista** NOUN
list
>la **lista de espera**
>the waiting list
>**pasar lista**
>to call the register

listo (FEM **lista**) ADJECTIVE
1 **clever**
>**Es una chica muy lista.**
>She's a very clever girl.
2 **ready**
>**¿Estás listo?**
>Are you ready?

la **litera** NOUN
bunk bed

la **literatura** NOUN
literature

el **litro** NOUN
litre

la **llama** NOUN
flame

la **llamada** NOUN
call
>**hacer una llamada telefónica**
>to make a phone call

llamar VERB
1 **to call**
>**Me llamaron mentiroso.**
>They called me a liar.
>**llamar a la policía**
>to call the police
>**llamar por teléfono a alguien**
>to phone somebody
>**Te llamaré por teléfono mañana.**
>I will phone you tomorrow.
2 **to ring**
3 **to knock**
>**llamar a la puerta**
>to knock at the door

¿Cómo te llamas?
What's your name?
Me llamo Adela.
My name's Adela.

llano (FEM **llana**) ADJECTIVE
flat

la **llave** NOUN
key
>**las llaves del coche**
>the car keys

el **llavero** NOUN
keyring

la **llegada** NOUN
1 **arrival**
2 **finish**

llegar VERB
1 **to arrive**
>**El avión llega a las dos.**
>The plane arrives at two o'clock.
>**Acabamos de llegar.**
>We've just arrived.
>**Llegamos tarde.**
>We were late.
2 **llegar a**
>to get to
>**Llegamos a León a las cinco.**
>We got to Leon at five o'clock.
>**¿A qué hora llegaste a casa?**
>What time did you get home?
3 **to reach**
>**No llego al estante de arriba.**
>I can't reach the top shelf.
>**El agua me llegaba hasta las rodillas.**
>The water came up to my knees.

llenar VERB
to fill
>**Llena la jarra de agua.**
>Fill the jug with water.

lleno (FEM **llena**) ADJECTIVE
full
>**Todos los hoteles están llenos.**
>All the hotels are full.

El restaurante estaba lleno de gente.
The restaurant was full of people.

llevar VERB

1 to take
¿Llevas los vasos a la cocina?
Can you take the glasses to the kitchen?
No llevará mucho tiempo.
It won't take long.

2 to wear
María llevaba un abrigo muy bonito.
María was wearing a nice coat.

3 to give a lift
Sofía nos llevó a casa.
Sofía gave us a lift home.

4 to carry
Yo te llevo la maleta.
I'll carry your case.

5 ¿Cuánto tiempo llevas aquí?
How long have you been here?
Llevo horas esperando aquí.
I've been waiting here for hours.
Mi hermana mayor me lleva ocho años.
My elder sister is eight years older than me.

■ **llevarse**

1 llevarse algo
to take something
Llévatelo.
Take it with you.
¿Le gusta? — Sí, me lo llevo.
Do you like it? — Yes, I'll take it.

2 Me llevo bien con mi hermano.
I get on well with my brother.
Nos llevamos muy mal.
We don't get on at all.

llorar VERB
to cry

llover VERB
to rain

llueve VERB ▷ *see* llover
Llueve mucho.
It's raining hard.

la lluvia NOUN
rain
bajo la lluvia
in the rain

lluvioso (FEM lluviosa) ADJECTIVE
rainy

lo

> **lo** can be an article or a pronoun.

A ARTICLE
Lo peor fue que no pudimos entrar.
The worst thing was we couldn't get in.
Pon en mi habitación lo de Diego.
Put Diego's things in my room.
Lo mío son las matemáticas.
Maths is my thing.
Olvida lo de ayer.
Forget what happened yesterday.
¡No sabes lo aburrido que es!
You don't know how boring he is!
lo que
what/whatever

LANGUAGE TIP

lo que has two meanings. Look at the examples.

Lo que más me gusta es nadar.
What I like most is swimming.

Ponte lo que quieras.
Wear whatever you like.
más de lo que
more than
Cuesta más de lo que crees.
It costs more than you think.

B PRONOUN

1 him
No lo conozco.
I don't know him.
Lo han despedido.
He's been sacked.

2 you
Yo a usted lo conozco.
I know you.

3 it
No lo veo.
I can't see it.
Voy a pensarlo.
I'll think about it.
No lo sabía.
I didn't know.
No parece lista pero lo es.
She doesn't seem clever but she is.

el **lobo** NOUN
wolf

local

A ADJECTIVE (FEM **local**)
local
un producto local
a local product

B MASC NOUN
premises PL
Lo echaron del local.
They threw him off the premises.

loco (FEM **loca**)

> **loco** can be an adjective or a noun.

A ADJECTIVE
mad
volver loco a alguien
to drive somebody mad
Me estás volviendo loco.
You're driving me mad.
volverse loco
to go mad
¿Estás loco?
Are you mad?
Está loco con su moto nueva.
He's mad about his new motorbike.
Me vuelve loco el marisco.
I'm mad about seafood.

B MASC/FEM NOUN
un loco
a madman
una loca
a madwoman

la **locura** NOUN
madness
Es una locura montar aquí en bici.
It's madness to ride a bike here.

lógico (FEM **lógica**) ADJECTIVE
natural
Es lógico que no quiera venir.
It's only natural he doesn't want to come.

lograr VERB
to manage
Logré escaparme de ellos.
I managed to get away from them.

la **longitud** NOUN
length
Tiene tres metros de longitud.
It's three metres long.

los

> **los** can be an article or a pronoun.

A ARTICLE
the
los barcos
the boats

los de las bufandas rojas
the people in the red scarves
Se lavaron los pies en el río.
They washed their feet in the river.
Abrochaos los abrigos.
Button up your coats.
Me gustan sus cuadros, pero prefiero los de Ana.
I like his paintings, but I prefer Ana's.
No me gustan los melocotones.
I don't like peaches.
Solo vienen los lunes.
They only come on Mondays.

B PRONOUN

1 **them**
Los vi por la calle.
I saw them in the street.
Los han despedido.
They've been sacked.

2 **you**
Los acompaño hasta la puerta, señores.
I'll see you to the door, gentlemen.

la **lotería** NOUN
lottery
Le tocó la lotería.
He won the lottery.

la **lucha** NOUN
fight
lucha libre
wrestling

luchar VERB
to fight

luego ADVERB

1 **then**
Primero se puso de pie y luego habló.
First he stood up and then he spoke.

2 **later**
Mi hermana viene luego.
My sister's coming later.

¡Hasta luego!
See you!

3 **desde luego**
of course

¡Desde luego que me gusta!
Of course I like it!

el **lugar** NOUN
place
Este lugar es muy bonito.
This is a lovely place.
Llegó en último lugar.
He came last.

el **lujo** NOUN
luxury
un apartamento de lujo
a luxury apartment

la **luna** NOUN
moon
la luna de miel
honeymoon

el **lunar** NOUN
mole

el **lunes** (PL los **lunes**) NOUN
Monday

LANGUAGE TIP
The days of the week are not spelled with a capital letter in Spanish.

La vi el lunes.
I saw her on Monday.

todos los lunes
every Monday
el lunes pasado
last Monday
el lunes que viene
next Monday

la **lupa** NOUN
magnifying glass

la **luz** (PL las **luces**) NOUN
light
Enciende la luz, por favor.
Put on the light please.

A
B
C
D
E
F
G
H
I
J
K
L
M
N
O
P
Q
R
S
T
U
V
W
X
Y
Z

146

los **macarrones** NOUN
macaroni
> **Me gustan los macarrones.**
> I like macaroni.

la **maceta** NOUN
flowerpot

macho ADJECTIVE, MASC NOUN
male
> **una rata macho**
> a male rat

la **madera** NOUN
wood
> **Está hecho de madera.**
> It's made of wood.
> **un juguete de madera**
> a wooden toy

la **madre**
NOUN
mother

la **madrugada** NOUN
early morning
> **a las cuatro de la madrugada**
> at four o'clock in the morning

madrugar VERB
to get up early

maduro (FEM **madura**) ADJECTIVE
1 ripe
2 mature

el **maestro**
la **maestra** NOUN
teacher
> **Mi tía es maestra.**
> My aunt's a teacher.

la **magia** NOUN
magic

mágico (FEM **mágica**) ADJECTIVE
magic
> **una varita mágica**
> a magic wand

majo (FEM **maja**) ADJECTIVE
nice

mal

> **mal** can be an adverb, a noun or an
> adjective.

A ADVERB
1 badly
> **Toca la guitarra muy mal.**
> He plays the guitar very badly.
> **Esta habitación huele mal.**
> This room smells bad.
> **Lo pasé muy mal.**
> I had a terrible time.
> **Me entendió mal.**
> He misunderstood me.

2 wrong
> **Han escrito mal mi apellido.**
> They've spelt my surname wrong.
> **Está mal mentir.**
> It's wrong to tell lies.

B MASC NOUN
> **evil**

C ADJECTIVE ▷ *see* **malo**

maleducado
(FEM **maleducada**)
ADJECTIVE
rude

la **maleta** NOUN
suitcase

> **hacer la maleta**
> to pack

el **maletero** NOUN
boot

malo (FEM **mala**)

> **malo** can be a noun or an adjective.

A MASC/FEM NOUN
el malo de la película
the villain in the film

B ADJECTIVE

LANGUAGE TIP
malo becomes **mal** before a
masculine singular noun.

1 bad
un mal día
a bad day
Este programa es muy malo.
This is a very bad programme.
**Soy muy mala para las
matemáticas.**
I'm very bad at maths.
Lo malo es que ...
The trouble is that ...

2 naughty
¿Por qué eres tan malo?
Why are you so naughty?

3 ill
Mi hija está mala.
My daughter's ill.
Se puso malo después de comer.
He started to feel ill after lunch.

la **mamá** (PL las **mamás**) NOUN
mum
¡Hola, mamá!
Hi Mum!

la **mancha** NOUN
stain

manchar VERB
to stain
El agua no mancha.
Water doesn't stain.
■ **mancharse**
to get dirty
No te manches la camisa.
Don't get your shirt dirty.

**Me he manchado el vestido de
tinta.**
I've got ink stains on my dress.

LANGUAGE TIP
In Spanish, the person is the direct
subject of the action.

mandar VERB
1 to tell
¿Qué te mandaron hacer?
What did they tell you to do?
Nos mandó callar.
He told us to be quiet.
Aquí mando yo.
I'm the boss here.
2 to send
**Se lo mandaremos por
correo.**
We'll send it to you by post.
**Me mandaron a hacer un
recado.**
They sent me on an errand.

el **mando** NOUN
el mando a distancia
the remote control
los mandos
the controls

manejar VERB
to operate

la **manera** NOUN
way
Lo hice a mi manera.
I did it my way.
**No hay manera de
convencerla.**
There's nothing one can do to
convince her.

la **manga** NOUN
sleeve
Súbete las mangas.
Roll your sleeves up.
de manga corta
short-sleeved
de manga larga
long-sleeved

English
Spanish
a
b
c
d
e
f
g
h
i
j
k
l
m
n
o
p
q
r
s
t
u
v
w
x
y
z

la **manía** NOUN

Tiene la manía de repetir todo lo que digo.
He has an irritating habit of repeating everything I say.
El profesor me tiene manía.
The teacher has it in for me.

la **mano** NOUN
hand

Dame la mano.
Give me your hand.
tener algo a mano
to have something to hand
Ahora no tengo ese libro a mano.
I don't have that book to hand right now.
hecho a mano
handmade
de segunda mano
secondhand

echar una mano
to lend a hand

la **manta** NOUN
blanket

el **mantel** NOUN
tablecloth

mantener VERB
to keep

Les mantendremos informados.
We'll keep you informed.
mantener la calma
to keep calm

la **mantequilla** NOUN
butter

mantuve VERB ▷ *see* **mantener**

Mantuve la calma.
I stayed calm.

la **manzana** NOUN
apple

mañana

mañana can be a noun or an adverb.

A FEM NOUN
morning

Llegó a las nueve de la mañana.
He arrived at nine o'clock in the morning.
Por la mañana voy al colegio.
In the mornings I go to school.
a media mañana
mid-morning

B ADVERB
tomorrow

¡Hasta mañana!
See you tomorrow!
pasado mañana
the day after tomorrow
mañana por la mañana
tomorrow morning
mañana por la noche
tomorrow night

el **mapa** NOUN
map

El pueblo no está en el mapa.
The village isn't on the map.

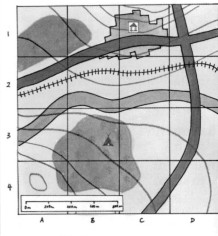

el **maquillaje** NOUN
make-up

maquillarse VERB
to put one's make-up on
   Está maquillándose.
   She's putting her make-up on.

la **máquina** NOUN
machine
   una máquina de coser
   a sewing machine
   una máquina de afeitar
   an electric razor
   una máquina fotográfica
   a camera

la **maquinilla** NOUN
razor
   una maquinilla eléctrica
   an electric razor

el **mar** NOUN
sea
   por mar
   by sea

LANGUAGE TIP
Note that in some set phrases, **mar** is feminine.

   Lo hizo la mar de bien.
   He did it really well.

la **maravilla** NOUN
   ¡Qué maravilla de casa!
   What a wonderful house!
   ser una maravilla
   to be wonderful
   Se llevan de maravilla.
   They get on wonderfully well together.

maravilloso (FEM **maravillosa**)
ADJECTIVE
marvellous

la **marca** NOUN
1 mark
   Había marcas de neumático en la arena.
   There were tyre marks in the sand.
2 make
   ¿De qué marca es tu tele?
   What make's your TV?

3 brand
   una conocida marca de chocolate
   a well-known brand of chocolate
   la ropa de marca
   designer clothes

el **marcador** NOUN
scoreboard

marcar VERB
1 to dial
2 to score

marcharse VERB
to leave

la **marea** NOUN
tide
   una marea negra
   an oil slick

mareado (FEM **mareada**) ADJECTIVE
   Estoy mareado.
   I feel dizzy./I feel sick.

LANGUAGE TIP
estoy mareado has two meanings.
It can be translated as **I feel dizzy** and **I feel sick**.

---

marear VERB
1 to make ... feel dizzy
   La altura me marea.
   Heights me feel dizzy.
2 to make ... feel sick
   Ese olor me marea.
   That smell makes me feel sick.
3 ¡No me marees!
   Stop going on!
■ **marearse**
1 to get dizzy
   Te marearás si das tantas vueltas.
   You'll get dizzy going round and round like that.
2 to get sick
   ¿Te mareas cuando vas en barco?
   Do you get seasick when you travel by boat?
   Siempre me mareo en coche.
   I always get carsick.

el mareo NOUN
1 **Le dio un mareo con el calor.**
The heat made him feel dizzy.
2 **car sickness**
3 **sea sickness**

la margarina NOUN
margarine

el margen (PL los **márgenes**) NOUN
margin
Escribe las notas al margen.
Write your notes in the margin.

el marido NOUN
husband

la mariposa NOUN
butterfly

el martes (PL los **martes**) NOUN
Tuesday

LANGUAGE TIP
The days of the week are not spelled with a capital letter in Spanish.

La vi el martes.
I saw her on Tuesday.

todos los martes
every Tuesday
el martes pasado
last Tuesday
el martes que viene
next Tuesday
Martes de Carnaval
Shrove Tuesday

DID YOU KNOW...?
During the week before Lent, all over Spain and Latin America there are fiestas and fancy-dress parades, with the main celebrations taking place on **Martes de Carnaval** (literally Carnival Tuesday).

marzo MASC NOUN
March

LANGUAGE TIP
Months are not spelled with a capital letter in Spanish.

---

en marzo
in March
Nació el diecisiete de marzo.
He was born on the seventeenth of March.

más ADJECTIVE, ADVERB
more
Ahora salgo más.
! go out more these days.
Últimamente nos vemos más.
We've been seeing more of each other lately.
¿Quieres más?
Would you like some more?
No tengo más dinero.
I haven't got any more money.
deprisa – más deprisa
quickly – more quickly
barato – más barato
cheap – cheaper
lejos – más lejos
far – further
grande – más grande
big – bigger
temprano – más temprano
early – earlier
caro – más caro
expensive – more expensive
Es más grande que el tuyo.
It's bigger than yours.
Corre más rápido que yo.
He runs faster than I do.
más de mil libros
more than a thousand books
más de lo que yo creía
more than I thought
el niño más joven
the youngest child
el coche más grande
the biggest car

el punto más lejano
the furthest point
el más inteligente de todos
the most intelligent of all of them
Pablo es el que come más.
Pablo's the one who eats the most.
Fue el que más trabajó.
He was the one who worked the hardest.
¿Qué más?
What else?
¡Qué perro más sucio!
What a filthy dog!
Por más que estudio no apruebo.
However hard I study I don't pass.
Dos más dos son cuatro.
Two plus two is four.

la **mascarilla** NOUN
facemask

masculino (FEM **masculina**) ADJECTIVE
1 **male**
el sexo masculino
the male sex
2 **men's**
la ropa masculina
men's clothing
3 **masculine**

masticar VERB
to chew

matar VERB
to kill
Mi padre me va a matar.
My dad will kill me.

las **matemáticas** NOUN
mathematics

la **materia** NOUN
subject
Es un experto en la materia.
He's an expert on the subject.

material ADJECTIVE, MASC NOUN
material

matricularse VERB
to enrol

máximo

máximo can be a noun or an adjective.

A MASC NOUN
maximum
un máximo de cincuenta euros
a maximum of fifty euros
como máximo
at the most/at the latest

LANGUAGE TIP
como máximo has two meanings. Look at the examples.

Te costará cinco libras como máximo.
It'll cost you five pounds at the most.
Llegaré a las diez como máximo.
I'll be there by ten o'clock at the latest.
B ADJECTIVE (FEM **máxima**)
maximum
la velocidad máxima
the maximum speed

mayo MASC NOUN
May

LANGUAGE TIP
Months are not spelled with a capital letter in Spanish.

en mayo
in May
Nació el veintiocho de mayo.
He was born on the twenty-eighth of May.

la **mayonesa** NOUN
mayonnaise

mayor (FEM **mayor**)

mayor can be an adjective, a pronoun or a noun.

A ADJECTIVE, PRONOUN
older
Marc es mayor que Nacho.
Marc is older than Nacho.
Es tres años mayor que yo.
He is three years older than me.
el hermano mayor
the older brother/the oldest brother

LANGUAGE TIP
el hermano mayor has two meanings. It can be translated as **the older brother** and **the oldest brother**.

Soy el mayor.
I'm the older./I'm the oldest.

LANGUAGE TIP
Soy el mayor has two meanings. It can be translated as **I'm the older (of the two)** and **I'm the oldest**.

Sus hijos ya son mayores.
Their children are grown-up now.
la gente mayor
the elderly

B MASC/FEM NOUN
un mayor de edad
an adult
los mayores
grown-ups

la **mayúscula** NOUN
capital letter
Empieza cada frase con mayúscula.
Start each sentence with a capital letter.
una M mayúscula
a capital M

me PRONOUN
1 me
Me quiere.
He loves me.
Me regaló una pulsera.
He gave me a bracelet.
Me lo dio.
He gave it to me.
¿Me echas esta carta?
Will you post this letter for me?
Me duelen los pies.
My feet hurt.
2 myself
No me hice daño.
I didn't hurt myself.
me dije a mí mismo
I said to myself

Me puse el abrigo.
I put my coat on.

la **medalla** NOUN
medal

la **media** NOUN
1 average
la media de edad
the average age
2 medias
stockings/tights

LANGUAGE TIP
medias has two meanings. It can be translated either as **stockings** or **tights**.

mediados PLURAL NOUN
a mediados de
around the middle of

la **medianoche** NOUN
midnight
a medianoche
at midnight

el **medicamento** NOUN
medicine

la **medicina** NOUN
medicine
Mi hermano estudia medicina en la universidad.
My brother's studying medicine at university.
¿Te has tomado ya la medicina?
Have you taken your medicine yet?

el médico
la médica NOUN
doctor
> **Quiere ser médica.**
> She wants to be a doctor.
> **el médico de cabecera**
> the family doctor

la medida NOUN
1 measure
> **medidas de seguridad**
> security measures
2 measurement
> **una unidad de medida**
> a unit of measurement
3 a medida que ...
> as ...
> **Dio un libro a cada alumno a medida que iban llegando.**
> She gave a book to each student as they arrived.

medio

> **medio** can be an adjective, an adverb or a noun.

A ADJECTIVE (FEM **media**)
1 half
> **medio litro**
> half a litre
> **Nos queda media botella de leche.**
> We've got half a bottle of milk left.
> **media hora**
> half an hour
> **una hora y media**
> an hour and a half
> **Son las ocho y media.**
> It's half past eight.
2 average
> **la temperatura media**
> the average temperature
B ADVERB
half
> **Estaba medio dormido.**
> He was half asleep.
C MASC NOUN
1 middle
> **Está en el medio.**
> It's in the middle.

2 means
> **un medio de transporte**
> a means of transport
> **los medios de comunicación**
> the media
> **el medio ambiente**
> the environment

el mediodía NOUN
> **al mediodía**
> at midday/at lunchtime

LANGUAGE TIP
al mediodía has two meanings. It can be translated as **at midday** and **at lunchtime**.

---

medir VERB
to measure
> **¿Has medido la ventana?**
> Have you measured the window?
> **¿Cuánto mides? — Mido un metro cincuenta.**
> How tall are you? — I'm one metre fifty.
> **¿Cuánto mide esta habitación? — Mide tres metros por cuatro.**
> How big is this room? — It measures three metres by four.

la mejilla NOUN
cheek

mejor

> **mejor** can be an adjective or an adverb.

A ADJECTIVE (FEM **mejor**)
1 better
> **Este es mejor que el otro.**
> This one is better than the other one.
> **Es el mejor de los dos.**
> He's the better of the two.
2 best
> **mi mejor amiga**
> my best friend

la mejor de la clase
the best in the class
Es el mejor de todos.
He's the best of the lot.

B ADVERB

1 better
La conozco mejor que tú.
I know her better than you do.

2 best
¿Quién lo hace mejor?
Who does it best?
Mejor nos vamos.
We had better go.

> **a lo mejor**
> probably

mejorar VERB
to improve
El tiempo está mejorando.
The weather's improving.
Han mejorado el servicio.
They have improved the service.

> **¡Que te mejores!**
> Get well soon!

la melena NOUN
long hair
Lleva una melena rubia.
She has long blond hair.

mellizo (FEM **melliza**) ADJECTIVE, NOUN
twin
Son mellizos.
They're twins.

el melocotón (PL los **melocotones**)
NOUN
peach

el melón (PL los **melones**)
NOUN
melon

la memoria NOUN
memory
tener mala memoria
to have a bad memory
aprender algo de memoria
to learn something by heart

menor (FEM **menor**)

> **menor** can be an adjective, a pronoun
> or a noun.

A ADJECTIVE, PRONOUN

1 younger
Es tres años menor que yo.
He's three years younger than me.
Alejandro es menor que Hassan.
Alejandro is younger than Hassan.
el hermano menor
the younger brother/the youngest
brother

LANGUAGE TIP
el hermano menor has two
meanings. It can be translated as **the
younger brother** and **the youngest
brother**.

Yo soy el menor.
I'm the younger./I'm the youngest.

LANGUAGE TIP
yo soy el menor has two meanings.
It can be translated as **I'm the
younger** and **I'm the youngest**.

2 smaller
una talla menor
a smaller size
No tiene la menor importancia.
It's not in the least important.

B MASC/FEM NOUN

un menor de edad
a minor
los menores
the under-18s

menos

> **menos** can be an adjective, an adverb
> or a preposition.

A ADJECTIVE, ADVERB

1 less

Ahora salgo menos.
I go out less these days.

Últimamente nos vemos menos.
We've been seeing less of each other recently.

menos caro
less expensive

menos harina
less flour

menos gatos
fewer cats

menos gente
fewer people

menos ... que
less ... than

Me gusta menos que el otro.
I like it less than the other one.

Trabaja menos que yo.
He doesn't work as hard as I do.

Es menos nerviosa que antes.
She's less nervous than she was.

menos de cincuenta cajas
fewer than fifty boxes

2 least

el chico menos desobediente de la clase
the least disobedient boy in the class

Fue el que menos trabajó.
He was the one who worked the least hard.

el examen con menos errores
the exam paper with the fewest mistakes

No quiero verle y menos hablar con él.
I don't want to see him, let alone talk to him.

¡Menos mal!
Thank goodness!

B PREPOSITION

1 except

todos menos él
everyone except him

2 minus

Cinco menos dos son tres.
Five minus two is three.

3 to

Son las dos menos cuarto.
It's quarter to two.

a menos que
unless

el **mensaje** NOUN

1 message

2 un mensaje de texto
a text message

mentir VERB

to lie

No me mientas.
Don't lie to me.

la **mentira** NOUN

lie

No digas mentiras.
Don't tell lies.

Parece mentira que aún no hayas terminado.
It's incredible that you still haven't finished.

una pistola de mentira
a toy pistol

el **mentiroso**
la **mentirosa** NOUN

liar

el **menú** (PL los **menús**) NOUN

menu

el menú del día
the set menu

menudo (FEM **menuda**) ADJECTIVE

¡Menudo lío!
What a mess!

a menudo
often

el **meñique** NOUN

little finger

English

Spanish

a
b
c
d
e
f
g
h
i
j
k
l
m
n
o
p
q
r
s
t
u
v
w
x
y
z

el mercado NOUN
market

merecer VERB
to deserve
> **Mereces que te castiguen.**
> You deserve to be punished.

> **merece la pena**
> it's worthwhile

merendar VERB
to have tea

la merienda NOUN
tea

el mes (PL los **meses**) NOUN
month

> **el mes que viene**
> next month

la mesa NOUN
table

> **poner la mesa**
> to lay the table

el metal NOUN
metal

meter VERB
to put
> **¿Dónde has metido las llaves?**
> Where have you put the keys?
> ■ **meterse**
> **meterse con alguien**
> to pick on somebody
> **No te metas con tu hermano.**
> Don't pick on your brother.
> **meterse en**
> to go into

Se metió en la cueva.
He went into the cave.
No te metas donde no te llaman.
Don't poke your nose in where it doesn't belong.

el metro NOUN
1 underground
> **coger el metro**
> to take the underground
2 metre
> **Mide tres metros de largo.**
> It's three metres long.

la mezcla NOUN
mixture

mezclar VERB
to mix
> **Hay que mezclar el azúcar y la harina.**
> You have to mix the sugar and the flour.

mi (FEM **mi**, PL **mis**) ADJECTIVE
my
> **mis hermanas**
> my sisters

mí PRONOUN
me
> **para mí**
> for me
> **Para mí que ...**
> I think that ...
> **Por mí no hay problema.**
> There's no problem as far as I'm concerned.

el micrófono NOUN
microphone

el microondas (PL los **microondas**) NOUN
microwave

un horno microondas
a microwave oven

el **microscopio** NOUN
microscope

midiendo VERB ▷ see **medir**
Estaba midiendo la habitación.
I was measuring the room.

el **miedo** NOUN
fear
el miedo a la oscuridad
fear of the dark

tener miedo
to be afraid
Le tenía miedo a su padre.
He was afraid of his father.
Tengo miedo a caerme.
I'm afraid of falling over.
dar miedo a
to scare
Me daba miedo hacerlo.
I was scared of doing it.

la **miel** NOUN
honey

el/la **miembro** NOUN
member

mientras ADVERB, CONJUNCTION
1 **while**
Lava tú mientras yo seco.
You wash while I dry.

mientras tanto
meanwhile

2 **Seguiré jugando al fútbol
mientras pueda.**
I'll carry on playing football for as long
as I can.

el **miércoles** (PL los **miércoles**) NOUN
Wednesday

LANGUAGE TIP
The days of the week are not spelled
with a capital letter in Spanish.

La vi el miércoles.
I saw her on Wednesday.

todos los miércoles
every Wednesday
el miércoles pasado
last Wednesday
el miércoles que viene
next Wednesday

mil (FEM **mil**) ADJECTIVE, PRONOUN
thousand
miles de personas
thousands of people
dos mil euros
two thousand euros

el **milagro** NOUN
miracle
**No nos hemos matado de
milagro.**
It was a miracle we weren't
killed.

el **milímetro**
NOUN
millimetre

el **millón**
(PL los **millones**) NOUN
million
millones de personas
millions of people
mil millones
a billion

el **millonario**
la **millonaria** NOUN
millionaire

mimado (FEM **mimada**) ADJECTIVE
spoiled

mineral ADJECTIVE, MASC NOUN
mineral

mínimo

> **mínimo** can be a noun or an adjective.

A MASC NOUN
minimum
un mínimo de diez euros
a minimum of ten euros
lo mínimo que puede hacer
the least he can do
Como mínimo podrías haber llamado.
You could at least have called.

B ADJECTIVE (FEM **mínima**)
minimum
la puntuación mínima
the minimum score
No tienes ni la más mínima idea.
You haven't the faintest idea.

la **minoría** NOUN
minority
las minorías étnicas
ethnic minorities

la **minúscula** NOUN
small letter

el **minuto** NOUN
minute
Espera un minuto.
Wait a minute.

mío (FEM **mía**) ADJECTIVE, PRONOUN
mine
Esos patines son míos.
Those skates are mine.
¿De quién es esta bufanda? — Es mía.
Whose scarf is this? — It's mine.
El mío está en el armario.
Mine's in the cupboard.
Este es el mío.
This one's mine.
un amigo mío
a friend of mine

la **mirada** NOUN
look
con una mirada de odio
with a look of hatred
echar una mirada a algo
to have a look at something
¿Le has echado una mirada a mi informe?
Have you had a look at my report?

mirar VERB
to look
¡Mira! Un ratón.
Look! A mouse.
Mira a ver si está ahí.
Look and see if he is there.
mirar algo
to look at something
Mira esta foto.
Look at this photo.
mirar por la ventana
to look out of the window
mirar algo fijamente
to stare at something
¡Mira que es tonto!
What an idiot!

■ **mirarse**
mirarse al espejo
to look at oneself in the mirror
Se miraron asombrados.
They looked at each other in amazement.

la **misa** NOUN
mass

mismo

> **mismo** can be an adjective, an adverb or a pronoun.

A ADJECTIVE (FEM **misma**)
1 same
Nos gustan los mismos libros.
We like the same books.
Vivo en su misma calle.
I live in the same street as him.
2 yo mismo
myself
Lo hice yo mismo.
I did it myself.

B ADVERB

Hoy mismo le escribiré.
I'll write to him today.
Nos podemos encontrar aquí mismo.
We can meet right here.

C PRONOUN

1 lo mismo
the same
Yo tomaré lo mismo.
I'll have the same.

Da lo mismo.
It doesn't matter.

2 No ha llamado pero lo mismo viene.
He hasn't phoned but he may well come.

el **misterio** NOUN
mystery

la **mitad** NOUN
half
Se comió la mitad del pastel.
He ate half the cake.
más de la mitad de los alumnos
more than half the pupils
La mitad son chicas.
Half of them are girls.
a mitad de precio
half-price
a mitad de camino
halfway there
Corta el pan por la mitad.
Cut the loaf in half.

mixto (FEM **mixta**) ADJECTIVE
mixed
una escuela mixta
a mixed school

la **mochila** NOUN
rucksack

el **moco** NOUN
Límpiate los mocos.
Wipe your nose.

tener mocos
to have a runny nose

la **moda** NOUN
fashion
estar de moda
to be in fashion
pasado de moda
old-fashioned

los **modales** NOUN
manners
buenos modales
good manners

modelo (FEM **modelo**) ADJECTIVE, NOUN
model
una niña modelo
a model child
Quiero ser modelo.
I want to be a model.

moderno (FEM **moderna**) ADJECTIVE
modern

modesto (FEM **modesta**) ADJECTIVE
modest

el **modo** NOUN
way
Le gusta hacerlo todo a su modo.
She likes to do everything her own way.
de modo que
so/so that

LANGUAGE TIP
de modo que has two meanings.
Look at the examples.

No has hecho los deberes, de modo que no puedes salir.
You haven't done your homework so you can't go out.
Mueve la tele de modo que todos la podamos ver.
Move the TV so that we can all see it.
modo de empleo
instructions for use
de todos modos
anyway

mojado (FEM **mojada**) ADJECTIVE
wet

mojar VERB
to get ... wet

A
B
C
D
E
F
G
H
I
J
K
L
M
N
O
P
Q
R
S
T
U
V
W
X
Y
Z

¡No mojes la alfombra!
Don't get the carpet wet!
Me he mojado las mangas.
I got my sleeves wet.
Moja el pan en la salsa.
Dip the bread in the sauce.
■ **mojarse**
  to get wet

molar VERB
  Me mola hacer skate.
  I like skateboarding.

molestar VERB
  1 to bother
    ¿Te molesta la radio?
    Is the radio bothering you?
    Siento molestarle.
    I'm sorry to bother you.
  2 to disturb
    No me molestes, que estoy trabajando.
    Don't disturb me, I'm working.
  ■ **molestarse**
    to get upset
    Se molestó por algo que dije.
    She got upset because of something I said.

el **momento** NOUN
  moment
    Espera un momento.
    Wait a moment.
    en este momento
    at the moment
    Tenemos mucho trabajo en este momento.
    We've got a lot of work at the moment.
    de un momento a otro
    any moment now
    Llegarán de un momento a otro.
    They'll be here any moment now.
    Llegó el momento de irnos.
    The time came for us to go.

la **moneda** NOUN
  coin
    una moneda de dos euros
    a two-euro coin

el **monedero** NOUN
  purse

mono (FEM **mona**)

| **mono** can be an adjective or a noun. |

A ADJECTIVE
  pretty
    ¡Qué piso tan mono!
    What a pretty flat!
    ¡Qué niña tan mona!
    What a sweet little girl!
B MASC/FEM NOUN
  monkey

el **monopatín**
  (PL los **monopatines**)
  NOUN
  skateboard

el **monstruo** NOUN
  monster

la **montaña** NOUN
  mountain
    Fuimos de vacaciones a la montaña.
    We went to the mountains on holiday.
    la montaña rusa
    the roller coaster

montar VERB
  1 to ride

  montar en bici
  to ride a bike

  2 to assemble
  3 to put up
  ■ **montarse**
    to get on
    Se montó en el autobús.
    He got on the bus.

el **montón** (PL los **montones**) NOUN
  pile
    Puso el montón de libros sobre la mesa.
    He put the pile of books on the table.
    un montón de ...
    loads of ...
    un montón de gente
    loads of people
    un montón de dinero
    loads of money

la **moral** NOUN
morale
levantar la moral a alguien
to cheer somebody up

morder VERB
to bite
morderse las uñas
to bite one's nails
No te muerdas las uñas.
Don't bite your nails.

el **mordisco** NOUN
bite
Dame un mordisco de tu bocadillo.
Let me have a bite of your sandwich.
dar un mordisco
to bite
Me dio un mordisco.
He bit me.

moreno (FEM **morena**) ADJECTIVE
dark
Es moreno.
He has dark hair./He is dark-skinned.

LANGUAGE TIP
Es moreno has two meanings. It can be translated as **he has dark hair** and **he is dark-skinned**.

ponerse moreno
to get brown

morir VERB
to die
¿Cuándo murió?
When did he die?
¡Me muero de hambre!
I'm starving!
Me muero de vergüenza.
I'm so embarrassed.
Me muero de ganas de ir a nadar.
I'm dying to go for a swim.

la **mosca** NOUN
fly

el **mosquito** NOUN
mosquito

el **mostrador** NOUN
counter

mostrar VERB
to show
Nos mostró el camino.
He showed us the way.

el **mote** NOUN
nickname

el **motivo** NOUN
reason
¿Cuál es el motivo de tu comportamiento?
What's the reason for your behaviour?

la **moto** NOUN
motorbike

el **motor** NOUN
engine

el/la **motorista** NOUN
motorcyclist

mover VERB
to move
Mueve un poco las cajas para que podamos pasar.
Move the boxes a bit so that we can get past.
■ **moverse**
to move
¡No te muevas!
Don't move!

el **móvil** NOUN
mobile
un móvil con cámara
a camera phone

el **movimiento** NOUN
movement

el **MP3** NOUN
MP3
un reproductor de MP3
an MP3 player

la **muchacha** NOUN
girl

el **muchacho** NOUN
boy

mucho (FEM **mucha**)

mucho can be an adjective, a pronoun or an adverb.

161

Spanish ~ English

A B C D E F G H I J K L **M** N O P Q R S T U V W X Y Z

A ADJECTIVE

1 a lot of
Había mucha gente.
There were a lot of people.
Tiene muchas plantas.
He has got a lot of plants.

2 much
No tenemos mucho tiempo.
We haven't got much time.
¿Conoces a mucha gente?
Do you know many people?
Muchas personas creen que ...
Many people think that ...
no hace mucho tiempo
not long ago
Hace mucho calor.
It's very hot.
Tengo mucho frío.
I'm very cold.
Tengo mucha hambre.
I'm very hungry.
Tengo mucha sed.
I'm very thirsty.

B PRONOUN

1 a lot
Tengo mucho que hacer.
I've got a lot to do.
¿Cuántos había? — Muchos.
How many were there? — A lot.

2 much
No tengo mucho que hacer.
I haven't got much to do.
¿Hay manzanas? — Sí, pero no muchas.
Are there any apples? — Yes, but not many.
¿Vinieron muchos?
Did many people come?
Muchos dicen que ...
Many people say that ...

C ADVERB

1 very much
Te quiero mucho.
I love you very much.
No me gusta mucho la carne.
I don't like meat very much.
Me gusta mucho la música.
I really like music.

2 a lot
Come mucho.
He eats a lot.
mucho más
a lot more
mucho antes
long before
No tardes mucho.
Don't be long.

mudarse VERB
to move
mudarse de casa
to move house

el **mueble** NOUN
un mueble
a piece of furniture
seis muebles
six pieces of furniture
los muebles
furniture

la **muela** NOUN
tooth
una muela del juicio
a wisdom tooth

el **muelle** NOUN
1 spring
2 quay

muerdo VERB ▷ see **morder**
Me duele cuando muerdo.
It hurts when I bite.

la **muerte** NOUN
death
Nos dio un susto de muerte.
He nearly frightened us to death.

muerto (FEM **muerta**)

> **muerto** can be an adjective or a noun.

A ADJECTIVE
dead
Está muerto de cansancio.
(*informal*) He's dead tired.

B MASC/FEM NOUN
un muerto
a dead man

una muerta
a dead woman
los muertos
the dead
Hubo tres muertos.
Three people were killed.

la **muestra** NOUN
sign
dar muestras de
to show signs of

muestro VERB ▷ *see* **mostrar**
Ahora te muestro cómo se hace.
I'll show you now how it's done.

muevo VERB ▷ *see* **mover**
Yo no me muevo de aquí.
I'm not moving from here.

la **mujer** NOUN
1 **woman**
Me ayudó una mujer.
A woman helped me.
2 **wife**
la mujer del médico
the doctor's wife

la **multa** NOUN
fine
una multa de cincuenta euros
a fifty-euro fine

multiplicar VERB
to multiply
Hay que multiplicarlo por cinco.
You have to multiply it by five.
la tabla de multiplicar
the times tables

mundial

> **mundial** can be an adjective or a noun.

A ADJECTIVE (FEM **mundial**)
1 **world**
un récord mundial
a world record
2 **worldwide**
B MASC NOUN
world championship
el Mundial
the World Cup

el **mundo** NOUN
world
todo el mundo
everybody
Se lo ha dicho a todo el mundo.
He has told everybody.
No lo cambiaría por nada del mundo.
I wouldn't change it for anything in the world.

la **muñeca** NOUN
1 **wrist**
2 **doll**

el **muñeco** NOUN
doll
un muñeco de peluche
a soft toy
un muñeco de nieve
a snowman

el **museo** NOUN
museum
un museo de arte
an art gallery

la **música** NOUN
music
la música pop
pop music

muy ADVERB
very
muy bonito
very pretty

A
B
C
D
E
F
G
H
I
J
K
L
M
N
O
P
Q
R
S
T
U
V
W
X
Y
Z

164

nacer VERB
to be born
>**Nació en 1964.**
>He was born in 1964.

nacional (FEM **nacional**) ADJECTIVE
national
>**vuelos nacionales**
>domestic flights

nada

> **nada** can be a pronoun or an adverb.

A PRONOUN
1 **nothing**
>**¿Qué has comprado? — Nada.**
>What have you bought? — Nothing.
>**No hace nada.**
>He does nothing.
2 **anything**
>**No quiero nada.**
>I don't want anything.
>**No dijo nada más.**
>He didn't say anything else.
>**Encendió la tele nada más llegar.**
>He turned on the TV as soon as he came in.
>**No sabe nada de español.**
>He knows no Spanish at all.

>**¡Gracias! — De nada.**
>Thanks! — You're welcome!

B ADVERB
at all
>**Esto no me gusta nada.**
>I don't like this at all.

el **nadador**
la **nadadora** NOUN
swimmer

nadar VERB
to swim

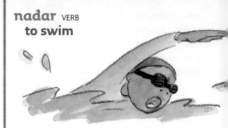

nadie PRONOUN
1 **nobody**
>**Nadie habló.**
>Nobody spoke.
>**No había nadie.**
>There was nobody there.
2 **anybody**
>**No quiere ver a nadie.**
>He doesn't want to see anybody.

naranja

> **naranja** can be an adjective or a noun.

A ADJECTIVE
orange

LANGUAGE TIP
The colour **naranja** never changes its ending no matter what it describes.

>**un anorak naranja**
>an orange anorak

B FEM NOUN
orange (*fruit*)
C MASC NOUN
orange (*colour*)

la **nariz** (PL las **narices**)
NOUN
nose

la **nata** NOUN
cream

la **natación** NOUN
swimming

natural (FEM **natural**) ADJECTIVE
natural

la **naturaleza** NOUN
nature

las **náuseas** NOUN
  tener náuseas
  to feel sick

la **navaja** NOUN
  penknife

la **nave** NOUN
  ship
  una nave espacial
  a spaceship

el **navegador** NOUN
  browser
  ¿Qué navegador usas?
  Which browser do you use?

navegar VERB
  to sail

  navegar por internet
  to surf the Net

la **Navidad** NOUN
  Christmas

  ¡Feliz Navidad!
  Happy Christmas!

necesario (FEM **necesaria**) ADJECTIVE
  necessary
  No es necesario.
  It isn't necessary.
  Ya tenemos los materiales necesarios para hacer el collage.
  We now have all the materials we need to make the collage.
  No es necesario que vengas.
  You don't have to come.

la **necesidad** NOUN
  need
  No hay necesidad de hacerlo.
  There is no need to do it.

necesitar VERB
  to need
  Necesito cien euros.
  I need a hundred euros.
  Necesito sacar buena nota en el examen.
  I need to get a good mark in the exam.

Necesito que me ayudes.
I need you to help me.
"Se necesita camarero"
'Waiter wanted'

negar VERB
  1 to deny
  No lo puedes negar.
  You can't deny it.
  Negó con la cabeza.
  He shook his head.
  2 to refuse
  Se negó a hacer las compras.
  He refused to do the shopping.

negativo (FEM **negativa**) ADJECTIVE
  negative

negro

  negro can be an adjective or a noun.

  A ADJECTIVE (FEM **negra**)
    black
  B MASC NOUN
    black (colour)

el **neopreno** NOUN
  neoprene
  un traje de neopreno
  a wetsuit

el **nervio** NOUN
  nerve
  Me pone de los nervios.
  She gets on my nerves.

nervioso (FEM **nerviosa**) ADJECTIVE
  nervous
  Me pongo muy nervioso en los exámenes.
  I get very nervous during exams.
  ¡Me pone nervioso!
  He gets on my nerves!

nevar VERB
  to snow
  Está nevando.
  It's snowing.

la **nevera** NOUN
  refrigerator

ni CONJUNCTION
neither
Ella no fue, ni yo tampoco.
She didn't go and neither did I.
ni ... ni
neither ... nor
No vinieron ni Carlos ni Sofía.
Neither Carlos nor Sofía came.
No me gustan ni el bacalao ni el hígado.
I don't like either cod or liver.
No compré ni uno ni otro.
I didn't buy either of them.
Ni siquiera me saludó.
He didn't even say hello.

el **nido** NOUN
nest

la **niebla** NOUN
fog
Hay niebla.
It's foggy.

niego VERB ▷ see **negar**
No niego que esté enfadado.
I'm not denying I'm angry.

la **nieta** NOUN
granddaughter

el **nieto** NOUN
grandson
mis nietos
my grandsons/my grandchildren

LANGUAGE TIP
mis nietos has two meanings. It can be translated as **my grandsons** or **my grandchildren**.

nieva VERB ▷ see **nevar**

la **nieve** NOUN
snow

ningún PRONOUN ▷ see **ninguno**
No tengo ningún caramelo.
I don't have any sweets.

ninguno (FEM **ninguna**)

ninguno can be an adjective or a pronoun.

A ADJECTIVE

ninguno becomes **ningún** before a masculine singular noun.

1 **no**
No hay ninguna prisa.
There's no hurry.
2 **any**
No vimos a ningún amigo en las vacaciones.
We didn't see any friends in the holidays.
No lo encuentro por ningún sitio.
I can't find it anywhere.

B PRONOUN
none
¿Cuál eliges? — Ninguno.
Which one do you want? — None of them.
No me queda ninguno.
I have none left.
Ninguno de nosotros va a ir a la fiesta.
None of us is going to the party.
ninguno de los dos
neither of them/either of them

LANGUAGE TIP
ninguno de los dos has two meanings. Look at the examples.

A ninguna de las dos les gusta la leche.
Neither of them likes milk.
No me gusta ninguno de los dos.
I don't like either of them.

la **niña** NOUN
girl

el **niño** NOUN
boy
los niños
the boys/the children

LANGUAGE TIP

los niños has two meanings. It can be translated as **the boys** or **the children**.

---

el nivel NOUN

1 level
el nivel del agua
the water level

2 standard
el nivel de vida
the standard of living

no ADVERB

no

¿Quieres venir? — No.
Do you want to come? — No.
¿Te gusta? — No mucho.
Do you like it? — Not really.
No me gusta.
I don't like it.
María no habla inglés.
María doesn't speak English.
No puedo venir esta noche.
I can't come tonight.
No tengo tiempo.
I haven't got time.
No debes preocuparte.
You mustn't worry.
No hace frío.
It isn't cold.
No conozco a nadie.
I don't know anyone.
Esto es tuyo, ¿no?
This is yours, isn't it?
Fueron al cine, ¿no?
They went to the cinema, didn't they?
¿Puedo ver la tele? — ¡Que no!
Can I watch TV? — I said no!
los no fumadores
non-smokers

la noche NOUN

night

Pasó la noche sin dormir.
He had a sleepless night.
¡Buenas noches!
Good evening!/Good night!

LANGUAGE TIP

¡buenas noches! has two meanings. It can be translated as **good evening!** and **good night!**

Era de noche cuando llegamos a casa.
It was night time when we got home.

el sábado por la noche
on Saturday night
esta noche
tonight
por la noche
at night

la Nochebuena NOUN
Christmas Eve

la Nochevieja NOUN
New Year's Eve

nombrar VERB
to mention
Te nombró en la conversación.
He mentioned you in the conversation.

el nombre NOUN
1 name
nombre de pila
first name
nombre y apellidos
full name
2 noun

noreste MASC NOUN, ADJECTIVE
northeast

English

Spanish

LANGUAGE TIP
The adjective **noreste** never changes its ending, no matter what it describes.

la **noria** NOUN
big wheel

la **norma** NOUN
rule

normal (FEM **normal**) ADJECTIVE
normal
una persona normal
a normal person
Es normal que quiera divertirse.
It's natural that he should want to enjoy himself.

noroeste MASC NOUN, ADJECTIVE
northwest

LANGUAGE TIP
The adjective **noroeste** never changes its ending, no matter what it describes.

norte MASC NOUN, ADJECTIVE
north
el norte del país
the north of the country

LANGUAGE TIP
The adjective **norte** never changes its ending, no matter what it describes.

en la costa norte
on the north coast

norteamericano
(FEM **norteamericana**) ADJECTIVE, NOUN
American

nos PRONOUN
1 us
Nos vinieron a ver.
They came to see us.
Nos dio un consejo.
He gave us some advice.
Nos lo dio.
He gave it to us.
Nos tienen que arreglar el ordenador.
They have to fix the computer for us.

2 ourselves
Tenemos que defendernos.
We must defend ourselves.
Nos levantamos a las ocho.
We got up at eight o'clock.
Nos dolían los pies.
Our feet were hurting.
Nos pusimos los abrigos.
We put our coats on.
3 each other
No nos hablamos desde hace tiempo.
We haven't spoken to each other for a long time.

la **nota** NOUN
1 mark
Saca muy malas notas.
He gets very bad marks.
2 note
Tomó muchas notas en la conferencia.
He took a lot of notes during the lecture.

notar VERB
1 to notice
Notó que le seguían.
He noticed they were following him.
2 to feel
Con este abrigo no noto el frío.
I don't feel the cold with this coat on.
Se nota que has estudiado mucho este trimestre.
You can tell that you've studied a lot this term.

la **noticia** NOUN
news
Tengo una buena noticia que darte.
I've got some good news for you.
Vi las noticias de las nueve.
I watched the nine o'clock news.
Fue una noticia excelente para la escuela.
It was an excellent piece of news for the school.

el **novato**
la **novata** NOUN
beginner

novecientos (FEM **novecientas**)
ADJECTIVE, PRONOUN
nine hundred

la **novedad** NOUN
las últimas novedades en moda infantil
the latest in children's fashions

la **novela** NOUN
novel

noveno (FEM **novena**) ADJECTIVE, PRONOUN
ninth
Vivo en el noveno.
I live on the ninth floor.

noventa (FEM **noventa**) ADJECTIVE, PRONOUN
ninety
el noventa aniversario
the ninetieth anniversary

la **novia** NOUN
1 girlfriend
2 bride

noviembre MASC NOUN
November

en noviembre
in November
Nació el treinta de noviembre.
He was born on the thirtieth of November.

los **novillos** NOUN
hacer novillos
to play truant

el **novio** NOUN
1 boyfriend
2 bridegroom
los novios
the bride and groom

la **nube** NOUN
cloud

nublado (FEM **nublada**) ADJECTIVE
cloudy

nublarse VERB
to cloud over

la **nuca** NOUN
nape

nuclear ADJECTIVE
nuclear
una central nuclear
a nuclear power station

el **nudo** NOUN
knot

nuestro (FEM **nuestra**) ADJECTIVE, PRONOUN
1 our
nuestro perro
our dog
nuestras bicicletas
our bicycles
2 ours
¿De quién es esto? — Es nuestro.
Whose is this? — It's ours.
La nuestra es blanca.
Ours is white.
un amigo nuestro
a friend of ours

nueve (FEM **nueve**) ADJECTIVE, PRONOUN
nine
Son las nueve.
It's nine o'clock.

a
b
c
d
e
f
g
h
i
j
k
l
m
n
o
p
q
r
s
t
u
v
w
x
y
z

A
B
C
D
E
F
G
H
I
J
K
L
M
N
O
P
Q
R
S
T
U
V
W
X
Y
Z

el nueve de marzo
the ninth of March
Nació el nueve de marzo.
He was born on the ninth of March.

nuevo (FEM **nueva**) ADJECTIVE
new
Necesito un ordenador nuevo.
I need a new computer.
Tuve que leer el libro de nuevo.
I had to read the book again.

la **nuez** (PL las **nueces**) NOUN
walnut

el **número** NOUN
1 **number**
Calle Aribau, sin número.
Aribau street, no number.
número de teléfono
telephone number
2 **size** (of shoe)

nunca ADVERB
1 **never**

No viene nunca.
He never comes.
No la veré nunca más.
I'll never see her again.
2 **ever**
Ninguno de nosotros había esquiado nunca.
Neither of us had ever skied before.
Casi nunca me escribe.
He hardly ever writes to me.

ñoño (FEM **ñoña**)

> **ñoño** can be an adjective or a noun.

A ADJECTIVE
wet
Me parece algo ñoña.
I think she's a bit wet.
B MASC/FEM NOUN
drip
Tu hermano es un ñoño.
Your brother's a drip.

LANGUAGE TIP
The Spanish alphabet has an extra letter in it: **ñ**. Not many words begin with it but you will see it in lots of common words e.g. **niño**, **cariño**.

O CONJUNCTION
or
¿Quieres té o café?
Would you like tea or coffee?
¿Vas a ayudarme o no?
Are you going to help me or not?
o ... o ...
either ... or ...
O ha salido o no coge el teléfono.
Either he's out or he's not answering
the phone.

obedecer VERB
to obey

obediente (FEM **obediente**) ADJECTIVE
obedient

el **objeto** NOUN
object
un objeto metálico
a metal object

obligar VERB
to force
Nadie te obliga a ir.
Nobody's forcing you to go.

obligatorio (FEM **obligatoria**) ADJECTIVE
compulsory

la **obra** NOUN
1 work
una obra de arte
a work of art
una obra de teatro
a play
2 building site
"obras"
'roadworks'

observar VERB
to observe

el **obstáculo** NOUN
obstacle

obtener VERB
to obtain

obvio (FEM **obvia**) ADJECTIVE
obvious

la **ocasión** (PL las **ocasiones**) NOUN
opportunity
**Esta es la ocasión que
esperábamos.**
This is the opportunity we've been
waiting for.

el **océano** NOUN
ocean
el océano Atlántico
the Atlantic Ocean

ochenta (FEM **ochenta**) ADJECTIVE, PRONOUN
eighty
Tiene ochenta años.
He's eighty.
el ochenta aniversario
the eightieth anniversary

ocho (FEM **ocho**) ADJECTIVE, PRONOUN
eight
Son las ocho.
It's eight o'clock.

el ocho de agosto
the eighth of August
Nació el ocho de agosto.
He was born on the eighth of August.

ochocientos (FEM **ochocientas**)
ADJECTIVE, PRONOUN
eight hundred

octavo (FEM **octava**) ADJECTIVE, PRONOUN
eighth
Vivo en el octavo.
I live on the eighth floor.

octubre MASC NOUN
October

LANGUAGE TIP
Months are not spelled with a capital
letter in Spanish.

en octubre
in October
Nació el tres de octubre.
He was born on the third of October.

ocupado (FEM **ocupada**) ADJECTIVE
1 **busy**
Estoy muy ocupado.
I'm very busy.
2 **engaged**
La línea está ocupada.
The line's engaged.
"ocupado"
'engaged'
¿Está ocupado este asiento?
Is this seat taken?

ocupar VERB
to take up
Ocupa casi todo mi tiempo.
It takes up almost all my time.
Los espectadores ocuparon sus asientos.
The spectators took their seats.
■ **ocuparse**
ocuparse de algo
to look after something
Joel se ocupa de las ventas.
Joel looks after sales.

ocurrir VERB
to happen
¿Qué ocurrió?
What happened?
¿Qué te ocurre?
What's the matter?
Se nos ocurrió una idea brillante.
We had a brilliant idea.

odiar VERB
to hate
Odio tener que levantarme pronto.
I hate having to get up early.

oeste MASC NOUN, ADJECTIVE
west
el oeste del país
the west of the country

LANGUAGE TIP
The adjective **oeste** never changes its ending, no matter what it describes.

en la costa oeste
on the west coast

la **oferta** NOUN
offer

estar de oferta
to be on special offer

la **oficina** NOUN
office
la oficina de turismo
the tourist office
la oficina de correos
the post office
la oficina de objetos perdidos
the lost property office

ofrecer VERB
to offer
Nos ofrecieron un refresco.
They offered us something to drink.
Me ofrecí para ayudar.
I offered to help.

el **oído** NOUN
1 **ear**
2 **hearing**

oír VERB
1 **to hear**
He oído un ruido.
I heard a noise.
¿Me oyes bien desde ahí?
Can you hear me all right from there?
2 **to listen to**
Óyeme bien.
Listen to me.
oír la radio
to listen to the radio
¡Oye!
Hey!
¡Oiga, por favor!
Excuse me!

ojalá EXCLAMATION
I hope
¡Ojalá Toni venga hoy!
I hope Toni comes today!

el **ojo** NOUN
  eye
    Tengo algo en el ojo.
    I've got something in my eye.
    ¡Ojo! Es muy mentiroso.
    Watch out! He's a real liar.

la **ola** NOUN
  wave

oler VERB
  to smell
    Huele a menta.
    It smells of mint.
    Esta salsa huele muy bien.
    This sauce smells very good.
    ¡Qué mal huelen estos zapatos!
    These shoes smell awful!

el **olfato** NOUN
  sense of smell

la **oliva** NOUN
  olive
    el aceite de oliva
    olive oil

la **olla** NOUN
  pot
    una olla a presión
    a pressure cooker

el **olor** NOUN
  smell
    un olor a tabaco
    a smell of cigarette smoke
    ¡Qué mal olor!
    What a horrible smell!

olvidar VERB
  1 to forget
    No olvides comprar el pan.
    Don't forget to buy the bread.
    Se me olvidó por completo.
    I completely forgot.
  2 to leave
    Olvidé el libro en casa.
    I left the book at home.

once (FEM **once**) ADJECTIVE, PRONOUN
  eleven
    Tengo once años.
    I'm eleven.
    Son las once.
    It's eleven o'clock.
    el once de agosto
    the eleventh of August
    Nació el once de agosto.
    He was born on the eleventh of August.

la **onda** NOUN
  wave

la **operación** (PL **operaciones**) NOUN
  operation
    una operación de estómago
    a stomach operation

operar VERB
    Lo tienen que operar.
    He has to have an operation.
  ■ **operarse**
    to have an operation
    Me tengo que operar de la rodilla.
    I have to have a knee operation.

opinar VERB
  to think
    ¿Y tú qué opinas del nuevo gimnasio?
    So what do you think about the new gym?

la **opinión** (PL las **opiniones**) NOUN
  opinion

la **oportunidad** NOUN
  chance
    No tuvo la oportunidad de hacerlo.
    He didn't have a chance to do it.

opuesto (FEM **opuesta**) ADJECTIVE
  opposite

oral (FEM **oral**) ADJECTIVE
  oral
    un examen oral
    an oral exam

a
b
c
d
e
f
g
h
i
j
k
l
m
n
o
p
q
r
s
t
u
v
w
x
y
z

orden

> **orden** can be a masculine or a feminine noun.

A MASC NOUN (PL los **órdenes**)
order
en orden alfabético
in alphabetical order
B FEM NOUN (PL las **órdenes**)
order
¡Es una orden!
That's an order!

el **ordenador** NOUN
computer
un ordenador portátil
a laptop

ordenar VERB
1 **to tidy**
¿Por qué no ordenas tu habitación?
Why don't you tidy your room?
2 **to order**
El policía nos ordenó que saliéramos del edificio.
The police officer ordered us to leave the building.

ordinario (FEM **ordinaria**) ADJECTIVE
ordinary
los acontecimientos ordinarios
ordinary events

la **oreja** NOUN
ear

organizar VERB
to organize

orgulloso (FEM **orgullosa**) ADJECTIVE
proud

el **origen** (PL los **orígenes**) NOUN
origin

original (FEM **original**) ADJECTIVE
original

la **orilla** NOUN
1 **shore**
un paseo a la orilla del mar
a walk along the seashore
2 **bank**
a orillas de
on the shores of/on the banks of

> **LANGUAGE TIP**
> **a orillas de** has two meanings. It can be translated as **on the shores of** and **on the banks of**.

el **oro** NOUN
gold
un collar de oro
a gold necklace

la **orquesta** NOUN
orchestra
una orquesta de jazz
a jazz band

la **ortografía** NOUN
spelling

os PRONOUN
1 **you**
No os oigo.
I can't hear you.
Os he comprado un libro a cada uno.
I've bought each of you a book.
Os lo doy.
I'll give it to you.
¿Os han arreglado ya el ordenador?
Have they fixed your computer yet?
2 **yourselves**
¿Os habéis hecho daño?
Did you hurt yourselves?
Os tenéis que levantar antes de las ocho.
You have to get up before eight.
Lavaos las manos.
Wash your hands.

3 each other
Quiero que os pidáis perdón.
I want you to say sorry to each other.

oscurecer VERB
to get dark

la **oscuridad** NOUN
dark
Estaban hablando en la oscuridad.
They were talking in the dark.

oscuro (FEM **oscura**) ADJECTIVE
dark
una habitación muy oscura
a very dark room
azul oscuro
dark blue

a oscuras
in the dark

el **oso**
la **osa** NOUN
bear
un oso de peluche
a teddy bear

el **otoño** NOUN
autumn

en otoño
in autumn

otro (FEM **otra**)

otro can be an adjective or a pronoun.

A ADJECTIVE
1 another
otro coche
another car
¿Me das otra manzana, por favor?
Can I have another apple, please?
¿Hay alguna otra manera de hacerlo?
Is there any other way of doing it?

otra vez
again

2 other
Tengo otros planes.
I have other plans.

B PRONOUN
1 another one
¿Has perdido el lápiz? — No importa, tengo otro.
Have you lost your pencil? — It doesn't matter, I've got another one.
el otro/la otra
the other one
No quiero éste, quiero el otro.
I don't want this one, I want the other one.

2 other
Tengo otros planes.
I have other plans.

la **oveja** NOUN
sheep

el **oxígeno** NOUN
oxygen

oyendo VERB ▷ *see* oír
¿Estás oyendo lo que te dice?
Are you listening to what she's saying?

Spanish – English

P p

la **paciencia** NOUN
patience

paciente (FEM **paciente**) ADJECTIVE, NOUN
patient

pacífico (FEM **pacífica**) ADJECTIVE
peaceful

el **padre** NOUN
father
mis padres
my parents

el **padrino** NOUN
godfather
mis padrinos
my godparents

DID YOU KNOW...?
At a wedding, the **padrino** is the person
who escorts the bride down the aisle
and gives her away, usually her father.

---

la **paga** NOUN
pocket money
Me dan la paga los domingos.
I get my pocket money on Sundays.

pagar VERB
1 to pay
¿Dónde pago?
Where do I pay?
2 to pay for
Tengo que pagar las entradas.
I have to pay for the tickets.

la **página** NOUN
page
Está en la página diez.
It's on page ten.

una página web
a Web page

el **país** (PL los **países**) NOUN
country
el País Vasco
the Basque Country

el **paisaje** NOUN
landscape
el paisaje de Castilla
the Castilian landscape

la **paja** NOUN
straw
**un sombrero
de paja**
a straw hat

el **pájaro**
NOUN
bird

la **pajita** NOUN
straw

la **pala** NOUN
1 spade
2 shovel

la **palabra** NOUN
word

pálido (FEM **pálida**) ADJECTIVE
pale
Se puso pálida.
She turned pale.

la **palma** NOUN
palm

el **palo** NOUN
stick
Le pegó con un palo.
He hit him with a stick.
una cuchara de palo
a wooden spoon

la **paloma** NOUN
pigeon

las **palomitas** NOUN
las palomitas de maíz
popcorn

el paloselfi NOUN
selfie stick
> **La plaza estaba llena de gente con paloselfis.**
> The square was full of people with selfie sticks.

el pan NOUN
1 **bread**
pan integral
wholemeal bread
pan de molde
sliced bread
una barra de pan
a baguette
2 **loaf**
Compré dos panes.
I bought two loaves.

la panadería NOUN
bakery

la pandilla NOUN
gang

el pánico NOUN
panic
> **en un momento de pánico**
> in a moment of panic
> **Me entró pánico.**
> I panicked.
> **Les tengo pánico a las arañas.**
> I'm terrified of spiders.

la pantalla NOUN
screen
> **una pantalla plana**
> a flat screen

los pantalones NOUN
trousers
> **unos pantalones**
> a pair of trousers
> **pantalones cortos**
> shorts

pantalones vaqueros
jeans

el pañal NOUN
nappy

el paño NOUN
cloth
> **un paño de cocina**
> a dishcloth

el pañuelo NOUN
handkerchief

el papa NOUN
pope
> **el Papa**
> the Pope

el papá (PL los **papás**) NOUN
dad

mis papás
my mum
and dad
Papá Noel
Father Christmas

el papel NOUN
1 **paper**
una bolsa de papel
a paper bag
papel de aluminio
foil
papel higiénico
toilet paper
2 **piece of paper**
Lo escribí en un papel.
I wrote it on a piece of paper.

English | **Spanish**

A
B
C
D
E
F
G
H
I
J
K
L
M
N
O
P
Q
R
S
T
U
V
W
X
Y
Z

178

la **papelera** NOUN
  1 **wastepaper bin**
  2 **litter bin**

el **paquete** NOUN
  1 **packet**
  2 **parcel**
  Me mandaron un paquete por correo.
  I got a parcel in the post.

par

> **par** can be a noun or an adjective.

  A MASC NOUN
  1 **couple**
  un par de horas al día
  a couple of hours a day
  2 **pair**
  un par de calcetines
  a pair of socks
  Abrió la ventana de par en par.
  He opened the window wide.
  B ADJECTIVE (FEM **par**)
  un número par
  an even number

para PREPOSITION
  1 **for**
  Es para ti.
  It's for you.
  Tengo muchos deberes para mañana.
  I have a lot of homework to do for tomorrow.
  ¿Para qué lo quieres?
  What do you want it for?
  ¿Para qué sirve?
  What's it for?
  2 **to**
  Estoy ahorrando para comprarme una bici.
  I'm saving up to buy a bike.

  3 **para que te acuerdes de mí**
  so that you remember me

la **parada** NOUN
  stop
  una parada de autobús
  a bus stop
  una parada de taxis
  a taxi rank

parado (FEM **parada**) ADJECTIVE
  1 **No te quedes ahí parado.**
  Don't just stand there.
  2 **out of work**
  Hace seis meses que está parada.
  She's been out of work for six months.

el **paraguas** (PL los **paraguas**) NOUN
  umbrella

parar VERB
  to stop
  Paramos a poner gasolina.
  We stopped to get some petrol.
  No paró de llover en toda la noche.
  It didn't stop raining all night.
  ▪ **pararse**
  to stop
  El reloj se ha parado.
  The clock has stopped.

parecer VERB
  1 **to seem**
  Parece muy simpática.
  She seems very nice.
  2 **to look**
  Esos zapatos no parecen muy cómodos.
  Those shoes don't look very comfortable.
  Parece una modelo.
  She looks like a model.

Parece que va a llover.
It looks as if it's going to rain.
3 to think
¿Qué te pareció la película?
What did you think of the film?

Me parece que sí.
I think so.
Me parece que no.
I don't think so.

■ **parecerse**
to look alike
María y Ana se parecen mucho.
María and Ana look very much alike.
parecerse a
to look like
Te pareces mucho a tu madre.
You look very like your mother.

parecido (FEM **parecida**) ADJECTIVE
similar
Tu blusa es parecida a la mía.
Your blouse is similar to mine.

la **pared** NOUN
wall

la **pareja** NOUN
1 couple
Había varias parejas bailando.
There were several couples dancing.
2 pair
En este juego hay que formar parejas.
For this game you have to get into pairs.

el **paréntesis** (PL los **paréntesis**) NOUN
bracket

entre paréntesis
in brackets

el/la **pariente** NOUN
relative
Es pariente mío.
He's a relative of mine.

LANGUAGE TIP
Be careful! **pariente** does not mean **parent**.

el **parking** (PL los **parkings**) NOUN
car park

LANGUAGE TIP
Be careful! **parking** does not mean **parking**.

el **parque** NOUN
park
un parque de atracciones
an amusement park
un parque zoológico
a zoo

el **párrafo** NOUN
paragraph

la **parrilla** NOUN
grill
carne a la parrilla
grilled meat

la **parte** NOUN
1 part
¿De qué parte de Inglaterra eres?
What part of England are you from?
la mayor parte de los españoles
most Spanish people
la parte delantera
the front
la parte de atrás
the back
la parte de arriba
the top
la parte de abajo
the bottom
alguna parte
somewhere
Tengo que haberlo dejado en alguna parte.
I must have left it somewhere.
por todas partes
everywhere
¡Hay gatos por todas partes!
There are cats everywhere!
2 ¿De parte de quién?
Who's calling please?

179

participar VERB
 to take part
  Voy a participar en un concurso.
  I'm going to take part in a competition.

el **participio** NOUN
 participle

la **partícula** NOUN
 particle
  una partícula de polvo
  a dust particle

particular (FEM **particular**) ADJECTIVE
 private
  clases particulares
  private classes

la **partida** NOUN
 game
  echar una partida de cartas
  to have a game of cards

el **partido** NOUN
 1 match
 2 party

partir VERB
 1 to cut
 2 to crack
 3 to break off

  a partir de ahora
  from now on

 ■ **partirse**
  to break
  El remo se partió en dos.
  The oar broke in two.

la **pasada** NOUN
  ¡Ese coche es una pasada!
  This car is amazing!

pasado

 pasado can be an adjective or a noun.

 A ADJECTIVE (FEM **pasada**)
 1 last
  el verano pasado
  last summer

 2 after
  Pasado el semáforo, verás un cine.
  After the traffic lights you'll see a cinema.

  pasado mañana
  the day after tomorrow

 B MASC NOUN
  past
  en el pasado
  in the past

el **pasajero**
la **pasajera** NOUN
 passenger

el **pasaporte** NOUN
 passport

pasar VERB
 1 to happen
  Por suerte no le pasó nada.
  Luckily nothing happened to him.
  ¿Qué le pasa a Toni?
  What's the matter with Toni?
  ¿Qué pasa?
  What's the matter?
 2 to go
  Pasaron cinco años.
  Five years went by.
 3 to go past
  Pasaron varios coches.
  Several cars went past.
 4 to spend
  Voy a pasar unos días con ella.
  I'm going to spend a few days with her.
  Me pasé el fin de semana estudiando.
  I spent the weekend studying.
 5 to pass
  ¿Me pasas la sal, por favor?
  Can you pass me the salt, please?
  Cuando termines pásasela a Daniela.
  When you've finished pass it on to Daniela.
  Un momento, te paso con Pablo.
  Just a moment, I'll put you on to Pablo.

6 Hemos pasado mucho frío.
We were very cold.

> **pasarlo bien**
> to have a good time
> **¡Pase, por favor!**
> Please come in.

el **pasatiempo** NOUN
hobby

la **Pascua** NOUN
Easter

> **¡Felices Pascuas!**
> Happy Christmas!

pasear VERB
to walk
> **ir a pasear**
> to go for a walk

el **paseo** NOUN
walk
> **Salimos a dar un paseo.**
> We went out for a walk.
> **un paseo en barco**
> a boat trip
> **un paseo en bicicleta**
> a bike ride

> **dar un paseo**
> to go for a walk

el **pasillo** NOUN
1 **corridor**
2 **aisle**

pasmado (FEM **pasmada**) ADJECTIVE
amazed
> **Cuando me enteré, me quedé pasmado.**
> I was amazed when I found out.

el **paso** NOUN
1 **step**
> **Dio un paso hacia atrás.**
> He took a step backwards.

He oído pasos.
I heard footsteps.
2 **way**
> **Han cerrado el paso.**
> They've blocked the way.
> **Tu casa me pilla de paso.**
> Your house is on my way.
> **un paso de peatones**
> a pedestrian crossing
> **un paso de cebra**
> a zebra crossing

la **pasta** NOUN
1 **pasta**

2 **pasta de dientes**
toothpaste

el **pastel** NOUN
cake

la **pastelería** NOUN
cake shop

la **pastilla** NOUN
pill
> **pastillas para la tos**
> cough sweets

la **pata** NOUN
leg
> **saltar a la pata coja**
> to hop

la **patada** NOUN
> **Me dio una patada.**
> He kicked me.

la **patata** NOUN
potato
> **un filete con patatas fritas**
> steak and chips
> **una bolsa de patatas fritas**
> a bag of crisps

el **patín** (PL los **patines**) NOUN
1 **roller skate**
> **los patines en línea**
> Rollerblades®
2 **skate**

el **patinaje** NOUN
  1 roller skating
  2 ice skating

patinar VERB
  1 to roller-skate
  2 to skate

el **patinete** NOUN
  scooter

el **patio** NOUN
  playground
    el patio de
    recreo
    the playground

el **pato** NOUN
  duck

el **payaso**
la **payasa** NOUN
  clown
    Deja de hacer el payaso.
    Stop clowning around.

la **paz** (PL las **paces**) NOUN
  peace

> **¡Déjame en paz!**
> Leave me alone!

el **PC** ABBREVIATION
  PC

el **peatón** (PL los **peatones**) NOUN
  pedestrian

la **peca** NOUN
  freckle

el **pecho** NOUN
  chest

pedalear VERB
  to pedal

el **pedazo** NOUN
  piece
    un pedazo de pan
    a piece of bread
    hacer pedazos
    to smash

pedir VERB
  to ask for
    Le pedí dinero a mi padre.
    I asked my father for some money.
    He pedido hora para el médico.
    I've asked for a doctor's appointment.
    ¿Te puedo pedir un favor?
    Can I ask you a favour?
    pedir disculpas a alguien
    to apologize to somebody
    Le pedí disculpas.
    I apologized to him.
    Tuve que pedir dinero prestado.
    I had to borrow some money.

el **pegamento** NOUN
  glue

pegar VERB
  1 to hit
    Andrés me ha pegado.
    Andrés hit me.
    La pelota pegó en el árbol.
    The ball hit the tree.
  2 to stick
    Lo puedes pegar con celo.
    You can stick it on with sellotape.
    Tengo que pegar las fotos en el álbum.
    I have to stick the photos in the album.
  3 to give
    Le pegó una bofetada.
    She gave him a slap.
    ¡Qué susto me has pegado!
    What a fright you gave me!
    Pegó un grito.
    He shouted.

la **pegatina** NOUN
  sticker

peinar VERB
    peinar a alguien
    to comb somebody's hair
    Péinate antes de salir.
    Comb your hair before you go out.

el **peine** NOUN
  comb

p.ej. ABBREVIATION
(= **por ejemplo**)
e.g.

pelar VERB
1 to peel
2 Se me está pelando la espalda.
My back is peeling.

la **pelea** NOUN
1 fight
Hubo una pelea en el patio.
There was a fight in the playground.
2 argument
Tuvo una pelea con su novio.
She had an argument with her boyfriend.

pelear VERB
1 to fight
¡Deja de pelear con tu hermano!
Stop fighting with your brother!
2 to argue
Pelean por cualquier tontería.
They argue over the slightest thing.

la **película** NOUN
film
A las ocho ponen una película.
There's a film on at eight.

el **peligro** NOUN
danger

peligroso (FEM **peligrosa**) ADJECTIVE
dangerous

pelirrojo (FEM **pelirroja**) ADJECTIVE
Es pelirroja.
She has red hair.

pellizcar VERB
to pinch
Me pellizcó el brazo.
He pinched my arm.

el **pellizco** NOUN
pinch
un pellizco en la mejilla
a pinch on the cheek

el **pelo** NOUN
hair
Tiene el pelo rizado.
He has curly hair.
No perdimos el avión por un pelo.
We only just caught the plane.
Se me pusieron los pelos de punta.
It made my hair stand on end.
Me estás tomando el pelo.
You're pulling my leg.

la **pelota** NOUN
ball
jugar a la pelota
to play ball

peludo (FEM **peluda**) ADJECTIVE
hairy

la **peluquería** NOUN
hairdresser's

el **peluquero**
la **peluquera** NOUN
hairdresser

la **pena** NOUN
shame
Es una pena que no puedas venir.
It's a shame you can't come.
Me dio tanta pena el pobre animal.
I felt so sorry for the poor animal.
Me da pena tener que marcharme.
I'm so sad to have to go away.

Vale la pena.
It's worth it.
¡Qué pena!
What a shame!

el **penalti** (PL los **penaltis**) NOUN
penalty

el **pendiente** NOUN
earring

A
B
C
D
E
F
G
H
I
J
K
L
M
N
O
P
Q
R
S
T
U
V
W
X
Y
Z

184

la **pendiente** NOUN
slope

pensar VERB
to think
> **Piénsalo bien antes de contestar.**
> Think carefully before you answer.
> **¿Piensas que vale la pena?**
> Do you think it's worth it?
> **¿Qué piensas de Adrián?**
> What do you think of Adrián?
> **Tengo que pensarlo.**
> I'll have to think about it.

la **pensión** (PL las **pensiones**) NOUN
pension
> **pensión completa**
> full board
> **media pensión**
> half board

penúltimo (FEM **penúltima**)

> **penúltimo** can be an adjective or a noun.

A ADJECTIVE
> **la penúltima estación**
> the last station but one
B MASC/FEM NOUN
> **Soy el penúltimo.**
> I'm second to last.

peor ADJECTIVE, ADVERB

> **peor** can be an adjective or an adverb.

1 worse
> **Su situación es peor que la nuestra.**
> Their situation is worse than ours.
> **Hoy me siento peor.**
> I feel worse today.
2 worst
> **el peor día de mi vida**
> the worst day of my life
> **Sacó la peor nota de toda la clase.**
> He got the worst mark in the whole class.

el **pepino** NOUN
cucumber
> **Me importa un pepino lo que piense.**
> I couldn't care less what he thinks.

la **pepita** NOUN
pip

pequeño (FEM **pequeña**) ADJECTIVE
small
> **un niño pequeño**
> a small child
> **Estos zapatos me quedan pequeños.**
> These shoes are too small for me.
> **¿Cuál prefieres? — El pequeño.**
> Which would you prefer? — The small one.
> **mi hermana pequeña**
> my younger sister

la **pera** NOUN
pear

el **perdedor**
la **perdedora** NOUN
loser
> **Eres mal perdedor.**
> You're a bad loser.

perder VERB
1 to lose
> **He perdido el monedero.**
> I've lost my purse.
> **Está intentando perder peso.**
> He's trying to lose weight.
> **perder el conocimiento**
> to lose consciousness
> **Perdimos dos a cero.**
> We lost two nil.
2 to miss
> **Date prisa o perderás el tren.**
> Hurry up or you'll miss the train.
> **No quiero perder esta oportunidad.**
> I don't want to miss this opportunity.
■ **perderse**
to get lost
> **Tenía miedo de perderme.**
> I was afraid of getting lost.

la **pérdida** NOUN
1 **loss**
2 **Fue una pérdida de tiempo.**
It was a waste of time.

perdido (FEM **perdida**) ADJECTIVE
lost

el **perdón** NOUN
Le pedí perdón.
I apologized to him.
¡Perdón!
Sorry!/Excuse me!

LANGUAGE TIP
¡perdón! has two meanings. It can be translated as **sorry!** and **excuse me!**

---

perdonar VERB
to forgive
¿Me perdonas?
Will you forgive me?
¡Perdona! ¿Tienes hora?
Excuse me, do you have the time?
¡Perdona! ¿Te he hecho daño?
I'm so sorry! Did I hurt you?

la **pereza** NOUN
laziness
¡Qué pereza tengo!
I feel so lazy!
Me da pereza levantarme.
I can't be bothered to get up.

perezoso (FEM **perezosa**) ADJECTIVE
lazy

perfecto (FEM **perfecta**) ADJECTIVE
perfect

el **periódico** NOUN
newspaper

el **periodo** NOUN
period
un periodo de tres meses
a three-month period

el **permiso** NOUN
permission
Tengo que pedirles permiso a mis padres.
I have to ask my parents' permission.

permitir VERB
to allow
No nos permiten llevar zapatillas de deporte.
We're not allowed to wear trainers.
No me lo puedo permitir.
I can't afford it.

pero CONJUNCTION
but
Me gustaría, pero no puedo.
I'd like to, but I can't.

el **perro**
la **perra** NOUN
dog
un perro callejero
a stray dog
Es una perra muy buena.
She's a very good dog.
¿Es perra o perro?
Is it a bitch or a dog?
un perro pastor
a sheepdog

perseguir VERB
to chase
Mi perro persigue a los gatos.
My dog chases cats.
Me persigue la policía.
The police are after me.

persiguiendo VERB ▷ see **perseguir**
Me venían persiguiendo por la calle.
They were chasing me down the street.

la **persona** NOUN
person
Es una persona encantadora.
He's a really nice person.
personas
people
Había unas diez personas en la sala.
There were about ten people in the hall.

el personaje NOUN
character
> **los personajes de la novela**
> the characters in the novel

personal (FEM **personal**) ADJECTIVE
personal

pertenecer VERB
> **pertenecer a**
> to belong to
> **Este reloj perteneció a su abuelo.**
> This watch belonged to his grandfather.

la pesa NOUN
weight

la pesadilla NOUN
nightmare

pesado (FEM **pesada**)

> **pesado** can be an adjective or a noun.

A ADJECTIVE
1 heavy
2 ¡No seas pesado!
> Don't be a pain!
B MASC/FEM NOUN
> **Mi primo es un pesado.**
> My cousin is a pain.
> **Mi hermana es una pesada.**
> My sister is a pain.

pesar VERB
1 to weigh
> **El paquete pesaba dos kilos.**
> The parcel weighed two kilos.
> **¿Cuánto pesas?**
> How much do you weigh?
> **Tengo que pesarme.**
> I must weigh myself.
2 to be heavy
> **Esta maleta pesa mucho.**
> This suitcase is very heavy.
> **¡No pesa nada!**
> It isn't heavy at all!
3 a pesar de
> in spite of

> **a pesar del mal tiempo**
> in spite of the bad weather
> **a pesar de que la quiero**
> even though I love her

la pesca NOUN
fishing

la pescadería NOUN
fishmonger's

el pescado NOUN
fish
> **Quiero comprar pescado.**
> I want to buy some fish.

el pescador NOUN
fisherman
> **Mi tío es pescador.**
> My uncle is a fisherman.

pescar VERB
1 to fish
> **Los domingos íbamos a pescar.**
> On Sundays we used to go fishing.
2 to catch
> **Pescamos varias truchas.**
> We caught several trout.

el peso NOUN
weight
> **ganar peso**
> to put on weight
> **Ha perdido mucho peso.**
> He's lost a lot of weight.

la pestaña NOUN
eyelash

la peste NOUN
stink
> **¡Qué peste hay aquí!**
> There's a real stink in here!

el **pestillo** NOUN
 1 **bolt**
 2 **latch**

petado (FEM **petada**) ADJECTIVE
 crashed
  El ordenador se ha quedado petado.
  The computer has crashed.

petar VERB
 to crash
  El ordenador me ha vuelto a petar.
  My computer has crashed again.
  a petar
  packed
  El estadio estaba a petar.
  The stadium was packed.

el **petardo** NOUN
 banger

la **petición** (PL las **peticiones**) NOUN
 request

el **petróleo** NOUN
 oil

el **pez** (PL los **peces**) NOUN
 fish
  Cogimos tres peces.
  We caught three fish.
  un pez de colores
  a goldfish

el **piano** NOUN
 piano

la **picadura** NOUN
 1 **bite**
 2 **sting**

picante (FEM **picante**) ADJECTIVE
 spicy

picar VERB
 1 **to bite**

  Me ha picado algo.
  I've been bitten by something.
 2 **to sting**
 3 **to chop up**
  Luego picas un poquito de jamón.
  Then you chop up a bit of ham.
 4 **to be itchy**
  Me pica la espalda.
  I've got an itchy back.
 5 **to be hot**
  La salsa pica bastante.
  The sauce is quite hot.
 6 **to nibble**
  Saqué algunas cosas para picar.
  I put out some nibbles.

el **pico** NOUN
  Eran las tres y pico.
  It was just after three.
  doscientos y pico euros
  just over two hundred euros

pidiendo VERB ▷ *see* **pedir**
  Siempre anda pidiendo algo.
  She's always asking for something.

el **pie** NOUN
 foot
  Fuimos a pie.
  We went on foot.
  Estaba de pie junto a mi cama.
  She was standing next to my bed.

  ponerse de pie
  to stand up

la **piedra** NOUN
 stone
  Nos tiraban piedras.
  They were throwing stones at us.

la **piel** NOUN
 1 **skin**
  Tengo la piel grasa.
  I have greasy skin.
 2 **peel**
 3 **fur**
  un abrigo de pieles
  a fur coat

English

Spanish

A
B
C
D
E
F
G
H
I
J
K
L
M
N
O
P
Q
R
S
T
U
V
W
X
Y
Z

188

4 leather
un bolso de piel
a leather bag

pienso VERB ▷ see **pensar**
Pienso que sí.
I think so.

pierdo VERB ▷ see **perder**
Siempre pierdo.
I always lose.

la **pierna** NOUN
leg

la **pieza** NOUN
piece
una pieza del rompecabezas
a piece of the jigsaw puzzle

el **pijama** NOUN
pyjamas
un pijama
a pair of pyjamas

la **pila** NOUN
1 battery
Funciona con pilas.
It runs on batteries.
2 pile
una pila de revistas
a pile of magazines

pillar VERB
to catch
Pillaron al ladrón.
They caught the thief.
Lo pillé haciendo trampa.
I caught him cheating.

pillo (FEM **pilla**) ADJECTIVE
1 crafty
2 naughty

el/la **piloto** NOUN
pilot

la **pimienta** NOUN
pepper
pimienta negra
black pepper

el **pimiento** NOUN
pepper

el **pincel** NOUN
paintbrush

pinchar VERB
1 to prick
Me pinché con un alfiler.
I pricked myself on a pin.
Me pincharon en el brazo.
They gave me an injection in
the arm.
2 to burst
El clavo pinchó la pelota.
The nail burst the ball.
Se me pinchó una rueda.
I had a puncture.

el **pinchazo** NOUN
puncture
Tuvimos un pinchazo en la
autopista.
We got a puncture on the motorway.

el **ping-pong** NOUN
table tennis
jugar al ping-pong
to play table tennis

el **pino** NOUN
pine tree

hacer el pino
to do a headstand

la **pinta** NOUN
tener buena pinta
to look good
La paella tiene muy buena
pinta.
The paella looks delicious.
Con esas gafas tienes pinta
de maestra.
You look like a teacher with those
glasses on.

el **pintalabios** NOUN (PL los
  pintalabios)
  lipstick

pintar VERB
  1 to paint
  **Quiero pintar la habitación de
  azul.**
  I want to paint the room blue.
  Me estoy pintando las uñas.
  I'm painting my nails.
  2 to colour in
  Dibujó un árbol y lo pintó.
  He drew a tree and coloured it in.

el **pintor**
la **pintora** NOUN
  painter
  Soy pintor.
  I'm a painter.

la **pintura** NOUN
  1 paint
  Tengo que comprar más pintura.
  I've got to buy some more paint.
  2 painting
  varias pinturas al óleo
  several oil paintings

la **pinza** NOUN
  1 clothes peg
  2 hairgrip

la **piña** NOUN
  pineapple

la **pipa** NOUN
  1 pipe

Fuma en pipa.
  He smokes a pipe.
  2 seed
  comer pipas
  to eat sunflower seeds

DID YOU KNOW...?
pipas are a common snack which
both children and adults enjoy.

---

el/la **pirata** NOUN
  pirate

  un pirata informático
  a hacker

la **pisada** NOUN
  1 footprint
  2 footstep

pisar VERB
  1 to walk on
  **¿Se puede pisar el suelo de la
  cocina?**
  Can I walk on the kitchen floor?
  2 to tread on
  Perdona, te he pisado.
  Sorry, I trod on your toe.

la **piscina** NOUN
  swimming pool

el **piso** NOUN
  1 flat
  Vivimos en un piso céntrico.
  We live in a flat in the town centre.
  2 floor
  **Su oficina está en el segundo
  piso.**
  His office is on the second floor.

a
b
c
d
e
f
g
h
i
j
k
l
m
n
o
p
q
r
s
t
u
v
w
x
y
z

189

la **pista** NOUN
1 **clue**
¿Te doy una pista?
Shall I give you a clue?
2 **court**
la pista de aterrizaje
the runway
la pista de esquí
the ski slope
la pista de patinaje
the ice rink

la **pistola** NOUN
pistol

pitar VERB
to blow one's whistle
El policía nos pitó.
The policeman blew his whistle at us.

el **pito** NOUN
whistle

la **pizarra** NOUN
board
una pizarra interactiva
an interactive whiteboard

la **pizca** NOUN
pinch
una pizca de sal
a pinch of salt

el **plan** NOUN
plan
¿Qué planes tienes para este verano?
What are your plans for the summer?
Lo dije en plan de broma.
I said it as a joke.

la **plancha** NOUN
1 **iron**
2 **riddle**
pescado a la plancha
grilled fish

planchar VERB
1 **to iron**
Tengo que planchar esta camisa.
I've got to iron this shirt.
2 **to do the ironing**
¿Quieres que planche?
Do you want me to do the ironing?

el **planeta** NOUN
planet

el **plano** NOUN
street plan
en primer plano
in close-up

la **planta** NOUN
1 **plant**
Tengo que regar las plantas.
I have to water the plants.
2 **floor**
El edificio tiene tres plantas.
The building has three floors.
la planta baja
the ground floor

plantar VERB
to plant

el **plástico** NOUN
plastic
cubiertos de plástico
plastic cutlery

la **plata** NOUN
silver

el **plátano** NOUN
banana

el **plato** NOUN
1 **plate**
¿Me pasas un plato?
Could you pass me a plate?
2 **dish**
un plato típico de Galicia
a typical Galician dish
el plato del día
the dish of the day

3 course
¿Qué hay de segundo plato?
What's for the main course?

la **playa** NOUN
1 beach
Los niños jugaban en la playa.
The children were playing on the beach.
2 seaside
Prefiero la playa a la montaña.
I prefer the seaside to the mountains.

la **plaza** NOUN
square
la plaza del pueblo
the town square
la plaza mayor
the main square
una plaza de toros
a bullring

el **plazo** NOUN
period
en un plazo de diez días
within a period of ten days
El viernes se cumple el plazo.
Friday is the deadline.

pleno (FEM **plena**) ADJECTIVE
en pleno verano
in the middle of summer
a plena luz del día
in broad daylight

el **pliegue** NOUN
fold

el **plomo** NOUN
1 lead
gasolina sin plomo
unleaded petrol
2 fuse
Se han fundido los plomos.
The fuses have blown.

la **pluma** NOUN
1 feather
2 pen
una pluma estilográfica
a fountain pen

plural ADJECTIVE, MASC NOUN
plural

la **población** (PL las **poblaciones**) NOUN
1 population
2 town

pobre (FEM **pobre**) ADJECTIVE
poor
Somos pobres.
We're poor.
los pobres
the poor

la **pobreza** NOUN
poverty

poco

> **poco** can be an adjective, an adverb or a pronoun.

A ADJECTIVE (FEM **poca**)
not much
Hay poca leche.
There isn't much milk.
Tenemos muy poco tiempo.
We haven't got much time.
pocos
not many
Tiene pocos amigos.
He hasn't got many friends.
B ADVERB
1 Sus libros son poco conocidos.
His books are not very well known.
2 por poco
nearly
Por poco me caigo.
I nearly fell.
C PRONOUN (FEM **poca**)
unos pocos
a few
Me llevé unos pocos.
I took a few with me.
un poco
a bit
¿Tienes frío? — Un poco.
Are you cold? — A bit.
¿Me das un poco?
Can I have a bit?

Tomé un poco de zumo.
I had a bit of juice.

dentro de poco
soon
hace poco
not long ago

poder VERB
1 **can**
   Yo puedo ayudarte.
   I can help you.
   ¿Puedo usar tu teléfono?
   Can I use your phone?
   Aquí no se puede jugar.
   You can't play here.
   ¡Me lo podías haber dicho!
   You could have told me!
   ¡No puede ser!
   That's impossible!
2 **to be able to**
   Mañana no podré ir.
   I won't be able to come tomorrow.
3 **Puede que llegue mañana.**
   He may arrive tomorrow.

poderoso (FEM **poderosa**) ADJECTIVE
powerful

podrido (FEM **podrida**) ADJECTIVE
rotten

la **poesía** NOUN
1 **poetry**
   Me gusta la poesía.
   I like poetry.
2 **poem**
   una poesía de Machado
   a poem by Machado

el/la **poeta** NOUN
poet

policía

policía can be a masculine or a feminine noun.

A MASC NOUN
   police officer
   Es policía.
   He's a police officer.

B FEM NOUN
1 **police**
   Llamamos a la policía.
   We called the police.
2 **police officer**
   Soy policía.
   I'm a police officer.

el **polideportivo** NOUN
sports centre

la **política** NOUN
1 **politics**
   Hablaban de política.
   They were talking about politics.
2 **politician**

político

político can be an adjective or a noun.

A ADJECTIVE (FEM **política**)
   political
B MASC NOUN
   politician
   Soy político.
   I'm a politician.

el **pollo** NOUN
chicken
   pollo asado
   roast chicken

el **polo** NOUN
1 **ice lolly**
2 **polo shirt**

el **polvo** NOUN
dust
   quitar el polvo
   to do the dusting
   quitar el polvo a algo
   to dust something
   polvos de talco
   talcum powder

Estoy hecho polvo.
I'm shattered.

pondrá VERB ▷ *see* **poner**
Ya lo pondrá en su sitio cuando acabe.
He'll put it back when he's finished.

poner VERB
1 **to put**
¿Dónde pongo mis cosas?
Where shall I put my things?
2 **to put on**
Me puse el abrigo.
I put my coat on.
¿Pongo música?
Shall I put some music on?
Pon el radiador.
Put the heater on.
No sé que ponerme.
I don't know what to wear.
¿Ponen alguna película esta noche?
Is there a film on tonight?
3 **to set**
La maestra nos puso un examen.
Our teacher set us an exam.
Puse el despertador para las siete.
I set the alarm for seven o'clock.
poner la mesa
to lay the table
4 **to get**
¿Qué te pongo?
What can I get you?
5 **¿Me pone con el Sr. García, por favor?**
Could you put me through to Mr García, please?
■ **ponerse**
1 **to sit**
Se puso a mi lado en clase.
He sat down beside me in class.
2 **Cuando se lo dije se puso muy triste.**
He was very sad when I told him.
3 **ponerse a hacer algo**
to start doing something
Se puso a llorar.
He started crying.

pongo VERB ▷ *see* **poner**
¿Lo pongo aquí?
Shall I put it here?

por PREPOSITION
1 **for**
Lo hice por mis padres.
I did it for my parents.
Lo vendió por cien euros.
He sold it for a hundred euros.
Me castigaron por mentir.
I was punished for lying.
2 **through**
Pasamos por Valencia.
We went through Valencia.
3 **by**
Fueron apresados por la policía.
They were captured by the police.
Me agarró por el brazo.
He grabbed me by the arm.
4 **along**
Paseábamos por la playa.
We were walking along the beach.
5 **per**
cien kilómetros por hora
a hundred kilometres per hour
diez euros por persona
ten euros per person

por la mañana
in the morning
por la noche
at night
¿Por qué?
Why?

la **porción** (PL las **porciones**) NOUN
portion

porque CONJUNCTION
because
No fuimos porque llovía.
We didn't go because it was raining.

la **porquería** NOUN
comer porquerías
to eat rubbish
Este juguete es una porquería.
This toy's rubbish.

English
Spanish

a
b
c
d
e
f
g
h
i
j
k
l
m
n
o
p
q
r
s
t
u
v
w
x
y
z

Spanish — English

la **portada** NOUN
 1 **front page**
 2 **cover**

el **portal** NOUN
 1 **hallway**
  Los buzones están en el portal.
  The letterboxes are in the hallway.
  el portal de Belén
  the nativity scene
 2 **portal**

portarse VERB
 to behave
  ¡Pórtate bien!
  Behave yourself!
  Se está portando muy mal.
  He's behaving very badly.

portátil

> **portátil** can be an adjective or a noun.

 A ADJECTIVE (FEM **portátil**)
  portable
 B MASC NOUN
  laptop

el **portazo** NOUN
  Dio un portazo.
  He slammed the door.

la **portería** NOUN
 goal
  El balón entró en la portería.
  The ball went into the goal.

el **portero**
 la **portera** NOUN
 1 **caretaker**
 2 **goalkeeper**
  un portero automático
  an entryphone

poseer VERB
 to possess

la **posibilidad** NOUN
 1 **possibility**
  Es una posibilidad.
  It's a possibility.

 2 **chance**
  Tendrás la posibilidad de viajar.
  You'll have the chance to travel.
  Tiene muchas posibilidades de ganar.
  He has a good chance of winning.

posible (FEM **posible**) ADJECTIVE
 possible
  Es posible.
  It's possible.
  Haremos todo lo posible.
  We'll do everything we can.
  Es posible que ganen.
  They might win.

la **posición** (PL las **posiciones**) NOUN
 position
  una posición estratégica
  a strategic position
  Está en primera posición.
  He's in first place.

positivo (FEM **positiva**) ADJECTIVE
 positive
  El test dio positivo.
  The test was positive.

la **postal** NOUN
 postcard

el **poste** NOUN
 post

el **póster** (PL los **pósters**) NOUN
 poster

el **postre** NOUN
 dessert
  De postre tomé un helado.
  I had ice cream for dessert.
  ¿Qué hay de postre?
  What's for dessert?

potable (FEM **potable**) ADJECTIVE
 agua potable
 drinking water

potente (FEM **potente**) ADJECTIVE
powerful

el **pozo** NOUN
well

la **práctica** NOUN
practice
No tengo mucha práctica.
I haven't had much practice.

practicar VERB
to practise
Tengo que practicar un poco más.
I need to practise a bit more.
No practico ningún deporte.
I don't do any sports.

práctico (FEM **práctica**) ADJECTIVE
practical

el **precio** NOUN
price
Han subido los precios.
Prices have gone up.

precioso (FEM **preciosa**) ADJECTIVE
beautiful
¡Es precioso!
It's beautiful!

preciso (FEM **precisa**) ADJECTIVE
1 **precise**
en ese preciso momento
at that precise moment
2 **accurate**
un reloj muy preciso
a very accurate watch
No es preciso que vengas.
There's no need for you to come.

preferido (FEM **preferida**) ADJECTIVE
favourite

preferir VERB
to prefer
Prefiero un buen libro a una película.
I prefer a good book to a film.
Prefiero ir mañana.
I'd rather go tomorrow.

prefiero VERB ▷ see **preferir**
Prefiero el verde.
I prefer the green one.

la **pregunta** NOUN
question
hacer una pregunta
to ask a question

preguntar VERB
to ask
Siempre me preguntas lo mismo.
You're always asking me the same question.
Me preguntó por ti.
He asked after you.
Me pregunto si estará enterado.
I wonder if he's heard yet.

el **premio** NOUN
prize
llevarse un premio
to get a prize

preocupado (FEM **preocupada**) ADJECTIVE
worried
Estoy preocupado por el examen.
I'm worried about the exam.

preocupar VERB
Me preocupa el examen.
I'm worried about the exam.
■ **preocuparse**
to worry
No te preocupes.
Don't worry.
preocuparse por algo
to worry about something
Se preocupa por sus gatitos.
She worries about her kittens.
Si llego un poco tarde se preocupa.
If I arrive a bit late he gets worried.

preparar VERB
1 **to prepare**
No he preparado el discurso.
I haven't prepared my talk.
2 **to prepare for**
¿Te has preparado el examen?
Have you prepared for the exam?
3 **to cook**
Mi madre estaba preparando la cena.
My mother was cooking dinner.
■ **prepararse**
to get ready
Me estaba preparando para salir.
I was getting ready to go out.

el **presentador**
la **presentadora** NOUN
presenter

presentar VERB
1 **to introduce**
Me presentó a sus padres.
He introduced me to his parents.
2 **to hand in**
Mañana tengo que presentar un trabajo.
I have to hand in an essay tomorrow.
■ **presentarse**
1 **to turn up**
Se presentó en mi casa sin avisar.
He turned up at my house without warning.
presentarse a un examen
to sit an exam
2 **to introduce oneself**
Me voy a presentar.
Let me introduce myself.

presente

> **presente** can be an adjective or a noun.

A ADJECTIVE (FEM **presente**)
present
Juan no estaba presente en la reunión.
Juan was not present at the meeting.

¡Presente!
Here!

B MASC NOUN
el presente
the present
los presentes
those present

el **presidente**
la **presidenta** NOUN
president

el **preso**
la **presa** NOUN
prisoner

prestado (FEM **prestada**) ADJECTIVE
La camiseta no es mía, es prestada.
It's not my T-shirt, somebody lent it to me.
Le pedí prestada la bicicleta.
I asked if I could borrow his bicycle.
Me dejó el boli prestado.
He lent me his pen.

prestar VERB
to lend
Un amigo me prestó el diccionario.
A friend lent me the dictionary.
¿Me prestas el boli?
Can I borrow your pen?
Tienes que prestar atención.
You must pay attention.

presumido (FEM **presumida**) ADJECTIVE
vain

presumir VERB
to show off
Lleva ropa cara para presumir.
He wears expensive clothes just to show off.

pretender VERB
1 **to intend**
Pretendo sacar al menos un notable.
I intend to get at least a B.
2 **to expect**
¡No pretenderás que lo haga yo todo!
You're not expecting me to do everything, are you?

¿Qué pretendes decir con eso?
What do you mean by that?

LANGUAGE TIP
Be careful! **pretender** does not mean
to pretend.

---

prevenir VERB
  to prevent
    prevenir un accidente
    to prevent an accident

previsto (FEM **prevista**) ADJECTIVE
    Tengo previsto volver mañana.
    I plan to return tomorrow.
    **El avión tiene prevista su llegada
    a las dos.**
    The plane is due in at two o'clock.
    Como estaba previsto, ganó él.
    As expected, he won.

la **primavera** NOUN
  spring
    en primavera
    in spring

primero (FEM **primera**) ADJECTIVE, PRONOUN
  first

LANGUAGE TIP
primero becomes **primer** before a
masculine singular noun.

---

    el primer día
    the first day
    la primera planta
    the first floor
    Primero vamos a comer.
    Let's eat first.
    en primera fila
    in the front row
    **En primer lugar, vamos a
    ponernos en grupos.**

Firstly, let's get into groups.
    Vivo en el primero.
    I live on the first floor.
    Fui la primera en llegar.
    I was the first to arrive.
    Juan es el primero de la clase.
    Juan is top of the class.
    **El examen será a primeros de
    mayo.**
    The exam will be at the beginning of
    May.

el **primo**
  la **prima** NOUN
    cousin

la **princesa** NOUN
  princess

principal (FEM **principal**) ADJECTIVE
    main
    el personaje principal
    the main character
    Lo principal es que estás mejor.
    The main thing is that you're better.

principalmente ADVERB
    mainly

el **príncipe** NOUN
    prince

el/la **principiante** NOUN
    beginner

el **principio** NOUN
    beginning
    El principio me gustó.
    I liked the beginning.
    Al principio parecía fácil.
    It seemed easy at first.

la **prisa** NOUN
    rush
    **Con las prisas me olvidé el
    paraguas.**
    In the rush I forgot my umbrella.

    ¡Date prisa!
    Hurry up!
    Tengo prisa.
    I'm in a hurry.

la **prisión** (PL las **prisiones**) NOUN
prison

el **prisionero**
la **prisionera** NOUN
prisoner

los **prismáticos** NOUN
binoculars

privado (FEM **privada**) ADJECTIVE
private
un colegio privado
a private school

probable (FEM **probable**) ADJECTIVE
likely
Es muy probable.
It's very likely.
Es probable que llegue tarde.
He'll probably arrive late.

probablemente ADVERB
probably

el **probador** NOUN
changing room

probar VERB
1 **to try**
Pruébalo antes para ver si
funciona bien.
Try it first and see if it works properly.
Me probé un vestido.
I tried on a dress.
2 **to prove**
La policía no pudo probarlo.
The police could not prove it.
3 **to taste**
Probé la salsa para ver si era
picante.
I tasted the soup to see if it needed
more salt.

el **problema** NOUN
problem

la **procesión** (PL las **procesiones**) NOUN
procession

el **proceso** NOUN
process

procurar VERB
to try

Procura terminarlo mañana.
Try to finish it tomorrow.

la **producción** (PL las **producciones**)
NOUN
production

producir VERB
to produce
No producen lo suficiente.
They are not producing enough.
■ **producirse**
¿Cómo se produjo el accidente?
How did the accident happen?

el **producto** NOUN
product
productos de limpieza
cleaning products
productos lácteos
dairy products

la **profesión** (PL las **profesiones**) NOUN
profession

profesional (FEM **profesional**) ADJECTIVE,
NOUN
professional

el **profesor**
la **profesora** NOUN
teacher
Amelia es profesora de inglés.
Amelia is an English teacher.
mi profesor particular
my private tutor

LANGUAGE TIP
Be careful! **profesor** does not mean
professor.

la **profundidad** NOUN
depth
la profundidad de la piscina
the depth of the pool
Tiene dos metros de profundidad.
It's two metres deep.

profundo (FEM **profunda**) ADJECTIVE
deep
una piscina poco profunda
a shallow pool

el programa NOUN
1 **programme**
un programa de televisión
a television programme

un programa-concurso
a quiz show
2 **program**
un programa informático
a computer program

el progreso NOUN
progress
Carmen ha hecho muchos progresos este trimestre.
Carmen has made great progress this term.

prohibir VERB
to ban
Le prohibieron la entrada en el edificio.
He was banned from entering the building.
terminantemente prohibido
strictly forbidden

el promedio NOUN
average

la promesa NOUN
promise

prometer VERB
to promise
Prometió llevarnos al cine.
He promised to take us to the cinema.

la promoción (PL **promociones**) NOUN
promotion
Está en promoción.
It's on offer.

el pronombre NOUN
pronoun

el pronóstico NOUN
el pronóstico del tiempo
the weather forecast

pronto ADVERB
1 **soon**
Los invitados llegarán pronto.
The guests will be here soon.
2 **early**
¿Por qué has llegado tan pronto?
Why are you so early?
Hoy me he levantado muy pronto.
I got up very early this morning.
De pronto, empezó a nevar.
All of a sudden it began to snow.

¡Hasta pronto!
See you soon!

pronunciar VERB
to pronounce
¿Cómo se pronuncia esta palabra?
How do you pronounce this word?

la propina NOUN
tip
¿Vamos a dejar propina?
Shall we leave a tip?

propio (FEM **propia**) ADJECTIVE
1 **own**
Tengo mi propia habitación.
I have my own room.
2 **himself**
Lo dijo el propio director del colegio.
The headmaster himself said it.
3 **un nombre propio**
a proper noun

proponer VERB
to suggest
Nos propuso ir al cine..
He suggested that we should go to the cinema.
■ **proponerse**
Se ha propuesto adelgazar.
He's decided to lose some weight.

el **propósito** NOUN
purpose
¿Cuál es el propósito de su visita?
What is the purpose of your visit?
A propósito, ya tengo los billetes.
By the way, I've got the tickets.
Lo hizo a propósito.
He did it deliberately.

propuesto VERB ▷ see **proponer**
He propuesto ayudarles.
I've suggested helping them.

el/la **protagonista** NOUN
main character
El protagonista no muere en la película.
The main character doesn't die in the film.
La protagonista es Emma Watson.
Emma Watson plays the lead.

proteger VERB
to protect
El muro le protegió de las balas.
The wall protected him from the bullets.
Nos protegimos de la lluvia en la cabaña.
We sheltered from the rain in the hut.

protestar VERB
1 **to protest**
Protestaron contra la subida de la gasolina.
They protested against the rise in petrol prices.
2 **to complain**
Cómete la verdura y no protestes.
Eat your vegetables and don't complain.

el **provecho** NOUN
¡Buen provecho!
Enjoy your meal!
Sacó mucho provecho del curso.
He got a lot out of the course.

provocar VERB
1 **to provoke**
No quería pegarle pero me provocó.
I didn't mean to hit him but he provoked me.

2 **to cause**
La lluvia ha provocado graves inundaciones.
The rain caused serious flooding.
El incendio fue provocado.
The fire was started deliberately.

próximo (FEM **próxima**) ADJECTIVE
next
Lo haremos la próxima semana.
We'll do it next week.
la próxima calle a la izquierda
the next street on the left

la próxima vez
next time

el **proyecto** NOUN
project

prueba

prueba can be a noun or part of the verb **probar**.

A FEM NOUN
1 **test**
El médico me hizo más pruebas.
The doctor did some more tests.
2 **proof**
Eso es la prueba de que lo hizo él.
This is the proof that he did it.
B VERB ▷ see **probar**
Prueba esto.
Try this.

pruebo VERB ▷ see **probar**
A ver, que pruebo yo.
Let me try.

la **publicidad** NOUN
advertising
una campaña de publicidad
an advertising campaign

público

público can be an adjective or a noun.

A ADJECTIVE (FEM **pública**)
public

B MASC NOUN
1 public
cerrado al público
closed to the public
2 spectators

pude VERB ▷ *see* **poder**
No pude hacerlo.
I couldn't do it.

el **pueblo** NOUN
1 village
2 town

puedo VERB ▷ *see* **poder**
Yo puedo ayudarte.
I can help you.

el **puente** NOUN
bridge

hacer puente
to make a long weekend of it

DID YOU KNOW...?
When a public holiday falls on a
Tuesday or Thursday people often take
off Monday or Friday as well to give
themselves a long weekend.

la **puerta** NOUN
door
Llaman a la puerta.
There's somebody at the door.
Lidia me acompañó a la puerta.
Lidia saw me out.

el **puerto** NOUN
port
un puerto pesquero
a fishing port
un puerto de montaña
a mountain pass

pues CONJUNCTION
1 then
**Tengo sueño. –– ¡Pues vete a la
cama!**
I'm tired. — Then go to bed!
2 well
Pues, como te iba contando ...
Well, as I was saying ...
¡Pues no lo sabía!
Well I didn't know!

¡Pues claro!
Yes, of course!

puesto

puesto can be a noun or part of the
verb **poner**.

A MASC NOUN
1 place
Acabé en primer puesto.
I finished in first place.
2 un puesto de trabajo
a job
B VERB ▷ *see* **poner**
**Han puesto un
cartel en la ventana.**
They've put a sign in
the window.

el **pulgar** NOUN
thumb

el **pulmón**
(PL los **pulmones**) NOUN
lung

pulsar VERB
to press

la **pulsera** NOUN
bracelet
un reloj de pulsera
a wrist watch

el **pulso** NOUN
1 pulse
El doctor le tomó el pulso.
The doctor took his pulse.
Tengo muy mal pulso.
My hand is very unsteady.

2 Echamos un pulso y le gané.
We had an arm-wrestling match and I won.

la **punta** NOUN
1 tip
2 point
Sácale punta al lápiz.
Sharpen your pencil.
la hora punta
the rush hour

la **puntería** NOUN
tener buena puntería
to be a good shot

la **puntilla** NOUN
andar de puntillas
to tiptoe
ponerse de puntillas
to stand on tiptoe

el **punto** NOUN
1 point
Perdieron por tres puntos.
They lost by three points.
Ese es un punto importante.
That's an important point.
2 stitch
3 dot
Mi correo es loveday arroba collins punto es (loveday@collins.es).
My email address is loveday at collins dot E-S (loveday@collins.es).
4 full stop
punto y seguido
full stop, new sentence
punto y aparte
full stop, new paragraph
punto y coma
semi-colon
dos puntos
colon

puntos suspensivos
dot, dot, dot
5 **Estábamos a punto de salir cuando llamaste.**
We were about to go out when you phoned.
Estuve a punto de perder el tren.
I very nearly missed the train.

a la una en punto
at one o'clock sharp

la **puntuación** (PL las **puntuaciones**) NOUN
1 punctuation
los signos de puntuación
punctuation marks
2 score
Recibió una puntuación alta.
He got a high score.

el **puñado** NOUN
handful
un puñado de arena
a handful of sand

el **puñetazo** NOUN
punch
un puñetazo en la cara
a punch in the face
Le pegó un puñetazo.
He punched him.

el **puño** NOUN
fist

el **puré** (PL los **purés**) NOUN
puré de verduras
vegetable soup
puré de patatas
mashed potato

puro (FEM **pura**) ADJECTIVE
pure
pura lana
pure wool
Es la pura verdad.
That's the absolute truth.

puse VERB ▷ see **poner**
Yo lo puse allí.
I put it there.

English **Spanish**

A B C D E F G H I J K L M N O P Q R S T U V W X Y Z

Qq

English

Spanish

a
b
c
d
e
f
g
h
i
j
k
l
m
n
o
p
q
r
s
t
u
v
w
x
y
z

el **quad** NOUN
   quad bike

que

> **que** can be a conjunction or a pronoun.

A CONJUNCTION
1 than
   Es más alto que tú.
   He's taller than you.
2 that
   Bruno sabe que estás aquí.
   Bruno knows that you're here.
   Dijo que vendría.
   He said he'd come.
   Dile que me llame.
   Ask her to call me.
   ¡Que te mejores!
   Get well soon!
B PRONOUN
1 which
   la película que ganó el premio
   the film which won the award
   el juego que te compraste ayer
   the game you bought yesterday
2 who
   el hombre que vino ayer
   the man who came yesterday
   la chica que conocí
   the girl I met

qué ADJECTIVE, ADVERB, PRONOUN
1 what
   ¿Qué haces?
   What are you doing?
   ¿Qué hora es?
   What's the time?

2 which
   ¿Qué película quieres ver?
   Which film do you want to see?
   ¿Qué tal?
   How are things?
   No lo he hecho.
   ¿Y qué?
   I haven't done it.
   So what?
   ¡Qué asco!
   How revolting!

quedar VERB
1 to be left
   Quedan dos manzanas.
   There are two apples left.
   Me quedan diez euros.
   I've got ten euros left.
2 to be
   Eso queda muy lejos de aquí.
   That's a long way from here.
3 to suit
   No te queda bien ese vestido.
   That dress doesn't suit you.
4 to arrange to meet
   Hemos quedado en el cine.
   We've arranged to meet at the cinema.
   ■ **quedarse**
1 to stay
   Ve tú, yo me quedo.
   You go, I'll stay.
2 quedarse con algo
   to keep something
   Quédese con el cambio.
   Keep the change.

la **queja** NOUN
   complaint

quejarse VERB
   to complain
   quejarse de algo
   to complain about something
   Se quejan de la comida.
   They complain about the food.

quejarse de que ...
to complain that ...
Pablo se queja de que nadie lo escucha.
Pablo complains that nobody listens to him.

quemado (FEM **quemada**) ADJECTIVE
burnt
El arroz estaba quemado.
The rice was burnt.
quemado por el sol
sunburnt

quemar VERB
to burn
He quemado la camisa con la plancha.
I burned my shirt with the iron.
Esta sopa quema.
This soup's boiling hot.
■ **quemarse**
to burn oneself
Me quemé con una cerilla.
I burned myself with a match.

quepa VERB ▷ *see* **caber**
No creo que quepa ahí.
I don't think it will fit in there.

querer VERB
1 **to want**
No quiero jugar.
I don't want to play.
¿Quieres un bocadillo?
Would you like a sandwich?
2 **to love**
Te quiero.
I love you.
3 **to mean**
No quería hacerte daño.
I didn't mean to hurt you.
Lo hice sin querer.
It was an accident.
querer decir
to mean
¿Qué quieres decir?
What do you mean?

querido (FEM **querida**) ADJECTIVE
dear
Querido Sr. Lobos
Dear Mr Lobos

querré VERB ▷ *see* **querer**
Jamás querré ir allí.
I'll never want to go there.

el **queso** NOUN
cheese

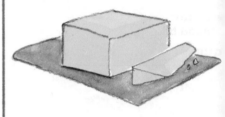

un bocadillo de queso
a cheese sandwich

quien PRONOUN
who
Fue Iker quien nos lo dijo.
It was Iker who told us.
Vi al chico con quien sales.
I saw the boy you're going out with.

quién PRONOUN
who
¿Quién es esa?
Who's that?
¿A quién viste?
Who did you see?
¿De quién es ... ?
Whose is...?
¿De quién es este libro?
Whose is this book?
¿Quién es?
Who's there?/Who's he?

___

LANGUAGE TIP
¿Quién es? has two meanings. It can be translated as **Who's there?** when there's somebody at the door and **Who is he/she?** if you want to find out who someone is.

quiero VERB ▷ *see* **querer**
Quiero un bocadillo.
I want a sandwich.

quieto (FEM **quieta**) ADJECTIVE
still
¡Estáte quieto!
Keep still!

la **química** NOUN
1 chemistry
clase de química
chemistry class
2 chemist
Es química.
She's a chemist.

el **químico** NOUN
chemist
Es químico.
He's a chemist.

quince (FEM **quince**) ADJECTIVE, PRONOUN
fifteen
quince euros
fifteen euros
Mi hermano tiene quince años.
My brother's fifteen.

el quince de enero
the fifteenth of January
Nació el quince de enero.
He was born on the fifteenth of
January.

quinientos (FEM **quinientas**) ADJECTIVE,
PRONOUN
five hundred

quinto (FEM **quinta**) ADJECTIVE, PRONOUN
fifth

Vivo en el quinto.
I live on the fifth floor.

el **quiosco** NOUN
un quiosco de periódicos
a news stand

DID YOU KNOW...?
In Spain, people traditionally buy their
newspapers, lottery tickets etc from the
quioscos that are dotted around a
town.

quise VERB ▷ *see* **querer**
No quise ir al cine con él.
I didn't want to go to the cinema with
him.

quisquilloso (FEM **quisquillosa**)
ADJECTIVE
fussy
**No soy quisquillosa con la
comida.**
I'm not fussy about what I eat.

quitar VERB
to take away
Su hermana le quitó la pelota.
His sister took the ball away from him.
Me han quitado la cartera.
I've had my wallet stolen.
■ **quitarse**
to take off
Juan se quitó la chaqueta.
Juan took his jacket off.
¡Quítate de en medio!
Get out of the way!

quizás ADVERB
perhaps

English

Spanish

a
b
c
d
e
f
g
h
i
j
k
l
m
n
o
p
q
r
s
t
u
v
w
x
y
z

la **rabia** NOUN
> **Me da mucha rabia.**
> It's really annoying.

la **rabieta** NOUN
> **tantrum**
>> **agarrarse una rabieta**
>> to throw a tantrum

el **rabo** NOUN
> **tail**
>> **Ese perro tiene un rabo muy corto.**
>> That dog has a very short tail.

la **racha** NOUN
>> **una racha de buen tiempo**
>> a spell of good weather
>> **pasar una mala racha**
>> to go through a bad patch

el **racimo** NOUN
> **bunch**
>> **un racimo de uvas**
>> a bunch of grapes

la **ración** (PL las **raciones**) NOUN
> **portion**
>> **una ración de patatas fritas**
>> a portion of chips

la **radio** NOUN
> **radio**
>> **El abuelo escucha la radio.**
>> Granddad listens to the radio.
>> **Lo oí por la radio.**
>> I heard it on the radio.
>> **la radio digital**
>> digital radio

el **radio** NOUN
> **radius**
>> **en un radio de cincuenta kilómetros**
>> within a fifty-kilometre radius

la **radiografía** NOUN
> **X-ray**
>> **Tengo que hacerme una radiografía.**
>> I've got to have an X-ray.

la **raíz** (PL las **raíces**) NOUN
> **root**
>> **a raíz de**
>> as a result of

rallar VERB
> **to grate**
>> **Primero rallas el queso.**
>> First you grate the cheese.

la **rama** NOUN
> **branch**

el **ramo** NOUN
> **bunch**
>> **un ramo de rosas**
>> a bunch of roses

rápidamente ADVERB
> **quickly**

rápido

> **rápido** can be an adjective or an adverb.

A ADJECTIVE (FEM **rápida**)
> **fast**
>> **un coche muy rápido**
>> a very fast car
>> **Fue una visita muy rápida.**
>> It was a very quick visit.

B ADVERB
> **fast**
>> **Conduces demasiado rápido.**
>> You drive too fast.
>> **Lo hice tan rápido como pude.**
>> I did it as quickly as I could.
>> **¡Rápido!**
>> Hurry up!

la raqueta NOUN
 1 **racket**
 2 **bat**

raro (FEM **rara**) ADJECTIVE
  strange
   Es una cosa muy rara.
   It's a very strange thing.
   ¡Qué raro!
   How strange!
   Sabe un poco raro.
   It tastes a bit funny.
   Es raro que haga tan buen tiempo.
   It's unusual to have such good weather.

rascar VERB
  to scratch
   ¿Me rascas la espalda?
   Could you scratch my back for me?
 ■ **rascarse**
   to scratch
   No deja de rascarse.
   He can't stop scratching.

el rastro NOUN
  trail
   seguir el rastro de alguien
   to follow somebody's trail

la rata NOUN
  rat

el rato NOUN
  while
   después de un rato
   after a while
   hace un rato
   a little while ago
   al poco rato
   shortly after
   Pasamos un buen rato.
   We had a good time.
   Pasamos un mal rato.
   We had a dreadful time.
   en mis ratos libres
   in my free time
   Tengo para rato con los deberes.
   My homework's going to take me quite a while.

el ratón (PL los **ratones**) NOUN
  mouse

   dos ratones blancos
   two white mice

la raya NOUN
 1 **line**
   trazar una raya
   to draw a line
   pasarse de la raya
   to overstep the mark
   un jersey a rayas
   a striped jumper
 2 **parting**
   Me hago la raya en medio.
   I have a middle parting.

rayar VERB
  to scratch

el rayo NOUN
 1 **lightning**
   Cayó un rayo en la iglesia.
   The church was struck by lightning.
 2 **ray**
   los rayos del sol
   the sun's rays

la raza NOUN
  race
   la raza humana
   the human race
   ¿De qué raza es tu perro?
   What breed's your dog?

la razón (PL las **razones**) NOUN
  reason
   la razón de su visita
   the reason for his visit
   Iván tiene razón.
   Iván's right.
   no tener razón
   to be wrong

la reacción (PL las **reacciones**) NOUN
  reaction

English

Spanish

A
B
C
D
E
F
G
H
I
J
K
L
M
N
O
P
Q
R
S
T
U
V
W
X
Y
Z

reaccionar VERB
to react

real (FEM **real**) ADJECTIVE
real
> **en la vida real**
> in real life
> **la familia real**
> the royal family

la **realidad** NOUN
reality
> **en realidad**
> actually
> **Parece mayor, pero en realidad es menor que yo.**
> He looks older but actually he's younger than I am.
> **Mi sueño se hizo realidad.**
> My dream came true.

realista (FEM **realista**) ADJECTIVE
realistic

el **reality** (PL los **realitys**) NOUN
reality show

realmente ADVERB
really
> **un problema realmente difícil**
> a really difficult problem

la **rebaja** NOUN
discount
> **Me hizo una rebaja.**
> He gave me a discount.
> **las rebajas**
> the sales
> **Las tiendas están de rebajas.**
> The sales are on.

rebajar VERB
to reduce

Han rebajado los abrigos.
Coats have been reduced.

la **rebanada** NOUN
slice
> **una rebanada de pan**
> a slice of bread

rebelde (FEM **rebelde**) ADJECTIVE
rebellious

rebotar VERB
to bounce
> **La pelota rebotó en el poste.**
> The ball bounced off the post.

el **recado** NOUN
errand
> **Ha ido a hacer unos recados.**
> She's gone to do some errands.

el **recambio** NOUN
refill

la **receta** NOUN
1 recipe
> **Me dio la receta de las galletas.**
> He gave me the recipe for the biscuits.
2 prescription

LANGUAGE TIP
Be careful! **receta** does not mean **receipt**.

---

recetar VERB
to prescribe

rechazar VERB
to reject
> **Rechazaron mi sugerencia.**
> They rejected my suggestion.

recibir VERB
to receive
> **No he recibido tu carta.**
> I haven't received your letter.
> **Recibí muchos regalos.**
> I got a lot of presents.

el **recibo** NOUN
receipt
> **No te lo devuelven sin recibo.**
> They won't give you a refund without a receipt.

reciclar VERB
 to recycle

recién ADVERB
 just
  El comedor está recién pintado.
  The dining room has just been painted.
  un recién nacido
  a newborn baby

reciente (FEM **reciente**) ADJECTIVE
 recent

recientemente ADVERB
 recently

el **recipiente** NOUN
 container

la **reclamación**
 (PL las **reclamaciones**) NOUN
 complaint
  hacer una reclamación
  to make a complaint

reclamar VERB
 to complain
  Fuimos a reclamar al director.
  We went and complained to the manager.

recoger VERB
 to pick up
  Me agaché para recoger la cuchara.
  I bent down to pick up the spoon.
  Me recogen en la estación.
  They pick me up at the station.
  Recógelo todo antes de marcharte.
  Clear up everything before you leave.
  recoger la mesa
  to clear the table

recomendar VERB
 to recommend
  ¿Qué nos recomienda?
  What do you recommend?

la **recompensa** NOUN
 reward

reconocer VERB
 to recognize
  No lo reconocí con las gafas.
  I didn't recognize him with his glasses on.

el **récord** (PL los **récords**) NOUN
 record
  el récord mundial de salto de altura
  the world record in the high jump
  batir el récord
  to break the record

recordar VERB
 1 **to remember**
  No recuerdo dónde lo puse.
  I can't remember where I put it.
 2 **to remind**
  Me recuerda a su padre.
  He reminds me of his father.

LANGUAGE TIP
Be careful! **recordar** does not mean **to record**.

---

recorrer VERB
 to travel around
  Recorrimos toda Francia.
  We travelled all around France.

recortar VERB
 to cut out
  Lo recorté de una revista.
  I cut it out from a magazine.

el **recreo** NOUN
 break
  Tenemos veinte minutos de recreo.
  We have a twenty-minute break.
  Salimos al recreo a las once.
  We have a break at eleven o'clock.
  a la hora del recreo
  at playtime

rectangular (FEM **rectangular**)
 ADJECTIVE
 rectangular

el **rectángulo** NOUN
 rectangle

English

Spanish

a
b
c
d
e
f
g
h
i
j
k
l
m
n
o
p
q
r
s
t
u
v
w
x
y
z

A
B
C
D
E
F
G
H
I
J
K
L
M
N
O
P
Q
R
S
T
U
V
W
X
Y
Z
210

recto
  A ADJECTIVE (FEM **recta**)
   straight
   una línea recta
   a straight line
  B ADVERB
   straight
   Siga todo recto.
   Go straight on.

el **recuadro** NOUN
  box

recuerdo

> **recuerdo** can be a noun or part of the verb **recordar**.

  A MASC NOUN
  1 memory
   Me trae buenos recuerdos.
   It brings back happy memories.
  2 souvenir
   una tienda de recuerdos
   a souvenir shop
  3 Dale recuerdos de mi parte.
   Give him my regards.
  B VERB ▷ see **recordar**
   No recuerdo su nombre.
   I can't remember his name.

recuperar VERB
  to get back
   Nunca recuperó la maleta.
   She never got her suitcase back.
   Se está recuperando de la operación.
   He's recovering from the operation.

la **red** NOUN
  1 net
   La pelota dio contra la red.
   The ball went into the net.
  2 la Red
   the Net
   las redes sociales
   social media

redondo (FEM **redonda**) ADJECTIVE
  round
   una mesa redonda
   a round table

   Todo salió redondo.
   Everything worked out perfectly.

reducir VERB
  to reduce
   Reduzca la velocidad.
   Reduce speed.

referirse VERB
  referirse a
  to refer to
   ¿Te refieres a mí?
   Are you referring to me?
   ¿A qué te refieres con eso?
   What exactly do you mean by that?

reflejar VERB
  to reflect

el **refresco** NOUN
  soft drink

el **refugio** NOUN
  refuge
   un refugio de montaña
   a mountain refuge

la **regadera** NOUN
  watering can

regalar VERB
  to give
   ¿Y si le regalamos un libro?
   What about giving him a book?
   Me lo regalaron para mi cumpleaños.
   I got it for my birthday.

el **regalo** NOUN
  present
   un regalo de Navidad
   a Christmas present
   hacer un regalo a alguien
   to give somebody a present
   papel de regalo
   wrapping paper
   de regalo
   free
   Te dan un CD de regalo.
   They give you a free CD.

regañar VERB
to tell off
Me regañó por llegar tarde.
He told me off for being late.

regar VERB
to water

el **régimen** (PL los **regímenes**) NOUN
diet
estar a régimen
to be on a diet
ponerse a régimen
to go on a diet

la **región** (PL las **regiones**) NOUN
region

la **regla** NOUN
1 ruler
Trazó la línea con una regla.
He drew the line with a ruler.
2 rule
saltarse las reglas
to break the rules

regresar VERB
to go back
Regresó a casa a por el paraguas.
He went back home for his umbrella.
Regresamos tarde.
We got back late.

el **regreso** NOUN
return
el viaje de regreso
the return journey
de regreso
on the way back
De regreso paramos en Ávila.
On the way back we stopped in Ávila.

regular

> **regular** can be an adjective or an adverb.

A ADJECTIVE (FEM **regular**)
regular
un verbo regular
a regular verb
B ADVERB
El examen me fue regular.
My exam didn't go brilliantly.

Me encuentro regular.
I'm not too bad.

la **reina** NOUN
queen

el **Reino Unido** NOUN
the United Kingdom

reír VERB
to laugh
No te rías.
Don't laugh.
echarse a reír
to burst out laughing
Siempre nos reímos con él.
We always have a good laugh with him.
reírse de
to laugh at
¿De qué te ríes?
What are you laughing at?

la **relación** (PL las **relaciones**) NOUN
1 link
la relación entre los dos casos
the link between the two cases
2 relationship
una relación de amistad
a friendly relationship
con relación a
in relation to

relajar VERB
to relax
¡Relájate!
Relax!
La música clásica la relaja mucho.
She finds classical music really relaxing.

el relámpago NOUN
flash of lightning
> **Vimos un relámpago.**
> We saw a flash of lightning.
> **No me gustan los relámpagos.**
> I don't like lightning.

relativo (FEM **relativa**)
ADJECTIVE
relative
> **un pronombre relativo**
> a relative pronoun
> **Eso es muy relativo.**
> That's all relative.

religión (PL **religiones**) NOUN
religion

rellenar VERB
to fill in
> **Tienes que rellenar un impreso.**
> You have to fill in a form.

relleno (FEM **rellena**) ADJECTIVE
stuffed
> **aceitunas rellenas**
> stuffed olives

el reloj NOUN
1 **clock**
> **El reloj de la cocina va atrasado.**
> The kitchen clock's slow.
> **un reloj despertador**
> an alarm clock
> **contra reloj**
> against the clock
2 **watch**
> **Se me ha parado el reloj.**
> My watch has stopped.
> **un reloj sumergible**
> a waterproof watch

remar VERB
to row

el remedio NOUN
remedy
> **un remedio contra la tos**
> a cough remedy

> **No tuve otro remedio.**
> I had no other choice.

el remolque NOUN
trailer

remover VERB
to stir
> **Remueve la leche con una cuchara.**
> Stir the milk with a spoon.

rendirse VERB
1 **to give up**
> **No sé la respuesta; me rindo.**
> I don't know the answer; I give up.
2 **to surrender**
> **El enemigo se rindió.**
> The enemy surrendered.

el renglón (PL **los renglones**) NOUN
line

reñir VERB
1 **to tell somebody off**
> **Mis padres me riñeron.**
> My parents told me off.
2 **to quarrel**
> **Mi hermana y yo siempre estamos riñendo.**
> My sister and I are always quarrelling.

repartir VERB
1 **to hand out**
> **El profesor repartió los exámenes.**
> The teacher handed out the exam papers.
2 **to share out**
> **Nos repartimos los caramelos.**
> We shared out the sweets between us.

repasar VERB
1 **to check**
> **Repasa la ortografía.**
> Check the spelling.
2 **to revise**
> **repasar para un examen**
> to revise for an exam

el repaso NOUN
revision
> **Tengo que darle un repaso a los apuntes.**
> I have to revise my notes.

repente ADVERB
de repente
suddenly

repetir VERB
1 **to repeat**
¿Podría repetirlo, por favor?
Could you repeat that, please?
2 **to have seconds**
Todavía tengo hambre. Voy a repetir.
I'm still hungry. I'm going to have seconds.

repitiendo VERB ▷ *see* **repetir**
Repitiendo las tablas se aprenden.
Repeating your tables helps you learn them.

representar VERB
1 **to represent**
Van a representar a España.
They will be representing Spain.
2 **to put on**
Vamos a representar una obra de teatro.
We're going to put on a play.

reproducirse VERB
to reproduce

el **reproductor** NOUN
player
un reproductor de CD
a CD player
un reproductor de MP3
an MP3 player

el **reptil** NOUN
reptile

repugnante (FEM **repugnante**) ADJECTIVE
revolting

la **reputación** (PL las **reputaciones**) NOUN
reputation

tener buena reputación
to have a good reputation

resbalar VERB
to be slippery
Este suelo resbala.
This floor's slippery.
■ **resbalarse**
to slip
Me resbalé y me caí.
I slipped and fell down.

rescatar VERB
to rescue

el/la **reserva** NOUN
reserve

reservar VERB
to reserve

resfriado

> **resfriado** can be an adjective or a noun.

A ADJECTIVE (FEM **resfriada**)
estar resfriado
to have a cold
Estaba muy resfriado.
I had a bad cold.
B MASC NOUN
cold
agarrarse un resfriado
to catch a cold

resfriarse VERB
to catch a cold

la **residencia** NOUN
residence
la residencia del primer ministro
the prime minister's residence

resistir VERB
1 **to resist**
No pude resistir la tentación.
I couldn't resist the temptation.
2 **to stand**
No puedo resistir este frío.
I can't stand this cold.

resolver VERB
to solve

A
B
C
D
E
F
G
H
I
J
K
L
M
N
O
P
Q
R
S
T
U
V
W
X
Y
Z

respetar VERB
to respect
Hay que respetar a los ancianos.
We should respect old people.

el **respeto** NOUN
respect
tener respeto a alguien
to respect somebody
No le faltes al respeto.
Don't be disrespectful to him.

la **respiración** NOUN
quedarse sin respiración
to be out of breath
la respiración boca a boca
the kiss of life
Le hicieron la respiración boca a
boca.
They gave him the kiss of life.

respirar VERB
to breathe

responder VERB
1 **to answer**
Tienes que responder sí o no.
You have to answer yes or no.
2 **to reply**
No han respondido a mi carta.
They haven't replied to my letter.

la **responsabilidad** NOUN
responsibility

responsable (FEM **responsable**)

> **responsable** can be an adjective or a
> noun.

A ADJECTIVE
responsible
No parece muy responsable.
She doesn't seem very responsible.
Todos somos responsables de
nuestros actos.
We are all responsible for our actions.
hacerse responsable de algo
to take responsibility for something
B MASC/FEM NOUN
Tú eres la responsable de lo
ocurrido.
You're responsible for what happened.

Raúl es el responsable de la
cocina.
Raúl is in charge of the kitchen.

la **respuesta** NOUN
answer

la **resta** NOUN
subtraction

restar VERB
to subtract
Está aprendiendo a restar.
He's learning to subtract.
Tienes que restar tres de ocho.
You have to take three away from eight.

el **restaurante** NOUN
restaurant

el **resto** NOUN
rest
Yo haré el resto.
I'll do the rest.
Juan se comió los restos.
Juan ate the leftovers.

resuelto VERB ▷ see **resolver**
El problema ha quedado resuelto.
The problem has been solved.

resuelvo VERB ▷ see **resolver**
Yo te resuelvo el problema.
I'll solve the problem for you.

el **resultado** NOUN
result
el resultado de los exámenes
the exam results

resultar VERB
to turn out
Al final resultó que él tenía razón.
In the end it turned out that he was
right.

el **resumen** (PL los **resúmenes**) NOUN
summary
un resumen de las noticias
a news summary
hacer un resumen de algo
to summarize something
en resumen
in short

retirarse VERB
  1 to withdraw
    Se retiraron del torneo.
    They withdrew from the tournament.
  2 to retire
    Mi abuelo se retira el año que viene.
    My granddad will be retiring next year.

retorcer VERB
  to twist
    Me retorció el brazo.
    He twisted my arm.

retrasado (FEM **retrasada**) ADJECTIVE
  1 slow
    Este reloj va retrasado.
    This clock is slow.
  2 delayed
    Todos los vuelos iban retrasados.
    All flights were delayed.

retrasar VERB
  to postpone
    Retrasaron el viaje.
    They postponed the trip.
  ▪ **retrasarse**
    to be late
    El tren de las nueve se retrasó.
    The nine o'clock train was late.

el **retraso** NOUN
    Date prisa que vamos con retraso.
    Hurry up, we're running late.
    El autobús lleva una hora de retraso.
    The bus is an hour late.

retuerzo VERB ▷ see **retorcer**
    Suéltame o te retuerzo el brazo.
    Let go of me or I'll twist your arm.

reunir VERB
  1 to gather together
    Reunió a los niños en el patio.
    She gathered the children together in the playground.
  2 to raise
    Estamos reuniendo dinero para el viaje.
    We're raising money for the trip.

▪ **reunirse**
  1 to get together
    En Navidad nos reunimos toda la familia.
    The whole family gets together at Christmas.
  2 to meet
    Los profesores se reúnen una vez a la semana.
    The teachers meet once a week.

reventar VERB
  to burst
    No revientes los globos.
    Don't burst the balloons.

el **revés** NOUN
    al revés
    the wrong way round
    Lo tienes puesto al revés.
    You've got it on the wrong way round.
    El dibujo está al revés.
    The picture's upside down.

reviento VERB
  ▷ see **reventar**
    Reviento de ganas de decírselo.
    I'm bursting to tell him.

revisar VERB
  to check
    Revisa que esté bien la cuenta.
    Check the sum is right.

la **revista** NOUN
  magazine
    una revista de modas
    a fashion magazine

revuelto

> **revuelto** can be an adjective or part of the verb **revolver**.

A ADJECTIVE (FEM **revuelta**)
  in a mess

Todo estaba revuelto.
Everything was in a mess.
Tengo el estómago revuelto.
I've got an upset stomach.
B VERB ▷ *see* **revolver**
Eso me ha revuelto el estómago.
That's turned my stomach.

el **rey** (PL los **reyes**) NOUN
king
Los reyes visitaron China.
The King and Queen visited China.
los Reyes Magos
the Three Wise Men

DID YOU KNOW...?
As part of the Christmas festivities, the
Spanish celebrate **el día de Reyes**
(Epiphany) on the 6th of January, when
the Three Wise Men bring presents for
children.

---

rezar VERB
to pray
rezar por algo
to pray for something

rico (FEM **rica**)

rico can be an adjective or a noun.

A ADJECTIVE
1 rich
Son muy ricos.
They're very rich.
2 delicious
¡Qué rico está esto!
This is delicious!
B MASC/FEM NOUN
un rico
a rich man
una rica
a rich woman
los ricos
the rich

ridículo (FEM **ridícula**) ADJECTIVE
ridiculous
¿A que suena ridículo?
Doesn't it sound ridiculous?
hacer el ridículo
to make a fool of oneself

poner a alguien en ridículo
to make a fool of somebody

riendo VERB ▷ *see* **reír**
Se estaba riendo de mí.
He was laughing at me.

el **riesgo** NOUN
risk
correr riesgos
to take risks
No quiero correr ese riesgo.
I don't want to take that risk.

la **rifa** NOUN
raffle

el **rincón** (PL los **rincones**) NOUN
corner
Pon la silla en ese rincón.
Put the chair in that corner.

riñendo VERB ▷ *see* **reñir**
La profesora le estaba riñendo.
The teacher was telling him off.

río

río can be a noun or part of the verb
reír.

A MASC NOUN
river
el río Támesis
the River Thames
B VERB ▷ *see* **reír**
No me río.
I'm not laughing.

la **risa** NOUN
laugh
una risa contagiosa
an infectious laugh
Me da risa.
It makes me laugh.
Daba risa cómo lo explicaba.
It was so funny the way he told it.
¡Qué risa!
What a laugh!

el **ritmo** NOUN
rhythm

rival (FEM **rival**) ADJECTIVE, NOUN
rival

rizado (FEM **rizada**) ADJECTIVE
curly
> **Tiene el pelo rizado.**
> He has curly hair.

rizar VERB
to curl
> **Se riza el pelo.**
> She curls her hair.

robar VERB
to steal
> **Le robaba dinero a su amigo.**
> He was stealing money from his friend.
> **¡Nos han robado!**
> We've been robbed!

el **robo** NOUN
theft
> **un robo de banco**
> a bank robbery

la **roca** NOUN
rock

la **rodaja** NOUN
slice
> **cortar algo en rodajas**
> to cut something into slices

rodar VERB
1 to roll
> **La pelota rodó por la calle.**
> The ball rolled down the street.
2 to shoot
> **rodar una película**
> to shoot a film

rodear VERB
to surround
> **El bosque rodea el palacio.**
> The forest surrounds the palace.
> **rodeado de**
> surrounded by

la **rodilla** NOUN
knee
> **ponerse de rodillas**
> to kneel down

rogar VERB
to beg

rojo
A ADJECTIVE (FEM **roja**)
red

> **ponerse rojo de vergüenza**
> to go red with embarrassment
B MASC NOUN
red
> **Va vestida de rojo.**
> She's wearing red.

el **rollo** NOUN
1 roll
> **un rollo de papel higiénico**
> a roll of toilet paper
2 ¡Qué rollo de película!
> What a boring film!
> **Nos soltó el rollo de siempre.**
> He gave us the same old lecture.

el **rompecabezas**
(PL los **rompecabezas**)
NOUN
jigsaw

romper VERB
1 to break
> **Me rompí el brazo.**
> I broke my arm.
2 to tear up
> **Rompió la carta en pedazos.**
> He tore the letter up.
> **Se me han roto los pantalones.**
> I've torn my trousers.

roncar VERB
to snore

la **ropa** NOUN
clothes
> **Voy a cambiarme de ropa.**
> I'm going to change my clothes.
> **la ropa interior**
> underwear
> **ropa de deporte**
> sportswear

a b c d e f g h i j k l m n o p q r s t u v w x y z

English Spanish

English · **Spanish**

rosa

> **rosa** can be an adjective or a noun.

A ADJECTIVE
pink

LANGUAGE TIP
The colour **rosa** never changes its ending no matter what it describes.

Compramos unos calcetines rosa.
We bought pink socks.

B FEM NOUN
rose
una rosa amarilla
a yellow rose

C MASC NOUN
pink
Pintaron la silla de rosa.
They painted the chair pink.

el **roscón** (PL los **roscones**) NOUN
cake

DID YOU KNOW...?
In Spain it's traditional to eat **el roscón de Reyes** on 6th January. Hidden in this fruit-studded ring-shaped cake is a little figure or other surprise that is meant to bring good luck to the person that finds it.

roto

> **roto** can be an adjective or a part of the verb **romper**.

A ADJECTIVE (FEM **rota**)
broken
un vaso roto
a broken glass

Llevas la camisa rota.
Your shirt is torn.

B VERB ▷ *see* **romper**
Se ha roto.
It's broken.

el **rotulador** NOUN
felt-tip pen

rubio (FEM **rubia**) ADJECTIVE
fair
Diego tiene el pelo rubio.
Diego has got fair hair.
De pequeña era rubia.
She had fair hair when she was little.
Quiero teñirme el pelo de rubio.
I want to dye my hair blond.

la **rueda** NOUN
wheel
la rueda delantera
the front wheel
Se nos pinchó la rueda.
We got a puncture.

ruego VERB ▷ *see* **rogar**
Te lo ruego.
I'm begging you.

el **ruido** NOUN
noise
Hacen mucho ruido.
They make a lot of noise.

ruidoso (FEM **ruidosa**) ADJECTIVE
noisy

la **ruina** NOUN
las ruinas
the ruins
El castillo está en ruinas.
The castle is in ruins.

la **ruta** NOUN
route

la **rutina** NOUN
routine
la rutina diaria
the daily routine

Ss

el **sábado** NOUN
Saturday

LANGUAGE TIP
Days are not spelled with a capital letter in Spanish.

Jugamos los sábados.
We play on Saturdays.

todos los sábados
every Saturday
el sábado pasado
last Saturday
el sábado que viene
next Saturday

la **sábana** NOUN
sheet

saber VERB
1 to know
No lo sé.
I don't know.
Sabe mucho de ordenadores.
She knows a lot about computers.
No sé nadar.
I can't swim.
¿Sabes inglés?
Can you speak English?
Se sabe la lista de memoria.
He knows the list off by heart.
2 to taste
Sabe a pescado.
It tastes of fish.

el **sabor** NOUN
1 taste
Tiene un sabor muy raro.
It's got a very strange taste.

2 flavour
¿De qué sabor lo quieres?
What flavour do you want?

sabré VERB ▷ see **saber**
Pronto lo sabré.
I'll soon know.

sabroso (FEM **sabrosa**) ADJECTIVE
tasty

el **sacapuntas** (PL los **sacapuntas**) NOUN
pencil sharpener

sacar VERB
1 to take out
Sacó las llaves del bolsillo.
He took the keys out of his pocket.
sacar la basura
to take the rubbish out
sacar al perro a pasear
to take the dog out for a walk
sacarse las botas
to take off one's boots
2 to get
Hoy sacaremos las entradas.
We'll get the tickets today.
sacar buenas notas
to get good marks
3 to take
Le sacamos una foto a Jaime.
We took a photo of Jaime.

el **saco** NOUN
sack
un saco de patatas
a sack of potatoes
un saco de dormir
a sleeping bag

sacudir VERB
to shake
Hay que sacudir la alfombra.
The carpet needs shaking.

la **sal** NOUN
salt

la **sala** NOUN
room
sala de estar
living room
sala de espera
waiting room

sala de profesores
staffroom

salado (FEM **salada**) ADJECTIVE
salty

la **salchicha** NOUN
sausage

el **salchichón** (PL los **salchichones**)
NOUN
spiced salami sausage

saldré VERB ▷ *see* **salir**
Saldré después de almorzar.
I'm going out after lunch.

salgo VERB ▷ *see* **salir**
Siempre salgo los sábados por la tarde.
I always go out on Saturday afternoons.

la **salida** NOUN
exit
salida de emergencia
emergency exit

salir VERB
1 **to come out**
Salió a jugar con nosotros.
She came out to play with us.
Sal del coche.
Get out of the car.
2 **to go out**
Ha salido a la tienda.
He's gone out to the shop.
Mi hermana está saliendo con Juan.
Mi sister's going out with Juan.
3 **to leave**
El autocar sale a las ocho.
The coach leaves at eight.
Sale a quince euros por persona.
It works out at fifteen euros each.
Todo salió bien.
Everything worked out well.

el **salón** (PL los **salones**) NOUN
living room

salpicar VERB
to splash

la **salsa** NOUN
sauce
salsa de tomate
tomato sauce

saltar VERB
to jump
saltar por la ventana
to jump out of the window
Te has saltado una página.
You've skipped a page.

el **salto** NOUN
jump
salto de altura
high jump
salto de longitud
long jump
dar un salto
to jump

salud

> **salud** can be a noun or an exclamation.

A FEM NOUN
health
B EXCLAMATION
bless you!

saludable (FEM **saludable**) ADJECTIVE
healthy

saludar VERB
to say hello
Entramos a saludarla.
We went in to say hello to her.

el **saludo** NOUN
greeting

saludos
best wishes

salvaje (FEM **salvaje**) ADJECTIVE
wild

salvar VERB
to save
Me has salvado la vida.
You saved my life.
He salvado el archivo.
I've saved the file.

la **sandalia** NOUN
sandal
unas sandalias
a pair of sandals

la **sandía** NOUN
watermelon

el **sándwich** (PL los **sándwiches**) NOUN
sandwich
un sándwich de queso
a cheese sandwich

la **sangre** NOUN
blood

sano (FEM **sana**) ADJECTIVE
healthy
una dieta sana
a healthy diet

santo (FEM **santa**)

> **santo** can be a noun or an adjective.

A MASC/FEM NOUN
saint
Santa Clara
Saint Clara
Mañana es mi santo.
Tomorrow is my saint's day.

DID YOU KNOW...?
Besides birthdays, some Spaniards also
celebrate the feast day of the saint they
are named after.

B ADJECTIVE
holy
un lugar santo
a holy place

el **sapo** NOUN
toad

la **sartén** (PL las **sartenes**) NOUN
frying pan

satisfecho (FEM **satisfecha**) ADJECTIVE
satisfied

se PRONOUN

LANGUAGE TIP
When **se** is an indirect object and
appears in a sentence with another
pronoun, it means **him**, **her**, **them** or
you, when it refers to **él**, **ella**, **ellos**,
ellas and **usted** or **ustedes**.

**Pedro necesitaba la calculadora y
se la dejé.**
Pedro needed the calculator and I lent
it to him.
Rosa no lo sabe. No se lo digas.
Rosa doesn't know. Don't tell her.

LANGUAGE TIP
When the object is repeated, **se** isn't
translated.

No se lo digas a Susana.
Don't tell Susana.
**¿Se lo has preguntado a tus
padres?**
Have you asked your parents?

LANGUAGE TIP
When **se** is reflexive, it means
himself, **herself**, **itself**,
themselves, **yourself** o **yourselves**
when it refers to **él**, **ella**, **ellos**, **ellas**
and **usted** or **ustedes**.

Se ha cortado con un cristal.
She cut herself on a piece of broken
glass.
¿Se ha hecho usted daño?
Have you hurt yourself?

LANGUAGE TIP
When it refers to parts of the body or
clothes you wear, **se** isn't translated.

Pablo se lavó los dientes.
Pablo brushed his teeth.
Me puse los guantes.
I put my gloves on.

LANGUAGE TIP
When **se** is reciprocal, it is translated
by **each other**.

Se dieron un beso.
They gave each other a kiss.

LANGUAGE TIP
When **se** is impersonal it is usually translated by **it** or **you**.

Eso pasa cuando se come tan deprisa.
That's what happens when you eat so fast.

sé VERB ▷ *see* **saber**
No sé.
I don't know.

sea VERB ▷ *see* **ser**
siempre que sea razonable
as long as it's reasonable

el **secador** NOUN
hair dryer

secar VERB
to dry
Voy a secarme el pelo.
I'm going to dry my hair.
■ **secarse**
to dry oneself
Sécate con la toalla.
Dry yourself with the towel.

la **sección** NOUN
1 **section**
Lo leí en la sección de deportes.
I read it in the sports section.
2 **department**
la sección de zapatos
the shoes department

seco (FEM **seca**) ADJECTIVE
dry
La pintura ya está seca.
The paint's dry already.
flores secas
dried flowers

el **secretario**
la **secretaria** NOUN
secretary
Es secretaria.
She's a secretary.

secreto

> **secreto** can be a noun or an adjective.

A MASC NOUN
secret
Te voy a contar un secreto.
I'm going to tell you a secret.
en secreto
in secret
B ADJECTIVE (FEM **secreta**)
secret
un agente secreto
a secret agent

la **sed** NOUN
thirst
apagar la sed
to quench one's thirst
Tengo sed.
I'm thirsty.

la **seda** NOUN
silk
una camisa de seda
a silk shirt

seguido (FEM **seguida**) ADJECTIVE
in a row
tres días seguidos
three days in a row
en seguida
straight away
Vino en seguida.
He came straight away.
todo seguido
straight on
Vaya todo seguido hasta la plaza.
Go straight on until the square.

seguir VERB
1 **to carry on**
¡Sigue, no pares!
Carry on, don't stop!
Siguió hablando.
She carried on talking.
Sigue lloviendo.
It's still raining.
2 **to follow**
Tú ve primero que yo te sigo.
You go first and I'll follow you.

seguir adelante
to go ahead
Siguieron adelante con su plan.
They went ahead with their plan.

según PREPOSITION
1 according to
Según el testigo, el coche no paró.
According to the witness, the car didn't stop.
2 depending on
Iremos o no, según esté el tiempo.
We might go, depending on the weather.

segundo

> **segundo** can be an adjective, pronoun or noun.

A ADJECTIVE, PRONOUN (FEM **segunda**)
second
el segundo plato
the second course
la segunda planta
the second floor
Vive en el segundo.
He lives on the second floor.
B MASC NOUN
second
Es un segundo nada más.
It'll only take a second.

seguramente ADVERB
probably
Seguramente llegarán mañana.
They'll probably arrive tomorrow.

seguro (FEM **segura**) ADJECTIVE
1 safe
Aquí estaremos seguros.
We'll be safe here.
2 sure
¿Estás seguro?
Are you sure?
seguro que
it's bound to
Seguro que llueve.
It's bound to rain.

seis (FEM **seis**) ADJECTIVE, PRONOUN
six

Tiene seis años.
She's six.

> **Son las seis.**
> It's six o'clock.
> **el seis de enero**
> the sixth of January

seiscientos (FEM **seiscientas**) ADJECTIVE, PRONOUN
six hundred

la **selección** (PL las **selecciones**) NOUN
1 selection
una selección de juguetes
a selection of toys
2 team
la selección nacional
the national team

el **selfi** NOUN
selfie

Siempre está mandándonos selfis.
He's always sending us selfies.

el **sello** NOUN
stamp
Colecciono sellos.
I collect stamps.

la **selva** NOUN
jungle

el **semáforo** NOUN
traffic lights
El semáforo está en rojo.
The lights are red.

la **semana** NOUN
week
dentro de una semana
in a week's time
una vez a la semana
once a week

a b c d e f g h i j k l m n o p q r s t u v w x y z

223

English

Spanish

A
B
C
D
E
F
G
H
I
J
K
L
M
N
O
P
Q
R
S
T
U
V
W
X
Y
Z

la **semilla** NOUN
seed

sencillo (FEM **sencilla**) ADJECTIVE
simple
> **Es muy sencillo.**
> It's really simple.

sensible (FEM **sensible**) ADJECTIVE
sensitive
> **Es un chico muy sensible.**
> He's a very sensitive boy.

LANGUAGE TIP
Be careful! **sensible** does not mean **sensible**.

---

sentar VERB
1 **to suit**
> **Ese vestido te sienta muy bien.**
> That dress really suits you.
2 **to agree with**
> **La paella no me sentó bien.**
> The paella didn't agree with me.
> **Le sentó mal lo que dije.**
> He didn't like what I said.
■ **sentarse**
to sit down
> **Me senté en el banco.**
> I sat down on the bench.

el **sentido** NOUN
sense
> **Eso no tiene sentido.**
> That doesn't make sense.
> **sentido común**
> common sense
> **Eso es de sentido común.**
> That's common sense.
> **sentido del humor**
> sense of humour
> **No tiene sentido del humor.**
> He doesn't have a sense of humour.

el **sentimiento** NOUN
feeling

sentir VERB
1 **to feel**
> **Sentí un dolor en la pierna.**
> I felt a pain in my leg.

2 **to be sorry**
> **Lo siento mucho.**
> I'm very sorry.
> **Siento llegar tarde.**
> I'm sorry I'm late.
■ **sentirse**
to feel
> **No me siento bien.**
> I don't feel well.

la **seña** NOUN
sign
> **Nos comunicamos por señas.**
> We communicate by signs.

la **señal** NOUN
1 **sign**
> **Eso es mala señal.**
> That's a bad sign.
> **una señal de tráfico**
> a road sign
2 **signal**
> **Yo daré la señal.**
> I'll give the signal.

señalar VERB
to mark
> **Señálalo con un bolígrafo rojo.**
> Mark it with a red pen.
> **señalar con el dedo**
> to point

el **señor** NOUN
1 **man**
> **¿Quién es ese señor?**
> Who's that man?
> **¿Qué le pongo, señor?**
> What would you like, sir?

LANGUAGE TIP
Señor is a handy way of attracting somebody's attention. Look at the example.

¡Señor! ¡Se le ha caído el billete!
Excuse me! You've dropped your ticket!

2 Mr
el señor Delgado
Mr Delgado
Muy señor mío: ...
Dear Sir, ...

la **señora** NOUN

1 lady
Deja pasar a esta señora.
Let the lady past.
¿Qué le pongo, señora?
What would you like, madam?

LANGUAGE TIP
Señora is a handy way of attracting somebody's attention. Look at the example.

¡Señora! ¡Se ha dejado las gafas!
Excuse me! You've forgotten your glasses!

2 Mrs
la señora Delgado
Mrs Delgado

3 wife
Vino con su señora.
He came with his wife.

la **señorita** NOUN

1 young lady
Hay una señorita esperando.
There's a young lady waiting.

2 Miss
la señorita Delgado
Miss Delgado

sepa VERB ▷ see **saber**
Que yo sepa no.
Not as far as I know.

separado (FEM **separada**) ADJECTIVE

1 separate
Ponlos en dos montones separados.
Put them in two separate piles.

2 separated
Sus padres están separados.
His parents are separated.

separar VERB
to separate

septiembre NOUN
September

LANGUAGE TIP
Months are not spelled with a capital letter in Spanish.

en septiembre
in September
Nació el once de septiembre.
He was born on the eleventh of September.

séptimo (FEM **séptima**) ADJECTIVE, PRONOUN
seventh
Vivo en el séptimo.
I live on the seventh floor.

ser

ser can be a verb or a noun.

A VERB
to be
Juan es muy alto.
Juan is very tall.
Es médico.
He's a doctor.
Era de noche.
It was night.
Soy Lucía.
It's Lucía.
Son las seis y media.
It's half past six.
Éramos cinco en el coche.
There were five of us in the car.
Es de Carla.
It's Carla's.
¿De dónde eres?
Where are you from?
Soy de Barcelona.
I'm from Barcelona.
Es de plástico.
It's made of plastic.
a no ser que ...
unless ...

a no ser que vayamos mañana
unless we go tomorrow

B MASC NOUN
being
Son seres humanos.
They're human beings.

serio (FEM **seria**) ADJECTIVE
serious
No te pongas tan serio.
Don't look so serious.
No hablaba en serio.
I didn't mean it.

en serio
seriously

la **serpiente** NOUN
snake

el **servicio** NOUN
1 service
2 toilet
Está en el servicio.
He's in the toilet.
el servicio de caballeros
the gents'
el servicio de señoras
the ladies'

la **servilleta** NOUN
napkin

servir VERB
to be useful for
Estas cajas sirven para muchas cosas.
These boxes are useful for a lot of things.
¿Para qué sirve esto?
What's this for?
no servir para nada
to be useless
Este mapa no sirve para nada.
This map is useless.

sesenta (FEM **sesenta**) ADJECTIVE, PRONOUN
sixty

Tiene sesenta años.
He's sixty.

la **seta** NOUN
mushroom

setecientos (FEM **setecientas**) ADJECTIVE, PRONOUN
seven hundred

setenta (FEM **setenta**) ADJECTIVE, PRONOUN
seventy
Tiene setenta años.
He's seventy.

sexto (FEM **sexta**) ADJECTIVE, PRONOUN
sixth
Vivo en el sexto.
I live on the sixth floor.

si CONJUNCTION
1 if
Si quieres te dejo mi bici.
I'll lend you my bike if you like.
¿Y si llueve?
And what if it rains?
2 whether
No sé si ir o no.
I don't know whether to go or not.
si no
otherwise/if not

LANGUAGE TIP
si no has two meanings. Look at the examples.

Ponte crema. Si no, te quemarás.
Put some cream on, otherwise you'll get sunburned.
Avísame si no puedes venir.
Let me know if you can't come.

sí

sí can be an adverb or a pronoun.

A ADVERB
yes
¿Quieres un helado? — Sí, gracias.
Do you want an ice-cream? — Yes, please.
¿Te gusta? — Sí.
Do you like it? — Yes, I do.

Él no quiere pero yo sí.
He doesn't want to but I do.
Creo que sí.
I think so.
B PRONOUN
Solo piensa en sí misma.
She only thinks about herself.
Hablaban entre sí.
They were talking among themselves.
Es mejor aprender las cosas por sí mismo.
It's better to learn things by yourself.

siempre ADVERB
always
Siempre llega tarde.
She always arrives late.

para siempre
forever

siendo VERB ▷ see **ser**
Sigue siendo feliz.
She's still happy.

siento VERB ▷ see **sentir**
Siento pena por ellos.
I feel sorry for them.

Lo siento.
I'm sorry.

la **siesta** NOUN
nap
echarse la siesta
to have a nap
A mi abuela le gusta echarse la siesta.
My grandma likes to have an afternoon nap.

siete (FEM **siete**) ADJECTIVE, PRONOUN
seven
Tiene siete años.
She's seven.

Son las siete.
It's seven o'clock.
el siete de marzo
the seventh of March
Nació el siete de marzo.
He was born on the seventh of March.

el **siglo** NOUN
century
el siglo veintiuno
the twenty-first century

el **significado** NOUN
meaning

significar VERB
to mean
¿Qué significa "wild"?
What does 'wild' mean?
No sé lo que significa.
I don't know what it means.

el **signo** NOUN
1 sign
Eso es signo de buena salud.
That's a sign of good health.
¿De qué signo eres?
What star sign are you?
2 mark
signo de admiración
exclamation mark
signo de interrogación
question mark

DID YOU KNOW...?
Don't forget that in Spanish you also need an upside-down exclamation mark or question mark at the beginning of your phrase or question.

siguiendo VERB ▷ see **seguir**
Nos están siguiendo.
We're being followed.

siguiente (FEM **siguiente**) ADJECTIVE
next
Al día siguiente visitamos Toledo.
The next day we visited Toledo.
¡Que pase el siguiente, por favor!
Next please!

silbar VERB
to whistle

el **silencio** NOUN
silence
guardar silencio
to keep quiet

En la biblioteca hay que guardar silencio.
You need to keep quiet in the library.

¡Silencio!
Quiet!

la **silla** NOUN
chair

silla de paseo
pushchair
silla de ruedas
wheelchair

el **sillón** (PL los **sillones**) NOUN
armchair

el **símbolo** NOUN
symbol

simpático (FEM **simpática**) ADJECTIVE
nice
Amanda es muy simpática.
Amanda is very nice.
Me cae simpático.
I think he's really nice.

LANGUAGE TIP
Be careful! **simpático** does not mean **sympathetic**.

simple (FEM **simple**) ADJECTIVE
simple

simplemente ADVERB
simply

sin PREPOSITION
without
Salió sin abrigo.
She went out without a coat.
sin hacer ruido
without making a noise

singular ADJECTIVE, MASC NOUN
singular
en singular
in the singular

sino CONJUNCTION
but
No son ingleses sino galeses.
They're not English, but Welsh.

sintiendo VERB ▷ see **sentir**
¿Te sigues sintiendo mal?
Do you still feel ill?

siquiera ADVERB
ni siquiera
not even
Ni siquiera se despidió.
She didn't even say goodbye.

sirviendo VERB ▷ see **servir**
Estas clases no me están sirviendo para nada.
I'm not finding these classes at all useful.

el **sitio** NOUN
1 place
Es un sitio tranquilo.
It's a quiet place.
¿Me puedo cambiar de sitio?
Can I change places?

en cualquier sitio
anywhere
en algún sitio
somewhere

2 room
Hay sitio de sobra.
There's room to spare.
Hacedme sitio.
Can you make some room for me?
un sitio web
a website

la **situación** (PL las **situaciones**) NOUN
situation

el **SMS** NOUN
text message
enviar un SMS
to send a text
enviarle un SMS a alguien
to text somebody

sobra FEM NOUN
Tenemos comida de sobra.
We've got more than enough food.

English
Spanish

A
B
C
D
E
F
G
H
I
J
K
L
M
N
O
P
Q
R
S
T
U
V
W
X
Y
Z

sobrar VERB
1 **to be left over**
   Ha sobrado mucha comida.
   There's plenty of food left over.
2 **Con diez euros sobrará.**
   Ten euros will be more than enough.

sobre

> **sobre** can be a preposition or a noun.

A PREPOSITION
1 **on**
   Deja el dinero sobre la mesa.
   Leave the money on the table.
2 **about**
   información sobre hoteles
   information about hotels

   sobre las seis
   at about six o'clock

3 **sobre todo**
   above all
   Me gustan los deportes, sobre todo la natación.
   I like sport, especially swimming.
B MASC NOUN
   envelope

el sobresaliente NOUN
   distinction
   He sacado sobresaliente en matemáticas.
   I got top marks in maths.

sobrevivir VERB
   to survive

la sobrina NOUN
   niece

el sobrino NOUN
   nephew
   mis sobrinos
   my nephews/my nieces and nephews

   LANGUAGE TIP
   mis sobrinos has two meanings. It can be translated as **my nephews** or **my nephews and nieces**.

la sociedad NOUN
   society

el socio
   la socia NOUN
1 **partner**
2 **member**

el/la socorrista NOUN
   lifeguard

el socorro NOUN
   help
   pedir socorro
   to ask for help
   La mujer pedía socorro.
   The woman was asking for help.

   ¡Socorro!
   Help!

el sofá (PL los **sofás**) NOUN
   sofa

   un sofá-cama
   a sofa bed

sois VERB ▷ *see* **ser**
   ¿Sois hermanas?
   Are you sisters?

el sol NOUN
   sun
   estar al sol
   to be in the sun
   Hace sol.
   It's sunny.
   tomar el sol
   to sunbathe

solamente ADVERB
   only

el soldado NOUN
   soldier

A
B
C
D
E
F
G
H
I
J
K
L
M
N
O
P
Q
R
S
T
U
V
W
X
Y
Z

soler VERB

> **LANGUAGE TIP**
> In the present, English normally uses the adverb **usually** to translate **soler**.

> **Suele salir a las ocho.**
> He usually leaves at eight.

> **LANGUAGE TIP**
> In the past, English normally uses the structure **used to** to translate **soler**.

> **Solíamos ir a la playa.**
> We used to go to the beach.

solo

> solo can be an adjective or an adverb.

A ADJECTIVE (FEM **sola**)
1 **alone**
  Me quedé solo.
  I was left alone.
  ¿Estás solo?
  Are you on your own?
  Lo hice yo solo.
  I did it on my own.
  Había un solo problema.
  There was just one problem.
2 **lonely**
  A veces me siento solo.
  Sometimes I feel lonely.
B ADVERB
  only
  Solo cuesta diez libras.
  It only costs ten pounds.
  no solo ... sino ...
  not only ... but ...
  No solo es bonito, sino barato.
  It's not only nice, but cheap.

> **LANGUAGE TIP**
> You may sometimes see **sólo** written with an accent when it is an adverb.

soltar VERB
  to let go of
  No sueltes la cuerda.
  Don't let go of the rope.
  ¡Suéltame!
  Let go of me!

soltero (FEM **soltera**) ADJECTIVE
  single
  Es soltero.
  He's single.

la **solución** (PL las **soluciones**) NOUN
  solution

solucionar VERB
  to solve

la **sombra** NOUN
1 **shade**
  Prefiero quedarme a la sombra.
  I prefer to stay in the shade.
2 **shadow**
  Solo vi una sombra.
  I only saw a shadow.
  sombra de ojos
  eye shadow

el **sombrero** NOUN
  hat

la **sombrilla** NOUN
  sunshade

sonar VERB
1 **to sound**
  Sonaba un poco triste.
  She sounded a bit sad.
  Se escribe tal y como suena.
  It's written as it sounds.
2 **to ring**
  Sonó el timbre.
  The bell rang.
3 **sonarse la nariz**
  to blow one's nose

el **sonido** NOUN
  sound

sonreír VERB
  to smile
  Me sonrió.
  She smiled at me.

la **sonrisa** NOUN
  smile

soñar VERB
  to dream
  Ayer soñé con él.
  I dreamed about him yesterday.

la **sopa** NOUN
soup

soplar VERB
to blow
¡Sopla con fuerza!
Blow hard!
Soplaba un viento fuerte.
A strong wind was blowing.

soportar VERB
to stand
No la soporto.
I can't stand her.

LANGUAGE TIP
Be careful! **soportar** does not mean
to support.
---

sordo (FEM **sorda**) ADJECTIVE
deaf

sorprender VERB
to surprise
No me sorprende.
It doesn't surprise me.
Me sorprendí al verlos.
I was surprised to see them.

la **sorpresa** NOUN
surprise
¡Qué sorpresa!
What a surprise!
Me pilló de sorpresa.
It took me by surprise.

el **sorteo** NOUN
draw

soso (FEM **sosa**) ADJECTIVE
1 dull
Es un poco soso.
He's a bit dull.
2 bland
estar soso
to need more salt
Estas patatas fritas están sosas.
These chips need more salt.

sospechar VERB
to suspect
Sospechan de Sofía.
They suspect Sofía.

sospechoso (FEM **sospechosa**) ADJECTIVE
suspicious

sostener VERB
1 to support
Está sostenido por dos columnas.
It is supported by two columns.
2 to hold
Sostenían la caja entre los dos.
They held the box between the two of
them.

soy VERB ▷ see ser
Soy española.
I'm Spanish.

Sr. ABBREVIATION
Mr

Sra. ABBREVIATION
Mrs

Sres. ABBREVIATION
Messrs

Srta. ABBREVIATION
Miss

su ADJECTIVE
1 his
su mochila
his backpack
Antonio y sus padres
Antonio and his parents
2 her
su falda
her skirt
Marta y sus amigas
Marta and her friends
3 its
un oso y su cachorro
a bear and its cub

English

Spanish

4 **their**
mis padres y sus amigos
my parents and their friends
5 **your**
No olviden sus paraguas.
Don't forget your umbrellas.

suave (FEM **suave**) ADJECTIVE
1 **gentle**
2 **soft**

subir VERB
1 **to go up**
Subimos las escaleras.
We went up the stairs.
La gasolina ha subido.
Petrol's gone up.
2 **to come up**
Sube, que te voy a enseñar una cosa.
Come up, I've got something to show you.
3 **to take up**
Ayúdame a subir las maletas.
Help me take the cases up.
4 **to turn up**
Sube la tele, que no se oye.
Turn the TV up. I can't hear it.

LANGUAGE TIP
subirse a has several meanings.
Look at the examples.

---

subirse al coche
to get into the car
subirse al tren
to get on the train
subirse a la bici
to get onto the bike
subirse a un árbol
to climb a tree

subrayar VERB
to underline

el **suceso** NOUN
incident
El suceso ocurrió sobre las tres de la tarde.
The incident happened at around three in the afternoon.

LANGUAGE TIP
Be careful! **suceso** does not mean **success**.

---

sucio (FEM **sucia**) ADJECTIVE
dirty
Tienes las manos sucias.
You've got dirty hands.

sudamericano (FEM **sudamericana**)
ADJECTIVE, NOUN
South American

sudar VERB
to sweat

sudeste MASC NOUN, ADJECTIVE
southeast

LANGUAGE TIP
The adjective **sudeste** never changes its ending, no matter what it describes.

---

sudoeste MASC NOUN, ADJECTIVE
southwest

LANGUAGE TIP
The adjective **sudoeste** never changes its ending, no matter what it describes.

---

el **sudor** NOUN
sweat

la **suegra** NOUN
mother-in-law

el **suegro** NOUN
father-in-law

los **suegros** PLURAL NOUN
in-laws

el **sueldo** NOUN
salary

suelo

---

suelo can be a noun or part of the verb **soler**.

A MASC NOUN
1 **floor**
un suelo de madera
a wooden floor

2 ground
El suelo está mojado.
The ground is wet.
Me caí al suelo.
I fell over.

B VERB ▷ *see* **soler**
Suelo ir al cine los domingos.
I usually go to the cinema on Sundays.

suelto

suelto can be an adjective, a noun or part of the verb **soltar**.

A ADJECTIVE (FEM **suelta**)
loose
Tiene varias hojas sueltas.
Some of the pages are loose.
Lleva el pelo suelto.
She wears her hair loose.

B MASC NOUN
change
No llevo suelto.
I don't have any change on me.

C VERB ▷ *see* **soltar**
Si lo suelto, se cae.
If I let go, it will fall.

sueno VERB ▷ *see* **sonar**
Sueno rara cuando hablo inglés.
I sound strange when I speak English.

sueño

sueño can be a noun or part of the verb **soñar**.

A MASC NOUN
dream
Anoche tuve un mal sueño.
I had a bad dream last night.

Tengo sueño.
I'm sleepy.

B VERB ▷ *see* **soñar**
Siempre sueño.
I always dream.

la **suerte** NOUN
luck
No tiene mucha suerte.
She doesn't have much luck.
Tuvo suerte.
She was lucky.
por suerte
luckily

¡Buena suerte!
Good luck!
¡Qué suerte!
How lucky!

suficiente (FEM **suficiente**) ADJECTIVE
enough
No tenía dinero suficiente.
I didn't have enough money.

sufrir VERB
to suffer
Sufre de artritis.
He suffers from arthritis.

la **sugerencia** NOUN
suggestion
hacer una sugerencia
to make a suggestion

sugerir VERB
to suggest
Sugirió que fuéramos al cine.
She suggested going to the cinema.

sugiero VERB ▷ *see* **sugerir**
Sugiero que lo dejemos para mañana.
I suggest we leave it until tomorrow.

sujetar VERB
to hold
Sujeta la escalera.
Hold the ladder.
Sujeta al perro, que no se escape.
Hold on to the dog so it doesn't get away.

la **suma** NOUN
sum
hacer una suma
to do a sum

English

Spanish

A
B
C
D
E
F
G
H
I
J
K
L
M
N
O
P
Q
R
S
T
U
V
W
X
Y
Z

sumar VERB
to add up

supe VERB ▷ *see* **saber**
Siempre lo supe.
I always knew it.

el **supermercado** NOUN
supermarket

el/la **superviviente** NOUN
survivor

suponer VERB
to suppose
Supongo que vendrá.
I suppose she'll come.

Supongo que sí.
I suppose so.
Supongo que no.
I suppose not.

supuesto VERB ▷ *see* **suponer**

por supuesto
of course

supuse VERB ▷ *see* **suponer**
Ya supuse que no vendría.
I thought he wouldn't come.

sur MASC NOUN, ADJECTIVE
south
el sur del país
the south of the country

LANGUAGE TIP
The adjective **sur** never changes its
ending, no matter what it describes.

sureste MASC NOUN, ADJECTIVE
southeast

LANGUAGE TIP
The adjective **sureste** never changes
its ending, no matter what it
describes.

el **surf** NOUN
surfing
surf a vela
windsurfing
practicar el surf
to surf

surgir VERB
to come up
Ha surgido un problema.
A problem has come up.

suroeste MASC NOUN, ADJECTIVE
southwest

LANGUAGE TIP
The adjective **suroeste** never
changes its ending, no matter what
it describes.

la **suscripción** (PL las **suscripciones**)
NOUN
subscription

suspender VERB
1 **to fail**
He suspendido Matemáticas.
I've failed maths.
2 **to call off**
Suspendieron el partido.
They called off the match.

suspirar VERB
to sigh

el **sustantivo** NOUN
noun

el **susto** NOUN
fright
dar un susto a alguien
to give somebody a fright
Me has dado un susto.
You gave me a fright.

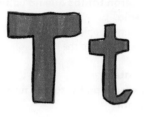

el tabaco NOUN
1 tobacco
2 cigarettes

la tabla NOUN
plank
El agujero estaba cubierto con tablas.
The hole was covered with planks.
la tabla de multiplicar
the multiplication table
una tabla de cocina
a chopping board
la tabla de surf
the surfboard

el tablero NOUN
board
el tablero de ajedrez
the chessboard

la tableta NOUN
1 tablet
2 bar

tachar VERB
to cross out
No lo taches, bórralo.
Don't cross it out, rub it out.

el taco NOUN
1 stud
2 cube
3 swearword
soltar tacos
to swear

el tacón (PL los **tacones**) NOUN
heel
zapatos de tacón
high-heeled shoes

tal (FEM **tal**) ADJECTIVE, PRONOUN
such
En tales casos es mejor consultar con un médico.
In such cases it's better to see a doctor.
Lo dejé tal como estaba.
I left it just as it was.
con tal de que
as long as
con tal de que regreséis antes de las once
as long as you get back before eleven
¿Qué tal has dormido?
How did you sleep?

¿Qué tal?
How are things?
tal vez
perhaps

la talla NOUN
size
¿Tienen esta camisa en la talla cuatro?
Do you have this shirt in a size four?

el taller NOUN
garage
Tenemos el coche en el taller.
Our car is in the garage.

el tamaño NOUN
size
¿Qué tamaño tiene?
What size is it?

también ADVERB
1 also
Canta flamenco y también baila.
He sings flamenco and also dances.
2 too
Mi hermana también viene.
My sister is coming too.
3 Tengo hambre. — Yo también.
I'm hungry. — So am I.
Yo estoy de acuerdo. — Nosotros también.
I agree. — So do we.

el **tambor**
NOUN
drum

tampoco
ADVERB
1 **either**
Yo tampoco lo compré.
I didn't buy it either.
2 **neither**
Yo no la vi. — Yo tampoco.
I didn't see her. — Neither did I.
Nunca he estado en París. — Yo tampoco.
I've never been to Paris. — Neither have I.

tan ADVERB
so
No creí que fueras a venir tan pronto.
I didn't think you'd come so soon.
¡No es tan difícil!
It's not so difficult!
¡Qué hombre tan amable!
What a kind man!
tan ... como ...
as ... as ...
No es tan guapa como su madre.
She's not as pretty as her mother.
Vine tan pronto como pude.
I came as soon as I could.
tan ... que ...
so ... that ...
Habla tan deprisa que no la entiendo.
She talks so fast I can't understand her.

tanto

tanto can be an adjective, an adverb, a pronoun or a noun.

A ADJECTIVE, PRONOUN (FEM **tanta**)
so much
Ahora no bebo tanta leche.
I don't drink so much milk now.
¡Tengo tantos ejercicios que hacer hoy!
I have so many exercises to do today!

Vinieron tantos que no cabían en la sala.
So many people came that they couldn't fit into the room.
B ADVERB
1 **so much**
Se preocupa tanto que no puede dormir.
He worries so much that he can't sleep.
¡No corras tanto!
Don't run so fast!
tanto tú como yo
both you and I
2 **so often**
Ahora no la veo tanto.
I don't see her so often these days.
C MASC NOUN
goal
Juárez marcó el segundo tanto.
Juárez scored the second goal.
un tanto por ciento
a percentage
Había cuarenta y tantos invitados.
There were forty-odd guests.

la **tapa** NOUN
1 **lid**
2 **top**
3 **cover**
4 **tapa**
Pedimos unas tapas en el bar.
We ordered some tapas in the bar.

tapar VERB
to cover
La tapé con una manta.
I covered her with a blanket.
Tapa la olla.
Put the lid on the pan.
Tápate bien que hace frío.
Wrap up well as it's cold.

el **tapón** (PL los **tapones**) NOUN
1 **plug**
2 **top**

la **taquilla** NOUN
1 **box office**
2 **ticket office**

tardar VERB
1 **to be late**
Te espero a las ocho. No tardes.
I expect you at eight. Don't be late.
2 **to take**
Tardaron una semana en contestar.
They took a week to reply.
En avión se tarda dos horas.
The plane takes two hours.

tarde

tarde can be a noun or an adverb.

A FEM NOUN
1 **afternoon**
a las tres de la tarde
at three in the afternoon
¡Buenas tardes!
Good afternoon!
por la tarde
in the afternoon
hoy por la tarde
this afternoon
2 **evening**
a las ocho de la tarde
at eight in the evening
¡Buenas tardes!
Good evening!
por la tarde
in the evening
hoy por la tarde
this evening
B ADVERB
late
Se está haciendo tarde.
It's getting late.
más tarde
later
Llegaré a las nueve como muy tarde.
I'll arrive at nine at the latest.

tarde o temprano
sooner or later

la **tarea** NOUN
task

Una de sus tareas es repartir las pinturas.
One of his tasks is to hand out the crayons.
las tareas domésticas
housework

la **tarjeta** NOUN
card
Me mandó una tarjeta de Navidad.
He sent me a Christmas card.
una tarjeta de crédito
a credit card
una tarjeta telefónica
a phonecard
una tarjeta de embarque
a boarding card

el **tarro** NOUN
jar

la **tarta** NOUN
1 **cake**
una tarta de cumpleaños
a birthday cake
2 **tart**

el **tatuaje** NOUN
tattoo

el **taxi** NOUN
taxi
Cogimos un taxi.
We got a taxi.

el/la **taxista** NOUN
taxi driver

la **taza** NOUN
1 **cup**
Mis padres tomaron una taza de café.
My parents had a cup of coffee.
2 **cupful**
una taza de arroz
a cupful of rice
3 **bowl**

el **tazón** (PL los **tazones**) NOUN
bowl

English

Spanish

a b c d e f g h i j k l m n o p q r s t u v w x y z

237

te PRONOUN
1 you
Te quiero.
I love you.
Te voy a dar un consejo.
I'm going to give you some advice.
Me gustaría comprártelo.
I'd like to buy it for you.
2 yourself
¿Te has hecho daño?
Have you hurt yourself?
¿Te duelen los pies?
Do your feet hurt?
No te has lavado los dientes.
You haven't brushed your teeth.

el **té** (PL los **tés**) NOUN
tea
Me hice un té.
I made myself a cup of tea.

DID YOU KNOW...?
People don't tend to drink as much tea in Spain as in Britain, and tea with lemon and herbal teas are more common.

---

el **teatro** NOUN
theatre
Por la noche fuimos al teatro.
At night we went to the theatre.
una obra de teatro
a play

el **tebeo** NOUN
comic

el **techo** NOUN
ceiling
El techo está pintado de blanco.
The ceiling is painted white.

la **tecla** NOUN
key
pulsar una tecla
to press a key

el **teclado** NOUN
keyboard

teclear VERB
to type

la **técnica** NOUN
1 technique
2 technician
Mi hermana es técnica de laboratorio.
My sister is a laboratory technician.
3 engineer
La técnica me arregló la lavadora.
The engineer fixed my washing machine.

técnico

> **técnico** can be a noun or an adjective.

A MASC NOUN
1 technician
Es técnico de laboratorio.
He is a laboratory technician.
2 engineer
El técnico me arregló la lavadora.
The engineer fixed my washing machine.
B ADJECTIVE (FEM **técnica**)
technical

la **tecnología** NOUN
technology
tecnología punta
state-of-the-art technology

el **tejado** NOUN
roof

la **tela** NOUN
fabric

la **telaraña** NOUN
cobweb

la **tele** NOUN
TV

Estábamos viendo la tele.
We were watching TV.

el **telediario** NOUN
news
    el telediario de las nueve
    the nine o'clock news

el **teléfono** NOUN
telephone
    No tengo teléfono.
    I don't have a telephone.
    Está hablando
    por teléfono.
    He's on the phone.
    un teléfono móvil
    a mobile phone

la **telenovela** NOUN
soap opera

el **telesilla** NOUN
chairlift

la **televisión** (PL las **televisiones**) NOUN
television
    Dieron la noticia por la televisión.
    They gave the news on the television.
    ¿Qué ponen en la televisión esta
    noche?
    What's on the television tonight?
    la televisión por cable
    cable television
    la televisión digital
    digital TV

el **televisor** NOUN
television set

el **tema** NOUN
1 **topic**
    El tema de la redacción era "Las
    vacaciones".
    The topic of the essay was 'The
    holidays'.
2 **subject**
    Luego hablaremos de ese tema.
    We'll talk about that subject later.

temblar VERB
to tremble
    Me temblaban las manos.
    My hands were trembling.

    temblar de miedo
    to tremble with fear
    temblar de frío
    to shiver

temer VERB
1 **to be afraid**
    No temas.
    Don't be afraid.
2 **to be afraid of**
    Le teme al profesor.
    He's afraid of the teacher.

el **temor** NOUN
fear
    por temor a equivocarme
    for fear of making a mistake

la **temperatura** NOUN
temperature
    El médico le tomó la temperatura.
    The doctor took his temperature.

la **temporada** NOUN
season
    la temporada alta
    the high season
    la temporada baja
    the low season

el **temporal** NOUN
storm

temprano ADVERB
early
    por la mañana temprano
    early in the morning

ten VERB ▷ see **tener**
    Ten el mío si quieres.
    Have mine if you like.

tender VERB
to hang out
    Marta estaba tendiendo la ropa.
    Marta was hanging out the washing.
    ■ **tenderse**
    tenderse en el sofá
    to lie down on the sofa

tendrá VERB ▷ see **tener**
    Tendrá que hacerlo.
    She'll have to do it.

el tenedor NOUN
fork

tener VERB
to have

> **Tengo dos hermanas.**
> I have two sisters.
> **¿Tienes dinero?**
> Do you have any money?
> **Tiene el pelo rubio.**
> He has blond hair.
> **Mi tía va a tener un niño.**
> My aunt's going to have a baby.
> **¿Cuántos años tienes?**
> How old are you?
> **Tiene cinco metros de largo.**
> It's five metres long.
> **Ten cuidado.**
> Be careful.
> **tener que hacer algo**
> to have to do something
> **Tengo que llamar a mi padre.**
> I have to call my father.

tenga VERB ▷ see **tener**

> **No creo que tenga tiempo.**
> I don't think I'll have time.

el tenis NOUN
tennis

> **¿Juegas al tenis?**
> Do you play tennis?
> **tenis de mesa**
> table tennis

el/la tenista NOUN
tennis player

la tentación
(PL las **tentaciones**) NOUN
temptation

el tentempié (PL los **tentempiés**) NOUN
snack

teñir VERB
to dye

> **Se ha teñido el pelo.**
> He's dyed his hair.

la teoría NOUN
theory

> **En teoría es fácil.**
> In theory it's easy.

tercero (FEM **tercera**)

LANGUAGE TIP
tercero becomes **tercer** before a masculine singular noun. ADJECTIVE, PRONOUN

---

third

> **la tercera vez**
> the third time
> **la tercera planta**
> the third floor
> **Llegué el tercero.**
> I arrived third.
> **una tercera parte de la población**
> a third of the population
> **Vivo en el tercero.**
> I live on the third floor.

el tercio NOUN
third

terco (FEM **terca**) ADJECTIVE
obstinate

terminar VERB
1 **to finish**

> **He terminado el libro.**
> I've finished the book.
> **cuando terminó de hablar**
> when he finished talking

2 **to end**

> **¿A qué hora termina la clase?**
> At what time does the class end?
> **Terminaron peleándose.**
> They ended up fighting.
> **Se nos ha terminado la leche.**
> We've run out of milk.
> **Ha terminado con Mario.**
> She's broken up with Mario.

la ternera NOUN
veal

la terraza NOUN
1 **balcony**
2 **roof terrace**

el terremoto NOUN
earthquake

el **terreno** NOUN
1 **land**
una granja con mucho terreno
a farm with a lot of land
2 **un terreno**
a plot of land
Mis padres han comprado un terreno.
My parents have bought a plot of land.
3 **field**
terrenos plantados de naranjos
fields planted with orange trees
el terreno de juego
the pitch

terrestre (FEM **terrestre**) ADJECTIVE
land
los animales terrestres
land animals

terrible (FEM **terrible**) ADJECTIVE
terrible
Fue una experiencia terrible.
It was a terrible experience.

el **texto** NOUN
text
un libro de texto
a textbook

ti PRONOUN
you
una llamada para ti
a call for you
Solo piensas en ti mismo.
You only think of yourself.

la **tía** NOUN
1 **aunt**
mi tía
my aunt
2 **girl**
Es una tía majísima.
She's a really nice girl.

tiemblo VERB ▷ *see* **temblar**
Tiemblo de miedo.
I'm shaking with fear.
Tiemblo de frío.
I'm shivering.

el **tiempo** NOUN
1 **time**

No tengo tiempo.
I don't have time.
¿Qué haces en tu tiempo libre?
What do you do in your spare time?
Me llevó bastante tiempo.
It took me quite a long time.
¿Cuánto tiempo hace que vives aquí?
How long have you been living here?
Hace mucho tiempo que no la veo.
I haven't seen her for a long time.
al mismo tiempo
at the same time
a tiempo
in time
Llegamos a tiempo de ver la película.
We got there in time to see the film.
2 **weather**
¿Qué tiempo hace ahí?
What's the weather like there?
Hace mal tiempo.
The weather's bad.
Hizo buen tiempo.
The weather was fine.

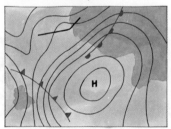

3 **half**
Metieron el gol durante el segundo tiempo.
They scored the goal during the second half.

perder el tiempo
to waste time

la **tienda** NOUN
1 **shop**
una tienda de ropa
a clothes shop

ir de tiendas
to go shopping

2 una tienda de campaña
a tent

tiendo VERB ▷ *see* **tender**
En el verano tiendo la ropa fuera.
I hang out the washing outside in the summer.

tiene VERB ▷ *see* **tener**
Tiene dos hermanas.
She has two sisters.

la **tierra** NOUN
1 land
2 la Tierra
the Earth

tieso (FEM **tiesa**) ADJECTIVE
1 stiff
quedarse tieso de frío
to be frozen stiff
2 straight
Ponte tiesa.
Stand up straight.

el **tigre** NOUN
tiger

las **tijeras** NOUN
scissors
Es más fácil cortarlo con las tijeras.
It's easier to cut it with scissors.
¿Tienes unas tijeras?
Do you have a pair of scissors?

el **timbre** NOUN
bell
Ya ha sonado el timbre.
The bell has already gone.

llamar al timbre
to ring the bell

tímido (FEM **tímida**) ADJECTIVE
shy

el **timo** NOUN
1 con
2 rip off
¡Vaya timo!
What a rip-off!

la **tinta** NOUN
ink

el **tinto** NOUN
red wine

tiñendo VERB ▷ *see* **teñir**
Mamá se está tiñendo el pelo.
Mum is dyeing her hair.

el **tío** NOUN
1 uncle
mis tíos
my uncles/my uncle and aunt

LANGUAGE TIP
mis tíos has more than one meaning. It can be translated as **my uncles** or **my uncle and aunt**.

2 guy
Es un tío muy simpático.
He's a really nice guy.
Oye, tío, me alegro de verte.
Hey, man, nice to see you.

el **tiovivo** NOUN
merry-go-round

típico (FEM **típica**) ADJECTIVE
typical
Eso es muy típico de ella.
That's very typical of her.

el **tipo** NOUN
1 kind
No me gusta este tipo de fiestas.
I don't like this kind of party.
todo tipo de ...
all sorts of ...
2 figure
Alba tiene un tipo muy bonito.
Alba has a lovely figure.

la **tira** NOUN
1 strip

una tira de papel
a strip of paper
una tira cómica
a comic strip
2 **Hace la tira de tiempo que no la veo.**
I haven't seen her for ages.

tirado (FEM **tirada**) ADJECTIVE
1 **dirt-cheap**
2 **dead easy**

tirar VERB
1 **to throw**
Tírame la pelota.
Throw me the ball.
2 **to throw away**
No tires la comida.
Don't throw away the food.
tirar algo a la basura
to throw something out
3 **to knock down**
Queremos tirar esta pared.
We want to knock this wall down.
tirar de la cadena
to pull the chain
■ **tirarse**
1 **Se tiró al suelo.**
He threw himself to the ground.
tirarse al agua
to plunge into the water
tirarse de cabeza
to dive in head first

2 **Se tiró toda la mañana estudiando.**
He spent the whole morning studying.

la **tirita** NOUN
plaster

el **tiro** NOUN
shot
Oímos un tiro.
We heard a shot.
un tiro libre
a free kick

la **tirolina** NOUN
zipwire
El camping tiene una tirolina.
The campsite has a zipwire.

titularse VERB
to be called
La novela se titula "Marcianos".
The novel is called 'Marcianos'.

el **título** NOUN
title
Necesito un título para el poema.
I need a title for the poem.

la **tiza** NOUN
chalk
una tiza
a piece of chalk

la **toalla** NOUN
towel
una toalla de baño
a bath towel

el **tobillo** NOUN
ankle
Me he torcido el tobillo.
I've twisted my ankle.

el **tobogán**
(PL los **toboganes**) NOUN
slide

tocar VERB
1 **to touch**
Si lo tocas te quemarás.
If you touch it you'll burn yourself.
2 **to play**
Toca el violín.
He plays the violin.
3 **Te toca fregar los platos.**
It's your turn to do the dishes.
Le tocó la lotería.
He won the lottery.

todavía ADVERB
1 **still**
¿Todavía estás en la cama?
Are you still in bed?
¡Y todavía se queja!
And he still complains!
2 **yet**

Todavía no han llegado.
They haven't arrived yet.
¿Todavía no has comido?
Haven't you eaten yet?
Todavía no.
Not yet.

todo (FEM **toda**) ADJECTIVE, PRONOUN
  1 all
   todos los niños
   all the children
   Todos son caros.
   They're all expensive.
   toda la noche
   all night
   todos vosotros
   all of you
  2 every
   todos los días
   every day
  3 the whole
   Me he aprendido toda la canción.
   I've learnt the whole song.
  4 everything
   Lo sabemos todo.
   We know everything.
  5 everybody
   Todos estaban de acuerdo.
   Everybody agreed.
   Todo el mundo lo sabe.
   Everybody knows.

tomar VERB
  1 to take
   En clase tomamos apuntes.
   We take notes in class.
  2 to have
   ¿Qué quieres tomar?
   What are you going to have?
   De postre tomé un helado.
   I had an ice cream for dessert.
   Toma, esto es tuyo.
   Here, this is yours.
   tomar el pelo a alguien
   to pull somebody's leg
   ¡Me estás tomando el pelo!
   You're pulling my leg!

tomar el sol
to sunbathe

el **tomate** NOUN
  tomato

el **tono** NOUN
  1 tone
   **Lo dijo en
   tono cariñoso.**
   He said it in an affectionate tone.
   un tono de llamada
   a ringtone
  2 shade
   un tono un poco más oscuro
   a slightly darker shade

la **tontería** NOUN
  silly thing
   Se pelearon por una tontería.
   They fell out over a silly thing.
   tonterías
   nonsense
   ¡Eso son tonterías!
   That's nonsense!
   ¡No digas tonterías!
   Don't talk nonsense!

tonto (FEM **tonta**)

tonto can be an adjective or a noun.

A ADJECTIVE
  silly
   ¡Qué error más tonto!
   What a silly mistake!
B MASC/FEM NOUN
  fool

hacer el tonto
to mess around

el **tope** NOUN
  El autobús iba a tope.
  The bus was packed.

el **toque** NOUN
  dar los últimos toques a algo
  to put the finishing touches to
  something

torcer VERB
  1 to twist
   ¡Me estás torciendo el brazo!
   You're twisting my arm!

Se torció el tobillo.
He sprained his ankle.
2 **to turn**
torcer a la derecha
to turn right
torcer la esquina
to turn the corner

la **tormenta** NOUN
storm
Hubo tormenta.
There was a storm.
un día de tormenta
a stormy day

el **torneo** NOUN
tournament

el **tornillo** NOUN
screw

el **toro** NOUN
bull
los toros
(*espectáculo*) bullfighting

torpe (FEM **torpe**) ADJECTIVE
1 **clumsy**
2 **dim**

la **torre** NOUN
tower
la torre de control
the control tower

la **torta** NOUN
small flat cake

la **tortilla** NOUN
omelette
una tortilla de patatas
a Spanish omelette

la **tos** (PL las **toses**) NOUN
cough
Tengo mucha tos.
I have a bad cough.

toser VERB
to cough

la **tostada** NOUN
piece of toast
¿Quieres una tostada?
Do you want a piece of toast?

tostadas
toast
Tomé café con tostadas.
I had coffee and toast.

tostar VERB
to toast

total

> **total** can be an adjective, a noun or an adverb.

A ADJECTIVE (FEM **total**)
total
B MASC NOUN
El total son cuarenta y cinco euros con cincuenta.
The total is forty-five euros fifty.
En total éramos catorce.
There were fourteen of us altogether.
C ADVERB
Total, que perdimos.
So, anyway, we lost.

totalmente ADVERB
totally
Mario es totalmente distinto a Carlos.
Mario is totally different from Carlos.
Estoy totalmente de acuerdo.
I completely agree.
¿Estás seguro? — Totalmente.
Are you sure? — Absolutely.

tóxico (FEM **tóxica**) ADJECTIVE
toxic

el **trabajador**
la **trabajadora** NOUN
worker

trabajar VERB
to work
No trabajes tanto.
Don't work so hard.
¿En qué trabajas?
What's your job?
Trabajo de camarero.
I work as a waiter.

el **trabajo** NOUN
1 **work**

Tengo mucho trabajo.
I have a lot of work.
2 job
Mi hermano no encuentra trabajo.
My brother can't find a job.
3 essay
Tengo que entregar dos trabajos mañana.
I have to hand in two essays tomorrow.

la **tradición** (PL las **tradiciones**) NOUN
tradition

tradicional (FEM **tradicional**) ADJECTIVE
traditional

la **traducción** (PL las **traducciones**) NOUN
translation
una traducción del español al inglés
a translation from Spanish into English

traducir VERB
to translate
traducir del inglés al español
to translate from English into Spanish

traer VERB
to bring
He traído el paraguas por si acaso.
I've brought the umbrella just in case.

el **tráfico** NOUN
traffic
un accidente de tráfico
a road accident

tragar VERB
1 to swallow
Traga esta pastilla.
Swallow this tablet.
2 to stand
No la trago.
I can't stand her.

la **tragedia** NOUN
tragedy

el **traidor**
la **traidora** NOUN
traitor

traigo VERB ▷ see **traer**
¿Te traigo un vaso de leche?
Shall I bring you a glass of milk?

el **traje** NOUN
1 suit
Lucas llevaba un traje gris.
Lucas was wearing a grey suit.
2 un traje de baño
a pair of swimming trunks/a swimsuit

LANGUAGE TIP
un traje de baño can mean either
a pair of swimming trunks or
a swimsuit.

---

la **trampa** NOUN
trap
caer en la trampa
to fall into the trap

hacer trampa
to cheat

el **tramposo**
la **tramposa** NOUN
cheat

tranquilamente ADVERB
calmly
Háblale tranquilamente.
Speak to him calmly.

la **tranquilidad** NOUN
peace and quiet
Necesito un poco de tranquilidad.
I need a little peace and quiet.

tranquilizar VERB
to calm down
¡Tranquilízate!
Calm down!

tranquilo (FEM **tranquila**) ADJECTIVE
1 calm
El día del examen estaba bastante tranquilo.
On the day of the exam I was quite calm.
2 peaceful

transgénico (FEM **transgénica**)
ADJECTIVE
genetically modified

la **transmisión** (PL las **transmisiones**)
NOUN
broadcast
una transmisión en directo
a live broadcast

transmitir VERB
to transmit

transparente (FEM **transparente**)
ADJECTIVE
transparent

el **transporte** NOUN
transport
el transporte público
public transport

el **trapo** NOUN
cloth
Lo limpié con un trapo.
I wiped it with a cloth.
un trapo de cocina
a tea towel
Pásale un trapo al espejo.
Give the mirror a wipe.
el trapo del polvo
the duster

tras PREPOSITION
after
Salimos corriendo tras ella.
We ran out after her.
semana tras semana
week after week

el **trasero** NOUN
bum

el **trasto** NOUN
piece of junk
El desván está lleno de trastos.
The loft is full of junk.

trastornado (FEM **trastornada**)
ADJECTIVE
disturbed

tratar VERB
1 **to treat**
Su padrastro los trata muy bien.
Their stepfather treats them really well.
2 **tratar de**
to try/to be about

LANGUAGE TIP
tratar de has two meanings. Look at
the examples.

Trataré de llegar pronto.
I'll try to arrive early.
**La película trata de un
adolescente en Nueva York.**
The film is about a teenager in New
York.

¿De qué se trata?
What's it about?

el **trato** NOUN
deal
hacer un trato
to make a deal

¡Trato hecho!
It's a deal!

través PREPOSITION
a través de
across/through

LANGUAGE TIP
a través de has two meanings. Look
at the examples.

Nadó a través del río.
He swam across the river.
**Se enteraron a través de un
amigo.**
They found out through a friend.

English

Spanish

A
B
C
D
E
F
G
H
I
J
K
L
M
N
O
P
Q
R
S
T
U
V
W
X
Y
Z

248

travieso (FEM **traviesa**) ADJECTIVE
naughty

el **trayecto** NOUN
  1 **journey**
  2 **way**
      ¿Qué trayecto hace ese autobús?
      What way does that bus go?

el **trébol** NOUN
  clover

trece (FEM **trece**) ADJECTIVE, PRONOUN
  thirteen
      Tengo trece años.
      I'm thirteen.

      el trece de enero
      the thirteenth of January
      Nació el trece de enero.
      He was born on the thirteenth of
      January.

treinta (FEM **treinta**) ADJECTIVE, PRONOUN
  thirty
      Tiene treinta años.
      He's thirty.
      el treinta de enero
      the thirtieth of January
      Nació el treinta de enero.
      He was born on the thirtieth of January.

tremendo (FEM **tremenda**) ADJECTIVE
  1 **terrible**
      **Tenía un tremendo dolor de
      cabeza.**
      I had a terrible headache.
      Hacía un frío tremendo.
      It was terribly cold.
  2 **tremendous**
      **La película tuvo un éxito
      tremendo.**
      The film was a tremendous success.

el **tren** NOUN
  train
      viajar en tren
      to travel by train

la **trenza** NOUN
  plait
      Le hice una trenza.
      I put her hair up in a plait.

tres (FEM **tres**) ADJECTIVE, PRONOUN
  three

      Son las tres.
      It's three o'clock.
      el tres de febrero
      the third of February
      Nació el tres de febrero.
      He was born on the third of
      February.

trescientos (FEM **trescientas**) ADJECTIVE,
PRONOUN
  three hundred

el **triángulo** NOUN
  triangle

el **trimestre** NOUN
  term

el **trineo** NOUN
  1 **sledge**
  2 **sleigh**

el **trío** NOUN
  trio

la **tripa** NOUN
  gut

el **triple** NOUN
      **Esta habitación es el triple de
      grande.**
      This room is three times as big.
      Gastan el triple que nosotros.
      They spend three times as much as
      we do.

la **tripulación** (PL las **tripulaciones**)
NOUN
  crew

triste (FEM **triste**) ADJECTIVE
  sad
      **Me puse muy triste cuando me
      enteré.**
      I was very sad when I heard.

la **tristeza** NOUN
  sadness

triunfar VERB
  to triumph

el **triunfo** NOUN
triumph

el **trofeo** NOUN
trophy

la **trompeta** NOUN
trumpet

tronar VERB
to thunder
Ha estado tronando toda la
noche.
It has been thundering all night.

troncharse VERB
Yo me tronchaba de risa.
I was killing myself laughing.

el **tronco** NOUN
1 **trunk**
2 **log**

el **trono** NOUN
throne

tropezar VERB
to trip
Tropecé y me caí.
I tripped and fell.
tropezar contra un árbol
to bump into a tree

el **tropezón** (PL los **tropezones**) NOUN
trip

tropical (FEM **tropical**) ADJECTIVE
tropical

tropiece VERB ▷ *see* **tropezar**
Mira que no tropiece con la
puerta.
Make sure it doesn't bang into
the door.

el **trozo** NOUN
piece
un trozo de madera
a piece of wood
Dame un trocito solo.
Just give me a small piece.

la **trucha** NOUN
trout

el **truco** NOUN
trick
Ya le he cogido el truco.
I've got the hang of it already.

truena VERB ▷ *see* **tronar**
Truena.
It's thundering.

el **trueno** NOUN
Oímos un trueno.
We heard a clap of thunder.
Me despertaron los truenos.
The thunder woke me up.

tu ADJECTIVE
your
tu bicicleta
your bicycle
tus familiares
your relations

tú PRONOUN
you
Cuando tú quieras.
Whenever you like.

la **tubería** NOUN
pipe
Ha reventado una tubería.
A pipe has burst.

el **tubo** NOUN
1 **pipe**
2 **tube**
un tubo de crema para las
manos
a tube of hand cream

tuerzo VERB ▷ *see* **torcer**
Si no me sueltas, te tuerzo
el brazo.
Let go or I'll twist your arm.

tuitear VERB
to tweet
Se metió en problemas por tuitear insultos.
He got into trouble for posting insults.

el **tuitero**
la **tuitera** NOUN
Twitter® user
La cantante es también una entusiasta tuitera.
The singer is also an enthusiastic Twitter user.

la **tumba** NOUN
grave

tumbar VERB
to knock down
El perro me tumbó.
The dog knocked me down.

■ **tumbarse**
to lie down
Me tumbé en el sofá.
I lay down on the sofa.

el **túnel** NOUN
tunnel

el **turismo** NOUN
tourism
El turismo es importante para nuestra economía.
Tourism is important for our economy.
turismo rural
rural tourism

el/la **turista** NOUN
tourist

turístico (FEM **turística**) ADJECTIVE
tourist

turnarse VERB
to take it in turns

Nos turnamos para fregar los platos.
We take it in turns to do the washing-up.

el **turno** NOUN
turn
cuando me tocó el turno
when it was my turn

el **turrón** (PL los **turrones**) NOUN
nougat

DID YOU KNOW…?
There is a wide range of **turrones** in Spain which people traditionally eat at Christmas.

---

tutear VERB

DID YOU KNOW…?
In Spanish there are two ways of addressing people. You can use the familiar **tú** form to talk to friends and people you know, and this is known as **tutear**. You should use the more formal **usted** form to talk to people you don't know, especially if they are adults.

Se tutean con el profesor.
They address their teacher in familiar terms.

el **tutor**
la **tutora** NOUN
tutor

tuve VERB ▷ see **tener**
Tuve fiebre.
I had a temperature.

tuyo (FEM **tuya**) ADJECTIVE, PRONOUN
yours
¿Es tuyo este abrigo?
Is this coat yours?
La tuya está en el armario.
Yours is in the cupboard.
mis amigos y los tuyos
my friends and yours
un amigo tuyo
a friend of yours

Uu

u CONJUNCTION

or

LANGUAGE TIP

u is used instead of **o** before words starting with **o-** or **ho-**.

¿Minutos u horas?
Minutes or hours?

Ud. ABBREVIATION = **usted**

la **UE** ABBREVIATION
(= **Unión Europea**)
EU

uf EXCLAMATION
1 **phew!**
2 **ugh!**

últimamente ADVERB
recently

último (FEM **última**)

> **último** can be an adjective or a noun.

A ADJECTIVE
1 **last**
la última vez que hablé con ella
the last time I spoke to her
2 **top**
No llego al último estante.
I can't reach the top shelf.
3 **back**
Nos sentamos en la última fila.
We sat in the back row.
la última moda
the latest fashion
llegar en último lugar
to come last

a última hora
at the last minute

B MASC/FEM NOUN
the last one

a últimos de mes
towards the end of the month
por último
lastly

un
una ARTICLE
1 **a**
una silla
a chair
2 **an**
un paraguas
an umbrella
3 **some**
Fui con unos amigos.
I went with some friends.
Había unas veinte personas.
There were about twenty people.
Me he comprado unas deportivas muy chulas.
I've bought a pair of really cool trainers.

undécimo (FEM **undécima**)
ADJECTIVE, PRONOUN
eleventh
Vivo en el undécimo piso.
I live on the eleventh floor.

único (FEM **única**)

> **único** can be an adjective or a noun.

A ADJECTIVE
only
el único día que tengo libre
the only day I have free

A
B
C
D
E
F
G
H
I
J
K
L
M
N
O
P
Q
R
S
T
U
V
W
X
Y
Z

Soy hija única.
I'm an only child.
Lo único que no me gusta ...
The only thing I don't like ...
B MASC/FEM NOUN
el único/la única
the only one
el único que me queda
the only one I've got left

la **unidad** NOUN
unit
una unidad de peso
a unit of weight

unido (FEM **unida**) ADJECTIVE
close
**una familia muy
unida**
a very close family

el **uniforme** NOUN
uniform
**Llevaba el uniforme
del colegio.**
He was wearing
his school uniform.

la **unión**
(PL las **uniones**) NOUN
union
la Unión Europea
the European Union

unir VERB
1 to link
**Este pasaje une
los dos edificios.**
This passage links
the two buildings.
2 to join
**Unió los dos extremos con
una cuerda.**
He joined the two ends with
some string.
3 unirse a algo
to join something
**Olivia se unió a la
expedición.**
Olivia joined the expedition.

la **universidad** NOUN
university
Mi hermana va a la universidad.
My sister's at university.

el **universo** NOUN
universe

uno (FEM **una**) ADJECTIVE, PRONOUN
one
Vivo en el número uno.
I live at number one.
Uno de ellos era mío.
One of them was mine.
Entraron uno a uno.
They came in one by one.

el uno de abril
the first of April
Es la una.
It's one o'clock.

untar VERB
untar algo con algo
to spread something on something
**Primero hay que untar el pan con
mantequilla.**
First you have to spread the butter on
the bread.
**Te has untado las manos de
chocolate.**
You've got chocolate all over your hands.

la **uña** NOUN
nail

la **urbanización** (PL las
urbanizaciones) NOUN
housing estate

la **urgencia** NOUN
emergency
los servicios de urgencia
the emergency services
urgencias
accident and emergency department

urgente (FEM **urgente**) ADJECTIVE
urgent

usado (FEM **usada**) ADJECTIVE
1 secondhand

ropa usada
secondhand clothes

2 worn
Estas zapatillas están ya muy usadas.
These slippers are very worn now.

usar VERB

1 to use
¿Usaste el grande o el pequeño?
Did you use the small one or the big one?

2 to wear
Esta falda está sin usar.
This skirt has never been worn.
¿Qué número de zapato usas?
What size shoe do you take?

el **uso** NOUN

use
instrucciones de uso
instructions for use

usted PRONOUN

you
Quisiera hablar con usted en privado.
I'd like to speak to you in private.

útil (FEM **útil**) ADJECTIVE
useful

utilizar VERB
to use

la **uva** NOUN
grape

DID YOU KNOW...?
in Spain, people celebrate the start of the New Year by eating twelve grapes, one with each of the twelve chimes, representing a month's luck for each grape that is eaten.

Spanish English

a
b
c
d
e
f
g
h
i
j
k
l
m
n
o
p
q
r
s
t
u
v
w
x
y
z

va VERB ▷ *see* **ir**
> **Va a la escuela del barrio.**
> He goes to the local school.

la **vaca** NOUN
> **1 cow**
> **2 beef**
> **No como carne de vaca.**
> I don't eat beef.

las **vacaciones** NOUN
> **holidays**
> **las vacaciones de Navidad**
> the Christmas holidays
> **La secretaria está de vacaciones.**
> The secretary is on holiday.
> **En agosto me voy de vacaciones.**
> I'm going on holiday in August.

vaciar VERB
> **to empty**
> **Ayúdame a vaciar este cajón.**
> Help me empty this drawer.

vacío (FEM **vacía**) ADJECTIVE
> **empty**

el **vagabundo**
la **vagabunda** NOUN
> **tramp**

vago (FEM **vaga**) ADJECTIVE
> **lazy**

el **vagón** (PL los **vagones**) NOUN
> **carriage**

la **vainilla** NOUN
> **vanilla**
> **un helado de vainilla**
> a vanilla ice cream

el **vale** NOUN
> **voucher**
> **un vale de regalo**
> a gift voucher

valer VERB
> **1 to cost**
> **¿Cuánto vale?**
> How much does it cost?
> **2 to be worth**
> **El terreno vale más que la casa.**
> The land is worth more than the house.
> **vale la pena**
> it's worth it
> **no vale la pena**
> it's not worth it
> **No vale la pena gastar tanto dinero.**
> It's not worth spending that much money.
> **Este cuchillo no vale para nada.**
> This knife is useless.
> **Vamos a jugar. — ¡Vale!**
> Let's play. — OK!

> **¡Eso no vale!**
> That's not fair!
> **¿Vale?**
> OK?

válido (FEM **válida**) ADJECTIVE
> **valid**

valiente (FEM **valiente**) ADJECTIVE
> **brave**

la **valla** NOUN
> **fence**

el **valle** NOUN
> **valley**

el **valor** NOUN
> **1 value**
> **valor sentimental**
> sentimental value
> **objetos de valor**
> valuables
> **2 courage**
> **armarse de valor**
> to pluck up courage

el **vapor** NOUN
steam
 al vapor
 steamed

el **vaquero** NOUN
 1 **cowboy**
  una película
  de vaqueros
  a western
 2 **vaqueros**
  jeans (*pantalones*)
  Llevaba unos
  vaqueros negros.
  He was
  wearing
  black jeans.

variado (FEM **variada**) ADJECTIVE
varied
 Tenemos un programa muy
 variado.
 Our timetable is really varied.

variar VERB
to vary
 Los precios varían según las
 tallas.
 Prices vary according to size.
 Decidí ir en tren, para variar.
 I decided to go by train for a change.

la **variedad** NOUN
variety

varios (FEM **varias**) ADJECTIVE, PRONOUN
several
 Estuve enfermo varios días.
 I was ill for several days.
 Le hicimos un regalo entre varios.
 Several of us clubbed together to get
 him a present.

varón (PL **varones**)

> **varón** can be an adjective or a noun.

A ADJECTIVE
 male
B MASC NOUN
 Tiene dos hembras y un varón.
 She has two girls and a boy.

 Sexo: varón.
 Sex: male.

vasco (FEM **vasca**)

> **vasco** can be an adjective or a noun.

A ADJECTIVE
 Basque
 el País Vasco
 the Basque Country
B MASC/FEM NOUN
 vasco/vasca
 Basque
C MASC NOUN
 Basque
 Hablamos vasco.
 We speak Basque.

el **vaso** NOUN
glass
 Bebí un vaso de leche.
 I drank a glass of milk.
 un vaso de plástico
 a plastic cup

el **váter** NOUN
loo

vaya VERB ▷ *see* **ir**
 ¿Quieres que vaya contigo?
 Do you want me to go with you?

Vd. ABBREVIATION = **usted**

ve VERB ▷ *see* **ir**, **ver**
 Ve con él.
 Go with him.
 Mi perro no ve bien.
 My dog can't see very well.

el **vecindario** NOUN
neighbourhood

el **vecino**
la **vecina** NOUN
neighbour
 los vecinos de al lado
 the next door neighbours

vegetal ADJECTIVE, MASC NOUN
vegetable
 aceite vegetal
 vegetable oil

English | **Spanish**

el **vehículo** NOUN
vehicle

veinte (FEM **veinte**) ADJECTIVE, PRONOUN
twenty

> **Tiene veinte años.**
> He's twenty.
> **el veinte de enero**
> the twentieth of January
> **Nació el veinte de enero.**
> He was born on the twentieth of January.
> **el siglo veinte**
> the twentieth century

la **vejez** NOUN
old age

la **vela** NOUN
1 candle
> **Encendimos una vela.**
> We lit a candle.

2 sail

el **velo** NOUN
1 veil
> **La novia llevaba un velo de encaje.**
> The bride was wearing a lace veil.

2 headscarf
> **Se colocó bien el velo para tapar el pelo.**
> She moved her headscarf so it was covering her hair.

la **velocidad** NOUN
speed
> **Pasó una moto a toda velocidad.**
> A motorbike went past at full speed.
> **¿A qué velocidad ibas?**
> How fast were you going?

veloz (FEM **veloz**, PL **veloces**) ADJECTIVE
swift

ven VERB ▷ see **ir**, **ver**
> **Ven conmigo.**
> Come with me.
> **Sus padres no ven el problema.**
> Her parents can't see the problem.

la **vena** NOUN
vein

vencer VERB
1 to defeat
2 to overcome

la **venda** NOUN
bandage
> **Me pusieron una venda en el brazo.**
> They bandaged my arm.

vendar VERB
to bandage
> **Me vendaron el codo.**
> They bandaged my elbow.
> **vendar los ojos a alguien**
> to blindfold somebody

vender VERB
to sell
> **He vendido la bici.**
> I've sold my bike.

> **"se vende"**
> 'for sale'

vendré VERB ▷ see **venir**
> **Mañana vendré de nuevo.**
> I'll come again tomorrow.

el **veneno** NOUN
poison

venenoso (FEM **venenosa**) ADJECTIVE
poisonous

vengo VERB ▷ see **venir**
> **No vengo aquí mucho.**
> I don't come here much.

venir VERB
1 to come
> **Vino en taxi.**
> He came by taxi.
> **Vinieron a verme al hospital.**
> They came to see me in hospital.
> **¡Ven aquí!**
> Come here!

2 to be
> **La noticia venía en el periódico.**
> The news was in the paper.

¿Te viene bien el sábado?
Is Saturday all right for you?

el año que viene
next year
¡Venga, vámonos!
Come on, let's go!
¡Venga ya!
Come off it!

la **ventaja** NOUN
advantage
Tiene la ventaja de que está cerca de casa.
It has the advantage of being close to home.

la **ventana** NOUN
window

la **ventanilla** NOUN
window
Baja la ventanilla.
Open the window.

ver VERB
1 to see
Te vi en el parque.
I saw you in the park.
¡Cuánto tiempo sin verte!
I haven't seen you for ages!
No he visto esa película.
I haven't seen that film.
¿Ves? Ya te lo dije.
See? I told you so.
Eso no tiene nada que ver.
That has nothing to do with it.
¡No la puede ver!
He can't stand her!
Se ve que no tiene idea de informática.
It's clear he's got no idea about computers.
2 to watch
¿Te apetece ver la tele?
Do you feel like watching TV?

A ver ...
Let's see ...

el **verano** NOUN
summer
En verano hace mucho calor.
It's very hot in summer.
las vacaciones de verano
the summer holidays

en verano
in summer

el **verbo** NOUN
verb

la **verdad** NOUN
truth
Les dije la verdad.
I told them the truth.
La verdad es que no tengo ganas.
I don't really feel like it.
De verdad que yo no dije eso.
I didn't say that, honestly.
Es bonito, ¿verdad?
It's pretty, isn't it?
No te gusta, ¿verdad?
You don't like it, do you?

LANGUAGE TIP
Use **¿verdad?** to check information where in English we'd say **don't you?**, **doesn't he?, isn't it?** etc.

¿De verdad?
Really?

verdadero (FEM **verdadera**) ADJECTIVE
real
No me dijo la verdadera razón.
He didn't tell me the real reason.

English
Spanish

A
B
C
D
E
F
G
H
I
J
K
L
M
N
O
P
Q
R
S
T
U
V
W
X
Y
Z

verde

> **verde** can be an adjective or a noun.

A ADJECTIVE (FEM **verde**)
green
Tiene los ojos verdes.
She has green eyes.
Estos plátanos están todavía verdes.
These bananas are still green.

B MASC NOUN
green

la **verdura** NOUN
vegetables
Comemos mucha verdura.
We eat a lot of vegetables.

vergonzoso (FEM vergonzosa)
ADJECTIVE
1 shy
Es muy vergonzosa.
She is very shy.
2 disgraceful
Es vergonzoso cómo los trataron.
It's disgraceful the way they were treated.

la **vergüenza** NOUN
1 embarrassment
Casi me muero de vergüenza.
I almost died of embarrassment.
¡Qué vergüenza!
How embarrassing!
Le da vergüenza pedirle ayuda.
He's embarrassed to ask her for help.
2 shame
No tienen vergüenza.
They have no shame.
¡Es una vergüenza!
It's disgraceful!

la **versión** (PL las **versiones**) NOUN
version

vertical (FEM **vertical**) ADJECTIVE
vertical
Ponlo vertical.
Put it upright.

vestido

> **vestido** can be a noun or an adjective.

A MASC NOUN
dress
B ADJECTIVE
(FEM **vestida**)
Iba vestida de negro.
She was dressed in black.
Yo iba vestido de payaso.
I was dressed as a clown.

vestir VERB
to wear
Vestía pantalones vaqueros y una camiseta.
He was wearing jeans and a T-shirt.
▪ **vestirse**
to get dressed
Se está vistiendo.
He's getting dressed.
Se vistió de superheroína de cómic.
She dressed up as a princess.

el **veterinario**
la **veterinaria** NOUN
vet

la **vez** (PL las **veces**) NOUN
time
¿Cuántas veces al año?
How many times a year?
¿La has visto alguna vez?
Have you ever seen her?
una vez
once
La veo una vez a la semana.
I see her once a week.
dos veces
twice

a veces
sometimes
algunas veces
sometimes
de vez en cuando
from time to time
en vez de
instead of
otra vez
again
tal vez
maybe

vi VERB ▷ *see* **ver**
  Lo vi ayer.
  I saw him yesterday.

viajar VERB
  to travel
  viajar en autocar
  to travel by coach

el **viaje** NOUN
  1 trip
  ¡Buen viaje!
  Have a good trip!
  2 journey
  Es un viaje muy largo.
  It's a very long journey.

  estar de viaje
  to be away

el **viajero**
  la **viajera** NOUN
  passenger

la **vida** NOUN
  life
  He vivido aquí toda mi vida.
  I've lived here all my life.

el **vídeo** NOUN
  video

la **videocámara** NOUN
  video camera

el **videojuego** NOUN
  video game

el **vidrio** NOUN
  glass
  botellas de vidrio
  glass bottles
  Me corté el dedo con un vidrio.
  I cut my finger on a piece of glass.

viejo (FEM **vieja**)

  viejo can be an adjective or a noun.

A ADJECTIVE
  old
  un viejo amigo mío
  an old friend of mine
  Estos zapatos ya están muy viejos.
  These shoes are very old now.
B MASC/FEM NOUN
  un viejo
  an old man
  una vieja
  an old woman
  los viejos
  old people

viene VERB ▷ *see* **venir**
  ¿Viene o no?
  Is she coming or not?

el **viento** NOUN
  wind

el **vientre** NOUN
  stomach

el **viernes** (PL los **viernes**) NOUN
  Friday

LANGUAGE TIP
Days are not spelled with a capital letter in Spanish.

La vi el viernes.
I saw her on Friday.
Viernes Santo
Good Friday

todos los viernes
every Friday
el viernes pasado
last Friday
el viernes que viene
next Friday

vigilar VERB
1 **to guard**
Un policía vigilaba al preso.
A policeman was guarding the prisoner.
2 **to watch**
Nos vigilan.
They're watching us.

el **vinagre** NOUN
vinegar

vine VERB ▷ *see* venir
Vine sola.
I came on my own.

viniendo VERB ▷ *see* venir
¿Nos veías viniendo por la montaña?
Could you see us coming down the mountain?

el **vino** NOUN
wine
vino blanco
white wine
vino tinto
red wine

la **violencia** NOUN
violence

violento (FEM **violenta**) ADJECTIVE
violent

el **violín** (PL los **violines**) NOUN
violin

el/la **violinista**
NOUN
violinist

el **virus** (PL los **virus**) NOUN
virus

visible (FEM **visible**) ADJECTIVE
visible

la **visión** (PL las **visiones**) NOUN
vision
la visión nocturna
night vision

la **visita** NOUN
1 **visit**
hacer una visita a alguien
to visit somebody
Hice una visita a mi abuela.
I visited my grandmother.
2 **visitor**
Tienes visita.
You've got visitors.
horario de visita
visiting hours

visitar VERB
to visit
Fuimos a visitar a mis tíos.
We went to visit my aunt and uncle.

la **víspera** NOUN
the day before
la víspera del partido
the day before the match

la **vista** NOUN
1 **sight**

conocer a alguien de vista
to know somebody by sight
La conozco de vista.
I know her by sight.
2 **view**
una habitación con vistas al mar
a room with a sea view

¡Hasta la vista!
See you!

el **vistazo** NOUN
echar un vistazo a algo
to have a look at something
Échale un vistazo a esta revista.
Have a look at this magazine.

vistiendo VERB ▷ see **vestir**
Se está vistiendo.
She's getting dressed.

visto (FEM **vista**)

visto can be an adjective or part of the verb **ver**.

A ADJECTIVE
Está visto que ...
It's clear that ...

por lo visto
apparently

B VERB ▷ see **ver**
¿Has visto a Elena?
Have you seen Elena?

viuda

viuda can be an adjective or a noun.

A ADJECTIVE
Es viuda.
She's a widow.
B FEM NOUN
widow

viudo

viudo can be an adjective or a noun.

A ADJECTIVE
Es viudo.
He's a widower.

B MASC NOUN
widower

vivir VERB
1 **to live**
¿Dónde vives?
Where do you live?
2 **to be alive**
¿Todavía vive?
Is he still alive?

¡Viva!
Hurray!

vivo (FEM **viva**) ADJECTIVE
1 **alive**
Estaba vivo.
He was alive.
en vivo
live
una retransmisión en vivo
a live broadcast
2 **bright**

el **vocabulario** NOUN
vocabulary

la **vocal** NOUN
vowel

el **volante** NOUN
steering wheel

volar VERB
to fly
El helicóptero volaba muy bajo.
The helicopter was flying very low.
Se me pasó la semana volando.
The week just flew by.
Tuvimos que ir volando al hospital.
We had to rush to the hospital.

el **voleibol** NOUN
volleyball

la **voltereta** NOUN
somersault
dar una voltereta
to do a somersault

el **volumen** (PL los **volúmenes**) NOUN
volume
bajar el volumen
to turn the volume down
subir el volumen
to turn the volume up

la **voluntad** NOUN
1 **will**
Lo hizo contra mi voluntad.
He did it against my will.
2 **willpower**
Le cuesta, pero tiene mucha voluntad.
It's difficult for him, but he has a lot of willpower.

voluntario (FEM **voluntaria**)

> **voluntario** can be an adjective or a noun.

A ADJECTIVE
voluntary
B MASC/FEM NOUN
volunteer

volver VERB
1 **to come back**
2 **to go back**
3 **to turn**
Me volvió la espalda.
He turned away from me.
Me volví para ver quién era.
I turned round to see who it was.
4 **to become**
Se ha vuelto muy cariñoso.
He's become very affectionate.
5 **volver a hacer algo**
to do something again
Volví a abrir la puerta.
I opened the door again.

vomitar VERB
to be sick
Ha vomitado dos veces.
He's been sick twice.
Vomitó todo lo que había comido.
He threw up everything he'd eaten.

votar VERB
to vote
Voté por Alcántara.
I voted for Alcántara.

voy VERB ▷ see **ir**
Voy al parque.
I'm going to the park.

la **voz** (PL las **voces**) NOUN
voice
No tengo buena voz.
I don't have a very good voice.

vuelo

> **vuelo** can be a noun or part of the verb **volar**.

A MASC NOUN
flight
B VERB ▷ see **volar**
Esta vez vuelo en primera clase.
I'm flying first class this time.

la **vuelta** NOUN
1 **return**
un billete de ida y vuelta
a return ticket
2 **lap**
Di tres vueltas a la pista.
I did three laps of the track.
3 **change**
Quédese con la vuelta.
Keep the change.
Vive a la vuelta de la esquina.
He lives round the corner.
dar una vuelta
to go for a walk/to go for a drive

LANGUAGE TIP
dar una vuelta has two meanings. It can be translated as **to go for a walk** and **to go for a drive**.

vuelto VERB ▷ see **volver**
Ya ha vuelto del viaje.
He's back from his trip already.

vuelvo VERB ▷ *see* **volver**
    Mañana vuelvo.
    I'll be back tomorrow.

vuestro (FEM **vuestra**)

> **vuestro** can be an adjective or a pronoun.

A ADJECTIVE
    your
    vuestra casa
    your house
    vuestros amigos
    your friends

    un amigo vuestro
    a friend of yours

B PRONOUN
    yours
    ¿Son vuestros?
    Are they yours?
    ¿Es ésta la vuestra?
    Is this one yours?
    ¿Y los bocadillos? — Los vuestros están aquí.
    Where are the sandwiches? — Yours are over here.

English

Spanish

a
b
c
d
e
f
g
h
i
j
k
l
m
n
o
p
q
r
s
t
u
v
w
x
y
z

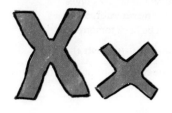

English

Spanish

el **wáter** NOUN
loo

LANGUAGE TIP
Be careful! **wáter** does not mean **water**.

---

la **web** NOUN
1 **website**
2 **(World Wide) Web**

la **webcam** NOUN
webcam

el **windsurf** NOUN
windsurfing

WWW ABBREVIATION
(= World Wide Web)
WWW

el **xilófono** NOUN
xylophone

A
B
C
D
E
F
G
H
I
J
K
L
M
N
O
P
Q
R
S
T
U
V
W
X
Y
Z

Yy

y CONJUNCTION
and
Andrés y su novia.
Andrés and his girlfriend.
Yo quiero una ensalada. ¿Y tú?
I'd like a salad. What about you?
Son las tres y cinco.
It's five minutes past three.

ya ADVERB
already
Ya se han ido.
They've already left.
¿Ya has terminado?
Have you finished already?
ya no
not ... any more
Ya no salimos juntos.
We aren't going out together any more.

> **ya que**
> since
> **Ya lo sé.**
> I know.
> **¡Ya voy!**
> I'm coming!

el yate NOUN
yacht

la yema NOUN
1 **yolk**
2 **fingertip**

yendo VERB ▷ *see* ir
Llevo todo el día yendo y viniendo.
I've spent all day coming and going.

el yeso NOUN
plaster

yo PRONOUN
1 **I**
Carlos y yo no fuimos.
Carlos and I didn't go.
2 **me**
¿Quién ha visto la película?
— Ana y yo.
Who's seen the film? — Ana and me.
Es más alta que yo.
She's taller than me.
Soy yo, María.
It's me, María.
yo mismo
myself
Lo hice yo misma.
I did it myself.

> **¡Yo también!**
> Me too!
> **yo que tú**
> if I were you

el yoga NOUN
yoga

el yogur NOUN
yoghurt

a
b
c
d
e
f
g
h
i
j
k
l
m
n
o
p
q
r
s
t
u
v
w
x
y
z

English

Spanish

A
B
C
D
E
F
G
H
I
J
K
L
M
N
O
P
Q
R
S
T
U
V
W
X
Y
Z

Z z

zamparse VERB
to wolf down
> **Se zampó todas las galletas.**
> He wolfed down all the biscuits.

la **zanahoria** NOUN
carrot

la **zancadilla** NOUN
> **Me puso la zancadilla.**
> He tripped me up.

la **zanja** NOUN
ditch

la **zapatería** NOUN
shoe shop

la **zapatilla** NOUN
slipper
> **Tráeme las zapatillas.**
> Bring me my slippers.
> **zapatillas de ballet**
> ballet shoes
> **zapatillas de deporte**
> trainers

el **zapato** NOUN
shoe
> **zapatos cómodos**
> comfortable shoes
> **zapatos de tacón**
> high-heeled shoes

el **zapping** NOUN
channel hopping
> **hacer zapping**
> to channel-hop

la **zona** NOUN
area
> **Viven en una zona muy tranquila.**
> They live in a very quiet area.
> **una zona peatonal**
> a pedestrian precinct
> **una zona verde**
> a green space

el **zoo** NOUN
zoo

el **zoológico** NOUN
zoo

el **zorro** NOUN
fox

zumbar VERB
to buzz
> **Me zumban los oídos.**
> My ears are buzzing.

el **zumo** NOUN
juice
> **zumo de naranja**
> orange juice

zurdo (FEM **zurda**) ADJECTIVE
1 **left-handed**
2 **left-footed**

zurrar VERB
to thrash

Language Plus

Contents

Animals   270
The body   273
Clothes   275
Colours   278
Family   279
Days and dates   281
The weather   282
Seasons   283
Places   284
Food   287
Fruit and vegetables   291
Drinks   293
In the home   294
Instruments   296
Jobs   297
Sports   301
At school   303
School subjects   306
Phones and computing   307
The environment   308
Numbers   309
Time   310
Spanish verbs   311

Animals | Los animales

Pets | Los animales domésticos

budgie NOUN el **periquito**

canary NOUN el **canario**

cat NOUN el **gato**

dog NOUN el **perro**

ferret NOUN el **hurón**

gerbil NOUN el **jerbo**

goldfish NOUN el **pez de colores** (PL los **peces de colores**)

guinea pig NOUN el **conejillo de Indias**

hamster NOUN el **hámster** (PL los **hámsters**)

kitten NOUN el **gatito**

mouse NOUN el **ratón** (PL los **ratones**)

parrot NOUN el **loro**

poodle NOUN el **caniche**

puppy NOUN el **cachorro**

rabbit NOUN el **conejo**

tortoise NOUN la **tortuga**

Farm animals | Los animales de la granja

bull NOUN el **toro**

calf NOUN el **ternero**

chick NOUN el **polluelo**

chicken NOUN el **pollo**

cock NOUN el **gallo**

cow NOUN la **vaca**

donkey NOUN el **burro**

duck NOUN el **pato**

goat NOUN la **cabra**

goose NOUN la **oca**

hen NOUN la **gallina**

horse NOUN el **caballo**

lamb NOUN el **cordero**

mare NOUN la **yegua**

peacock NOUN el **pavo real**

pheasant NOUN el **faisán** (PL los **faisanes**)

pig NOUN el **cerdo**

pony NOUN el **poni** (PL los **ponis**)

ram NOUN el **carnero**

sheep NOUN la **oveja**

sheepdog NOUN el **perro pastor**

turkey NOUN el **pavo**

Other animals | Otros animales

ant NOUN la **hormiga**

ape NOUN el **simio**

bat NOUN el **murciélago**

bear NOUN el **oso**

bee NOUN la **abeja**

beetle NOUN el **escarabajo**

bird NOUN el **pájaro**

butterfly NOUN la **mariposa**

camel NOUN el **camello** (*two humps*)

camel NOUN el **dromedario**
(*one hump*)

cheetah NOUN el **guepardo**

crab NOUN el **cangrejo**

crocodile NOUN el **cocodrilo**

cub NOUN el **cachorro**

deer NOUN el **ciervo**

dinosaur NOUN el **dinosaurio**

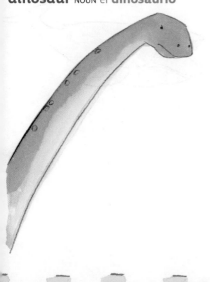

dolphin NOUN el **delfín**
(PL los **delfines**)

dragon NOUN el **dragón**

duck NOUN el **pato**

elephant NOUN el **elefante**

fish NOUN el **pez** (PL los **peces**)

fly NOUN la **mosca**

fox NOUN el **zorro**

frog NOUN la **rana**

giraffe NOUN la **jirafa**

gorilla NOUN el **gorila**

hare NOUN la **liebre**

hedgehog NOUN el **erizo**

hippo NOUN el **hipopótamo**

insect NOUN el **insecto**

jellyfish NOUN la **medusa**

kangaroo NOUN el **canguro**

koala NOUN el **koala**

ladybird NOUN la **mariquita**

leopard NOUN el **leopardo**

lion NOUN el **león** (PL los **leones**)

lioness NOUN la **leona**

lizard NOUN el **lagarto**

mammoth NOUN el **mamut**

midge NOUN el **mosquito**

mole NOUN el **topo**

monkey NOUN el **mono**

mosquito NOUN el **mosquito**

moth NOUN la **polilla**

octopus NOUN el **pulpo**

ostrich NOUN el **avestruz**
(PL los **avestruces**)

owl NOUN el **búho**

panther NOUN la **pantera**

peacock NOUN el **pavo real**

penguin NOUN el **pingüino**

pigeon NOUN la **paloma**

polar bear NOUN el **oso polar**

rat NOUN la **rata**

raven NOUN el **cuervo**

reindeer NOUN el **reno**

reptile NOUN el **reptil**

rhino NOUN el **rinoceronte**

robin NOUN el **petirrojo**

seagull NOUN la **gaviota**

seal NOUN la **foca**

shark NOUN el **tiburón**
(PL los **tiburones**)

slug NOUN la **babosa**

snail NOUN el **caracol**

snake NOUN la **serpiente**

sparrow NOUN el **gorrión**
(PL los **gorriones**)

spider NOUN la **araña**

squirrel NOUN la **ardilla**

swallow NOUN la **golondrina**

swan NOUN el **cisne**

tadpole NOUN el **renacuajo**

tiger NOUN el **tigre**

toad NOUN el **sapo**

trout NOUN la **trucha**

turtle NOUN la **tortuga de mar**

wasp NOUN la **avispa**

whale NOUN la **ballena**

wolf NOUN el **lobo**

worm NOUN el **gusano**

zebra NOUN la **cebra**

Remember that if the word has **la** in front of it, it is feminine, if it has **el** in front of it, it is masculine.

The body | El cuerpo humano

ankle NOUN el **tobillo**

arm NOUN el **brazo**

back NOUN la **espalda**

beard NOUN la **barba**

blood NOUN la **sangre**

body NOUN el **cuerpo**

bottom NOUN el **culo**

brain NOUN el **cerebro**

cheek NOUN la **mejilla**

chest NOUN el **pecho**

chin NOUN la **barbilla**

ear NOUN la **oreja**

elbow NOUN el **codo**

eye NOUN el **ojo**

eyebrow NOUN la **ceja**

eyelash NOUN la **pestaña**

eyelid NOUN el **párpado**

face NOUN la **cara**

finger NOUN el **dedo** (**de la mano**)

fist NOUN el **puño**

foot NOUN el **pie**

forehead NOUN la **frente**

freckles NOUN las **pecas**

fringe NOUN el **flequillo**

hair NOUN el **pelo**

hand NOUN la **mano**

head NOUN la **cabeza**

heart NOUN el **corazón**
(PL los **corazones**)

heel NOUN el **talón**
(PL los **talones**)

hip NOUN la **cadera**

jaw NOUN la **mandíbula**

kidney NOUN el **riñón**
(PL los **riñones**)

knee NOUN la **rodilla**

leg NOUN la **pierna**

lip NOUN el **labio**

liver NOUN el **hígado**

lung NOUN el **pulmón** (PL los **pulmones**)

moustache NOUN el **bigote**

mouth NOUN la **boca**

muscle NOUN el **músculo**

nail NOUN la **uña**

neck NOUN el **cuello**

nerve NOUN el **nervio**

nose NOUN la **nariz** (PL las **narices**)

organ NOUN el **órgano**

palm NOUN la **palma**

rib NOUN la **costilla**

shin NOUN la **tibia**

shoulder NOUN el **hombro**

skeleton NOUN el **esqueleto**

skin NOUN la **piel**

skull NOUN el **cráneo**

spine NOUN la **columna vertebral**

stomach NOUN el **estómago**

thigh NOUN el **muslo**

throat NOUN la **garganta**

thumb NOUN el **pulgar**

toe NOUN el **dedo** (del pie)

tongue NOUN la **lengua**

tonsils NOUN PL las **amígdalas**

tooth NOUN el **diente**

tummy NOUN la **barriga**

waist NOUN la **cintura**

wrist NOUN la **muñeca**

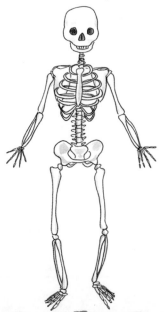

Remember that if the word has **la** in front of it, it is feminine, if it has **el** in front of it, it is masculine.

Clothes | La ropa

anorak NOUN el **anorak**

apron NOUN el **delantal**

ballet shoes NOUN PL
las **zapatillas de ballet**

baseball cap NOUN la **gorra de béisbol**

belt NOUN el **cinturón**
(PL los **cinturones**)

beret NOUN la **boina**

bikini NOUN el **bikini**

blazer NOUN el **blazer**

blouse NOUN la **blusa**

boots NOUN PL las **botas**

bow tie NOUN la **pajarita**

boxer shorts NOUN el **boxer**

bra NOUN el **sujetador**

cagoule NOUN el **chubasquero**

cap NOUN la **gorra**

cardigan NOUN la **rebeca**

clothes NOUN la **ropa**

coat NOUN el **abrigo**

dress NOUN el **vestido**

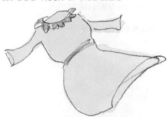

dressing gown NOUN
la **bata**

dungarees NOUN el **peto**

fleece NOUN el **forro polar**

flippers NOUN PL las **aletas**

football boots NOUN PL
las **botas de fútbol**

football shirt NOUN
la **camiseta de fútbol**

glasses NOUN PL
las **gafas**

glove NOUN el **guante**

goggles NOUN PL las **gafas de piscina**

hat NOUN el **sombrero**

helmet NOUN el **casco**

hood NOUN la **capucha**

hoodie NOUN la **sudadera con capucha**

jacket NOUN la **chaqueta**

jeans NOUN PL los **vaqueros**

jumper NOUN el **jersey**

kilt NOUN la **falda escocesa**

knickers NOUN PL las **bragas**

leather jacket NOUN la **chaqueta de cuero**

leggings NOUN PL las **mallas**

miniskirt NOUN PL la **minifalda**

nightie NOUN el **camisón**

overall NOUN la **bata**

overalls NOUN PL el **mono (de trabajo)**

pants NOUN PL las **bragas** (*women's*)

pants NOUN PL los **calzoncillos** (*men's*)

plimsolls NOUN PL las **bailarinas**

polo neck NOUN el **polo**

polo shirt NOUN el **polo**

pullover NOUN el **jersey**

pyjamas NOUN el **pijama**

raincoat NOUN el **impermeable**

sandals NOUN PL las **sandalias**

scarf NOUN la **bufanda**

shirt NOUN la **camisa**

shoes NOUN PL los **zapatos**

shorts NOUN PL los **pantalones cortos**

ski boots NOUN PL las **botas de esquí**

skirt NOUN la **falda**

slippers NOUN PL las **zapatillas**

sock NOUN el **calcetín**
(PL los **calcetines**)

suit NOUN el **traje**

sunglasses NOUN PL las **gafas de sol**

sweater NOUN la **suéter**

sweatshirt NOUN la **sudadera**

swimming costume NOUN el **bañador (de mujer)**

swimsuit NOUN el **bañador**

tie NOUN la **corbata**

tights NOUN las **medias**

top NOUN el **top**

tracksuit NOUN el **chándal**
(PL los **chándals**)

trainers NOUN PL las **zapatillas de deporte**

trousers NOUN PL los **pantalones**

trunks NOUN PL el **bañador (de hombre)**

T-shirt NOUN la **camiseta**

underpants NOUN PL los **calzoncillos**

underwear NOUN la **ropa interior**

uniform NOUN el **uniforme**

vest NOUN la **camiseta**

waistcoat NOUN el **chaleco**

wellingtons NOUN PL las **botas de agua**

wetsuit NOUN el **traje de neopreno**

Colours | Los colores

beige ADJ beige
(FEM, PL **beige**)

black ADJ negro (FEM **negra**)

blonde ADJ rubio
(FEM **rubia**)

blue ADJ azul (FEM **azul**)

brown ADJ marrón
(FEM **marrón**)

cream ADJ crema
(FEM, PL **crema**)

green ADJ verde (FEM **verde**)

grey ADJ gris (FEM **gris**)

maroon ADJ burdeos
(FEM, PL **burdeos**)

navy blue ADJ azul
marino (FEM, PL **azul marino**)

orange ADJ naranja
(FEM, PL **naranja**)

pink ADJ rosa (FEM, PL **rosa**)

purple ADJ morado
(FEM **morada**)

red ADJ rojo (FEM **roja**)

turquoise ADJ turquesa
(FEM, PL **turquesa**)

white ADJ blanco
(FEM **blanca**)

yellow ADJ amarillo
(FEM **amarilla**)

Family | La familia

aunt NOUN la **tía**
baby NOUN el **bebé**
brother NOUN el **hermano**
brother-in-law NOUN el **cuñado**
child NOUN la **niña** (girl)
child NOUN el **niño** (boy)
cousin NOUN la **prima** (girl)
cousin NOUN el **primo** (boy)
dad NOUN el **papá**

daughter NOUN la **hija**
daughter-in-law NOUN la **nuera**
family NOUN la **familia**
father NOUN el **padre**
father-in-law NOUN el **suegro**
fiancé NOUN el **prometido**
fiancée NOUN la **prometida**

godfather NOUN el **padrino**
godmother NOUN la **madrina**
grandchildren NOUN PL los **nietos**
granddad NOUN el **abuelo**
granddaughter NOUN la **nieta**
grandfather NOUN el **abuelo**
grandma NOUN la **abuela**

grandmother NOUN la **abuela**
grandpa NOUN el **abuelo**
grandparents NOUN PL los **abuelos**
grandson NOUN el **nieto**
granny NOUN la **abuela**
half-brother NOUN el **hermanastro**
half-sister NOUN la **hermanastra**
husband NOUN el **marido**
in-laws NOUN PL los **suegros**
mother NOUN la **madre**
mother-in-law NOUN la **suegra**
mum NOUN la **mamá**

nephew NOUN el **sobrino**

niece NOUN la **sobrina**

parent NOUN el **padre** (*man*)

parent NOUN la **madre** (*woman*)

parents NOUN los **padres**

sister NOUN la **hermana**

sister-in-law NOUN la **cuñada**

son NOUN el **hijo**

son-in-law NOUN el **yerno**

stepbrother NOUN el **hermanastro**

stepdaughter NOUN la **hijastra**

stepfather NOUN el **padrastro**

stepmother NOUN la **madrastra**

stepsister NOUN la **hermanastra**

stepson NOUN el **hijastro**

twins NOUN PL los **mellizos**
(*not identical*)

twins NOUN PL los **gemelos**
(*identical*)

uncle NOUN el **tío**

wife NOUN la **mujer**

Remember that if the word has **la** in front of it, it is feminine, if it has **el** in front of it, it is masculine.

Days and dates | Los días y la fecha

Days of the week | Los días de la semana

Monday el lunes

Tuesday el martes

Wednesday el miércoles

Thursday el jueves

Friday el viernes

Saturday el sábado

Sunday el domingo

Months of the year | Los meses del año

January enero

February febrero

March marzo

April abril

May mayo

June junio

July julio

August agosto

September septiembre

October octubre

November noviembre

December diciembre

Special days | Fiestas señaladas

Christmas NOUN la Navidad

Christmas Eve NOUN la Nochebuena

Diwali NOUN el Diwali

Easter NOUN la Semana Santa

Father's Day NOUN el Día del Padre

Hanukkah NOUN la Janucá

Mother's Day NOUN el Día de la Madre

New Year's Day NOUN el Día de Año Nuevo

New Year's Eve NOUN la Nochevieja

Pancake Day NOUN el martes de Carnaval

Ramadan NOUN el Ramadán

Valentine's Day NOUN el Día de San Valentín

The weather | El tiempo

It's chilly. Hace fresco.

It's cloudy. Está nublado.

It's cold.
Hace frío.

It's foggy.
Hay niebla.

It's freezing.
Hace mucho frío.

It's frosty. Hay escarcha.

It's hot. Hace calor.

It's icy. Hay hielo.

It's misty. Hay neblina.

It's nice. Hace buen tiempo.

It's overcast. El cielo está nublado.

It's raining. Llueve.

It's snowing. Nieva.

It's stormy. Hay tormenta.

It's sunny. Hace sol.

It's warm. Hace calor.

It's windy.
Hace viento.

Seasons | Las estaciones del año

spring NOUN
la **primavera**

summer NOUN
el **verano**

autumn NOUN
el **otoño**

winter NOUN
el **invierno**

Places | Los lugares

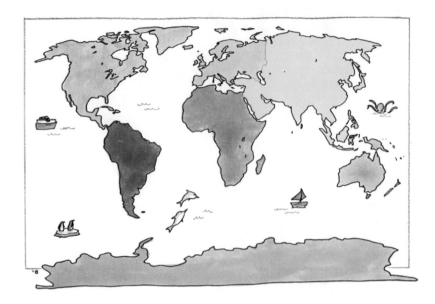

Africa NOUN África

Albania NOUN Albania

Algeria NOUN Argelia

America NOUN América

Asia NOUN Asia

Australia NOUN Australia

Austria NOUN Austria

Belgium NOUN Bélgica

Brazil NOUN Brasil

Brussels NOUN Bruselas

Bulgaria NOUN Bulgaria

Canada NOUN Canadá

Central America NOUN
América Central

China NOUN China

Cornwall NOUN Cornualles

Corsica NOUN Córcega

Croatia NOUN Croacia

Cyprus NOUN Chipre

Czech Republic NOUN
la República Checa

Denmark NOUN Dinamarca

Dublin NOUN Dublín

Edinburgh NOUN Edimburgo

Egypt NOUN Egipto

Eire NOUN la República de Irlanda

England NOUN Inglaterra

Estonia NOUN Estonía

Ethiopia NOUN Etiopía
Europe NOUN Europa
Far East NOUN Extremo Oriente
Finland NOUN Finlandia
France NOUN Francia

Germany NOUN Alemania
Great Britain NOUN Gran Bretaña
Greece NOUN Grecia
Greenland NOUN Groenlandia
Holland NOUN Holanda
Hungary NOUN Hungría
Iceland NOUN Islandia
India NOUN India
Iran NOUN Irán
Iraq NOUN Irak
Ireland NOUN Irlanda
Israel NOUN Israel
Italy NOUN Italia
Japan NOUN Japón
Jordan NOUN Jordania
Korea NOUN Corea
Lapland NOUN Laponia

Latin America NOUN América Latina
Latvia NOUN Letonia
Lebanon NOUN Líbano
Libya NOUN Libia
Lithuania NOUN Lituania
London NOUN Londres
Luxembourg NOUN Luxemburgo
Majorca NOUN Mallorca
Malaysia NOUN Malasia
Malta NOUN Malta
Mexico NOUN México
Middle East NOUN Oriente Medio
Milan NOUN Milán
Monaco NOUN Mónaco
Morocco NOUN Marruecos
Naples NOUN Nápoles
New Zealand NOUN Nueva Zelanda
North America NOUN América del Norte
Northern Ireland NOUN Irlanda del Norte
North Korea NOUN Corea del Norte
Norway NOUN Noruega
Orkney NOUN las Órcadas
Pakistan NOUN Paquistán
Palestine NOUN Palestina
Paris NOUN París
Poland NOUN Polonia

Portugal NOUN Portugal

Romania NOUN Rumania

Rome NOUN Roma

Russia NOUN Rusia

Sardinia NOUN Cerdeña

Saudi Arabia NOUN Arabia Saudí

Scandinavia NOUN los países escandinavos

Scotland NOUN Escocia

Shetland NOUN las Shetland

Sicily NOUN Sicilia

Slovakia NOUN Eslovaquia

Slovenia NOUN Eslovenia

South Africa NOUN Sudáfrica

South America NOUN Sudamérica

South Korea NOUN Corea del Sur

Spain NOUN España

Sweden NOUN Suecia

Switzerland NOUN Suiza

Syria NOUN Siria

the Alps NOUN PL los Alpes

the Atlantic NOUN el Atlántico

the British Isles las Islas Británicas

the Caribbean NOUN el Caribe

the Czech Republic NOUN la República Checa

the English Channel NOUN el Canal de la Mancha

the Mediterranean NOUN el Mediterráneo

the Netherlands NOUN PL los Países Bajos

the North Pole NOUN el Polo Norte

the North Sea NOUN el Mar del Norte

the South Pole NOUN el Polo Sur

the Thames NOUN el Támesis

the UK NOUN el Reino Unido

the United Kingdom NOUN el Reino Unido

the United States NOUN PL los Estados Unidos

the US NOUN los EE. UU.

the West Indies NOUN PL las Antillas

Tunisia NOUN Túnez

Turkey NOUN Turquía

Vietnam NOUN Vietnam

Wales NOUN Gales

Food | Los alimentos

Savoury | Alimentos salados

bacon NOUN la **panceta**

baked potato NOUN la **patata asada (con piel)**

beans NOUN PL las **alubias**

beef NOUN la **carne de vaca**

beefburger NOUN la **hamburguesa**

biscuit NOUN la **galleta**

bread NOUN el **pan**

burger NOUN la **hamburguesa**

butter NOUN la **mantequilla**

cereal NOUN los **cereales**

cheese NOUN el **queso**

chicken NOUN el **pollo**

chips NOUN la **patatas fritas**

chop NOUN la **chuleta**

cod NOUN el **bacalao**

corn on the cob NOUN la **mazorca de maíz**

cracker NOUN la **galleta salada**

cream NOUN la **nata**

cream cheese NOUN el **queso para untar**

crisps NOUN las **patatas fritas (de bolsa)**

egg NOUN el **huevo**

fish NOUN el **pescado**

fish fingers NOUN PL los **palitos de pescado**

French fries NOUN PL las **patatas fritas**

fried egg NOUN el **huevo frito**

garlic NOUN el **ajo**

gravy NOUN el **jugo de carne**

ham NOUN el **jamón**

hard-boiled egg NOUN el **huevo cocido**

herbs NOUN PL las **hierbas aromáticas**

hot dog NOUN el **perrito caliente**

ketchup NOUN el **ketchup**

kidney NOUN el **riñón** (PL los **riñones**)

lamb NOUN el **cordero**

lamb chop NOUN la **chuleta de cordero**

lentils NOUN PL las **lentejas**

liver NOUN el **hígado**

loaf of bread NOUN el **pan**

lobster NOUN la **langosta**

macaroni NOUN los **macarrones**

mackerel NOUN la **caballa**

margarine NOUN la **margarina**

mashed potatoes NOUN el **puré de patatas**

mayonnaise NOUN la **mayonesa**

meat NOUN la **carne**

mince NOUN la **carne picada**

muesli NOUN el **muesli**

mussel NOUN el **mejillón** (PL los **mejillones**)

mustard NOUN la **mostaza**

noodles NOUN PL los **fideos**

oats NOUN la **avena**

oil NOUN el **aceite**

olive NOUN la **aceituna**

olive oil NOUN el **aceite de oliva**

omelette NOUN la **tortilla**

oyster NOUN la **ostra**

parsley NOUN el **perejil**

pasta NOUN la **pasta**

pâté NOUN el **paté**

pepper NOUN la **pimienta**

pizza NOUN la **pizza**

pork NOUN la **carne de cerdo**

potato NOUN la **patata**

prawn NOUN la **gamba**

rice NOUN el **arroz**

roast potatoes NOUN las **patatas asadas**

roll NOUN el **bollo**

rye NOUN el **centeno**

rye bread NOUN el **pan de centeno**

salad NOUN la **ensalada**

salad dressing NOUN el **aliño**

salami NOUN el **salami**

salmon NOUN el **salmón**

salt NOUN la **sal**

sandwich NOUN el **bocadillo**

sardine NOUN la **sardina**

sauce NOUN la **salsa**

sausage NOUN la **salchicha**

scampi NOUN las **gambas rebozadas**

scrambled eggs NOUN PL los **huevos revueltos**

seafood NOUN el **marisco**

shellfish NOUN el **marisco**

shrimps NOUN PL los **camarones**

soft-boiled egg NOUN el **huevo pasado por agua**

soup NOUN la **sopa**

soy sauce NOUN la **salsa de soja**

spaghetti NOUN los **espaguetis**

steak NOUN el **bistec**

stew NOUN el **estofado**

sweetcorn NOUN el **maíz (dulce)**

thyme NOUN el **tomillo**

toast NOUN las **tostadas**

toasted sandwich NOUN el **sándwich caliente**

trout NOUN la **trucha**

tuna NOUN el **atún**

turkey NOUN el **pavo**

veal NOUN la **ternera**

vinegar NOUN el **vinagre**

wheat NOUN el **trigo**

wholemeal bread NOUN el **pan integral**

Sweet | Alimentos dulces

apple tart NOUN la **tarta de manzana**

biscuit NOUN la **galleta**

cake NOUN el **pastel** (*small*)

cake NOUN la **tarta** (*big*)

candyfloss NOUN el **algodón de azúcar**

caramel NOUN el **caramelo líquido**

chewing gum NOUN el **chicle**

chocolate NOUN el **chocolate**

chocolate mousse NOUN la **mousse de chocolate**

cone NOUN el **cucurucho**

cream NOUN la **nata**

cream cake NOUN la **tarta de nata**

crème caramel NOUN el **flan**

custard NOUN las **natillas**

dessert NOUN el **postre**

doughnut NOUN el **dónut**

fruit salad NOUN la **macedonia**

honey NOUN la **miel**

ice cream NOUN el **helado**

ice lolly NOUN el **polo**

jam NOUN la **mermelada**

jelly NOUN la **gelatina**

lollipop NOUN el **pirulí**

marmalade NOUN la **mermelada de naranja**

marzipan NOUN el **mazapán**

meringue NOUN el **merengue**

mint NOUN el **caramelo de menta**

mousse NOUN la **mousse**

pancake NOUN la **tortita**

popcorn NOUN las **palomitas**

pudding NOUN el **postre**

rice pudding NOUN el **arroz con leche**

sponge cake NOUN el **bizcocho**

sugar NOUN el **azúcar**

sweet NOUN el **caramelo**

tart NOUN la **tarta**

vanilla NOUN la **vainilla**

whipped cream NOUN la **nata montada**

yoghurt NOUN el **yogur**

Remember that if the word has **la** in front of it, it is feminine, if it has **el** in front of it, it is masculine.

Fruit and vegetables | La fruta y la verdura

apple NOUN la **manzana**

apricot NOUN el **albaricoque**

aubergine NOUN la **berenjena**

avocado NOUN el **aguacate**

banana NOUN
el **plátano**

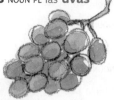

beetroot NOUN
la **remolacha**

blackberry NOUN la **mora**

blackcurrant NOUN la **grosella negra**

blueberry NOUN el **arándano**

broccoli NOUN el **brécol**

Brussels sprouts NOUN PL
las **coles de Bruselas**

cabbage NOUN la **col**

carrot NOUN la **zanahoria**

cauliflower NOUN la **coliflor**

celery NOUN el **apio**

cherry NOUN la **cereza**

chestnut NOUN la **castaña**

clementine NOUN
la **clementina**

coconut NOUN el **coco**

courgette NOUN el **calabacín**
(PL los **calabacines**)

cress NOUN el **berro**

cucumber NOUN el **pepino**

currant NOUN la **pasa de Corinto**

French beans NOUN PL
las **judías verdes**

fruit NOUN la **fruta**

fruit salad NOUN la **macedonia**

gooseberry NOUN la **grosella espinosa**

grapefruit NOUN el **pomelo**

grapes NOUN PL las **uvas**

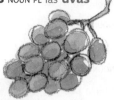

hazelnut NOUN la **avellana**

leek NOUN el **puerro**

lemon NOUN el **limón** (PL los **limones**)

lettuce NOUN la **lechuga**

lime NOUN la **lima**

mango NOUN el **mango**

melon NOUN el **melón** (PL los **melones**)

mushroom NOUN el **champiñón**
(PL los **champiñones**)

mushroom NOUN la **seta** (*open-cup*)

onion NOUN la **cebolla**

orange NOUN la **naranja**

pea NOUN el **guisante**

peach NOUN el **melocotón**
(PL los **melocotones**)

peanut NOUN el **cacahuete**

pear NOUN la **pera**

pepper NOUN el **pimiento**

pineapple NOUN la **piña**

plum NOUN la **ciruela**

potato NOUN la **patata**

pumpkin NOUN la **calabaza**

radish NOUN el **rábano**

raisin NOUN la **pasa**

raspberry NOUN
la **frambuesa**

redcurrant NOUN la **grosella roja**

spinach NOUN
las **espinacas**

strawberry NOUN
la **fresa**

sultana NOUN
la **pasa sultana**

sweetcorn NOUN
el **maíz (dulce)**

tangerine NOUN la **mandarina**

tomato NOUN el **tomate**

turnip NOUN el **nabo**

vegetables NOUN PL las **verduras**

walnut NOUN la **nuez**

watermelon NOUN la **sandía**

Drinks | Las bebidas

apple juice NOUN el **zumo de manzana**

beer NOUN la **cerveza**

black coffee NOUN el **café solo**

champagne NOUN el **champán**

cocoa NOUN el **cacao**

coffee NOUN el **café**

Coke® NOUN la **Coca-Cola®**

decaffeinated coffee NOUN el **café descafeinado**

fruit juice NOUN el **zumo de fruta**

hot chocolate NOUN el **chocolate caliente**

juice NOUN el **zumo**

latte NOUN el **café con leche**

lemonade NOUN la **gaseosa**

milk NOUN la **leche**

milkshake NOUN el **batido**

mineral water NOUN el **agua mineral**

orange juice NOUN el **zumo de naranja**

peach juice NOUN el **zumo de melocotón**

pineapple juice NOUN el **zumo de piña**

soft drink NOUN el **refresco**

tea NOUN el **té**

tomato juice NOUN el **zumo de tomate**

water NOUN el **agua**

wine NOUN el **vino**

Remember that if the word has **la** in front of it, it is feminine, if it has **el** in front of it, it is masculine.

In the home | En casa

Rooms | Las habitaciones

attic NOUN el **desván**

basement NOUN el **sótano**

bedroom NOUN el **dormitorio**

dining room NOUN el **comedor**

garage NOUN el **garaje**

hall NOUN la **entrada**

kitchen NOUN la **cocina**

library NOUN la **biblioteca**

living room NOUN la **sala de estar**

lounge NOUN el **salón**
(PL los **salones**)

office NOUN la **oficina**

staircase NOUN la **escalera**

study NOUN el **despacho**

toilet NOUN el **baño**

Furniture | Los muebles

armchair NOUN el **sillón**
(PL los **sillones**)

bath tub NOUN la **bañera**

bed NOUN la **cama**

bench NOUN el **banco**

bookcase NOUN la **librería**

bookshelf NOUN la **estantería**

bunk beds NOUN PL las **camas literas**

chair NOUN la **silla**

chest of drawers NOUN la **cómoda**

coffee table NOUN la **mesa de centro**

cooker NOUN la **cocina**

couch NOUN el **sofá**

cupboard NOUN el **armario**

curtain NOUN la **cortina**

cushion NOUN el **cojín**
(PL los **cojines**)

deck chair NOUN la **tumbona**

sofa NOUN el **sofá**

dishwasher NOUN el **lavavajillas**
(PL los **lavavajillas**)

double bed NOUN la **cama de matrimonio**

easy chair NOUN la **butaca**

freezer NOUN el **congelador**

fridge NOUN la **nevera**

microwave NOUN el **microondas**
(PL los **microondas**)

oven NOUN el **horno**

picture NOUN el **cuadro**

refrigerator NOUN el **frigorífico**

rug NOUN la **alfombra**

settee NOUN el **sofá**

sink NOUN el **fregadero**

table NOUN la **mesa**

television NOUN la **televisión**

tumble dryer NOUN la **secadora**

wardrobe NOUN el **armario**

washing machine NOUN
la **lavadora**

Remember that if the word has **la** in front of it, it is feminine, if it has **el** in front of it, it is masculine.

Instruments | Los instrumentos

accordion NOUN el **acordeón**

bagpipes NOUN PL la **gaita**

bass drum NOUN el **bombo**

bass guitar NOUN el **bajo**

bassoon NOUN el **fagot**

cello NOUN el **violonchelo**

clarinet NOUN el **clarinete**

cornet NOUN la **corneta**

double bass NOUN el **contrabajo**

drum NOUN el **tambor**

drums NOUN la **batería**

electric guitar NOUN la **guitarra eléctrica**

horn NOUN la **trompa**

keyboards NOUN el **teclado**

mouth organ NOUN la **armónica**

oboe NOUN el **oboe**

organ NOUN el **órgano**

percussion NOUN la **percusión**

piano NOUN el **piano**

pipes NOUN PL la **gaita**

recorder NOUN la **flauta dulce**

flute NOUN la **flauta**

guitar NOUN la **guitarra**

saxophone NOUN el **saxofón**

trombone NOUN el **trombón**

trumpet NOUN la **trompeta**

tuba NOUN la **tuba**

viola NOUN la **viola**

violin NOUN el **violín**

Jobs | Las profesiones

Where the article is shown as el/la, it means that the same noun works for both males and females, eg el/la **contable** (**accountant**). Where two translations are given, the one that starts with el is the masculine form while the one that starts with la is the feminine form.

accountant NOUN el/la **contable**

actor NOUN el **actor**, la **actriz**

actress NOUN la **actriz**

architect NOUN el **arquitecto**, la **arquitecta**

artist NOUN el/la **artista**

athlete NOUN el/la **atleta**

au pair NOUN el/la **au pair**

author NOUN el **autor**, la **autora**

baker NOUN el **panadero**, la **panadera**

builder NOUN el/la **albañil**

bus driver NOUN el **conductor de autobús**, la **conductora de autobús**

butcher NOUN el **carnicero**, la **carnicera**

caretaker NOUN el **guardián**, la **guardiana**

carpenter NOUN el **carpintero**, la **carpintera**

chef NOUN el/la **chef**

child minder NOUN el/la **canguro**

cleaner NOUN el **limpiador**, la **limpiadora**

computer programmer NOUN el **programador**, la **programadora**

cook NOUN el **cocinero**, la **cocinera**

dancer NOUN el **bailarín** (PL los **bailarines**), la **bailarina**

dentist NOUN el/la **dentista**

detective NOUN el/la **detective**

disc jockey NOUN el/la **disc jockey**

doctor NOUN el **médico**, la **médica**

drummer NOUN el/la **batería**

electrician NOUN el/la **electricista**

engineer NOUN el **ingeniero**, la **ingeniera**

farmer NOUN el **agricultor**, la **agricultora**

film star NOUN la **estrella de cine**

firefighter NOUN el **bombero**, la **bombera**

fisherman NOUN el **pescador**

flight attendant NOUN el/la **auxiliar de vuelo**

florist NOUN el/la **florista**

footballer NOUN el/la **futbolista**

gardener NOUN el **jardinero**, la **jardinera**

goalkeeper NOUN el **portero**, la **portera**

hairdresser NOUN el **peluquero**, la **peluquera**

headteacher NOUN el **director de colegio**, la **directora de colegio**

imam NOUN el **imán**

instructor NOUN el **instructor**, la **instructora**

interior designer NOUN el **diseñador de interiores**, la **diseñadora de interiores**

interpreter NOUN el/la **intérprete**

interviewer NOUN el **entrevistador**, la **entrevistadora**

janitor NOUN el/la **conserje**

jockey NOUN el/la **jockey**

joiner NOUN el **carpintero**, la **carpintera**

journalist NOUN el/la **periodista**

judge NOUN el **juez**, la **jueza**

lawyer NOUN el **abogado**, la **abogada**

lecturer NOUN el **profesor universitario**, la **profesora universitaria**

librarian NOUN el **bibliotecario**, la **bibliotecaria**

lorry driver NOUN el **camionero**, la **camionera**

mayor NOUN el **alcalde**, la **alcaldesa**

mechanic NOUN el **mecánico**, la **mecánica**

midwife NOUN la **comadrona**

miner NOUN el **minero**, la **minera**

minister NOUN el **ministro**, la **ministra**

model NOUN el/la **modelo**

monk NOUN el **monje**

MP NOUN el **diputado**, la **diputada**

musician NOUN el **músico**, la **música**

nanny NOUN la **niñera**

nurse NOUN el **enfermero,** la **enfermera**

optician NOUN el **óptico,** la **óptica**

painter NOUN el **pintor,** la **pintora**

paperboy NOUN el **repartidor de periódicos**

papergirl NOUN la **repartidora de periódicos**

pharmacist NOUN el **farmacéutico,** la **farmacéutica**

physiotherapist NOUN el/la **fisioterapeuta**

pianist NOUN el/la **pianista**

pilot NOUN el/la **piloto**

plumber NOUN el **fontanero,** la **fontanera**

police officer NOUN el/la **policía**

postman NOUN el **cartero**

priest NOUN el **sacerdote**

professor NOUN el **catedrático,** la **catedrática**

programmer NOUN el **programador,** la **programadora**

psychiatrist NOUN el/la **psiquiatra**

psychologist NOUN el **psicólogo,** la **psicóloga**

rabbi NOUN el **rabino,** la **rabina**

receptionist NOUN el/la **recepcionista**

rep NOUN el/la **representante**

reporter NOUN el **reportero,** la **reportera**

sailor NOUN el **marinero,** la **marinera**

sales rep NOUN el/la **comercial**

scientist NOUN el **científico,** la **científica**

security guard NOUN el/la **guardia de seguridad**

shop assistant NOUN el **dependiente,** la **dependienta**

shopkeeper NOUN el/la **comerciante**

social worker NOUN el/la **asistente social**

soldier NOUN el/la **soldado**

solicitor NOUN el **notario**, la **notaria**

supply teacher NOUN el **maestro suplente**, la **maestra suplente** (*primary school*)

surgeon NOUN el **cirujano**, la **cirujana**

taxi driver NOUN el/la **taxista**

teacher NOUN el **maestro**, la **maestra** (*primary school*)

technician NOUN el **técnico**, la **técnica**

translator NOUN el **traductor**, la **traductora**

vet NOUN el **veterinario**, la **veterinaria**

vicar NOUN el **párroco**, la **párroca**

waiter NOUN el **camarero**

waitress NOUN la **camarera**

writer NOUN el **escritor**, la **escritora**

Remember that if the word has **la** in front of it, it is feminine, if it has **el** in front of it, it is masculine.

Sports | Los deportes

aerobics NOUN el **aerobic**

athletics NOUN el **atletismo**

badminton NOUN el **bádminton**

baseball NOUN el **béisbol**

basketball NOUN el **baloncesto**

bowling NOUN los **bolos**

boxing NOUN el **boxeo**

cricket NOUN el **críquet**

cycling NOUN el **ciclismo**

dancing NOUN el **baile**

fishing NOUN la **pesca**

football NOUN el **fútbol**

golf NOUN el **golf**

gymnastics NOUN la **gimnasia**

handball NOUN el **balonmano**

high jump NOUN el **salto de altura**

hockey NOUN el **hockey**

ice-skating NOUN el **patinaje sobre hielo**

judo NOUN el **judo**

karate NOUN el **kárate**

long jump NOUN el **salto de longitud**

motor racing NOUN el **automovilismo**

mountaineering NOUN el **alpinismo**

netball NOUN el **netball**

pool NOUN el **billar americano**

riding NOUN la **equitación**

roller-blading NOUN el **patinaje en línea**

roller-skating NOUN el **patinaje sobre ruedas**

rugby NOUN el **rugby**

running NOUN la **carrera**

sailing NOUN la **vela**

skateboarding NOUN el **skateboard**

skating NOUN el **patinaje**

skiing NOUN el **esquí**

soccer NOUN el **fútbol**

squash NOUN el **squash**

surfing NOUN el **surf**

swimming NOUN la **natación**

table tennis NOUN el **ping-pong**

tennis NOUN el **tenis**

tenpin bowling NOUN los **bolos**

trampolining NOUN la **gimnasia en trampolín**

volleyball NOUN el **vóleibol**

water-skiing NOUN el **esquí acuático**

windsurfing NOUN el **windsurf**

wrestling NOUN la **lucha**

Remember that if the word has **la** in front of it, it is feminine, if it has **el** in front of it, it is masculine.

At school | En el colegio

absent ADJECTIVE **ausente**

assembly hall NOUN el **salón de actos**

atlas NOUN el **atlas**

bell NOUN la **campana**

Biro® NOUN el **bolígrafo**

board NOUN la **pizarra**

book NOUN el **libro**

break time NOUN el **recreo**

calculator NOUN la **calculadora**

canteen NOUN el **comedor**

chair NOUN la **silla**

chalk NOUN la **tiza**

changing room NOUN el **vestuario**

chart NOUN el **gráfico**

class NOUN la **clase**

classroom NOUN el **aula** *(fem)*

clock NOUN el **reloj**

computer NOUN el **ordenador**

corridor NOUN el **pasillo**

curriculum NOUN el **programa**

deputy head NOUN el **subdirector**, la **subdirectora**

desk NOUN la **mesa**

diagram NOUN el **esquema**

dictionary NOUN el **diccionario**

door NOUN la **puerta**

drawing NOUN el **dibujo**

drawing pin NOUN la **chincheta**

essay NOUN la **redacción** (PL las **redacciones**)

exam NOUN el **examen** (PL los **exámenes**)

exercise NOUN el **ejercicio**

exercise book NOUN
el **cuaderno**

felt-tip pen NOUN el **rotulador**

folder NOUN la **carpeta**

general knowledge NOUN
la **cultura general**

grammar NOUN la **gramática**

gym NOUN el **gimnasio**

gym kit NOUN la **ropa de gimnasia**

head teacher NOUN el **director**,
la **directora**

homework NOUN los **deberes**

ink NOUN la **tinta**

interactive board NOUN la **pizarra
interactiva**

interval NOUN el **recreo**

jotter NOUN el **bloc de notas**

language laboratory NOUN
el **laboratorio de idiomas**

lesson NOUN la **clase**

library NOUN la **biblioteca**

mouse NOUN el **ratón** (PL los **ratones**)

mousemat NOUN la **alfombrilla del
ratón**

packed lunch NOUN la **bolsa del
almuerzo**

page NOUN la **página**

pen NOUN la **pluma**

pencil NOUN el **lápiz** (PL los **lápices**)

pencil case NOUN el **lapicero**

pencil sharpener NOUN
el **sacapuntas** (PL los **sacapuntas**)

photocopier NOUN
la **fotocopiadora**

photocopy NOUN la **fotocopia**

playground NOUN el **patio de
recreo**

playtime NOUN el **recreo**

primary school NOUN el **colegio
de primaria**

printer NOUN la **impresora**

projector NOUN el **proyector**

pupil NOUN el **alumno**,
la **alumna**

rubber NOUN la **goma**

ruler NOUN la **regla**

school NOUN el **colegio**

schoolbag NOUN la **cartera**

schoolboy NOUN el **colegial**

schoolgirl NOUN la **colegiala**

school uniform NOUN el **uniforme**

secondary school NOUN
el **instituto de secundaria**

sharpener NOUN el **sacapuntas**

teacher NOUN el **maestro,**
la **maestra** (primary school)

team NOUN el **equipo**

test NOUN la **prueba**

textbook NOUN el **libro de texto**

toilets NOUN los **aseos**

whiteboard NOUN la **pizarra blanca**

window NOUN la **ventana**

worksheet NOUN la **hoja de ejercicios**

Remember that if the word has **la** in front of it, it is feminine, if it has **el** in front of it, it is masculine.

School subjects | Las asignaturas

art NOUN la **plástica**

biology NOUN la **biología**

chemistry NOUN la **química**

drama NOUN el **teatro**

English NOUN el **inglés**

French NOUN el **francés**

geography NOUN la **geografía**

gym NOUN la **gimnasia**

history NOUN la **historia**

ICT NOUN la **informática**

literacy NOUN la **lengua**

literature NOUN la **literatura**

maths NOUN las **matemáticas**

music NOUN la **música**

numeracy NOUN las **matemáticas**

PE NOUN la **educación física**

physics NOUN la **física**

science NOUN las **ciencias**

Phones and computing | Teléfonos e informática

app NOUN la **aplicación**

charger NOUN el **cargador**

connection NOUN la **conexión**

game controller NOUN
el **controlador de videojuegos**

games console NOUN la **consola de juegos**

icon NOUN el **icono**

laptop NOUN el **(ordenador) portátil**

mobile phone NOUN
el **(teléfono) móvil**

password NOUN la **contraseña**

PC NOUN el **PC**

SIM card NOUN
la **tarjeta SIM**

smartphone NOUN el **smartphone**

social media NOUN PL las **redes sociales**

tablet NOUN la **tablet**

username NOUN el **nombre de usuario**

video game NOUN el **videojuego**

Wi-Fi NOUN el **wifi**

The environment | El medio ambiente

air NOUN el **aire**

climate change NOUN el **cambio climático**

eco-friendly ADJECTIVE **ecológico** (*fem* **ecológica**)

energy NOUN la **energía**

fire NOUN el **incendio**

flood NOUN la **inundación**

forest NOUN el **bosque**

global warming NOUN el **calentamiento global**

greenhouse effect NOUN el **efecto invernadero**

nature NOUN la **naturaleza**

ocean NOUN el **océano**

plastic bag NOUN la **bolsa de plástico**

pollution NOUN la **contaminación**

recyclable ADJECTIVE **reciclable** (*fem* **reciclable**)

recycling NOUN el **reciclaje**

river NOUN el **río**

sea NOUN el **mar**

solar panel NOUN el **panel solar**

tree NOUN el **árbol**

wind turbine NOUN el **aerogenerador**

Numbers | Los números

1	uno
2	dos
3	tres
4	cuatro
5	cinco
6	seis
7	siete
8	ocho
9	nueve
10	diez
11	once
12	doce
13	trece
14	catorce
15	quince
16	dieciséis
17	diecisiete
18	dieciocho
19	diecinueve
20	veinte
21	veintiuno
22	veintidós
30	treinta
40	cuarenta
50	cincuenta
60	sesenta
70	setenta
80	ochenta
90	noventa
100	cien
101	ciento uno
200	doscientos
250	doscientos cincuenta
1,000	mil
2,000	dos mil
1,000,000	un millón

Time | La hora

What time is it? ¿Qué hora es?		It's... Es .../Son ...

one o'clock
la una

ten past one
la una y diez

quarter past one
la una y cuarto

half past one
la una y media

twenty to two
las dos menos veinte

quarter to two
las dos menos cuarto

What time...?		¿A qué hora ... ?

at midnight
a medianoche

at midday
a mediodía

**at one o'clock
(in the afternoon)**
a la una (de la tarde)

**at eight o'clock
(at night)**
a las ocho
(de la noche)

**at quarter past eleven
(in the morning)**
a las once y cuarto
(de la mañana)

**at quarter to nine
(at night)**
a las nueve menos cuarto
(de la noche)

Spanish verbs | Los verbos españoles

In Spanish, the ending of the verb varies according to the person, which means that the form of the verb that goes with **yo** is different from the form that goes with **tú**, **él**, etc.

Spanish has several words for 'you'. Here you will see the forms **tú** and **vosotros**: **tú** is used when talking to one person that you know well, or someone your own age. **vosotros** is used in Spain when talking to more than one person you know well.

The tables that follow show how some common Spanish verbs work in the **present tense**.

At the end of each table, there are some useful phrases which require other tenses. The examples throughout the dictionary use a variety of basic tenses that children and teachers alike will find useful.

A verb form that is of particular interest to teachers is the **imperative**. In English, **Look!**, **Listen!**, **Don't do that!** can be used to a single child, or to the whole class. In Spanish there are different forms of the verb, depending on whether one, or more than one person is being spoken to. It also depends on whether you are telling someone to do something or not to do something, and whether you know the person or people well.

The first three verbs given (**hablar**, **comer** and **vivir**) can be used as models for any other regular verb ending in **-ar**, **-er** or **-ir**.

hablar
to speak/to talk

(yo) hablo	I speak
	I talk
(tú) hablas	you speak
	you talk
(él/ella) habla	he/she speaks
	he/she talks
(nosotros/nosotras)	we speak
hablamos	we talk
(vosotros/vosotras)	you speak
habláis	you talk
(ellos/ellas) hablan	they speak
	they talk

PRESENT
Olivia **habla** un español perfecto.
Olivia speaks perfect Spanish.

No **se hablan.**
They don't talk to each other.

PAST
Hoy **he hablado** con mi hermana.
I've spoken to my sister today.

Nadie **habló.**
Nobody spoke.

FUTURE
Hablaré con ella.
I'll speak to her.

IMPERATIVE
Habla con ella mañana, Oscar.
Speak to her tomorrow, Oscar.

No hables tan alto, Poppy.
Don't talk so loud, Poppy.

comer
to eat

(yo) como	I eat
(tú) comes	you eat
(él/ella) come	he/she eats
(nosotros/nosotras)	
comemos	we eat
(vosotros/vosotras)	
coméis	you eat
(ellos/ellas) comen	they eat

PRESENT
No **come** carne.
He doesn't eat meat.

Comemos mucha verdura.
We eat a lot of vegetables.

PAST
Se lo **ha comido** todo.
He's eaten it all.

Casi no **comí.**
I hardly ate

FUTURE
Comeremos en casa de Sophie.
We'll eat at Sophie's.

IMPERATIVE
Come lo que quieras, Theo.
Eat what you want, Theo.

No comas tan deprisa, Alice.
Don't eat so fast, Alice.

vivir
to live

(yo) **vivo**	I live
(tú) **vives**	you live
(él/ella) **vive**	he/she lives
(nosotros/nosotras) **vivimos**	we live
(vosotros/vosotras) **vivís**	you live
(ellos/ellas) **viven**	they live

PRESENT
¿Dónde **vives**?
Where do you live?

Viven en Newcastle.
They live in Newcastle.

PAST
Vivimos dos años en Australia.
We lived in Australia for two years.

FUTURE
Viviremos en el centro de la ciudad.
We'll live in the city centre.

IMPERATIVE
Vive la vida.
Live your life.

estar
to be

(yo) **estoy**	I am
(tú) **estás**	you are
(él/ella) **está**	he/she is
(nosotros/nosotras) **estamos**	we are
(vosotros/vosotras) **estáis**	you are
(ellos/ellas) **están**	they are

PRESENT
Estoy cansado.
I'm tired.

¿Dónde **está** tu abrigo?
Where is your coat?

PAST
Nunca **he estado** allí.
I have never been there.

Estuvimos en casa de mi tía.
We went to my aunt's.

FUTURE
¿A qué hora **estarás** en casa?
What time will you be home?

IMPERATIVE
¡**Estáte** quieto, Harry!
Keep still, Harry!

No estés triste, Lucas.
Don't be sad, Lucas.

ser
to be

(yo) soy	I am
(tú) eres	you are
(él/ella) es	he/she is
(nosotros/nosotras) somos	we are
(vosotros/vosotras) sois	you are
(ellos/ellas) son	they are

PRESENT

Soy español.
I'm Spanish.

Qué inteligente **eres**, Ella.
You are so intelligent, Ella.

PAST

¿**Fuiste** tú el que llamó?
Was it you who phoned?

Era de noche.
It was dark.

FUTURE

Pronto **será** mi cumpleaños.
It will soon be my birthday.

IMPERATIVE

No seas tan egoísta, Leo.
Don't be so selfish, Leo.

¡**Sed** buenos!
Behave yourselves!

ir
to go

(yo) voy	I go
(tú) vas	you go
(él/ella) va	he/she goes
(nosotros/nosotras) vamos	we go
(vosotros/vosotras) vais	you go
(ellos/ellas) van	they go

PRESENT

Voy al colegio del barrio.
I go to the local school.

¿Dónde **vas**?
Where are you going?

PAST

Ayer **fuimos** al cine.
We went to the cinema yesterday.

Sam **se ha ido** sin esperarnos.
Sam's gone without waiting for us.

FUTURE

El domingo **iré** a la piscina.
I'll go to the swimming pool on Sunday.

IMPERATIVE

Vete a hacer los deberes, George.
Go and do your homework, George.

No te **vayas** sin despedirte, Emily.
Don't go without saying goodbye, Emily.

¡**Vamos** al parque!
Let's go to the park!

tener

to have

(yo) tengo	I have
(tú) tienes	you have
(él/ella) tiene	he/she has
(nosotros/nosotras) tenemos	we have
(vosotros/vosotras) tenéis	you have
(ellos/ellas) tienen	they have

PRESENT

Tengo dos hermanos.
I have two brothers.

¿Cuántos años **tienes**?
How old are you?

Tengo que hacer los deberes.
I have to do my homework.

PAST

Grace **ha tenido** una gripe muy fuerte.
Grace has had very bad flu.

Anoche **tuve** un mal sueño.
I had a bad dream last night.

FUTURE

Tendrás que pagarlo tú.
You'll have to pay for it yourself.

IMPERATIVE

Ten cuidado, Mia.
Be careful, Mia.

No tengas miedo, Noah.
Don't be afraid, Noah.

haber

to have
[auxiliary, used when forming other tenses]

(yo) he	I have
(tú) has	you have
(él/ella) ha	he/she has
(nosotros/nosotras) hemos	we have
(vosotros/vosotras) habéis	you have
(ellos/ellas) han	they have

PRESENT

¿Lo **has** hecho ya, James?
Have you done it yet, James?

Charlie **ha** roto el espejo.
Charlie has broken the mirror.

PAST

No lo **había** visto.
I hadn't seen it.

FUTURE

Habrá que decírselo a Chloe.
We'll have to tell Chloe.

IMPERATIVE

This verb is not used much in the imperative.

decir
to say/tell

(yo) digo	I say
	I tell
(tú) dices	you say
	you tell
(él/ella) dice	he/she says
	he/she tells
(nosotros/nosotras)	we say
decimos	we tell
(vosotros/vosotras)	you say
decís	you tell
(ellos/ellas) dicen	they say
	they tell

PRESENT
Pero ¿qué **dices**?
What are you saying?

Patrick **dice** que es fácil.
Patrick says it's easy.

PAST
Lily me lo **dijo** ayer.
Lily told me yesterday.

¿Te **ha dicho** Carter lo del profesor?
Has Carter told you about the teacher?

FUTURE
Se lo **diré** a tu hermano.
I'll tell your brother.

IMPERATIVE
Dime quién lo hizo, Emma.
Tell me who did it, Emma.

Decid las palabras otra vez, niños.
Say the words again, children.

No digas nada, Oliver.
Don't say anything, Oliver.

dar
to give

(yo) doy	I give
(tú) das	you give
(él/ella) da	he/she gives
(nosotros/nosotras)	
damos	we give
(vosotros/vosotras)	
dais	you give
(ellos/ellas) dan	they give

PRESENT
¿Me **das** otra hoja de papel, por favor?
Can you give me another sheet of paper, please?

Me **da** miedo la oscuridad.
I'm scared of the dark.

PAST
Zoe me **ha dado** un buen consejo.
Zoe gave me a good piece of advice.

Le **dieron** una entrada gratis.
They gave him a free ticket.

FUTURE
Te **daré** el número de mi móvil.
I'll give you my mobile phone number.

IMPERATIVE
Dame el libro, por favor, Daniel.
Give me the book, please, Daniel.

¡Vamos chicos, **daos** prisa!
Hurry up, you guys!

English-Spanish

Aa

a ARTICLE
un *masc*
una *fem*

> **LANGUAGE TIP**
> Use **un** for masculine nouns and **una** for feminine nouns.

a book
un libro
a girl
una chica

> **LANGUAGE TIP**
> **a** isn't always translated by **un** and **una**.

He's a mechanic.
Es mecánico.
It costs ten pence a packet.
Cuesta diez peniques el paquete.
a hundred pounds
cien libras

able ADJECTIVE
to be able to
poder
Will you be able to come?
¿Podrás venir?
I won't be able to help you.
No podré ayudarte.

about ADVERB, PREPOSITION
1 **alrededor de** (*approximately*)
about fifty euros
alrededor de cincuenta euros
at about eleven o'clock
alrededor de las once
2 **sobre** (*concerning*)
a programme about lions
un programa sobre los leones

How about a game of cards?
¿Por qué no jugamos a las cartas?
I'm hungry, how about you?
Yo tengo hambre, ¿y tú?
We're about to go out.
Estamos a punto de salir.

above PREPOSITION

> **LANGUAGE TIP**
> When something is located above something, use **encima de**. When there is movement involved, use **por encima de**.

1 **encima de**
There's a picture above the fireplace.
Hay un cuadro encima de la chimenea.
2 **por encima de**
Throw the ball above your head.
Lanza el balón por encima de la cabeza.

> **LANGUAGE TIP**
> In Spanish you usually use an article like **el**, **la** or **los**, **las** with parts of the body.

3 **más de** (*more than*)
above thirty degrees
más de treinta grados

abroad ADVERB
1 **en el extranjero** (*in a foreign country*)
They live abroad.
Viven en el extranjero.
2 **al extranjero** (*to a foreign country*)
We're going abroad this year.
Vamos al extranjero este año.

absent ADJECTIVE
Who's absent today?
¿Quién falta hoy?
Tom's absent.
Falta Tom.

absurd ADJECTIVE
absurdo *masc*
absurda *fem*
That's absurd!
¡Eso es absurdo!

academy NOUN
la **academia** *fem*

Spanish

English

A
B
C
D
E
F
G
H
I
J
K
L
M
N
O
P
Q
R
S
T
U
V
W
X
Y
Z

accent NOUN
 el **acento** *masc*
  He's got a good accent.
  Tiene buen acento.

accident NOUN
 el **accidente** *masc*
  It was an accident.
  Fue un accidente.
  a car accident
  un accidente de coche
  by accident
  por casualidad/sin querer

  LANGUAGE TIP
  by accident has two translations.
  Look at the examples.

  They discovered it by accident.
  Lo descubrieron por casualidad.
  The player touched the ball by accident.
  El jugador tocó el balón sin querer.

ace NOUN
 el **as** *masc*
  the ace of hearts
  el as de corazones

ache VERB
  My leg's aching.
  Me duele la pierna.

  LANGUAGE TIP
  In Spanish you usually use an article like **el**, **la** or **los**, **las** with parts of the body.

across PREPOSITION
 al **otro lado de**
  It's across the road.
  Está al otro lado de la calle.
  You mustn't run across the road.
  No debes cruzar la calle corriendo.

act VERB
 actuar
  He's acting in a play.
  Actúa en una obra de teatro.

activity NOUN
 la **actividad** *fem*
  outdoor activities
  actividades al aire libre

actor NOUN
 el **actor** *masc*
 la **actriz** *fem* (PL las **actrices**)
  He's an actor.
  Es actor.

  LANGUAGE TIP
  In Spanish, you do not use an article with people's jobs.

actress NOUN
 la **actriz** *fem* (PL las **actrices**)

actually ADVERB
 en realidad
  Actually, it's good fun.
  En realidad, es bastante divertido.

  LANGUAGE TIP
  Be careful! The translation of **actually** is not **actualmente**.

AD ABBREVIATION
 (= **Anno Domini**)
  d.C. (= *después de Cristo*)
  in 800 AD
  en el 800 d.C.

add VERB
 añadir
  Add some sugar.
  Añade un poco de azúcar.

add up VERB
 sumar
  You have to add the figures up.
  Hay que sumar las cantidades.

address NOUN
 la **dirección** *fem* (PL las **direcciones**)
  What's your address, Emma?
  ¿Cuál es tu dirección, Emma?

adjective NOUN
 el **adjetivo** *masc*

admission NOUN
 la **entrada** *fem*
  'admission free'
  "entrada libre"

adopted ADJECTIVE
  I'm adopted.
  Soy adoptado.

adult NOUN
el **adulto** *masc*
la **adulta** *fem*
> **two adults and one child**
> dos adultos y un menor

advantage NOUN
la **ventaja** *fem*
> **It's an advantage to be able to speak English.**
> Es una ventaja saber hablar inglés.

adventure NOUN
la **aventura** *fem*
> **Harry has lots of adventures.**
> A Harry le suceden muchas aventuras.

adverb NOUN
el **adverbio** *masc*

advert NOUN
el **anuncio** *masc*
> **They put an advert in the newspaper.**
> Pusieron un anuncio en el periódico.

advice NOUN
los **consejos** *masc pl*
> **Can you give me some advice?**
> ¿Puedes darme algunos consejos?
> **That's good advice.**
> Es un buen consejo.
> **a piece of advice**
> un consejo

LANGUAGE TIP
Be careful! The translation of **advice** is not **aviso**.

---

aerobics NOUN
el **aerobic** *masc*

aeroplane NOUN
el **avión** *masc* (PL los **aviones**)
> **on an aeroplane**
> en un avión

affectionate ADJECTIVE
cariñoso *masc*
cariñosa *fem*
> **My cat is very affectionate.**
> Mi gato es muy cariñoso.

afford VERB
permitirse
> **I can't afford a new pair of jeans.**
> No puedo permitirme comprar unos vaqueros nuevos.

LANGUAGE TIP
There isn't really a verb that translates **afford** in Spanish. You need to use a phrase with **permitirse comprar**.

---

afraid ADJECTIVE
> **to be afraid**
> tener miedo
> **I'm afraid.**
> Tengo miedo.
> **I'm afraid of spiders.**
> Me dan miedo las arañas.
> **Are you afraid of the dark?**
> ¿Te da miedo la oscuridad?

after PREPOSITION
después de
> **after break**
> después del recreo
> **after lunch**
> después de comer

afternoon NOUN
la **tarde** *fem*
> **In the morning or in the afternoon?**
> ¿Por la mañana o por la tarde?

at three o'clock in the afternoon
a las tres de la tarde
I'm playing football on Saturday afternoon.
Voy a jugar al fútbol el sábado por la tarde.

this afternoon
esta tarde
in the afternoon
por la tarde
Good afternoon!
¡Buenas tardes!

afters PL NOUN
el **postre** *masc*
What do you want for afters?
¿Qué quieres de postre?

again ADVERB
otra vez
I'd like to hear it again.
Quiero escucharlo otra vez.
Try again!
¡Inténtalo otra vez!

LANGUAGE TIP
You can also use **volver a** followed by the main verb to translate **again**.

Try again!
¡Vuelve a intentarlo!

against PREPOSITION
contra
You mustn't lean your chair against the wall.
No debes apoyar la silla contra la pared.

age NOUN
la **edad** *fem*
Write your name and age.
Escribe tu nombre y tu edad.
at the age of thirteen
a la edad de trece años
I am the same age as you.
Tengo la misma edad que tú.

LANGUAGE TIP
Note that in Spanish you use the verb **tener** to talk about somebody's age.

ago ADVERB
I bought it six months ago.
Lo compré hace seis meses.

a week ago
hace una semana
a long time ago
hace mucho tiempo

agree VERB
estar de acuerdo
I agree.
Estoy de acuerdo.
I agree with Monika.
Estoy de acuerdo con Monika.

ahead ADVERB
Look straight ahead!
¡Mira hacia adelante!
The red team is five points ahead.
El equipo rojo lleva cinco puntos de ventaja.
There were a lot of people ahead of us in the queue.
Había mucha gente delante de nosotros en la cola.

air NOUN
el **aire** *masc*
Throw the ball into the air.
Lanza el balón al aire.
I prefer to travel by air.
Prefiero viajar en avión.

air-conditioned ADJECTIVE
climatizado *masc*
climatizada *fem*

airmail NOUN
by airmail
por avión

airport NOUN
el **aeropuerto** *masc*

alarm clock NOUN
el **despertador** *masc*

album NOUN
el **álbum** *masc*

alcohol NOUN
el **alcohol** *masc*
I don't drink alcohol.
No bebo alcohol.

A levels PL NOUN
el **bachillerato** *masc*
My brother is doing his A levels.
Mi hermano está haciendo el bachillerato.

DID YOU KNOW...?
The **bachillerato** is the Spanish equivalent of **A levels**.

---

alive ADJECTIVE
vivo *masc*
viva *fem*
They're still alive.
Todavía siguen vivos.

all ADJECTIVE, PRONOUN
todo *masc*
toda *fem*
all the time
todo el tiempo
all night
toda la noche
all my friends
todos mis amigos
all the girls
todas las chicas
The score is five all.
El marcador está empatado a cinco.

Is that all?
¿Eso es todo?

allergic ADJECTIVE
alérgico *masc*
alérgica *fem*
I'm allergic to cats.
Soy alérgica a los gatos.

allergy NOUN
la **alergia** *fem*
Have you got any allergies?
¿Tienes alguna alergia?

allowed ADJECTIVE
permitido *masc*
permitida *fem*
It's not allowed.
No está permitido.
We're not allowed to use calculators in the exam.
No se nos permite usar calculadora en el examen.

all right ADVERB, ADJECTIVE
1 **bien** (*not bad*)
Are you all right?
¿Estás bien?
Is that all right?
¿Está bien así?
Do you like school? — It's all right.
¿Te gusta ir al colegio? — Regular.
2 **de acuerdo** (*when agreeing*)
I'd like a coffee. — All right.
Quiero un café. — De acuerdo.

almost ADVERB
casi
Are you ready? — Almost.
¿Estás lista? — Casi.

alone ADJECTIVE
1 **solo** *masc*
sola *fem*

to be alone
estar solo
He was alone in the house.
Estaba solo en la casa.
She lives alone.
Vive sola.
2 **tranquilo** *masc*
tranquila *fem* (*in peace*)

Ethan, leave Paul alone!
¡Ethan, deja tranquilo a Paul!
Leave him alone!
¡Déjalo tranquilo!
Leave me alone!
¡Déjame tranquilo!
Leave my things alone!
¡No toques mis cosas!

along PREPOSITION
por
> **a walk along the beach**
> un paseo por la playa

aloud ADVERB
en voz alta
> **Read the words aloud, children.**
> Leed las palabras en voz alta, niños.
> **Read the words aloud, Richard.**
> Lee las palabras en voz alta, Richard.

alphabet NOUN
el **alfabeto** masc

alphabetical order NOUN
> **in alphabetical order**
> por orden alfabético

already ADVERB
ya
> **I've already done it.**
> Ya lo he hecho.
> **Have you finished already?**
> ¿Ya has terminado?

also ADVERB
también
> **I also play the flute.**
> También toco la flauta.

alternate ADJECTIVE
> **on alternate days**
> un día sí y otro no

alternative NOUN
la **alternativa** fem
> **You have no alternative.**
> No tienes alternativa.

altogether ADVERB
en total
> **That's twenty pounds altogether.**
> Son veinte libras en total.

always ADVERB
siempre
> **The bus is always late.**
> El autobús siempre llega tarde.

am VERB ▷ see **be**

a.m. ABBREVIATION
de la mañana
> **at four a.m.**
> a las cuatro de la mañana

amazing ADJECTIVE
1 **increíble** masc/fem (surprising)
> **That's amazing!**
> ¡Eso es increíble!
2 **excelente** masc/fem (excellent)
> **Vivian's an amazing cook.**
> Vivian es una cocinera excelente.

ambulance NOUN
la **ambulancia** fem

America NOUN
los **Estados Unidos** masc pl
> **We're going to America.**
> Vamos a Estados Unidos.

American

> **American** can be an adjective or a noun.

A ADJECTIVE
americano masc
americana fem
> **American food**
> la cocina americana

> **He's American.**
> Es americano.
> **She's American.**
> Es americana.

B NOUN
el **americano** masc
la **americana** fem
> **the Americans**
> los americanos

LANGUAGE TIP
americano is not spelled with a
capital letter in Spanish.

amount NOUN
la **cantidad** *fem*
a huge amount of rice
una enorme cantidad de arroz
a large amount of money
una gran suma de dinero

amusement arcade NOUN
el **salón recreativo** *masc* (PL los **salones recreativos**)

an ARTICLE
un *masc*
una *fem*

LANGUAGE TIP
Use **un** for masculine nouns and **una** for feminine nouns.

---

an animal
un animal
an apple
una manzana

LANGUAGE TIP
Sometimes the article **an** isn't translated.

He's an actor.
Es actor.
ten kilometres an hour
diez kilómetros por hora

and CONJUNCTION
y
my brother and me
mi hermano y yo
Two and two are four.
Dos y dos son cuatro.

LANGUAGE TIP
Use **e** instead of **y** before words beginning with **i-** or **hi-** but not **hie-**.

Miguel and Ignacio
Miguel e Ignacio

LANGUAGE TIP
Don't translate **and** in numbers.

---

two hundred and fifty
doscientos cincuenta

angel NOUN
el **ángel** *masc*

LANGUAGE TIP
Even though **ángel** is a masculine word, you can use it to refer to a woman or girl.

You're an angel!
¡Eres un ángel!

angry ADJECTIVE
enfadado *masc*
enfadada *fem*
He's very angry.
Está muy enfadado.
to get angry
enfadarse
Mum gets angry if I'm late.
Mi madre se enfada si llego tarde.

animal NOUN
el **animal** *masc*

anniversary NOUN
el **aniversario** *masc*
my parents' wedding anniversary
el aniversario de boda de mis padres

Happy anniversary!
¡Feliz aniversario!

LANGUAGE TIP
Have you noticed the upside-down exclamation mark at the start of Spanish exclamations?

---

announcement
NOUN
el **anuncio** *masc*
an important announcement
un anuncio importante

anorak NOUN
el **anorak** *masc*
my new anorak
mi anorak nuevo

Spanish

English

another ADJECTIVE, PRONOUN
otro *masc*
otra *fem*
> **Would you like another sandwich?**
> ¿Quieres otro sándwich?
> **There are plenty of apples. Would you like another one?**
> Hay muchas manzanas. ¿Quieres otra?

answer

> **answer** can be a verb or a noun.

A VERB
> **to answer**
> **contestar**
> **Isabel, you have to answer yes or no.**
> Isabel, tienes que contestar sí o no.
> **Think before you answer.**
> Piensa antes de contestar.
> **to answer a question**
> contestar a una pregunta
> **Who can answer the question?**
> ¿Quién puede contestar a la pregunta?

B NOUN
> la **respuesta** *fem*
> **the right answer**
> la respuesta correcta

ant NOUN
la **hormiga** *fem*

anthem NOUN
> **the national anthem**
> el himno nacional

any

> **any** can be an adjective or a pronoun.

A ADJECTIVE

> **LANGUAGE TIP**
> You usually don't translate **any** in questions.

> **Do you want any bread?**
> ¿Quieres pan?
> **Have you got any brothers or sisters?**
> ¿Tienes hermanos?

> **LANGUAGE TIP**
> However, you can use **algún** with a masculine singular noun and **alguna** with a feminine singular noun when the emphasis is on each individual person or thing.

> **Do you have any hobbies?**
> ¿Tienes algún pasatiempo?

> **LANGUAGE TIP**
> Similarly, you usually don't translate **any** in negative sentences.

> **I don't want any bread.**
> No quiero pan.
> **There aren't any oranges.**
> No hay naranjas.

> **LANGUAGE TIP**
> However, you can use **ningún** with a masculine singular noun and **ninguna** with a feminine singular noun when **not ... any** is equivalent to **not a single**.

> **I haven't got any CDs left.**
> No me queda ningún CD.
> **I can't see any flowers.**
> No veo ninguna flor.

> **Have you got any money?**
> ¿Tienes dinero?
> **Have you got any pets?**
> ¿Tienes alguna mascota?
> **There isn't any milk.**
> No hay leche.

B PRONOUN
1 **alguno** *masc*
alguna *fem* (in questions)
> **I need a stamp. Have you got any left?**
> Necesito un sello. ¿Te queda alguno?

I fancy some soup. Have we got any?
Me apetece sopa. ¿Tenemos?
I need some oil. Is there any?
Necesito aceite. ¿Hay?

2 ninguno *masc*
ninguna *fem* (*in negatives*)
I don't like any of them.
No me gusta ninguno.
A stamp? Sorry, I haven't got any.
¿Un sello? Lo siento, no tengo ninguno.

I prefer apple juice, but we haven't got any.
Prefiero zumo de manzana, pero no tenemos.
I don't want any more.
No quiero más.

anybody PRONOUN
1 alguien (*in questions*)
Does anybody want a sweet?
¿Alguien quiere un caramelo?
2 nadie (*in negatives*)
I didn't see anybody.
No vi a nadie.

anyone PRONOUN
1 alguien (*in questions*)
Does anyone want to try?
¿Alguien quiere probar?
2 nadie (*in negatives*)
I can't see anyone.
No veo a nadie.

anything PRONOUN
1 algo (*in questions*)
Do you want anything to eat?
¿Quieres comer algo?
2 nada (*in negatives*)
I don't want anything.
No quiero nada.

anywhere PRONOUN
1 en algún sitio (*in questions*)
Have you seen my pen anywhere?
¿Has visto mi bolígrafo en algún sitio?
Are you going anywhere?
¿Vas a algún sitio?
2 en ningún sitio (*in negatives*)
I can't find it anywhere.
No lo encuentro en ningún sitio.
I'm not going anywhere.
No voy a ningún sitio.

apart ADVERB
Stand with your feet apart.
Ponte de pie con los pies separados.

apart from
aparte de
Apart from that, everything's fine.
Aparte de eso, todo va bien.

apartment NOUN
el **piso** *masc*

apostrophe NOUN
el **apóstrofo** *masc*
Don't forget the apostrophe!
¡Que no se te olvide el apóstrofo!

app NOUN
la **aplicación** *fem*

apple NOUN
la **manzana** *fem*
a big red apple
una manzana grande y roja

a
b
c
d
e
f
g
h
i
j
k
l
m
n
o
p
q
r
s
t
u
v
w
x
y
z

apple juice NOUN
el **zumo de manzana** *masc*

apple pie NOUN
el **pastel de manzana** *masc*

appointment NOUN
la **cita** *fem*
I've got a dental appointment.
Tengo cita con el dentista.

April NOUN
abril *masc*
My birthday's in April.
Mi cumpleaños es en abril.
It's the fifth of April today.
Hoy es cinco de abril.

> **in April**
> en abril
> **on the ninth of April**
> el nueve de abril

LANGUAGE TIP
Months are not spelled with a capital letter in Spanish.

April Fool NOUN
April Fool!
¡Inocente!

April Fools' Day NOUN
el **día de los inocentes** *masc*

DID YOU KNOW...?
In Spanish-speaking countries the day people play practical jokes on each other is 28 December, which is called **el día de los inocentes**.

---

apron NOUN
el **delantal** *masc*
a white apron
un delantal blanco

are VERB ▷ *see* **be**

area NOUN
la **zona** *fem*
a mountainous area of Spain
una zona montañosa de España

argue VERB
discutir
Stop arguing!
¡Dejad de discutir!

arm NOUN
el **brazo** *masc*
I've hurt my arm.
Me he hecho daño en el brazo.

LANGUAGE TIP
In Spanish you usually use an article like **el**, **la** or **los**, **las** with parts of the body.

---

armchair NOUN
el **sillón** *masc* (PL los **sillones**)

army NOUN
el **ejército** *masc*
He's in the army.
Está en el ejército.

around PREPOSITION
1 **alrededor de**
The pupils are sitting around the teacher.
Los alumnos están sentados alrededor del profesor.
I go to bed around ten o'clock.
Me voy a la cama alrededor de las diez.
2 **por** (*near*)
around here
por aquí
Is there a chemist's around here?
¿Hay una farmacia por aquí?

arrive VERB
llegar
What time does the train arrive?
¿A qué hora llega el tren?

arrow NOUN
la **flecha** *fem*
Follow the arrows.
Siga las flechas.

art NOUN
1 el **dibujo** *masc* (at school)
   Art is my favourite subject.
   El dibujo es mi asignatura preferida.
2 el **arte** *masc* (artwork)
   modern art
   el arte moderno

art gallery NOUN
el **museo** *masc*
   The art gallery is closed.
   El museo está cerrado.

artist NOUN
el/la **artista** *masc/fem*

as CONJUNCTION, PREPOSITION
1 **como** (since)
   Ava, as it's your birthday you can choose.
   Ava, como es tu cumpleaños, puedes elegir.
2 **de** (in the role of)
   He works as a waiter in the holidays.
   Trabaja de camarero en las vacaciones.
   as ... as
   tan ... como
   Marco's as tall as David.
   Marco es tan alto como David.
   Write to me as soon as possible.
   Escríbeme lo antes posible.

ashamed ADJECTIVE
avergonzado *masc*
avergonzada *fem*
   He's ashamed.
   Está avergonzado.
   You should be ashamed of yourself!
   ¡Debería darte vergüenza!

ashtray NOUN
el **cenicero** *masc*

ask VERB
1 **preguntar** (make inquiry)
   Ask his name.
   Pregúntale el nombre.
   Ask your friend.
   Pregúntale a tu amigo.

LANGUAGE TIP
Don't forget the personal **a** in examples like this one.

   Who wants to ask a question?
   ¿Quién quiere hacer una pregunta?
   Ask the question.
   Haz la pregunta.
2 **pedir** (request)
   If you need help, ask!
   Si necesitas ayuda, ¡pídela!
3 **invitar** (invite)
   Are you going to ask Matthew to the party?
   ¿Vas a invitar a Matthew a la fiesta?

LANGUAGE TIP
Don't forget the personal **a** in examples like this one.

---

ask for VERB
pedir
   Ask for some chips and a drink.
   Pide patatas fritas y una bebida.

asleep ADJECTIVE
dormido *masc*
dormida *fem*
   to be asleep
   estar dormido
   Are you asleep?
   ¿Estás dormido?

assembly NOUN
la **reunión de los profesores y alumnos** *fem*

DID YOU KNOW...?
There is not normally **assembly** in Spanish schools.

---

assistant NOUN
1 el **dependiente** *masc*
   la **dependienta** *fem* (shop assistant)
   Ask the assistant.
   Pregúntale a la dependienta.
2 el/la **ayudante** *masc/fem* (helper)
   my assistant
   mi ayudante

asthma NOUN
el **asma** *fem*
I've got asthma.
Tengo asma.

LANGUAGE TIP
Even though it's a feminine noun, remember that you use **el** with **asma**.

astronomy NOUN
la **astronomía** *fem*

at PREPOSITION
1 **en** (*with place, festival*)
at the café
en el café
at Christmas
en Navidad
2 **a** (*with time, speed*)
at four o'clock
a las cuatro
at fifty kilometres an hour
a cincuenta kilómetros por hora
What time did you arrive at the station?
¿A qué hora llegaste a la estación?

LANGUAGE TIP
a combines with **el** to form **al**.

What time did you arrive at the airport?
¿A qué hora llegaste al aeropuerto?
3 la **arroba** *fem* (*at sign*)
My email address is loveday at collins dot co dot U-K (loveday@collins.co.uk).
Mi e-mail es loveday arroba collins punto co punto U-K (loveday@collins.co.uk).

at night
por la noche
What are you doing at the weekend?
¿Qué vas a hacer el fin de semana?
at school
en el colegio
at home
en casa

two at a time
dos a la vez

ate VERB ▷ *see* **eat**

athlete NOUN
el/la **atleta** *masc/fem*

Atlantic NOUN
el **Atlántico** *masc*

atlas NOUN
el **atlas** *masc* (PL los **atlas**)

attention NOUN
la **atención** *fem*
Pay attention, everyone!
¡Prestad atención todos!
Pay attention, Mark!
¡Presta atención, Mark!

attic NOUN
el **desván** *masc* (PL los **desvanes**)

attractive ADJECTIVE
atractivo *masc*
atractiva *fem*
She's very attractive.
Es muy atractiva.

August NOUN
agosto *masc*
My birthday's in August.
Mi cumpleaños es en agosto.
It's the tenth of August today.
Hoy es diez de agosto.

in August
en agosto
on the fifth of August
el cinco de agosto

LANGUAGE TIP
Months are not spelled with a capital letter in Spanish.

aunt NOUN
la **tía** *fem*
my aunt
mi tía
my aunt and uncle
mis tíos

au pair NOUN
el/la **au pair** *masc/fem* (PL los/las **au pair**)
She's working as an au pair in London.
Está de au pair en Londres.

Australia NOUN
Australia *fem*

Australian

> **Australian** can be an adjective or a noun.

A ADJECTIVE
australiano *masc*
australiana *fem*

He's Australian.
Es australiano.
She's Australian.
Es australiana.

B NOUN
el **australiano** *masc*
la **australiana** *fem*

LANGUAGE TIP
australiano is not spelled with a capital letter in Spanish.

---

author NOUN
1 el **autor** *masc*
la **autora** *fem* (*of particular book*)
the author of the book
el autor del libro
2 el **escritor** *masc*
la **escritora** *fem* (*as a job*)
a famous author
un escritor famoso

autumn
NOUN
el **otoño** *masc*
in autumn
en otoño

avatar NOUN
el **avatar** *masc*

avenue NOUN
la **avenida** *fem*

average

> **average** can be a noun or an adjective.

A NOUN
la **media** *fem*
on average
de media
above average
por encima de la media

B ADJECTIVE
medio *masc*
media *fem*
the average age
la edad media
I'm average height.
Soy de estatura media.

away ADVERB
fuera
He's away on a business trip.
Está fuera en viaje de negocios.
He'll be away for a week.
Estará fuera una semana.

awful ADJECTIVE
horroroso *masc*
horrorosa *fem*
The food's awful.
La comida está horrorosa.
That's awful!
¡Eso es horroroso!
I feel awful.
Me siento fatal.

Bb

baby NOUN
el **bebé** *masc*

LANGUAGE TIP
The masculine form **el bebé** applies to both boys and girls.

The baby's asleep.
El bebé está durmiendo.
She's going to have a baby.
Va a tener un niño.
Don't be a baby!
¡No seas crío!
my baby sister
mi hermanita

babysit VERB
hacer de canguro
I babysit at the weekends.
Hago de canguro los fines de semana.

babysitter NOUN
el/la **canguro** *masc/fem*

DID YOU KNOW...?
Did you know that **un canguro** is also a kangaroo?

---

back

┌─────────────────────────────────────┐
│ **back** can be a noun or an adjective. │
└─────────────────────────────────────┘

A NOUN
1 la **espalda** *fem* (*of person*)
My back hurts.
Me duele la espalda.

LANGUAGE TIP
In Spanish you usually use an article like **el**, **la** or **los**, **las** with parts of the body.

Lie on your back!
¡Túmbate de espaldas!
2 el **fondo** *masc* (*of room*)
at the back
al fondo
Tony and I sit at the back.
Tony y yo nos sentamos al fondo.
at the back of the house
en la parte de atrás de la casa
3 el **final** *masc* (*of book*)
The verb tables are at the back of the book.
Las conjugaciones verbales están al final del libro.

B ADJECTIVE
trasero *masc*
trasera *fem*
the back seat
el asiento trasero
He came in the back door.
Entró por la puerta de atrás.

backache NOUN
I've got backache.
Me duele la espalda.

background NOUN
el **fondo** *masc*
a house in the background
una casa en el fondo

backstroke NOUN
la **espalda** *fem*
I can do the backstroke.
Sé nadar a espalda.

backwards ADVERB
hacia atrás
Take a step backwards!
¡Da un paso hacia atrás!

bacon NOUN
el **beicon** *masc*
bacon and eggs
huevos con beicon

Spanish
English

A
B
C
D
E
F
G
H
I
J
K
L
M
N
O
P
Q
R
S
T
U
V
W
X
Y
Z

bad ADJECTIVE
1 **malo** *masc*
  mala *fem (awful)*
  a bad film
  una película mala
  Smoking is bad for you.
  Fumar es malo para la salud.

LANGUAGE TIP
Shorten **malo** to **mal** before a masculine singular noun.

  bad weather
  mal tiempo

LANGUAGE TIP
mal is also used in some phrases.

  That's not bad.
  No está mal.
  I'm bad at drawing.
  Se me da mal el dibujo.
2 **grave** *masc/fem (serious)*
  a bad accident
  un accidente grave
3 **travieso** *masc*
  traviesa *fem (naughty)*
  You bad boy!
  ¡Eres un chico travieso!

  Bad luck!
  ¡Mala suerte!

badge NOUN
la **chapa** *fem*

badly ADVERB
mal
  He behaved badly.
  Se portó mal.

badminton NOUN
el **bádminton** *masc*
  I play badminton.
  Juego al bádminton.

LANGUAGE TIP
In Spanish, you need to include **al** or **a la** before the names of sports or games when talking about playing them.

bag NOUN
1 la **bolsa** *fem*
  a plastic bag
  una bolsa de plástico
2 el **bolso** *masc (handbag)*

bagpipes PL NOUN
la **gaita** *fem*
  Jimmy plays the bagpipes.
  Jimmy toca la gaita.

baked beans PL NOUN
las **alubias con tomate** *fem pl*
  I like baked beans.
  Me gustan las alubias con tomate.

baked potato NOUN
la **patata asada** *fem*

baker's NOUN
la **panadería** *fem*

bakery NOUN
la **panadería** *fem*

balcony NOUN
el **balcón** *masc* (PL los **balcones**)

bald ADJECTIVE
calvo *masc*
calva *fem*
  My grandfather is bald.
  Mi abuelo es calvo.

ball NOUN
1 la **pelota** *fem*
  (for tennis, golf, cricket)
  Hit the ball!
  ¡Dale a la pelota!
2 el **balón** *masc*
  (PL los **balones**)
  (for football, rugby)
  Pass the ball!
  ¡Pasa el balón!

ballet NOUN
el **ballet** *masc*
  I do ballet.
  Hago ballet.

ballet dancer NOUN
el **bailarín** *masc* (PL los **bailarines**)
la **bailarina** *fem*

ballet shoes PL NOUN
las **zapatillas de ballet** *fem pl*

balloon NOUN
el **globo** *masc*
a red balloon
un globo rojo

banana NOUN
el **plátano** *masc*

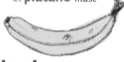

band NOUN
1 el **grupo de rock** *masc* (*rock band*)
2 la **banda de música** *fem* (*brass band*)

bandage NOUN
la **venda** *fem*
He's got a bandage round his arm.
Lleva una venda en el brazo.

LANGUAGE TIP
In Spanish you usually use an article like **el**, **la** or **los**, **las** with parts of the body.

---

bang

| **bang** can be a noun or a verb. |

A NOUN
el **golpe** *masc*
I heard a bang.
Oí un golpe.
I got a nasty bang on my head.
Me di un golpe fuerte en la cabeza.
The door shut with a bang.
La puerta se cerró de un portazo.
B VERB
to bang
golpear
Mind you don't bang your head!
¡Cuidado no te vayas a golpear la cabeza!

Don't bang the door!
¡No des un portazo!

banger NOUN
la **salchicha** *fem* (*sausage*)
bangers and mash
salchichas con puré de patatas

bank NOUN
1 el **banco** *masc* (*for money*)
She works in a bank.
Trabaja en un banco.
2 la **orilla** *fem* (*of river, lake*)
the banks of the Thames
las orillas del Támesis

bank holiday NOUN
el **día festivo** *masc*
It's a bank holiday today.
Hoy es día festivo.

bar NOUN
1 (*piece*)
a bar of chocolate
una tableta de chocolate
a bar of soap
una pastilla de jabón
2 el **bar** *masc* (*place*)
She works in a bar.
Trabaja en un bar.

barbecue NOUN
la **barbacoa** *fem*

barber's NOUN
la **barbería** *fem*
at the barber's
en la barbería

bare ADJECTIVE
desnudo *masc*
desnuda *fem*
She had bare arms.
Tenía los brazos desnudos.
Don't run about in bare feet.
No andes por ahí descalzo.

bargain NOUN
la **ganga** *fem*
It's a bargain!
¡Es una ganga!

bark VERB
ladrar
>**My dog barks a lot.**
>Mi perro ladra mucho.

baseball NOUN
el **béisbol** *masc*
>**I play baseball.**
>Juego al béisbol.

LANGUAGE TIP
In Spanish, you need to include **al** or **a la** before the names of sports or games when talking about playing them.

---

baseball cap NOUN
la **gorra de béisbol** *fem*

basement NOUN
el **sótano** *masc*

basin NOUN
el **lavabo** *masc* (*washbasin*)

basket NOUN
la **cesta** *fem*

basketball NOUN
el **baloncesto** *masc*
>**Do you play basketball?**
>¿Juegas al baloncesto?

LANGUAGE TIP
In Spanish, you need to include **al** or **a la** before the names of sports or games when talking about playing them.

---

bat NOUN
1 el **bate** *masc* (*for cricket, rounders*)
2 la **raqueta** *fem* (*for table tennis*)
3 el **murciélago** *masc* (*animal*)

bath NOUN
1 el **baño** *masc* (*wash*)
>**a hot bath**
>un baño caliente
>**to have a bath**
>bañarse
>**I have a bath every night.**
>Me baño todas las noches.
2 la **bañera** *fem* (*tub*)
>**There's a spider in the bath!**
>¡Hay una araña en la bañera!

LANGUAGE TIP
Don't confuse **la bañera** (the bathtub) with **el baño** (the wash you have in it).

bathroom NOUN
el **cuarto de baño** *masc*

battery NOUN
1 la **pila** *fem* (*for torch, toy*)
>**I need a battery.**
>Necesito una pila.
2 la **batería** *fem* (*for car*)
>**The battery's flat.**
>La batería está descargada.

battle NOUN
la **batalla** *fem*

BC ABBREVIATION
(= **before Christ**)
a.C. (= *antes de Cristo*)
>**in 200 BC**
>en el 200 a.C.

be VERB

LANGUAGE TIP
There are two main verbs **ser** and **estar** for **to be** in Spanish.

---

1 ser

LANGUAGE TIP
Use **ser** to talk about size, shape, colour and characteristics which are generally permanent.

I'm quite tall.
Soy bastante alto.
She's blonde.
Es rubia.
It's green.
Es verde.
It isn't very big.
No es muy grande.
It's round.
Es redondo.
They're wooden.
Son de madera.
It's easy.
Es fácil.

LANGUAGE TIP
Use **ser** to talk about where someone's from.

I'm English.
Soy inglesa.
I'm from Manchester.
Soy de Manchester.

LANGUAGE TIP
Use **ser** with a following noun (naming word) to say what someone or something is.

He's a teacher.
Es profesor.
It's a table.
Es una mesa.
It's the 28th of October today.
Hoy es 28 de octubre.

It's me.
Soy yo.

2 estar

LANGUAGE TIP
Use **estar** to talk about where people, places and objects are.

I'm at home.
Estoy en casa.
Lima is in Peru.
Lima está en Perú.
Where are the keys?
¿Dónde están las llaves?

LANGUAGE TIP
Use **estar** with adjectives (describing words) to talk about passing or temporary states.

I'm tired.
Estoy cansado.
Are you ready?
¿Estás listo?
The coffee's cold.
El café está frío.
He's ill today.
Hoy está enfermo.

LANGUAGE TIP
Use **estar** when talking about what someone is doing now.

I'm writing a letter.
Estoy escribiendo una carta.
What are you doing?
¿Qué estás haciendo?

3 tener

LANGUAGE TIP
Use **tener** when saying you're 'hot', 'cold', 'hungry', 'thirsty' or 'sleepy'.

I'm hot.
Tengo calor.
I'm cold.
Tengo frío.
I'm hungry.
Tengo hambre.
I'm thirsty.
Tengo sed.
I'm sleepy.
Tengo sueño.

LANGUAGE TIP
Use **tener** when talking about somebody's age.

I'm eleven.
Tengo once años.
My brother is thirteen.
Mi hermano tiene trece años.

4 hacer

LANGUAGE TIP
Use **hacer** when talking about the weather.

It's cold.
Hace frío.
It's hot.
Hace calor.
It's a nice day.
Hace buen día.

beach NOUN
la **playa** fem

beans PL NOUN
1 las **alubias con tomate** fem pl (baked beans)
Would you like some beans?
¿Quieres unas alubias con tomate?
2 las **judías verdes** fem pl (green beans)

beard NOUN
la **barba** fem
Our teacher's got a beard.
Nuestro profesor tiene barba.

beat VERB
ganar a (in game)
We're going to beat you!
¡Os vamos a ganar!

beautiful ADJECTIVE
1 **precioso** masc
preciosa fem (thing, place)
Your garden is beautiful.
Tu jardín es precioso.
2 **guapo** masc
guapa fem (person)
Emma is very beautiful.
Emma es muy guapa.

because CONJUNCTION
porque
We can't play outside because it's too cold.
No podemos jugar fuera porque hace mucho frío.

LANGUAGE TIP
The Spanish translations for **why** and **because** are very similar. When it is used to ask a question, **¿por qué?** is two separate words and has an accent on the **qué**.

Why don't you eat meat?
— Because I don't like it.
¿Por qué no comes carne? — Porque no me gusta.
I can't sleep because of the noise.
No puedo dormir por el ruido.
because of the weather
debido al mal tiempo
because of you
por ti

become VERB
hacerse
He became a footballer.
Se hizo futbolista.

LANGUAGE TIP
In Spanish, you do not use an article with people's jobs.

bed NOUN
la **cama** fem
in bed
en la cama
to go to bed
acostarse
I go to bed at ten o'clock.
Me acuesto a las diez.
What time do you go to bed?
¿A qué hora te acuestas?

bed and breakfast NOUN
la **pensión** fem (PL las **pensiones**)

bedroom NOUN
la **habitación** fem (PL las **habitaciones**)
my bedroom
mi habitación

bedtime NOUN
Ten o'clock is my usual bedtime.
Casi siempre me acuesto a las diez.
Bedtime!
¡A la cama!

bee NOUN
la **abeja** *fem*

beef NOUN
la **ternera** *fem*
Would you like beef or chicken?
¿Quieres ternera o pollo?
roast beef
el rosbif

been VERB ▷ *see* **be**

beer NOUN
la **cerveza** *fem*
a can of beer
una lata de cerveza

beetle NOUN
el **escarabajo** *masc*

before

> **before** can be a preposition, conjunction or adverb.

A PREPOSITION
antes de
before three o'clock
antes de las tres

B CONJUNCTION
Think before you answer, Rosa!
¡Piensa antes de contestar, Rosa!

C ADVERB
antes
Why didn't you say so before?
¿Por qué no lo has dicho antes?
I've never been to Scotland before.
Nunca había estado en Escocia.

begin VERB
empezar
It begins with 'b'.
Empieza por "b".
It's beginning to get cold.
Está empezando a hacer frío.

beginner NOUN
el/la **principiante** *masc/fem*
I'm a beginner.
Soy principiante.

beginning NOUN
el **principio** *masc*
at the beginning
al principio

begun VERB ▷ *see* **begin**

behave VERB
portarse
He behaves badly.
Se porta mal.
She's behaving like an idiot.
Se está portando como una idiota.
Behave!
¡Pórtate bien!

behind PREPOSITION
detrás de
It's behind the television.
Está detrás del televisor.
one behind the other
uno detrás del otro

beige

> **beige** can be an adjective or a noun.

A ADJECTIVE
beige *masc/fem*
It's beige.
Es beige.
a beige skirt
una falda beige

LANGUAGE TIP
Colour adjectives come after the noun in Spanish.

B NOUN
el **beige** *masc*

believe VERB
creer
I don't believe you.
No te creo.

bell NOUN

1 la **campana** *fem (at school, in church)*
The bell rang.
Sonó la campana.
2 el **timbre** *masc (at door, on reception)*
Ring the bell.
Llama al timbre.
3 el **cascabel** *masc (small bell)*
My cat has a bell on its collar.
Mi gato lleva un cascabel en el collar.

belong VERB
pertenecer
to belong to somebody
pertenecer a alguien
That belongs to me.
Eso me pertenece a mí.
Does this belong to you?
¿Es tuyo esto?
Who does it belong to?
¿De quién es?
The ball belongs to Amira.
El balón es de Amira.

below PREPOSITION
bajo
below ground
bajo tierra
ten degrees below freezing
diez grados bajo cero

belt NOUN
el **cinturón** *masc (PL los **cinturones**)*

bench NOUN
el **banco** *masc*

bend

> **bend** can be a noun or a verb.

A NOUN
la **curva** *fem*
a dangerous bend
una curva peligrosa
B VERB
to bend
doblar
Bend your legs!
¡Dobla las piernas!

LANGUAGE TIP
In Spanish you usually use an article like **el**, **la** or **los**, **los** with parts of the body.

---

beneath PREPOSITION
debajo de
beneath the table
debajo de la mesa

bent VERB ▷ see bend

beside PREPOSITION
al lado de
beside the television
al lado del televisor
Sit beside me.
Siéntate a mi lado.

best

> **best** can be an adjective, noun or adverb.

A ADJECTIVE
mejor *masc/fem*
Francis is my best friend.
Francis es mi mejor amigo.
Mary and Olga are my best friends.
Mary y Olga son mis mejores amigas.
the best team in the world
el mejor equipo del mundo
B NOUN
el/la **mejor** *masc/fem*
He's the best in the class.
Es el mejor de la clase.

C ADVERB
mejor
Priya sings best.
Priya es la que canta mejor.

Best wishes!
¡Saludos cordiales!

LANGUAGE TIP
Have you noticed the upside-down exclamation mark at the start of Spanish exclamations?

best man NOUN
el **padrino de boda** *masc*

better

better can be an adjective or an adverb.

A ADJECTIVE
mejor *masc/fem*
The ice cream is better than the cake.
El helado está mejor que el pastel.
That's better!
¡Eso está mejor!

B ADVERB
mejor
I can sing better than you.
Yo canto mejor que tú.

Get better soon!
¡Que te mejores pronto!

LANGUAGE TIP
Have you noticed the upside-down exclamation mark at the start of Spanish exclamations?

between PREPOSITION
entre
Think of a number between one and twelve.
Piensa en un número entre uno y doce.

Bible NOUN
la **Biblia** *fem*

bicycle NOUN
la **bicicleta** *fem*
by bicycle
en bicicleta

big ADJECTIVE
grande *masc/fem*
a big garden
un jardín grande
a big house
una casa grande
Have you got it in a bigger size?
¿Tiene una talla más grande?

LANGUAGE TIP
Shorten **grande** to **gran** before a singular noun.

a big problem
un gran problema
my big brother
mi hermano mayor
her big sister
su hermana mayor

bike NOUN
1 la **bici** *fem* (*bicycle*)
by bike
en bici

2 la **moto** *fem* (*motorbike*)

LANGUAGE TIP
Even though it ends in **-o**, **la moto** is a feminine noun.

bikini NOUN
el **bikini** *masc*

bill NOUN
  la **cuenta** fem (in restaurant, hotel)
    Can we have the bill, please?
    ¿Nos puede traer la cuenta, por favor?

billion NOUN
  mil millones masc pl
    a billion dollars
    mil millones de dólares

    LANGUAGE TIP
    Be careful! The translation of **billion** is
    not **billón**.

bin NOUN
  1 la **papelera** fem (wastepaper basket)
    Put your chewing gum in the bin.
    Tira el chicle a la papelera.
  2 el **cubo de la basura** masc
    The bin is in the kitchen.
    El cubo de la basura está en la cocina.

bingo NOUN
  el **bingo** masc
    We're going to play bingo.
    Vamos a jugar al bingo.

    LANGUAGE TIP
    In Spanish, you need to include **al** or **a
    la** before the names of sports or games
    when talking about playing them.

biology NOUN
  la **biología** fem

bird NOUN
  el **pájaro**
    masc

Biro®
  NOUN
  el **boli** masc

birthday NOUN
  el **cumpleaños**
    masc
    (PL los **cumpleaños**)
    My birthday is the third of May.
    Mi cumpleaños es el tres de mayo.
    When's your birthday?
    ¿Cuándo es tu cumpleaños?

    Happy Birthday!
    ¡Feliz cumpleaños!

    LANGUAGE TIP
    Have you noticed the upside-down
    exclamation mark at the start of
    Spanish exclamations?

birthday cake NOUN
  la **tarta de cumpleaños** fem

birthday card NOUN
  la **tarjeta de cumpleaños** fem

birthday party NOUN
  la **fiesta de cumpleaños** fem
    **Would you like to come to my
    birthday party?**
    ¿Quieres venir a mi fiesta de
    cumpleaños?

biscuit NOUN
  la **galleta** fem
    Would you like a biscuit?
    ¿Quieres una galleta?

bit NOUN
    a bit
    un poco
    I'm a bit tired.
    Estoy un poco cansado.

bite VERB
  1 **morder** (with teeth)
    My dog doesn't bite.
    Mi perro no muerde.
    Stop biting your nails!
    ¡Deja de morderte las uñas!
  2 **picar** (insect)
    I've been bitten by a mosquito.
    Me ha picado un mosquito.

black

  black can be an adjective or a noun.

A ADJECTIVE
  negro masc
  negra fem
    She's Black.
    Es negra.
    a black jacket
    una chaqueta negra

LANGUAGE TIP
Colour adjectives come after the noun in Spanish.

B NOUN
el **negro** *masc*
He's dressed in black.
Va vestido de negro.

blackberry NOUN
la **mora** *fem*
We picked blackberries.
Cogimos moras.

blackboard NOUN
la **pizarra** *fem*
Look at the blackboard!
¡Mira la pizarra!

black coffee NOUN
1 el **café solo** *masc* (small)
2 el **café americano** *masc* (large)

DID YOU KNOW...?
un café solo is a very small strong black coffee while **un café americano** is a mug of weaker black coffee.

blackcurrant NOUN
la **grosella negra** *fem*
blackcurrant jam
mermelada de grosella negra

blank

blank can be an adjective or a noun.

A ADJECTIVE
en blanco
a blank sheet of paper
un folio en blanco
B NOUN
el **espacio en blanco** *masc*
Fill in the blanks.
Rellena los espacios en blanco.

blanket NOUN
la **manta** *fem*

blazer NOUN
el **blazer** *masc*
a navy blazer
un blazer azul marino

bless VERB
Bless you!
¡Salud!

DID YOU KNOW...?
People say **isalud!** when someone sneezes in Spain.

blew VERB ▷ *see* **blow**

blind

blind can be an adjective or a noun.

A ADJECTIVE
ciego *masc*
ciega *fem*
My grandfather is blind.
Mi abuelo es ciego.
a blind man
un ciego
B NOUN
la **persiana** *fem*
Open the blinds!
¡Sube las persianas!

blindfold VERB
I'm going to blindfold you.
Te voy a vendar los ojos.

block NOUN
a block of flats
un bloque de pisos

blog NOUN
el **blog** *masc* (PL los **blogs**)

blogpost NOUN
la **entrada de blog** *fem*

blonde ADJECTIVE
rubio *masc*
rubia *fem*
She's got blonde hair.
Tiene el pelo rubio.

blood NOUN
la **sangre** *fem*

blouse NOUN
la **blusa** *fem*
a white blouse
una blusa blanca

blow VERB
soplar
The wind is blowing.
Está soplando el viento.
Stop when I blow the whistle!
¡Para cuando toque el silbato!
Blow your nose!
¡Suénate la nariz!

LANGUAGE TIP
In Spanish you usually use an article like **el**, **la** or **los**, **las** with parts of the body.

Blow out the candles!
¡Apaga las velas!

blue

> **blue** can be an adjective or a noun.

A ADJECTIVE
azul *masc/fem*
The sky is blue.
El cielo es azul.
a blue dress
un vestido azul

LANGUAGE TIP
Colour adjectives come after the noun in Spanish.

B NOUN
el **azul** *masc*
Blue is my favourite colour.
El azul es mi color preferido.

board NOUN
la **pizarra** *fem* (*blackboard, whiteboard*)
on the board
en la pizarra

board game NOUN
el **juego de mesa** *masc*

boarding school NOUN
el **internado** *masc*
I go to boarding school.
Voy a un internado.

boat NOUN
1 el **barco** *masc* (*ferry, liner*)
by boat
en barco
2 el **bote** *masc* (*rowing boat, dinghy*)

body NOUN
el **cuerpo** *masc*

boiled ADJECTIVE
cocido *masc*
cocida *fem*
boiled potatoes
patatas cocidas
a boiled egg
un huevo pasado por agua

bomb NOUN
la **bomba** *fem*

bonfire NOUN
la **hoguera** *fem*

DID YOU KNOW...?
The Spanish do not celebrate **Bonfire Night** though it is traditional in many places in Spain to celebrate **la noche de San Juan** (Saint John's Eve) with a public bonfire on the 23rd of June.

---

book

> **book** can be a noun or a verb.

A NOUN
1 el **libro** *masc* (*printed*)
Open your books at page ten.
Abrid los libros por la página diez.
2 el **cuaderno** *masc* (*exercise book*)
Write the words in your books.
Escribid las palabras en los cuadernos.

A
B
C
D
E
F
G
H
I
J
K
L
M
N
O
P
Q
R
S
T
U
V
W
X
Y
Z

B VERB
to book
reservar
I want to book a seat.
Quiero reservar un asiento.

bookcase NOUN
la **librería** *fem*

LANGUAGE TIP
Did you know that **la librería** is also
the word for **bookshop** in Spanish?

booklet NOUN
el **folleto** *masc*

bookshelf NOUN
la **estantería** *fem*
on the bookshelves
en las estanterías

bookshop NOUN
la **librería** *fem*

boot NOUN
1 la **bota** *fem*
I like your boots!
¡Me gustan tus botas!
football boots
botas de fútbol
2 el **maletero** *masc* (*of car*)
It's in the boot.
Está en el maletero.

border NOUN
la **frontera** *fem* (*of country*)

bored ADJECTIVE
aburrido *masc*
aburrida *fem*
I'm bored.
Estoy aburrido.

boring ADJECTIVE
aburrido *masc*
aburrida *fem*
a boring programme
un programa aburrido
**This game is pretty boring,
isn't it?**
Este juego es bastante aburrido,
¿verdad?

born ADJECTIVE
I was born in 2000.
Nací en el 2000.

borrow VERB
Can I borrow your pen?
¿Me dejas tu boli?

LANGUAGE TIP
Notice how the action is reversed in
Spanish. You would normally use **¿me
dejas...?** or **¿me prestas...?** when you
want to borrow something.

boss NOUN
el **jefe** *masc*
la **jefa** *fem*

bossy ADJECTIVE
mandón *masc* (PL **mandones**)
mandona *fem*

both PRONOUN, ADJECTIVE
los **dos** *masc pl*
las **dos** *fem pl*
**Anna and Manuel, you're both
late!**
Anna y Manuel, ¡habéis llegado tarde
los dos!
**Peter and Laura have both got a
rabbit.**
Tanto Peter como Laura tienen un
conejo.

bother VERB
molestar
I'm sorry to bother you.
Siento molestarle.

Don't bother!
¡No te preocupes!

bottle NOUN
la **botella** *fem*
**a bottle of
mineral
water**
una botella
de agua
mineral

bottom NOUN
1 la **parte de abajo** *fem* (*of page, list*)
   Look at the bottom of the page.
   Mira en la parte de abajo de la página.
2 el **fondo** *masc* (*of container, bag, sea*)
   My pen's at the bottom of my bag.
   Mi boli está en el fondo del bolso.
3 el **trasero** *masc* (*bum*)

bought VERB ▷ *see* **buy**

bow

> **bow** can be a noun or a verb.

A NOUN
1 el **lazo** *masc* (*in ribbon, string*)
   Tie a bow!
   ¡Haz un lazo!
   She's wearing a pink bow in her hair.
   Lleva un lazo rosa en el pelo.
2 el **arco** *masc* (*for archery*)
   a bow and arrow
   un arco y una flecha
B VERB
   to bow
   hacer una reverencia

bowl NOUN
el **tazón** *masc* (PL los **tazones**)
   a bowl of soup
   un tazón de sopa

bowling NOUN
los **bolos** *masc pl*
   Do you want to come bowling?
   ¿Quieres venir a jugar a los bolos?

LANGUAGE TIP
In Spanish, you need to include **a los** before **bolos** when using it with the verb **jugar**.

box NOUN
1 la **caja** *fem* (*container*)
   a box of matches
   una caja de cerillas
   a cardboard box
   una caja de cartón
2 la **casilla** *fem* (*in questionnaire*)
   Tick the boxes.
   Marca las casillas.

boxer NOUN
el **boxeador** *masc*

boxer shorts PL NOUN
los **bóxers** *masc pl*

boxing NOUN
el **boxeo** *masc*
   I don't like boxing.
   No me gusta el boxeo.

Boxing Day NOUN
el **día después de Navidad** *masc*
   on Boxing Day
   el día después de Navidad

DID YOU KNOW...?
Boxing Day is not celebrated in Spain.
---

boy NOUN
1 el **niño** *masc* (*young*)
   a boy of six
   un niño de seis años
2 el **chico** *masc* (*older*)
   Well done, boys!
   ¡Muy bien, chicos!

boyfriend NOUN
el **novio** *masc*
   Have you got a boyfriend?
   ¿Tienes novio?

bra NOUN
el **sujetador** *masc*

brace NOUN
los **brákets** *masc pl*
   She wears a brace.
   Lleva brákets.

bracelet NOUN
la **pulsera** *fem*

bracket NOUN
el **paréntesis** *masc* (PL los **paréntesis**)
in brackets
entre paréntesis

brain NOUN
el **cerebro** *masc*

brainy ADJECTIVE
listo *masc*
lista *fem*
Marina is very brainy.
Marina es muy lista.

branch NOUN
la **rama** *fem* (of tree)

brand-new ADJECTIVE
flamante *masc/fem*
It's brand-new.
Es flamante.

brass band NOUN
la **banda de música** *fem*

brave ADJECTIVE
valiente *masc/fem*
Be brave!
¡Sé valiente!

bread NOUN
el **pan** *masc*
Would you like some bread?
¿Quieres pan?
bread and butter
pan con mantequilla

break

> **break** can be a noun or a verb.

A NOUN
1 el **descanso** *masc* (in activity)
2 el **recreo** *masc* (at school)
during morning break
durante el recreo de la mañana
B VERB
to break
romper
You're going to break it.
Lo vas a romper.
Who broke the window?
¿Quién rompió el cristal?

Richard has broken his arm.
Richard se ha roto el brazo.

LANGUAGE TIP
In Spanish you usually use an article like **el**, **la** or **los**, **las** with parts of the body.

---

break down VERB
averiarse
The bus has broken down.
El autobús se ha averiado.
Our car broke down.
Se nos averió el coche.

break up VERB
We break up next Wednesday.
Empezamos las vacaciones el miércoles que viene.

breakfast NOUN
el **desayuno** *masc*
Breakfast is at eight o'clock.
El desayuno es a las ocho.
I have cereal for breakfast.
Tomo cereales para el desayuno.
to have breakfast
desayunar
When do you have breakfast?
¿A qué hora desayunas?

break time NOUN
el **recreo** *masc*
at break time
en el recreo

breaststroke NOUN
la **braza** *fem*
I can do the breaststroke.
Sé nadar a braza.

breath NOUN
Take a deep breath!
¡Respira hondo!

brick NOUN
el **ladrillo** *masc*
a brick wall
una pared de ladrillo

bride NOUN
la **novia** *fem*
the bride and groom
los novios

bridegroom NOUN
el **novio** *masc*

bridesmaid NOUN
la **dama de honor** *fem*

bridge NOUN
el **puente** *masc*

bright ADJECTIVE
vivo *masc*
viva *fem*
a bright colour
un color vivo
bright blue
azul vivo
a bright blue shirt
una camisa azul vivo

LANGUAGE TIP
When you describe something as
bright blue, **bright red** and so on,
neither the colour nor **vivo** changes its
ending to agree with the noun.

brilliant ADJECTIVE
estupendo *masc*
estupenda *fem*
**We're going to London.
— Brilliant!**
Nos vamos a Londres. — ¡Estupendo!

bring VERB
traer
**Could you bring me a glass of
water?**
¿Me podrías traer un vaso de agua?
Bring the money tomorrow.
Trae el dinero mañana.

bring back VERB
devolver
**You must bring them back
tomorrow.**
Tienes que devolverlos mañana.

Britain NOUN
Gran Bretaña *fem*
in Britain
en Gran Bretaña

British

British can be an adjective or a noun.

A ADJECTIVE
británico *masc*
británica *fem*
She's British.
Es británica.
B NOUN
the British
los británicos

LANGUAGE TIP
británico is not spelled with a capital
letter in Spanish.

British Isles PL NOUN
las **Islas Británicas** *fem pl*

broccoli NOUN
el **brécol** *masc*
Would you like some broccoli?
¿Quieres brécol?

brochure NOUN
el **folleto** *masc*

broke VERB ▷ *see* **break**

broken
A ADJECTIVE
roto *masc*
rota *fem*

A
B
C
D
E
F
G
H
I
J
K
L
M
N
O
P
Q
R
S
T
U
V
W
X
Y
Z

It's broken.
Está roto.
He's got a broken arm.
Tiene un brazo roto.
B VERB ▷ see **break**

bronze NOUN
el **bronce** *masc*
the bronze medal
la medalla de bronce

brother NOUN
el **hermano** *masc*
my big brother
mi hermano mayor
**I've got one brother and two
sisters.**
Tengo un hermano y dos hermanas.
**I haven't got any brothers or
sisters.**
No tengo hermanos.

> **Have you got any brothers or
> sisters?**
> ¿Tienes hermanos?

brought VERB ▷ see **bring**
brown

> **brown** can be an adjective or a noun.

A ADJECTIVE
1 **marrón** *masc/fem* (PL **marrones**)
My shoes are brown.
Mis zapatos son marrones.
I've got brown eyes.
Tengo los ojos marrones.

LANGUAGE TIP
Colour adjectives come after the noun
in Spanish.

2 **castaño** *masc*
castaña *fem* (hair)
I've got brown hair.
Tengo el pelo castaño.
She's got light brown hair.
Tiene el pelo castaño claro.
3 **moreno** *masc*
morena *fem* (tanned)
Sabrina is very brown.
Sabrina está muy morena.
B NOUN
el **marrón** *masc*
**Do you have these shoes in
brown?**
¿Tiene estos zapatos en marrón?

brown bread NOUN
el **pan integral** *masc*

Brownie NOUN
la **exploradora** *fem*
I'm a Brownie.
Soy exploradora.

bruise NOUN
el **moretón** *masc* (PL los **moretones**)
You've got a bruise.
Tienes un moretón.

brush

> **brush** can be a noun or a verb.

A NOUN
el **cepillo** *masc*
a brush and comb
un cepillo y un peine
B VERB
to brush
cepillar
I brush my pony.
Cepillo a mi pony.
I brush my hair.
Me cepillo el pelo.
I brush my teeth every night.
Me cepillo los dientes todas las noches.

LANGUAGE TIP
In Spanish you usually use an article like **el**, **la** or **los**, **las** with parts of the body.

bubble gum NOUN
el **chicle** *masc*

bucket NOUN
el **cubo** *masc*
my bucket and spade
mi cubo y mi pala

bug NOUN
el **virus** *masc* (PL los **virus**)
Amy's got a bug.
Amy tiene un virus.

buggy NOUN
la **sillita de paseo** *fem*

build VERB
construir
My dad is building a garage.
Mi padre está construyendo un garaje.

building NOUN
el **edificio** *masc*
a tall building
un edificio alto

built VERB ▷*see* **build**

bull NOUN
el **toro** *masc*
There's a bull in the field.
Hay un toro en el prado.

bully
A NOUN
el **abusón** *masc* (PL los **abusones**)
la **abusona** *fem*
B VERB
to bully
acosar

bullying NOUN
el **acoso** *masc*

bum NOUN
el **trasero** *masc*

bun NOUN
el **bollo** *masc*
I'd like a bun.
Quiero un bollo.

bunch NOUN
el **ramo** *masc*
a bunch of flowers
un ramo de flores

bunches PL NOUN
las **coletas** *fem pl*
She has bunches.
Lleva coletas.

bunk beds PL NOUN
las **literas** *fem pl*

burger NOUN
la **hamburguesa** *fem*
a burger and chips
una hamburguesa y patatas fritas

burglar NOUN
el **ladrón** *masc* (PL los **ladrones**)
la **ladrona** *fem*

burqua NOUN
la **burka** *fem*
She is wearing a burqua.
Lleva burka.

bus NOUN
el **autobús** *masc* (PL los **autobuses**)
I go to school by bus.
Voy al colegio en autobús.
the school bus
el autobús escolar

by bus
en autobús

bus driver NOUN
el **conductor de autobús** *masc*
la **conductora de autobús** *fem*
My uncle's a bus driver.
Mi tío es conductor de autobús.

LANGUAGE TIP
In Spanish, you do not use an article with people's jobs.

Spanish

English

A
B
C
D
E
F
G
H
I
J
K
L
M
N
O
P
Q
R
S
T
U
V
W
X
Y
Z

business NOUN
1 los **negocios** *masc pl* (*activity*)
He's away on business.
Está en viaje de negocios.
a business trip
un viaje de negocios
2 la **empresa** *fem* (*company*)
My mum has her own business.
Mi madre tiene su propia empresa.

bus station NOUN
la **estación de autobuses** *fem*
(PL las **estaciones de autobuses**)

bus stop NOUN
la **parada de autobús** *fem*

busy ADJECTIVE
ocupado *masc*
ocupada *fem*
My mother is always busy.
Mi madre siempre está ocupada.

but CONJUNCTION
pero
Thanks, but I'm not hungry.
Gracias, pero no tengo hambre.

butcher's NOUN
la **carnicería** *fem*

butter NOUN
la **mantequilla** *fem*

butterfly NOUN
la **mariposa** *fem*

button NOUN
el **botón** *masc* (PL los **botones**)

buy VERB
comprar
What are you going to buy?
¿Qué vas a comprar?
I'm going to buy a present for Tim.
Voy a comprar un regalo para Tim.

by PREPOSITION
1 **por** (*person*)
a meal prepared by Helen
una comida preparada por Helen
2 **de** (*artist*)
a painting by Picasso
un cuadro de Picasso
a book by J.K. Rowling
un libro de J.K. Rowling
3 **al lado de** (*place*)
Where's the library? — It's by the post office.
¿Dónde está la biblioteca? — Está al lado de Correos.
4 **en** (*transport*)
We're going by car.
Vamos en coche.

by car
en coche
by train
en tren
by bus
en autobús

bye EXCLAMATION
¡**adiós**!

Cc

cab NOUN
el **taxi** *masc*

cabbage NOUN
la **col** *fem*

café NOUN
la **cafetería** *fem*

DID YOU KNOW…?
Spanish cafés are a bit different from the ones in Britain. They tend to stay open at night and can serve alcoholic drinks throughout the day.

---

cafeteria NOUN
el **restaurante autoservicio** *masc*
(PL los **restaurantes autoservicio**)

cage NOUN
la **jaula** *fem*

cagoule NOUN
el **chubasquero** *masc*

cake NOUN
1 el **pastel** *masc* (*individual*)
2 la **tarta** *fem* (*bigger*)
I'm going to bake a cake.
Voy a hacer una tarta.
a piece of cake
un trozo de tarta

calculator NOUN
la **calculadora** *fem*

calendar NOUN
el **calendario** *masc*

calf NOUN
el **ternero** *masc*

call

> **call** can be a verb or a noun.

A VERB
to call
llamar
Everyone calls her Fi.
Todos la llaman Fi.
Call this number.
Llama a este número.
Call the police!
¡Llama a la policía!
My cat is called Fluffy.
Mi gato se llama Fluffy.
What's your cat called?
¿Cómo se llama tu gato?
What are your brothers called?
¿Cómo se llaman tus hermanos?

What are you called?
¿Cómo te llamas?
I'm called Helen.
Me llamo Helen.
I am going to call the register.
Voy a pasar lista.

B NOUN
la **llamada** *fem*
Thanks for your call.
Gracias por tu llamada.
Give me a call.
Llámame.

call back VERB
volver a llamar
I'll call you back later.
Te volveré a llamar más tarde.

call centre NOUN
el **servicio de atención telefónica** *masc*

Spanish
English
a
b
c
d
e
f
g
h
i
j
k
l
m
n
o
p
q
r
s
t
u
v
w
x
y
z

A
B
C
D
E
F
G
H
I
J
K
L
M
N
O
P
Q
R
S
T
U
V
W
X
Y
Z

calm ADJECTIVE
  tranquilo *masc*
  tranquila *fem*

calm down VERB
  Calm down, Paul!
  ¡Tranquilo, Paul!
  Calm down, Elsa!
  ¡Tranquila, Elsa!
  Calm down, children!
  ¡Tranquilos, niños!

calves PL NOUN
  los **terneros** *masc pl* (*young cattle*)

camcorder NOUN
  la **videocámara** *fem*

came VERB ▷ *see* **come**

camera NOUN
  la **cámara** *fem*
    I've got a new camera.
    Tengo una cámara nueva.

camp NOUN
  el **campamento** *masc*

camping NOUN
  to go camping
  ir de camping
  We're going camping.
  Vamos a ir de camping.

LANGUAGE TIP
Note that in Spanish the word
camping on its own means
campsite. To talk about the activity,
you need to say **ir de camping**.

---

campsite NOUN
  el **camping** *masc* (PL los **campings**)
  **The campsite is next to the
  river.**
  El camping está al lado del río.

can

> **can** can be a noun or a verb.

A NOUN
  la **lata** *fem*
  a can of Coke
  una lata de Coca-Cola

B VERB
1 **poder** (*be able to*)
  I can't go.
  No puedo ir.
  Can I come in?
  ¿Puedo entrar?
  Can you open the door?
  ¿Puedes abrir la puerta?

LANGUAGE TIP
You don't always translate **can**.

  I can't see it.
  No lo veo.
  **Can you speak English? — No, I
  can't.**
  ¿Hablas inglés? — No.

  I can.
  Puedo.
  I can't.
  No puedo.
  Can you?
  ¿Puedes?

2 **saber** (*know how to*)
  I can swim.
  Sé nadar.
  I can't ride a bike.
  No sé montar en bici.

Canada NOUN
  Canadá *masc*

Canadian

> **Canadian** can be an adjective or a
> noun.

A ADJECTIVE
  canadiense *masc/fem*

  She's Canadian
  Es canadiense.

B NOUN
el/la **canadiense** *masc/fem*

---

canal NOUN
el **canal** *masc*

cancel VERB
cancelar
**We've got to cancel our trip to
London.**
Tenemos que cancelar nuestro viaje a
Londres.

cancer NOUN
el **cáncer** *masc*
He's got cancer.
Tiene cáncer.

candle NOUN
la **vela** *fem*

canoe NOUN
la **canoa** *fem*

canoeing NOUN
to go canoeing
hacer piragüismo
We're going canoeing.
Vamos a hacer piragüismo.

can-opener NOUN
el **abrelatas** *masc* (PL los **abrelatas**)

can't VERB ▷ *see* **can**

canteen NOUN
la **cafetería** *fem*
I eat in the canteen.
Yo como en la cafetería.

cap NOUN
la **gorra** *fem*

capital NOUN
1 la **capital** *fem* (*city*)
Madrid is the capital of Spain.
Madrid es la capital de España.
2 la **mayúscula** *fem* (*letter*)
Write your address in capitals.
Escribe tu dirección en mayúsculas.

capital letter NOUN
la **mayúscula** *fem*

captain NOUN
el **capitán** *masc* (PL los **capitanes**)
la **capitana** *fem*
She's captain of the hockey team.
Es capitana del equipo de hockey.

caption NOUN
la **leyenda** *fem*

car NOUN
el **coche** *masc*
We've got a new car.
Tenemos un coche nuevo.
by car
en coche
We're going there by car.
Vamos allí en coche.

caravan NOUN
la **caravana** *fem*

caravan site NOUN
el **camping de caravanas** *masc*

card NOUN
1 la **carta** *fem* (*playing card*)
They are playing cards.
Están jugando a las cartas.

---

a
b
c
d
e
f
g
h
i
j
k
l
m
n
o
p
q
r
s
t
u
v
w
x
y
z

2 la **tarjeta** *fem* (*for birthday, Christmas*)
I got lots of cards.
He recibido muchas tarjetas.

DID YOU KNOW...?
Spanish people don't generally send as many cards as we do in Britain.

cardboard NOUN
el **cartón** *masc*

card game NOUN
el **juego de cartas** *masc*

cardigan NOUN
la **rebeca** *fem*
a green cardigan
una rebeca verde

care

> **care** can be a noun or a verb.

A NOUN
el **cuidado** *masc*
with care
con cuidado
B VERB
to care
I don't care!
¡No me importa!

careful ADJECTIVE
to be careful
tener cuidado
Be careful, Gordon!
¡Ten cuidado, Gordon!

carefully ADVERB
con cuidado
Fold the paper carefully.
Dobla el papel con cuidado.
Think carefully, Hazel!
¡Piénsatelo bien, Hazel!
Listen carefully, children!
¡Escuchad con atención, niños!

careless ADJECTIVE
a careless mistake
un error por descuido

caretaker NOUN
el **bedel** *masc*

LANGUAGE TIP
In Spanish, you do not use an article with people's jobs.

carol NOUN
a Christmas carol
un villancico

car park NOUN
el **parking** *masc* (PL los **parkings**)

carpet NOUN
la **moqueta** *fem* (*fitted*)
My bedroom carpet is blue.
La moqueta de mi habitación es azul.

carriage NOUN
el **vagón** *masc* (PL los **vagones**)

carrier bag NOUN
la **bolsa de asas** *fem*

carrot NOUN
la **zanahoria** *fem*

carry VERB
llevar
I'll carry your bag.
Yo te llevo la bolsa.

carry on VERB
seguir
Carry on, Jaya!
¡Sigue, Jaya!

carton NOUN
el **cartón** *masc* (PL los **cartones**)
a carton of milk
un cartón de leche

cartoon NOUN
1 los **dibujos animados** *masc pl* (*on television*)
I watch cartoons on Saturdays.
Veo los dibujos animados los sábados.
2 la **viñeta** *fem* (*strip cartoon*)

case NOUN
la **maleta** *fem* (*suitcase*)
That's my case!
¡Esa es mi maleta!

casserole NOUN
el **guiso** *masc*

castle NOUN
  el **castillo** *masc*
    Dover Castle
    el castillo de Dover

casual ADJECTIVE
  informal *masc/fem*
    I prefer casual clothes.
    Prefiero la ropa informal.

cat NOUN
  el **gato** *masc*
  la **gata** *fem*
    **Have you
    got a cat?**
    ¿Tienes gato?

catch VERB
  coger
    Catch!
    ¡Cógelo!
    Which bus do you catch?
    ¿Qué autobús coges tú?
    My cat catches birds.
    Mi gato atrapa pájaros.

cathedral NOUN
  la **catedral** *fem*

Catholic

> **Catholic** can be an adjective or a
> noun.

A ADJECTIVE
  católico *masc*
  católica *fem*
B NOUN
  el **católico** *masc*
  la **católica** *fem*
    I'm a Catholic.
    Soy católico.

LANGUAGE TIP
católico is not spelled with a capital
letter in Spanish.

---

cauliflower NOUN
  la **coliflor** *fem*

cave NOUN
  la **cueva** *fem*

CD NOUN
  el **CD** *masc* (PL los **CDs**)

ceiling NOUN
  el **techo** *masc*

DID YOU KNOW...?
Did you know that **el techo** can also
be the word for **roof**?

---

celebrate VERB
  celebrar
    Let's celebrate!
    ¡Vamos a celebrarlo!

celery NOUN
  el **apio** *masc*

cellar NOUN
  el **sótano** *masc*
    The cellar is damp.
    El sótano está húmedo.
    a wine cellar
    una bodega

cello NOUN
  el **violonchelo** *masc*
    I play the cello.
    Toco el violonchelo.

cemetery NOUN
  el **cementerio** *masc*

cent NOUN
el **céntimo** masc (division of euro)
two euros and twenty cents
dos euros y veinte céntimos

centigrade ADJECTIVE
centígrado masc
centígrada fem
twenty degrees centigrade
veinte grados centígrados

centimetre NOUN
el **centímetro** masc

central heating NOUN
la **calefacción central** fem

centre NOUN
el **centro** masc
in the centre
en el centro
The cinema is in the centre of town.
El cine está en el centro de la ciudad.
a sports centre
un polideportivo

century NOUN
el **siglo** masc
the twenty-first century
el siglo veintiuno

cereal NOUN
los **cereales** masc pl
I have cereal for breakfast.
Desayuno cereales.

certain ADJECTIVE
1 **cierto** masc
cierta fem
a certain person
una cierta persona
2 **seguro** masc
segura fem (sure)
I'm not certain.
No estoy seguro.

certainly ADVERB
Certainly!
¡Por supuesto!
Certainly not!
¡Por supuesto que no!

certificate NOUN
el **certificado** masc

chain NOUN
la **cadena** fem
a silver chain
una cadena de plata

chair NOUN
1 la **silla** fem
There's a table and four chairs in the kitchen.
Hay una mesa y cuatro sillas en la cocina.

2 el **sillón** masc (PL los **sillones**)
(armchair)
There are two chairs and a sofa in the lounge.
Hay dos sillones y un sofá en el salón.

chalk NOUN
la **tiza** fem
a piece of chalk
una tiza

champagne NOUN
el **champán** masc
a glass of champagne
una copa de champán

champion NOUN
el **campeón** masc (PL los **campeones**)
la **campeona** fem
Mike is the champion!
¡Mike es el campeón!

championship NOUN
el **campeonato** masc

chance NOUN
la **oportunidad** fem
I'll give you another chance.
Te daré otra oportunidad.
No chance!
¡Ni en broma!
You're taking a chance!
¡Te estás arriesgando!

change

change can be a verb or a noun.

A VERB
to change
1 **cambiar**
I'd like to change fifty pounds.
Quiero cambiar cincuenta libras.
How you've changed!
¡Cuánto has cambiado!
2 **cambiar de** (swap)
Change places!
¡Cambiad de sitio!
I want to change my cards.
Quiero cambiar de cartas.
I've changed my mind.
He cambiado de idea.
3 **cambiarse** (get changed)
I must go and change.
Tengo que ir a cambiarme.
B NOUN
el **cambio** masc
I haven't got any change.
No tengo cambio.

changeable ADJECTIVE
variable masc/fem
The weather is changeable.
El tiempo está variable.

changing room NOUN
1 el **vestuario** masc (in school)
2 el **probador** masc (in shop)

Channel NOUN
the English Channel
el canal de la Mancha

channel NOUN
la **cadena** fem (on TV)
There's football on the other channel.
Hay fútbol en la otra cadena.

Channel Islands PL NOUN
the Channel Islands
las islas del canal de la Mancha

Channel Tunnel NOUN
the Channel Tunnel
el Eurotúnel masc

chapter NOUN
el **capítulo** masc

character NOUN
el **personaje** masc
Harriet is the main character.
Harriet es el personaje principal.

LANGUAGE TIP
Even though **el personaje** is a masculine noun, you can use it to refer to a woman or girl.

---

charge NOUN
an extra charge
un suplemento
There's no charge.
No hay que pagar nada.
to be in charge
ser el responsable
Who is in charge?
¿Quién es el responsable?

charity NOUN
la **organización benéfica** fem
(PL las **organizaciones benéficas**)
We give the money to charity.
Donamos el dinero a una organización benéfica.

chart NOUN
el **gráfico** masc
We're making a chart.
Estamos haciendo un gráfico.

charter flight NOUN
el **vuelo chárter** masc

chase VERB
perseguir
My dog chases cats.
Mi perro persigue a los gatos.

chat VERB
  charlar
    Rafa chats a lot.
    Rafa charla mucho.
    Stop chatting.
    Dejad de charlar.

cheap ADJECTIVE
  barato *masc*
  barata *fem*
    It's cheaper by bus.
    Es más barato en autobús.

cheat

> **cheat** can be a verb or a noun.

A VERB
  to cheat
  hacer trampa
    You're cheating!
    ¡Estás haciendo trampa!
B NOUN
  el **tramposo** *masc*
  la **tramposa** *fem*
    Patrick, you're a cheat!
    ¡Patrick, eres un tramposo!

check VERB
  comprobar
    Check your spelling.
    Comprobad la ortografía.

check in VERB
  facturar (*at airport*)
    What time do I have to check in?
    ¿A qué hora tengo que facturar?

checked ADJECTIVE
  de cuadros
    a checked shirt
    una camisa de cuadros

checkout NOUN
  la **caja** *fem*
    at the checkout
    en la caja

cheek NOUN
  la **mejilla** *fem*
    He kissed her on the cheek.
    Le dio un beso en la mejilla.

cheeky ADJECTIVE
  descarado *masc*
  descarada *fem*
    Don't be cheeky, Isaac!
    ¡No seas descarado, Isaac!

cheer

> **cheer** can be a noun or a verb.

A NOUN
  There was a loud cheer.
  Hubo una fuerte ovación.
  Three cheers for the captain!
  ¡Viva el capitán!
  Cheers!
  ¡Salud!/¡Gracias!

LANGUAGE TIP
Translate **cheers!** as **¡salud!** when making a toast. Use **¡gracias!** instead when thanking someone.

  Cheers, everyone!
  ¡Salud, por todos!
  Cheers, Max! That's very kind of you.
  ¡Gracias, Max! Eres muy amable.
B VERB
  to cheer
  gritar entusiasmado
    The crowd was cheering.
    La multitud estaba gritando entusiasmada.

> **Cheer up!**
> ¡Anímate!

cheerful ADJECTIVE
  alegre *masc/fem*

cheerio EXCLAMATION
  ¡hasta luego!

cheese NOUN
  el **queso** *masc*
    a cheese sandwich
    un sándwich de queso

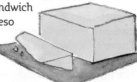

chef NOUN
  el **chef** *masc*

chemist NOUN
  1 la **farmacia** *fem* (*shop*)
  You get it from the chemist.
  Lo compras en la farmacia.
  the chemist's
  la farmacia

DID YOU KNOW...?
Spanish chemists are identifiable by
a red or green cross outside the shop.
Go to a **perfumería** instead if you
want to buy cosmetics or toiletries.

---

  2 el **farmacéutico** *masc*
  la **farmacéutica** *fem* (*pharmacist*)

chemistry NOUN
  la **química** *fem*
  the chemistry teacher
  el profesor de química

cherry NOUN
  la **cereza** *fem*
  I love cherries.
  Me encantan
  las cerezas.

chess NOUN
  el **ajedrez** *masc*
  I can play chess.
  Sé jugar al ajedrez.

LANGUAGE TIP
In Spanish, you need to include **al** or **a
la** before the names of sports or games
when talking about playing them.

---

chest NOUN
  el **pecho** *masc*

chest of drawers NOUN
  la **cómoda** *fem*

chewing gum NOUN
  el **chicle** *masc*
  **Put your chewing gum in
  the bin!**
  ¡Tira el chicle a la papelera!

chick NOUN
  el **pollito**
  masc

chicken NOUN
  el **pollo** *masc*
  Chicken and chips, please.
  Pollo con patatas fritas,
  por favor.

chickenpox NOUN
  la **varicela** *fem*
  Paul has got chickenpox.
  Paul tiene varicela.

child NOUN
  1 el **niño** *masc*
  la **niña** *fem* (*boy, girl*)
  Goodbye children!
  ¡Adiós, niños!
  2 el **hijo** *masc*
  la **hija** *fem* (*son, daughter*)
  They've got three children.
  Tienen tres hijos.

child minder NOUN
  el **cuidador de niños** *masc*
  la **cuidadora de niños** *fem*

children PL NOUN
  1 los **niños** *masc pl* (*boys and girls*)
  Where are the children?
  ¿Dónde están los niños?
  2 los **hijos** *masc pl* (*sons and
  daughters*)
  They've got three children.
  Tienen tres hijos.

chilly ADJECTIVE
  It's chilly today.
  Hace frío hoy.

chip NOUN
  la **patata frita** *fem*
  **I'd like
  some
  chips.**
  Quiero
  patatas
  fritas.

Spanish

English

a b c d e f g h i j k l m n o p q r s t u v w x y z

Spanish

English

A
B
C
D
E
F
G
H
I
J
K
L
M
N
O
P
Q
R
S
T
U
V
W
X
Y
Z

chocolate NOUN
1 el **chocolate** *masc*
I love chocolate.
Me encanta el chocolate.
a chocolate cake
una tarta de chocolate
a chocolate ice cream
un helado de chocolate
2 el **bombón** *masc* (PL los **bombones**)
(*sweet*)
a box of chocolates
una caja de bombones

choice NOUN
la **elección** *fem*
I had no choice.
No tenía elección.
You have to make a choice.
Tienes que elegir.

choir NOUN
el **coro** *masc*
I sing in the school choir.
Canto en el coro de la escuela.

choose VERB
elegir
It's difficult to choose.
Es difícil elegir.

chop NOUN
la **chuleta** *fem*
a pork chop
una chuleta de cerdo

chose VERB ▷ *see* choose

chosen VERB ▷ *see* choose

christening NOUN
el **bautizo** *masc*

Christmas NOUN
la **Navidad** *fem*
at Christmas
en Navidad

Happy Christmas!
¡Feliz Navidad!

LANGUAGE TIP
Have you noticed the upside-down
exclamation mark at the start of
Spanish exclamations?

Christmas cake NOUN
el **pastel de Navidad** *masc*

DID YOU KNOW...?
In Spain it's traditional to eat **el
roscón de Reyes** on 6th January.
Hidden in this fruit-studded ring-
shaped cake is a little figure or other
surprise that is meant to bring good
luck to the person that finds it.

Christmas card NOUN
la **tarjeta de Navidad** *fem*

Christmas Day NOUN
el **día de Navidad** *masc*

Christmas dinner NOUN
la **comida de Navidad** *fem*

DID YOU KNOW...?
In Spain, people usually have their
special Christmas meal on Christmas Eve.

Christmas Eve NOUN
la **Nochebuena** *fem*

DID YOU KNOW...?
In Spain, it's often **los Reyes Magos**
(the Three Kings) rather than **Papá
Noel** (Father Christmas) who bring
children their presents. They come on
5th January rather than on 24th
December.

Christmas present NOUN
el **regalo de Navidad** *masc*

Christmas tree NOUN
el **árbol de Navidad** masc

church NOUN
la **iglesia** fem

cider NOUN
la **sidra** fem

cigarette NOUN
el **cigarrillo** masc

cinema NOUN
el **cine** masc
I'm going to the cinema this evening.
Voy a ir al cine esta noche.

circle NOUN
el **círculo** masc
Stand in a circle.
Poneos de pie formando un círculo.

circus NOUN
el **circo** masc

citizenship NOUN
la **ciudadanía** fem

city NOUN
la **ciudad** fem
I live in a city.
Vivo en una ciudad.
the city centre
el centro de la ciudad
It's in the city centre.
Está en el centro de la ciudad.

clap

clap can be a verb or a noun.

A VERB
to clap
aplaudir
The audience was clapping.
El público estaba aplaudiendo.
Clap your hands!
¡Haced palmas!
B NOUN
Give Emma a clap.
Dadle un aplauso a Emma.

clarinet NOUN
el **clarinete** masc
I play the clarinet.
Toco el clarinete.

class NOUN
la **clase** fem
Javier is in my class.
Javier está en mi clase.
I go to dancing classes.
Voy a clases de baile.

classroom NOUN
el **aula** fem

LANGUAGE TIP
Even though it's a feminine noun, remember that you use **el** and **un** with **aula**.

classroom assistant NOUN
el **profesor de apoyo** masc
la **profesora de apoyo** fem

clean

clean can be an adjective or a verb.

A ADJECTIVE
limpio masc
limpia fem
a clean shirt
una camisa limpia
The bath isn't very clean.
La bañera no está muy limpia.
B VERB
to clean
limpiar
I'm cleaning the cooker.
Estoy limpiando la cocina.
Clean the board please!
¡Borrad la pizarra, por favor!
I clean my teeth twice a day.
Me lavo los dientes dos veces al día.

LANGUAGE TIP
In Spanish you usually use an article like **el**, **la** or **los**, **las** with parts of the body.

cleaner NOUN
el **señor de la limpieza** *masc*
la **señora de la limpieza** *fem*

clear ADJECTIVE
claro *masc*
clara *fem*
a clear explanation
una explicación clara

clementine NOUN
la **mandarina** *fem*

clever ADJECTIVE
listo *masc*
lista *fem*
Diane is very clever.
Diane es muy lista.

click VERB
hacer clic
Click on the icon.
Haz clic en el icono.

climate NOUN
el **clima** *masc*

LANGUAGE TIP
Even though it ends in **-a**, **el clima**
is a masculine noun.

We have a terrible climate.
Tenemos un clima espantoso.

climate change NOUN
el **cambio climático** *masc*

climb VERB
1 **escalar** (*mountain*)
I want to climb that mountain.
Quiero escalar esa montaña.
2 **subirse a** (*tree, wall*)
Can you climb that tree?
¿Puedes subirte a ese árbol?

cloakroom NOUN
1 el **guardarropa** *masc* (*for coats*)

LANGUAGE TIP
Even though it ends in **-a**, **el
guardarropa** is a masculine
noun.

---
2 el **servicio** *masc* (*toilet*)

clock NOUN
el **reloj** *masc*
Look at the clock.
Mira al reloj.

LANGUAGE TIP
Did you know that
reloj is also the
word for a **watch**?

---

close

close can be a verb or an adverb.

A VERB
to close
cerrar
Please close the door.
Por favor, cierra la puerta.
Close your books, children.
Cerrad los libros, niños.
What time does the pool close?
¿A qué hora cierra la piscina?
B ADVERB
cerca
The shops are very close.
Las tiendas están muy cerca.
My house is close to the school.
Mi casa está cerca del colegio.
Come closer, Daniel.
Acércate más, Daniel.

closed ADJECTIVE
cerrado *masc*
cerrada *fem*
The door's closed.
La puerta está cerrada.

clothes PL NOUN
la **ropa** *fem*
**I'd like to
buy some
new clothes.**
Quiero comprarme
ropa nueva.

LANGUAGE TIP
Even though **clothes** is a plural word
in English, you use **ropa** in the
singular in Spanish.

---

cloud NOUN
la **nube** *fem*
There are some black clouds.
Hay nubarrones.

cloudy ADJECTIVE
nublado *masc*
nublada *fem*
It's cloudy today.
Está nublado hoy.

clown NOUN
el **payaso** *masc*
la **payasa** *fem*

club NOUN
1 el **club** *masc* (*organization*)
a football club
un club de fútbol
2 (*in cards*)
clubs
los tréboles *masc pl*
the ace of clubs
el as de tréboles

coach NOUN
1 el **autocar** *masc* (*vehicle*)
by coach
en autocar
We're going by coach.
Vamos en autocar.
2 el **entrenador** *masc*
la **entrenadora** *fem* (*person*)

coach station NOUN
la **estación de autobuses** *fem*
(PL las **estaciones de autobuses**)

coal NOUN
el **carbón** *masc*

coast NOUN
la **costa** *fem*
It's on the west coast of Scotland.
Está en la costa oeste de Escocia.

coat NOUN
el **abrigo** *masc*
**I'm wearing
a blue coat.**
Llevo un
abrigo azul.

cocoa NOUN
el **cacao** *masc*

coconut NOUN
el **coco** *masc*

coffee NOUN
el **café** *masc*
I like coffee.
Me gusta el café.
I'd like a white coffee.
Quiero un café con leche.

coin NOUN
la **moneda** *fem*
a two-euro coin
una moneda de dos euros

Coke® NOUN
la **Coca-Cola**® *fem*
a can of Coke
una lata de Coca-Cola

cold

cold can be an adjective or a noun.

A ADJECTIVE
frío *masc*
fría *fem*
The water's cold.
El agua está fría.

It's cold today.
Hace frío hoy.
I'm cold.
Tengo frío.
I'm not cold.
No tengo frío.
Are you cold?
¿Tienes frío?

B NOUN
(*illness*)
I've got a cold.
Estoy resfriado.
Julie's got a cold.
Julie está resfriada.

coleslaw NOUN
la **ensalada de col, zanahoria,
cebolla y mayonesa**

Spanish
English

A
B
C
D
E
F
G
H
I
J
K
L
M
N
O
P
Q
R
S
T
U
V
W
X
Y
Z

collar NOUN
1 el **cuello** masc (on clothing)
2 el **collar** masc (for dog, cat)

collect VERB
1 **recoger** (pick up)
Collect the books please, Ryan.
Recoge los libros, por favor, Ryan.
2 **coleccionar** (as hobby)
I collect football cards.
Colecciono cromos de fútbol.

collection NOUN
la **colección** fem (PL las **colecciones**)

college NOUN
la **universidad** fem (university)
Do you want to go to college?
¿Quieres ir a la universidad?
a technical college
una escuela técnica

colour

> **colour** can be a noun or a verb.

A NOUN
el **color** masc
What colour are the curtains?
¿De qué color son las cortinas?
What colour eyes has he got?
¿De qué color tiene los ojos?

> **What colour is it?**
> ¿De qué color es?

B VERB
to colour
pintar
I'm going to colour the house yellow.
Voy a pintar la casa de amarillo.

comb

> **comb** can be a noun or a verb.

A NOUN
el **peine** masc
B VERB
to comb
peinar
to comb one's hair
peinarse

I comb my hair every day.
Me peino todos los días.
I'm combing my hair.
Me estoy peinando.

come VERB
1 **venir**
Come with me, June.
Ven conmigo, June.

> **LANGUAGE TIP**
> Use **ir** (go) rather than **venir** when you tell someone you're coming to join them.

Can I come too?
¿Puedo ir yo también?
I'll come with you.
Iré contigo.
2 **llegar** (arrive)
The bus is coming.
Ya llega el autobús.
The letter came this morning.
La carta llegó esta mañana.

> **I'm coming!**
> ¡Ya voy!
> **Come on!**
> ¡Vamos!

come back VERB
volver
Come back, Basil!
¡Vuelve, Basil!

come from VERB
ser de
Where do you come from?
¿De dónde eres?

come in VERB
entrar
Can I come in?
¿Puedo entrar?

> **Come in!**
> ¡Pasa!

comfortable ADJECTIVE
cómodo masc
cómoda fem (person, shoes, chair)

Make yourself comfortable.
Ponte cómodo.

comic NOUN
el **cómic** *masc* (PL los **cómics**)
(*magazine*)

comma NOUN
la **coma** *fem*

common ADJECTIVE
común *masc/fem* (PL **comunes**)
'Davies' is a very common surname.
"Davies" es un apellido muy común.

compared ADJECTIVE
compared with
en comparación con
Oxford is small compared with London.
Oxford es pequeño en comparación con Londres.

competition NOUN
el **concurso** *masc*

competitor NOUN
el/la **concursante** *masc/fem*

complete

> **complete** can be an adjective or a verb.

A ADJECTIVE
completo *masc*
completa *fem*
B VERB
to complete
completar
Complete the following phrases.
Completa las frases siguientes.

completely ADVERB
completamente

complicated ADJECTIVE
complicado *masc*
complicada *fem*

comprehension NOUN
el **ejercicio de comprensión** *masc*

comprehensive school NOUN
el **instituto de secundaria** *masc*

computer NOUN
el **ordenador** *masc*

computer game NOUN
el **juego de ordenador** *masc*
I like computer games.
Me gustan los juegos de ordenador.

computer room NOUN
la **sala de informática** *fem*

concert NOUN
el **concierto** *masc*

cone NOUN
el **cucurucho** *masc*
an ice-cream cone
un cucurucho de helado

congratulations PL NOUN
la **enhorabuena** *fem*
Congratulations!
¡Enhorabuena!

conservatory NOUN
la **habitación acristalada** *fem* (PL las **habitaciones acristaladas**)

constant ADJECTIVE
constante *masc/fem*

contact lens NOUN
la **lentilla** *fem*
I wear contact lenses.
Llevo lentillas.

container NOUN
el **recipiente** *masc*
a plastic container
un recipiente de plástico

contest NOUN
el **concurso** *masc*

A
B
C
D
E
F
G
H
I
J
K
L
M
N
O
P
Q
R
S
T
U
V
W
X
Y
Z

contestant NOUN
el/la **concursante** *masc/fem*

continent NOUN
el **continente** *masc*
How many continents are there?
¿Cuántos continentes hay?
the Continent
Europa
on the Continent
en Europa

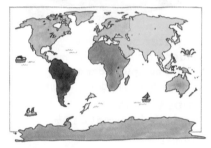

continental breakfast NOUN
el **desayuno europeo** *masc*

continue VERB
seguir
Continue with your work, children!
¡Seguid con vuestro trabajo, niños!

conversation NOUN
la **conversación** *fem*
(PL las **conversaciones**)

cook

> **cook** can be a verb or a noun.

A VERB
to cook
1 **cocinar**
I can cook.
Sé cocinar.
I can't cook.
No sé cocinar.
2 **cocer**
(*potatoes, rice etc*)
Cook the pasta for ten minutes.
Cocer la pasta durante diez minutos.

B NOUN
el **cocinero** *masc*
la **cocinera** *fem*
Matthew's an excellent cook.
Matthew es un excelente cocinero.

cookbook NOUN
el **libro de cocina** *masc*

cooked ADJECTIVE
cocido *masc*
cocida *fem*

cooker NOUN
la **cocina** *fem*
a gas cooker
una cocina de gas

cooking NOUN
la **cocina** *fem*
I like cooking.
Me gusta la cocina.

cool ADJECTIVE
1 **fresquito** *masc*
fresquita *fem* (*quite cold*)
It's cooler in the shade.
Hace más fresquito en la sombra.
2 **guay** (*super*)
Cool!
¡Guay!
What a cool T-shirt!
¡Qué camiseta más guay!

copy

> **copy** can be a noun or a verb.

A NOUN
la **copia** *fem*
I'll make a copy.
Haré una copia.
B VERB
to copy
copiar
Copy the words off the board.
Copiad las palabras de la pizarra.

cork NOUN
el **corcho** *masc*

corkscrew NOUN
el **sacacorchos** *masc*
(PL los **sacacorchos**)

corner NOUN
1 el **rincón** *masc* (PL los **rincones**)
(*in room*)
in a corner of the room
en un rincón de la habitación
2 la **esquina** *fem* (*of street*)
on a street corner
en una esquina de la calle

cornflakes PL NOUN
los **copos de maíz** *masc pl*

correct

> **correct** can be an adjective or a verb.

A ADJECTIVE
correcto *masc*
correcta *fem*
That's correct.
Eso es correcto.
the correct answer
la respuesta correcta
B VERB
to correct
corregir
I have to correct the spelling.
Tengo que corregir la ortografía.

correction NOUN
la **corrección** *fem* (PL las **correcciones**)

correctly ADVERB
correctamente

corridor NOUN
el **pasillo** *masc*
in the corridor
en el pasillo

cost VERB
costar
It costs two euros.
Cuesta dos euros.

> **How much does it cost?**
> ¿Cuánto cuesta?

costume NOUN
el **disfraz** *masc* (PL los **disfraces**)
(*fancy-dress*)
Mum's making me a clown costume.
Mi madre me está haciendo un disfraz de payaso.

cottage NOUN
la **casa de campo** *fem*

cotton NOUN
el **algodón** *masc*
a cotton shirt
una camisa de algodón

couch NOUN
el **sofá** *masc*

cough

> **cough** can be a noun or a verb.

A NOUN
la **tos** *fem*
I've got a cough.
Tengo tos.
B VERB
to cough
toser
I can't stop coughing.
No dejo de toser.

could VERB
Could I make a phone call?
¿Puedo hacer una llamada?
Could you open the door?
¿Puedes abrir la puerta?
Could I have a kilo of potatoes?
¿Me da un kilo de patatas?
Could I have an orange juice?
¿Me pone un zumo de naranja?

> **Could I...?**
> ¿Puedo...?
> **Could you...?**
> ¿Puedes...?

a b c d e f g h i j k l m n o p q r s t u v w x y z

Spanish

English

A
B
C
D
E
F
G
H
I
J
K
L
M
N
O
P
Q
R
S
T
U
V
W
X
Y
Z

count VERB
contar
Count from one to twenty.
Cuenta del uno al veinte.

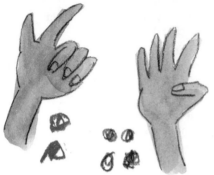

counter NOUN
1 el **mostrador** *masc (in shop)*
2 la **ficha** *fem (in game)*
Take ten yellow counters.
Coge diez fichas amarillas.

country NOUN
1 el **país** *masc (Spain, Britain etc)*
Spain is a big country.
España es un país grande.
the border between the two countries
la frontera entre los dos países
2 el **campo** *masc (countryside)*
I live in the country.
Vivo en el campo.

countryside NOUN
el **campo** *masc*
in the countryside
en el campo

couple NOUN
a couple of
un par de
a couple of days
un par de días
a young couple
una pareja joven

courgette NOUN
el **calabacín** *masc*
(PL los **calabacines**)

course NOUN
1 el **plato** *masc (of meal)*
the main course
el plato principal
the first course
el primer plato
2 el **curso** *masc (lessons)*
an English course
un curso de inglés

of course
claro

Do you love me? — Of course I do!
¿Me quieres? — ¡Claro que sí!
Of course not!
¡Claro que no!

court NOUN
la **pista** *fem*
There are two tennis courts.
Hay dos pistas de tenis.

cousin NOUN
el **primo** *masc*
la **prima** *fem*

cover

cover can be a noun or a verb.

A NOUN
1 la **funda** *fem (of duvet)*
2 la **tapa** *fem (of book)*
B VERB
to cover
cubrir
The roof is covered with snow.
El techo está cubierto de nieve.

cow NOUN
la **vaca** *fem*

crab NOUN
el **cangrejo** *masc*

cracker NOUN
la **galleta salada**
fem (biscuit)

DID YOU KNOW...?
The Spanish don't pull crackers at Christmas.

crash NOUN
el **accidente** masc
 a car crash
 un accidente de coche

crawl NOUN
crol masc
 I can do the crawl.
 Sé nadar a crol.

crazy ADJECTIVE
loco masc
loca fem
 Are you crazy?
 ¿Estás loco?

cream

> **cream** can be a noun or an adjective.

A NOUN
la **nata** fem
strawberries and cream
fresas con nata
B ADJECTIVE
de color crema (cream-coloured)
a cream shirt
una camisa de color crema

cream cake NOUN
el **pastel de nata** masc
 two cream cakes
 dos pasteles de nata

credit card NOUN
la **tarjeta de crédito** fem

cress NOUN
los **berros** masc pl
 I'm growing cress.
 Estoy cultivando berros.

cricket NOUN
el **críquet** masc
 I play cricket.
 Juego al críquet.

LANGUAGE TIP
In Spanish, you need to include **al** or **a la** before the names of sports or games when talking about playing them.

---

cricket bat NOUN
el **bate de críquet** masc

crisps PL NOUN
las **patatas fritas** fem pl
 a bag of crisps
 una bolsa de patatas fritas

cross

> **cross** can be a verb, noun or adjective.

A VERB
to cross
cruzar
Cross the road at the lights.
Cruza la calle por el semáforo.
B NOUN
la **cruz** fem (PL las **cruces**)
Put a tick or a cross.
Poned una señal o una cruz.
C ADJECTIVE
enfadado masc
enfadada fem
She is cross.
Está enfadada.

crossing NOUN
la **travesía** fem
 the crossing from Plymouth to Santander
 la travesía de Plymouth a Santander

crossroads NOUN
el **cruce** masc
 at the crossroads
 en el cruce

crossword NOUN
el **crucigrama** masc
 I like doing crosswords.
 Me gusta hacer crucigramas.

LANGUAGE TIP
Even though it ends in **-a**, **el crucigrama** is a masculine noun.

---

crowd NOUN
la **multitud** fem

Spanish

English

A
B
C
D
E
F
G
H
I
J
K
L
M
N
O
P
Q
R
S
T
U
V
W
X
Y
Z

crowded ADJECTIVE
lleno de gente *masc*
llena de gente *fem*
> **The pool is crowded on Saturdays.**
> La piscina está llena de gente los sábados.

crown NOUN
la **corona** *fem*

crutch NOUN
la **muleta** *fem*

cry VERB
llorar *(weep)*
> **Why are you crying?**
> ¿Por qué lloras?

cub NOUN
1 el **cachorro** *masc (young animal)*
> **a lion cub**
> un cachorro de león
> **a bear cub**
> un osezno

2 el **lobato** *masc (scout)*

cube NOUN
el **cubo** *masc*

cucumber NOUN
el **pepino** *masc*

cup NOUN
1 la **taza** *fem*
> **a cup of tea**
> una taza de té
> **a paper cup**
> un vaso de papel
2 la **copa** *fem (trophy)*

cupboard NOUN
el **armario** *masc*
> **What's in the cupboard?**
> ¿Qué hay en el armario?

curious ADJECTIVE
curioso *masc*
curiosa *fem*

curly ADJECTIVE
rizado *masc*
rizada *fem*
> **She's got curly hair.**
> Tiene el pelo rizado.

currant NOUN
la **pasa** *fem*
> **I don't like currants.**
> No me gustan las pasas.

curriculum NOUN
el **programa de estudios** *masc*

LANGUAGE TIP
Even though it ends in **-a**, **el programa** is a masculine noun.

---

curry NOUN
el **curry** *masc*
> **chicken curry**
> el pollo al curry

curtain NOUN
la **cortina** *fem*
> **Draw the curtains, please.**
> Corre las cortinas, por favor.

cushion NOUN
el **cojín** *masc* (PL los **cojines**)

custard NOUN
las **natillas** *fem pl*

custom NOUN
  la **costumbre** *fem*
    It's an old custom.
    Es una vieja costumbre.

customer NOUN
  el **cliente** *masc*
  la **clienta** *fem*

cut VERB
  cortar
    I'll cut the cake.
    Yo cortaré la tarta.
    Mind you don't cut yourself!
    ¡Ten cuidado de no cortarte!

cutlery NOUN
  los **cubiertos** *masc pl*

cyberbullying NOUN
  el **ciberacoso** *masc*

cycle VERB
  montar en bici

I like cycling.
Me gusta montar en bici.
I cycle to school.
Voy en bici al colegio.

cycle lane NOUN
  el **carril-bici** *masc*
    (PL los **carriles-bici**)

cycling NOUN
  el **ciclismo** *masc*

cyclist NOUN
  el/la **ciclista** *masc/fem*

A
B
C
D
E
F
G
H
I
J
K
L
M
N
O
P
Q
R
S
T
U
V
W
X
Y
Z

Dd

dad NOUN
1 el **padre** *masc*
my dad
mi padre
my mum and dad
mis padres

2 el **papá** *masc* (*used as a name*)
Let's ask Dad.
¡Vamos a preguntarle a papá!

daddy NOUN
el **papá** *masc*
Hello, Daddy!
¡Hola, papá!

daffodil NOUN
el **narciso** *masc*

daily ADVERB
diariamente
The pool is open daily.
La piscina está abierta diariamente.

damn EXCLAMATION
¡maldita sea!

damp ADJECTIVE
húmedo *masc*
húmeda *fem*

dance

> **dance** can be a noun or a verb.

A NOUN
el **baile** *masc*
It's a new dance.
Es un nuevo baile.
Are you going to the dance tonight, Michael?
¿Vas a ir al baile esta noche, Michael?

B VERB
to dance
bailar
Can you dance?
¿Sabes bailar?
I like dancing.
Me gusta bailar.

dancer NOUN
el **bailarín** *masc* (PL los **bailarines**)
la **bailarina** *fem*

danger NOUN
el **peligro** *masc*
in danger
en peligro
His life is in danger.
Su vida está en peligro.

dangerous ADJECTIVE
peligroso *masc*
peligrosa *fem*

dark

> **dark** can be an adjective or a noun.

A ADJECTIVE
oscuro *masc*
oscura *fem*
She's got dark hair.
Tiene el pelo oscuro.
We wear dark green skirts.
Llevamos unas faldas verde oscuro.

LANGUAGE TIP
When you describe something as **dark green**, **dark blue** and so on, neither the colour nor **oscuro** changes its ending to agree with the noun.

some dark blue curtains
unas cortinas azul oscuro
It's dark in here.
Está oscuro aquí dentro.
It's dark at six o'clock.
Es de noche a las seis.
It's getting dark.
Se está haciendo de noche.
B NOUN
la **oscuridad** *fem*
I'm afraid of the dark.
Me da miedo la oscuridad.

darling NOUN
cariño *masc*
Thank you, darling!
¡Gracias, cariño!

LANGUAGE TIP
cariño still ends in **-o** even when it
refers to a woman or girl.

---

dart NOUN
el **dardo** *masc*
Do you want to play darts?
¿Quieres jugar a los dardos?

LANGUAGE TIP
In Spanish, you need to include **a los**
before **dardos** when talking about
playing darts.

---

date NOUN
la **fecha** *fem* (day)
What's the date on the letter?
¿Qué fecha pone en la carta?
my date of birth
mi fecha de nacimiento

What's the date today?
¿A cuántos estamos hoy?

daughter NOUN
la **hija** *fem*

day NOUN
el **día** *masc*
**I'm going to London for three
days.**
Voy a ir tres días a Londres.
during the day
durante el día
**It's Richard's birthday the day
after tomorrow.**
Pasado mañana es el cumpleaños de
Richard.
It's my day off.
Es mi día libre.

the days of the week
los días de la semana
every day
todos los días
all day
todo el día
What day is it today?
¿Qué día es hoy?
the day after tomorrow
pasado mañana
the day before yesterday
antes de ayer

LANGUAGE TIP
Even though it ends in **-a**, **el día** is a
masculine noun.

---

dead ADJECTIVE
muerto *masc*
muerta *fem*
He's dead.
Está muerto.

deaf ADJECTIVE
sordo *masc*
sorda *fem*
She's deaf.
Es sorda.

deal

deal can be a noun or a verb.

A NOUN
el **trato** *masc*

Spanish | **English**

A B C D E F G H I J K L M N O P Q R S T U V W X Y Z

It's a deal!
¡Trato hecho!
a great deal
mucho
a great deal of money
mucho dinero
B VERB
to deal
repartir (*cards*)
It's your turn to deal.
Te toca repartir a ti.

dear ADJECTIVE
1 **querido** *masc*
querida *fem* (*in letters to friends*)
Dear Julia, ...
Querida Julia: ...
Dear Mum and Dad, ...
Queridos papás: ...
2 **estimado** *masc*
estimada *fem* (*in formal letters*)
Dear Mrs Blanco, ...
Estimada Sra. Blanco: ...

LANGUAGE TIP
Did you notice that there's a colon (:) at the end of the opening line of a letter in Spanish, not a comma?

---

death NOUN
la **muerte** *fem*

December NOUN
diciembre *masc*
My birthday's in December.
Mi cumpleaños es en diciembre.
It's the sixth of December today.
Hoy es seis de diciembre.

in December
en diciembre
on the fifth of December
el cinco de diciembre

LANGUAGE TIP
Months are not spelled with a capital letter in Spanish.

---

decide VERB
decidir
I have decided to go to the party.
He decidido ir a la fiesta.
I can't decide.
No puedo decidirme.

decision NOUN
la **decisión** *fem* (PL las **decisiones**)
We need to take a decision.
Tenemos que tomar una decisión.

deck NOUN
la **cubierta** *fem*
on deck
en cubierta

deckchair NOUN
la **tumbona** *fem*

decorate VERB
1 **decorar** (*with decorations*)
We decorate the classroom for Christmas.
Decoramos la clase para la Navidad.
2 **pintar** (*paint*)
Mum's going to decorate my bedroom.
Mi madre va a pintar mi habitación.
3 **empapelar** (*paper*)
Mum's going to decorate my bedroom.
Mi madre va a empapelar mi habitación.

LANGUAGE TIP
There's no single verb meaning both 'to paint' and 'to paper' in Spanish. Use one or the other or **pintar y empapelar** together if you mean both.

---

decorations PL NOUN
los **adornos** *masc pl*
Christmas decorations
adornos de Navidad

deep ADJECTIVE
profundo *masc*
profunda *fem (water, hole, cut)*
Is it deep?
¿Es profundo?
Take a deep breath, girls!
¡Respirad hondo, chicas!

deer NOUN
el **ciervo** *masc*

defence NOUN
la **defensa** *fem*
I play in defence.
Juego en la defensa.

defender NOUN
el/la **defensa** *masc/fem (in sport)*

definite ADJECTIVE
1 **definitivo** *masc*
definitiva *fem (fixed)*
I haven't got any definite plans.
No tengo ningún plan definitivo.
2 **seguro** *masc*
segura *fem (certain)*
Maybe, it's not definite.
Quizás, no es seguro.

definitely ADVERB
sin duda
He's definitely the best player.
Es sin duda el mejor jugador.
Definitely!
¡Claro que sí!

degree NOUN
1 el **grado** *masc (measurement)*
a temperature of thirty degrees
una temperatura de treinta grados
2 la **licenciatura** *fem (qualification)*
a degree in maths
una licenciatura en matemáticas

delayed ADJECTIVE
retrasado *masc*
retrasada *fem*
All flights are delayed.
Todos los vuelos están retrasados.

delicatessen NOUN
la **tienda gourmet** *fem*

delicious ADJECTIVE
buenísimo *masc*
buenísima *fem*
The chocolate mousse is delicious!
¡La mousse de chocolate está buenísima!

deliver VERB
1 **repartir** *(mail, newspapers)*
I deliver newspapers.
Yo reparto periódicos.
2 **entregar** *(order, goods)*
They'll deliver my new bed on Friday.
Me van a entregar la cama nueva el viernes.

denim NOUN
a denim jacket
una cazadora vaquera

dentist NOUN
el/la **dentista** *masc/fem*
I'm going to the dentist.
Voy a ir al dentista.
Ellie is a dentist.
Ellie es dentista.

LANGUAGE TIP
Did you notice that **dentista** still ends in **-a** even when referring to a man? Remember that in Spanish, you do not use an article with people's jobs.

---

department NOUN
1 la **sección** *fem* (PL las **secciones**)
(in shop)
the shoe department
la sección de calzado
2 el **departamento** *masc (of school, university)*
He works in the English department.
Trabaja en el departamento de inglés.

department store NOUN
los **grandes almacenes** *masc pl*
This is my favourite department store.
Estos son mis grandes almacenes favoritos.

Spanish

English

a
b
c
d
e
f
g
h
i
j
k
l
m
n
o
p
q
r
s
t
u
v
w
x
y
z

departure NOUN
la **salida** *fem*

departure lounge NOUN
la **sala de embarque** *fem*

depend VERB
It depends.
Depende.
depending on the weather
dependiendo del tiempo

LANGUAGE TIP
Even though we say **to depend on** in English, remember that in Spanish they say **depender de**.

---

deposit NOUN
1 la **señal** *fem* (*part payment*)
You have to pay a deposit when you book.
Hay que dejar una señal para hacer la reserva.
2 el **depósito** *masc* (*when hiring something*)
You get the deposit back when you return the bike.
Recuperas el depósito cuando devuelves la bici.

depressed ADJECTIVE
deprimido *masc*
deprimida *fem*
I feel depressed.
Me encuentro deprimido.

deputy head NOUN
el **subdirector** *masc*
la **subdirectora** *fem*

describe VERB
describir
Can you describe the man you saw?
¿Puedes describir al hombre que viste?

LANGUAGE TIP
Don't forget the personal **a** in examples like this last one.

Describe yourself.
Descríbete.

description NOUN
la **descripción** *fem* (PL las **descripciones**)

LANGUAGE TIP
Have you noticed that words ending in **-tion** in English often have Spanish counterparts ending in **-ción**?

---

desert NOUN
el **desierto** *masc*

desert island NOUN
la **isla desierta** *fem*

deserve VERB
merecerse
You deserve a prize, Beth.
Te mereces un premio, Beth.

design

> **design** can be a noun or a verb.

A NOUN
el **modelo** *masc*
a simple design
un modelo simple
B VERB
to design
diseñar

designer NOUN
el **diseñador** *masc*
la **diseñadora** *fem*

designer clothes PL NOUN
la **ropa de diseño** *fem*

LANGUAGE TIP
Even though we always talk about clothes in the plural in English, in Spanish they use **la ropa** in the singular.

---

desk NOUN
1 la **mesa** *fem* (*in school, office*)
my desk
mi mesa
2 el **mostrador** *masc* (*in hotel, at airport*)

dessert NOUN
  el **postre** *masc*
  for dessert
  de postre

destination NOUN
  el **destino** *masc*

detached house NOUN
  la **casa independiente** *fem*

detail NOUN
  el **detalle** *masc*
  in detail
  con detalle

detective NOUN
  el/la **detective** *masc/fem*

detective story NOUN
  la **novela policíaca** *fem*

detention NOUN
  You'll get a detention!
  ¡Te vas a quedar castigado después de clase!

develop VERB
  desarrollarse

diabetic NOUN
  el **diabético** *masc*
  la **diabética** *fem*
    I'm a diabetic.
    Soy diabética.

diagonal ADJECTIVE
  diagonal *masc/fem*

diagram NOUN
  el **diagrama** *masc*

LANGUAGE TIP
Even though it ends in **-a**, **el diagrama** is a masculine noun.

---

dial VERB
  marcar
    Dial the number.
    Marca el número.

dialogue NOUN
  el **diálogo** *masc*

diamond NOUN
  el **diamante** *masc*
    a diamond ring
    un anillo de diamantes
    the ace of diamonds
    el as de diamantes

diary NOUN
  1 la **agenda** *fem* (for appointments)
    I've got her phone number in my diary.
    Tengo su número de teléfono en mi agenda.
  2 el **diario** *masc* (personal record)
    I keep a diary.
    Estoy escribiendo un diario.

dice NOUN
  el **dado** *masc*
    Throw the dice, Sonia.
    Tira los dados, Sonia.

dictionary NOUN
  el **diccionario** *masc*
    Look in the dictionary.
    Mira en el diccionario.

did VERB ▷ *see* **do**

didn't (= did not) ▷ *see* **do**

die VERB
  morir
    He died last year.
    Murió el año pasado.
    She's dying.
    Se está muriendo.

diesel NOUN
  el **gasoil** *masc*

diet

  diet can be a noun or a verb.

  A NOUN
    la **dieta** *fem*
    a healthy diet
    una dieta sana
    My dad's on a diet.
    Mi padre está a dieta.

B VERB
to diet
estar a dieta
My mum's dieting.
Mi madre está a dieta.

difference NOUN
la **diferencia** *fem*
What's the difference?
¿Cuál es la diferencia?
the difference between Barcelona and Madrid
la diferencia entre Barcelona y Madrid

different ADJECTIVE
diferente *masc/fem*
We are very different.
Somos muy diferentes.
Dublin is different from London.
Dublín es diferente de Londres.

LANGUAGE TIP
Don't forget that there's only one **f** in the Spanish word **diferente**.

---

difficult ADJECTIVE
difícil *masc/fem*
It's difficult.
Es difícil.
a difficult question
una pregunta difícil

LANGUAGE TIP
Don't forget that there's only one **f** in the Spanish word **difícil**.

---

difficulty NOUN
la **dificultad** *fem*
without difficulty
sin dificultad

dig VERB
cavar
My dog digs lots of holes.
Mi perro cava muchos hoyos.
The children are digging in the sand.
Los niños están haciendo hoyos en la arena.

digital ADJECTIVE
digital *masc/fem*
a digital camera
una cámara digital
digital radio
la radio digital
digital television
la televisión digital

dinghy NOUN
a rubber dinghy
una lancha neumática

dining room NOUN
el **comedor** *masc*

dinner NOUN
1 la **comida** *fem* (*midday meal*)
Dinner's ready!
¡La comida está lista!
We always go home for dinner.
Siempre vamos a comer a casa.
We usually have dinner at one o'clock.
Normalmente comemos a la una.

LANGUAGE TIP
Only use **la comida** and the verb **comer** when talking about a midday meal.

---

2 la **cena** *fem* (*evening meal*)
There's a good film on after dinner.
Echan una película buena después de la cena.
What are we having for dinner tonight?
¿Qué hay para cenar esta noche?
We usually have dinner at seven o'clock.
Normalmente cenamos a las siete.

LANGUAGE TIP
Only use **la cena** and the verb **cenar** when talking about an evening meal.

---

dinner lady NOUN
  la **señora que ayuda en el comedor** fem

dinner time NOUN
  1 la **hora de comer** fem (for midday meal)
  2 la **hora de cenar** fem (for evening meal)

DID YOU KNOW...?
The Spanish tend to have their meals much later than in Britain, with the lunchtime meal around 2 p.m. and the evening meal around 9 p.m. or 10 p.m.

---

dinosaur NOUN
  el **dinosaurio** masc

direct ADJECTIVE
  directo masc
  directa fem
    the most direct route
    la ruta más directa

direction NOUN
  la **dirección** fem (PL las **direcciones**)
    We're going in the wrong direction.
    Vamos en la dirección equivocada.
    Let's ask somebody for directions.
    Vamos a pedirle a alguien que nos indique el camino.

LANGUAGE TIP
Have you noticed that words ending in **-tion** in English often have Spanish counterparts ending in **-ción**?

---

dirty ADJECTIVE
  sucio masc
  sucia fem
    The house is very dirty.
    La casa está muy sucia.

disabled ADJECTIVE
  discapacitado masc
  discapacitada fem
    disabled people
    personas discapacitadas

disagree VERB
    I disagree!
    ¡No estoy de acuerdo!
    He disagrees with me.
    No está de acuerdo conmigo.

disappointed ADJECTIVE
  decepcionado masc
  decepcionada fem
    We are very disappointed.
    Estamos muy decepcionados.

disappointment NOUN
  la **decepción** fem (PL las **decepciones**)

disaster NOUN
  el **desastre** masc
    It's a disaster!
    ¡Es un desastre!

discipline NOUN
  la **disciplina** fem

disco NOUN
  el **baile** masc
    There's a disco at school tonight.
    Hay un baile en el colegio esta noche.
    disco music
    la música disco

discussion NOUN
  la **discusión** fem (PL las **discusiones**)

disguise VERB
  disfrazar
    He was disguised as a police officer.
    Iba disfrazado de policía.

disgusting ADJECTIVE
asqueroso *masc*
asquerosa *fem*
It looks disgusting.
Tiene un aspecto asqueroso.

dish NOUN
el **plato** *masc* (*meal, plate*)
a vegetarian dish
un plato vegetariano
to wash the dishes
fregar los platos
I always wash the dishes.
Yo siempre friego los platos.

dishwasher NOUN
el **lavavajillas** *masc* (PL los **lavavajillas**)

disk NOUN
el **disco** *masc*

dislike NOUN
my likes and dislikes
lo que me gusta y lo que no

distance NOUN
la **distancia** *fem*
a distance of ten kilometres
una distancia de diez kilómetros
in the distance
a lo lejos

distract VERB
distraer
Don't distract him, Poppy.
No lo distraigas, Poppy.

district NOUN
1 el **barrio** *masc* (*of town*)
2 la **región** *fem* (PL las **regiones**) (*of country*)

disturb VERB
molestar
I'm sorry to disturb you.
Siento molestarte.
'Do not disturb'
"No molestar"

dive VERB
tirarse de cabeza
I like diving.
Me gusta tirarme de cabeza.
He dived into the water.
Se tiró al agua de cabeza.

divide VERB
dividir
Divide the pastry in half.
Divide la masa en dos.
Twelve divided by three is four.
Doce dividido entre tres son cuatro.
Divide into two groups!
¡Dividíos en dos grupos!

diving board NOUN
el **trampolín** *masc* (PL los **trampolines**)

divorced ADJECTIVE
divorciado *masc*
divorciada *fem*
My parents are divorced.
Mis padres están divorciados.

DIY NOUN
el **bricolaje** *masc*
He likes doing DIY.
Le gusta hacer bricolaje.

dizzy ADJECTIVE
mareado *masc*
mareada *fem*
I feel dizzy.
Estoy mareada.

DJ NOUN
el/la **disc-jockey** *masc/fem*
(PL los/las **disc-jockeys**)

do VERB
hacer
What are you going to do this evening?
¿Qué vas a hacer esta noche?
My brother does judo.
Mi hermano hace yudo.
I haven't done my homework.
No he hecho mis deberes.
Who did that?
¿Quién hizo eso?
That'll do, thanks.
Así está bien, gracias.

LANGUAGE TIP
You often use **do** to form questions in English. Don't use **hacer** like this in Spanish. Just use the normal form of the verb and make your voice go up at the end. Don't forget the opening and closing question marks in written Spanish.

Do you speak English? — Yes, I do.
¿Hablas inglés? — Sí.
Do you like horses? — No, I don't.
¿Te gustan los caballos? — No.
Where does he live?
¿Dónde vive?
What do you do in your free time?
¿Qué haces en tu tiempo libre?

LANGUAGE TIP
Just use **no** to make sentences negative.

I don't understand.
No entiendo.
She doesn't like dogs.
No le gustan los perros.

LANGUAGE TIP
Use **¿no?** to check information where in English we'd say **don't you?**, **doesn't he?** and so on.

You go swimming on Fridays, don't you?
Tú vas a nadar los viernes, ¿no?

LANGUAGE TIP
You can also use **¿verdad?** to check information.

It doesn't matter, does it?
No importa, ¿verdad?

What are you doing?
¿Qué estás haciendo?
I'm not doing anything.
No estoy haciendo nada.
... don't you?
... ¿no?
... do you?
... ¿verdad?

do up VERB
1 **atarse** (*tie*)
Do up your shoes!
¡Átate los cordones!
2 **abrocharse** (*fasten*)
Do up your coat!
¡Abróchate el abrigo!
Do up your zip!
¡Súbete la cremallera!

LANGUAGE TIP
In Spanish you usually use an article like **el**, **la** or **los**, **las** with clothes you are wearing.

doctor NOUN
el **médico** *masc*
la **médica** *fem*
I'd like to be a doctor.
Me gustaría ser médico.

LANGUAGE TIP
In Spanish, you do not use an article with people's jobs.

She's a doctor.
Es médica.
I need to see a doctor.
Tengo que ver a un médico.

LANGUAGE TIP
Don't forget the personal **a** in
examples like this one.

---

dodgems PL NOUN
los **coches de choque** *masc pl*

does VERB ▷ *see* **do**

doesn't (= does not) ▷ *see* **do**

dog NOUN
el **perro** *masc*
**Have you got
a dog?**
¿Tienes perro?

doll NOUN
la **muñeca** *fem*

dollar NOUN
el **dólar** *masc*

dolphin NOUN
el **delfín** *masc*
(PL los **delfines**)

dominoes PL NOUN
Let's have a game of dominoes.
Vamos a echar una partida al dominó.

done VERB ▷ *see* **do**

donkey NOUN
el **burro** *masc*
la **burra** *fem*

don't (= do not) ▷ *see* **do**

door NOUN
la **puerta** *fem*
the first door on the right
la primera puerta a la derecha

dormitory NOUN
el **dormitorio** *masc*

dot NOUN
el **punto** *masc*
**My email address is loveday at
collins dot co dot U-K (loveday@
collins.co.uk).**
Mi dirección de correo es loveday
arroba collins punto co punto U-K
(loveday@collins.co.uk).

double ADJECTIVE
doble *masc/fem*
a double helping
una ración doble

double bed NOUN
la **cama de matrimonio** *fem*

double-decker bus NOUN
el **autobús de dos pisos** *masc*
(PL los **autobuses de dos pisos**)

double room NOUN
la **habitación doble** *fem*
(PL las **habitaciones dobles**)

doubt VERB
dudar
I doubt it.
Lo dudo.

doughnut NOUN
el **donut** (PL los **donuts**)

down

> **down** can be an adverb, preposition
> or adjective.

A ADVERB
abajo
It's down in the cellar.
Está abajo en el sótano.
It's down there.
Está ahí abajo.
Don't look down!
¡No mires hacia abajo!
B PREPOSITION
He ran down the road.
Corrió calle abajo.
I live just down the road.
Vivo aquí cerca en esta calle.

C ADJECTIVE
I'm feeling a bit down.
Me siento un poco deprimido.
The computer's down.
El ordenador no funciona.

download VERB
descargar
You can download the file.
Puedes descargar el archivo.

downstairs ADVERB
abajo
The bathroom's downstairs.
El baño está abajo.
I'm downstairs!
¡Estoy abajo!

dozen NOUN
la **docena** *fem*
two dozen
dos docenas
a dozen eggs
una docena de huevos

dragon NOUN
el **dragón** *masc* (PL los **dragones**)

drama NOUN
el **teatro** *masc*
Drama is my favourite subject.
Teatro es mi asignatura favorita.

drank VERB ▷ *see* **drink**

draughts NOUN
las **damas** *fem pl*
Do you want to play draughts?
¿Quieres jugar a las damas?

LANGUAGE TIP
In Spanish, you need to include **a las**
before **damas** when talking about
playing draughts.
---

draw

| draw can be a verb or a noun. |

A VERB
to draw
1 **dibujar** (*with pencil, pen*)
I can't draw.
No sé dibujar.

Draw a house, everyone.
Dibujad todos una casa.
I'm drawing a picture.
Estoy haciendo un dibujo.
2 **empatar** (*in game*)
We drew two all.
Empatamos a dos.
B NOUN
el **empate** *masc* (*in game*)
**It's a draw between the boys and
the girls.**
Es un empate entre los niños y las
niñas.

drawer NOUN
el **cajón** *masc* (PL los **cajones**)

drawing NOUN
1 el **dibujo** *masc* (*picture*)
2 (*activity*)
I like drawing.
Me gusta dibujar.

drawing pin NOUN
la **chincheta** *fem*

dream

| dream can be a noun or a verb. |

A NOUN
el **sueño** *masc*
Sweet dreams, darling!
¡Felices sueños, cariño!
a bad dream
un mal sueño
B VERB
to dream
soñar

dress

| dress can be a noun or a verb. |

A NOUN
el **vestido** *masc*

Spanish · **English**

Sophie is wearing a white dress.
Sophie lleva un vestido blanco.

B VERB

to get dressed
vestirse
I'm getting dressed.
Me estoy vistiendo.
Go and get dressed.
Ve a vestirte.

dress up VERB
disfrazarse
I'm going to dress up
as a princess.
Voy a disfrazarme
de princesa.

dressed ADJECTIVE
vestido *masc*
vestida *fem*
I'm not dressed yet.
Todavía no estoy vestido.
How was he dressed?
¿Cómo iba vestido?
She was dressed in a green
sweater and jeans.
Iba vestida con un jersey verde y unos
vaqueros.

drew VERB ▷ *see* **draw**

drink

drink can be a verb or a noun.

A VERB

to drink
beber
What would you like to drink?
¿Qué quieres beber?

B NOUN
la **bebida** *fem*
a cold drink
una bebida fría
a hot drink
una bebida caliente
Would you like a drink?
¿Quieres beber algo?

drive

drive can be a noun or a verb.

A NOUN

1 (*in car*)
Let's go for a drive.
Vamos a dar una vuelta en el coche.
**It's a twenty-minute drive to
school.**
El colegio está a veinte minutos en
coche.

2 (*of house*)
**You can park your car in the
drive.**
Puedes aparcar en la entrada de la
casa.

B VERB

to drive

1 **conducir** (*as skill*)
She's learning to drive.
Está aprendiendo a conducir.
Can you drive?
¿Sabes conducir?

2 **ir en coche** (*go by car*)
**Are you going by train? — No,
we're driving.**
¿Vais en tren? — No, vamos en coche.

3 **llevar en coche** (*take by car*)
My mother drives me to school.
Mi madre me lleva en coche al colegio.

driver NOUN
el **conductor** *masc*
la **conductora** *fem*
She's an excellent driver.
Es una conductora excelente.

driving licence NOUN
el **carnet de conducir** *masc*
(PL los **carnets de conducir**)

drone NOUN
el **dron** *masc*

drop

> **drop** can be a noun or a verb.

A NOUN
la **gota** *fem*
a drop of water
una gota de agua

B VERB
to drop
dejar caer
Don't drop that glass, will you!
No dejes caer ese vaso, ¿vale?

drove VERB ▷ *see* **drive**

drug NOUN
1 la **medicina** *fem* (*medicine*)
They need food and drugs.
Necesitan alimentos y medicinas.
2 la **droga** *fem* (*illegal*)
It's crazy to take drugs.
Es una locura drogarse.

drum NOUN
el **tambor** *masc*
an African drum
un tambor africano
I play drums.
Toco la batería.

drum kit NOUN
la **batería** *fem*

drummer NOUN
el/la **batería** *masc/fem*

drunk ADJECTIVE
borracho *masc*
borracha *fem*

dry

> **dry** can be an adjective or a verb.

A ADJECTIVE
1 **seco** *masc*
seca *fem* (*not wet*)
The paint isn't dry yet.
La pintura no está seca todavía.
2 **sin lluvias** (*without rain*)
a long dry period
una larga temporada sin lluvias

B VERB
to dry
1 **secar**

LANGUAGE TIP
Use **secar** to talk about drying objects, animals and babies.

Can you dry the dishes?
¿Puedes secar los platos?
2 **secarse**

LANGUAGE TIP
Use **secarse** when something dries.

Let the glue dry.
Deja que se seque el pegamento.

LANGUAGE TIP
Use **secarse** when someone dries themselves or their own hair, hands, feet, etc.

Dry yourself on this towel.
Sécate con esta toalla.
I need to dry my hair.
Tengo que secarme el pelo.
Have you dried your hands?
¿Te has secado las manos?

A
B
C
D
E
F
G
H
I
J
K
L
M
N
O
P
Q
R
S
T
U
V
W
X
Y
Z

duck NOUN
el **pato**
masc

due ADJECTIVE
1 The plane is due in half an hour.
El avión llegará dentro de media hora.
When's the baby due?
¿Para cuándo nacerá el niño?

2 due to
debido a
We can't go out due to the bad weather.
No podemos salir debido al mal tiempo.

dug VERB ▷ *see* **dig**

dull ADJECTIVE
It's dull today.
Hace un día gris hoy.

dummy NOUN
el **chupete** *masc* (*for baby*)

dungeon NOUN
la **mazmorra** *fem*

during PREPOSITION
durante
during the day
durante el día

dustbin NOUN
el **cubo de la basura** *masc*

duty-free shop NOUN
la **tienda libre de impuestos** *fem*

duvet NOUN
el **edredón nórdico** *masc* (PL los **edredones nórdicos**)

DVD NOUN
el **DVD** *masc* (PL los **DVDs**)
I've got that film on DVD.
Tengo esa película en DVD.

DVD player NOUN
el **reproductor de DVD** *masc*

dyslexia NOUN
la **dislexia** *fem*
Two of her friends have dyslexia.
Dos de sus amigos tienen dislexia.

dyspraxia NOUN
la **dispraxia** *fem*

Ee

each

> **each** can be an adjective or a pronoun.

A ADJECTIVE
cada *masc/fem*
each day
cada día

LANGUAGE TIP
Even though **cada** ends in **-a**, you can use it with a masculine noun.

B PRONOUN
cada uno *masc*
cada una *fem*
They have ten points each.
Tienen diez puntos cada uno.
The towels cost five pounds each.
Las toallas cuestan cinco libras cada una.
Take one card each.
Coged una carta cada uno.
We write to each other.
Nos escribimos.

ear NOUN
1 la **oreja** *fem* (*outer part*)
I want to have my ears pierced.
Quiero hacerme agujeros en las orejas.
2 el **oído** *masc* (*inner part*)
My ears are aching.
Me duelen los oídos.

earache NOUN
I've got earache.
Me duele el oído.

early ADVERB
1 **temprano** (*early in the day*)
I get up early.
Me levanto temprano.

I go to bed early.
Me acuesto temprano.
2 **pronto** (*ahead of time*)
Come early to get a good seat.
Llega pronto para conseguir un buen sitio.

earn VERB
ganar
She earns ten pounds an hour.
Gana diez libras a la hora.

earring NOUN
el **pendiente** *masc*
diamond earrings
pendientes de diamantes
a pair of earrings
unos pendientes

earth NOUN
la **tierra** *fem*

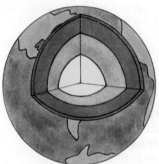

east

> **east** can be an adjective or a noun.

A ADJECTIVE
este

LANGUAGE TIP
When it means 'east', **este** never changes its ending no matter what it describes. Adjectives that behave like this are called 'invariable adjectives'.

---

the east coast
la costa este
B NOUN
el **este** *masc*
in the east
en el este

Spanish

English

A
B
C
D
E
F
G
H
I
J
K
L
M
N
O
P
Q
R
S
T
U
V
W
X
Y
Z

Easter NOUN
la **Semana Santa** *fem*
at Easter
en Semana Santa
the Easter holidays
las vacaciones de Semana Santa
Easter Saturday
el Sábado Santo
Easter Sunday
el Domingo de Resurrección

Happy Easter!
¡Felices Pascuas!

DID YOU KNOW...?
Many places in Spain have festivals
during **Semana Santa** (Easter week).
These usually involve religious floats
and processions of people wearing
robes and hoods which cover their
faces.

Easter egg NOUN
el **huevo de Pascua** *masc*
a big Easter egg
un gran huevo de Pascua

easy ADJECTIVE
fácil *masc/fem*
It's easy!
¡Es fácil!

eat VERB
comer
I eat a lot of sweets.
Como muchos caramelos.
Would you like something to eat?
¿Quieres comer algo?

edge NOUN
el **borde** *masc*
on the edge of the table
en el borde de la mesa

Edinburgh NOUN
Edimburgo *masc*
Andrew lives in Edinburgh.
Andrew vive en Edimburgo.

education NOUN
la **educación** *fem*

effect NOUN
el **efecto** *masc*

effort NOUN
el **esfuerzo** *masc*
You have to make an effort.
Tienes que hacer un esfuerzo.

e.g. ABBREVIATION
p.ej. (= *por ejemplo*)

egg NOUN
el **huevo** *masc*

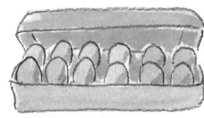

a boiled egg
un huevo pasado por agua
a hard-boiled egg
un huevo cocido
scrambled eggs
huevos revueltos
a fried egg
un huevo frito

eight NUMBER
ocho
eight euros
ocho euros

She's eight.
Tiene ocho años.

LANGUAGE TIP
In English you can say **she's eight** or
she's eight years old. In Spanish you
can only say **tiene ocho años**. Have
you noticed that in Spanish you need
to use the verb **tener** to talk about
somebody's age?

---

eighteen NUMBER
dieciocho
eighteen euros
dieciocho euros

He's eighteen.
Tiene dieciocho años.

LANGUAGE TIP
In English you can say **he's eighteen** or **he's eighteen years old**. In Spanish you can only say **tiene dieciocho años**. Have you noticed that in Spanish you need to use the verb **tener** to talk about somebody's age?

eighteenth NUMBER
dieciocho
> **on the eighteenth floor**
> en el piso dieciocho
> **It's my brother's eighteenth birthday on Saturday.**
> Mi hermano cumple dieciocho años el sábado.
> **My birthday's the eighteenth of August.**
> Mi cumpleaños es el dieciocho de agosto.
> **Today's the eighteenth of May.**
> Hoy es dieciocho de mayo.

> **on the eighteenth of June**
> el dieciocho de junio

LANGUAGE TIP
Use the same set of numbers that you use for counting (**uno**, **dos**, **tres** and so on) when giving Spanish dates.

eighth NUMBER
octavo masc
octava fem
> **on the eighth floor**
> en el octavo piso
> **My birthday's the eighth of May.**
> Mi cumpleaños es el ocho de mayo.
> **It's the eighth of June today.**
> Hoy es ocho de junio.

> **on the eighth of April**
> el ocho de abril

LANGUAGE TIP
Use the same set of numbers that you use for counting (**uno**, **dos**, **tres** and so on) when giving Spanish dates.

eighty NUMBER
ochenta
> **My grandmother is eighty.**
> Mi abuela tiene ochenta años.

LANGUAGE TIP
In English you can say **she's eighty** or **she's eighty years old**. In Spanish you can only say **tiene ochenta años**. Have you noticed that in Spanish you need to use the verb **tener** to talk about somebody's age?

Éire NOUN
la **República de Irlanda** fem

either ADVERB, CONJUNCTION, PRONOUN
tampoco
> **I don't like milk, and I don't like eggs either.**
> No me gusta la leche ni tampoco me gustan los huevos.
> **I haven't got any money.**
> **— I haven't either.**
> No tengo dinero. — Ni yo tampoco.
> **I don't like either of them.**
> No me gusta ninguno de los dos.
> **either ... or ...**
> o ... o ...
> **You can have either ice cream or yoghurt.**
> Puedes tomar o helado o yogur.

elastic band NOUN
la **goma elástica** fem

elbow NOUN
el **codo** masc
> **I've hurt my elbow.**
> Me he hecho daño en el codo.

LANGUAGE TIP
In Spanish you usually use an article like **el**, **la** or **los**, **las** with parts of the body.

Spanish

English

A
B
C
D
E
F
G
H
I
J
K
L
M
N
O
P
Q
R
S
T
U
V
W
X
Y
Z

elder ADJECTIVE
mayor *masc/fem*
my elder sister
mi hermana mayor

elderly ADJECTIVE
mayor *masc/fem*
an elderly gentleman
un señor mayor
the elderly
los ancianos

eldest ADJECTIVE
mayor *masc/fem*
my eldest brother
mi hermano mayor
He's the eldest.
Él es el mayor.

election NOUN
la **elección** *fem*
(PL las **elecciones**)
the election of the new mayor
la elección del nuevo alcalde
The elections will be in May.
Las elecciones serán en mayo.

electric ADJECTIVE
eléctrico *masc*
eléctrica *fem*
an electric guitar
una guitarra eléctrica

electrician NOUN
el/la **electricista** *masc/fem*
He's an electrician.
Es electricista.

LANGUAGE TIP
In Spanish, you do not use an article
with people's jobs.

electricity NOUN
la **electricidad** *fem*

electronic ADJECTIVE
electrónico *masc*
electrónica *fem*

elegant ADJECTIVE
elegante *masc/fem*

elephant NOUN
el **elefante** *masc*

eleven NUMBER
once
eleven euros
once euros

I'm eleven.
Tengo once años.

LANGUAGE TIP
In English you can say **I'm eleven** or
I'm eleven years old. In Spanish you
can only say **tengo once años**. Have
you noticed that in Spanish you need
to use the verb **tener** to talk about
somebody's age?

eleventh NUMBER
undécimo *masc*
undécima *fem*
on the eleventh floor
en el undécimo piso
**My birthday's the eleventh of
June.**
Mi cumpleaños es el once de
junio.
**It's the eleventh of December
today.**
Hoy es once de diciembre.

on the eleventh of January
el once de enero

LANGUAGE TIP
Use the same set of numbers that you
use for counting (**uno**, **dos**, **tres** and
so on) when giving Spanish dates.

else ADVERB
más
nobody else
nadie más
nothing else
nada más
Would you like anything else?
¿Quieres algo más?
I don't want anything else.
No quiero nada más.
somebody else
otra persona

email

email can be a noun or a verb.

A NOUN
el **correo electrónico** masc
by email
por correo electrónico
Send your friend an email.
Envíale un correo a tu amigo.
B VERB
to email
mandar un correo electrónico a
I'll email you.
Te mandaré un correo.

email address NOUN
el **e-mail** masc (PL los **e-mails**)
My email address is hello at collins.com (hello@collins.com).
Mi dirección de correo es hello arroba collins punto com(hello@collins.com).

embarrassed ADJECTIVE
I was really embarrassed.
Me dio mucha vergüenza.

embarrassing ADJECTIVE
incómodo masc
incómoda fem
an embarrassing situation
una situación incómoda

emergency NOUN
la **emergencia** fem
This is an emergency!
¡Es una emergencia!

in an emergency
en caso de emergencia

emergency exit NOUN
la **salida de emergencia** fem

emoji NOUN
el **emoji** masc

empty

empty can be an adjective or a verb.

A ADJECTIVE
vacío masc
vacía fem
The cage is empty.
La jaula está vacía.
B VERB
to empty
vaciar
Can you empty the wastepaper basket?
¿Puedes vaciar la papelera?

encourage VERB
animar
Encourage your team!
¡Anima a tu equipo!

encyclopedia NOUN
la **enciclopedia** fem

end

end can be a noun or a verb.

A NOUN
el **final** masc
the end of the lesson
el final de la clase
at the end of the street
al final de la calle

in the end
al final

B VERB
to end
terminar
What time does the lesson end?
¿A qué hora termina la clase?

A
B
C
D
E
F
G
H
I
J
K
L
M
N
O
P
Q
R
S
T
U
V
W
X
Y
Z

ending NOUN
el **final** *masc*
> **It's a great film, especially the ending.**
> Es una película estupenda, sobre todo el final.

enemy NOUN
el **enemigo** *masc*
la **enemiga** *fem*

energetic ADJECTIVE
lleno de energía *masc*
llena de energía *fem*

energy NOUN
la **energía** *fem*

engaged ADJECTIVE
1 **ocupado** *masc*
ocupada *fem* (*busy*)
> **The toilet is engaged.**
> El baño está ocupado.
> **Her phone is always engaged.**
> Su teléfono está siempre comunicando.
2 **prometido** *masc*
prometida *fem* (*to be married*)
> **My brother is engaged.**
> Mi hermano está prometido.
> **She's engaged to Rob.**
> Está prometida con Rob.

engagement NOUN
el **compromiso** *masc* (*to be married*)

engagement ring NOUN
el **anillo de compromiso** *masc*

engine NOUN
1 el **motor** *masc* (*of car, machine*)
2 la **locomotora** *fem* (*train*)

engineer NOUN
el **ingeniero** *masc*
la **ingeniera** *fem*
> **He's an engineer.**
> Es ingeniero.

LANGUAGE TIP
In Spanish, you do not use an article with people's jobs.

England NOUN
Inglaterra *fem*
> **I live in England.**
> Vivo en Inglaterra.
> **Are you coming to England?**
> ¿Vienes a Inglaterra?

English

> **English** can be an adjective or a noun.

A ADJECTIVE
inglés *masc* (PL **ingleses**)
inglesa *fem*
> **I'm English.**
> Soy inglés.
> **English food is different.**
> La comida inglesa es diferente.
> **English people**
> los ingleses

> **He's English.**
> Es inglés.
> **She's English.**
> Es inglesa.

B NOUN
el **inglés** *masc*
> **Do you speak English?**
> ¿Hablas inglés?
> **the English**
> los ingleses

LANGUAGE TIP
inglés is not spelled with a capital letter in Spanish.

Englishman NOUN
el **inglés** *masc* (PL los **ingleses**)
> **an Englishman**
> un inglés

LANGUAGE TIP
inglés is not spelled with a capital letter in Spanish.

Englishwoman NOUN
la **inglesa** *fem* (PL las **inglesas**)
    an Englishwoman
    una inglesa

LANGUAGE TIP
inglesa is not spelled with a capital letter in Spanish.

---

enjoy VERB
    I enjoy learning English.
    Me gusta aprender inglés.
    Did you enjoy the film?
    ¿Te gustó la película?
    to enjoy oneself
    divertirse
    Did you enjoy yourself?
    ¿Te divertiste?

enjoyable ADJECTIVE
    agradable *masc/fem*

enormous ADJECTIVE
    enorme *masc/fem*

enough

---

enough can be an adjective, pronoun or adverb.

A ADJECTIVE
    suficiente *masc/fem*
    enough time
    tiempo suficiente
    I haven't got enough money.
    No tengo dinero suficiente.

LANGUAGE TIP
You can also use **bastante**, which goes before the noun.

    I haven't got enough money.
    No tengo bastante dinero.
B PRONOUN
    bastante *masc/fem*
    Have you got enough?
    ¿Tienes bastante?
    I've had enough!
    ¡Ya está bien!

    That's enough.
    Ya basta.

C ADVERB
    This hat isn't big enough.
    Este sombrero no es lo suficientemente grande.
    Is your coffee hot enough?
    ¿Tu café está lo suficientemente caliente?

enter VERB
    I'm going to enter the competition.
    Voy a participar en el concurso.

enthusiasm NOUN
    el **entusiasmo** *masc*

enthusiastic ADJECTIVE
    entusiasta *masc/fem*

entrance NOUN
    la **entrada** *fem*
    I'll wait for you by the entrance.
    Te esperaré en la entrada.

entrance exam NOUN
    la **prueba de acceso** *fem*

entry NOUN
    la **entrada** *fem*
    'no entry'
    "prohibida la entrada"

entry phone NOUN
    el **portero automático** *masc*

envelope NOUN
    el **sobre** *masc*

envious ADJECTIVE
    envidioso *masc*
    envidiosa *fem*

environment NOUN
    el **medio ambiente** *masc*

episode NOUN
    el **capítulo** *masc*

equal

> **equal** can be an adjective or a verb.

A ADJECTIVE
igual *masc/fem*
Cut the pizza into six equal pieces.
Corta la pizza en seis trozos iguales.

B VERB
to equal
ser igual a
Two times three equals six.
Dos por tres es igual a seis.

equalize VERB
empatar
Henry has equalized.
Henry ha empatado.

equipment NOUN
el **equipo** *masc*
lots of equipment
mucho equipo

e-reader NOUN
el **lector electrónico** *masc*

error NOUN
el **error** *masc*
a small error
un pequeño error

escalator NOUN
la **escalera mecánica** *fem*
Is there an escalator?
¿Hay escalera mecánica?

escape VERB
escaparse
My mouse has escaped.
Se ha escapado mi ratón.

especially ADVERB
sobre todo
It's very hot, especially in summer.
Hace mucho calor, sobre todo en verano.

essay NOUN
el **trabajo** *masc*
a history essay
un trabajo de historia

essential ADJECTIVE
esencial *masc/fem*
It's essential to bring warm clothes.
Es esencial traer ropa de abrigo.

euro NOUN
el **euro** *masc*

Europe NOUN
Europa *fem*

European ADJECTIVE
europeo *masc*
europea *fem*

> **LANGUAGE TIP**
> **europeo** is not spelled with a capital letter in Spanish.

even

> **even** can be an adverb or an adjective.

A ADVERB
incluso
I like all animals, even snakes.
Me gustan todos los animales, incluso las serpientes.

B ADJECTIVE
an even number
un número par

evening NOUN
1 la **tarde** *fem* (*early evening*)

> **LANGUAGE TIP**
> Use **la tarde** in the early evening while it's still light.

at six o'clock in the evening
a las seis de la tarde

this evening at about six thirty
esta tarde, a eso de las seis y media
2 la **noche** *fem* (*after dark*)

LANGUAGE TIP
Use **la noche** for later in the evening,
particularly after dark.

at nine o'clock in the evening
a las nueve de la noche
tomorrow evening
mañana por la noche
yesterday evening
ayer por la noche
Good evening!
¡Buenas noches!

LANGUAGE TIP
Change **noche** and **noches** to **tarde**
and **tardes** if it's very early in the
evening.

evening class NOUN
la **clase nocturna** *fem*
**My mother goes to an evening
class.**
Mi madre va a una clase nocturna.

event NOUN
el **acontecimiento** *masc*
an important event
un acontecimiento importante

ever ADVERB
1 **alguna vez** (*in questions*)
Have you ever been to France?
¿Has estado alguna vez en Francia?
2 **nunca**
Nothing ever happens.
Nunca pasa nada.
3 **for the first time ever**
por primera vez

every ADJECTIVE
every pupil
todos los alumnos
I talk to her every day.
Hablo con ella todos los días.
I do judo every week.
Hago yudo todas las semanas.

every time
cada vez

every day
todos los días
every night
todas las noches
every week
todas las semanas

everybody PRONOUN
todos *masc pl*
todas *fem pl*
Good morning, everybody!
¡Buenos días a todos!
Is everybody here?
¿Están todos?
Everybody likes sweets.
A todo el mundo le gustan los
caramelos.

everyone PRONOUN
todos *masc pl*
todas *fem pl masc pl*
Good morning, everyone!
¡Buenos días a todos!
Is everyone here?
¿Están todos?
Everyone likes sweets.
A todo el mundo le gustan los
caramelos.

everything PRONOUN
todo *masc*
Everything's fine!
¡Todo está bien!
Is that everything?
¿Eso es todo?

everywhere ADVERB
por todas partes
**I looked everywhere, but I
couldn't find it.**
Miré por todas partes, pero no lo
encontré.
There are cats everywhere!
¡Hay gatos por todas partes!

exact ADJECTIVE
exacto *masc*
exacta *fem*

Spanish

English

a
b
c
d
e
f
g
h
i
j
k
l
m
n
o
p
q
r
s
t
u
v
w
x
y
z

exactly ADVERB
exactamente
Our trainers are exactly the same.
Nuestras zapatillas de deporte son
exactamente iguales.
not exactly
no exactamente
It's exactly ten o'clock.
Son las diez en punto.

LANGUAGE TIP
Have you noticed that the Spanish
equivalent of the English **-ly** ending is
-mente? It's added to the feminine
form of the adjective.

---

exam NOUN
el **examen** *masc* (PL los **exámenes**)
an English exam
un examen de inglés

example NOUN
el **ejemplo** *masc*
for example
por ejemplo

excellent ADJECTIVE
excelente *masc/fem*
Excellent!
¡Excelente!

except PREPOSITION
excepto
everyone except me
todos menos yo

exchange VERB
cambiar
**I want to exchange the book for
a toy.**
Quiero cambiar el libro por un juguete.

excited ADJECTIVE
entusiasmado *masc*
entusiasmada *fem*

exciting ADJECTIVE
emocionante *masc/fem*
an exciting film
una película emocionante

exclamation mark NOUN
el **signo de admiración** *masc*

excuse VERB

> **Excuse me!**
> ¡Perdón!

exercise NOUN
el **ejercicio** *masc*

exercise book NOUN
el **cuaderno** *masc*

exhausted ADJECTIVE
agotado *masc*
agotada *fem*
Clare is exhausted.
Clare está agotada.

exhibition NOUN
la **exposición** *fem* (PL las
exposiciones)

exit NOUN
la **salida** *fem*
Where is the exit?
¿Dónde está la salida?

expect VERB
1 **esperar** (*wait for*)
I'm expecting a phone call.
Estoy esperando una llamada.
She's expecting a baby.
Está esperando un niño.
2 **imaginarse** (*imagine*)
I expect he'll be late.
Me imagino que llegará tarde.

expedition NOUN
la **expedición** *fem* (PL las
expediciones)

expensive ADJECTIVE
caro *masc*
cara *fem*
It's too expensive.
Es demasiado caro.

experience NOUN
la **experiencia** *fem*
an interesting experience
una experiencia interesante

experiment NOUN
el **experimento** *masc*

expert NOUN
el **experto** *masc*
la **experta** *fem*
She's a computer expert.
Es una experta en informática.
Jay is an expert cook.
Jay es un experto cocinero.

explain VERB
explicar
I'll explain it in English.
Te lo explicaré en inglés.

explanation NOUN
la **explicación** *fem* (PL las **explicaciones**)
a clear explanation
una explicación clara

explode VERB
explotar
It's going to explode!
¡Va a explotar!

explosion NOUN
la **explosión** *fem* (PL las **explosiones**)

extension NOUN
1 la **extensión** *fem* (PL las **extensiones**) (phone)
Extension 3137, please.
Con la extensión 3137, por favor.
2 (of building)
We're having an extension built.
Nos están construyendo una ampliación de la casa.

extra

extra can be an adjective or an adverb.

A ADJECTIVE
1 (additional)
an extra blanket
una manta más
2 (not included)
Breakfast is extra.
El desayuno no está incluido.
B ADVERB
to pay extra
pagar más
You have to pay extra for a room with a sea view.
Si quieres una habitación con vistas al mar tienes que pagar más.
It costs extra.
Lleva un suplemento aparte.

extremely ADVERB
sumamente

eye NOUN
el **ojo** *masc*
I've got blue eyes.
Tengo los ojos azules.
What colour eyes has he got?
¿De qué color tiene los ojos?
She opened her eyes.
Abrió los ojos.

LANGUAGE TIP
In Spanish you usually use an article like **el**, **la** or **los**, **las** with parts of the body.

eyebrow NOUN
la **ceja** *fem*

eyelash NOUN
la **pestaña** *fem*
She's got very long eyelashes.
Tiene las pestañas muy largas.

eyelid NOUN
el **párpado** *masc*

eyesight NOUN
la **vista** *fem*

fabulous ADJECTIVE
fantástico *masc*
fantástica *fem*

face NOUN
la **cara** *fem*

She has a freckly face.
Tiene la cara pecosa.

LANGUAGE TIP
In Spanish you usually use an article like **el**, **la** or **los**, **las** with parts of the body.

---

face cloth NOUN
la **toallita** *fem*

face mask NOUN
la **mascarilla** *fem*

facilities PL NOUN
las **instalaciones** *fem pl*

fact NOUN
el **hecho** *masc*
an interesting fact
un hecho interesante
in fact
en realidad

factory NOUN
la **fábrica** *fem*

fail VERB
suspender
She's going to fail her exams.
Va a suspender los exámenes.

fair

---
fair can be an adjective or a noun.

A ADJECTIVE
1 **justo** *masc*
justa *fem* (*right*)
That's not fair.
Eso no es justo.
2 **rubio** *masc*
rubia *fem* (*blonde*)
He's got fair hair.
Tiene el pelo rubio.
B NOUN
la **feria** *fem*
Are you going to the fair?
¿Vas a ir a la feria?

fair-haired ADJECTIVE
Nina is fair-haired.
Nina tiene el pelo rubio.

fairly ADVERB
bastante
That's fairly good.
Eso está bastante bien.

fairy NOUN
el **hada** *fem*

LANGUAGE TIP
Even though it's a feminine noun, remember that you use **el** and **un** with **hada**.

---

fairy tale NOUN
el **cuento de hadas** *masc*

fall VERB
1 **caerse**
Mind you don't fall!
¡Ten cuidado de no caerte!
2 **to fall asleep**
quedarse dormido
I'm falling asleep.
Me estoy quedando dormido.

fall off VERB
caerse de
   He's going to fall off the wall.
   Se va a caer del muro.

false ADJECTIVE
falso *masc*
falsa *fem*
   True or false?
   ¿Verdadero o falso?

family NOUN
la **familia** *fem*
   my family
   mi familia
   the whole family
   toda la familia
   the Crooks family
   la familia Crooks

famous ADJECTIVE
famoso *masc*
famosa *fem*

fan NOUN
  1 el **ventilador** *masc* (*electric*)
  2 el **abanico** *masc* (*hand-held*)
  3 el/la **hincha** *masc/fem* (*enthusiast*)
   football fans
   los hinchas de fútbol

fancy VERB
   Do you fancy an ice cream?
   ¿Te apetece un helado?
   I fancy watching a film.
   Me apetece ver una película.
   I fancy that girl.
   Me gusta esa chica.

fantastic ADJECTIVE
fantástico *masc*
fantástica *fem*

far ADVERB
  1 **lejos** (*distant*)
   It isn't very far.
   No está muy lejos.
   far from
   lejos de
   It isn't far from here.
   No está lejos de aquí.

   Is it far?
   ¿Está lejos?
   No, it isn't far.
   No, no está lejos.
   It's too far.
   Está demasiado lejos.

  2 **mucho** (*much*)
   That's far better!
   ¡Eso está mucho mejor!

farm NOUN
la **granja** *fem*

farmer NOUN
el **agricultor** *masc*
la **agricultora** *fem*
   He's a farmer.
   Es agricultor.

LANGUAGE TIP
In Spanish, you do not use an article
with people's jobs.

---

farmhouse NOUN
la **granja** *fem*

fashion NOUN
la **moda** *fem*
   These shoes are in fashion.
   Estos zapatos están de moda.

fashionable ADJECTIVE
de moda
   This style is very fashionable.
   Este estilo está muy de moda.
   Jane wears fashionable clothes.
   Jane se viste a la moda.

fashion show NOUN
el **desfile de moda** *masc*

fast

    fast can be an adverb or an adjective.

  A ADVERB
   rápido
   You walk fast.
   Andas rápido.
  B ADJECTIVE
   rápido *masc*
   rápida *fem*

a fast car
un coche rápido
fast food
la comida rápida

fasten VERB
abrocharse
> **Fasten your seat belts, please.**
> Abróchense los cinturones de seguridad, por favor.

fat ADJECTIVE
gordo *masc*
gorda *fem*
> **They're both fat.**
> Los dos están gordos.

father NOUN
el **padre** *masc*
> **my father**
> mi padre
> **my mother and father**
> mis padres

Father Christmas NOUN
Papá Noel *masc*

DID YOU KNOW...?
In Spain it's often **los Reyes Magos** (the Three Kings) who bring children their presents. And instead of Christmas Eve they come on the night of the fifth of January, so children open their presents on the sixth.

Father's Day NOUN
el **día del Padre** *masc*

LANGUAGE TIP
Even though it ends in **-a**, **el día** is a masculine noun.

---

fault NOUN
la **culpa** *fem*
> **It's your fault!**
> ¡Es culpa tuya!
> **It wasn't my fault.**
> No fue culpa mía.

favour NOUN
el **favor** *masc*
> **Could you do me a favour?**
> ¿Me podrías hacer un favor?

favourite ADJECTIVE
favorito *masc*
favorita *fem*
> **Blue's my favourite colour.**
> El azul es mi color favorito.

fear NOUN
el **miedo** *masc*

feather NOUN
la **pluma** *fem*

February NOUN
febrero *masc*
> **My birthday's the fourteenth of February.**
> Mi cumpleaños es el catorce de febrero.
> **It's the eighth of February today.**
> Hoy es ocho de febrero.

in February
en febrero
on the fifth of February
el cinco de febrero

LANGUAGE TIP
Months are not spelled with a capital letter in Spanish.

---

feed VERB
dar de comer a
> **I'm going to feed the cat.**
> Voy a darle de comer al gato.

feel VERB
1 sentirse

I don't feel well.
No me siento bien.
2 I feel like ...
Me apetece ...
I feel like going for a walk.
Me apetece dar un paseo.
Do you feel like an ice cream?
¿Te apetece un helado?

feet PL NOUN
los **pies** *masc pl*
My feet are cold.
Tengo los pies fríos.

LANGUAGE TIP
In Spanish you usually use an article like **el**, **la** or **los**, **las** with parts of the body.

---

fell VERB ▷ *see* **fall**

felt-tip pen NOUN
el **rotulador** *masc*
Can I borrow your felt-tip pens?
¿Me dejas tus rotuladores?

female NOUN
la **hembra** *fem*
Is it a male or a female?
¿Es macho o hembra?

feminine ADJECTIVE
femenino *masc*
femenina *fem*

fence NOUN
la **valla** *fem*

ferret
NOUN
el **hurón**
masc
(PL los **hurones**)

ferry NOUN
el **ferri** *masc* (PL los **ferris**)

fetch VERB
ir a buscar
Can you fetch my bag?
¿Puedes ir a buscar mi bolso?

Mum always fetches us from school.
Mamá siempre nos va a buscar al colegio.

few ADJECTIVE, PRONOUN
a few
unos pocos

LANGUAGE TIP
Remember to change **unos pocos** to **unas pocas** when describing or referring to a feminine noun.

---

a few hours
unas pocas horas
How many potatoes do you want? — Just a few.
¿Cuántas patatas quieres? — Solo unas pocas.
quite a few people
bastante gente
I've got fewer sweets than Jim.
Tengo menos caramelos que Jim.
Who's got the fewest cards?
¿Quién tiene menos cartas?

fiancé NOUN
el **prometido** *masc*
He's her fiancé.
Es su prometido.

fiancée NOUN
la **prometida** *fem*
She's his fiancée.
Es su prometida.

field NOUN
el **campo** *masc*
a football field
un campo de fútbol
a field of wheat
un campo de trigo

fifteen NUMBER
quince
fifteen euros
quince euros

I'm fifteen.
Tengo quince años.

fifteenth NUMBER
quince
on the fifteenth floor
en el piso quince
Today's the fifteenth of July.
Hoy es quince de julio.
**My birthday's the fifteenth of
August.**
Mi cumpleaños es el quince de agosto.

on the fifteenth of November
el quince de noviembre

fifth NUMBER
quinto masc
quinta fem
on the fifth floor
en el quinto piso
Today's the fifth of April.
Hoy es cinco de abril.
My birthday's the fifth of March.
Mi cumpleaños es el cinco de marzo.

on the fifth of August
el cinco de agosto

fifty NUMBER
cincuenta
My aunt is fifty.
Mi tía tiene cincuenta años.

fight

fight can be a noun or a verb.

A NOUN
la **pelea** fem
B VERB
to fight
pelearse
Two tigers are fighting.
Dos tigres se están peleando.

figure NOUN
la **cifra** fem
**Shall I write it in figures or in
words?**
¿Lo escribo en cifras o en
palabras?

file NOUN
1 la **carpeta** fem (folder)
Keep the leaflets in your file.
Guarda los folletos en tu carpeta.
2 el **archivo** masc (on computer)

fill VERB
llenar
Can you fill the glasses?
¿Puedes llenar las copas?

fill in VERB
rellenar
**You have to fill in the gaps in
the sentences.**
Hay que rellenar los huecos de las
frases.

filling NOUN
el **empaste** masc (in tooth)

film NOUN
la **película** fem (movie)
Is it a good film?
¿Es una buena película?

film star NOUN
la **estrella de cine** *fem*
Eddie Murphy is a film star.
Eddie Murphy es una estrella de cine.

> **LANGUAGE TIP**
> Even though **una estrella** is a feminine word, you can use it to refer to a man or boy.

final

> **final** can be an adjective or a noun.

A ADJECTIVE
último *masc*
última *fem*
the final minutes
los últimos minutos

B NOUN
la **final** *fem*
The final is tomorrow.
La final es mañana.

finally ADVERB
finalmente

find VERB
encontrar
My brother wants to find a job.
Mi hermano quiere encontrar trabajo.

fine ADJECTIVE
bien

> **LANGUAGE TIP**
> **bien** never changes its ending no matter what it describes.

That's fine, thanks.
Eso está bien, gracias.
How are you? — I'm fine.
¿Qué tal estás? — Estoy bien.

finger NOUN
el **dedo** *masc*
my little finger
mi dedo meñique
My finger is hurting.
Me duele el dedo.

> **LANGUAGE TIP**
> In Spanish you usually use an article like **el**, **la** or **los**, **las** with parts of the body.

fingernail NOUN
la **uña** *fem*

finish VERB
terminar
I've got to finish my homework.
Tengo que terminar los deberes.
I've finished!
¡He terminado!
Is it finished?
¿Está terminado?

fire NOUN
1 el **fuego** *masc*
You mustn't play with fire.
No hay que jugar con el fuego.
2 el **incendio** *masc* (*accidental*)
There's a fire in the wood.
Hay un incendio en el bosque.

fire engine NOUN
el **coche de bomberos** *masc*

fire extinguisher NOUN
el **extintor** *masc*

firefighter NOUN
el **bombero** *masc*
la **bombera** *fem*
She's a firefighter.
Es bombera.

> **LANGUAGE TIP**
> In Spanish, you do not use an article with people's jobs.

fireplace NOUN
la **chimenea** *fem*

fire station NOUN
el **parque de bomberos** *masc*

fireworks PL NOUN
los **fuegos artificiales** *masc pl*
There are fireworks this evening.
Hay fuegos artificiales esta noche.

A
B
C
D
E
F
G
H
I
J
K
L
M
N
O
P
Q
R
S
T
U
V
W
X
Y
Z

first

> **first** can be an adjective, noun or adverb.

A ADJECTIVE
primero *masc*
primera *fem*
the first time
la primera vez

LANGUAGE TIP
Shorten **primero** to **primer** before a masculine singular noun.

---

the first day
el primer día
to come first
quedar primero
Rachel came first in the race.
Rachel quedó primera en la carrera.
Who's first?
¿Quién va primero?
Me first!
¡Yo primero!

B NOUN
at first
al principio
It's easy at first.
Es fácil al principio.
My birthday's the first of October.
Mi cumpleaños es el uno de octubre.
Today's the first of June.
Hoy es uno de junio.

on the first of September
el uno de septiembre

LANGUAGE TIP
Use the same set of numbers that you use for counting (**uno**, **dos**, **tres** and so on) when giving Spanish dates.

C ADVERB
primero
First write your names.
Primero escribid vuestros nombres.
first of all
en primer lugar

first aid NOUN
los **primeros auxilios** *masc pl*

first name NOUN
el **nombre de pila** *masc*

fish

> **fish** can be a noun or a verb.

A NOUN
1 el **pescado** *masc* (as food)
I don't like fish.
No me gusta el pescado.
2 el **pez** *masc* (PL los **peces**) (animal)
I caught three fish.
Pesqué tres peces.

B VERB
to go fishing
ir a pescar
Let's go fishing.
Vamos a pescar.

fish fingers PL NOUN
las **varitas de merluza** *fem pl*

fishing NOUN
la **pesca** *fem*
I like fishing.
Me gusta la pesca.

fishing boat NOUN
la **barca de pesca** *fem*

fishing rod NOUN
la **caña de pescar** *fem*

fish tank NOUN
el **acuario** *masc*

fit

> **fit** can be a verb or an adjective.

A VERB
to fit
caber
It doesn't fit in the kitchen.
No cabe en la cocina.
These trousers don't fit me.
Estos pantalones no me están bien.

B ADJECTIVE
en forma (*healthy*)
He's fit.
Está en forma.

five NUMBER
cinco
five euros
cinco euros

She's five.
Tiene cinco años.

LANGUAGE TIP
In English you can say **she's five** or **she's five years old**. In Spanish you can only say **tiene cinco años**. Have you noticed that in Spanish you need to use the verb **tener** to talk about somebody's age?

fix VERB
arreglar
Can you fix my bike?
¿Me puedes arreglar la bici?

fizzy ADJECTIVE
con gas
I don't like fizzy drinks.
No me gustan las bebidas con gas.

flag NOUN
la **bandera** *fem*

flame NOUN
la **llama** *fem*

flan NOUN
1 la **tarta** *fem* (*sweet*)
a raspberry flan
una tarta de frambuesa

LANGUAGE TIP
Be careful! The translation of **flan** is not **flan**.

2 el **quiche** *masc* (*savoury*)
a cheese and onion flan
un quiche de queso y cebolla

flannel NOUN
la **toallita** *fem*

flash NOUN
a flash of lightning
un relámpago

flask NOUN
el **termo** *masc*

flat

> **flat** can be an adjective or a noun.

A ADJECTIVE
1 **plano** *masc*
plana *fem* (*level*)
a flat roof
un tejado plano
flat shoes
zapatos planos
2 **pinchado** *masc*
pinchada *fem* (*tyre*)
I've got a flat tyre.
Tengo una rueda pinchada.

B NOUN
el **piso** *masc*
She lives in a flat.
Vive en un piso.

flavour NOUN
el **sabor** *masc*
Which flavour of ice cream would you like?
¿De qué sabor quieres el helado?

fleece NOUN
el **forro polar** *masc*

flew VERB ▷ see **fly**

flight NOUN
el **vuelo** masc
What time is the flight to London?
¿A qué hora es el vuelo a Londres?

floor NOUN
1 el **suelo** masc (of room)
on the floor
en el suelo
Sit on the floor, Jenny.
Siéntate en el suelo, Jenny.
2 la **planta** fem (storey)
the ground floor
la planta baja
the first floor
la primera planta
on the third floor
en la tercera planta

florist NOUN
el/la **florista** masc/fem
He's a florist.
Es florista.
a florist's
una floristería

LANGUAGE TIP
Did you notice that **florista** still ends in **-a** even when referring to a man? Remember that in Spanish, you do not use an article with people's jobs.

---

flour NOUN
la **harina** fem

flower NOUN
la **flor** fem

flu NOUN
la **gripe** fem
Nathan has got flu.
Nathan tiene gripe.

fluent ADJECTIVE
My sister speaks fluent Spanish.
Mi hermana habla español con fluidez.

flush VERB
to flush the toilet
tirar de la cadena

flute NOUN
la **flauta** fem
I play the flute.
Toco la flauta.

fly

> **fly** can be a verb or a noun.

A VERB
to fly
1 **ir en avión** (go by plane)
I'm going to fly to Florida.
Voy a ir a Florida en avión.
2 **volar** (with wings)
A bee was flying around the room.
Había una abeja volando por la habitación.
B NOUN
la **mosca** fem

fog NOUN
la **niebla** fem

foggy ADJECTIVE
a foggy day
un día de niebla

It's foggy.
Hay niebla.

fold VERB
doblar
Fold the paper in half.
Dobla el papel por la mitad.

folder NOUN
la **carpeta** fem

follow VERB
seguir
Follow me, Yan.
Sígueme, Yan.
How many people do you follow?
¿A cuántas personas sigues?

follower NOUN
el **seguidor** masc
la **seguidora** fem

following ADJECTIVE
siguiente masc/fem
the following day
el día siguiente

food NOUN
la **comida** *fem*
  I like Spanish food.
  Me gusta la comida española.
  We need to buy some food.
  Necesitamos comprar comida.

food processor NOUN
el **robot de cocina** *masc*

foot NOUN
el **pie** *masc*
  My feet are hurting.
  Me duelen los pies.

LANGUAGE TIP
In Spanish you usually use an article like **el**, **la** or **los**, **las** with parts of the body.

---

  on foot
  a pie
  Richard is six foot tall.
  Richard mide seis pies de altura.

football NOUN
1 el **fútbol** *masc* (*game*)
  I like playing football.
  Me gusta jugar al fútbol.
  Do you want to play football, boys?
  ¿Queréis jugar al fútbol, niños?

LANGUAGE TIP
In Spanish, you need to include **al** or **a la** before the names of sports or games when talking about playing them.

---

2 el **balón** *masc* (PL los **balones**) (*ball*)
  Aman's got a new football.
  Aman tiene un balón nuevo.

football boots PL NOUN
las **botas de fútbol** *fem pl*

footballer NOUN
el/la **futbolista** *masc/fem*
  He's a footballer.
  Es futbolista.

LANGUAGE TIP
Did you notice that **futbolista** still ends in **-a** even when referring to a man? Remember that in Spanish, you do not use an article with people's jobs.

---

football player NOUN
el **jugador de fútbol** *masc*
la **jugadora de fútbol** *fem*
  David Beckham is a famous football player.
  David Beckham es un jugador de fútbol famoso.

football shirt NOUN
la **camiseta de fútbol** *fem*

footpath NOUN
el **sendero** *masc*

footstep NOUN
el **paso** *masc*

for PREPOSITION
1 **para** (*intended for, destined for*)
  a present for me
  un regalo para mí
  the train for London
  el tren para Londres
  I'll do it for you.
  Yo te lo haré.
  What's the Spanish for 'lion'?
  ¿Cómo se dice "lion" en español?
  It's time for lunch.
  Es la hora de comer.

A
B
C
D
E
F
G
H
I
J
K
L
M
N
O
P
Q
R
S
T
U
V
W
X
Y
Z

What's it for?
¿Para qué es?
B for Barcelona
B de Barcelona

2 por (*in exchange for*)
I'll give it to you for five pounds.
Te lo doy por cinco libras.
He bought it for ten euros.
Lo compró por diez euros.
3 (*for a period of*)
We're going there for three weeks.
Vamos a pasar ahí tres semanas.

LANGUAGE TIP
You can often use the verb **llevar** to talk about how long you've been doing something.

I have been learning Spanish for six months.
Llevo seis meses aprendiendo español.

LANGUAGE TIP
But there are other ways of saying how long you've been doing something.

I haven't seen her for two years.
No la veo desde hace dos años.

forbidden ADJECTIVE
prohibido *masc*
prohibida *fem*
Smoking is forbidden.
Está prohibido fumar.

forecast NOUN
el **pronóstico** *masc*
the weather forecast
el pronóstico del tiempo
What's the forecast for today?
¿Cuál es el pronóstico para hoy?

forehead NOUN
la **frente** *fem*

foreign ADJECTIVE
extranjero *masc*
extranjera *fem*

foreigner NOUN
el **extranjero** *masc*
la **extranjera** *fem*
He's a foreigner.
Es extranjero.

forest NOUN
1 el **bosque** *masc* (*wood*)
2 la **selva** *fem* (*tropical*)

forget VERB
olvidarse

LANGUAGE TIP
To say **I've forgotten …** use **se me ha olvidado …** when you've forgotten one thing and **se me han olvidado …** when you've forgotten two or more things.

I've forgotten his name.
Se me ha olvidado su nombre.
I've forgotten my keys.
Se me han olvidado las llaves.
Don't forget!
¡Que no se te olvide!
to forget to do something
olvidarse de hacer algo
I forgot to post the letter.
Me olvidé de echar la carta.

fork NOUN
el **tenedor** *masc*

form NOUN
el **impreso** *masc*
You have to fill in the form.
Tienes que rellenar el impreso.

fortnight NOUN
a fortnight
dos semanas
I'm going on holiday for a fortnight.
Me voy dos semanas de vacaciones.

fortunately ADVERB
afortunadamente

forty NUMBER
cuarenta
My father is forty.
Mi padre tiene cuarenta años.

LANGUAGE TIP
In English you can say **he's forty** or **he's forty years old**. In Spanish you can only say **tiene cuarenta años**. Have you noticed that in Spanish you need to use the verb **tener** to talk about somebody's age?

forward ADVERB
hacia adelante
   a step forward
   un paso hacia adelante
   to move forward
   avanzar
   Move forward two spaces.
   Avanza dos casillas.

fought VERB
   ▷ see **fight**

found VERB
   ▷ see **find**

fountain
NOUN
   la **fuente**
   fem

fountain pen NOUN
   la **pluma estilográfica** *fem*

four NUMBER
cuatro
   four euros
   cuatro euros

   He's four.
   Tiene cuatro años.

LANGUAGE TIP
In English you can say **he's four** or **he's four years old**. In Spanish you can only say **tiene cuatro años**. Have you noticed that in Spanish you need to use the verb **tener** to talk about somebody's age?

fourteen NUMBER
catorce
   fourteen euros
   catorce euros

   I'm fourteen.
   Tengo catorce años.

LANGUAGE TIP
In English you can say **I'm fourteen** or **I'm fourteen years old**. In Spanish you can only say **tengo catorce años**. Have you noticed that in Spanish you need to use the verb **tener** to talk about somebody's age?

fourteenth NUMBER
catorce
   on the fourteenth floor
   en el piso catorce
   My birthday's the fourteenth of January.
   Mi cumpleaños es el catorce de enero.
   Today's the fourteenth of July.
   Hoy es catorce de julio.

   on the fourteenth of August
   el catorce de agosto

LANGUAGE TIP
Use the same set of numbers that you use for counting (**uno**, **dos**, **tres** and so on) when giving Spanish dates.

fourth NUMBER
   cuarto *masc*
   cuarta *fem*
   on the fourth floor
   en el cuarto piso
   My birthday's the fourth of December.
   Mi cumpleaños es el cuatro de diciembre.
   Today's the fourth of October.
   Hoy es cuatro de octubre.

   on the fourth of June
   el cuatro de junio

LANGUAGE TIP
Use the same set of numbers that you use for counting (**uno**, **dos**, **tres**, **cuatro** and so on) when giving Spanish dates.

fox NOUN
  el **zorro** *masc*

frame NOUN
  el **marco** *masc*
    a photo frame
    un marco de fotos

freckles PL NOUN
  las **pecas** *fem pl*

free ADJECTIVE
  1 **gratis** (*free of charge*)

LANGUAGE TIP
gratis never changes its ending no matter what it describes.

  a free brochure
  un folleto gratis
  2 **libre** *masc/fem* (*not taken*)
    Excuse me, is this seat free?
    Perdón, ¿está libre este asiento?

freezer NOUN
  el **congelador** *masc*

freezing ADJECTIVE
  helado *masc*
  helada *fem*
    I'm freezing!
    ¡Estoy helado!
    It's absolutely freezing!
    ¡Hace un frío que pela!

French beans PL NOUN
  las **judías verdes** *fem pl*

French fries PL NOUN
  las **patatas fritas** *fem pl*

fresh ADJECTIVE
  fresco *masc*
  fresca *fem*
    I need some fresh air.
    Necesito un poco de aire fresco.

Friday NOUN
  el **viernes** *masc*
    It's Friday today.
    Hoy es viernes.

  on Friday
  el viernes
  on Fridays
  los viernes
  every Friday
  todos los viernes
  last Friday
  el viernes pasado
  next Friday
  el viernes que viene

LANGUAGE TIP
Days are not spelled with a capital letter in Spanish.

fridge NOUN
  el **frigorífico** *fem*

fried ADJECTIVE
  frito *masc*
  frita *fem*
    a fried egg
    un huevo frito

friend NOUN
  el **amigo** *masc*
  la **amiga** *fem*
    my friend George
    mi amigo George
    my friend Natasha
    mi amiga Natasha

friendly ADJECTIVE
  simpático *masc*
  simpática *fem*
    She's very friendly.
    Es muy simpática.

frightened ADJECTIVE
    to be frightened
    tener miedo
    I'm not frightened.
    No tengo miedo.
    Kali is frightened of spiders.
    A Kali le dan miedo las arañas.

I'm frightened!
¡Tengo miedo!

fringe NOUN
el **flequillo** *masc*
He's got a fringe.
Lleva flequillo.

Frisbee® NOUN
el **disco volador** *masc*

frog NOUN
la **rana** *fem*

from PREPOSITION
de
She comes from Bristol.
Es de Bristol.
a letter from my friend
una carta de mi amiga

LANGUAGE TIP
de combines with **el** to form **del**.

We aren't very far from the centre.
No estamos muy lejos del centro.
from ... to ...
desde ... hasta ...
from London to New York
desde Londres hasta Nueva York
the numbers from one to ten
los números del uno al diez

Where are you from?
¿De dónde eres?
I'm from Birmingham.
Soy de Birmingham.

front

front can be a noun or an adjective.

A NOUN
la **parte delantera** *fem*
the front of the house
la parte delantera de la casa
in front of
delante de
in front of the house
delante de la casa
B ADJECTIVE
de delante
the front row
la fila de delante

front door NOUN
la **puerta principal** *fem*

frontier NOUN
la **frontera** *fem*

frost NOUN
la **helada** *fem*

frosty ADJECTIVE
a frosty morning
una mañana de helada

It's frosty today.
Ha helado hoy.

frozen ADJECTIVE
1 **congelado** *masc*
congelada *fem (food)*
frozen peas
guisantes congelados
2 **helado** *masc*
helada *fem (lake, fingers)*
I'm frozen.
Estoy helado.

fruit NOUN
la **fruta** *fem*
I like fruit.
Me gusta la fruta.
a piece of fruit
una fruta

fruit juice NOUN
el **zumo de fruta** *masc*

fruit salad NOUN
la **macedonia** fem

fry NOUN
freír

frying pan NOUN
la **sartén** fem (PL las **sartenes**)

full ADJECTIVE
lleno masc
llena fem
> The bottle's full.
> La botella está llena.
> I'm full.
> Estoy lleno.

full stop NOUN
el **punto** masc

fun NOUN
> to have fun
> pasárselo bien
> Are you having fun?
> ¿Te lo estás pasando bien?

> It's fun!
> ¡Es divertido!
> Have fun!
> ¡Que te diviertas!

funfair NOUN
la **feria** fem

funny ADJECTIVE
divertido masc
divertida fem
> It was very funny.
> Fue muy divertido.

fur NOUN
1 la **piel** fem (used in clothing)
> a fur coat
> un abrigo de piel
2 el **pelo** masc (of animal)
> the dog's fur
> el pelo del perro

furious ADJECTIVE
furioso masc
furiosa fem
> Dad is furious with me.
> Papá está furioso conmigo.

furniture NOUN
los **muebles** masc pl
> We've got new furniture.
> Tenemos muebles nuevos.
> a piece of furniture
> un mueble

LANGUAGE TIP
Use **un mueble** to refer to one piece of furniture and **muebles** in the plural to talk about **furniture** in general.

future NOUN
el **futuro** masc
> What are your plans for the future?
> ¿Qué planes tienes para el futuro?
> Be more careful in future.
> De ahora en adelante ten más cuidado.

Gg

game NOUN
1 el **juego** *masc*
   Let's play a game.
   Vamos a jugar a algún juego.
   a game of chess
   una partida de ajedrez
2 el **partido** *masc* (*match*)
   The game is tomorrow.
   El partido es mañana.
   a game of football
   un partido de fútbol

games PL NOUN
la **educación física** *fem* (*at school*)
   I like games.
   Me gusta la educación física.

gang NOUN
1 la **banda** *fem* (*of thieves, troublemakers, bullies*)
2 la **pandilla** *fem* (*of friends*)

gap NOUN
el **hueco** *masc*
   You have to fill in the gaps in the sentences.
   Hay que rellenar los huecos de las frases.

garage NOUN
el **garaje** *masc*

garbage NOUN (US)
la **basura** *fem*

garden NOUN
el **jardín** *masc* (PL los **jardines**)
   We haven't got a garden.
   No tenemos jardín.

gardener NOUN
el **jardinero** *masc*
la **jardinera** *fem*

gardening NOUN
la **jardinería** *fem*

garlic NOUN
el **ajo** *masc*
   I don't like garlic.
   No me gusta el ajo.
   a clove of garlic
   un diente de ajo

gas NOUN
el **gas** *masc*

gas cooker NOUN
la **cocina de gas** *fem*

gate NOUN
1 el **portón** *masc* (PL los **portones**) (*wooden*)
   Please close the gate.
   Por favor, cierre el portón.
2 la **verja** *fem* (*metal*)
   There's a cow by the gate.
   Hay una vaca al lado de la verja.
3 la **puerta** *fem* (*at airport*)
   Please go to gate seven.
   Diríjanse a la puerta siete.

gave VERB ▷ *see* **give**

gay ADJECTIVE
gay
   His big brother is gay.
   Su hermano mayor es gay.

GCSE NOUN
el **Título de Graduado en Educación Secundaria** *masc*

DID YOU KNOW...?
Exams in Spain are different from British ones. There, the qualification

A
B
C
D
E
F
G
H
I
J
K
L
M
N
O
P
Q
R
S
T
U
V
W
X
Y
Z

you can get at sixteen is the **Título de Graduado en Educación Secundaria**.

general knowledge NOUN
la **cultura general** fem
a general knowledge quiz
un concurso de cultura general

generous ADJECTIVE
generoso masc
generosa fem
That's very generous of you.
Eso es muy generoso de tu parte.

genius NOUN
el **genio** masc
She's a genius!
¡Es un genio!

LANGUAGE TIP
Did you notice that you still use the masculine **un genio** even when referring to a woman or girl?

gentleman NOUN
el **caballero** masc

gents NOUN
el **baño de caballeros** masc
Where is the gents, please?
¿Dónde está el baño de caballeros, por favor?

geography NOUN
la **geografía** fem
I like geography.
Me gusta la geografía.

gerbil NOUN
el **gerbo** masc

get VERB
1 **recibir** (receive)
He always gets lots of presents.
Siempre recibe muchos regalos.
What did you get for your birthday?
¿Qué te regalaron para tu cumpleaños?
How much pocket money do you get?
¿Cuánto te dan de paga?

I get five pounds a week.
Me dan cinco libras a la semana.
2 **comprar** (buy)
Can you get me a smoothie?
¿Me puedes comprar un batido?
Mum's getting me a PlayStation.
Mamá me va a comprar una play.
3 **conseguir** (obtain)
We couldn't get any tickets for the match.
No logramos conseguir entradas para el partido.
4 **ir a buscar** (fetch)
I'll get my coat.
Voy a buscar el abrigo.
5 **llegar** (arrive)
How do you get to the castle, please?
¿Cómo se llega al castillo, por favor?
What time do we get there?
¿A qué hora llegamos allí?
6 **to have got** ▷ see got

get away VERB
escaparse
Quick! He's getting away!
¡Rápido! ¡Que se escapa!

get back VERB
volver
What time will you get back?
¿A qué hora volverás?

get in VERB
entrar
Get in, boys!
¡Entrad, chicos!
Get in the car, Olivia.
Entra en el coche, Olivia.

get off VERB
bajarse de
Where do we get off the train?
¿Dónde nos bajamos del tren?

get on VERB
1 **subirse a** (bus, train)
I get on the bus at the station.
Me subo al autobús en la estación.

2 montarse en (*bike*)
I got on my bike.
Me monté en mi bici.

How are you getting on?
¿Cómo te va?

get out VERB
1 salir (*of room, building, car*)
Get out!
¡Salid!
2 sacar (*book, object*)
Get your book out, Darren.
Saca tu libro, Darren.

get up VERB
levantarse
What time do you get up?
¿A qué hora te levantas?
I get up early.
Me levanto temprano.

ghost NOUN
el **fantasma** *masc*

LANGUAGE TIP
Even though it ends in **-a**, **el fantasma** is a masculine noun.

giant NOUN
el **gigante** *masc*
la **giganta** *fem*

gift NOUN
el **regalo** *masc*
Christmas gifts
regalos de Navidad

gift shop NOUN
la **tienda de regalos** *fem*

gigantic ADJECTIVE
gigantesco *masc*
gigantesca *fem*

ginger ADJECTIVE
I've got ginger hair.
Soy pelirrojo.

LANGUAGE TIP
If you're a girl, say **soy pelirroja** instead.

giraffe NOUN
la **jirafa** *fem*

girl NOUN
1 la niña *fem* (*young*)
a five-year-old girl
una niña de cinco años
2 la chica *fem* (*older*)
a sixteen-year-old girl
una chica de dieciséis años

girlfriend NOUN
la **novia** *fem*
She's his girlfriend.
Es su novia.

give VERB
1 dar
Give me the book, please.
Dame el libro, por favor.
Give the books to Lisa.
Dale los libros a Lisa.
2 regalar (*as gift*)
What are you giving Carlos?
¿Qué le vas a regalar a Carlos?
My parents gave me a bike.
Mis padres me regalaron una bici.

give out VERB
repartir
Will you give out the books, please, Mike?
¿Quieres repartir los libros, por favor, Mike?

given VERB ▷ *see* **give**

glad ADJECTIVE
contento *masc*
contenta *fem*

She's glad she's won.
Está contenta de haber ganado.

glass NOUN

1 el **vaso** *masc* (*beaker*)
   I'd like a glass of milk.
   Quiero un vaso de leche.
2 la **copa** *fem* (*with stem*)
   a glass of wine
   una copa de vino
3 el **vidrio** *masc* (*material*)

glasses PL NOUN

las **gafas** *fem pl*
   I wear glasses.
   Llevo gafas.

globe NOUN

el **globo terráqueo** *masc*
   We've got a globe in the classroom.
   Tenemos un globo terráqueo en la clase.

glove NOUN

el **guante** *masc*
   a pair of gloves
   unos guantes

glue NOUN

el **pegamento** *masc*

go

> **go** can be a noun or a verb.

A NOUN
   It's my go.
   Me toca a mí.
   Whose go is it?
   ¿A quién le toca?

B VERB
   to go
   ir
   I don't want to go to school.
   No quiero ir al colegio.
   I don't go to school on Saturdays.
   No voy al colegio los sábados.
   Where are you going?
   ¿Adónde vas?
   I went to London.
   Fui a Londres.

Where did you go yesterday?
¿Dónde fuiste ayer?
He's gone.
Se ha ido.

LANGUAGE TIP
In the same way that we say **I'm going to** and **we're going to** and so on to talk about the future, in Spanish they use **voy a** and **vamos a** and so on.

I'm going to win.
Voy a ganar.
We're going to visit our cousins on Friday.
Vamos a visitar a nuestros primos el viernes.
I'm not going to play.
No voy a jugar.

go away VERB

irse
   Go away!
   ¡Vete!

go back VERB

1 **retroceder** (*in game*)
   Go back three spaces.
   Retrocede tres casillas.
2 **volver** (*return*)
   Go back to your seats, boys!
   ¡Volved a vuestro sitio, chicos!
   Let's go back to the beginning.
   Volvamos al principio.

go down VERB

bajar
   Let's go down to the cellar.
   Vamos a bajar al sótano.

go forward VERB

avanzar
   Go forward three spaces, James.
   Avanza tres casillas, James.

go in VERB

entrar
   Let's go in.
   Vamos a entrar.

go on VERB
  1 **seguir** (*continue*)
    Shall I go on?
    ¿Sigo?
    Go on, don't stop.
    Sigue, no pares.
  2 **pasar** (*happen*)
    What's going on?
    ¿Qué está pasando?

go out VERB
  salir
    Are you going out tonight?
    ¿Vas a salir esta noche?
    Alex is going out with Riley.
    Alex está saliendo con Riley.

go past VERB
  pasar por
    We're going past the cathedral.
    Estamos pasando por la catedral.
    Go past the station and turn right.
    Pasa la estación y gira a la derecha.

go up VERB
  subir
    I'm going up to my room.
    Voy a subir a mi habitación.

goal NOUN
  el **gol** *masc*
    It's a goal!
    ¡Es un gol!
    He's scored a goal!
    ¡Ha marcado un gol!

goalkeeper NOUN
  el **portero** *masc*
  la **portera** *fem*
    He's the goalkeeper.
    Es el portero.

goat NOUN
  la **cabra** *fem*

God NOUN
  Dios *masc*

godfather NOUN
  el **padrino** *masc*
    my godfather
    mi padrino

godmother NOUN
  la **madrina** *fem*
    my godmother
    mi madrina

goggles PL NOUN
  las **gafas de natación** *fem pl* (*for swimming*)
    I've got new goggles.
    Tengo unas gafas de natación nuevas.

gold

> **gold** can be a noun or an adjective.

A NOUN
  el **oro** *masc*
B ADJECTIVE
  de oro
    a gold necklace
    un collar de oro

goldfish NOUN
  el **pez de colores** *masc*
    (PL los **peces de colores**)
    I've got five goldfish.
    Tengo cinco peces de colores.

golf NOUN
  el **golf** *masc*
    My dad plays golf.
    Mi padre juega al golf.

LANGUAGE TIP
In Spanish, you need to include **al** or **a la** before the names of sports or games when talking about playing them.

---

golf club NOUN
  1 el **palo de golf**
    masc (*stick*)
  2 el **club de golf**
    masc (*place*)

a
b
c
d
e
f
g
h
i
j
k
l
m
n
o
p
q
r
s
t
u
v
w
x
y
z

A
B
C
D
E
F
G
H
I
J
K
L
M
N
O
P
Q
R
S
T
U
V
W
X
Y
Z

golf course NOUN
el **campo de golf** *masc*

gone VERB ▷ *see* go

good ADJECTIVE
bueno *masc*
buena *fem*
That's a good idea.
Esa es una buena idea.
It's a very good film.
Es una película muy buena.

LANGUAGE TIP
Shorten **bueno** to **buen** before a
masculine singular noun.

We've got a good teacher.
Tenemos un buen profesor.
Pablo's very good at English.
Pablo es muy bueno en inglés.
Be good, Andrew!
¡Pórtate bien, Andrew!

It's good.
Es bueno.
Good morning!
¡Buenos días!
Good morning, everyone!
¡Buenos días a todos!
Good afternoon!
¡Buenas tardes!
Good evening!
¡Buenas tardes!/
¡Buenas noches!
Good night!
¡Buenas noches!
Good luck!
¡Buena suerte!

LANGUAGE TIP
If you want to wish someone a
good evening in the early evening,
use **¡buenas tardes!** instead of
¡buenas noches!

goodbye EXCLAMATION
¡adiós!

Good Friday NOUN
el **Viernes Santo** *masc*

good-looking ADJECTIVE
guapo *masc*
guapa *fem*
Wayne is very good-looking.
Wayne es muy guapo.

goose NOUN
el **ganso** *masc*

gorgeous ADJECTIVE
1 **guapísimo** *masc*
guapísima *fem* (person)
Isn't she gorgeous!
¿Verdad que es guapísima?
2 **excelente** *masc/fem* (weather)
The weather's gorgeous.
El tiempo es excelente.

got VERB
1 **to have got**
tener
I've got a dog and two cats.
Tengo un perro y dos gatos.
I haven't got a mobile phone.
No tengo móvil.
Elena has got fair hair.
Elena tiene el pelo rubio.
How many have you got?
¿Cuántos tienes?

I've got a cat.
Tengo un gato.
I haven't got a dog.
No tengo perro.
Have you got a sister?
¿Tienes una hermana?
She's got long hair.
Tiene el pelo largo.

2 **to have got to**
tener que
I've got to go to the dentist.
Tengo que ir al dentista.
You've got to take a card, Christine.
Tienes que coger una carta, Christine.

You've got to be careful, children.
Tenéis que tener cuidado, niños.

3 ▷ see **get**

government NOUN
el **gobierno** masc

grade NOUN
la **nota** fem
very good grades
muy buenas notas

gradually ADVERB
poco a poco

graffiti NOUN
las **pintadas** fem pl
There's a lot of graffiti.
Hay muchas pintadas.

gram NOUN
el **gramo** masc
two hundred grams of cheese
doscientos gramos de queso

grammar NOUN
la **gramática** fem

grandchild NOUN
el **nieto** masc
la **nieta** fem
her grandchildren
sus nietos

granddad NOUN
el **abuelo** masc
my granddad
mi abuelo

granddaughter NOUN
la **nieta** fem
He has two granddaughters.
Tiene dos nietas.

grandfather NOUN
el **abuelo** masc
my grandfather
mi abuelo

grandma NOUN
la **abuela** fem
her grandma
su abuela

grandmother NOUN
la **abuela** fem
his grandmother
su abuela

grandpa NOUN
el **abuelo** masc
my grandpa
mi abuelo

grandparents PL NOUN
los **abuelos** masc pl
my grandparents
mis abuelos

grandson NOUN
el **nieto** masc
her grandsons
sus nietos

granny NOUN
la **abuela** fem
my granny
mi abuela

grapefruit NOUN
el **pomelo** masc
I don't like grapefruit.
No me gusta el pomelo.

grapes PL NOUN
las **uvas** fem pl
a kilo of grapes
un kilo de uvas

Spanish

English

a
b
c
d
e
f
g
h
i
j
k
l
m
n
o
p
q
r
s
t
u
v
w
x
y
z

419

grass NOUN
1 la **hierba** *fem* (*plant*)
2 el **césped** *masc* (*lawn*)
   The children are playing on the grass.
   Los niños están jugando en el césped.

grated ADJECTIVE
rallado *masc*
rallada *fem*
   grated cheese
   queso rallado

grateful ADJECTIVE
agradecido *masc*
agradecida *fem*
   We're very grateful.
   Le estamos muy agradecidos.

gravy NOUN
   I'd like some gravy.
   Quiero un poco de jugo de carne.

great ADJECTIVE
estupendo *masc*
estupenda *fem*
   We're going to New York. — Great!
   Vamos a ir a Nueva York.
   — ¡Estupendo!

   That's great!
   ¡Eso es estupendo!

Great Britain NOUN
Gran Bretaña *fem*
   We live in Great Britain.
   Vivimos en Gran Bretaña.

greedy ADJECTIVE
glotón *masc* (PL **glotones**)
glotona *fem*
   Don't be so greedy, Kira.
   No seas tan glotona, Kira.

green

> **green** can be an adjective or a noun.

A ADJECTIVE
verde *masc/fem*
It's green.
Es verde.

I've got green eyes.
Tengo los ojos verdes.

LANGUAGE TIP
Colour adjectives come after the noun in Spanish.

B NOUN
el **verde** *masc*
Green is my favourite colour.
El verde es mi color favorito.

green beans PL NOUN
las **judías verdes** *fem pl*

greengrocer's NOUN
la **verdulería** *fem*
   at the greengrocer's
   en la verdulería

greenhouse NOUN
el **invernadero** *masc*

grew VERB ▷ *see* **grow**

grey

> **grey** can be an adjective or a noun.

A ADJECTIVE
gris *masc/fem*
It's grey.
Es gris.
a grey skirt
una falda gris
She's got grey hair.
Tiene el pelo gris.

LANGUAGE TIP
Colour adjectives come after the noun in Spanish.

B NOUN
el **gris** *masc*
He's dressed in grey.
Va vestido de gris.

grin VERB
sonreír
Why are you grinning like that?
¿Por qué estás sonriendo de esa manera?

grocer's NOUN
la **tienda de comestibles** *fem*
I'm going to the grocer's.
Voy a la tienda de comestibles.

groom NOUN
el **novio** *masc*

ground NOUN
1 el **suelo** *masc*
We sat on the ground.
Nos sentamos en el suelo.
2 la **tierra** *fem* (earth)
The ground is wet.
La tierra está mojada.
3 el **campo** *masc* (sports ground)
Where's the football ground?
¿Dónde está el campo de fútbol?

on the ground
en el suelo

ground floor NOUN
la **planta baja** *fem*
This is the ground floor.
Esta es la planta baja.
The toilets are on the ground floor.
Los baños están en la planta baja.

on the ground floor
en la planta baja

group NOUN
el **grupo** *masc*
Get into groups of four.
Formad grupos de cuatro.

grow VERB
1 **crecer** (get bigger)
Grass grows fast.
La hierba crece rápido.
2 **cultivar** (gardener)
I'm growing a sunflower.
Estoy cultivando un girasol.

grow up VERB
What do you want to be when you grow up, Maria?
¿Qué quieres ser cuando seas mayor, Maria?

growl VERB
gruñir
My dog growls a lot.
Mi perro gruñe mucho.

grown VERB ▷ see **grow**

grown-up NOUN
el **adulto** *masc*
la **adulta** *fem*
the grown-ups
los adultos

guarantee NOUN
la **garantía** *fem*

guard dog NOUN
el **perro guardián** *masc* (PL los **perros guardianes**)

guess VERB
adivinar
Guess what this is!
¡Adivina lo que es esto!

guest NOUN
el **invitado** *masc*
la **invitada** *fem*
our Spanish guests
nuestros invitados españoles

guide NOUN
1 el/la **guía** *masc/fem* (tourist guide)
He works as a guide at the castle.
Trabaja de guía en el castillo.
2 la **exploradora** *fem* (girl guide)

guidebook NOUN
la **guía** *fem*

guide dog NOUN
el **perro guía** *masc*

guilty ADJECTIVE
culpable *masc/fem*
Innocent or guilty?
¿Inocente o culpable?
I feel guilty.
Me siento culpable.

Spanish

English

a b c d e f g h i j k l m n o p q r s t u v w x y z

421

guinea pig NOUN
el **conejillo de Indias** *masc*
I've got a guinea pig.
Tengo un conejillo de Indias.

guitar NOUN
la **guitarra** *fem*
I play the guitar.
Toco la guitarra.

gun NOUN
la **pistola** *fem*

guy NOUN
you guys
vosotros
What do you guys think?
¿Vosotros qué pensáis?

Hurry up, you guys!
¡Vamos chicos, daos prisa!

gym NOUN
1 la **gimnasia** *fem* (*school subject*)
We've got gym today.
Hoy tenemos gimnasia.
2 el **gimnasio** *masc* (*place*)
My mum goes to the gym.
Mi madre va al gimnasio.

gymnastics NOUN
la **gimnasia** *fem*
I like gymnastics.
Me gusta la gimnasia.
I do gymnastics.
Hago gimnasia.

Hh

had VERB ▷ *see* **have**

hadn't (= had not) ▷ *see* **have**

hail

> **hail** can be a noun or a verb.

A NOUN
el **granizo** *masc*

B VERB
to hail
granizar
It's hailing.
Está granizando.

hair NOUN
el **pelo** *masc*
He's got black hair.
Tiene el pelo negro.
My cat has long hair.
Mi gato tiene el pelo largo.
You've had your hair cut!
¡Te has cortado el pelo!
I want to wash my hair.
Quiero lavarme la cabeza.

LANGUAGE TIP
In Spanish you usually use an article
like **el**, **la** or **los**, **las** with parts of the
body.

---

hairbrush NOUN
el **cepillo** *masc*

haircut NOUN
el **corte de pelo** *masc*
That's a nice haircut!
¡Qué corte de pelo tan bonito!
to have a haircut
cortarse el pelo
I need to have a haircut.
Tengo que cortarme el pelo.

hairdresser NOUN
el **peluquero** *masc*
la **peluquera** *fem*
He's a hairdresser.
Es peluquero.

LANGUAGE TIP
In Spanish, you do not use an article
with people's jobs.

---

the hairdresser's
la peluquería
at the hairdresser's
en la peluquería

hairstyle NOUN
el **peinado**
masc
You've got
a new
hairstyle.
Llevas un
nuevo
peinado.

half

> **half** can be a noun, adjective or
> adverb.

A NOUN
1 la **mitad** *fem* (*fraction*)
half of the class
la mitad de la clase
to cut something in half
cortar algo por la mitad

two and a half
dos y medio
half an hour
media hora
half past ten
las diez y media
half a kilo
medio kilo

2 el **billete para niños**
masc (*ticket*)
A half to the town centre, please.
Un billete para niños para el centro,
por favor.

B ADJECTIVE
medio *masc*
media *fem*
a half portion
media ración

C ADVERB
medio
I'm half Scottish.
Soy medio escocés.

LANGUAGE TIP
When you use **medio** before an
adjective its ending never changes.

---

half-brother NOUN
el **hermanastro** *masc*
my half-brother
mi hermanastro

half-sister NOUN
la **hermanastra** *fem*
my half-sister
mi hermanastra

half-term NOUN
las **vacaciones de mitad de
trimestre** *fem*

DID YOU KNOW...?
Spanish students don't have half-term
as such. However in winter some
schools have **la semana blanca**, or
'white week' – the perfect opportunity
for many to take off for the ski slopes.

---

half-time NOUN
el **descanso** *masc*

hall NOUN
1 el **salón de actos** *masc* (*assembly
hall*)
2 la **entrada** *fem* (*entrance hall*)

Hallowe'en NOUN
la **víspera de Todos los Santos** *fem*

DID YOU KNOW...?
Hallowe'en is not celebrated in Spain,
but All Saints' Day (1st November) is a
public holiday and the day when
people often visit family graves. In

Latin America 1st/2nd November often
means colourful and fun fiestas with
skulls, skeletons and symbols of death
everywhere in honour of **el Día de los
Muertos** (**The Day of the Dead** or
All Souls' Day).

ham NOUN
el **jamón** *masc* (PL los **jamones**)
a ham sandwich
un sándwich de jamón de York

DID YOU KNOW...?
In Spain you'll come across two main
types of ham: **jamón serrano**, which
is the more expensive cured ham, and
the softer **jamón de York**, also known
as **jamón dulce**, which is boiled and
similar to British ham.

---

hamburger NOUN
la **hamburguesa** *fem*
I'd like a hamburger.
Quiero una hamburguesa.

hammer NOUN
el **martillo** *masc*

hamster NOUN
el **hámster** *masc*
(PL los **hámsters**)

hand NOUN
1 la **mano** *fem* (*of person*)

LANGUAGE TIP
Even though it ends in **-o**, **la mano** is
a feminine noun.

**Put up your hand if you know the
answer.**
Levantad la mano si sabéis la
respuesta.

LANGUAGE TIP
In Spanish you usually use an article
like **el**, **la** or **los**, **las** with parts of the
body.

Can you give me a hand?
¿Me puedes echar una mano?
2 la **aguja** *fem* (*of clock*)

hand in VERB
entregar
> **Hand in your books.**
> Entregad vuestros libros.

hand out VERB
repartir
> **Hand out the books, Ahmed.**
> Reparte los libros, Ahmed.

handbag NOUN
el **bolso** *masc*

handball NOUN
el **balonmano** *masc*
> **Can we play handball?**
> ¿Podemos jugar al balonmano?

LANGUAGE TIP
In Spanish, you need to include **al** or **a la** before the names of sports or games when talking about playing them.

---

handkerchief NOUN
el **pañuelo** *masc*
> **Have you got a handkerchief?**
> ¿Tienes un pañuelo?

handle NOUN
1 el **asa** *fem* (*of cup, briefcase*)

LANGUAGE TIP
Even though it's a feminine noun, remember that you use **el** and **un** with **asa**.

> **the handles**
> las asas
2 el **picaporte** *masc* (*of door*)

handsome ADJECTIVE
guapo *masc*
guapa *fem*
> **Paul is very handsome.**
> Paul es muy guapo.

handwriting NOUN
la **letra** *fem*
> **He has nice handwriting.**
> Tiene una letra bonita.

hang VERB
colgar

hang on VERB
esperar
> **Hang on a minute, please.**
> Espera un minuto, por favor.

hangman NOUN
el **ahorcado** *masc* (*game*)
> **to play hangman**
> jugar al ahorcado

LANGUAGE TIP
In Spanish, you need to include **al** or **a la** before the names of sports or games when talking about playing them.

---

happen VERB
pasar
> **What's happening?**
> ¿Qué está pasando?

happy ADJECTIVE
contento *masc*
contenta *fem*

> **Eve is happy.**
> Eve está contenta.
> **The children are happy.**
> Los niños están contentos.

> **Happy birthday!**
> ¡Feliz cumpleaños!
> **Happy Mother's Day!**
> ¡Feliz día de la Madre!
> **Happy Christmas!**
> ¡Feliz Navidad!
> **Happy New Year!**
> ¡Feliz Año Nuevo!

a
b
c
d
e
f
g
h
i
j
k
l
m
n
o
p
q
r
s
t
u
v
w
x
y
z

A
B
C
D
E
F
G
H
I
J
K
L
M
N
O
P
Q
R
S
T
U
V
W
X
Y
Z

426

LANGUAGE TIP
Have you noticed the upside-down exclamation mark at the start of Spanish exclamations?

harbour NOUN
el **puerto** masc

hard

> **hard** can be an adjective or an adverb.

A ADJECTIVE
1 **difícil** masc/fem (difficult)
This question's too hard for me.
Esta pregunta es demasiado difícil para mí.
2 **duro** masc
dura fem (not soft)
This chair is very hard.
Esta silla es muy dura.
B ADVERB
mucho
Shilpa works hard.
Shilpa trabaja mucho.

hard drive NOUN
el **disco duro** masc

hardly ADVERB
casi
hardly ever
casi nunca
hardly anything
casi nada

has VERB ▷ see **have**

hashtag NOUN
la **etiqueta** fem (on Twitter)

hasn't (= has not) ▷ see **have**

hat NOUN
1 el **sombrero** masc
2 el **gorro** masc (knitted)
a woolly hat
un gorro de lana

hate VERB
odiar
I hate maths.
Odio las matemáticas.

---

have VERB
1 **tener**
I have a bike.
Tengo una bici.
He has blue eyes.
Tiene los ojos azules.

LANGUAGE TIP
You also use **tener** to translate **have got**.

I've got a bike.
Tengo una bici.
He has got blue eyes.
Tiene los ojos azules.
I haven't got any pets.
No tengo mascota.
Have you got a sister? — Yes, I have.
¿Tienes una hermana? — Sí.
Have you got any sweets? — No, I haven't.
¿Tienes caramelos? — No.

I've got …
Tengo …
I haven't got …
No tengo …
Have you got …?
¿Tienes …?
Yes, I have.
Sí.
No, I haven't.
No.

LANGUAGE TIP
Just use **sí** and **no** to translate **yes, I have** and **no, I haven't**.

2 **haber** (used to form tenses)
I have done the shopping.
He hecho las compras.
He hasn't seen it.
No lo ha visto.
They've arrived.
Han llegado.
Have you done your homework? — Yes, I have.
¿Has hecho los deberes? — Sí.

LANGUAGE TIP
Just use **sí** and **no** to translate **yes, I have** and **no, I haven't**.

3 tomar (eat, drink)
What are you going to have?
¿Qué vas a tomar?
I'll have a white coffee.
Voy a tomar un café con leche.
What time do you have breakfast?
¿A qué hora desayunas?

4 to have a shower
ducharse
I have a shower every day.
Me ducho todos los días.
to have a bath
bañarse
I'll have a bath.
Me voy a bañar.

5 to have to
tener que
You have to be careful.
Tienes que tener cuidado.
She has to do her homework.
Tiene que hacer los deberes.
Do I have to?
¿Tengo que hacerlo?

You have to ...
Tienes que ...
You have got to ...
Tienes que ...

haven't (= have not) ▷ see **have**

hay fever NOUN
la **alergia al polen**
fem

hazelnut NOUN
la **avellana** *fem*

he PRONOUN
él
He's got a tablet but I haven't.
Él tiene una tablet pero yo no.

LANGUAGE TIP
he isn't usually translated unless it's emphatic.

He works in a bank.
Trabaja en un banco.

head NOUN
1 la **cabeza** *fem* (of person)
Mind your head!
¡Cuidado con la cabeza!

LANGUAGE TIP
In Spanish you usually use an article like **el**, **la** or **los**, **las** with parts of the body.

Heads or tails? — Heads.
¿Cara o cruz? — Cara.
2 el **director** *masc*
la **directora** *fem* (head teacher)

headache NOUN
I've got a headache.
Me duele la cabeza.

headmaster NOUN
el **director** *masc*

headmistress NOUN
la **directora** *fem*

head teacher NOUN
el **director** *masc*
la **directora** *fem*

health NOUN
la **salud** *fem*

healthy ADJECTIVE
sano *masc*
sana *fem*
a healthy diet
una dieta sana

hear VERB
oír
I can't hear.
No oigo.
I can't hear you.
No te oigo.
Can you hear the difference?
¿Notas la diferencia al oírlo?

heart NOUN
el **corazón** *masc* (PL los **corazones**)
the ace of hearts
el as de corazones

a
b
c
d
e
f
g
h
i
j
k
l
m
n
o
p
q
r
s
t
u
v
w
x
y
z

Spanish

English

A
B
C
D
E
F
G
H
I
J
K
L
M
N
O
P
Q
R
S
T
U
V
W
X
Y
Z

heat NOUN
el **calor** masc

heater NOUN
la **estufa** fem
an electric heater
una estufa eléctrica

heavy
ADJECTIVE
pesado
masc
pesada
fem

This bag's very heavy.
Esta bolsa es muy pesada.

he'd
(= **he had**) ▷ see **have**
(= **he would**) ▷ see **would**

hedgehog NOUN
el **erizo** masc

heel NOUN
1 el **tacón** masc (PL los **tacones**)
(of shoe)
high heels
tacones altos
2 el **talón** masc (PL los **talones**)
(of foot, sock)

height NOUN
1 la **estatura** fem (of person)
2 la **altura** fem (of object, person)

held VERB ▷ see **hold**

helicopter NOUN
el **helicóptero** masc

he'll (= **he will**) ▷ see **will**

hello EXCLAMATION
¡hola!

DID YOU KNOW...?
If you ring a Spanish person up, they'll probably answer the phone with **¿diga?** or **¿dígame?** They won't say **¡hola!**

helmet NOUN
el **casco** masc

help

help can be a verb or a noun.

A VERB
to help
ayudar
Can you help me?
¿Me puedes ayudar?
Help yourself!
¡Sírvete!

Help!
¡Socorro!

B NOUN
la **ayuda** fem
Do you need any help?
¿Necesitas ayuda?

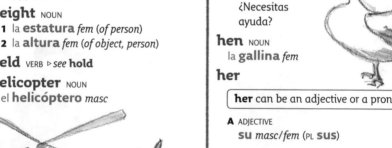

hen NOUN
la **gallina** fem

her

her can be an adjective or a pronoun.

A ADJECTIVE
su masc/fem (PL **sus**)

LANGUAGE TIP
Remember to use **su** before a singular noun and **sus** before a plural one.

her name
su nombre
her house
su casa

428

her cats
sus gatos
her aunts
sus tías

LANGUAGE TIP
You usually translate **her** using **el**, **la**, etc before parts of the body or clothes, particularly when using a reflexive verb.

She took off her coat.
Se quitó el abrigo.

B PRONOUN

1 **la** (direct object)
I love her.
La quiero.
Do you know her?
¿La conoces?
Look at her!
¡Mírala!

2 **le** (indirect object)

LANGUAGE TIP
Use **le** when **her** means **to her**.

I gave her a book.
Le di un libro.
What did you say to her?
¿Qué le dijiste?

LANGUAGE TIP
Change **le** to **se** when combining it with a direct object pronoun like **lo**.

I'll tell her.
Se lo diré.
We've already handed it over to her.
Ya se lo hemos entregado.

LANGUAGE TIP
Because **se** can mean **to him**, **to them** and **to you** as well as **to her**, you can add **a ella** (to her) after the verb for clarity.

I'm going to give it to her.
Voy a dárselo a ella.

3 **ella** (after prepositions)
It's for her.
Es para ella.

He's next to her.
Está al lado de ella.

LANGUAGE TIP
Use **ella** in comparisons.

I'm older than her.
Soy mayor que ella.

LANGUAGE TIP
Use **ella** after the verb **ser**.

It must be her.
Debe de ser ella.
It's her.
Es ella.

here ADVERB
aquí
I live here.
Yo vivo aquí.
Here he is!
¡Aquí está!
Here's Molly.
Aquí está Molly.
Here are the books.
Aquí tienes los libros.

hers PRONOUN
el **suyo** masc
la **suya** fem

LANGUAGE TIP
Remember that the choice of **el suyo**, **la suya**, **los suyos** or **las suyas** depends entirely on the thing or things referred to.

That's not Miranda's coat. Hers is here.
Aquél no es el abrigo de Miranda. El suyo está aquí.
Those aren't Marian's boots. Hers are here.
Aquéllas no son las botas de Marian. Las suyas están aquí.

LANGUAGE TIP
After **ser** you can usually just use **suyo**, **suya**, **suyos** or **suyas** to agree with the noun referred to.

Spanish

English

A
B
C
D
E
F
G
H
I
J
K
L
M
N
O
P
Q
R
S
T
U
V
W
X
Y
Z

Is this hers?
¿Es suyo esto?
These boots are hers.
Estas botas son suyas.
Whose is this? — It's hers.
¿De quién es esto? — Es suyo.

LANGUAGE TIP
Because **suyo** can also mean **his**, **theirs** and **yours**, you can avoid confusion by using **de ella** instead.

Whose is this? — It's hers.
¿De quién es esto? — Es de ella.

---

a friend of hers
un amigo suyo

herself PRONOUN
1 **se** (reflexive use)
   She's hurt herself.
   Se ha hecho daño.
   My cat washes herself a lot.
   Mi gata se lava mucho.
2 **sí misma** (after preposition)
   She talked about herself.
   Habló de sí misma.
3 **ella misma** (for emphasis)
   She did it herself.
   Lo hizo ella misma.
   She lives by herself.
   Ella vive sola.

by herself
sola

he's
(= **he is**) ▷ see **be**
(= **he has**) ▷ see **have**

hi EXCLAMATION
¡hola!

hiccups NOUN
el **hipo** masc
   I've got hiccups.
   Tengo hipo.

hide VERB
1 **esconder**
   Mum hides the biscuits.
   Mamá esconde las galletas.

2 **esconderse** (hide oneself)
   Hide!
   ¡Escóndete!
   Rhys is hiding under the bed.
   Rhys está escondido debajo de la cama.

hide-and-seek
NOUN
el **escondite** masc
   Let's play hide-and-seek!
   ¡Vamos a jugar al escondite!

LANGUAGE TIP
In Spanish, you need to include **al** or **a la** before the names of sports or games when talking about playing them.

high ADJECTIVE
alto masc
alta fem
   It's too high.
   Es demasiado alto.
   How high is Mount Everest?
   ¿Cuál es la altura del Everest?
   The wall is two metres high.
   El muro tiene dos metros de altura.

high jump NOUN
el **salto de altura** masc

high-rise NOUN
la **torre de pisos** fem
   I live in a high-rise.
   Vivo en una torre de pisos.

high school NOUN
el **instituto** masc

high street NOUN
la **calle principal** fem

hiking NOUN
  el **senderismo** *masc*
    We're going to go hiking.
    Vamos a ir a hacer senderismo.

hill NOUN
  la **colina** *fem*

him PRONOUN
 1 lo (*direct object*)
    I love him.
    Lo quiero.
    Do you know him?
    ¿Lo conoces?
    Look at him!
    Míralo.

  LANGUAGE TIP
  In some parts of Spain you'll hear people using **le** instead of **lo**.

 2 le (*indirect object*)

  LANGUAGE TIP
  Use **le** when **him** means **to him**.

    I gave him a book.
    Le di un libro.
    What did you say to him?
    ¿Qué le dijiste?

  LANGUAGE TIP
  Change **le** to **se** when combining it with a direct object pronoun like **lo**.

    I'll tell him.
    Se lo diré.
    We've already handed it over to him.
    Ya se lo hemos entregado.

  LANGUAGE TIP
  Because **se** can mean **to her**, **to them** and **to you** as well as **to him**, you can add **a él** (to him) after the verb for clarity.

    I'm going to give it to him.
    Voy a dárselo a él.

 3 él

  LANGUAGE TIP
  Use **él** after a preposition.

    It's for him.
    Es para él.
    She's next to him.
    Ella está al lado de él.

  LANGUAGE TIP
  Use **él** in comparisons.

    I'm older than him.
    Soy mayor que él.

  LANGUAGE TIP
  Use **él** after the verb **ser**.

    It must be him.
    Debe de ser él.
    It's him.
    Es él.

himself PRONOUN
 1 se (*reflexive use*)
    He's hurt himself.
    Se ha hecho daño.
    The cat is washing himself.
    El gato está lavándose.
 2 sí mismo (*after preposition*)
    He talked about himself.
    Habló de sí mismo.
 3 él mismo (*for emphasis*)
    He did it himself.
    Lo hizo él mismo.
    He lives by himself.
    Vive solo.

  by himself
  solo

hip NOUN
  la **cadera** *fem*

hippo NOUN
  el **hipopótamo** *masc*

hire VERB
  alquilar
    You can hire bikes.
    Se pueden alquilar bicis.

A
B
C
D
E
F
G
H
I
J
K
L
M
N
O
P
Q
R
S
T
U
V
W
X
Y
Z

his

> **his** can be an adjective or a pronoun.

A ADJECTIVE
su *masc/fem* (PL **sus**)

LANGUAGE TIP
Remember to use **su** with singular nouns and **sus** with plural ones.

---

his name
su nombre
his house
su casa
his cats
sus gatos
his aunts
sus tías

LANGUAGE TIP
You usually translate **his** using **el**, **la**, etc before parts of the body or clothes, particularly when using a reflexive verb.

He took off his coat.
Se quitó el abrigo.

B PRONOUN
el **suyo** *masc*
la **suya** *fem*

LANGUAGE TIP
Remember that the choice of **el suyo**, **la suya**, **los suyos** or **las suyas** depends entirely on the thing or things referred to.

That's not Mike's coat. His is here.
Aquél no es el abrigo de Mike. El suyo está aquí.
Those aren't Martin's boots. His are here.
Aquéllas no son las botas de Martin. Las suyas están aquí.

LANGUAGE TIP
After **ser** you can usually just use **suyo**, **suya**, **suyos** or **suyas** to agree with the noun referred to.

Is this his?
¿Esto es suyo?
These boots are his.
Estas botas son suyas.
Whose is this? — It's his.
¿De quién es esto? — Es suyo.

LANGUAGE TIP
Because **suyo** can also mean **hers**, **theirs** and **yours**, you can avoid confusion by using **de él** instead.

Whose is this? — It's his.
¿De quién es esto? — Es de él.

a friend of his
un amigo suyo

history NOUN
la **historia** *fem*
History is my favourite subject.
La historia es mi asignatura favorita.

hit

> **hit** can be a verb or a noun.

A VERB
to hit
pegar
Don't hit me!
¡No me pegues!
He's hitting his brother.
Le está pegando a su hermano.

LANGUAGE TIP
Don't forget the personal **a** in examples like this one.

B NOUN
1 el **éxito** *masc* (*success*)
Sam Smith's latest hit
el último éxito de Sam Smith
2 el **acierto** *masc* (*on internet*)
I got a lot of hits.
Tuve muchos aciertos.

hobby NOUN
la **afición** *fem* (PL las **aficiones**)
What are your hobbies?
¿Cuáles son tus aficiones?

hockey NOUN
el **hockey** masc
> **I play hockey.**
> Juego al hockey.

LANGUAGE TIP
In Spanish, you need to include **al** or **a la** before the names of sports or games when talking about playing them.

---

hold VERB
1 **sostener** (hold on to)
> **Can you hold the baby?**
> ¿Puedes sostener al niño?
2 **sujetar** (keep in position)
> **Can you hold the ladder?**
> ¿Puedes sujetar la escalera?
3 **llevar en la mano** (carry)
> **He's holding a spoon.**
> Lleva una cuchara en la mano.
> **Hold hands!**
> ¡Cogeos de la mano!

hold on VERB
esperar
> **Hold on a minute!**
> ¡Espera un momento!

hold up VERB
> **Hold up your hands.**
> Levantad las manos.

LANGUAGE TIP
In Spanish you usually use an article like **el**, **la** or **los**, **las** with parts of the body.

---

hole NOUN
el **agujero** masc

holiday NOUN
1 las **vacaciones** fem pl
> **our holiday in France**
> nuestras vacaciones en Francia
> **When are you going on holiday?**
> ¿Cuándo te vas de vacaciones?
> **We are on holiday.**
> Estamos de vacaciones.
> **in the school holidays**
> durante las vacaciones escolares

> **on holiday**
> de vacaciones
> **the school holidays**
> las vacaciones escolares

2 la **fiesta** fem (public holiday)
> **Monday is a holiday.**
> El lunes es fiesta.

holly NOUN
el **acebo** masc

home NOUN
la **casa** fem
> **Is Chris at home?**
> ¿Está Chris en casa?
> **What time do you get home?**
> ¿A qué hora llegas a casa?
> **I get home at five o'clock.**
> Llego a casa a las cinco.
> **to go home**
> irse a casa
> **I've got to go home.**
> Tengo que irme a casa.

> **at home**
> en casa
> **Let's go home.**
> Vámonos a casa.

homesick ADJECTIVE
> **I'm homesick.**
> Echo de menos mi casa.

homework NOUN
los **deberes** masc pl
> **We have too much homework.**
> Tenemos demasiados deberes.
> **my geography homework**
> mis deberes de geografía

honey NOUN
la **miel** fem

honeymoon NOUN
la **luna de miel** fem

hood NOUN
la **capucha** fem

A
B
C
D
E
F
G
H
I
J
K
L
M
N
O
P
Q
R
S
T
U
V
W
X
Y
Z

hook NOUN
el **gancho** masc

hooray EXCLAMATION
¡**hurra!**

hop VERB
saltar a la pata coja
> **Hop!**
> ¡Salta a la pata coja!
> **children hopping on one leg**
> niños saltando a la pata coja

hope VERB
esperar
> **I'm hoping to go to Spain.**
> Espero ir a España.
> **I hope that's okay.**
> Espero que eso esté bien.

> **I hope so.**
> Espero que sí.
> **I hope not.**
> Espero que no.

hopeless ADJECTIVE
> **I'm hopeless at maths.**
> Soy un negado para las matemáticas.
> **She's hopeless at biology.**
> Es una negada para la biología.
> **You're hopeless, Louise!**
> ¡No tienes remedio, Louise!

horrible ADJECTIVE
horrible masc/fem

horror film NOUN
la **película de terror** fem

horse NOUN
el **caballo** masc
> **I can ride a horse.**
> Sé montar a caballo.

hospital NOUN
el **hospital** masc
> **My grandmother is in hospital.**
> Mi abuela está en el hospital.

hot ADJECTIVE
1 caliente masc/fem
> **a hot bath**
> un baño caliente

> **I'm too hot.**
> Tengo mucho calor.
> **It's very hot today.**
> Hace mucho calor hoy.
> **The weather is hotter in Spain.**
> En España hace más calor.

> **I'm hot.**
> Tengo calor.

> **It's hot.**
> Hace calor.

2 picante (spicy)
> **a very hot curry**
> un curry muy picante

hot chocolate NOUN
el **chocolate caliente** masc

hot dog NOUN
el **perrito caliente** masc

hotel NOUN
el **hotel** masc
> **We're staying at a hotel near the beach.**
> Nos alojamos en un hotel cerca de la playa.

hour NOUN
la **hora** fem
> **an hour and ten minutes**
> una hora y diez minutos
> **an hour and a half**
> una hora y media

> **a quarter of an hour**
> un cuarto de hora
> **half an hour**
> media hora
> **two and a half hours**
> dos horas y media

house NOUN
la **casa** fem (building)
You've got a nice house.
Tienes una casa bonita.
Do you want to play at my house?
¿Quieres jugar en mi casa?

at my house
en mi casa

how ADVERB
cómo
How do you say 'apple' in Spanish?
¿Cómo se dice "apple" en español?
How do you spell your name?
¿Cómo se escribe tu nombre?
How many...?
¿Cuántos...?
How many pupils are there in the class?
¿Cuántos alumnos hay en la clase?
How many apples are there?
¿Cuántas manzanas hay?
How much...?
¿Cuánto...?
How much sugar would you like?
¿Cuánto azúcar quieres?
How much is it?
¿Cuánto es?
How old is your brother?
¿Cuántos años tiene tu hermano?

How are you?
¿Cómo estás?
How old are you?
¿Cuántos años tienes?
How many?
¿Cuántos?
How much?
¿Cuánto?

LANGUAGE TIP
Don't forget the accent on question words like **cómo** and **cuántos** nor the upside-down question mark at the start of questions.

hug

hug can be a noun or a verb.

A NOUN
el **abrazo** masc
a big hug
un fuerte abrazo
Give me a hug.
Dame un abrazo.

DID YOU KNOW...?
Spanish speakers sometimes end letters, postcards and emails to friends with **un abrazo** (a hug) or **un fuerte abrazo** (a big hug).

B VERB
to hug
abrazar

huge ADJECTIVE
enorme masc/fem

human ADJECTIVE
humano masc
humana fem
a human being
un ser humano

hundred NOUN
a hundred
cien

LANGUAGE TIP
When translating **a hundred** or **one hundred** use **cien** before words for things and people.

a hundred euros
cien euros
a hundred students
cien estudiantes

LANGUAGE TIP
Use **cien** before **mil** (thousand).

one hundred thousand
cien mil

LANGUAGE TIP
When translating **a hundred and** use **ciento**.

one hundred and one
ciento uno
one hundred and twenty-five
ciento veinticinco

LANGUAGE TIP
There are special words for two
hundred, three hundred and so on.

---

two hundred
doscientos
**three hundred and fifty
people**
trescientas cincuenta
personas
five hundred and one
quinientos uno
hundreds of people
cientos de personas

hung VERB ▷ *see* **hang**

hungry ADJECTIVE
to be hungry
tener hambre
Are you hungry?
¿Tienes hambre?

I'm hungry.
Tengo hambre.
I'm not hungry.
No tengo hambre.

hunting NOUN
la **caza** *fem*
I'm against hunting.
Estoy en contra de la caza.

hurry NOUN
to be in a hurry
tener prisa
I'm in a hurry!
¡Tengo prisa!

hurry up VERB
Hurry up, Caleb!
¡Date prisa, Caleb!
Hurry up, children!
¡Daos prisa, niños!

hurt VERB
You're hurting me!
¡Me estás haciendo daño!
Have you hurt yourself?
¿Te has hecho daño?
My leg hurts.
Me duele la pierna.

LANGUAGE TIP
In Spanish you usually use an article
like **el**, **la** or **los**, **las** with parts of the
body.

That hurts.
Eso duele.

husband NOUN
el **marido** *masc*

hut NOUN
la **cabaña** *fem*

hymn NOUN
el **himno** *masc*

hyphen NOUN
el **guión** *masc* (PL los **guiones**)

I PRONOUN

yo

He's got a bike but I haven't.
Él tiene una bici pero yo no.
Anja and I
Anja y yo

LANGUAGE TIP

I isn't usually translated before a verb unless it's emphatic.

I speak English.
Hablo inglés.
I play the flute.
Toco la flauta.

ice NOUN
el **hielo** masc

ice cream NOUN
el **helado** masc

Would you like an ice cream?
¿Quieres un helado?
vanilla ice cream
helado de vainilla

ice cube NOUN
el **cubito de hielo** masc

ice lolly NOUN
el **polo** masc

ice rink NOUN
la **pista de patinaje** fem

ice-skating NOUN
el **patinaje sobre hielo** masc
an ice-skating championship
un campeonato de patinaje sobre hielo
I like ice-skating.
Me gusta patinar sobre hielo.

icon NOUN
el **icono** masc
Click on the icon to open the app.
Haz clic en el icono para abrir la aplicación.

ICT NOUN (= **information and communications technology**)
la **informática** fem

icy ADJECTIVE
The roads are icy.
Las carreteras están cubiertas de hielo.

I'd
(= **I had**) ▷ see **have**
(= **I would**) ▷ see **would**

idea NOUN
la **idea** fem
Good idea!
¡Buena idea!
I have no idea.
No tengo ni idea.

identical ADJECTIVE
idéntico masc
idéntica fem
They're identical.
Son idénticos.

idiot NOUN
el/la **idiota** masc/fem

if CONJUNCTION
si
You can have it if you like.
Te lo puedes quedar si quieres.
Do you know if he's there?
¿Sabes si él está allí?
if I were you
yo que tú

ill ADJECTIVE
enfermo masc
enferma fem

English

a
b
c
d
e
f
g
h
i
j
k
l
m
n
o
p
q
r
s
t
u
v
w
x
y
z

Melissa is ill.
Melissa está enferma.

I'll (= I will) ▷ *see* **will**

I'm (= I am) ▷ *see* **be**

imagination NOUN
la **imaginación** *fem*

imagine VERB
imaginar
Imagine you have lots of money.
Imagina que tienes mucho dinero.

imitate VERB
imitar
Imitate the sound.
Imita el sonido.

immediately ADVERB
inmediatamente
I'll do it immediately.
Lo haré inmediatamente.

immigrant NOUN
el/la **inmigrante** *masc/fem*

impatient ADJECTIVE
impaciente *masc/fem*
Don't be so impatient, Sasha.
No seas tan impaciente, Sasha.

important ADJECTIVE
importante *masc/fem*
Today's an important day.
Hoy es un día importante.

impossible ADJECTIVE
imposible *masc/fem*
Sorry, it's impossible.
Lo siento, es imposible.

LANGUAGE TIP
Don't forget that there's only one **s** in the Spanish word **imposible**.

improve VERB
mejorar
You need to improve your work.
Tienes que mejorar tu trabajo.

in

in can be a preposition or an adverb.

A PREPOSITION
1 en
in the house
en la casa
What can you see in the picture?
¿Qué ves en la foto?
in England
en Inglaterra
in hospital
en el hospital
in 2019
en el 2019

in London
en Londres
in Spain
en España
in English
en inglés
in Spanish
en español

2 de
the tallest person in the family
la persona más alta de la familia
She's the oldest in the class.
Ella es la mayor de la clase.
at six o'clock in the morning
a las seis de la mañana
the boy in the blue shirt
el chico de la camisa azul
B ADVERB
He isn't in.
No está.

inbox NOUN
la **bandeja de entrada** *fem*

inch NOUN
la **pulgada** *fem*
six inches
seis pulgadas

DID YOU KNOW...?
Inches, **feet** and **yards** aren't used in Spain. Use **centímetros** (centimetres) and **metros** (metres) instead.

included ADJECTIVE
  incluido *masc*
  incluida *fem*
> **Service is not included.**
> La propina no está incluida.

including PREPOSITION

LANGUAGE TIP
including is often translated by **incluido**, which, as it's an adjective, changes to **incluida**, **incluidos** or **incluidas** to agree with the noun that goes with it.

> **Everybody came, including Jack.**
> Vinieron todos, incluido Jack.
> **Everybody came, including Sophie.**
> Vinieron todos, incluida Sophie.
> **There are fifteen people, not including me.**
> Hay quince personas, sin incluirme a mí.

incredible ADJECTIVE
  increíble *masc/fem*
> **That's incredible!**
> ¡Eso es increíble!

indeed ADVERB
> **Thank you very much indeed!**
> ¡Muchísimas gracias!

indoor ADJECTIVE
> **an indoor swimming pool**
> una piscina cubierta

indoors ADVERB
  dentro
> **They're indoors.**
> Están dentro.

inexpensive ADJECTIVE
  barato *masc*
  barata *fem*
> **an inexpensive hotel**
> un hotel barato

infant school NOUN
  la **primaria** *fem*
> **He's going to start infant school.**
> Va a empezar primaria.

infection NOUN
  la **infección** *fem* (PL las **infecciones**)
> **an ear infection**
> una infección de oído

information NOUN
  la **información** *fem*
> **I need some information.**
> Necesito información.
> **information about Ireland**
> información sobre Irlanda

ingredient NOUN
  el **ingrediente** *masc*
> **a list of ingredients**
> una lista de ingredientes

inhabitant NOUN
  el/la **habitante** *masc/fem*

inhaler NOUN
  el **inhalador** *masc*

initials PL NOUN
  las **iniciales** *fem pl*
> **My initials are G-A-C.**
> Mis iniciales son G-A-C.

injection NOUN
  la **inyección** *fem* (PL las **inyecciones**)

injure VERB
  herir
> **Was anyone injured?**
> ¿Resultó alguien herido?

injury NOUN
  la **herida** *fem*
> **a serious injury**
> una herida grave

ink NOUN
  la **tinta** *fem*

inquire VERB
  informarse
    I'm going to inquire about train times.
    Voy a informarme acerca del horario de los trenes.

inquisitive ADJECTIVE
  curioso *masc*
  curiosa *fem*

insect NOUN
  el **insecto** *masc*

inside

> **inside** can be an adverb or a preposition.

A ADVERB
  dentro
    They're inside.
    Están dentro.
B PREPOSITION
  dentro de
    inside the house
    dentro de la casa

inspector NOUN
  el **inspector** *masc*
  la **inspectora** *fem*

instance NOUN
    for instance
    por ejemplo

instantly ADVERB
  al instante

instead ADVERB
    instead of
    en vez de
    Eat fruit instead of sweets.
    Come fruta en vez de caramelos.
    instead of him
    en vez de él

LANGUAGE TIP
When **instead** is not followed by **of** it isn't always translated.

The pool was closed so we played tennis instead.
La piscina estaba cerrada así que jugamos al tenis.

There's no apple juice. Do you want orange juice instead?
No hay zumo de manzana. ¿Quieres de naranja?

instructions PL NOUN
  las **instrucciones** *fem pl*
    Follow the instructions.
    Sigue las instrucciones.

instructor NOUN
  el **monitor** *masc*
  la **monitora** *fem* (*swimming, skiing*)
    She's a skiing instructor.
    Es monitora de esquí.
    He's a driving instructor.
    Es profesor de autoescuela.

LANGUAGE TIP
In Spanish, you do not use an article with people's jobs.

---

instrument NOUN
  el **instrumento** *masc*
    Do you play an instrument?
    ¿Tocas algún instrumento?

intelligent ADJECTIVE
  inteligente *masc/fem*
    You're very intelligent.
    Eres muy inteligente.

LANGUAGE TIP
Don't forget that there's only one **l** in the Spanish word **inteligente**.

---

interest NOUN
  1 el **interés** *masc* (PL los **intereses**)
    to lose interest in something
    perder el interés por algo
    She shows interest in languages.
    Se interesa por los idiomas.
  2 la **afición** *fem* (PL las **aficiones**)
    My main interest is music.
    Mi mayor afición es la música.

interested ADJECTIVE
    I'm not interested.
    No me interesa.
    I'm not interested in football.
    No me interesa el fútbol.

A
B
C
D
E
F
G
H
I
J
K
L
M
N
O
P
Q
R
S
T
U
V
W
X
Y
Z

Are you interested?
¿Te interesa?

interesting ADJECTIVE
interesante *masc/fem*
It's a very interesting story.
Es una historia muy interesante.

international ADJECTIVE
internacional *masc/fem*
an international school
un colegio internacional

internet NOUN
the internet
internet
on the internet
en internet

interrupt VERB
interrumpir
Don't interrupt, Anthony!
¡No interrumpas, Anthony!

interval NOUN
el **descanso** *masc*
during the interval
durante el descanso

interview NOUN
la **entrevista** *fem*

interviewer NOUN
el **entrevistador** *masc*
la **entrevistadora** *fem*

into PREPOSITION
1 a (*to*)
I'm going into town.
Voy a la ciudad.

Translate it into English.
Tradúcelo al inglés.
2 en (*in*)
He got into the car.
Se metió en el coche.
Divide into two groups.
Dividíos en dos grupos.

introduce VERB
presentar
I'd like to introduce you to Julia.
Quiero presentarte a Julia.
Can you introduce yourselves?
¿Podéis presentaros vosotros mismos?

inventor NOUN
el **inventor** *masc*
la **inventora** *fem*

invisible ADJECTIVE
invisible *masc/fem*

invitation NOUN
la **invitación** *fem* (PL las
invitaciones)
Thank you for the invitation.
Gracias por la invitación.

invite VERB
invitar
Thank you for inviting me.
Gracias por invitarme.
I'm going to invite Sara to my party.
Voy a invitar a Sara a mi fiesta.

LANGUAGE TIP
Don't forget the personal **a** in
examples like this one.

Ireland NOUN
Irlanda *fem*
I live in Ireland.
Vivo en Irlanda.
I'm from Ireland.
Soy de Irlanda.

in Ireland
en Irlanda
I'm going to Ireland.
Voy a Irlanda.

Irish

> **Irish** can be an adjective or a noun.

A ADJECTIVE
irlandés *masc* (PL **irlandeses**)
irlandesa *fem*
I'm Irish.
Soy irlandés.
I like Irish music.
Me gusta la música irlandesa.
Irish people
los irlandeses

He's Irish.
Es irlandés.
She's Irish.
Es irlandesa.

B NOUN
el **irlandés** *masc* (language)
Do you speak Irish?
¿Hablas irlandés?
the Irish
los irlandeses

LANGUAGE TIP
irlandés is not spelled with a capital letter in Spanish.

Irishman NOUN
el **irlandés** *masc* (PL los **irlandeses**)

LANGUAGE TIP
irlandés is not spelled with a capital letter in Spanish.

Irishwoman NOUN
la **irlandesa** *fem*

LANGUAGE TIP
irlandesa is not spelled with a capital letter in Spanish.

---

iron

> **iron** can be a noun or a verb.

A NOUN
1 el **hierro** *masc* (metal)

an iron gate
un portón de hierro
2 la **plancha** *fem* (for clothes)
B VERB
to iron
planchar
I can iron a shirt.
Sé planchar una camisa.

ironing NOUN
to do the ironing
planchar

irritating ADJECTIVE
irritante *masc/fem*

is VERB ▷ *see* **be**

Islam NOUN
el **Islam** *masc*

island NOUN
la **isla** *fem*

isle NOUN
the Isle of Man
la Isla de Man
the Isle of Wight
la Isla de Wight

isn't (= **is not**) ▷ *see* **be**

it PRONOUN
1 (subject)

LANGUAGE TIP
When **it** is the subject of a verb, it isn't translated into Spanish.

Where's my book? — It's on the table.
¿Dónde está mi libro? — Está en la mesa.
Where's my notebook? — It's in your bag.
¿Dónde está mi libreta? — Está en tu bolsa.

It's easy.
Es fácil.
It's incredible!
¡Es increíble!

It's expensive.
Es caro.
It's one o'clock.
Es la una.
It's two o'clock.
Son las dos.
It's me.
Soy yo.
It's hot.
Hace calor.

2 **lo** *masc*
la *fem* (*direct object*)

LANGUAGE TIP
Remember to use **lo** to refer to a
masculine noun and **la** to refer to a
feminine one.

**There's one cake left. Do you
want it?**
Queda un pastel. ¿Lo quieres?
It's a good film. Have you seen it?
Es una buena película. ¿La has visto?
**This is my new jumper. Do you
like it?**
Éste es mi jersey nuevo. ¿Te gusta?

itch VERB
picar
My arm itches.
Me pica el brazo.

LANGUAGE TIP
In Spanish you usually use an article

like **el**, **la** or **los**, **las** with parts of
the body.

it'd
(= **it had**) ▷ *see* **have**
(= **it would**) ▷ *see* **would**

item NOUN
el **artículo** *masc*

it'll (= **it will**) ▷ *see* **will**

its ADJECTIVE
su *masc/fem* (PL **sus**)

LANGUAGE TIP
Remember to use **su** with singular
nouns and **sus** with plural ones.

Everything is in its place.
Cada cosa está en su sitio.
**This model has its
disadvantages.**
Este modelo tiene sus desventajas.
What's its name?
¿Cómo se llama?

it's
(= **it is**) ▷ *see* **be**
(= **it has**) ▷ *see* **have**

itself PRONOUN
by itself
solo
She left the cat by itself.
Dejó al gato solo.

LANGUAGE TIP
Don't forget the personal **a** in
examples like this one.

I've (= **I have**) ▷ *see* **have**

jab NOUN
la **inyección** *fem* (PL las **inyecciones**)

jack NOUN
la **jota** *fem*
> **the jack of hearts**
> la jota de corazones

jacket NOUN
la **chaqueta** *fem*
> **a white jacket**
> una chaqueta blanca

jacket potato NOUN
la **patata asada con piel** *fem*

jail NOUN
la **cárcel** *fem*
> **in jail**
> en la cárcel

jam NOUN
la **mermelada** *fem*
> **strawberry jam**
> mermelada de fresa

jam jar NOUN
el **tarro de mermelada** *masc*

janitor NOUN
el/la **conserje** *masc/fem*
> **He's a janitor.**
> Es conserje.

LANGUAGE TIP
In Spanish, you do not use an article with people's jobs.

January NOUN
enero *masc*
> **My birthday's in January.**
> Mi cumpleaños es en enero.

> **It's the sixth of January today.**
> Hoy es seis de enero.

> **in January**
> en enero
> **on the fifth of January**
> el cinco de enero

LANGUAGE TIP
Months are not spelled with a capital letter in Spanish.

---

jealous ADJECTIVE
celoso *masc*
celosa *fem*
> **Anne is jealous.**
> Anne está celosa.
> **She's jealous of Kate.**
> Le tiene envidia a Kate.

jeans PL NOUN
los **vaqueros** *masc pl*
> **I've got some new jeans.**
> Tengo unos vaqueros nuevos.
> **a pair of jeans**
> unos vaqueros

jelly NOUN
la **gelatina** *fem*

jersey NOUN
el **jersey** *masc*
(PL los **jerseys**)

Jew NOUN
el **judío** *masc*
la **judía** *fem*

jewel NOUN
la **joya** *fem*

jewellery NOUN
las **joyas** *fem pl*

Jewish ADJECTIVE
judío *masc*
judía *fem*

> **He's Jewish.**
> Es judío.
> **She's Jewish.**
> Es judía.

jigsaw NOUN
el **rompecabezas** *masc*
(PL los **rompecabezas**)
I like doing jigsaws.
Me gusta hacer rompecabezas.

job NOUN
el **trabajo** *masc*
He's got an interesting job.
Tiene un trabajo interesante.
She's looking for a job.
Está buscando trabajo.

jogging NOUN
el **footing** *masc*
She goes jogging.
Hace footing.

joke NOUN
1 el **chiste** *masc*
He told me a joke.
Me contó un chiste.
2 la **broma** *fem*
It was only a joke.
Era solo una broma.

jotter NOUN
el **bloc** *masc* (PL los **blocs**)

journalist NOUN
el/la **periodista** *masc/fem*
He's a journalist.
Es periodista.

journey NOUN
el **viaje** *masc*
I don't like long journeys.
No me gustan los viajes largos.

judge

judge can be a noun or a verb.

A NOUN
el **juez** *masc*
la **jueza** *fem*
B VERB
to judge
hacer de juez en
Who's going to judge the competition?
¿Quién va a hacer de juez en el concurso?

judo NOUN
el **yudo** *masc*
I do judo.
Hago yudo.

juggler NOUN
el/la **malabarista** *masc/fem*

juice NOUN
el **zumo** *masc*
I'd like some orange juice.
Quiero zumo de naranja.

July NOUN
julio *masc*
My birthday is in July.
Mi cumpleaños es en julio.
It's the fourth of July today.
Hoy es cuatro de julio.

in July
en julio
on the fourteenth of July
el catorce de julio

A
B
C
D
E
F
G
H
I
J
K
L
M
N
O
P
Q
R
S
T
U
V
W
X
Y
Z

jump VERB
  saltar
    Jump!
    ¡Salta!

jumper NOUN
  el **jersey** *masc* (PL los **jerseys**)
    a dark green jumper
    un jersey verde oscuro

June NOUN
  junio *masc*
    My birthday is in June.
    Mi cumpleaños es en junio.
    It's the eighteenth of June today.
    Hoy es dieciocho de junio.

  in June
  en junio
  on the fourth of June
  el cuatro de junio

  LANGUAGE TIP
  Months are not spelled with a capital letter in Spanish.
---

junior NOUN
  the juniors
  los alumnos de los primeros cursos

junior school NOUN
  el **colegio de primaria** *masc*

junk food NOUN
  la **comida basura** *fem*

just ADVERB
  1 justo
    just after Christmas
    justo después de Navidad
    just now
    en este momento
    I'm busy just now.
    Estoy ocupada en este momento.
    I'm just coming!
    ¡Ya voy!
  2 solo (*only*)
    It's just a suggestion.
    Es solo una sugerencia.
    Just a moment, please.
    Un momento, por favor.
  3 **to have just done something**
    acabar de hacer algo
    I've just done it.
    Acabo de hacerlo.
    He's just arrived.
    Acaba de llegar.

K k

kangaroo NOUN
el **canguro** *masc*

karaoke NOUN
el **karaoke** *masc*

karate NOUN
el **karate** *masc*
    I do karate.
    Hago karate.

keen ADJECTIVE
entusiasmado *masc*
entusiasmada *fem*
    He's not very keen.
    No está muy entusiasmado.
    I'm very keen on football.
    Me gusta mucho el fútbol.
    I'm not very keen on spinach.
    No me gustan mucho las espinacas.

LANGUAGE TIP
Remember that you use **me gusta ...**
to say that you're keen on one thing
and **me gustan ...** to say that you're
keen on two or more things.

---

keep VERB
1 quedarse con (*have*)
    You can keep it.
    Puedes quedarte con él.

Keep the receipt.
Quédate con el recibo.
2 quedarse (*stay*)
    Keep still!
    ¡Quédate quieto!
    Keep quiet!
    ¡Estaros callados!

keep on VERB
seguir
    Keep on singing.
    Seguid cantando.

keep-fit NOUN
la **gimnasia** *fem*
    The keep-fit class is on Tuesday.
    La clase de gimnasia es el martes.

kept VERB ▷ *see* **keep**

kettle NOUN
el **hervidor** *masc*

key NOUN
la **llave** *fem*
    Where are my keys?
    ¿Dónde están mis llaves?

keyboard NOUN
el **teclado** *masc*

kick

> **kick** can be a noun or a verb.

A NOUN
la **patada** *fem*
B VERB
to kick
dar una patada a
    He kicked me!
    ¡Me dio una patada!
    Kick the ball.
    Dale una patada al balón.

kid NOUN
el **niño** *masc*
la **niña** *fem* (*child*)
    the kids
    los niños

kill VERB
matar
    My cat kills birds.
    Mi gato mata pájaros.

kilo NOUN
el **kilo** *masc*
two euros a kilo
dos euros el kilo

kilometre NOUN
el **kilómetro** *masc*

kilt NOUN
la **falda escocesa** *fem*

kind

> **kind** can be an adjective or a noun.

A ADJECTIVE
amable *masc/fem*
She's a kind lady.
Es una señora amable.
That's very kind of you.
Es muy amable de tu parte.

B NOUN
el **tipo** *masc*
It's a kind of sausage.
Es un tipo de salchicha.

kindergarten NOUN
el **jardín de infancia** *masc*
(PL los **jardines de infancia**)

king NOUN
el **rey** *masc*
the king of hearts
el rey de corazones
the king and queen
los reyes

kiss

> **kiss** can be a noun or a verb.

A NOUN
el **beso** *masc*
Give me a kiss.
Dame un beso.

DID YOU KNOW...?
Did you know that Spanish speakers sometimes end emails, postcards and letters to friends with **un beso** (a kiss) or **besos** (kisses)?

B VERB
to kiss
besar
Kiss me.
Bésame.

kit NOUN
el **equipo** *masc*
Don't forget your gym kit.
Que no se te olvide el equipo de gimnasia.

kitchen NOUN
la **cocina** *fem*
He's in the kitchen.
Está en la cocina.

kite NOUN
la **cometa** *fem*

kitten NOUN
el **gatito** *masc*
la **gatita** *fem*

knee NOUN
la **rodilla** *fem*

kneel VERB
arrodillarse

knew VERB ▷ *see* **know**

knickers PL NOUN
las **bragas** *fem pl*
a pair of knickers
unas bragas

knife NOUN
el **cuchillo** *masc*

knit VERB
hacer punto
I can knit.
Sé hacer punto.
She's knitting a scarf.
Se está haciendo una bufanda de punto.

A B C D E F G H I J K L M N O P Q R S T U V W X Y Z

knives PL NOUN
  los **cuchillos** *masc pl*
    knives, forks and spoons
    cuchillos, tenedores y
    cucharas

knob NOUN
  1 el **pomo** *masc* (*on door*)
  2 el **botón** *masc* (PL los **botones**)
    (*on radio, TV*)

knock VERB
  llamar
    **Someone's
    knocking at
    the door.**
    Alguien está
    llamando a la
    puerta.

know VERB

LANGUAGE TIP
Use **saber** for knowing facts and
conocer for knowing people and
places.

---

  1 **saber** (*fact*)

It's a long way. — Yes, I know.
Está lejos. — Sí, ya lo sé.
Who knows the answer?
¿Quién sabe la respuesta?

> **I don't know.**
> No lo sé.

  2 **conocer** (*person, place*)
    I know her.
    La conozco.
    I don't know him.
    No lo conozco.

LANGUAGE TIP
Don't forget the personal **a** when you
name the person.

    Do you know Tom?
    ¿Conoces a Tom?
    I know Madrid well.
    Conozco bien Madrid.

knowledge NOUN
  el **conocimiento** *masc*

Koran NOUN
  el **Corán** *masc*

Spanish

English

A
B
C
D
E
F
G
H
I
J
K
L
M
N
O
P
Q
R
S
T
U
V
W
X
Y
Z

Ll

label NOUN
la **etiqueta** *fem*

lace NOUN
el **cordón** *masc* (PL los **cordones**) (*of shoe*)
Tie your laces.
Átate los cordones.

LANGUAGE TIP
In Spanish you usually use an article like **el**, **la** or **los**, **las** with clothes you are wearing.

---

ladder NOUN
la **escalera de mano** *fem*

lady NOUN
la **señora** *fem*
an old lady
una señora mayor
a young lady
una joven
Ladies and gentlemen ...
Señoras y caballeros ...
Where is the 'ladies'?
¿Dónde está el baño de señoras?

laid VERB ▷ *see* lay

lain VERB ▷ *see* lie

lake NOUN
el **lago** *masc*

lamb NOUN
el **cordero** *masc*
a newborn lamb
un cordero recién nacido

lamp NOUN
la **lámpara** *fem*

land

---

land can be a noun or a verb.

A NOUN
la **tierra** *fem*
on land
en tierra

B VERB
to land
aterrizar
The plane lands at nine o'clock.
El avión aterriza a las nueve.

lane NOUN
el **camino** *masc*
a country lane
un camino de campo
the fast lane
el carril de adelantamiento

language NOUN
el **idioma** *masc*
Spanish isn't a difficult language.
El español no es un idioma difícil.

LANGUAGE TIP
Even though it ends in **-a**, **el idioma** is a masculine noun.

---

lap NOUN
on my lap
en mi regazo

laptop NOUN
el **ordenador portátil** *masc*

large ADJECTIVE
grande *masc/fem*
a large house
una casa grande

a large dog
un perro grande

Spanish
English

LANGUAGE TIP
grande normally follows the noun when it means 'large'. However, when it does go before a singular noun, it is shortened to **gran**.

a large number of people
un gran número de personas

LANGUAGE TIP
Be careful! The translation of **large** is not **largo**.

last

last can be an adjective or an adverb.

A ADJECTIVE
último *masc*
última *fem*
the last time
la última vez
He arrived last night.
Llegó anoche.
We've got here at last!
¡Por fin hemos llegado!

last Friday
el viernes pasado
last week
la semana pasada
last year
el año pasado
last night
anoche
at last
por fin

B ADVERB
en último lugar (*in last place*)
He always comes last.
Siempre llega en último lugar.
I've lost my bag. — When did you last see it?
He perdido el bolso. — ¿Cuándo lo viste por última vez?

late ADVERB, ADJECTIVE
tarde
I go to bed late.
Me acuesto tarde.
to be late
llegar tarde
You're going to be late!
¡Vas a llegar tarde!
Sorry I'm late!
¡Siento llegar tarde!
I'm late for school.
Voy tarde para el colegio.

later ADVERB
más tarde
I'll do it later.
Lo haré más tarde.

See you later!
¡Hasta luego!

latest ADJECTIVE
último *masc*
última *fem*
their latest album
su último álbum

Latin NOUN
el **latín** *masc*
I do Latin.
Hago latín.

laugh VERB
reírse
Why are you laughing?
¿Por qué os reís?

lawn NOUN
el **césped** *masc*

lawnmower NOUN
la **cortadora de césped** *fem*

A
B
C
D
E
F
G
H
I
J
K
L
M
N
O
P
Q
R
S
T
U
V
W
X
Y
Z

lawyer NOUN
el **abogado** masc
la **abogada** fem
My mother's a lawyer.
Mi madre es abogada.

LANGUAGE TIP
In Spanish, you do not use an article with people's jobs.

lay VERB
1 **poner**
Lay your cards on the table.
Pon tus cartas sobre la mesa.
to lay the table
poner la mesa
It's Sylvia's turn to lay the table.
Le toca a Sylvia poner la mesa.
2 ▷ see **lie**

lazy ADJECTIVE
vago masc
vaga fem
My sister is very lazy.
Mi hermana es muy vaga.

lead

lead can be a noun or a verb.

A NOUN
1 **to be in the lead**
ir en cabeza
Our team is in the lead.
Nuestro equipo va en cabeza.
2 el **cable** masc (cable)
3 la **correa** fem (of dog)
B VERB
to lead
llevar
This street leads to the station.
Esta calle lleva a la estación.

leaf NOUN
la **hoja** fem

lean out VERB
asomarse
Don't lean out of the window.
No te asomes a la ventana.

lean over VERB
inclinarse
Don't lean over too far.
No te inclines demasiado.

leap year NOUN
el **año bisiesto** masc

learn VERB
aprender
I'm learning Spanish.
Estoy aprendiendo español.
I'm learning to ski.
Estoy aprendiendo a esquiar.

least ADVERB, ADJECTIVE, PRONOUN
menos

LANGUAGE TIP
menos never changes its ending.

the least expensive hotel
el hotel menos caro
the least expensive camera
la cámara menos cara
the least expensive hotels
los hoteles menos caros
Who's got the least money?
¿Quién tiene menos dinero?
It will cost at least two hundred pounds.
Costará al menos doscientas libras.

at least
al menos

leather NOUN
el **cuero** masc
It's made of leather.
Es de cuero.
a black leather jacket
una chaqueta de cuero negra

leave VERB
1 **dejar** (object)
Don't leave your bag in the car.
No dejes el bolso en el coche.
I've left my book at home.
Me he dejado el libro en casa.
2 **salir** (depart)
The bus leaves at eight.
El autobús sale a las ocho.

3 irse (*go away*)
He's already left.
Ya se ha ido.

leaves PL NOUN
las **hojas** *fem pl*

led VERB ▷*see* **lead**

leek NOUN
el **puerro** *masc*

left

> **left** can be an adjective, adverb, noun or verb.

A ADJECTIVE
1 izquierdo *masc*
izquierda *fem* (*not right*)
Stretch out your left arm.
Estira el brazo izquierdo.
on the left side of the road
en el lado izquierdo de la calle
2 (*remaining*)
I've got fifteen euros left.
Me quedan quince euros.
How many cards have you got left?
¿Cuántas cartas te quedan?
I haven't got any money left.
No me queda dinero.
B ADVERB
a la izquierda
Turn left.
Gira a la izquierda.
Take the next left.
Toma la siguiente a la izquierda.
C NOUN
la **izquierda** *fem*
It's on the left.
Está a la izquierda.
the house on the left
la casa de la izquierda
D VERB ▷*see* **leave**

left-hand ADJECTIVE
the left-hand side
la izquierda
It's on the left-hand side.
Está a la izquierda.

left-handed ADJECTIVE
zurdo *masc*
zurda *fem*
Tina is left-handed.
Tina es zurda.

left-luggage office NOUN
la **consigna** *fem*

leftovers PL NOUN
las **sobras** *fem pl*

leg NOUN
1 la **pierna** *fem* (*of person*)
She has a broken leg.
Tiene una pierna rota.
I've hurt my leg.
Me he hecho daño en la pierna.

LANGUAGE TIP
In Spanish you usually use an article like **el**, **la** or **los**, **las** with parts of the body.

---

2 la **pata** *fem* (*of animal, table*)
It's got a wobbly leg.
Tiene una pata que cojea.
a chicken leg
un muslo de pollo

leggings PL NOUN
las **mallas** *fem pl*

leisure centre NOUN
el **polideportivo** *masc*

lemon NOUN
el **limón** *masc*
(PL los **limones**)

lemonade NOUN
la **gaseosa** *fem*

lend VERB
dejar
Can you lend me a pencil?
¿Me puedes dejar un lápiz?

less ADJECTIVE, ADVERB, PRONOUN
menos

LANGUAGE TIP
menos never changes its ending.

Less noise, please!
¡Menos ruido, por favor!

A
B
C
D
E
F
G
H
I
J
K
L
M
N
O
P
Q
R
S
T
U
V
W
X
Y
Z

A bit less, please.
Un poco menos, por favor.

LANGUAGE TIP
You normally translate **less than** as
menos que.

I've got less than him!
¡Tengo menos que él!
I'm less nervous than I was.
Ahora estoy menos nervioso que
antes.

LANGUAGE TIP
Use **menos de** instead before
numbers.

It costs less than ten euros.
Cuesta menos de diez euros.

lesson NOUN
1 la **clase** *fem*
   an English lesson
   una clase de inglés
   Each lesson lasts forty minutes.
   Cada clase dura cuarenta minutos.
2 la **lección** *fem* (PL las **lecciones**)
   (*in book*)

let VERB
1 **dejar** (*allow*)
   Let me see.
   Déjame ver.
   Let me go!
   ¡Suéltame!
   I'll let you know.
   Ya te lo diré.
2 (*in suggestions*)

LANGUAGE TIP
let's ... is often translated by **vamos
a ...** when making a suggestion.

Let's send him an email!
¡Vamos a enviarle un correo!

LANGUAGE TIP
vamos is also used to mean **let's go**.

Let's go to the park!
¡Vamos al parque!

LANGUAGE TIP
Alternatively you can make
suggestions using **¿por qué no...?**,
which literally means 'why not...?'.

Let's send him an email!
¿Por qué no le enviamos un correo?
Let's go to the park!
¿Por qué no vamos al parque?

Let's go!
¡Vamos!
Let's start now!
¡Vamos a empezar ahora!

letter NOUN
1 la **carta** *fem* (*note*)
   I'm writing a letter to my friend.
   Le estoy escribiendo una carta a mi
   amigo.

2 la **letra** *fem* (*of alphabet*)
   It's a five-letter word.
   Es una palabra de cinco letras.

letterbox NOUN
el **buzón** *masc* (PL los **buzones**)

DID YOU KNOW...?
Spanish **letterboxes** tend to be metal
boxes in which the postman leaves any
mail rather than the hole in the door
that is common in the UK.

lettuce NOUN
la **lechuga** *fem*

level NOUN
el **nivel** *masc*

liar NOUN
el **mentiroso** *masc*
la **mentirosa** *fem*

library NOUN
la **biblioteca** *fem*

LANGUAGE TIP
Be careful! The translation of **library** is not **librería**.

---

licence NOUN
el **permiso** *masc*
a fishing licence
un permiso de pesca
a driving licence
un carnet de conducir

lick VERB
lamer
The dog is licking me.
El perro me está lamiendo.

lid NOUN
la **tapa** *fem*

lie

lie can be a verb or a noun.

A VERB
1 **mentir** (*tell lies*)
She's lying.
Está mintiendo.
2 **estar tumbado** (*lie down*)
He is lying on the sofa.
Está tumbado en el sofá.
B NOUN
la **mentira** *fem*
That's a lie!
¡Eso es mentira!

life NOUN
la **vida** *fem*

life jacket NOUN
el **chaleco salvavidas** *masc*
(PL los **chalecos salvavidas**)

lift

lift can be a verb or a noun.

A VERB
to lift
levantar
It's too heavy, I can't lift it.
Pesa demasiado, no puedo levantarlo.
B NOUN
1 el **ascensor** *masc* (*to another floor*)
The lift isn't working.
El ascensor no funciona.
2 (*in car*)
Can you give me a lift to the station?
¿Me puedes llevar a la estación?

light

light can be an adjective, noun or verb.

A ADJECTIVE
1 **ligero** *masc*
ligera *fem* (*in weight*)
as light as a feather
tan ligero como una pluma
2 **claro** *masc*
clara *fem* (*in colour*)
light blue socks
calcetines azul claro

LANGUAGE TIP
When you describe something as **light blue**, **light green** and so on, neither the colour nor **claro** changes its ending to agree with the noun.

---

some light green curtains
unas cortinas verde claro
B NOUN
la **luz** *fem* (PL las **luces**)
Switch on the light.
Enciende la luz.
Switch off the light.
Apaga la luz.
Turn right at the lights.
Gira a la derecha al llegar al semáforo.
C VERB
to light
encender
Let's light the fire.
Vamos a encender el fuego.

light bulb NOUN
la **bombilla** *fem*

lighter NOUN
el **mechero** *masc*

lighthouse
NOUN
el **faro**
masc

lightning
NOUN
los **relámpagos**
masc pl
There was thunder and lightning.
Había truenos y relámpagos.
a flash of lightning
un relámpago

like

> **like** can be a verb or a preposition.

A VERB
to like
1 I like ...
Me gusta .../Me gustan ...

LANGUAGE TIP
Remember that you use **me gusta ...** to say you like one thing and **me gustan ...** to say you like two or more things.

I like milk.
Me gusta la leche.
I don't like riding.
No me gusta montar a caballo.
I like cherries.
Me gustan las cerezas.
I don't like grapes.
No me gustan las uvas.
Do you like coffee?
¿Te gusta el café?
Do you like sweets?
¿Te gustan los caramelos?
I like Paul.
Paul me cae bien.

2 querer (*want*)
Yes, if you like.
Sí, si quieres.
I'd like an orange juice, please.
Quiero un zumo de naranja, por favor.
I'd like some chips.
Quiero patatas fritas.
What would you like for breakfast?
¿Qué quieres desayunar?
Would you like to go for a walk?
¿Quieres ir a dar un paseo?
What would you like, Madam?
¿Qué desea, señora?

I'd like ...
Quiero ...

B PREPOSITION
como
a city like London
una ciudad como Londres
I look like my brother.
Me parezco a mi hermano.
What's Madrid like?
¿Cómo es Madrid?

like this
así

likely ADJECTIVE
probable *masc/fem*
That's not very likely.
Eso no es muy probable.

line NOUN
la **línea** *fem*
a straight line
una línea recta

link NOUN
el **enlace** *masc*
This link will take you to the website.
Este enlace te lleva al sitio web.

lion NOUN
el **león** *masc*
(PL los **leones**)

lip NOUN
el **labio** masc

lipstick NOUN
la **barra de labios** fem

liquid NOUN
el **líquido** masc

list

> **list** can be a noun or a verb.

A NOUN
la **lista** fem
a shopping list
una lista de la compra
B VERB
to list
hacer una lista de
List your hobbies.
Haz una lista de tus aficiones.

listen VERB
escuchar
Are you listening, Sonia?
¿Estás escuchando, Sonia?
to listen to something
escuchar algo
Listen to this, everybody!
¡Escuchad todos esto!

Listen to me, children!
¡Escuchadme, niños!

LANGUAGE TIP
Have you noticed that in Spanish you don't need a preposition after the verb **escuchar**?

litre NOUN
el **litro** masc

litter NOUN
la **basura** fem
Don't leave litter.
No dejéis basura.

litter bin NOUN
la **papelera** fem

little

> **little** can be an adjective or a pronoun.

A ADJECTIVE
1 pequeño masc
pequeña fem (small)
a little girl
una niña pequeña
2 poco masc
poca fem (in quantity)
We've got very little time.
Tenemos muy poco tiempo.
B PRONOUN
a little
un poco
How much would you like?
— Just a little.
¿Cuánto quieres? — Solo un poco.
There's very little left.
Queda muy poco.

live VERB
vivir
Where do you live?
¿Dónde vives?
I live here.
Vivo aquí.
I live in Edinburgh.
Vivo en Edimburgo.
I live with my grandmother.
Vivo con mi abuela.
My parents don't live together any more.
Mis padres ya no viven juntos.

living room NOUN
la **sala de estar** fem

lizard NOUN
la **lagartija** fem

load

> **load** can be a noun or a verb.

A NOUN
loads of
un montón de

A
B
C
D
E
F
G
H
I
J
K
L
M
N
O
P
Q
R
S
T
U
V
W
X
Y
Z

loads of people
un montón de gente
loads of money
un montón de dinero
B VERB
to load
cargar

loaf NOUN
a loaf of bread
un pan

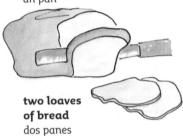

**two loaves
of bread**
dos panes
a French loaf
una barra de pan

lock

> **lock** can be a noun or a verb.

A NOUN
la **cerradura**
fem
**The lock is
broken.**
La cerradura
está rota.
B VERB
to lock
cerrar con llave
I must lock the door.
Tengo que cerrar la puerta con llave.

locker NOUN
la **taquilla** *fem*
Leave your books in your locker.
Deja los libros en la taquilla.

log NOUN
el **tronco** *masc*

log in VERB
conectarse
I can't log in.
No puedo conectarme.

log off VERB
desconectarse
I've forgotten how to log off.
He olvidado cómo desconectarme.

log on VERB
conectarse
Have you logged on yet?
¿Te has conectado ya?

log out VERB
desconectarse
Please log out now.
Por favor, desconéctate ahora.

lollipop NOUN
el **pirulí** *masc* (PL los **pirulís**)

> **DID YOU KNOW...?**
> Schools in Spain don't use a **lollipop
> man** or **lollipop lady**.

London NOUN
Londres *masc*
in London
en Londres
to London
a Londres
I'm from London.
Soy de Londres.

lonely ADJECTIVE
solo *masc*
sola *fem*
to feel lonely
sentirse solo
She feels lonely.
Se siente sola.

long ADJECTIVE
largo *masc*
larga *fem*
She's got long hair.
Tiene el pelo largo.
There's a long queue.
Hay una larga cola.

> **How long is the flight?**
> ¿Cuánto dura el vuelo?
> **How long does it take?**
> ¿Cuánto tiempo se tarda?

It takes a long time.
Se tarda mucho tiempo.
How long is it?
¿Cuánto mide de largo?
It's two hundred metres long.
Mide doscientos metros de largo.

loo NOUN
el **baño** *masc*
Where's the loo?
¿Dónde está el baño?
Can I go to the loo?
¿Puedo ir al baño?

look

> **look** can be a noun or a verb.

A NOUN
to have a look
echar un vistazo
Have a look at this!
¡Echa un vistazo a esto!
B VERB
to look
1 **mirar**
Look, children!
¡Mirad, niños!
to look at something
mirar algo
Look at the picture.
Mira la foto.
Look at me, Simon.
Mírame, Simon.
2 (*seem*)
That cake looks nice.
Esa tarta tiene buena pinta.

Look!
¡Mira!
Look at the board.
Mirad a la pizarra.
Look out!
¡Cuidado!

look after VERB
cuidar
I look after my little sister.
Cuido a mi hermana pequeña.

LANGUAGE TIP
Don't forget the personal **a** in
examples like this one.

---

look for VERB
buscar
What are you looking for?
¿Qué estás buscando?
I'm looking for my rubber.
Estoy buscando mi goma de borrar.
We're looking for Daniel.
Estamos buscando a Daniel.

LANGUAGE TIP
Don't forget the personal **a** in
examples like this one.

---

look up VERB
consultar
**You'll need to look up the words
in the dictionary.**
Tendrás que consultar las palabras en
el diccionario.

lorry NOUN
el **camión** *masc* (PL los **camiones**)

lorry driver NOUN
el **camionero** *masc*
la **camionera** *fem*
He's a lorry driver.
Es camionero.

LANGUAGE TIP
In Spanish, you do not use an article
with people's jobs.

---

lose VERB
perder
I've lost my purse.
He perdido mi monedero.

A
B
C
D
E
F
G
H
I
J
K
L
M
N
O
P
Q
R
S
T
U
V
W
X
Y
Z

460

Our team always loses.
Nuestro equipo siempre pierde.
to get lost
perderse
We got lost in the wood.
Nos perdimos en el bosque.

loser NOUN
el **perdedor** *masc*
la **perdedora** *fem*

lost VERB ▷ *see* **lose**

lot NOUN
a lot
mucho
She talks a lot.
Habla mucho.
Do you like football? — Not a lot.
¿Te gusta el fútbol? — No mucho.
**How many friends have you got?
— A lot.**
¿Cuántos amigos tienes? — Muchos.
a lot of
mucho
We haven't got a lot of time.
No tenemos mucho tiempo.

LANGUAGE TIP
Remember to change the ending of
mucho to agree with what it
describes.

She's got a lot of books.
Tiene muchos libros.
He's got lots of experience.
Tiene mucha experiencia.

Thanks a lot.
Muchas gracias.

lottery NOUN
la **lotería** *fem*
I hope I win the lottery.
Espero que me toque la lotería.
a lottery ticket
un billete de lotería

loud ADJECTIVE
alto *masc*
alta *fem*

The television is too loud.
La televisión está demasiado alta.
Speak louder!
¡Habla más alto!

lounge NOUN
el **salón** *masc* (PL los **salones**)

love

love can be a noun or a verb.

A NOUN
el **amor** *masc*
her love for animals
su amor por los animales
She's in love.
Está enamorada.
She's in love with Pierre.
Está enamorada de Pierre.
Give Emma my love.
Dale recuerdos a Emma de mi parte.
Love, Peter.
Un abrazo, Peter.

B VERB
to love
1 **querer** (*person*)
Do you love me?
¿Me quieres?
Everybody loves her.
Todos la quieren.
I love Renato.
Quiero a Renato.

LANGUAGE TIP
Don't forget the personal **a** in
examples like this one.

2 **encantar** (*thing*)
I love chocolate.
Me encanta el chocolate.
I love skiing.
Me encanta esquiar.
I love roses.
Me encantan las rosas.

LANGUAGE TIP
Remember that you use **me
encanta ...** to say you love one thing
and **me encantan ...** to say you love
two or more things.

Love from ...
Un abrazo de ...
I love you.
Te quiero.

lovely ADJECTIVE
precioso *masc*
preciosa *fem*
They've got a lovely house.
Tienen una casa preciosa.
It's a lovely day.
Hace un día bonito.
Have a lovely time!
¡Que lo paséis bien!

low ADJECTIVE
bajo *masc*
baja *fem*
a low price
un precio bajo

luck NOUN
la **suerte** *fem*
She doesn't have much luck.
No tiene mucha suerte.

Good luck!
¡Buena suerte!
Bad luck!
¡Qué mala suerte!

LANGUAGE TIP
Have you noticed the upside-down exclamation mark at the start of Spanish exclamations?

luckily ADVERB
afortunadamente

lucky ADJECTIVE
to be lucky
tener suerte
You're lucky!
¡Tienes suerte!
Sarah is lucky, she's going to Ireland.
Sarah tiene suerte, se va a Irlanda.
Black cats are lucky.
Los gatos negros traen suerte.
a lucky horseshoe
una herradura de la suerte

luggage NOUN
el **equipaje** *masc*
Have you got any luggage?
¿Tienes equipaje?

lump NOUN
1 el **trozo** *masc* (*piece*)
a lump of cheese
un trozo de queso
2 el **chichón** *masc* (PL los **chichones**)
(*bump*)
He's got a lump on his forehead.
Tiene un chichón en la frente.

LANGUAGE TIP
In Spanish you usually use an article like **el**, **la** or **los**, **las** with parts of the body.

lunch NOUN
la **comida** *fem*
Lunch is nearly ready.
La comida está casi lista.
I go home for lunch.
Voy a casa a comer.
It's time for lunch.
Es hora de comer.
to have lunch
comer
We have lunch at twelve thirty.
Comemos a las doce y media.

lying VERB ▷ *see* **lie**

Spanish

English

a
b
c
d
e
f
g
h
i
j
k
l
m
n
o
p
q
r
s
t
u
v
w
x
y
z

Spanish

English

A
B
C
D
E
F
G
H
I
J
K
L
M
N
O
P
Q
R
S
T
U
V
W
X
Y
Z

machine NOUN
la **máquina** *fem*

mad ADJECTIVE
1 **loco** *masc*
loca *fem* (*insane*)
You're mad!
¡Estás loco!
He's mad about football.
Está loco por el fútbol.
She's mad about horses.
Le encantan los caballos.
2 **furioso** *masc*
furiosa *fem* (*angry*)
He's mad at me for losing his watch.
Está furioso conmigo por haber perdido su reloj.

Madam NOUN
la **señora** *fem*
Excuse me, Madam.
Perdone, señora.

made VERB ▷ *see* **make**

Madrid NOUN
Madrid *masc*
in Madrid
en Madrid
to Madrid
a Madrid
Luis is from Madrid.
Luis es de Madrid.

magazine NOUN
la **revista** *fem*

magic

magic can be an adjective or a noun.

A ADJECTIVE
1 **mágico** *masc*
mágica *fem*
a magic wand
una varita mágica
a magic trick
un truco de magia
2 **fantástico** *masc*
fantástica *fem* (*brilliant*)
It was magic!
¡Fue fantástico!
B NOUN
la **magia** *fem*
by magic
por magia

magician NOUN
el **mago** *masc*
la **maga** *fem*

magnifying glass
NOUN
la **lupa** *fem*

mail

mail can be a noun or a verb.

A NOUN
el **correo** *masc*
You've got some mail.
Tienes correo.
by mail
por correo
B VERB
to mail
enviar un correo a (*email*)
I'll mail my friend.
Voy a enviar un correo a mi amigo.

main ADJECTIVE
principal *masc/fem*
the main problem
el problema principal

The hotel is on the main road.
El hotel está en la carretera principal.

major ADJECTIVE
muy importante
a major change
un cambio muy importante
a major problem
un problema serio

Majorca NOUN
Mallorca *fem*

make

> **make** can be a noun or a verb.

A NOUN
la **marca** *fem*
What make is that car?
¿De qué marca es ese coche?
B VERB
to make
1 **hacer**
I'm going to make a cake.
Voy a hacer una tarta.
They are making a lot of noise.
Están haciendo mucho ruido.
He made it himself.
Lo hizo él solo.
I make my bed every morning.
Me hago la cama todas las mañanas.
Two and two make four.
Dos y dos son cuatro.
Four take away two, what does that make?
Si a cuatro le quitamos dos, ¿cuánto queda?

made in Spain
fabricado en España
It's made of iron.
Es de hierro.

2 **ganar** (*earn*)
He makes a lot of money.
Gana mucho dinero.

make up VERB
inventar
You're making it up!
¡Te lo estás inventando!

make-up NOUN
el **maquillaje** *masc*

male ADJECTIVE
1 **macho** (*animal*)

LANGUAGE TIP
macho never changes its ending when it's used to describe a noun.
---

a male tortoise
una tortuga macho
2 **varón** *masc* (*on forms*)
Sex: male.
Sexo: varón.

man NOUN
el **hombre** *masc*
an old man
un hombre mayor

manage VERB
arreglárselas
It's okay, I can manage.
Está bien, yo me las arreglo.
I can't manage all that.
No puedo acabar con todo eso.
to manage to do something
conseguir hacer algo
I managed to fix my bike.
Conseguí arreglar mi bicicleta.

manager NOUN
1 el **director** *masc*
la **directora** *fem* (*of company*)
2 el **encargado** *masc*
la **encargada** *fem* (*of shop, restaurant*)
I'd like to speak to the manager.
Quiero hablar con el encargado.
3 el/la **gerente** *masc/fem* (*of hotel*)
4 el **entrenador** *masc*
la **entrenadora** *fem* (*of team*)

manageress NOUN
1 la **encargada** *fem* (*of shop, restaurant*)
2 la **gerente** *fem* (*of hotel*)

manners PL NOUN
los **modales** *masc pl*
> **good manners**
> buenos modales
> **Her manners are appalling.**
> Tiene muy malos modales.
> **It's bad manners to speak with your mouth full.**
> Es de mala educación hablar con la boca llena.

many ADJECTIVE, PRONOUN
muchos *masc pl*
muchas *fem pl*
> **He hasn't got many friends.**
> No tiene muchos amigos.
> **I haven't bought many magazines.**
> No he comprado muchas revistas.

> **How many?**
> ¿Cuántos?
> **Not many**
> No muchos.
> **too many**
> demasiados

> **How many...?**
> ¿Cuántos...?
> **How many sisters have you got?**
> ¿Cuántas hermanas tienes?

LANGUAGE TIP
Don't forget the accent on question words like **cuántos** nor the upside-down question mark at the start of questions.

> **That's too many.**
> Esos son demasiados.
> **You ask too many questions!**
> ¡Haces demasiadas preguntas!

map NOUN
1 el **mapa** *masc* (*of country, area*)
> **a map of Spain**
> un mapa de España

LANGUAGE TIP
Even though it ends in **-a**, **el mapa** is a masculine noun.

2 el **plano** *masc* (*of town*)
> **a map of London**
> un plano de Londres

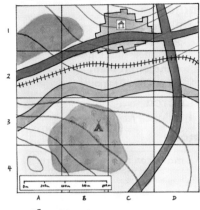

marathon NOUN
el **maratón** *masc* (PL los **maratones**)
> **the London marathon**
> el maratón de Londres

marbles PL NOUN
las **canicas** *fem pl*
> **Do you want to play marbles?**
> ¿Quieres jugar a las canicas?

LANGUAGE TIP
In Spanish, you need to include **a las** before **canicas** when talking about playing marbles.

March NOUN
marzo *masc*
> **My birthday's in March.**
> Mi cumpleaños es en marzo.
> **It's the twenty-ninth of March today.**
> Hoy es veintinueve de marzo.

> **in March**
> en marzo
> **on the fifth of March**
> el cinco de marzo

LANGUAGE TIP
Months are not spelled with a capital letter in Spanish.

Spanish

English

A
B
C
D
E
F
G
H
I
J
K
L
M
N
O
P
Q
R
S
T
U
V
W
X
Y
Z

margarine NOUN
la **margarina** *fem*

margin NOUN
el **margen** *masc* (PL los **márgenes**)
Write notes in the margin.
Escribid anotaciones en el margen.

mark

mark can be a noun or a verb.

A NOUN
1 la **nota** *fem* (*at school*)
I get good marks in English.
Saco buenas notas en inglés.
2 la **mancha** *fem* (*stain*)
You've got a mark on your shirt.
Tienes una mancha en la camisa.

On your marks, get set, go!
¡Preparados, listos, ya!

B VERB
to mark
corregir
She's got books to mark.
Tiene cuadernos para corregir.

market NOUN
el **mercado** *masc*

marmalade NOUN
la **mermelada de naranja** *fem*

LANGUAGE TIP
Don't forget to say **de naranja**
if you mean 'orange marmalade'.
La mermelada on its own just
means 'jam'.

marriage NOUN
el **matrimonio** *masc*

married ADJECTIVE
casado *masc*
casada *fem*
They are not married.
No están casados.
She's married to my cousin.
Está casada con mi primo.
to get married
casarse
They want to get married.
Quieren casarse.
My sister's getting married in June.
Mi hermana se va a casar en junio.
a married couple
un matrimonio

marry VERB
casarse con
He wants to marry her.
Quiere casarse con ella.

marvellous ADJECTIVE
estupendo *masc*
estupenda *fem*
She's a marvellous cook.
Es una cocinera estupenda.
The weather was marvellous.
Hizo un tiempo estupendo.

masculine ADJECTIVE
masculino *masc*
masculina *fem*

mashed potatoes PL NOUN
el **puré de patatas** *masc*
sausages and mashed potatoes
salchichas con puré de patatas

mask NOUN
la **máscara** *fem*

mass NOUN
1 el **montón** *masc* (PL los **montones**)
a mass of books and papers
un montón de libros y papeles
We've got masses of homework today.
Hoy tenemos montones de deberes.

2 la **misa** *fem* (*in church*)
We go to mass on Sundays.
Vamos a misa los domingos.

massive ADJECTIVE
enorme *masc/fem*

masterpiece NOUN
la **obra maestra** *fem*

mat NOUN
el **felpudo** *masc* (*doormat*)
Wipe your feet on the mat.
Límpiate los pies en el felpudo.

LANGUAGE TIP
In Spanish you usually use an article
like **el**, **la** or **los**, **las** with parts of the
body.

---

match

| **match** can be a noun or a verb. |

A NOUN
1 la **cerilla** *fem*
(*for striking*)
a box of matches
una caja de cerillas
2 el **partido** *masc*
(*game*)
a football match
un partido de fútbol
B VERB
to match
1 **hacer juego con** (*go with*)
The jacket matches the trousers.
La chaqueta hace juego con los
pantalones.
2 **hacer corresponder con** (*put
with*)
Match the words to the pictures.
Haz corresponder las palabras con las
imágenes.

matching ADJECTIVE
a juego
**My bedroom has matching
wallpaper and curtains.**
Mi habitación tiene el papel y las
cortinas a juego.

mate NOUN
el **amigo** *masc*
la **amiga** *fem* (*friend*)
He's my mate.
Es mi amigo.

material NOUN
la **tela** *fem* (*cloth*)
It's made of red material.
Está hecho de tela roja.

maths NOUN
las **matemáticas** *fem*

matter

| **matter** can be a noun or a verb. |

A NOUN
**What's the matter? Why are you
crying?**
¿Qué pasa? ¿Por qué estás llorando?
What's the matter with him?
¿Qué le pasa?
B VERB
to matter
importar
It doesn't matter.
No importa.

mattress NOUN
el **colchón** *masc* (PL los **colchones**)

maximum ADJECTIVE
máximo *masc*
máxima *fem*

May NOUN
mayo *masc*
My birthday's in May.
Mi cumpleaños es en mayo.
It's the eleventh of May today.
Hoy es once de mayo.

in May
en mayo
on the fifth of May
el cinco de mayo

LANGUAGE TIP
Months are not spelled with a capital
letter in Spanish.

may VERB
May I come in?
¿Puedo entrar?
She may not come.
Puede que no venga.

maybe ADVERB
a lo mejor
maybe not
a lo mejor no
Maybe she's at home.
A lo mejor está en casa.

mayonnaise NOUN
la **mayonesa** *fem*

mayor NOUN
el **alcalde** *masc*
la **alcaldesa** *fem*

maze NOUN
el **laberinto** *masc*

me PRONOUN
1 me
Do you love me?
¿Me quieres?
Can you help me?
¿Me puedes ayudar?
Wait for me!
¡Espérame!
Are you looking for me?
¿Me estás buscando?
Can you give it to me?
¿Me lo puedes dar?
He wants to talk to me.
Quiere hablar conmigo.
2 mí

LANGUAGE TIP
Use **mí** after a preposition.

Is it for me?
¿Es para mí?
You're after me.
Tú vas detrás de mí.

LANGUAGE TIP
Remember that **with me** translates as
conmigo.

He was with me.
Estaba conmigo.
3 yo

LANGUAGE TIP
Use **yo** after the verb **ser**.

It's me.
Soy yo.

LANGUAGE TIP
Use **yo** in comparisons.

He's taller than me.
Es más alto que yo.

It's me.
Soy yo.
Me too.
Yo también.
Excuse me!
¡Perdóname!

meal NOUN
la **comida** *fem*

mean

mean can be a verb or an adjective.

A VERB
to mean
significar
What does 'complete' mean?
¿Qué significa "complete"?
I don't know what it means.
No sé lo que significa.
What do you mean?
¿Qué quieres decir?
That's not what I mean.
Eso no es lo que quiero decir.

A
B
C
D
E
F
G
H
I
J
K
L
M
N
O
P
Q
R
S
T
U
V
W
X
Y
Z

What does it mean?
¿Qué significa?

B ADJECTIVE
1 **tacaño** *masc*
   tacaña *fem* (*with money*)
   He's too mean to buy presents.
   Es demasiado tacaño para comprar regalos.
2 **mezquino** *masc*
   mezquina *fem* (*unkind*)
   You're being mean to me.
   Estás siendo mezquina conmigo.

meaning NOUN
el **significado** *masc*

measles NOUN
el **sarampión** *masc*

measure VERB
medir
   Measure the length.
   Medid la longitud.

meat NOUN
la **carne** *fem*
   I don't eat meat.
   No como carne.

Mecca NOUN
La Meca *fem*

mechanic NOUN
el **mecánico** *masc*
la **mecánica** *fem*
   He's a mechanic.
   Es mecánico.

LANGUAGE TIP
In Spanish, you do not use an article with people's jobs.

---

medal NOUN
la **medalla** *fem*
   the gold medal
   la medalla de oro

medical

medical can be an adjective or a noun.

A ADJECTIVE
   She's a medical student.
   Es estudiante de medicina.
B NOUN
   You have to have a medical.
   Necesitas hacerte una revisión médica.

medicine NOUN
la **medicina** *masc*
   What's this medicine for?
   ¿Para qué es esta medicina?
   I want to study medicine.
   Quiero estudiar medicina.

Mediterranean NOUN
el **Mediterráneo** *masc*

medium ADJECTIVE
mediano *masc*
mediana *fem*
   a man of medium height
   un hombre de estatura mediana
   Small, medium or large?
   ¿Pequeño, mediano o grande?

medium-sized ADJECTIVE
de tamaño medio
   a medium-sized town
   una ciudad de tamaño medio

meet VERB
1 **encontrarse con** (*by chance*)
   I met Amos in town.
   Me encontré con Amos en el centro.
2 **quedar** (*by arrangement*)
   Let's meet in front of the museum.
   ¿Por qué no quedamos delante del museo?
   I'm meeting my friends at the swimming pool.
   He quedado con mis amigos en la piscina.
3 **conocer** (*get to know*)
   He met Jamie at a party.
   Conoció a Jamie en una fiesta.

LANGUAGE TIP
Don't forget the personal **a** after **conocer** when you name the person.

Have you met Amy?
¿Conoces a Amy?
Where did you two meet?
¿Dónde os conocisteis vosotros dos?
4 **recoger** (*pick up*)
I'll meet you at the station.
Te recogeré en la estación.

meeting NOUN
la **reunión** *fem* (PL las **reuniones**)
the club's first meeting
la primera reunión del club

melon NOUN
el **melón** *masc* (PL los **melones**)

melt VERB
derretirse
The snow is melting.
La nieve se está derritiendo.

member NOUN
el **socio** *masc*
la **socia** *fem*
a member of our club
un socio de nuestro club

meme NOUN
el **meme** *masc*
This is a very popular internet meme.
Este es un meme muy popular en internet.

memory NOUN
1 la **memoria** *fem* (*for facts, words*)
I haven't got a good memory.
No tengo buena memoria.
2 el **recuerdo** *masc* (*of past*)
some happy memories
algunos recuerdos felices

men PL NOUN
los **hombres** *masc pl*

mend VERB
arreglar
Can you mend it?
¿Puedes arreglarlo?

mention VERB
Thank you! — Don't mention it!
¡Gracias! — ¡De nada!

menu NOUN
1 la **carta** *fem* (*in restaurant*)
Could I have the menu please?
¿Me trae la carta por favor?
2 el **menú** *masc* (*on computer*)

merry ADJECTIVE

Merry Christmas!
¡Feliz Navidad!

LANGUAGE TIP
Have you noticed the upside-down exclamation mark at the start of Spanish exclamations?

merry-go-round NOUN
el **tiovivo** *masc*

mess NOUN
el **desorden** *masc*
What a mess!
¡Qué desorden!
My bedroom's in a mess.
Mi habitación está desordenada.

message NOUN
el **mensaje** *masc*

met VERB ▷ *see* **meet**

metal NOUN
el **metal** *masc*

method NOUN
el **método** *masc*

metre NOUN
el **metro** *masc*
I can swim two hundred metres.
Puedo nadar doscientos metros.
I'm one metre thirty tall.
Mido un metro treinta.

A
B
C
D
E
F
G
H
I
J
K
L
M
N
O
P
Q
R
S
T
U
V
W
X
Y
Z

470

metric ADJECTIVE
   métrico *masc*
   métrica *fem*

mice PL NOUN
   los **ratones** *masc pl*

microphone NOUN
   el **micrófono** *masc*

microscope NOUN
   el **microscopio** *masc*

microwave NOUN
   el **microondas** *masc*
   (PL los **microondas**)

midday NOUN
   el **mediodía** *masc*
     It's midday.
     Es mediodía.

> **at midday**
> al mediodía

> **LANGUAGE TIP**
> Even though it ends in **-a, el mediodía**, like **día**, is a masculine noun.

middle NOUN
   el **centro** *masc*
     Come into the middle, Anita.
     Ven al centro, Anita.
     in the middle of the road
     en medio de la carretera
     in the middle of the night
     en mitad de la noche

middle-aged ADJECTIVE
   de **mediana edad**
     a middle-aged man
     un hombre de mediana edad

middle name NOUN
   el **segundo nombre** *masc*
     It's my middle name.
     Es mi segundo nombre.

midge NOUN
   el **mosquito** *masc*

midnight NOUN
   la **medianoche** *fem*
     It's midnight.
     Es medianoche.

> **at midnight**
> a medianoche

might VERB
     I might, I might not.
     Puede que sí, puede que no.

> **LANGUAGE TIP**
> Literally, **puede que sí, puede que no** means 'maybe, maybe not'.

     It might rain.
     Puede que llueva.

migraine NOUN
   la **jaqueca** *fem*
     I've got a migraine.
     Tengo jaqueca.

mild ADJECTIVE
   suave *masc/fem*
     The winters are quite mild.
     Los inviernos son bastante suaves.
     It's mild today.
     No hace mucho frío hoy.

mile NOUN
   la **milla** *fem*
     It's five miles from here.
     Está a cinco millas de aquí.
     We walked miles!
     ¡Caminamos durante kilómetros!

> **DID YOU KNOW...?**
> In Spain distances are measured in kilometres. A mile is about 1.6 kilometres.

milk NOUN
  la **leche** *fem*
  tea with milk
  té con leche

milkman NOUN
  el **lechero** *masc*

LANGUAGE TIP
In Spanish, you do not use an article with people's jobs.

---

milk shake NOUN
  el **batido** *masc*

millimetre
NOUN
el **milímetro**
masc

million NOUN
  el **millón** *masc*
  (PL los **millones**)
  a million times
  un millón de veces
  two million
  dos millones

millionaire NOUN
  el **millonario** *masc*
  la **millonaria** *fem*

mince NOUN
  la **carne picada** *fem*

DID YOU KNOW...?
Mince pies are not eaten in Spain.

---

mind

mind can be a verb or a noun.

A VERB
  to mind
  Do you mind if I open the window?
  ¿Le importa si abro la ventana?
  Mind the step!
  ¡Cuidado con el escalón!

  I don't mind.
  No me importa.

  Never mind!
  ¡No importa!

B NOUN
  I've changed my mind.
  He cambiado de idea.
  Make your mind up!
  ¡Decídete ya!

mine

mine can be a pronoun or a noun.

A PRONOUN
  el **mío** *masc*
  la **mía** *fem*

LANGUAGE TIP
Remember that the choice of **el mío**, **la mía**, **los míos** or **las mías** depends entirely on the thing or things referred to and not on the person who owns it or them.

  That's not my coat. Mine is here.
  Ese no es mi abrigo. El mío está aquí.
  Those aren't my boots. Mine are here.
  Esas no son mis botas. Las mías están aquí.

LANGUAGE TIP
After **ser**, you can often just use **mío**, **mía**, **míos** or **mías** to agree with the noun referred to.

  This scarf is mine.
  Esta bufanda es mía.
  These books are mine.
  Estos libros son míos.

  a friend of mine
  una amigo mío
  It's mine.
  Es mío.

B NOUN
  la **mina** *fem*
  a coal mine
  una mina de carbón

Spanish

English

A
B
C
D
E
F
G
H
I
J
K
L
M
N
O
P
Q
R
S
T
U
V
W
X
Y
Z

472

mineral water NOUN
el **agua mineral** *fem*
A mineral water for me, please.
Para mí agua mineral, por favor.

LANGUAGE TIP
Even though it's a feminine noun,
remember that you use **el** and **un** with
agua.

minibus NOUN
el **microbús** *masc* (PL los
microbuses)

minimum ADJECTIVE
mínimo *masc*
mínima *fem*

miniskirt NOUN
la **minifalda** *fem*

minister NOUN
1 el **ministro** *masc*
la **ministra** *fem* (*in government*)
2 el **pastor** *masc*
la **pastora** *fem* (*in church*)

minor ADJECTIVE
de poca importancia
a minor problem
un problema de poca importancia
a minor injury
una herida leve

mint NOUN
1 el **caramelo de menta** *masc*
(*sweet*)
2 la **hierbabuena** *fem* (*plant*)
mint sauce
salsa de menta

minus PREPOSITION
menos
**Seventeen minus three is
fourteen.**
Diecisiete menos tres son catorce.
It's minus two degrees outside.
Fuera hace dos grados bajo cero.

minute NOUN
el **minuto** *masc*
Wait a minute!
¡Espera un minuto!

mirror NOUN
el **espejo** *masc*

misbehave VERB
portarse mal
She's misbehaving.
Se está portando mal.
Don't misbehave, Patrick!
¡No te portes mal, Patrick!

mischief NOUN
las **travesuras** *fem pl*
**My little sister's always up to
mischief.**
Mi hermana pequeña siempre está
haciendo travesuras.

miserable ADJECTIVE
1 **muy triste** *masc/fem* (*person*)
You're looking miserable.
Pareces muy triste.
2 **deprimente** *masc/fem*
(*weather*)
The weather was miserable.
El tiempo fue deprimente.

Miss NOUN
1 la **señorita** *fem*
Yes, Miss.
Sí, señorita.
2 **Srta.** (*in addresses*)
Miss Jones
Srta. Jones

LANGUAGE TIP
Don't forget the dot at the end of
Spanish abbreviations.

miss VERB
1 **perder**

Hurry or you'll miss the bus.
Date prisa o perderás el autobús.
Miss a turn.
Pierde un turno.
2 **echar de menos** (*long for*)
I miss you.
Te echo de menos.
He misses his family.
Echa de menos a su familia.

LANGUAGE TIP
Don't forget the personal **a** in examples like this one.

---

missing ADJECTIVE
perdido *masc*
perdida *fem*
   the missing piece
   la pieza perdida
   to be missing
   faltar
   My rucksack is missing.
   Falta mi mochila.
   Two children are missing.
   Faltan dos niños.

mist NOUN
   la **neblina** *fem*

mistake NOUN
   el **error** *masc*
   She only made two mistakes.
   Solo cometió dos errores.
   a spelling mistake
   una falta de ortografía
   by mistake
   por error
   I took his bag by mistake.
   Cogí su bolso por error.

mistletoe NOUN
   el **muérdago** *masc*

misty ADJECTIVE
   de neblina
   a misty morning
   una mañana de neblina

   It's misty.
   Hay neblina.

mix VERB
   mezclar
   Mix the flour with the sugar.
   Mezclar la harina con el azúcar.

mix up VERB
   confundir
   He always mixes me up with my sister.
   Siempre me confunde con mi hermana.

mixed ADJECTIVE
   mixto *masc*
   mixta *fem*
   a mixed school
   un colegio mixto

mixture NOUN
   la **mezcla** *fem*

mix-up NOUN
   el **lío** *masc*

mobile NOUN
   el **móvil** *masc*
   I haven't got a mobile.
   No tengo móvil.

model

> **model** can be a noun or an adjective.

A NOUN
1 la **maqueta** *fem* (*small version*)
   I'm making a model of the castle.
   Estoy haciendo una maqueta del castillo.
2 el/la **modelo** *masc/fem* (*person*)
   She's a famous model.
   Es una modelo famosa.

LANGUAGE TIP
Even though **modelo** ends in **-o**, you can use it to refer to a woman.

B ADJECTIVE
a model plane
una maqueta de avión
a model railway
una vía férrea en miniatura

modern ADJECTIVE
moderno *masc*
moderna *fem*

moment NOUN
el **momento** *masc*
Wait a moment, Mike.
Espera un momento, Mike.
Could you wait a moment?
¿Puedes esperar un momento?
in a moment
dentro de un momento
I'm a bit busy at the moment.
Estoy algo ocupado en este momento.

Just a moment!
¡Un momento!
at the moment
en este momento

Monday NOUN
el **lunes** *masc*
It's Monday today.
Hoy es lunes.

on Monday
el lunes
on Mondays
los lunes
every Monday
cada lunes
last Monday
el lunes pasado
next Monday
el lunes que viene

LANGUAGE TIP
Days are not spelled with a capital
letter in Spanish.

money NOUN
el **dinero** *masc*
I haven't got enough money.
No tengo suficiente dinero.

I need to change some money.
Necesito cambiar dinero.

monk NOUN
el **monje** *masc*

monkey NOUN
el **mono** *masc*

monster NOUN
el **monstruo** *masc*

month NOUN
el **mes** *masc*
two months
dos meses
**at the end of the
month**
a final de mes

this month
este mes
next month
el mes que viene
last month
el mes pasado
every month
cada mes
What month is it?
¿Qué mes es?

monument NOUN
el **monumento** *masc*

mood NOUN
el **humor** *masc*
She's in a bad mood.
Está de mal humor.
He's in a good mood.
Está de buen humor.

moon NOUN
la **luna** *fem*
the moon and the stars
la luna y las estrellas

moped NOUN
el **ciclomotor** *masc*

more ADVERB, ADJECTIVE, PRONOUN
más
more difficult
más difícil

Could you speak more slowly?
¿Puedes hablar más despacio?
There are more girls in the class.
Hay más chicas en la clase.
Do you want some more tea?
¿Quieres más té?
Would you like some more, Luke?
¿Quieres más, Luke?
There isn't any more.
Ya no queda más.
Two more minutes!
¡Dos minutos más!

LANGUAGE TIP
You normally translate **more than** using **más que**.

more than me
más que yo
He's more intelligent than me.
Es más inteligente que yo.
more than that
más que eso

LANGUAGE TIP
Use **más de** instead before numbers.

I've got more than fifty euros.
Tengo más de cincuenta euros.

a bit more
un poco más
more ... than
más ... que

morning NOUN
la **mañana** fem
on Saturday morning
el sábado por la mañana
all morning
toda la mañana
Are they staying all morning?
¿Se quedan toda la mañana?

this morning
esta mañana
tomorrow morning
mañana por la mañana
yesterday morning
ayer por la mañana

every morning
todas las mañanas
at seven o'clock in the morning
a las siete de la mañana

mosque NOUN
la **mezquita** fem
mosquito NOUN
el **mosquito** masc
a mosquito bite
una picadura de mosquito

most ADVERB, ADJECTIVE, PRONOUN

LANGUAGE TIP
When **most** goes with an adjective or verb, it usually translates as **más**.

the most expensive restaurant
el restaurante más caro
the most expensive restaurants
los restaurantes más caros
Stephen talks the most.
Stephen es el que más habla.
He got the most votes.
Fue él que sacó más votos.

LANGUAGE TIP
You can usually use **la mayoría de** to translate **most of** with a plural noun.

most of my friends
la mayoría de mis amigos
most of them
la mayoría
most Spanish people
la mayoría de los españoles

LANGUAGE TIP
Use **la mayor parte de** to translate **most of** with a singular noun.

most of the time
la mayor parte del tiempo
most of the class
la mayor parte de la clase
at the most
como máximo
two hours at the most
dos horas como máximo

A
B
C
D
E
F
G
H
I
J
K
L
M
N
O
P
Q
R
S
T
U
V
W
X
Y
Z

motel NOUN
el **motel** *masc*

moth NOUN
la **mariposa nocturna** *fem*

mother NOUN
la **madre** *fem*
my mother
mi madre
your mother
tu madre
my mother and father
mis padres

Mother's Day NOUN
el **día de la Madre**
It's Mother's Day on Sunday.
El domingo es el día de la Madre.

Happy Mother's Day!
¡Feliz día de la Madre!

LANGUAGE TIP
Have you noticed the upside-down
exclamation mark at the start of
Spanish exclamations?

motor NOUN
el **motor** *masc*

motorbike NOUN
la **moto** *fem*

LANGUAGE TIP
Even though it ends in **-o**, **la moto** is a
feminine noun.

motorboat NOUN
la **lancha motora** *fem*

motorcycle NOUN
la **motocicleta** *fem*

motorcyclist NOUN
el/la **motociclista** *masc/fem*

motorist NOUN
el/la **automovilista** *masc/fem*

motorway NOUN
la **autopista** *fem*
on the motorway
en la autopista

mountain NOUN
la **montaña** *fem*

mountain bike NOUN
la **bicicleta de montaña** *fem*

mouse NOUN
el **ratón** *masc* (PL los **ratones**)

mousse NOUN
la **mousse** *fem*
chocolate mousse
la mousse de chocolate

moustache NOUN
el **bigote** *masc*
He's got a moustache.
Tiene bigote.

mouth NOUN
la **boca** *fem*
Open your mouth.
Abre la boca.

LANGUAGE TIP
In Spanish you usually use an article
like **el**, **la** or **los**, **las** with parts of the
body.

move

move can be a noun or a verb.

A NOUN

el **turno** *masc*

It's your move.
Es tu turno.

Get a move on, Sebastian!
¡Muévete, Sebastian!

B VERB

to move

1 **mover** (*object*)

Could you move your stuff, please?
¿Puedes mover tus cosas, por favor?

2 **moverse** (*change position*)

Don't move!
¡No te muevas!

You moved!
¡Te has movido!

Move forward two spaces!
¡Adelanta dos casillas!

move over VERB

correrse

Could you move over a bit?
¿Puedes correrte un poco?

movement NOUN

el **movimiento** *masc*

movie NOUN

la **película** *fem*

an action movie
una película de acción

MP NOUN

el **diputado** *masc*
la **diputada** *fem*

She's an MP.
Es diputada.

LANGUAGE TIP
In Spanish, you do not use an article with people's jobs.

Mr NOUN

1 el **señor** *masc*

Good morning, Mr Jones.
¡Buenos días, señor Jones!

Mr Jones wants to see you.
El señor Jones quiere verte.

Mr and Mrs Carrasco are here.
Los señores Carrasco están aquí.

2 **Sr.** (*in addresses*)

Mr Silvestre
Sr. Silvestre

Mr and Mrs Ruiz
Srs. Ruiz

LANGUAGE TIP
Don't forget the dot at the end of Spanish abbreviations.

Mrs NOUN

1 la **señora** *fem*

Good morning, Mrs Jones.
¡Buenos días, señora Jones!

Mrs Jones wants to see you.
La señora Jones quiere verte.

2 **Sra.** (*in addresses*)

Mrs Silvestre
Sra. Silvestre

LANGUAGE TIP
Don't forget the dot at the end of Spanish abbreviations.

Ms NOUN

1 la **señora** *fem*

Ms Smith is here.
La señora Smith está aquí.

2 **Sra.** (*in addresses*)

DID YOU KNOW...?
There isn't a specific word for **Ms** in Spanish. Just use **Sra.**

---

much ADJECTIVE, ADVERB, PRONOUN

1 **mucho** *masc*
mucha *fem*

not much
no mucho

I haven't got much money.
No tengo mucho dinero.

I don't want very much milk.
No quiero mucha leche.

I don't like sport much.
No me gusta mucho el deporte.

I don't want much.
No quiero mucho.

I like England very much.
Me gusta muchísimo Inglaterra.

2 How much?
¿Cuánto?
How much money have you got?
¿Cuánto dinero tienes?
How much jam is left?
¿Cuánta mermelada queda?

LANGUAGE TIP
Don't forget the accent on question words like **cuánto** nor the upside-down question mark at the start of questions.

How much does it cost?
¿Cuánto cuesta?
How much do you want?
¿Cuánto quieres?
How much is it all together?
¿Cuánto es todo junto?
3 too much butter
demasiada mantequilla
It costs too much.
Cuesta demasiado.
That's too much!
¡Eso es demasiado!

not much
no mucho
How much?
¿Cuánto?
too much
demasiado
Thank you very much.
Muchas gracias.

mud NOUN
el **barro** masc

muddy ADJECTIVE
cubierto de barro masc
cubierta de barro fem

mug NOUN
el **tazón** masc (PL los **tazones**)
Do you want a cup or a mug?
¿Quieres una taza o un tazón?

multiply VERB
multiplicar
Multiply six by three.
Multiplica seis por tres.

Two multiplied by three is six.
Dos multiplicado por tres son seis.

mum NOUN
1 la **madre** fem
my mum
mi madre
my mum and dad
mis padres
2 la **mamá** fem
(used as name)
Hi, Mum.
Hola, mamá.
I'll ask Mum.
Se lo preguntaré
a mamá.

mummy NOUN
la **mamá** fem
Hello, Mummy!
¡Hola, mamá!

mumps NOUN
las **paperas** fem pl
Teresa has got mumps.
Teresa tiene paperas.

murder NOUN
el **asesinato** masc

muscle NOUN
el **músculo** masc

museum NOUN
el **museo** masc

mushroom NOUN
1 el **champiñón** masc
(PL los **champiñones**)
(button mushroom)
2 la **seta** fem
(open-cup mushroom)

music NOUN
la **música** fem
I like listening to music.
Me gusta escuchar música.

musical instrument NOUN
el **instrumento musical** *masc*
Can you play a musical instrument?
¿Sabes tocar algún instrumento musical?

musician NOUN
el **músico** *masc*
la **música** *fem*

Muslim NOUN
el **musulmán** *masc* (PL los **musulmanes**)
la **musulmana** *fem*
He's a Muslim.
Es musulmán.

LANGUAGE TIP
Remember that **musulmán** is not spelled with a capital letter in Spanish.

mussel NOUN
el **mejillón** *masc* (PL los **mejillones**)

must VERB
1 **tener que** (*have to*)
You must be careful, Conor.
Tienes que tener cuidado, Conor.
You must listen, children.
Tenéis que escuchar, niños.
2 **deber de** (*in guesses*)
You must be tired.
Debes de estar cansado.

mustard NOUN
la **mostaza** *fem*

mustn't (= must not) ▷ see **must**

my ADJECTIVE
mi *masc/fem* (PL **mis**)

LANGUAGE TIP
Remember to use **mi** before a singular noun and **mis** before a plural one.

my father
mi padre
my friend Alicia
mi amiga Alicia
my parents
mis padres

LANGUAGE TIP
In Spanish you usually use an article like **el**, **la** or **los**, **las** with parts of the body and clothes.

I wash my face in the morning.
Me lavo la cara por las mañanas.
I'm going to wear my shorts today.
Voy a llevar los pantalones cortos hoy.

myself PRONOUN
1 **me** (*reflexive use*)
I've hurt myself.
Me he hecho daño.
I like to look at myself in the mirror.
Me gusta mirarme en el espejo.
I'm enjoying myself.
Me estoy divirtiendo.
2 **mí** (*after preposition*)
I'll tell you about myself.
Te contaré sobre mí.
3 **yo mismo** *masc*
yo misma *fem* (*for emphasis*)
I made it myself.
Lo hice yo mismo.
4 **by myself**
solo *masc*
sola *fem*
I don't like travelling by myself.
No me gusta viajar solo.

mysterious ADJECTIVE
misterioso *masc*
misteriosa *fem*

mystery NOUN
el **misterio** *masc*

nail NOUN

1 la **uña** *fem (fingernail)*
Don't bite your nails!
¡No te muerdas las uñas!

LANGUAGE TIP
In Spanish you usually use an article like **el**, **la** or **los**, **las** with parts of the body.

2 el **clavo** *masc (for hammering)*

nailfile NOUN
la **lima de uñas** *fem*

nail varnish NOUN
el **esmalte de uñas** *masc*

naked ADJECTIVE
desnudo *masc*
desnuda *fem*

name NOUN
el **nombre** *masc*
a pretty name
un nombre bonito
What's your dog's name?
¿Cómo se llama tu perro?
His name's Max.
Se llama Max.

What's your name?
¿Cómo te llamas?
My name is Rosie.
Me llamo Rosie.

nanny NOUN

1 la **niñera** *fem*
She's a nanny.
Es niñera.

LANGUAGE TIP
In Spanish, you do not use an article with people's jobs.

2 la **abuela** *fem*

napkin NOUN
la **servilleta** *fem*

narrow ADJECTIVE
estrecho *masc*
estrecha *fem*
a narrow street
una calle estrecha

nasty ADJECTIVE

1 **malo** *masc*
mala *fem*
Don't be nasty!
¡No seas malo!

LANGUAGE TIP
Shorten **malo** to **mal** before a masculine singular noun.

a nasty smell
un mal olor
a nasty cold
un resfriado terrible
2 **He's a nasty man.**
Es un hombre con mala idea.

nationality NOUN
la **nacionalidad** *fem*

natural ADJECTIVE
natural *masc/fem*

nature NOUN
la **naturaleza** *fem*

naughty ADJECTIVE
travieso *masc*
traviesa *fem*
Naughty girl!
¡Qué chica más traviesa!
Don't be naughty!
¡No seas malo!

navy NOUN
la **armada** *fem*
> **He's in the navy.**
> Está en la armada.

navy-blue

> **navy-blue** can be an adjective or a
> noun.

A ADJECTIVE
azul marino

LANGUAGE TIP
azul marino never changes its endings
to agree with the noun it describes.

---

a navy-blue skirt
una falda azul marino
B NOUN
el **azul marino** *masc*

near

> **near** can be an adverb, adjective or
> preposition.

A ADVERB, ADJECTIVE
1 cerca

LANGUAGE TIP
Use **cerca** when saying that
something or someone is near. As it's
an adverb, it never changes its ending.

It's fairly near.
Está bastante cerca.
2 cercano *masc*
cercana *fem*

LANGUAGE TIP
Use the adjective **cercano, cercana,**
etc in noun phrases.

---

the nearest village
el pueblo más cercano
**Where's the nearest service
station?**
¿Dónde está la gasolinera más cercana?
**The nearest shops are three
kilometres away.**
Las tiendas más cercanas están a tres
kilómetros.

B PREPOSITION
cerca de (*close to*)
> **I live near Liverpool.**
> Vivo cerca de Liverpool.
> **near my house**
> cerca de mi casa
> **near here**
> cerca de aquí
> **Is there a bank near here?**
> ¿Hay un banco cerca de aquí?

LANGUAGE TIP
Another way of saying **near here** is
por aquí cerca.

> **Is there a supermarket near here?**
> ¿Hay un supermercado por aquí cerca?

nearby ADVERB
cerca
> **There's a supermarket nearby.**
> Hay un supermercado cerca.

nearly ADVERB
casi
> **Dinner's nearly ready.**
> La cena está casi lista.
> **I'm nearly ten.**
> Tengo casi diez años.

neat ADJECTIVE
1 ordenado *masc*
ordenada *fem* (*room, desk*)
> **a neat room**
> una habitación ordenada
2 claro *masc*
clara *fem* (*writing*)
> **She has very neat writing.**
> Tiene una letra muy clara.

necessary ADJECTIVE
necesario *masc*
necesaria *fem*

neck NOUN
el **cuello** *masc*
> **I've hurt my neck.**
> Me he hecho daño en el cuello.

LANGUAGE TIP
In Spanish you usually use an article
like **el, la** or **los, las** with parts of the
body.

---

necklace NOUN
el **collar**
masc

a **diamond necklace**
un collar de diamantes

need VERB
necesitar
I need a rubber.
Necesito una goma de borrar.
to need to
tener que
I need to wash the dishes.
Tengo que fregar los platos.

needle NOUN
la **aguja** fem

neighbour NOUN
el **vecino** masc
la **vecina** fem
the neighbours' garden
el jardín de los vecinos

neighbourhood NOUN
el **barrio** masc

neither PRONOUN, CONJUNCTION, ADVERB
ni una cosa ni otra
Carrots or peas? — Neither, thanks.
¿Zanahorias o guisantes? — Ni una cosa ni otra, gracias.
neither ... nor ...
ni ... ni ...
Neither Sarah nor Julia is coming to the party.
Ni Sarah ni Julia vienen a la fiesta.

Neither do I.
Yo tampoco.
Neither have I.
Yo tampoco.

nephew NOUN
el **sobrino** masc
her nephew
su sobrino

nerve NOUN
el **nervio** masc
She gets on my nerves.
Me pone de los nervios.

nervous ADJECTIVE
nervioso masc
nerviosa fem
I bite my nails when I'm nervous.
Cuando estoy nervioso me muerdo las uñas.

Net NOUN
the Net
internet
I like to surf the Net.
Me gusta navegar por internet.

netball NOUN

DID YOU KNOW...?
Netball is not played in Spain. The most similar game played there is **el baloncesto** (basketball).

never ADVERB
nunca
When are you going to phone him? — Never!
¿Cuándo vas a telefonearle? — ¡Nunca!
I never go to the cinema.
Nunca voy al cine.
We never see them.
No los vemos nunca.

LANGUAGE TIP
Don't forget to put **no** before the verb when putting **nunca** after it.

new ADJECTIVE
nuevo *masc*
nueva *fem*

> **LANGUAGE TIP**
> When **new** means **brand-new**, you usually put **nuevo** after the noun.

a new skirt
una falda nueva

> **LANGUAGE TIP**
> When **new** means **replacement** rather than **brand-new**, you usually put **nuevo** before the noun.

her new boyfriend
su nuevo novio

news NOUN
1 la **noticia** *fem*

> **LANGUAGE TIP**
> Use **noticia** in the singular when you're referring to a single piece of news.

That's wonderful news!
¡Eso es una noticia estupenda!
2 las **noticias** *fem pl*

> **LANGUAGE TIP**
> Use **noticias** in the plural when you're referring to more than one piece of news or to a news bulletin.

It was on the news.
Salió en las noticias.

newsagent's NOUN
la **tienda de periódicos** *fem*

> **DID YOU KNOW...?**
> In Spain you'll come across **kioscos**, newsstands on the street which sell newspapers, magazines and other items.

newspaper NOUN
el **periódico** *masc*

New Year NOUN
New Year's Day
el Día de Año Nuevo

New Year's Eve
la Nochevieja

Happy New Year!
¡Feliz Año Nuevo!

> **DID YOU KNOW...?**
> In Spain, it's traditional to see the New Year in by eating **doce uvas** (twelve grapes) for good luck as the clock strikes midnight.

next

> **next** can be an adjective or adverb.

A ADJECTIVE
1 **próximo** *masc*
próxima *fem* (*in sequence*)
the next time
la próxima vez
Who's next?
¿A quién le toca?
I'm next.
Me toca a mí.
2 **que viene** (*coming*)
next Saturday
el sábado que viene

next year
el año que viene
next week
la semana que viene
next summer
el verano que viene

3 **They live next door.**
Viven al lado.
the flat next door
el piso de al lado
B ADVERB
1 **después** (*afterwards*)
What shall I do next?
¿Qué hago después?
2 **next to**
al lado de
It's next to the bank.
Está al lado del banco.
I sit next to my friend.
Me siento al lado de mi amigo.

A
B
C
D
E
F
G
H
I
J
K
L
M
N
O
P
Q
R
S
T
U
V
W
X
Y
Z

next-door ADJECTIVE
 de al lado
  the next-door flat
  el piso de al lado

nice ADJECTIVE
 1 **simpático** *masc*
  simpática *fem* (*friendly*)
  Your parents are very nice.
  Tus padres son muy simpáticos.
 2 **amable** *masc/fem* (*kind*)
  She was always very nice to me.
  Siempre fue muy amable conmigo.
 3 **bonito** (*pretty*)
  Granada is a nice town.
  Granada es una ciudad bonita.
  What a nice dress!
  ¡Qué vestido más bonito!
 4 **bueno** (*good*)
  The soup is very nice.
  La sopa está muy buena.

LANGUAGE TIP
Shorten **bueno** to **buen** before a
masculine singular noun.

---

 nice weather
 buen tiempo

 Have a nice time!
 ¡Que te diviertas!
 It's a nice day.
 Hace buen día.

niece NOUN
 la **sobrina** *fem*
  his niece
  su sobrina

night NOUN
 la **noche** *fem*
  I want a room for two nights.
  Quiero una habitación para dos
  noches.
  We arrived last night.
  Llegamos anoche.

 last night
 anoche

tomorrow night
mañana por la noche

nightie NOUN
 el **camisón** *masc* (PL los **camisones**)

nightmare NOUN
 la **pesadilla** *fem*
  I have nightmares.
  Tengo pesadillas.

nil NOUN
 el **cero** *masc*
  We won two-nil.
  Ganamos dos a cero.

nine NUMBER
 nueve
  nine euros
  nueve euros

  She's nine.
  Tiene nueve años.

LANGUAGE TIP
In English you can say **she's nine** or
she's nine years old. In Spanish you
can only say **tiene nueve años**. Have
you noticed that in Spanish you need
to use the verb **tener** to talk about
somebody's age?

---

nineteen NUMBER
 diecinueve
  nineteen euros
  diecinueve euros

  She's nineteen.
  Tiene diecinueve años.

LANGUAGE TIP
In English you can say **she's nineteen**
or **she's nineteen years old**. In
Spanish you can only say **tiene
diecinueve años**. Have you noticed
that in Spanish you need to use the verb
tener to talk about somebody's age?

nineteenth NUMBER
  diecinueve
    on the nineteenth floor
    en la planta diecinueve
    **We break up on the nineteenth of
    December.**
    Empezamos las vacaciones el
    diecinueve de diciembre.
    **It's the nineteenth of February
    today.**
    Hoy es diecinueve de febrero.

    on the nineteenth of August
    el diecinueve de agosto

LANGUAGE TIP
Use the same set of numbers that you
use for counting (**uno**, **dos**, **tres** and
so on) when giving Spanish dates.

ninety NUMBER
  noventa
    My gran is ninety.
    Mi abuela tiene noventa años.

LANGUAGE TIP
In English you can say **he's ninety** or
he's ninety years old. In Spanish
you can only say **tiene noventa
años**. Have you noticed that in
Spanish you need to use the verb
tener to talk about somebody's age?

ninth NUMBER
  noveno *masc*
  novena *fem*
    on the ninth floor
    en la planta novena
    My birthday's the ninth of April.
    Mi cumpleaños es el nueve de abril.

    It's the ninth of July today.
    Hoy es nueve de julio.

    on the ninth of February
    el nueve de febrero

LANGUAGE TIP
Use the same set of numbers that you
use for counting (**uno**, **dos**, **tres** and
so on) when giving Spanish dates.

no

  no can be an adverb or an adjective.

A ADVERB
  no
    Are you coming? — No, I'm not.
    ¿Vienes? — No.
    Can you swim? — No, I can't.
    ¿Sabes nadar? — No.
B ADJECTIVE
    There are no trains on Sundays.
    No hay trenes los domingos.
    'no smoking'
    "prohibido fumar"

nobody PRONOUN
  nadie
    Who's going with you? — Nobody.
    ¿Quién va contigo? — Nadie.
    Nobody saw me.
    Nadie me vio.
    Nobody came.
    Nadie vino.

LANGUAGE TIP
nadie often goes before the verb. If
you're putting it after the verb, remember
to use the construction **no ... nadie**.

    There's nobody in the classroom.
    No hay nadie en la clase.

nod VERB
  decir que sí con la cabeza

noise NOUN
  el **ruido** *masc*
    Please make less noise.
    Por favor, haced menos ruido.

Spanish

English

noisy ADJECTIVE
ruidoso *masc*
ruidosa *fem*
the noisiest city in the world
la ciudad más ruidosa del mundo

none PRONOUN
1 **ninguno** *masc*
ninguna *fem*

LANGUAGE TIP
When **none** refers to things you can count, such as **girls** or **friends**, Spanish uses the singular **ninguno**.

How many girls? — None.
¿Cuántas chicas? — Ninguna.
None of these pens work.
No funciona ninguno de estos bolígrafos.
There are none left.
No queda ninguno.

LANGUAGE TIP
Don't forget to put **no** before the verb when putting **ninguno** after it.

---
2 **nada**

LANGUAGE TIP
When **none** refers to something you cannot count, such as **cheese** or **milk**, Spanish uses **nada**, which is also singular. Don't forget to put **no** before the verb when putting **nada** after it.

There's none left.
No queda nada.

nonsense NOUN
las **tonterías** *fem pl*
She talks a lot of nonsense.
Dice muchas tonterías.

noodles PL NOUN
los **fideos** *masc pl*

noon NOUN
las **doce del mediodía** *fem pl*
It's noon.
Son las doce del mediodía.

at noon
a las doce del mediodía

no one PRONOUN
nadie
Who's going with you? — No one.
¿Quién va contigo? — Nadie.
No one saw me.
Nadie me vio.
No one came.
Nadie vino.

LANGUAGE TIP
nadie often goes before the verb. If you're putting it after the verb, remember to use the construction **no ... nadie**.

There's no one in the classroom.
No hay nadie en la clase.

nor CONJUNCTION
neither ... nor
ni ... ni
neither Jack nor Jimmy
ni Jack ni Jimmy

Nor do I.
Yo tampoco.
Nor have I.
Yo tampoco.

normal ADJECTIVE
normal *masc/fem*
at the normal time
a la hora normal

north

north can be an adjective or a noun.

A ADJECTIVE
norte

A
B
C
D
E
F
G
H
I
J
K
L
M
N
O
P
Q
R
S
T
U
V
W
X
Y
Z

norte never changes its ending no matter what it describes. Did you know that adjectives that behave like this are called 'invariable adjectives'?

the north coast
la costa norte

B NOUN
el **norte** *masc*
in the north
en el norte

Northern Ireland NOUN
Irlanda del Norte *fem*
in Northern Ireland
en Irlanda del Norte
to Northern Ireland
a Irlanda del Norte
I'm from Northern Ireland.
Soy de Irlanda del Norte.

North Pole NOUN
el **Polo Norte** *masc*

North Sea NOUN
el **mar del Norte** *masc*

nose NOUN
la **nariz** *fem* (PL las **narices**)
My nose is blocked.
Tengo la nariz tapada.

In Spanish you usually use an article like **el**, **la** or **los**, **las** with parts of the body.

nosy ADJECTIVE
curioso *masc*
curiosa *fem*

not ADVERB
no
Are you coming or not?
¿Vienes o no?
It's not raining.
No está lloviendo.
I don't like cheese.
No me gusta el queso.
He can't drive.
No sabe conducir.

Sit down everybody! Not you, Lucas.
¡Sentaos todos! Tú no, Lucas.
Have you finished? — Not yet.
¿Has terminado? — Todavía no.

not yet
todavía no
not you
tú no
Thank you! — Not at all!
¡Gracias! — ¡De nada!

note NOUN
1 la **nota** *fem* (message)
I'll write her a note.
Le escribiré una nota.
2 el **billete** *masc* (banknote)

notebook NOUN
el **cuaderno** *masc*

notepad NOUN
el **bloc** *masc*
(PL los **blocs**)

nothing PRONOUN
nada
What's wrong? — Nothing.
¿Qué pasa? — Nada.

Don't forget to put **no** before the verb when putting **nada** after it.

Nothing's the matter.
No pasa nada.
He does nothing.
No hace nada.

notice

notice can be a noun or a verb.

A NOUN
el **anuncio** *masc*

Be careful! The translation of **notice** is not **noticia**.

B VERB
to notice
darse cuenta de

a
b
c
d
e
f
g
h
i
j
k
l
m
n
o
p
q
r
s
t
u
v
w
x
y
z

A
B
C
D
E
F
G
H
I
J
K
L
M
N
O
P
Q
R
S
T
U
V
W
X
Y
Z

Don't worry, he won't notice anything.
No te preocupes. No se dará cuenta de nada.

notice board NOUN
el **tablón de anuncios** *masc*
(PL los **tablones de anuncios**)

noun NOUN
el **sustantivo** *masc*

novel NOUN
la **novela** *fem*

November NOUN
noviembre *masc*
My birthday's in November.
Mi cumpleaños es en noviembre.
It's the eleventh of November today.
Hoy es once de noviembre.

in November
en noviembre
on the fifth of November
el cinco de noviembre

LANGUAGE TIP
Months are not spelled with a capital letter in Spanish.

now ADVERB
ahora
What are you doing now?
¿Qué estás haciendo ahora?
I'm rather busy just now.
Estoy bastante ocupado en este momento.

not now
ahora no
just now
en este momento
now and then
de vez en cuando
from now on
de ahora en adelante

nowhere ADVERB
a ningún sitio
Where did you go? — Nowhere.
¿Adónde fuiste? — A ningún sitio.
There's nowhere to go in the evenings.
No hay ningún sitio adonde ir por la noche.

number NOUN
1 el **número** *masc* (*of house, telephone*)
What's your phone number?
¿Cuál es tu número de teléfono?
2 la **cantidad** *fem* (*of people, things*)
a large number of people
una gran cantidad de personas
3 la **cifra** *fem* (*figure*)
the second number
la segunda cifra

nun NOUN
la **monja** *fem*

nurse NOUN
el **enfermero** *masc*
la **enfermera** *fem*
I want to be a nurse.
Quiero ser enfermera.

LANGUAGE TIP
In Spanish, you do not use an article with people's jobs.

nursery NOUN
la **guardería** *fem*
My sister goes to nursery.
Mi hermana va a la guardería.

nursery school NOUN
la **escuela infantil** *fem*
My little sister goes to nursery school.
Mi hermana pequeña va a la escuela infantil.

nut NOUN
el **fruto de cáscara** *masc*
I like nuts.
Me gustan los frutos de cáscara.
a bowl of nuts
un cuenco de frutos de cáscara

oats PL NOUN
la **avena** *fem*

> **LANGUAGE TIP**
> **avena** is a singular word.

obedient ADJECTIVE
obediente *masc/fem*

obey VERB
cumplir
You must obey the rules of the game.
Tienes que cumplir las reglas del juego.

object NOUN
el **objeto** *masc*

obstacle NOUN
el **obstáculo** *masc*

obvious ADJECTIVE
evidente *masc/fem*
That's obvious!
¡Eso es evidente!

occasion NOUN
la **ocasión** *fem* (PL las **ocasiones**)
a special occasion
una ocasión especial
on several occasions
en varias ocasiones

occasionally ADVERB
de vez en cuando

occupation NOUN
la **ocupación** *fem* (PL las **ocupaciones**)

ocean NOUN
el **océano** *masc*
the Atlantic Ocean
el océano Atlántico

the Pacific Ocean
el océano Pacífico

> **LANGUAGE TIP**
> **océano** is not spelled with a capital letter in names of oceans.

o'clock ADVERB
at four o'clock
a las cuatro

It's one o'clock.
Es la una.
It's five o'clock.
Son las cinco.

October NOUN
octubre *masc*
My birthday's in October.
Mi cumpleaños es en octubre.
It's the eleventh of October today.
Hoy es once de octubre.

in October
en octubre
on the fifth of October
el cinco de octubre

> **LANGUAGE TIP**
> Months are not spelled with a capital letter in Spanish.

odd ADJECTIVE
1 **raro** *masc*
rara *fem* (strange)
That's odd!
¡Eso es raro!
2 **impar** *masc/fem* (not even)
an odd number
un número impar

of PREPOSITION
de
a bottle of water
una botella de agua
a kilo of oranges
un kilo de naranjas
a boy of ten
un niño de diez años

the end of the film
el final de la película

LANGUAGE TIP
de combines with **el** to form **del**.

a photo of the school
una foto del colegio
Do you want some of them?
¿Quieres algunos de ellos?
a friend of mine
un amigo mío
That's very kind of you.
Eso es muy amable de tu parte.
There are three of us.
Somos tres.
There are seven of them.
Son siete.

off

off can be an adjective, preposition or adverb.

A ADJECTIVE
1 **apagado** *masc*
   apagada *fem* (*switched off*)
   The light is off.
   La luz está apagada.
2 **cerrado** *masc*
   cerrada *fem* (*turned off*)
   Is the tap off?
   ¿Está cerrado el grifo?
3 (*cancelled*)
   The match is off.
   El partido se ha cancelado.
4 (*absent*)
   He's off today.
   Hoy no ha venido.
   Dad's got the day off tomorrow.
   Papá no trabaja mañana.
5 (*not available*)
   The soup's off.
   No hay sopa.
6 **cortado** *masc*
   cortada *fem* (*milk*)
   The milk's off.
   La leche está cortada.

B PREPOSITION
He's off school.
No ha ido al colegio./No ha venido al colegio.

LANGUAGE TIP
he's off school has two translations depending on whether he hasn't gone to school or he hasn't come to school. Look at the examples.

David's upstairs, he's off school today.
David está arriba, hoy no ha ido al colegio.
Ryan isn't here, he's off school today.
Ryan no está aquí, hoy no ha venido al colegio.

C ADVERB
Off you go, Jack!
¡Hala Jack, vete!

offer

offer can be a verb or a noun.

A VERB
to offer
ofrecer
Can you offer Teresa something to drink?
¿Puedes ofrecerle a Teresa algo de beber?
B NOUN
la **oferta** *fem*
There's a special offer on dictionaries.
Hay una oferta especial de diccionarios.

office NOUN
la **oficina** *fem*
She works in an office.
Trabaja en una oficina.

often ADVERB
a menudo
We often go to London.
Vamos a menudo a Londres.

It often rains.
Llueve a menudo.
How often do you clean your teeth?
¿Con qué frecuencia te lavas los dientes?

oil NOUN
el **aceite** masc

OK EXCLAMATION, ADJECTIVE = **okay**

okay

> **okay** can be an exclamation or an adjective.

A EXCLAMATION
¡de acuerdo!
I'll go tomorrow. — Okay!
Iré mañana. — ¡De acuerdo!
B ADJECTIVE
bien

LANGUAGE TIP
bien never changes its ending.

I'm okay thanks.
Estoy bien, gracias.
Is everything okay?
¿Está todo bien?
Do you like school? — It's okay.
¿Te gusta el colegio? — No está mal.
Is that okay with you?
¿Estás de acuerdo con eso?

Okay!
¡De acuerdo!
Are you okay?
¿Estás bien?

old ADJECTIVE
viejo masc
vieja fem
an old dog
un perro viejo
an old house
una casa vieja

old shoes
zapatos viejos

LANGUAGE TIP
It sounds more polite if you describe someone as **mayor** rather than **viejo**.

an old man
un hombre mayor
an old lady
una señora mayor
old people
los mayores

LANGUAGE TIP
mayor can also mean **older** or **oldest** while **mayor que** means **older than**.

my older sister
mi hermana mayor
my oldest brother
mi hermano mayor
Damian's the oldest in the class.
Damian es el mayor de la clase.
I'm older than you.
Soy mayor que tú.
She's two years older than me.
Ella tiene dos años más que yo.

How old are you?
¿Cuántos años tienes?
He's ten years old.
Tiene diez años.

Olympic ADJECTIVE
olímpico masc
olímpica fem
the Olympic Games
los Juegos Olímpicos

omelette NOUN
la **tortilla** *fem*

on

> **on** can be an adjective or a preposition.

A ADJECTIVE
1 **encendido** *masc*
  encendida *fem (switched on)*
  The light is on.
  La luz está encendida.
2 **abierto** *masc*
  abierta *fem (tap)*
  The tap is on.
  El grifo está abierto.
B PREPOSITION
1 **en**
  Your books are on the table.
  Tus libros están en la mesa.
  on the wall
  en la pared
  I go to school on my bike.
  Voy al colegio en bici.
  Is there anything on television?
  ¿Hay algo en la televisión?
  I'm on the phone.
  Estoy hablando por teléfono.
2 **sobre** *(about)*
  a book on Gandhi
  un libro sobre Gandhi
3 *(with days and dates)*

LANGUAGE TIP
Just give **el** with a particular day or date.

on Monday
el lunes
on the fifteenth of June
el quince de junio

LANGUAGE TIP
To say **on Sundays**, **on Tuesdays**, and so on, use **los**.

---

on Sundays
los domingos
on Tuesdays
los martes
4 *(in expressions)*
  It's on the right.
  Está a la derecha.
  They're on holiday.
  Están de vacaciones.

on Friday
el viernes
on Fridays
los viernes
on June 20th
el 20 de junio
on Christmas Day
el día de Navidad
on holiday
de vacaciones
on the left
a la izquierda

once ADVERB
una vez
  once a week
  una vez por semana
  only once
  solo una vez
  Come here at once!
  ¡Ven aquí enseguida!
  Everybody answered at once.
  Todo el mundo contestó a la vez.
  once more
  otra vez

one NUMBER, PRONOUN
1 **un** *masc*
  una *fem (before noun)*

LANGUAGE TIP
Use **un** before a masculine noun and **una** before a feminine noun.

one day
un día
one hour
una hora
I've got one brother and one sister.
Tengo un hermano y una hermana.

She's one.
Tiene un año.

LANGUAGE TIP
In English you can say **she's one** or
she's one year old. In Spanish you
can only say **tiene un año.** Have you
noticed that in Spanish you need to
use the verb **tener** to talk about
somebody's age?

2 uno *masc*
una *fem (not before noun)*
**This sweater is too big, I need a
smaller one.**
Este jersey es demasiado grande.
Necesito uno más pequeño.
**This T-shirt is too small, I need
a bigger one.**
Esta camiseta es demasiado pequeña.
Necesito una más grande.
**Which packet do you want?
— The big one.**
¿Qué paquete quieres? — El grande.
**Which card do you want?
— The red one.**
¿Qué carta quieres? — La roja.
one, two, three, four, five ...
uno, dos, tres, cuatro, cinco ...
It's one o'clock.
Es la una.

onion NOUN
la **cebolla** *fem*

online ADJECTIVE
por internet
**You can order the
book online.**
Se puede comprar el libro
por internet.

only

only can be an adjective or an
adverb.

A ADJECTIVE
único *masc*
única *fem*

my only dress
mi único vestido
my only clean T-shirt
mi única camiseta limpia
I'm an only child.
Soy hijo único.
Tracy is an only child.
Tracy es hija única.
B ADVERB
solo
only ten euros
solo diez euros
I've only got two cards.
Sólo tengo dos cartas.
He's only three.
Solo tiene tres años.

LANGUAGE TIP
Traditionally, the adverb **sólo** was
written with an accent to distinguish it
from the unaccented adjective **solo**,
meaning 'alone'. Nowadays, you don't
have to give the accent unless the
sentence would be confusing
otherwise.

open

open can be an adjective or a verb.

A ADJECTIVE
abierto *masc*
abierta *fem*
**The supermarket is open on
Sunday mornings.**
El supermercado está abierto los
domingos por la mañana.
B VERB
to open
abrir
Can I open the window?
¿Puedo abrir la ventana?
Open your books.
Abrid vuestros libros.
What time does the bank open?
¿A qué hora abre el banco?

opening hours PL NOUN
el **horario de apertura** *masc*

Spanish

English

a
b
c
d
e
f
g
h
i
j
k
l
m
n
o
p
q
r
s
t
u
v
w
x
y
z

493

operation NOUN
la **operación** *fem* (PL las **operaciones**)
He is recovering from an operation.
Se está recuperando de una operación.
My mum's going to have an operation.
Van a operar a mi madre.

opinion NOUN
la **opinión** *fem* (PL las **opiniones**)
in my opinion
en mi opinión
What's your opinion?
¿Tú qué opinas?

opponent NOUN
el **adversario** *masc*
la **adversaria** *fem*

opportunity NOUN
la **oportunidad** *fem*
It's a good opportunity.
Es una buena oportunidad.

opposite

> **opposite** can be an adjective, noun, adverb or preposition.

A ADJECTIVE
contrario *masc*
contraria *fem*
It's in the opposite direction.
Está en la dirección contraria.
B NOUN
the opposite
lo contrario
the opposite of good
lo contrario de bueno
C ADVERB
enfrente
They live opposite.
Viven enfrente.
D PREPOSITION
enfrente de
the girl sitting opposite me
la niña que está sentada enfrente de mí

or CONJUNCTION
1 o
Would you like tea or coffee?
¿Quieres té o café?
Hurry up or you'll miss the bus.
Date prisa o perderás el autobús.

LANGUAGE TIP
Change **o** to **u** before words starting with **o-** or **ho-**.

seven or eight
siete u ocho
men or women
mujeres u hombres
2 ni (*in negatives*)
I don't eat meat or fish.
No como carne ni pescado.

oral NOUN
el **examen oral** *masc*
(PL los **exámenes orales**)
I've got my Spanish oral soon.
Tengo mi examen oral de español pronto.

orange

> **orange** can be a noun or an adjective.

A NOUN
1 la **naranja** *fem* (*fruit*)
a big orange
una naranja grande
2 el **naranja** *masc* (*colour*)
Orange is my favourite colour.
El naranja es mi color favorito.

LANGUAGE TIP
When it means the colour **orange**, **el naranja**, like all colours in Spanish, is masculine.

B ADJECTIVE
naranja

LANGUAGE TIP
The colour **naranja** never changes its ending no matter what it describes. Don't forget that colour adjectives come after the noun in Spanish.

orange curtains
cortinas naranja

orange juice NOUN
el **zumo de naranja** *masc*

orchard NOUN
el **huerto** *masc*

orchestra NOUN
la **orquesta** *fem*
I play in the school orchestra.
Toco en la orquesta del colegio.

order

> **order** can be a noun or a verb.

A NOUN

1 el **orden** *masc* (*sequence*)
Put the words in alphabetical order, children.
Poned las palabras en orden alfabético, niños.
The words are not in the right order.
Las palabras no están en el orden correcto.

2 (*in restaurant*)
The waiter took our order.
El camarero tomó nota de lo que queríamos.

3 la **orden** *fem* (PL las **órdenes**)
(*command*)

'out of order'
"no funciona"

B VERB
to order
pedir
Are you ready to order?
¿Ya saben lo que van a pedir?

ordinary ADJECTIVE
normal *masc/fem*
an ordinary day
un día normal

organize VERB
organizar
We are organizing a trip to London.
Estamos organizando un viaje a Londres.

original ADJECTIVE
original *masc/fem*
It's a very original idea.
Es una idea muy original.

orphan NOUN
el **huérfano** *masc*
la **huérfana** *fem*

other

> **other** can be an adjective or a pronoun.

A ADJECTIVE
otro *masc*
otra *fem*
on the other side of the street
al otro lado de la calle
the other day
el otro día

LANGUAGE TIP
The translation of **the other one** depends on whether you're referring to something masculine or feminine. Use **el otro** for something masculine and **la otra** for something feminine.

B PRONOUN
el **otro** *masc*
la **otra** *fem*
Get into twos, one behind the other.
Poneos de dos en dos, uno detrás del otro.
Where are the others?
¿Dónde están los otros?

ought VERB

> **LANGUAGE TIP**
> To translate **ought to**, you need to use the conditional tense of the verb **deber**.

I ought to phone my parents.
Debería llamar a mis padres.

our ADJECTIVE
nuestro *masc*
nuestra *fem*
our dog
nuestro perro
our house
nuestra casa
our friends
nuestros amigos
our plants
nuestras plantas

> **LANGUAGE TIP**
> You usually translate **our** using **el**, **la**, etc before parts of the body or clothes, particularly when using a reflexive verb.

We took off our coats.
Nos quitamos los abrigos.

ours PRONOUN
el **nuestro** *masc*
la **nuestra** *fem*

> **LANGUAGE TIP**
> Remember that the choice of **el nuestro**, **la nuestra**, **los nuestros** or **las nuestras** depends entirely on the thing or things referred to.

That's not our car. Ours is here.
Aquél no es nuestro coche. El nuestro está aquí.
Those aren't our backpacks. Ours are here.
Aquéllas no son nuestras mochilas. Las nuestras están aquí.

> **LANGUAGE TIP**
> After **ser** you can usually just use **nuestro**, **nuestra**, **nuestros** or **nuestras** to agree with the noun referred to.

Is this ours?
¿Es nuestro esto?
These cases are ours.
Estas maletas son nuestras.
Whose is this? — It's ours.
¿De quién es esto? — Es nuestro.

ourselves PRONOUN
1 **nos** (*reflexive*)
We enjoyed ourselves.
Nos divertimos.
2 **nosotros mismos** *masc pl*
nosotras mismas *fem pl* (*for emphasis*)
We did it ourselves!
¡Lo hicimos nosotros mismos!
by ourselves
solos
We want to do it by ourselves.
Queremos hacerlo solos.

out

> **out** can be an adverb or an adjective.

A ADVERB
1 **fuera** (*not at home*)
William's out.
William está fuera.
I'm going out.
Voy a salir.
He was coming out of the cinema.
Estaba saliendo del cine.
Can you get the paints out of the cupboard?
¿Puedes sacar las pinturas del armario?
2 **eliminado** *masc*
eliminada *fem* (*in game*)

> **LANGUAGE TIP**
> **eliminado** is an adjective, so remember that it needs to agree with the person it refers to.

You're out, Lucy!
¡Estás eliminada, Lucy!

> **'way out'**
> "salida"

B ADJECTIVE
apagado *masc*
apagada *fem (turned off)*
All the lights are out.
Todas las luces están apagadas.

outdoor ADJECTIVE
al aire libre
outdoor activities
actividades al aire libre
an outdoor swimming pool
una piscina exterior

outdoors ADVERB
al aire libre

outer space NOUN
el **espacio** *masc*
a monster from outer space
un monstruo del espacio

outside

> **outside** can be an adverb or a preposition.

A ADVERB
fuera
It's very cold outside.
Hace mucho frío fuera.
B PREPOSITION
fuera de
outside the school
fuera del colegio

oven NOUN
el **horno** *masc*

over

> **over** can be a preposition or an adjective.

A PREPOSITION
1 **más de** *(more than)*
There were over five hundred people at the concert.
Había más de quinientas personas en el concierto.
Are you over ten?
¿Tienes más de diez años?
The temperature is over thirty degrees.
La temperatura supera los treinta grados.
2 **durante** *(during)*
over Christmas
durante la Navidad
3 **al otro lado de** *(across)*
The baker's is over the road.
La panadería está al otro lado de la calle.
4 **encima de** *(above)*
There's a mirror over the washbasin.
Encima del lavabo hay un espejo.

LANGUAGE TIP
Use **por encima de** instead when there is movement **over** something.

The ball went over the wall.
La pelota pasó por encima del muro.
a bridge over the river
un puente sobre el río

> **over here**
> aquí
> **over there**
> allí
> **all over Scotland**
> por toda Escocia

B ADJECTIVE
(finished)
The match is over.
Se ha terminado el partido.

Spanish

English

overcast ADJECTIVE
cubierto *masc*
cubierta *fem*
> **The sky was overcast.**
> El cielo estaba cubierto.

overhead projector NOUN
el **retroproyector** *masc*

owe VERB
deber
> **He owes me five pounds.**
> Me debe cinco libras.

owl NOUN
el **búho** *masc*

own ADJECTIVE
propio *masc*
propia *fem*
> **I've got my own bathroom.**
> Tengo mi propio cuarto de baño.
> **I'd like a room of my own.**
> Quiero una habitación para mí solo.
> **He lives on his own.**
> Vive solo.

> **on his own**
> solo
> **on her own**
> sola

owner NOUN
el **propietario** *masc*
la **propietaria** *fem*

A
B
C
D
E
F
G
H
I
J
K
L
M
N
O
P
Q
R
S
T
U
V
W
X
Y
Z

P p

pack

> **pack** can be a verb or a noun.

A VERB
to pack
hacer las maletas
I have to pack.
Tengo que hacer las maletas.

B NOUN
1 el **pack** *masc* (*of goods*)
a pack of six
un pack de seis
2 el **paquete** *masc* (*packet*)
3 la **baraja** *fem* (*of cards*)
a pack of cards
una baraja de cartas

packed lunch NOUN
I take a packed lunch to school.
Me llevo la comida al colegio.

packet NOUN
el **paquete** *masc*
a packet of crisps
una bolsa de patatas fritas

page NOUN
la **página** *fem*
on page ten
en la página diez
Look at page six, everyone.
Mirad todos en la página seis.

paid VERB ▷ *see* **pay**

pain NOUN
1 el **dolor** *masc*
a terrible pain
un dolor horrible

2 **to be a pain**
ser un pesado
He's a pain.
Es un pesado.

LANGUAGE TIP
Change **un pesado** to **una pesada** if you're referring to a girl.

My sister is a pain.
Mi hermana es una pesada.

paint

> **paint** can be a noun or a verb.

A NOUN
la **pintura** *fem*
red paint
pintura roja
'wet paint'
"recién pintado"

B VERB
to paint
pintar
I'm going to paint it green.
Lo voy a pintar de verde.

paintbrush NOUN
1 el **pincel** *masc* (*for artwork*)
2 la **brocha** *fem* (*for walls, ceiling*)

painting NOUN
1 el **cuadro** *masc* (*picture*)
a painting by Picasso
un cuadro de Picasso
2 la **pintura** *fem* (*activity*)
I like painting.
Me gusta la pintura.

pair NOUN
el **par** *masc*
a pair of shoes
un par de zapatos
a pair of trousers
unos pantalones
two pairs of trousers
dos pantalones
a pair of jeans
unos vaqueros
in pairs
por parejas
We work in pairs.
Trabajamos por parejas.
Can you get into pairs?
¿Podéis colocaros por parejas?

pal NOUN
el **amigo** *masc*
la **amiga** *fem*

palace NOUN
el **palacio** *masc*

pale ADJECTIVE
1 **pálido** *masc*
pálida *fem*
She looks very pale.
Está muy pálida.
2 **claro** *masc*
clara *fem* (*in colour*)
pale blue
azul claro

LANGUAGE TIP
When you describe something as **pale blue**, **pale green** and so on, neither the colour nor **claro** changes its ending to agree with the noun.

some pale green curtains
unas cortinas verde claro

---

pan NOUN
1 la **cacerola** *fem* (*saucepan*)
2 la **sartén** *fem* (PL las **sartenes**)
(*frying pan*)

pancake NOUN
la **tortita** *fem*

Pancake Day NOUN
el **Martes de Carnaval** *masc*

DID YOU KNOW...?
During the week before Lent, all over Spain and Latin America there are fiestas and fancy-dress parades, with the main celebrations taking place on **Martes de Carnaval** (literally Carnival Tuesday).

---

panic VERB
Don't panic!
¡Tranquilo!

LANGUAGE TIP
Change **¡Tranquilo!** to **¡Tranquila!** if talking to a woman or girl.

---

pantomime NOUN
la **pantomima navideña** *fem*

DID YOU KNOW...?
There are no pantomime traditions in Spain.

---

pants PL NOUN
1 los **calzoncillos** *masc pl* (*for men, boys*)
a pair of pants
unos calzoncillos
2 las **braguitas** *fem pl* (*for women, girls*)
a pair of pants
unas braguitas

paper NOUN
1 el **papel** *masc*
Have you got a pencil and some paper?
¿Tienes lápiz y papel?
a paper towel
una servilleta de papel
a piece of paper
un papel
2 el **periódico** *masc* (*newspaper*)

paper boy NOUN
el **repartidor de periódicos** *masc*

paper girl NOUN
la **repartidora de periódicos** *fem*

parade NOUN
el **desfile** *masc*

paragraph NOUN
el **párrafo** *masc*

parcel NOUN
el **paquete** *masc*

pardon NOUN
Pardon?
¿Cómo?

parents PL NOUN
los **padres** *masc pl*
my parents
mis padres

LANGUAGE TIP
Be careful! The translation of **parents** is not **parientes**.

---

park

park can be a noun or a verb.

A NOUN
el **parque** *masc*
There's a nice park.
Hay un parque bonito.
B VERB
to park
aparcar
It's difficult to park.
Es difícil aparcar.

parking NOUN
'no parking'
"prohibido aparcar"

parrot NOUN
el **loro** *masc*

part NOUN
1 la **parte** *fem*
The first part is easy.
La primera parte es fácil.
2 **to take part in something**
participar en algo

I'm taking part in the competition.
Participo en el concurso.

partly ADVERB
en parte

partner NOUN
1 el **compañero** *masc*
la **compañera** *fem* (*in game, role play*)
2 la **pareja** *fem* (*in dance, relationship*)

LANGUAGE TIP
Even though **la pareja** is a feminine word, you can use it to refer to a man.

---

part-time ADJECTIVE, ADVERB
a tiempo parcial
a part-time job
un trabajo a tiempo parcial
She works part-time.
Trabaja a tiempo parcial.

party NOUN
la **fiesta** *fem*
I'm going to a party on Saturday.
Voy a una fiesta el sábado.
a birthday party
una fiesta de cumpleaños
a Christmas party
una fiesta de Navidad

pass VERB
1 **pasar** (*give*)
Pass the ball, Nina!
¡Pasa la pelota, Nina!
Could you pass me the salt?
¿Me puedes pasar la sal?
2 **pasar por delante de** (*go past*)
You pass the post office.
Pasas por delante de Correos.

passenger NOUN
el **pasajero** *masc*
la **pasajera** *fem*

Passover NOUN
la **Pascua Judía** *fem*
at Passover
en la Pascua Judía

A
B
C
D
E
F
G
H
I
J
K
L
M
N
O
P
Q
R
S
T
U
V
W
X
Y
Z

passport NOUN
el **pasaporte** *masc*
Have you got your passport?
¿Llevas tu pasaporte?

password NOUN
la **contraseña** *fem*

past

> **past** can be a preposition or a noun.

A PREPOSITION
1 después de (*after*)
It's on the right, just past the station.
Está a la derecha, justo después de la estación.
2 (*with times*)
It's quarter past one.
Es la una y cuarto.
It's half past ten.
Son las diez y media.
It's quarter past nine.
Son las nueve y cuarto.
It's ten past eight.
Son las ocho y diez.
at ten past five
a las cinco y diez

> **half past eight**
> las ocho y media
> **quarter past ten**
> las diez y cuarto

B NOUN
el **pasado** *masc*
in the past
en el pasado

pasta NOUN
la **pasta** *fem*
Pasta is easy to cook.
La pasta es fácil de cocinar.

path NOUN
1 el **camino** *masc* (*in garden, town*)
Follow the path.
Sigue el camino.
2 el **sendero** *masc* (*in woods*)

patience NOUN
la **paciencia** *fem*
He hasn't got much patience.
No tiene mucha paciencia.

patient

> **patient** can be a noun or an adjective.

A NOUN
el/la **paciente** *masc/fem*
B ADJECTIVE
paciente *masc/fem*
The teacher is very patient.
El maestro es muy paciente.
Be patient, Joshua.
Ten paciencia, Joshua.

patio NOUN
el **patio** *masc*

pattern NOUN
el **diseño** *masc*
a simple pattern
un diseño sencillo

pause NOUN
la **pausa** *fem*

pavement NOUN
la **acera** *fem*
on the pavement
en la acera

paw NOUN
la **pata** *fem*

pay

> **pay** can be a noun or a verb.

A NOUN
la **paga** *fem*
What is the pay?
¿Cuánto es la paga?
B VERB
to pay
pagar

Who's going to pay?
¿Quién va a pagar?
Where do I pay?
¿Dónde pago?
to pay for something
pagar algo
I've paid for my ticket.
He pagado mi entrada.
I paid ten euros for the book.
Pagué diez euros por el libro.
to pay attention
prestar atención

> **Pay attention, Hayley!**
> ¡Presta atención, Hayley!
> **Pay attention, everybody!**
> ¡Prestad todos atención!

PE NOUN
la **educación física** *fem*
We have PE twice a week.
Tenemos educación física dos veces
por semana.

pea NOUN
el **guisante** *masc*
a tin of peas
una lata de guisantes

peace NOUN
la **paz** *fem*

peach NOUN
el **melocotón** *masc*
(PL los **melocotones**)
a kilo of peaches
un kilo de melocotones

peanut NOUN
el **cacahuete**
masc
**a packet
of peanuts**
un paquete de
cacahuetes

peanut butter NOUN
la **mantequilla de cacahuete** *fem*
a peanut butter sandwich
un bocadillo de mantequilla de
cacahuete

pear NOUN
la **pera** *fem*
**Which would you like, a pear or
an apple?**
¿Qué es lo que quieres: una pera o una
manzana?

pebble NOUN
el **guijarro** *masc*

pedal NOUN
el **pedal** *masc*

peg NOUN
1 el **gancho** *masc* (*for coats*)
2 la **pinza de la ropa** *fem* (*clothes peg*)

pen NOUN
el **bolígrafo** *masc*
Can I borrow your pen?
¿Me dejas tu bolígrafo?

pence PL NOUN
los **peniques** *masc pl*

pencil NOUN
el **lápiz** *masc* (PL los **lápices**)
in pencil
a lápiz
coloured pencils
lápices de colores

pencil case NOUN
el **estuche** *masc*

pencil sharpener NOUN
el **sacapuntas** *masc* (PL los
sacapuntas)

penfriend NOUN
el **amigo por correspondencia**
masc
la **amiga por correspondencia** *fem*
**I'm Emma, your English
penfriend.**
Soy Emma, tu amiga por
correspondencia inglesa.

penknife NOUN
la **navaja** *fem*

a
b
c
d
e
f
g
h
i
j
k
l
m
n
o
p
q
r
s
t
u
v
w
x
y
z

penny NOUN
el **penique** *masc*

pensioner NOUN
el/la **pensionista** *masc/fem*

people PL NOUN
1 la **gente** *fem*
The people are nice.
La gente es simpática.
a lot of people
mucha gente
There are too many people here.
Aquí hay demasiada gente.

LANGUAGE TIP
Remember that **gente** is a singular word in Spanish.

---

2 las **personas** *fem pl* (*individuals*)
Four people can play.
Pueden jugar cuatro personas.
How many people are there in your family?
¿Cuántas personas forman tu familia?

LANGUAGE TIP
In English you can say **tall people**, **rich people** etc. In Spanish you say the equivalent of **the tall**, **the rich** etc.

---

tall people
los altos
rich people
los ricos
Spanish people
los españoles

pepper NOUN
1 la **pimienta** *fem* (*spice*)
Pass the pepper, please.
Pásame la pimienta, por favor.
2 el **pimiento** *masc* (*vegetable*)
a red pepper
un pimiento rojo

per PREPOSITION
por
per day
por día

per cent ADVERB
por ciento
fifty per cent
cincuenta por ciento

perfect ADJECTIVE
perfecto *masc*
perfecta *fem*
Raquel speaks perfect English.
Raquel habla un inglés perfecto.

performance NOUN
la **representación** *fem* (PL las **representaciones**)
The performance starts at two o'clock.
La representación empieza a las dos.

perfume NOUN
el **perfume** *masc*
a bottle of perfume
un frasco de perfume

perhaps ADVERB
a lo mejor
Perhaps he's ill.
A lo mejor está enfermo.

period NOUN
el **periodo** *masc*
the holiday period
el periodo de vacaciones

permission NOUN
el **permiso** *masc*
Have you got permission?
¿Tienes permiso?

person NOUN
la **persona** *fem*
She's a very nice person.
Es una persona muy simpática.

personality NOUN
la **personalidad** *fem*

pet NOUN
la **mascota** *fem*
Have you got a pet?
¿Tienes alguna mascota?

petrol NOUN
la **gasolina** *fem*
unleaded petrol
gasolina sin plomo

pet shop NOUN
la **tienda de animales** *fem*

phone

> **phone** can be a noun or a verb.

A NOUN
el **teléfono** *masc*
Where's the phone?
¿Dónde está el teléfono?
She's on the phone at the moment.
Ahora mismo está al teléfono.
Can I use the phone, please?
¿Puedo llamar por teléfono, por favor?

B VERB
to phone
llamar
I'll phone you tomorrow.
Mañana te llamo.
I have to phone my mum.
Tengo que llamar a mi madre.
Who are you phoning?
¿A quién llamas?

LANGUAGE TIP
Don't forget the personal **a** in examples like the last two.

phone box NOUN
la **cabina telefónica** *fem*

phone call NOUN
la **llamada** *fem*
She gets lots of phone calls.
Recibe muchas llamadas.
Can I make a phone call?
¿Puedo hacer una llamada?

phone number NOUN
el **número de teléfono** *masc*
What's your phone number?
¿Cuál es tu número de teléfono?

photo NOUN
la **foto** *fem*
This is a photo of my family.
Esta es una foto de mi familia.
I want to take some photos.
Quiero hacer unas fotos.
I want to take a photo of you.
Quiero hacerte una foto.

LANGUAGE TIP
Even though it ends in **-o**, **la foto** is a feminine noun.

photocopier NOUN
la **fotocopiadora** *fem*

photocopy

> **photocopy** can be a noun or a verb.

A NOUN
la **fotocopia** *fem*
It's only a photocopy.
Es solo una fotocopia.
B VERB
to photocopy
fotocopiar
You can photocopy it.
Puedes fotocopiarlo.

photograph NOUN
la **fotografía** *fem*

physics NOUN
la **física** *fem*
She teaches physics.
Ella da clases de física.

pianist NOUN
el/la **pianista** *masc/fem*

piano NOUN
el **piano** *masc*
I play the piano.
Toco el piano.
I have piano lessons.
Tomo clases de piano.

pick

> **pick** can be a noun or a verb.

A NOUN
Take your pick!
¡Escoge el que quieras!

a b c d e f g h i j k l m n o p q r s t u v w x y z

B VERB

to pick

1 escoger (*choose*)

Pick a card, Murray!

¡Escoge una carta, Murray!

Pick three girls and three boys.

Escoge a tres niños y tres niñas.

LANGUAGE TIP

Don't forget the personal **a** in examples like this one.

---

2 coger (*fruit, flowers*)

I like picking strawberries.

Me gusta coger fresas.

pick up VERB

1 recoger (*collect*)

We can come to the airport to pick you up.

Podemos ir al aeropuerto a recogerte.

2 coger (*take*)

Pick up another card, William!

¡Coge otra carta, William!

LANGUAGE TIP

Use **tomar** instead of **coger** if talking to someone from Latin America.

---

3 aprender (*learn*)

I hope I'll pick up some Spanish.

Espero aprender un poco de español.

picnic NOUN

el **pícnic** *masc*

I like picnics.

Me gustan los pícnics.

to have a picnic

hacer un pícnic

We had a picnic on the beach.

Hicimos un pícnic en la playa.

picture NOUN

1 la **foto** *fem* (*photo*)

This is a picture of my family.

Esta es una foto de mi familia.

LANGUAGE TIP

Even though it ends in **-o**, **la foto** is a feminine noun.

---

2 el **cuadro** *masc* (*painting*)

a famous picture

un cuadro famoso

3 el **dibujo** *masc* (*drawing*)

I'll draw a picture.

Haré un dibujo.

Draw a picture of your pet, Lisa.

Haz un dibujo de tu mascota, Lisa.

4 la **ilustración** *fem*

(PL las **ilustraciones**) (*illustration*)

Look at the picture.

Mira la ilustración.

pie NOUN

el **pastel** *masc*

an apple pie

un pastel de manzana

piece NOUN

el **trozo** *masc*

A small piece, please.

Un trozo pequeño, por favor.

pierced ADJECTIVE

I've got pierced ears.

Tengo los agujeros hechos en las orejas.

I want to get my ears pierced.

Quiero hacerme los agujeros en las orejas.

LANGUAGE TIP

In Spanish you usually use an article like **el**, **la** or **los**, **las** with parts of the body.

---

pig NOUN

el **cerdo** *masc*

pigeon NOUN

la **paloma** *fem*

piggy bank NOUN

la **hucha** *fem*

pigtail NOUN
la **trenza** *fem*
> **She's got pigtails.**
> Lleva trenzas.

pile NOUN
el **montón** *masc* (PL los **montones**)
> **a pile of books**
> un montón de libros

pill NOUN
la **píldora** *fem*

pillow NOUN
la **almohada** *fem*

pilot NOUN
el/la **piloto** *masc/fem*
> **She's a pilot.**
> Es piloto.

LANGUAGE TIP
Even though **piloto** ends in **-o**, you can use it to refer to a woman. Remember that in Spanish, you do not use an article with people's jobs.

pineapple NOUN
la **piña** *fem*

pink

> **pink** can be an adjective or a noun.

A ADJECTIVE
rosa

LANGUAGE TIP
The colour **rosa** never changes its ending no matter what it describes. Don't forget that colour adjectives come after the noun in Spanish.

a pink dress
un vestido rosa

B NOUN
el **rosa** *masc*

Pink is my favourite colour.
El rosa es mi color favorito.

LANGUAGE TIP
When it means the colour **pink**, **el rosa**, like all colours in Spanish, is masculine.

pint NOUN
la **pinta** *fem*
> **a pint of milk**
> una pinta de leche

DID YOU KNOW...?
In Spain liquids are measured in litres and centilitres. A pint is about 0.6 litres.

pipe NOUN
la **tubería** *fem* (*for water*)

pirate NOUN
el/la **pirata** *masc/fem*

pitch NOUN
el **campo** *masc*
> **a football pitch**
> un campo de fútbol

pity NOUN
> **What a pity she can't come!**
> ¡Qué pena que no pueda venir!

> **What a pity!**
> ¡Qué pena!

pizza NOUN
la **pizza** *fem*

place NOUN
el **sitio** *masc*
> **It's a quiet place.**
> Es un sitio tranquilo.

Spanish — **English**

There are a lot of interesting places to visit.
Hay un montón de sitios interesantes que visitar.
Can I change places?
¿Puedo cambiarme de sitio?
Carol, change places with Harry!
¡Carol, cámbiate de sitio con Harry!

plain ADJECTIVE
liso masc
lisa fem (not patterned)
a plain grey fabric
una tela gris lisa

plain chocolate NOUN
el **chocolate amargo** masc

plait NOUN
la **trenza** fem
She wears her hair in a plait.
Lleva el pelo recogido en una trenza.

LANGUAGE TIP
In Spanish you usually use an article like **el**, **la** or **los**, **las** with parts of the body.

---

plan

---
plan can be a noun or a verb.

A NOUN
1 el **plan** masc
Have you got any plans for the holidays?
¿Tienes planes para las vacaciones?
2 el **plano** masc (map)
a plan of the school
un plano del colegio
B VERB
to plan
planear
We're planning a trip to the States.
Estamos planeando hacer un viaje a Estados Unidos.

plane NOUN
el **avión** masc
(PL los **aviones**)
by plane
en avión

planet NOUN
el **planeta** masc

LANGUAGE TIP
Even though it ends in **-a**, **el planeta** is a masculine noun.

---

plant NOUN
la **planta** fem

plaster NOUN
la **tirita** fem (sticking plaster)

plastic

---
plastic can be a noun or an adjective.

A NOUN
el **plástico** masc
It's made of plastic.
Es de plástico.
B ADJECTIVE
de plástico
a plastic bag
una bolsa de plástico

plate NOUN
el **plato** masc

platform NOUN
el **andén** masc (PL los **andenes**)
I'll wait for you on the platform, OK?
Te espero en el andén, ¿vale?

DID YOU KNOW...?
At railway stations in Spain, it is the track rather than the platform that's numbered.

---

on platform seven
en la vía siete

play

---
play can be a verb or a noun.

A VERB
to play
1 jugar
He's playing with his friends.
Está jugando con sus amigos.
2 jugar a (*sport, game*)
I play football.
Juego al fútbol.
Can you play chess?
¿Sabes jugar al ajedrez?
3 tocar (*instrument*)
I play the guitar.
Toco la guitarra.
What sort of music do they play?
¿Qué tipo de música tocan?
4 poner (*CD*)
Why don't you play that CD that you like?
¿Por qué no pones ese CD que te gusta?
B NOUN
la **obra** *fem*
a play by Shakespeare
una obra de Shakespeare

player NOUN
el **jugador** *masc*
la **jugadora** *fem*
a football player
un jugador de fútbol

playground NOUN
1 el **patio de recreo** *masc* (*at school*)
2 el **parque infantil** *masc* (*in park*)

playgroup NOUN
la **guardería** *fem*

playing card NOUN
la **carta** *fem*

playing field NOUN
el **campo de deportes** *masc*

playtime NOUN
el **recreo** *masc*
at playtime
en el recreo

please EXCLAMATION
por favor
Two coffees, please.
Dos cafés, por favor.

DID YOU KNOW...?
In Spanish you don't use **por favor** as often as you'd say **please** in English. Speakers often show politeness by phrasing requests as a question.

I'd like a lemonade, please.
¿Me pone una gaseosa?
Can we have the bill, please?
¿Nos puede traer la cuenta?
Can you open the door for me, please?
¿Me puede abrir la puerta?

Yes, please!
¡Sí, por favor!

pleased ADJECTIVE
contento *masc*
contenta *fem*
My mother isn't pleased.
Mi madre no está contenta.

pleasure NOUN
el **gusto** *masc*
with pleasure
con mucho gusto

plenty NOUN
I've got plenty.
Tengo de sobra.
You've got plenty of time.
Tienes tiempo de sobra.

That's plenty, thanks.
Así está bien, gracias.

plug in VERB
enchufar
Is it plugged in?
¿Está enchufado?
It isn't plugged in.
No está enchufado.

plum NOUN
la **ciruela** *fem*

plum jam
mermelada de ciruela

plump ADJECTIVE
regordete *masc/fem*

plural NOUN
el **plural** *masc*
in the plural
en plural

plus PREPOSITION
más
Four plus three equals seven.
Cuatro más tres son siete.

p.m. ABBREVIATION
1 **de la tarde** (*in the afternoon or evening*)
at two p.m.
a las dos de la tarde
2 **de la noche** (*at night*)
at ten p.m.
a las diez de la noche

LANGUAGE TIP
Use **de la tarde** at times when it's still light and **de la noche** at times when it's dark.

---

poached egg NOUN
el **huevo escalfado** *masc*

pocket NOUN
el **bolsillo** *masc*
It's in my pocket.
Lo tengo en el bolsillo.

pocket money NOUN
la **paga** *fem*
I get two pounds a week pocket money.
Me dan dos libras a la semana de paga.

poem NOUN
el **poema** *masc*

LANGUAGE TIP
Even though it ends in **-a**, **el poema** is a masculine noun.

---

point

point can be a noun or a verb.

A NOUN
1 el **punto** *masc*
You've got five points.
Tienes cinco puntos.
What's the point?
¿Para qué?
What's the point of leaving so early?
¿Para qué vamos a salir tan pronto?
2 la **coma** *fem* (*in decimals*)
two point five (2.5)
dos coma cinco (2,5)

DID YOU KNOW...?
In Spanish you use a comma instead of a point in decimal numbers.

B VERB
to point
Which cake? Can you point to it?
¿Qué pastel? ¿Puedes señalarlo?
The guide pointed out the Columbus monument to us.
El guía nos señaló dónde estaba el monumento a Colón.

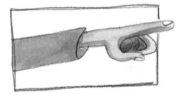

poison NOUN
el **veneno** *masc*

poisonous ADJECTIVE
venenoso *masc*
venenosa *fem*
a poisonous snake
una serpiente venenosa

police PL NOUN
la **policía** *fem*
The police are usually very helpful.
La policía suele ser de mucha ayuda.

LANGUAGE TIP
policía is a singular word in Spanish.

---

police car NOUN
el **coche de policía** *masc*

policeman NOUN
el **policía** *masc*
He's a policeman.
Es policía.

LANGUAGE TIP
In Spanish, you do not use an article
with people's jobs.

police officer NOUN
el **policía** *masc*
She's a police officer.
Es policía.

LANGUAGE TIP
In Spanish, you do not use an article
with people's jobs.

police station NOUN
la **comisaría** *fem*

policewoman NOUN
la **policía** *fem*
She's a policewoman.
Es policía.

LANGUAGE TIP
In Spanish, you do not use an article
with people's jobs.

polite ADJECTIVE
educado *masc*
educada *fem*
He's a very polite boy.
Es un chico muy educado.

polluted ADJECTIVE
contaminado *masc*
contaminada *fem*

pollution NOUN
la **contaminación** *fem*

polo shirt NOUN
el **polo** *masc*

pond NOUN
el **estanque** *masc*
There's a pond in our garden.
Hay un estanque en nuestro jardín.

pony NOUN
el **poni** *masc*

ponytail NOUN
la **coleta** *fem*
I've got a ponytail.
Llevo una coleta.

pony trekking NOUN
I go pony trekking.
Voy de excursión en poni.

pool NOUN
1 la **piscina** *fem* (*swimming pool*)
There's a pool.
Hay una piscina.
2 el **billar** *masc* (*game*)
Can you play pool?
¿Sabes jugar al billar?

poor ADJECTIVE
pobre *masc/fem*
They're very poor.
Son muy pobres.

LANGUAGE TIP
In noun phrases you put **pobre** before
the noun when you mean **unlucky**.

Poor David, he's very unlucky!
¡Pobre David, tiene muy mala suerte!

LANGUAGE TIP
You put **pobre** after the noun when
you mean **not wealthy**.

a poor family
una familia pobre

popcorn NOUN
las **palomitas de maíz** *fem*

Pope NOUN
el **Papa** *masc*

A
B
C
D
E
F
G
H
I
J
K
L
M
N
O
P
Q
R
S
T
U
V
W
X
Y
Z

pop group NOUN
el **grupo de pop** *masc*
What's your favourite pop group?
¿Cuál es tu grupo de pop favorito?

pop music NOUN
la **música pop** *fem*

poppy NOUN
la **amapola** *fem*

pop song NOUN
la **canción pop** *fem* (PL las **canciones pop**)

popular ADJECTIVE
She's a very popular girl.
Es una chica que le cae bien a todo el mundo.

porch NOUN
el **porche** *masc*

pork NOUN
la **carne de cerdo** *fem*
I don't eat pork.
No como carne de cerdo.
a pork chop
una chuleta de cerdo

port NOUN
el **puerto** *masc*

portable ADJECTIVE
portátil *masc/fem*
a portable TV
un televisor portátil

portion NOUN
la **ración** *fem* (PL las **raciones**)
a large portion of chips
una ración grande de patatas fritas

posh ADJECTIVE
de lujo
a posh hotel
un hotel de lujo

positive ADJECTIVE
seguro *masc*
segura *fem*
Are you positive, Kris?
¿Estás seguro, Kris?

possibility NOUN
It's a possibility.
Es posible.

possible ADJECTIVE
posible *masc/fem*
as soon as possible
lo antes posible

LANGUAGE TIP
Don't forget that there's only one **s** in the Spanish word **posible**.

---

post

> **post** can be a noun or a verb.

A NOUN
el **correo** *masc*
Is there any post for me?
¿Hay correo para mí?

B VERB
to post
1 **enviar por correo**
I've got some cards to post.
Tengo que enviar por correo algunas postales.
Can you post this letter for me?
¿Me echas esta carta al correo?

2 **publicar**
I posted the video on my blog.
Publiqué el vídeo en mi blog.

postbox NOUN
el **buzón** *masc* (PL los **buzones**)

postcard NOUN
la **postal** *fem*
Thank you for the postcard, Jodie.
Gracias por la postal, Jodie.

postcode NOUN
el **código postal** *masc*
What is your postcode?
¿Cuál es tu código postal?

poster NOUN
el **póster** *masc* (PL los **pósters**)
I've got posters on my bedroom walls.
Tengo pósters en las paredes de mi habitación.

postman NOUN
el **cartero** *masc*
He's a postman.
Es cartero.

LANGUAGE TIP
In Spanish, you do not use an article with people's jobs.

post office NOUN
la **oficina de Correos** *fem*
Where's the post office, please?
¿Dónde está la oficina de Correos, por favor?

potato NOUN
la **patata** *fem*
mashed potatoes
el puré de patatas
boiled potatoes
patatas cocidas
a baked potato
una patata asada

potato salad NOUN
la **ensaladilla de patatas** *fem*

pottery NOUN
la **cerámica** *fem*

pound NOUN
la **libra** *fem*
How many euros do you get for a pound?
¿Cuántos euros equivalen a una libra?
a pound of tomatoes
una libra de tomates

DID YOU KNOW...?
In Spain measurements are in grams and kilograms. One pound is about 450 grams.

pour VERB
1 **echar** (*pour out*)
She poured some water into the pan.
Echó un poco de agua en la olla.
2 **diluviar** (*with rain*)
It's pouring.
Está diluviando.

powerful ADJECTIVE
poderoso *masc*
poderosa *fem*

practically ADVERB
prácticamente
It's practically impossible.
Es prácticamente imposible.

practice NOUN
el **entrenamiento** *masc*
football practice
entrenamiento de fútbol
I've got to do my piano practice.
Tengo que hacer mis ejercicios de piano.

practise VERB
1 **practicar** (*instrument, language*)
I ought to practise more.
Debería practicar más.
I practise my flute every evening.
Practico con la flauta todas las noches.
I like practising my Spanish.
Me gusta poner en práctica el español.
2 **entrenar** (*do training*)
The team practises on Thursdays.
El equipo entrena los jueves.

prawn NOUN
la **gamba** *fem*

pray VERB
rezar
Let's pray for them.
Rezemos por ellos.
Let us pray.
Oremos.

prayer NOUN
la **oración** *fem* (PL las **oraciones**)

precisely ADVERB
at ten a.m. precisely
a las diez en punto de la mañana

prefer VERB
preferir
Which would you prefer?
¿Cuál prefieres?
Which do you prefer, tennis or football?
¿Qué prefieres, el tenis o el fútbol?
I prefer English to geography.
Prefiero el inglés a la geografía.

pregnant ADJECTIVE
embarazada *fem*
She's six months pregnant.
Está embarazada de seis meses.

prep NOUN
los **deberes** *masc pl*
history prep
los deberes de historia

prepare VERB
preparar
She's preparing dinner.
Está preparando la cena.

preposition NOUN
la **preposición** *fem* (PL las **preposiciones**)

prep school NOUN
el **colegio privado** *masc*

present

> **present** can be an adjective or a noun.

A ADJECTIVE
presente *masc/fem*
Ten present, two absent.
Diez presentes, dos faltas.
He was present at the party.
Asistió a la fiesta.
the present tense
el presente *masc*

B NOUN
1 el **regalo** *masc* (*gift*)
I'm going to give Julia a present.
Le voy a hacer un regalo a Julia.
I got lots of presents.
Me hicieron muchos regalos.

2 el **presente** *masc* (*time*)
the present and the future
el presente y el futuro

president NOUN
el **presidente** *masc*
la **presidenta** *fem*

pretend VERB
Pretend you are in a café.
Haz como si estuvieras en una cafetería.

LANGUAGE TIP
Be careful! The translation of **pretend** is not **pretender**.

pretty

> **pretty** can be an adjective or an adverb.

A ADJECTIVE
1 **guapo** *masc*
guapa *fem* (*good-looking*)
She's very pretty.
Es muy guapa.
Sarah is prettier than Irene.
Sarah es más guapa que Irene.
She's the prettiest girl in the class.
Es la chica más guapa de la clase.
2 **bonito** *masc*
bonita *fem* (*lovely*)
a pretty blouse
una blusa bonita

B ADVERB
bastante
It's pretty old.
Es bastante viejo.
The weather was pretty awful.
Hizo un tiempo bastante horrible.

previous ADJECTIVE
anterior *masc/fem*
the previous day
el día anterior

price NOUN
el **precio** *masc*

priest NOUN
el **sacerdote** *masc*

primary school NOUN
la **escuela primaria** *fem*
I am at primary school.
Estoy en la escuela primaria.

prince NOUN
el **príncipe** *masc*
the Prince of Wales
el Príncipe de Gales

princess NOUN
la **princesa** *fem*
Princess Anne
la princesa Ana

DID YOU KNOW...?
In Spain a princess who is not the heir
to the throne is called an **infanta**
rather than a **princesa** while a prince
who is not the heir to the throne is an
infante.

---

print VERB
1 escribir en letra de imprenta
(*write*)
Print your name.
Escribe tu nombre en letra de
imprenta.
2 imprimir (*on machine*)

printer NOUN
la **impresora** *fem*

prison NOUN
la **cárcel** *fem*

in prison
en la cárcel

private ADJECTIVE
privado *masc*
privada *fem*
a private letter
una carta privada
I have private lessons.
Tomo clases particulares.

private school NOUN
el **colegio privado** *masc*

prize NOUN
el **premio** *masc*
The prize is one hundred euros.
El premio son cien euros.
You can win a prize.
Puedes ganar un premio.

prize-giving NOUN
la **entrega de premios** *fem*

prizewinner NOUN
el **ganador** *masc*
la **ganadora** *fem*

probably ADVERB
probablemente
probably not
probablemente no

problem NOUN
el **problema** *masc*
Is there a problem?
¿Hay algún problema?

LANGUAGE TIP
Even though it ends in **-a**, **el
problema** is a masculine noun.

What's the problem?
¿Qué pasa?

No problem!
¡No importa!

procession NOUN
la **procesión** *fem* (PL las **procesiones**)

profession NOUN
la **profesión** *fem* (PL las **profesiones**)

professor NOUN
el **catedrático** *masc*
la **catedrática** *fem*

LANGUAGE TIP
Be careful! The translation of
professor is not **profesor**.

---

profit NOUN
el **beneficio** *masc*

program NOUN
el **programa** *masc*
a computer program
un programa informático

LANGUAGE TIP
Even though it ends in **-a**, **el**
programa is a masculine noun.

---

programme NOUN
el **programa** *masc*
my favourite TV programme
mi programa favorito de la tele
Would you like a programme?
¿Quieres un programa?

LANGUAGE TIP
Even though it ends in **-a**, **el**
programa is a masculine noun.

---

progress NOUN
You're making progress, Edward!
¡Estás progresando, Edward!

projector NOUN
el **proyector** *masc*

promise

> **promise** can be a noun or a verb.

A NOUN
la **promesa** *fem*
I'll make you a promise.
Te haré una promesa.
That's a promise!
¡Es una promesa!
B VERB
to promise
prometer
I promise!
¡Lo prometo!
I'll write, I promise!
¡Escribiré, lo prometo!

prompt

> **prompt** can be an adjective or an adverb.

A ADJECTIVE
rápido *masc*
rápida *fem*
a prompt reply
una rápida respuesta
B ADVERB
at eight o'clock prompt
a las ocho en punto

pronoun NOUN
el **pronombre** *masc*

pronounce VERB
pronunciar
How do you pronounce that word?
¿Cómo se pronuncia esa palabra?

pronunciation NOUN
la **pronunciación** *fem*
Your pronunciation is good!
¡Tienes una buena pronunciación!

proper ADJECTIVE
adecuado *masc*
adecuada *fem* (*suitable*)
the proper equipment
el equipo adecuado
You should eat a proper breakfast.
Deberías hacer un desayuno en
condiciones.

properly ADVERB
correctamente
> **I can't pronounce it properly.**
> No puedo pronunciarlo correctamente.

propose VERB
proponer
> **I propose a new plan.**
> Propongo un nuevo plan.

Protestant

> Protestant can be an adjective or a noun.

A ADJECTIVE
protestante *masc/fem*
B NOUN
el/la **protestante** *masc/fem*
> **I'm a Protestant.**
> Soy protestante.

LANGUAGE TIP
In Spanish **protestante** is not spelled with a capital letter. Remember that you do not use an article with people's religions in Spanish.

proud ADJECTIVE
orgulloso *masc*
orgullosa *fem*
> **Her parents are proud of her.**
> Sus padres están orgullosos de ella.

prune NOUN
la **ciruela pasa** *fem*

pub NOUN
el **pub** *masc*

public

> public can be a noun or an adjective.

A NOUN
el **público** *masc*
The castle is open to the public.
El castillo está abierto al público.
B ADJECTIVE
público *masc*
pública *fem*
a public swimming pool
una piscina pública

publicity NOUN
la **publicidad** *fem*

public school NOUN
el **colegio privado** *masc*

public transport NOUN
el **transporte público** *masc*
> **by public transport**
> en transporte público

pudding NOUN
el **postre** *masc*
> **Would you like a pudding?**
> ¿Quieres postre?
> **What's for pudding?**
> ¿Qué hay de postre?

pull VERB
tirar
> **Pull!**
> ¡Tira!

pullover NOUN
el **jersey** *masc* (PL los **jerseys**)
> **What colour is your pullover?**
> ¿De qué color es tu jersey?

pump NOUN
1 la **bomba** *fem* (for pumping)
> **a bicycle pump**
> una bomba de bicicleta
2 la **zapatilla de gimnasia** *fem* (shoe)
> **Have you got your pumps?**
> ¿Tienes tus zapatillas de gimnasia?

pump up VERB
inflar
> **Pump up your tyres!**
> ¡Infla tus ruedas!

pumpkin NOUN
la **calabaza** *fem*

Spanish

English

a
b
c
d
e
f
g
h
i
j
k
l
m
n
o
p
q
r
s
t
u
v
w
x
y
z

Spanish

English

A
B
C
D
E
F
G
H
I
J
K
L
M
N
O
P
Q
R
S
T
U
V
W
X
Y
Z

punch VERB
dar un puñetazo a
>**He punched me!**
>¡Me dio un puñetazo!

punctual ADJECTIVE
puntual *masc/fem*
>**Be punctual!**
>¡Sé puntual!

punctuation NOUN
la **puntuación** *fem*

punishment NOUN
el **castigo** *masc*

pupil NOUN
el **alumno** *masc*
la **alumna** *fem*
>**There are twenty-two pupils in my class.**
>Hay veintidós alumnos en mi clase.

puppet NOUN
la **marioneta** *fem*

puppy NOUN
el **cachorro** *masc*

pure ADJECTIVE
puro *masc*
pura *fem*
>**It's pure water.**
>Es agua pura.

purple

> **purple** can be an adjective or a noun.

A ADJECTIVE
morado *masc*
morada *fem*
a purple skirt
una falda morada

LANGUAGE TIP
Colour adjectives come after the noun in Spanish.

B NOUN
el **morado** *masc*
>**Purple is my favourite colour.**
>El morado es mi color favorito.

purpose NOUN
on purpose
a propósito
>**You're doing it on purpose.**
>Lo estás haciendo a propósito.

purr VERB
ronronear
>**The cat is purring.**
>El gato está ronroneando.

purse NOUN
el **monedero** *masc*
>**I've lost my purse.**
>He perdido mi monedero.

push VERB
empujar
>**Push!**
>¡Empuja!

pushchair NOUN
la **sillita de paseo** *fem*

put VERB
poner
>**Where shall I put my things?**
>¿Dónde pongo mis cosas?
>**Don't forget to put your name on the paper.**
>No te olvides de poner tu nombre en la hoja.
>**She's putting the baby to bed.**
>Está acostando al niño.
>**Put your chewing gum in the bin.**
>Tira el chicle a la papelera.

put away VERB
guardar
>**Put your things away, children.**
>Guardad vuestras cosas, niños.

put back VERB
poner en su sitio
>**Don't forget to put it back.**
>No te olvides de ponerlo en su sitio.

put down VERB
dejar (*stop holding*)
Put the bags down for a moment.
Deja las bolsas un momento.
Put down a card.
Deja una carta.
Put your hands down.
Bajad las manos.

LANGUAGE TIP
In Spanish you usually use an article like **el**, **la** or **los**, **las** with parts of the body.

---

put off VERB
1 **apagar** (*switch off*)
Shall I put the light off?
¿Apago la luz?
2 **distraer** (*distract*)
Stop putting me off!
¡Deja de distraerme!

put on VERB
1 **ponerse** (*clothes*)
I'll put my coat on.
Me pondré el abrigo.

LANGUAGE TIP
In Spanish you usually use an article like **el**, **la** or **los**, **las** with clothes you are wearing.

---

2 **encender** (*switch on*)
Shall I put the light on?
¿Enciendo la luz?

put up VERB
1 **colgar** (*hang*)
I'll put the poster up on my wall.
Colgaré el póster en la pared.
2 **subir** (*raise*)
They've put up the price.
Han subido el precio.
Put up your hand if you know the answer.
Que levante la mano el que sepa la respuesta.

puzzle NOUN
el **rompecabezas** *masc*
(PL los **rompecabezas**)

puzzled ADJECTIVE
perplejo *masc*
perpleja *fem*
You look puzzled.
Parece que te has quedado perplejo.

pyjamas PL NOUN
el **pijama** *masc*
my pyjamas
mi pijama
I've got some new pyjamas.
Tengo un pijama nuevo.
a pair of pyjamas
un pijama

LANGUAGE TIP
In Spanish **el pijama** is a singular word.

quad bike NOUN
el **quad** *masc*

quality NOUN
1 la **calidad** *fem (of work, product)*
good quality towels
toallas de buena calidad
2 la **cualidad** *fem (of person)*
She's got lots of good qualities.
Tiene un montón de buenas cualidades.

quantity NOUN
la **cantidad** *fem*

quarrel VERB
pelearse
They're always quarrelling.
Siempre se están peleando.

quarter NOUN
la **cuarta parte** *fem*
a quarter of the class
una cuarta parte de la clase
It's a quarter to one.
Es la una menos cuarto.
It's a quarter past six.
Son las seis y cuarto.
at a quarter to eight
a las ocho menos cuarto

three quarters
tres cuartos
a quarter of an hour
un cuarto de hora
three quarters of an hour
tres cuartos de hora
a quarter past ten
las diez y cuarto

a quarter to eleven
las once menos cuarto

queen NOUN
la **reina** *fem*
Queen Elizabeth
la reina Isabel

DID YOU KNOW...?
Did you know that Spanish speakers translate the names of the British royal family into Spanish?

the queen of hearts
la reina de corazones

question NOUN
1 la **pregunta** *fem (query)*
Are there any questions?
¿Hay alguna pregunta?
Can I ask a question?
¿Puedo hacer una pregunta?
2 la **cuestión** *fem* (PL las **cuestiones**) *(matter)*
That's a difficult question.
Esa es una cuestión complicada.

question mark NOUN
el **signo de interrogación** *masc*

questionnaire NOUN
el **cuestionario** *masc*

queue

queue can be a noun or a verb.

A NOUN
la **cola** *fem*
There's a very long queue.
Hay una cola muy larga.
B VERB
to queue
hacer cola
You have to queue.
Tienes que hacer cola.

quick ADJECTIVE
rápido *masc*
rápida *fem*
  a quick lunch
  una comida rápida
  It's quicker by train.
  Es más rápido en tren.
  Be quick, Laura!
  ¡Date prisa, Laura!
  Be quick, girls!
  ¡Daos prisa, niñas!

quickly ADVERB
rápido
  Am I speaking too quickly?
  ¿Estoy hablando demasiado
  rápido?

quiet ADJECTIVE
1 **callado** *masc*
  callada *fem* (*not chatty*)
  You're very quiet, Julia.
  Estás muy callada, Julia.

LANGUAGE TIP
When **be quiet** means 'fall silent',
you translate it using the verb
callarse.

  Be quiet all of you, I'm thinking!
  ¡Callaos todos, que estoy pensando!

  Be quiet, Jeremy!
  ¡Cállate, Jeremy!
  Quiet!
  ¡Silencio!

2 **tranquilo** *masc*
  tranquila *fem* (*peaceful*)

  a quiet place
  un lugar tranquilo
  a quiet weekend
  un fin de semana tranquilo

quietly ADVERB
1 **en voz baja** (*in a low voice*)
  Talk quietly.
  Hablad en voz baja.
2 **sin hacer ruido** (*noiselessly*)
  Shut the door quietly, Sophie.
  Cierra la puerta sin hacer ruido,
  Sophie.

quilt NOUN
  el **edredón** *masc* (PL los **edredones**)

quite ADVERB
1 **bastante** (*rather*)
  It's quite expensive.
  Es bastante caro.
  It's quite warm today.
  Hace bastante calor hoy.
  It's quite a long way.
  Está bastante lejos.
  quite a lot of money
  bastante dinero
2 **totalmente** (*completely*)
  I'm quite sure he's coming.
  Estoy totalmente seguro de que viene.
  Are you ready, Lorna? — Not quite.
  ¿Estás lista, Lorna? — No del todo.

  quite good
  bastante bueno

quiz NOUN
  el **concurso** *masc*

A
B
C
D
E
F
G
H
I
J
K
L
M
N
O
P
Q
R
S
T
U
V
W
X
Y
Z

Rr

rabbi NOUN
el **rabino** masc
la **rabina** fem

rabbit NOUN
el **conejo** masc

race NOUN
la **carrera** fem
a cycle race
una carrera ciclista
Let's have a race!
¡Vamos a echar una carrera!

racing car NOUN
el **coche de carreras** masc

racket NOUN
la **raqueta** fem
my tennis racket
mi raqueta de tenis

radiator NOUN
el **radiador** masc

radio NOUN
la **radio** fem
I heard it on the radio.
Lo escuché en la radio.

> **LANGUAGE TIP**
> Even though it ends in **-o**, **la radio** is a feminine noun.

raffle NOUN
la **rifa** fem

raffle ticket NOUN
la **papeleta para la rifa** fem
Do you want to buy a raffle ticket?
¿Quieres comprar una papeleta para la rifa?

rage NOUN
to be in a rage
estar furioso

> **LANGUAGE TIP**
> Change **furioso** to **furiosa** if it's a woman or girl who's in a rage.

She's in a rage.
Está furiosa.

rail NOUN
by rail
en tren

railway NOUN
el **ferrocarril** masc

railway line NOUN
la **línea de ferrocarril** fem

railway station NOUN
la **estación de trenes** fem (PL las **estaciones de trenes**)

rain

> **rain** can be a noun or a verb.

A NOUN
la **lluvia** fem
in the rain
bajo la lluvia
B VERB
to rain
llover
It's going to rain.
Va a llover.
It rains a lot here.
Llueve mucho aquí.

It's raining.
Está lloviendo.

rainbow NOUN
el **arco iris** masc

raincoat NOUN
el **impermeable** masc

rainforest NOUN
la **selva tropical** fem

rainy ADJECTIVE
lluvioso masc
lluviosa fem
a rainy day
un día lluvioso

raise VERB
1 **levantar**
Raise your left arm, everyone.
Levantad todos el brazo izquierdo.
2 **recaudar**
to raise money
recaudar fondos
We're raising money for a new gym.
Estamos recaudando fondos para un gimnasio nuevo.

raisin NOUN
la **pasa** fem

Ramadan NOUN
el **Ramadán** masc

ramp NOUN
la **rampa** fem

ran VERB ▷ see **run**

random ADJECTIVE
at random
al azar
Pick a card at random.
Escoge una carta al azar.

rang VERB ▷ see **ring**

range NOUN
la **gama** fem
There's a wide range of colours.
Hay una amplia gama de colores.

rap NOUN
el **rap** masc (poetry)

rare ADJECTIVE
1 **raro** masc
rara fem (unusual)
2 **poco hecho** masc
poco hecha fem (steak)

rarely ADVERB
raras veces

raspberry NOUN
la **frambuesa** fem
raspberry jam
mermelada de frambuesa

rat NOUN
la **rata** fem

rather ADVERB
1 **bastante** (quite)
Twenty pounds! That's rather expensive!
¡Veinte libras! ¡Eso es bastante caro!
2 **I'd rather ...**
Preferiría ...
I'd rather stay in tonight.
Preferiría no salir esta noche.
Would you like a sweet? — I'd rather have an apple.
¿Quieres un caramelo? — Preferiría una manzana.
Which would you rather have?
¿Cuál prefieres?
Would you rather have water or orange juice?
¿Prefieres agua o zumo de naranja?

ravenous ADJECTIVE
I'm ravenous!
¡Estoy muerto de hambre!

LANGUAGE TIP
Change **muerto** to **muerta** if you're a girl.

raw ADJECTIVE
crudo masc
cruda fem

razor NOUN
la **maquinilla de afeitar** fem

Spanish

English

A
B
C
D
E
F
G
H
I
J
K
L
M
N
O
P
Q
R
S
T
U
V
W
X
Y
Z

RE NOUN
la **religión** *fem*

reach

> **reach** can be a noun or a verb.

A NOUN
Mum keeps the biscuits out of reach.
Mi madre guarda las galletas fuera de nuestro alcance.
The hotel is within easy reach of the town centre.
El hotel está a poca distancia del centro de la ciudad.

B VERB
to reach
llegar a
We hope to reach London by five o'clock.
Esperamos llegar a Londres para las cinco.
I can't reach the top shelf.
No llego a la estantería de arriba.

read VERB
leer
I don't read much.
No leo mucho.
Have you read 'The Prisoner of Azkaban'?
¿Has leído "El prisionero de Azkaban"?

read out VERB
leer en voz alta
I'll read out the names.
Leeré en voz alta los nombres.

reading NOUN
la **lectura** *fem*
Reading is one of my hobbies.
La lectura es una de mis aficiones.

ready ADJECTIVE
listo *masc*
lista *fem*
Breakfast is ready.
El desayuno está listo.
She's nearly ready.
Está casi lista.
Are you ready, children?
¿Estáis listos, niños?

> **Ready, steady, go!**
> ¡Preparados, listos, ya!

real ADJECTIVE
1 **verdadero** *masc*
verdadera *fem* (*true*)
Her real name is Amina.
Su verdadero nombre es Amina.
2 **auténtico** *masc*
auténtica *fem* (*genuine*)
It's real leather.
Es piel auténtica.

realize VERB
darse cuenta de
Do you realize what time it is?
¿Te das cuenta de la hora que es?

really ADVERB
1 **muy** (*very*)
She's really nice.
Es muy simpática.
It's really hot today.
Hoy hace mucho calor.
2 **de verdad** (*genuinely*)
I'm learning German. — Really?
Estoy aprendiendo alemán. — ¿De verdad?
Do you want to go? — Not really.
¿Quieres ir? — La verdad es que no.

reason NOUN
la **razón** *fem* (PL las **razones**)

reasonable ADJECTIVE
razonable *masc/fem*
Be reasonable, Sam!
¡Sé razonable, Sam!

receipt NOUN
el **recibo** *masc*

Keep your receipt.
Guarda tu recibo.

LANGUAGE TIP
Be careful! The translation of **receipt** is not **receta**.

---

receive VERB
  recibir
  I received your letter yesterday.
  Recibí tu carta ayer.

recent ADJECTIVE
  reciente *masc/fem*

recently ADVERB
  recientemente
  He's been ill recently.
  Ha estado enfermo recientemente.

reception NOUN
  1 la **recepción** *fem* (*desk*)
  Please leave your key at reception.
  Por favor, deje su llave en recepción.
  2 la **celebración** *fem* (PL las **celebraciones**) (*party*)
  The reception will be at a big hotel.
  La celebración será en un gran hotel.

receptionist NOUN
  el/la **recepcionista** *masc/fem*
  She's a receptionist.
  Es recepcionista.

LANGUAGE TIP
In Spanish, you do not use an article with people's jobs.

---

recipe NOUN
  la **receta** *fem*
  a recipe book
  un libro de recetas

reckon VERB
  creer
  What do you reckon?
  ¿Tú qué crees?

recognize VERB
  reconocer

Do you recognize this boy?
¿Reconoces a este chico?

LANGUAGE TIP
Don't forget the personal **a** in examples like this one.

---

recommend VERB
  recomendar
  What do you recommend?
  ¿Qué me recomienda?
  I recommend the soup.
  Le recomiendo la sopa.

LANGUAGE TIP
In Spanish you usually say who you're recommending something to. Can you find words for 'to me' and 'to you' above?

---

record

> **record** can be a noun or a verb.

A NOUN
  el **récord** *masc* (*in sport*)
  the world record
  el récord mundial
B VERB
  to record
  grabar
  We're going to record the song.
  Vamos a grabar la canción.

LANGUAGE TIP
Be careful! The translation of **to record** is not **recordar**.

---

recorder NOUN
  la **flauta dulce** *fem*
  I play the recorder.
  Toco la flauta dulce.

rectangle NOUN
  el **rectángulo** *masc*

A
B
C
D
E
F
G
H
I
J
K
L
M
N
O
P
Q
R
S
T
U
V
W
X
Y
Z

recycle VERB
reciclar

red

> **red** can be an adjective or a noun.

A ADJECTIVE
rojo *masc*
roja *fem*
a red rose
una rosa roja

LANGUAGE TIP
Colour adjectives come after the noun
in Spanish.

The traffic lights are red.
El semáforo está en rojo.
Gerald's got red hair.
Gerald es pelirrojo.

B NOUN
el **rojo** *masc*
Red is my favourite colour.
El rojo es mi color favorito.

redecorate VERB
1 **empapelar de nuevo** (*with
wallpaper*)
I'd like to redecorate my room.
Quiero empapelar de nuevo mi
habitación.
2 **pintar de nuevo** (*with paint*)
I'd like to redecorate my room.
Quiero pintar de nuevo mi habitación.

LANGUAGE TIP
There's no single verb meaning both
'to paint' and 'to paper' in Spanish.

---

red-haired
ADJECTIVE
pelirrojo *masc*
pelirroja *fem*

redhead
NOUN
el **pelirrojo**
masc
la **pelirroja** *fem*

redo VERB
rehacer
I need to redo my homework.
Tengo que rehacer mis deberes.

reduced ADJECTIVE
at a reduced price
a un precio rebajado

reduction NOUN
la **rebaja** *fem*
a five-percent reduction
una rebaja del cinco por ciento

referee NOUN
el **árbitro** *masc*
la **árbitra** *fem*

reflexive ADJECTIVE
a reflexive verb
un verbo reflexivo

refrigerator NOUN
el **frigorífico** *masc*

refugee NOUN
el **refugiado** *masc*
la **refugiada** *fem*

refuse VERB
negarse
She's refusing to say anything.
Se niega a decir nada.

regards PL NOUN
los **recuerdos** *masc pl*
Give my regards to Lucy.
Dale recuerdos a Lucy.
Tim sends his regards.
Tim manda recuerdos.

region NOUN
la **región** *fem* (PL las **regiones**)
in this region
en esta región

register NOUN
I'm going to call the register.
Voy a pasar lista.

registration NOUN
after registration
después de pasar lista

regular ADJECTIVE
1 **regular** *masc/fem*
   at regular intervals
   a intervalos regulares
   a regular verb
   un verbo regular
   You should take regular exercise.
   Deberías hacer ejercicio con
   regularidad.
2 **normal** *masc/fem* (*medium*)
   a regular portion of fries
   una porción normal de patatas fritas

rehearsal NOUN
   el **ensayo** *masc*

reindeer NOUN
   el **reno** *masc*

relation NOUN
   el/la **pariente** *masc/fem*
   my relations
   mis parientes
   I've got relations in London.
   Tengo parientes en Londres.

relative NOUN
   el/la **pariente** *masc/fem*
   all her relatives
   todos sus parientes
   I've got relatives in Manchester.
   Tengo parientes en Manchester.

relax VERB
   relajarse
   Mum's relaxing in front of the TV.
   Mi madre se está relajando delante de
   la tele.
   Relax! Everything's fine.
   ¡Tranquilo! No pasa nada.

   LANGUAGE TIP
   Change **tranquilo** to **tranquila** if
   talking to a woman or girl.

relaxed ADJECTIVE
   relajado *masc*
   relajada *fem*

relaxing ADJECTIVE
   relajante *masc/fem*
   Cooking is very relaxing.
   Cocinar es muy relajante.

relay race NOUN
   la **carrera de relevos** *fem*
   We won the relay race.
   Ganamos la carrera de relevos.

reliable ADJECTIVE
   fiable *masc/fem*
   a reliable car
   un coche fiable
   He's not very reliable.
   No te puedes fiar de él.

relief NOUN
   el **alivio** *masc*
   What a relief!
   ¡Qué alivio!

religion NOUN
   la **religión** *fem* (PL las **religiones**)
   What religion are you?
   ¿De qué religión eres?

religious ADJECTIVE
   religioso *masc*
   religiosa *fem*

rely on VERB
   confiar en
   I'm relying on you.
   Confío en ti.

remark NOUN
   el **comentario** *masc*

remember VERB
   acordarse de
   I can't remember his name.
   No me acuerdo de su nombre.
   Sorry, I can't remember.
   Lo siento, no me acuerdo.
   **Did you remember to lock the
   door?**
   ¿Te acordaste de cerrar la puerta con
   llave?

   LANGUAGE TIP
   In Spanish you often say **no te olvides**
   (don't forget) instead of **remember**.

   **Remember to write your names
   on the form.**
   No os olvidéis de escribir vuestro
   nombre en el impreso.

remind VERB
recordar
> **Remind me to speak to Daniel.**
> Recuérdame que hable con Daniel.
> **She reminds me of you.**
> Me recuerda a ti.

remote control NOUN
el **mando a distancia** *masc*

remove VERB
quitar
> **Please remove your bag from my seat.**
> Por favor, quita tu bolsa de mi asiento.

rent

> rent can be a noun or a verb.

A NOUN
> el **alquiler** *masc*
> **She has to pay the rent.**
> Tiene que pagar el alquiler.

B VERB
> **to rent**
> **alquilar**
> **We are going to rent a villa.**
> Vamos a alquilar un chalet.

repair VERB
arreglar
> **Can you repair them?**
> ¿Puedes arreglarlos?

repeat VERB
repetir
> **Can you repeat that, please?**
> ¿Puedes repetir eso, por favor?
> **Repeat after me, everyone.**
> Repetid todos después de mí.

reply

> reply can be a noun or a verb.

A NOUN
> la **respuesta** *fem*
> **I got no reply to my letter.**
> No recibí respuesta a mi carta.

B VERB
> **to reply**
> **contestar**

> **I hope you will reply soon.**
> Espero que contestes pronto.
> **She always replies to my letters.**
> Siempre contesta a mis cartas.

report NOUN
1 el **boletín de evaluación** *masc* (PL los **boletines de evaluación**)
(*school report*)

LANGUAGE TIP
Although **el boletín de evaluación** is the Spanish for **school report**, Spanish children usually just talk about their **notas**, literally 'marks'.

> **I usually get a good report.**
> Normalmente saco buenas notas.
2 el **reportaje** *masc* (*news report*)

request NOUN
la **solicitud** *fem*

reservation NOUN
la **reserva** *fem*
> **I've got a reservation.**
> Tengo una reserva.
> **I'd like to make a reservation.**
> Quisiera hacer una reserva.

reserve

> reserve can be a noun or a verb.

A NOUN
> el/la **suplente** *masc/fem*
> **I was a reserve in the game last Saturday.**
> Estaba de suplente en el partido del sábado.

B VERB
> **to reserve**
> **reservar**
> **I'd like to reserve a table for tomorrow evening.**
> Quisiera reservar una mesa para mañana por la noche.

reserved ADJECTIVE
reservado *masc*
reservada *fem*
> **This seat is reserved.**
> Este asiento está reservado.

resolution NOUN
> **Have you made any New Year's resolutions?**
> ¿Tienes buenos propósitos para el Año Nuevo?

resort NOUN
> el **centro turístico** *masc*
> **It's a resort on the Costa del Sol.**
> Es un centro turístico de la Costa del Sol.
> **a ski resort**
> una estación de esquí

responsibility NOUN
> la **responsabilidad** *fem*
> **It's your responsibility.**
> Es tu responsabilidad.

LANGUAGE TIP
Have you noticed that **responsabilidad** has an 'a' in it in Spanish?

---

responsible ADJECTIVE
> **responsable** *masc/fem*

LANGUAGE TIP
Remember that the Spanish word ends in 'able' rather than 'ible'.

> **He's responsible for booking the tickets.**
> Es responsable de reservar las entradas.
> **It's a responsible job.**
> Es un puesto de responsabilidad.

rest

> **rest** can be a noun or a verb.

A NOUN
1 el **descanso** *masc* (break)
> **five minutes' rest**
> cinco minutos de descanso
> **Can we have a rest?**
> ¿Podemos descansar?
> **I need a rest.**
> Necesito descansar.

2 (remainder)
> **the rest**
> el resto
> **I'll do the rest.**
> Yo haré el resto.
> **the rest of the money**
> el resto del dinero

B VERB
> **to rest**
> **descansar**

restaurant NOUN
> el **restaurante** *masc*
> **We don't often go to restaurants.**
> No solemos ir a restaurantes.

result NOUN
> el **resultado** *masc*
> **my exam results**
> los resultados de los exámenes

LANGUAGE TIP
Change **los exámenes** to **el examen** if you're talking about only one exam.

> **What was the result? — One-nil.**
> ¿Cuál fue el resultado? — Uno a cero.

retire VERB
> **jubilarse**
> **He's going to retire.**
> Va a jubilarse.

retired ADJECTIVE
> **jubilado** *masc*
> **jubilada** *fem*
> **She's retired.**
> Está jubilada.

retirement NOUN
la **jubilación** *fem*

return

> **return** can be a noun or a verb.

A NOUN
1 la **vuelta** *fem*
after our return
después de nuestra vuelta
the return journey
el viaje de vuelta
2 la **ida y vuelta** *fem* (*ticket*)
A return to Glasgow, please.
Una ida y vuelta a Glasgow,
por favor.

Many happy returns!
¡Que cumplas muchos más!

LANGUAGE TIP
Have you noticed the upside-down
exclamation mark at the start of
Spanish exclamations?

B VERB
to return
1 **volver** (*come back*)
I've just returned from holiday.
Acabo de volver de vacaciones.
2 **devolver** (*give back*)
**I've got to return this book to the
library.**
Tengo que devolver este libro a la
biblioteca.

reverse ADJECTIVE
inverso *masc*
inversa *fem*
in reverse order
en orden inverso

revise VERB
estudiar para un examen
**I haven't started revising for my
exams yet.**
Todavía no he empezado a estudiar
para los exámenes.

revision NOUN
**Have you done a lot of maths
revision?**
¿Has estudiado mucho para el examen
de matemáticas?

reward NOUN
la **recompensa** *fem*
There's a thousand-euro reward.
Hay una recompensa de mil euros.

rhubarb NOUN
el **ruibarbo** *masc*

rhythm NOUN
el **ritmo** *masc*

rib NOUN
la **costilla** *fem*

ribbon NOUN
la **cinta** *fem*

rice NOUN
el **arroz** *masc*
**Would you like
some rice?**
¿Quieres arroz?

rich ADJECTIVE
rico *masc*
rica *fem*
He's very rich.
Es muy rico.

rid VERB
to get rid of
deshacerse de
I need to get rid of my chewing gum.
Necesito deshacerme del chicle.

ride

> **ride** can be a noun or a verb.

A NOUN
(*on horse*)
to go for a ride
ir a montar a caballo
Would you like to go for a ride?
¿Te gustaría ir a montar a caballo?
I'm going for a ride on my bike.
Voy a ir a dar una vuelta en bici.

B VERB
1 to ride
montar a caballo (*on horse*)
I'm learning to ride.
Estoy aprendiendo a montar a caballo.
2 to ride a bike
montar en bici
Can you ride a bike?
¿Sabes montar en bici?

rider NOUN
1 el **jinete** *masc* (*man, boy*)
He's a good rider.
Es un buen jinete.
2 la **amazona** *fem* (*woman, girl*)
She's a good rider.
Es una buena amazona.

ridiculous ADJECTIVE
ridículo *masc*
ridícula *fem*
Don't be ridiculous, Fiona!
¡No seas ridícula, Fiona!

riding NOUN
I like riding.
Me gusta montar a caballo.

riding school NOUN
la **escuela de equitación** *fem*

right

> **right** can be an adjective, adverb or noun.

A ADJECTIVE
1 correcto *masc*
correcta *fem* (*correct*)
That's the right answer!
¡Ésa es la respuesta correcta!
It isn't the right size.
No es la talla correcta.
We're on the right train.
Estamos en el tren correcto.
2 (*true*)
That's right!
¡Es verdad!
You're right, Luke.
Tienes razón, Luke.
3 derecho *masc*
derecha *fem* (*not left*)

Hold out your right hand.
Extiende la mano derecha.
B ADVERB
1 correctamente (*correctly*)
Am I pronouncing it right?
¿Lo pronuncio correctamente?
2 a la derecha (*to the right*)
Turn right at the traffic lights.
Gira a la derecha en el semáforo.
C NOUN
on the right
a la derecha
a step to the right
un paso a la derecha

> **You're right.**
> Tienes razón.

> **Right! Let's get started.**
> ¡Bueno! ¡Empecemos!

> **Turn right.**
> Gira a la derecha.

right-hand ADJECTIVE
the right-hand side
la derecha
It's on the right-hand side.
Está a la derecha.

right-handed ADJECTIVE
diestro *masc*
diestra *fem*
Tom is right-handed.
Tom es diestro.

ring

> **ring** can be a noun or a verb.

A NOUN
1 el **anillo** *masc*
(*for finger*)
a gold ring
un anillo de oro
a diamond ring
un anillo de
diamantes
a wedding ring
una alianza de boda

2 el **círculo** *masc* (*circle*)
Stand in a ring.
Poneos formando un círculo.
B VERB
to ring
1 **llamar** (*phone*)
You can ring me at home.
Me puedes llamar a casa.
2 **sonar** (*make sound*)
The phone's ringing.
El teléfono está sonando.

rink NOUN
1 la **pista de hielo** *fem*
(*for ice-skating*)
2 la **pista de patinaje** *fem*
(*for roller-skating*)

ripe ADJECTIVE
maduro *masc*
madura *fem*
a ripe peach
un melocotón maduro

rise VERB
subir

risk NOUN
el **riesgo** *masc*
It's a big risk.
Es un gran riesgo.

rival

rival can be a noun or an adjective.

A NOUN
el/la **rival** *masc/fem*
our rivals
nuestros rivales
B ADJECTIVE
rival *masc/fem*
a rival gang
una banda rival

river NOUN
el **río** *masc*
across the river
al otro lado del río
the River Amazon
el río Amazonas

LANGUAGE TIP
In Spanish **río** is not spelled with a capital letter in names of rivers.

road NOUN
1 la **carretera** *fem*
There's a lot of traffic on the roads.
Hay mucho tráfico en las carreteras.
2 la **calle** *fem* (*street*)
They live across the road.
Viven al otro lado de la calle.

road sign NOUN
la **señal de tráfico** *fem*

roadworks PL NOUN
las **obras** *fem pl*

roast ADJECTIVE
asado *masc*
asada *fem*
roast chicken
pollo asado
roast potatoes
patatas asadas

DID YOU KNOW...?
In Spanish you translate both **roast potatoes** and **baked potatoes** the same. If you want to specify, you can say **patatas asadas con la piel** for **baked potatoes**.

rob VERB
robar (*person*)
I've been robbed!
¡Me han robado!
to rob a bank
asaltar un banco
They're robbing the bank!
¡Están asaltando el banco!

robber NOUN
el **ladrón** *masc* (PL los **ladrones**)
la **ladrona** *fem*
a bank robber
un ladrón de bancos

robbery NOUN
el **robo** *masc*

There have been a lot of robberies in my neighbourhood.
Ha habido muchos robos en mi barrio.
a bank robbery
un asalto a un banco

rock NOUN
1 la **roca** *fem* (*boulder*)
2 el **rock** *masc* (*music*)
   a rock concert
   un concierto de rock
   He's a rock star.
   Es una estrella del rock.
3 (*sweet*)
   a stick of rock
   un palo de caramelo

rocket NOUN
el **cohete** *masc*

rod NOUN
la **caña** *fem*
   (*for fishing*)

rode VERB
▷ *see* **ride**

role play NOUN
el **juego de rol** *masc*
   We're going to do a role play.
   Vamos a hacer un juego de rol.

roll

| roll can be a noun or a verb. |

A NOUN
   el **bollito** *masc* (*of bread*)
   a ham roll
   un bollito con jamón
B VERB
   to roll
   Roll the dice.
   Lanza los dados.

Rollerblades® PL NOUN
los **patines en línea** *masc pl*
   a pair of Rollerblades
   unos patines en línea

rollercoaster NOUN
la **montaña rusa** *fem*

roller skates PL NOUN
los **patines de ruedas** *masc pl*

roller-skating NOUN
   to go roller-skating
   ir a patinar
   Do you want to go roller-skating?
   ¿Quieres ir a patinar?

Roman Catholic NOUN
el **católico** *masc*
la **católica** *fem*
   He's a Roman Catholic.
   Es católico.

LANGUAGE TIP
católico is not spelled with a capital letter. Remember that you do not use an article with people's religions in Spanish.

---

romantic ADJECTIVE
romántico *masc*
romántica *fem*

roof NOUN
el **tejado** *masc*

room NOUN
1 la **habitación** *fem*
   (PL las **habitaciones**) (*in house*)
   My room is the smallest.
   Mi habitación es la más pequeña.
   a single room
   una habitación individual
   a double room
   una habitación doble
   the biggest room in the house
   la habitación más grande de la casa

LANGUAGE TIP
You can also use **el cuarto** to refer to a room.

My room is the smallest.
Mi cuarto es el más pequeño.
2 el **aula** *fem (in school)*

___

LANGUAGE TIP
Even though it's a feminine noun,
remember that you use **el** and **un** with
aula.

___

the music room
el aula de música
3 el **sitio** *masc (space)*
Is there room for me?
¿Hay sitio para mí?

rope NOUN
la **cuerda** *fem*

rose NOUN
la **rosa** *fem*
a bouquet of roses
un ramo de rosas

rough ADJECTIVE
áspero *masc*
áspera *fem*

roughly ADVERB
aproximadamente
It weighs roughly twenty kilos.
Pesa unos veinte kilos
aproximadamente.

round

> **round** can be an adjective,
> preposition or noun.

A ADJECTIVE
redondo *masc*
redonda *fem*
a round table
una mesa redonda
B PREPOSITION
alrededor de
Sit round the table.
Sentaos alrededor de la mesa.
It's just round the corner.
Está aquí a la vuelta de la esquina.
round here
por aquí cerca
Is there a chemist's round here?
¿Hay una farmacia por aquí cerca?

C NOUN
la **vuelta** *fem (of tournament)*
the next round
la siguiente vuelta
a round of golf
un partido de golf

roundabout NOUN
1 el **tiovivo** *masc (merry-go-round)*
2 la **rotonda** *fem (at road junction)*

rounders NOUN

___

DID YOU KNOW...?
Rounders isn't played in Spain. The
nearest game for which there is a
Spanish translation is **el béisbol**
(baseball).

___

row

> **row** can be a noun or a verb.

A NOUN
1 la **hilera** *fem*
a row of houses
una hilera de casas
2 la **fila** *fem (of seats)*
Our seats are in the front row.
Nuestros asientos están en la primera
fila.
3 el **jaleo** *masc (noise)*
What a row!
¡Menudo jaleo!
B VERB
to row
remar
I can row.
Sé remar.

rowing boat NOUN
la **barca de remos** *fem*

royal ADJECTIVE
real *masc/fem*

rubber NOUN
la **goma de borrar** *fem*
Can I borrow your rubber?
¿Me dejas tu goma de borrar?

rubber band NOUN
la **goma elástica** *fem*

rubbish

> **rubbish** can be a noun or an adjective.

A NOUN

1 la **basura** *fem* (*garbage*)
Where shall I put the rubbish?
¿Dónde pongo la basura?

2 las **estupideces** *fem pl* (*nonsense*)
Don't talk rubbish!
¡No digas estupideces!

B ADJECTIVE
(*useless*)
They're a rubbish team!
¡Son un equipo que no vale nada!
The film was rubbish.
La película no valía nada.

rucksack NOUN
la **mochila** *fem*

rude ADJECTIVE
grosero *masc*
grosera *fem*
Don't be rude!
¡No seas grosero!
a rude word
una palabrota

rug NOUN

1 la **alfombra** *fem* (*carpet*)

2 la **manta de viaje** *fem* (*travelling rug*)

rugby NOUN
el **rugby** *masc*
I play rugby.
Juego al rugby.

LANGUAGE TIP
In Spanish, you need to include **al** or **a la** before the names of sports or games when talking about playing them.

---

ruin

> **ruin** can be a noun or a verb.

A NOUN
la **ruina** *fem*
the ruins of the castle
las ruinas del castillo

B VERB
to ruin
estropear
You'll ruin your shoes.
Te vas a estropear los zapatos.

LANGUAGE TIP
In Spanish you usually use an article like **el**, **la** or **los**, **las** with clothes you are wearing.

---

rule NOUN

1 la **regla** *fem* (*of game*)
the rules of the game
las reglas del juego

2 (*regulations*)
the rules
las normas
It's against the rules.
Va contra las normas.

ruler NOUN
la **regla** *fem*
Can I borrow your ruler?
¿Me dejas tu regla?

run

> **run** can be a noun or a verb.

A NOUN
to go for a run
ir a correr
Do you want to go for a run?
¿Quieres ir a correr?
I did a ten-kilometre run.
Corrí diez kilómetros.

B VERB
to run

1 **correr** (*move fast*)
Run!
¡Corre!
I ran two kilometres.
Corrí dos kilómetros.

She's running.
Está corriendo.
2 organizar (*organize*)
They run English courses.
Organizan cursos de inglés.

rung VERB ▷ *see* **ring**

runner NOUN
el **corredor** *masc*
la **corredora** *fem*

runner-up NOUN
el **segundo** *masc*
la **segunda** *fem*

running NOUN
Running is my favourite sport.
Correr es mi deporte favorito.

rush

rush can be a noun or a verb.

A NOUN
la **prisa** *fem*
I'm in a rush.
Tengo prisa.
B VERB
to rush
apurarse
There's no need to rush.
No hay por qué apurarse.

rush hour NOUN
la **hora punta** *fem*
in the rush hour
en la hora punta

S s

Sabbath NOUN
el **sábado** masc (Jewish)

sack NOUN
el **saco** masc

sad ADJECTIVE
triste masc/fem
Don't be sad.
No estés triste.

sadly ADVERB
1 **lamentablemente** (unfortunately)
Sadly, we haven't got time.
Lamentablemente, no tenemos tiempo.
2 **con tristeza** (sorrowfully)
'She's gone,' he said sadly.
"Se ha ido", dijo con tristeza.

safe ADJECTIVE
seguro masc
segura fem
This car isn't safe.
Este coche no es seguro.
We're safe here.
Aquí estamos seguros.
Put it in a safe place.
Ponlo en un lugar seguro.
Don't worry, it's perfectly safe.
No te preocupes, no tiene el menor peligro.
You're safe now.
Ya estás a salvo.

safety NOUN
la **seguridad** fem

safety pin NOUN
el **imperdible** masc

said VERB ▷ see **say**

sailing NOUN
la **vela** fem
His hobby is sailing.
Es aficionado a la vela.
to go sailing
hacer vela
I'd like to go sailing.
Me gustaría hacer vela.

sailing boat NOUN
el **barco de vela** masc

sailor NOUN
el **marinero** masc

saint NOUN
el **santo** masc
la **santa** fem

LANGUAGE TIP
The masculine form **Santo** is shortened to **San** before names other than **Domingo** and **Tomás**.

Saint John
San Juan
Saint Thomas
Santo Tomás

salad NOUN
la **ensalada** fem
Would you like some salad?
¿Quieres ensalada?

salad cream NOUN
la **mayonesa** fem

salad dressing NOUN
la **vinagreta** fem

salary NOUN
el **sueldo** masc

A
B
C
D
E
F
G
H
I
J
K
L
M
N
O
P
Q
R
S
T
U
V
W
X
Y
Z

sale NOUN
1 la **venta** *fem* (*transaction*)
'for sale'
"a la venta"
2 las **rebajas** *fem pl* (*with bargains*)
There's a sale on this week.
Hay rebajas esta semana.

salmon NOUN
el **salmón** *masc* (PL los **salmones**)

salt NOUN
la **sal** *fem*

same

| same can be an adjective or pronoun. |

A ADJECTIVE
mismo *masc*
misma *fem*
the same class
la misma clase
We've got the same colour T-shirts.
Tenemos las camisetas del mismo color.

B PRONOUN
They're exactly the same.
Son exactamente iguales.
Our trainers are the same.
Nuestras zapatillas son iguales.
It's not the same.
No es lo mismo.

sand NOUN
la **arena** *fem*

sandal NOUN
la **sandalia** *fem*
a pair of sandals
unas sandalias

sandcastle NOUN
el **castillo de arena** *masc*

sandwich NOUN
el **sándwich** *masc*
a cheese sandwich
un sándwich de queso

sang VERB ▷ *see* sing

Santa Claus NOUN
Papá Noel *masc*

satchel NOUN
la **cartera** *fem*

satellite NOUN
el **satélite** *masc*

satisfied ADJECTIVE
satisfecho *masc*
satisfecha *fem*

Saturday NOUN
el **sábado** *masc*
It's Saturday today.
Hoy es sábado.
I've got a Saturday job.
Tengo un trabajo los sábados.

on Saturday
el sábado
on Saturdays
los sábados
every Saturday
todos los sábados
last Saturday
el sábado pasado
next Saturday
el sábado que viene

LANGUAGE TIP
Days are not spelled with a capital letter in Spanish.

sauce NOUN
la **salsa** *fem*

saucepan NOUN
el **cazo** *masc*

saucer NOUN
el **platito** *masc*

sausage NOUN
la **salchicha** *fem*

sausages and chips
salchichas con patatas fritas

save VERB
1 **ahorrar** (*money, time*)
I'm saving for a new bike.
Estoy ahorrando para una bici nueva.
It'll save time.
Ahorrará tiempo.
2 **salvar** (*rescue*)
He saved my life.
Me salvó la vida.
3 **guardar** (*on computer*)
Don't forget to save the file.
No te olvides de guardar el archivo.

save up VERB
ahorrar
I'm saving up for a new bike.
Estoy ahorrando para una bici nueva.

savoury ADJECTIVE
salado *masc*
salada *fem*
Is it sweet or savoury?
¿Es dulce o salado?

saw VERB ▷ *see* **see**

say VERB
decir
Say hello, Matthew.
Di hola, Matthew.
What did you say?
¿Qué dijiste?
I said no.
Dije que no.
Could you say that again, please?
¿Puedes repetir eso, por favor?
I don't know how to say it in Spanish.
No sé cómo se dice en español.

> **How do you say 'hello' in Spanish?**
> ¿Cómo se dice "hello" en español?

scar NOUN
la **cicatriz** *fem* (PL las **cicatrices**)
He's got a scar on his face.
Tiene una cicatriz en la cara.

LANGUAGE TIP
In Spanish you usually use an article like **el**, **la** or **los**, **las** with parts of the body.

---

scared ADJECTIVE
to be scared
tener miedo
Don't be scared.
No tengas miedo.
I'm scared of dogs.
Me dan miedo los perros.

> **I'm scared!**
> ¡Tengo miedo!

scarf NOUN
la **bufanda** *fem*

scary ADJECTIVE
It was really scary.
Daba mucho miedo.
a scary film
una película de miedo

scenery NOUN
el **paisaje** *masc*

school NOUN
el **colegio** *masc*
I love school.
Me encanta el colegio.
The children are at school.
Los niños están en el colegio.
I go to school by bike.
Voy al colegio en bici.
the school library
la biblioteca del colegio
There's no school next week.
La semana que viene no hay clase.

> **at school**
> en el colegio

schoolbag NOUN
la **cartera** *fem*

schoolboy NOUN
el **escolar** *masc*

schoolchildren PL NOUN
los **escolares** *masc pl*

schoolgirl NOUN
la **escolar** *fem*

school holidays PL NOUN
las **vacaciones escolares** *fem pl*

school uniform NOUN
el **uniforme del colegio** *masc*

science NOUN
la **ciencia** *fem*

scientist NOUN
el **científico** *masc*
la **científica** *fem*

scissors PL NOUN
las **tijeras** *fem pl*
a pair of scissors
unas tijeras

scooter NOUN
1 el **patinete** *masc* (*child's toy*)
2 la **Vespa**® *fem* (*motorcycle*)

score

> **score** can be a noun or a verb.

A NOUN
What's the score?
¿Cómo va el partido?
The score was three nil.
El partido acabó tres a cero.

B VERB
to score
1 **marcar** (*goal*)
I scored a goal.
Marqué un gol.
2 **obtener** (*point*)
City School scored fifty points.
El colegio City obtuvo cincuenta puntos.

3 **llevar el tanteo** (*keep score*)
Who's going to score?
¿Quién va a llevar el tanteo?

Scot NOUN
el **escocés** *masc* (PL los **escoceses**)
la **escocesa** *fem*

Scotland NOUN
Escocia *fem*
Glasgow is in Scotland.
Glasgow está en Escocia.
I'm from Scotland.
Soy de Escocia.

Scotsman NOUN
el **escocés** *masc* (PL los **escoceses**)

LANGUAGE TIP
escocés is not spelled with a capital letter in Spanish.

Scotswoman NOUN
la **escocesa** *fem*

LANGUAGE TIP
escocesa is not spelled with a capital letter in Spanish.

Scottish ADJECTIVE
escocés *masc* (PL **escoceses**)
escocesa *fem*
He's Scottish.
Es escocés.

LANGUAGE TIP
escocés is not spelled with a capital letter in Spanish.

Scout NOUN
el **boy scout** *masc*
la **girl scout** *fem*
I'm in the Scouts.
Estoy en los scouts.

scrambled eggs PL NOUN
los **huevos revueltos** *masc pl*

scrapbook NOUN
el **álbum de recortes** *masc*

scream VERB
chillar

screen NOUN
la **pantalla** fem

screw NOUN
el **tornillo** masc

screwdriver NOUN
el **destornillador** masc

scroll VERB
deslizar
to scroll up/down
deslizar hacia arriba/abajo

sea NOUN
el **mar** masc
I live by the sea.
Vivo al lado del mar.

LANGUAGE TIP
mar is usually masculine but you may
come across some expressions where
it's feminine.

---

seafood NOUN
el **pescado y marisco** masc

seagull NOUN
la **gaviota** fem

seashore NOUN
la **orilla del mar** fem
on the seashore
a la orilla del mar

seasick ADJECTIVE
to get seasick
marearse en barco
I get seasick.
Me mareo en barco.

seaside NOUN
la **playa** fem
at the seaside
en la playa

season NOUN
la **estación del año** fem
(PL las **estaciones del año**)
What's your favourite season?
¿Cuál es tu estación del año preferida?

season ticket NOUN
el **abono de temporada** masc

seat NOUN
el **asiento** masc
I'd like a seat by the window.
Quiero un asiento al lado de la
ventana.
Go back to your seat, Mike!
¡Vuelve a tu sitio, Mike!

second

> **second** can be an adjective or a
> noun.

A ADJECTIVE
segundo masc
segunda fem
on the second page
en la segunda página
Rosa came second.
Rosa llegó el segundo.
B NOUN
el **segundo** masc
It'll only take a second.
Solo tardará un segundo.
My birthday's the second of July.
Mi cumpleaños es el dos de julio.
Today's the second of June.
Hoy es dos de junio.

on the second of March
el dos de marzo

LANGUAGE TIP
Use the same set of numbers that you
use for counting (**uno**, **dos**, **tres** and
so on) when giving Spanish dates.

---

secondary school NOUN
el **instituto** masc

secret

> **secret** can be a noun or an adjective.

Spanish

English

A
B
C
D
E
F
G
H
I
J
K
L
M
N
O
P
Q
R
S
T
U
V
W
X
Y
Z

A NOUN
> el **secreto** *masc*
> **It's a secret.**
> Es un secreto.
> **Can you keep a secret?**
> ¿Me guardas un secreto?

> **in secret**
> en secreto

B ADJECTIVE
> **secreto** *masc*
> **secreta** *fem*
> **a secret passage**
> un pasadizo secreto

secretary NOUN
> el **secretario** *masc*
> la **secretaria** *fem*
> **She's a secretary.**
> Es secretaria.

> **LANGUAGE TIP**
> In Spanish, you do not use an article
> with people's jobs.

secretly ADVERB
> en secreto

see VERB
> ver
> **We're going to see Granny and
> Grandpa.**
> Vamos a ir a ver a los abuelos.
> **I can't see her car.**
> No veo su coche.
> **I can't see anything.**
> No veo nada.
> **Can you see the difference?**
> ¿Ves la diferencia?

> **LANGUAGE TIP**
> Don't forget the personal **a** in
> examples like the following.

> **I saw Catriona yesterday.**
> Vi a Catriona ayer.
> **Have you seen Paul?**
> ¿Has visto a Paul?

> **See you!**
> ¡Hasta luego!
> **See you tomorrow!**
> ¡Hasta mañana!
> **See you soon!**
> ¡Hasta pronto!

seed NOUN
> la **semilla** *fem*
> **poppy seeds**
> semillas de amapola
> **sunflower seeds**
> pipas de girasol

> **DID YOU KNOW...?**
> Did you know that sunflower seeds,
> often referred to just as **pipas**, are a
> popular Spanish snack?

seem VERB
> parecer
> **She seems tired.**
> Parece cansada.
> **There seems to be a problem.**
> Parece que hay un problema.

seen VERB ▷ *see* see

seesaw NOUN
> el **balancín** *masc* (PL los **balancines**)

selfie NOUN
> el **selfi** *masc*
> **We send each
> other selfies.**
> Nos mandamos
> selfis entre nosostros.

selfie stick NOUN
> el **paloselfi** *masc*

selfish ADJECTIVE
> **egoísta** *masc/fem*

Don't be so selfish, Charles.
No seas tan egoísta, Charles.

LANGUAGE TIP
Even though **egoísta** ends in **-a**, you can use it to describe a man or boy.

self-service ADJECTIVE
autoservicio

LANGUAGE TIP
autoservicio never changes its ending no matter what it describes.

The café is self-service.
La cafetería es autoservicio.
a self-service restaurant
un autoservicio

sell VERB
vender
He's selling his car.
Vende su coche.
The tickets are sold out.
Las entradas están agotadas.

Sellotape® NOUN
el **celo** masc

semicircle NOUN
el **semicírculo** masc
Get into a semicircle.
Formad un semicírculo.

semicolon NOUN
el **punto y coma** masc

semi-final NOUN
la **semifinal** fem

send VERB
enviar
I'm going to send Sally a postcard.
Voy a enviarle una postal a Sally.
Send me an email.
Envíame un correo.
My friend has sent me some photos.
Mi amigo me ha enviado algunas fotos.

senior school NOUN
el **instituto de enseñanza secundaria** masc

sense of humour NOUN
el **sentido del humor** masc
Our teacher has a sense of humour.
Nuestro profesor tiene sentido del humor.
He has no sense of humour.
No tiene sentido del humor.

sensible ADJECTIVE
sensato masc
sensata fem
Be sensible, Amy!
¡Sé sensata, Amy!

LANGUAGE TIP
Be careful! The translation of **sensible** is not **sensible**.

sent VERB ▷ see **send**

sentence NOUN
la **oración** fem (PL las **oraciones**)
What does this sentence mean?
¿Qué significa esta oración?

separate ADJECTIVE
aparte masc/fem
Put the green cards in a separate pile.
Pon las tarjetas verdes en una pila aparte.

September NOUN
septiembre masc
My birthday's in September.
Mi cumpleaños es en septiembre.
It's the twelfth of September today.
Hoy es doce de septiembre.

in September
en septiembre
on the fifth of September
el cinco de septiembre

LANGUAGE TIP
Months are not spelled with a capital letter in Spanish.

Spanish

English

a b c d e f g h i j k l m n o p q r s t u v w x y z

543

sequence NOUN
el **orden** masc (PL los **órdenes**)
Put the pictures in sequence, Peter.
Pon las fotos en orden, Peter.

series NOUN
la **serie** fem
a TV series
una serie de TV

serious ADJECTIVE
serio masc
seria fem
You look very serious.
Estás muy serio.
Are you serious?
¿En serio?

serve VERB
servir
They're serving lunch now.
Están sirviendo la comida ahora.
It serves you right.
Te está bien empleado.

service NOUN
1 el **servicio** masc (in restaurant)
Service is included.
El servicio está incluido.
2 el **oficio religioso** masc (in church)

service station NOUN
la **estación de servicio** fem
(PL las **estaciones de servicio**)

serviette NOUN
la **servilleta** fem

set VERB
1 **poner**
I normally set the alarm for seven.
Normalmente pongo el despertador para las siete.
Could you set the table?
¿Puedes poner la mesa?
2 **ponerse** (sun)
The sun is setting.
El sol se está poniendo.

set off VERB
salir

What time are you setting off?
¿A qué hora sales?

settee NOUN
el **sofá** masc

settle down VERB
calmarse
Settle down, children!
¡Calmaos, niños!

seven NUMBER
siete
seven euros
siete euros
I get up at seven o'clock.
Me levanto a las siete.

She's seven.
Tiene siete años.

LANGUAGE TIP
In English you can say **she's seven** or **she's seven years old**. In Spanish you can only say **tiene siete años**. Have you noticed that in Spanish you need to use the verb **tener** to talk about somebody's age?

seventeen NUMBER
diecisiete
seventeen euros
diecisiete euros

He's seventeen.
Tiene diecisiete años.

LANGUAGE TIP
In English you can say **he's seventeen** or **he's seventeen years old**. In Spanish you can only say **tiene diecisiete años**. Have you noticed that in Spanish you need to use the verb **tener** to talk about somebody's age?

seventeenth NUMBER
diecisiete
on the seventeenth floor
en la planta diecisiete

We break up on the seventeenth of December.
Empezamos las vacaciones el diecisiete de diciembre.
Today's the seventeenth of March.
Hoy es diecisiete de marzo.

on the seventeenth of January
el diecisiete de enero

LANGUAGE TIP
Use the same set of numbers that you use for counting (**uno**, **dos**, **tres** and so on) when giving Spanish dates.

seventh NUMBER
séptimo *masc*
séptima *fem*
on the seventh floor
en la séptima planta
My birthday's the seventh of February.
Mi cumpleaños es el siete de febrero.
It's the seventh of April today.
Hoy es siete de abril.

on the seventh of August
el siete de agosto

LANGUAGE TIP
Use the same set of numbers that you use for counting (**uno**, **dos**, **tres** and so on) when giving Spanish dates.

seventy NUMBER
setenta
My grandma is seventy.
Mi abuela tiene setenta años.

LANGUAGE TIP
In English you can say **she's seventy** or **she's seventy years old**. In Spanish you can only say **tiene setenta años**. Have you noticed that in Spanish you need to use the verb **tener** to talk about somebody's age?

several ADJECTIVE
varios *masc pl*
varias *fem pl*
Several children are absent.
Varios niños no han venido.

sewing NOUN
la **costura** *fem*
I like sewing.
Me gusta la costura.

shade NOUN
la **sombra** *fem*
It was thirty-five degrees in the shade.
Hacía treinta y cinco grados a la sombra.

shadow NOUN
la **sombra** *fem*
my shadow
mi sombra

shake VERB
1 **temblar** (*tremble*)
My hands are shaking.
Me tiemblan las manos.

LANGUAGE TIP
In Spanish you usually use an article like **el**, **la** or **los**, **las** with parts of the body.

2 **sacudir** (*on purpose*)
She shook the rug.
Sacudió la alfombra.
to shake hands with somebody
darle la mano a alguien
Shake hands with your best friend!
¡Dale la mano a tu mejor amigo!
Spanish people shake hands a lot.
Los españoles se dan mucho la mano.

shall VERB

LANGUAGE TIP
You can usually translate **shall I...?** using the present tense of the main verb.

a
b
c
d
e
f
g
h
i
j
k
l
m
n
o
p
q
r
s
t
u
v
w
x
y
z

545

Shall I shut the window?
¿Cierro la ventana?
Shall I go first?
¿Empiezo yo?
Shall I put the light on?
¿Enciendo la luz?

shame NOUN

What a shame!
¡Qué pena!

shampoo NOUN
el **champú** masc
a bottle of shampoo
un bote de champú

shape NOUN
la **forma** fem

share VERB
compartir
I share a room with my brother.
Comparto la habitación con mi hermano.

shark NOUN
el **tiburón** masc (PL los **tiburones**)

sharp ADJECTIVE
afilado masc
afilada fem
Be careful, it's sharp.
Ten cuidado que está afilado.

she PRONOUN
ella
She's got a radio but I haven't.
Ella tiene una radio pero yo no.

LANGUAGE TIP
she isn't usually translated unless it's emphatic.

She's very nice.
Es muy simpática.

she'd
(= **she had**) ▷ see **have**
(= **she would**) ▷ see **would**

sheep NOUN
la **oveja** fem

LANGUAGE TIP
When **sheep** refers to more than one animal, use **ovejas** in the plural.

sheet NOUN
la **sábana** fem
clean sheets
sábanas limpias
a sheet of paper
una hoja de papel

shelf NOUN
el **estante** masc
the top shelf
el estante de arriba

shell NOUN
la **concha** fem

she'll (= **she will**) ▷ see **will**

shelves PL NOUN
los **estantes** masc pl

she's
(= **she is**) ▷ see **be**
(= **she has**) ▷ see **have**

Shetland Islands PL NOUN
las **Islas Shetland** fem pl

shine VERB
brillar
The sun is shining.
El sol brilla.

ship NOUN
el **barco** masc

shirt NOUN
la **camisa** *fem*
a white shirt
una camisa blanca

shocking ADJECTIVE
escandaloso *masc*
escandalosa *fem*
It's shocking!
¡Es escandaloso!

shoe NOUN
el **zapato** *masc*
I've got new shoes.
Tengo unos zapatos nuevos.
Put on your shoes.
Ponte los zapatos.

LANGUAGE TIP
In Spanish you usually use an article
like **el**, **la** or **los**, **las** with clothes you
are wearing.

shoelace NOUN
el **cordón** *masc* (PL los **cordones**)

shoe shop NOUN
la **zapatería** *fem*

shop NOUN
la **tienda** *fem*
The shop is shut.
La tienda está cerrada.
a sports shop
una tienda de deportes

shop assistant NOUN
el **dependiente** *masc*
la **dependienta** *fem*
She's a shop assistant.
Es dependienta.

LANGUAGE TIP
In Spanish, you do not use an article
with people's jobs.

shopkeeper NOUN
el **tendero** *masc*
la **tendera** *fem*

shopping NOUN
la **compra** *fem*

I do the shopping for my granny.
Le hago la compra a mi abuela.
I go shopping with my friends.
Me voy de compras con mis amigas.
**Can you get the shopping from
the car?**
¿Puedes traer las bolsas de la compra
del coche?

shopping bag NOUN
la **bolsa de la compra** *fem*

shopping centre NOUN
el **centro comercial** *masc*

short ADJECTIVE
1 **corto** *masc*
corta *fem* (*not long*)
a short skirt
una falda corta
short hair
el pelo corto
a short walk
un paseo corto
2 **bajo** *masc*
baja *fem* (*not tall*)
She's quite short.
Es bastante baja.

shorts PL NOUN
los **pantalones cortos** *masc pl*
My shorts are green.
Mis pantalones cortos son verdes.
a pair of shorts
unos pantalones cortos

short-sighted ADJECTIVE
miope *masc/fem*

should VERB
You should try it.
Deberías intentarlo.
You shouldn't do that.
No deberías hacer eso.

shoulder NOUN
el **hombro** *masc*

shout VERB
gritar
Don't shout, children!
¡Niños, no gritéis!

Spanish · English

a b c d e f g h i j k l m n o p q r s t u v w x y z

547

show VERB
enseñar
Show me!
¡Enséñame!
Shall I show you the photos?
¿Te enseño las fotos?

shower NOUN
1 la **ducha** *fem*
(*for washing*)
She's in the shower.
Está en la ducha.
to have a shower
ducharse
I'm going to have a shower.
Voy a ducharme.
2 el **chaparrón**
masc (PL los **chaparrones**) (*rain*)
It's just a shower.
Es solo un chaparrón.

Shrove Tuesday NOUN
el **Martes de Carnaval** *masc*

DID YOU KNOW...?
During the week before Lent, all over Spain and Latin America there are fiestas and fancy-dress parades, with the main celebrations taking place on **Martes de Carnaval** (literally 'Carnival Tuesday').

shrug VERB
to shrug one's shoulders
encogerse de hombros
She shrugged her shoulders.
Se encogió de hombros.

shuffle VERB
You have to shuffle the cards.
Tienes que barajar las cartas.

shut

shut can be a verb or an adjective.

A VERB
to shut
cerrar

What time do the shops shut?
¿A qué hora cierran las tiendas?
Shut your eyes and hold out your hands.
Cierra los ojos y extiende las manos.

LANGUAGE TIP
In Spanish you usually use an article like **el**, **la** or **los**, **las** with parts of the body.

B ADJECTIVE
cerrado *masc*
cerrada *fem*
The door is shut.
La puerta está cerrada.

shy ADJECTIVE
tímido *masc*
tímida *fem*
He's very shy.
Es muy tímido.

sick ADJECTIVE
1 **enfermo** *masc*
enferma *fem* (*unwell*)
He is sick.
Está enfermo.
2 **I'm going to be sick.**
Voy a devolver.
I feel sick.
Tengo ganas de devolver.

side NOUN
1 el **lado** *masc* (*of object, building, street*)
on this side
en este lado
It's on this side of the street.
Está en este lado de la calle.
2 el **equipo** *masc* (*team*)
He's on my side.
Está en mi equipo.

sightseeing NOUN
We're going to go sightseeing.
Vamos a ir a visitar monumentos.

sign

sign can be a noun or a verb.

A NOUN
la **señal** *fem*

548

a road sign
una señal de tráfico

B VERB
to sign
firmar
Sign here, please.
Firma aquí, por favor.

signal NOUN
la **señal** *fem*

signature NOUN
la **firma** *fem*

sign language NOUN
el **lenguaje de signos** *masc*

silence NOUN
el **silencio** *masc*

silk

> **silk** can be a noun or an adjective.

A NOUN
la **seda** *fem*
B ADJECTIVE
de seda
a silk scarf
un pañuelo de seda

silly ADJECTIVE
tonto *masc*
tonta *fem*
Don't be silly, Ian!
¡No seas tonto, Ian!

silver

> **silver** can be a noun or an adjective.

A NOUN
la **plata** *fem*
gold and silver
oro y plata
B ADJECTIVE
de plata
a silver chain
una cadena de plata
a silver medal
una medalla de plata

similar ADJECTIVE
parecido *masc*
parecida *fem*
His sweater's similar to mine.
Su jersey es parecido al mío.

simple ADJECTIVE
sencillo *masc*
sencilla *fem*
It's very simple.
Es muy sencillo.

since

> **since** can be a preposition or a conjunction.

A PREPOSITION
desde
since Christmas
desde Navidad
since then
desde entonces
B CONJUNCTION
desde que
since I arrived
desde que llegué

sincerely ADVERB
Yours sincerely …
Le saluda atentamente …

LANGUAGE TIP
Use **Le saluda atentamente** when writing to one person. Use **Les saluda atentamente** when writing to more than one person.

sing VERB
cantar
I sing in the choir.
Canto en el coro.

singer NOUN
el/la **cantante**
masc/fem

Spanish

English

A
B
C
D
E
F
G
H
I
J
K
L
M
N
O
P
Q
R
S
T
U
V
W
X
Y
Z

single

single can be an adjective or a noun.

A ADJECTIVE
individual *masc/fem*
a single room
una habitación individual
a single bed
una cama individual

B NOUN
el **billete de ida** *masc*
A single to Barcelona, please.
Uno de ida a Barcelona, por favor.

singular NOUN
in the singular
en singular

sink NOUN
el **fregadero** *masc* (*kitchen sink*)

sir NOUN
el **señor** *masc*
Yes, sir.
Sí, señor.

sister NOUN
la **hermana** *fem*
my little sister
mi hermana pequeña

my big sister
mi hermana mayor
I've got one sister.
Tengo una hermana.
I haven't got any sisters.
No tengo hermanas.

Have you got any brothers or sisters?
¿Tienes hermanos?

sit VERB
sentarse
I want to sit next to my friend.
Quiero sentarme al lado de mi amigo.
Can I sit here?
¿Puedo sentarme aquí?
Brian is sitting next to Megan.
Brian está sentado al lado de Megan.

LANGUAGE TIP
Change **está sentado** to **está sentada** if it's a girl or woman who is sitting somewhere.

---

sit down VERB
sentarse
Sit down, Anthony.
Siéntate, Anthony.

Sit down, children.
Niños, sentaos.

site NOUN
1 el **sitio web** *masc* (*website*)
2 el **camping** *masc* (*campsite*)

sitting room NOUN
el **salón** *masc* (PL los **salones**)

situation NOUN
la **situación** *fem* (PL las **situaciones**)

six NUMBER
seis
six euros
seis euros

She's six.
Tiene seis años.

LANGUAGE TIP
In English you can say **she's six** or **she's six years old**. In Spanish you can only say **tiene seis años**. Have you noticed that in Spanish you need to use the verb **tener** to talk about somebody's age?

sixteen NUMBER
dieciséis
  sixteen euros
  dieciséis euros

  He's sixteen.
  Tiene dieciséis años.

  LANGUAGE TIP
  In English you can say **he's sixteen** or
  he's sixteen years old. In Spanish
  you can only say **tiene dieciséis
  años**. Have you noticed that in
  Spanish you need to use the verb
  tener to talk about somebody's age?

sixteenth NUMBER
dieciséis
  on the sixteenth floor
  en la planta dieciséis
  **We break up on the sixteenth of
  December.**
  Empezamos las vacaciones el dieciséis
  de diciembre.
  Today's the sixteenth of January.
  Hoy es dieciséis de enero.

  on the sixteenth of August
  el dieciséis de agosto

  LANGUAGE TIP
  Use the same set of numbers that you
  use for counting (**uno**, **dos**, **tres** and
  so on) when giving Spanish dates.

sixth NUMBER
sexto masc
sexta fem
  on the sixth floor
  en la sexta planta
  My birthday's the sixth of October.
  Mi cumpleaños es el seis de octubre.
  **It's the sixth of November
  today.**
  Hoy es seis de noviembre.

  on the sixth of August
  el seis de agosto

  LANGUAGE TIP
  Use the same set of numbers that you
  use for counting (**uno**, **dos**, **tres** and
  so on) when giving Spanish dates.

sixty NUMBER
sesenta
  My aunt is sixty.
  Mi tía tiene sesenta años.

  LANGUAGE TIP
  In English you can say **she's sixty** or
  she's sixty years old. In Spanish you
  can only say **tiene sesenta años**.
  Have you noticed that in Spanish you
  need to use the verb **tener** to talk
  about somebody's age?

size NOUN
  la **talla** fem
  It's the right size.
  Es la talla correcta.

skate VERB
  1 **patinar** (roller-skate)
  I can't skate.
  No sé patinar.
  2 **patinar sobre hielo** (ice-skate)
  I like skating.
  Me gusta patinar sobre hielo.

skateboard NOUN
  el **monopatín** masc (PL los
  monopatines)

skateboarding NOUN
  el **skateboard** masc
  I like skateboarding.
  Me gusta el skateboard.
  **I'm going skateboarding
  with Olivia.**
  Voy a hacer skateboard con
  Olivia.

a b c d e f g h i j k l m n o p q r s t u v w x y z

A
B
C
D
E
F
G
H
I
J
K
L
M
N
O
P
Q
R
S
T
U
V
W
X
Y
Z

skating NOUN
I go skating every Saturday.
Voy a patinar todos los sábados.

skeleton NOUN
el **esqueleto** masc

ski

> **ski** can be a verb or a noun.

A VERB
to ski
esquiar
Can you ski?
¿Sabes esquiar?

B NOUN
el **esquí** masc (PL los **esquís**)

ski boots PL NOUN
las **botas de esquí** fem pl

skiing NOUN
Do you like skiing?
¿Te gusta esquiar?
I'm going on a skiing holiday.
Voy a ir de vacaciones a esquiar.

ski lift NOUN
el **telesilla** masc

> **LANGUAGE TIP**
> Even though it ends in **-a**, **el telesilla**
> is a masculine noun.

skin NOUN
la **piel** fem

skinny ADJECTIVE
flaco masc
flaca fem

skipping rope NOUN
la **comba** fem

skirt NOUN
la **falda** fem
a blue skirt
una falda azul

ski slope NOUN
la **pista de esquí** fem

sky NOUN
el **cielo** masc
The sky is blue.
El cielo es azul.

Skype® VERB
hablar por Skype
**Every week we Skype our
grandparents.**
Todas las semanas hablamos por
Skype con nuestros abuelos.

slam VERB
Don't slam the door.
No des portazos.

sledge NOUN
el **trineo** masc

sledging NOUN
Let's go sledging!
¡Vamos a montarnos en trineo!

sleep VERB
dormir
My cat sleeps in a box.
Mi gato duerme en una caja.
Did you sleep well, Sonia?
¿Dormiste bien, Sonia?

sleeping bag NOUN
el **saco de dormir** masc

sleepover NOUN
**My friend is coming for a
sleepover tonight.**
Mi amigo viene a dormir a mi casa esta
noche.
**We're going to Camilla's for a
sleepover.**
Vamos a quedarnos a dormir en casa
de Camilla.

sleepy ADJECTIVE
   I'm sleepy.
   Tengo sueño.

sleeve NOUN
   la **manga** *fem*
   a shirt with long sleeves
   una camisa de manga larga
   a shirt with short sleeves
   una camisa de manga corta

slept VERB ▷ *see* **sleep**

slice NOUN
   1 la **rebanada**
   fem (of bread)
   2 el **trozo**
   masc (of cake)

slide NOUN
   1 el **tobogán** *masc*
   (PL los **toboganes**)
   (in playground)
   2 el **pasador del
   pelo** *masc*
   (hair slide)

slight ADJECTIVE
   ligero *masc*
   ligera *fem*
   a slight fever
   una ligera fiebre
   a slight problem
   un pequeño problema

slightly ADVERB
   ligeramente

slim

   slim can be an adjective or a verb.

   A ADJECTIVE
   delgado *masc*
   delgada *fem*
   She's slimmer now.
   Ahora está más delgada.
   B VERB
   to slim
   adelgazar
   I'm trying to slim.
   Estoy intentando adelgazar.

slipper NOUN
   la **zapatilla** *fem*
   a pair of slippers
   unas zapatillas
   Put on your slippers.
   Ponte las zapatillas.

   LANGUAGE TIP
   In Spanish you usually use an article
   like **el**, **la** or **los**, **las** with clothes you
   are wearing.

slow ADJECTIVE
   lento *masc*
   lenta *fem*
   The music is too slow.
   La música es demasiado
   lenta.

slowly ADVERB
   despacio
   **Could you speak more
   slowly?**
   ¿Puedes hablar más despacio?

smack

   smack can be a noun or a verb.

   A NOUN
   el **cachete** *masc*
   B VERB
   to smack
   dar un cachete a

small ADJECTIVE
   pequeño *masc*
   pequeña *fem*
   **This skirt is too small
   for me.**
   Esta falda me está demasiado
   pequeña.

smart ADJECTIVE
   1 **elegante** *masc/fem (elegant)*
   smart clothes
   ropa elegante
   2 **listo** *masc*
   lista *fem (clever)*
   She's very smart.
   Es muy lista.

A
B
C
D
E
F
G
H
I
J
K
L
M
N
O
P
Q
R
S
T
U
V
W
X
Y
Z

smell

> **smell** can be a noun or a verb.

A NOUN
el **olor** *masc*
a nice smell
un buen olor

B VERB
to smell
oler
Mmm, that smells nice!
¡Uy, qué bien huele eso!

smile

> **smile** can be a noun or a verb.

A NOUN
la **sonrisa** *fem*
a beautiful smile
una bonita sonrisa

B VERB
to smile
sonreír
Why are you smiling?
¿Por qué sonríes?

smoke VERB
fumar
I don't smoke.
Yo no fumo.
He's smoking.
Está fumando.

smoking NOUN
Smoking is bad for you.
Fumar es malo para la salud.
'no smoking'
"prohibido fumar"

smoothie NOUN
el **batido de frutas** *masc*

snack NOUN
You can get a snack in the canteen.
Puedes picar algo en la cafetería.

snail NOUN
el **caracol** *masc*

snake NOUN
la **serpiente** *fem*

sneeze VERB
estornudar

snooker NOUN
el **billar** *masc*
I play snooker.
Juego al billar.

LANGUAGE TIP
In Spanish, you need to include **al** or **a la** before the names of sports or games when talking about playing them.

snore VERB
roncar
He's snoring.
Está roncando.

snow

> **snow** can be a noun or a verb.

A NOUN
la **nieve** *fem*

B VERB
to snow
nevar
It's going to snow.
Va a nevar.
It snows a lot in the mountains.
Nieva mucho en las montañas.

It's snowing.
Está nevando.

snowball NOUN
la **bola de nieve** *fem*

snowboarding NOUN
el **snowboard** *masc*
I like snowboarding.
Me gusta hacer snowboard.

snowflake NOUN
el **copo de nieve** *masc*

nowman NOUN
el **muñeco de nieve** *masc*

I'm going to make a snowman.
Voy a hacer un muñeco de nieve.

so

> **so** can be an adverb or a conjunction.

A ADVERB
tan

You talk so fast.
Hablas tan rápido.
It's so difficult.
Es tan difícil.
so much
tanto
I love you so much.
Te quiero tanto.
I've got so many things to do today.
Tengo tantas cosas que hacer hoy.

B CONJUNCTION
así que

It's Raymond's birthday, so I've got him a present.
Es el cumpleaños de Raymond, así que tengo un regalo para él.
I play football. — So do I.
Yo juego al fútbol. — Yo también.
Is Lisa winning? — I think so.
¿Va ganando Lisa? — Creo que sí.

> **so do I**
> yo también
> **so have I**
> yo también
> **so am I**
> yo también

I think so.
Creo que sí.
I don't think so.
Creo que no.
I hope so.
Eso espero.

soap NOUN
el **jabón** *masc*
a bar of soap
una pastilla de jabón

soccer NOUN
el **fútbol** *masc*

social media NOUN
las **redes sociales** *fem pl*

sock NOUN
el **calcetín** *masc* (PL los **calcetines**)
I'm wearing white socks.
Llevo calcetines blancos.
a pair of socks
un par de calcetines

sofa NOUN
el **sofá** *masc*

soft ADJECTIVE
1 **suave** *masc/fem* (*voice, texture*)
2 **blando** *masc*
blanda *fem* (*pillow, bed, ball*)

soft drink NOUN
el **refresco** *masc*

soil NOUN
la **tierra** *fem*

sold VERB ▷ *see* **sell**

soldier NOUN
  el **soldado** *masc*
  He's a soldier.
  Es soldado.

LANGUAGE TIP
In Spanish, you do not use an article with people's jobs.

sold out ADJECTIVE
  agotado *masc*
  agotada *fem*
  The tickets are sold out.
  Las entradas están agotadas.

some

some can be an adjective or a pronoun.

A ADJECTIVE
1 **algunos** *masc pl*
  algunas *fem pl* (*a few*)

LANGUAGE TIP
When **some** refers to something plural and means the same as 'a few', you can use **algunos** or **algunas** depending on whether the word is masculine or feminine.

Some children are absent.
Algunos niños no están.
I need some nails.
Necesito algunos clavos.
I've got some sweets.
Tengo algunos caramelos.

LANGUAGE TIP
However, when **some** is followed by a plural word, it is often not translated.

I need some nails.
Necesito clavos.
I've got some sweets.
Tengo caramelos.
2 (*a little*)

LANGUAGE TIP
When **some** refers to something you can't count, it usually isn't translated.

Would you like some bread?
¿Quieres pan?
I need some Sellotape.
Necesito celo.
3 **algún** *masc*
  alguna *fem* (*one*)
  some day
  algún día
B PRONOUN
1 **algunos** *masc pl*
  algunas *fem pl* (*a few*)
  some of my friends
  algunos de mis amigos
  Have you got all her books?
  — I've got some of them.
  ¿Tienes todos sus libros? — Tengo algunos.
  I've got some, but not many.
  Tengo algunos, pero no muchos.

LANGUAGE TIP
When the number of things referred to is unimportant, **some** usually isn't translated.

Chips? — No thanks, I've still got some.
¿Patatas fritas? — No, gracias, todavía tengo.
2 (*a little*)

LANGUAGE TIP
When **some** refers to something you can't count, it usually isn't translated.

Would you like some coffee?
— No thanks, I've already got some.
¿Quieres café? — No gracias, ya tengo.

LANGUAGE TIP
However, you can often use **un poco**, which literally means 'a little'.

I've got a bar of chocolate.
Would you like some?
Tengo una tableta de chocolate.
¿Quieres un poco?

556

I've got some.
Tengo.
Would you like some?
¿Quieres?

somebody PRONOUN
alguien
Somebody asked after you.
Alguien preguntó por ti.

someone PRONOUN
alguien
Someone asked after you.
Alguien preguntó por ti.

something PRONOUN
algo
Are you looking for something?
¿Estás buscando algo?
I can see something green.
Veo algo verde.

sometimes ADVERB
a veces
sometimes, but not very often
a veces, pero no muy a menudo

somewhere ADVERB
en alguna parte
It's somewhere in the classroom.
Está en alguna parte de la clase.
I've got to go somewhere.
Tengo que ir a un sitio.

son NOUN
el **hijo** masc
her son
su hijo

song NOUN
la **canción** fem
(PL las **canciones**)
**We're going to
sing a song.**
Vamos a
cantar
una
canción.

soon ADVERB
pronto
It'll soon be lunchtime.
Pronto será la hora de comer.
very soon
muy pronto
Please tell me as soon as possible.
Por favor, dímelo lo antes posible.

as soon as possible
lo antes posible
Write soon!
¡Escribe pronto!

sore ADJECTIVE
It's sore.
Duele.
My head is sore.
Me duele la cabeza.

LANGUAGE TIP
In Spanish you usually use an article
like **el**, **la** or **los**, **las** with parts of the
body.

sorry EXCLAMATION
Lo siento
I'm really sorry.
Lo siento mucho.
I'm sorry, I can't.
Lo siento, no puedo.
I'm sorry I'm late.
Siento llegar tarde.

Sorry!
¡Lo siento!

sort NOUN
el **tipo** masc
What sort of bike have you got?
¿Qué tipo de bici tienes?

sound

sound can be a noun or a verb.

A NOUN
1 el **ruido** masc (noise)
the sound of footsteps
el ruido de pasos

Spanish

English

a
b
c
d
e
f
g
h
i
j
k
l
m
n
o
p
q
r
s
t
u
v
w
x
y
z

A
B
C
D
E
F
G
H
I
J
K
L
M
N
O
P
Q
R
S
T
U
V
W
X
Y
Z

Don't make a sound!
¡No hagas ruido!
2 el **volumen** *masc* (*volume*)
Can I turn the sound down?
¿Puedo bajar el volumen?
B VERB
to sound
parecer
That sounds interesting.
Eso parece interesante.
That sounds like a good idea.
Eso parece una buena idea.

soup NOUN
la **sopa** *fem*
vegetable soup
sopa de verduras

sour ADJECTIVE
agrio *masc*
agria *fem*

south

> **south** can be an adjective or a noun.

A ADJECTIVE
sur

LANGUAGE TIP
sur never changes its ending no
matter what it describes. Did you know
that adjectives that behave like this are
called 'invariable adjectives'?

---

the south coast
la costa sur
B NOUN
el **sur** *masc*
in the south
en el sur
the south of Spain
el sur de España
Málaga is in the south of Spain.
Málaga está en el sur de España.

southern ADJECTIVE
southern England
el sur de Inglaterra

South Pole NOUN
the South Pole
el Polo Sur *masc*

souvenir NOUN
el **recuerdo** *masc*
a souvenir shop
una tienda de recuerdos

space NOUN
1 el **sitio** *masc* (*room*)
There's a lot of space.
Hay mucho sitio.
Leave a space for a drawing.
Deja un sitio para un dibujo.
2 el **espacio** *masc* (*outer space*)

3 la **casilla** *fem* (*in game*)
Go back three spaces.
Retrocede tres casillas.

spaceship NOUN
la **nave espacial** *fem*

spade NOUN
1 la **pala** *fem*
a bucket and spade
un cubo y una pala

LANGUAGE TIP
Be careful! The translation of **spade** is
not **espada**.

---

2 (*in cards*)
spades
las **picas** *fem pl*
the ace of spades
el as de picas

spaghetti NOUN
los **espaguetis** *masc pl*

Spain NOUN
España *fem*
Seville is in Spain.
Sevilla está en España.

He lives in Spain.
Vive en España.
We're going to Spain.
Vamos a ir a España.
They are from Spain.
Son de España.

Spanish

Spanish can be an adjective or a noun.

A ADJECTIVE
español *masc*
española *fem*
a Spanish girl
una chica española
our Spanish teacher
nuestro profesor de español
my Spanish book
mi libro de español
Spanish people
los españoles

He's Spanish.
Es español.
She's Spanish.
Es española.

B NOUN
el **español** *masc*
Do you speak Spanish?
¿Hablas español?

DID YOU KNOW...?
Did you know that Spanish is also called **el castellano** because it originated in **Castilla** in central Spain? Depending where you are in the country, you'll also hear other languages, such as **el catalán**, **el gallego** and **el vasco**, but **el castellano** is understood and used throughout the country too.

the Spanish
los españoles

LANGUAGE TIP
español is not spelled with a capital letter in Spanish.

spare room NOUN
la **habitación de invitados** *fem*
(PL las **habitaciones de invitados**)

spare time NOUN
el **tiempo libre** *masc*
What do you do in your spare time?
¿Qué haces en tu tiempo libre?

sparkling ADJECTIVE
con gas
sparkling water
agua con gas
sparkling wine
vino espumoso

speak VERB
hablar
Could you speak more slowly, please?
¿Puedes hablar más despacio, por favor?

I speak English.
Hablo inglés.
Do you speak English?
¿Hablas inglés?

special ADJECTIVE
especial *masc/fem*

speciality NOUN
la **especialidad** *fem*

specially ADVERB
sobre todo
It rains a lot, specially in winter.
Llueve mucho, sobre todo en invierno.

spectator NOUN
el **espectador** *masc*
la **espectadora** *fem*

speech NOUN
el **discurso** *masc*
The headmaster made a speech.
El director dio un discurso.

speed NOUN
la **velocidad** *fem*
a ten-speed bike
una bici de diez velocidades

a b c d e f g h i j k l m n o p q r s t u v w x y z

speedboat NOUN
la **lancha motora** *fem*

spell

> **spell** can be a verb or a noun.

A VERB

1 **escribir** (*in writing*)
How do you spell that?
¿Cómo se escribe eso?

2 **deletrear** (*out loud*)
Can you spell that please?
¿Puedes deletrear eso, por favor?

B NOUN
el **hechizo** *masc* (*magic*)

spelling NOUN
la **ortografía** *fem*
a spelling mistake
una falta de ortografía

spend VERB

1 **gastar** (*money*)
I spent twenty pounds on presents.
Gasté veinte libras en regalos.

2 **pasar** (*time*)
We are going to spend two weeks in Scotland.
Vamos a pasar dos semanas en Escocia.

spicy ADJECTIVE
picante *masc/fem*

spider NOUN
la **araña** *fem*

spinach NOUN
las **espinacas** *fem pl*
I don't like spinach.
No me gustan las espinacas.

spite NOUN
in spite of
a pesar de
in spite of the weather
a pesar del tiempo

split VERB

1 **dividirse** (*separate*)
Split into two groups.
Dividíos en dos grupos.

2 **compartir** (*share*)
Let's split the money between us.
Vamos a compartir el dinero entre nosotros.

spoiled ADJECTIVE
mimado *masc*
mimada *fem*
a spoiled child
un niño mimado

spoilsport NOUN
el/la **aguafiestas** *masc/fem*
(PL los/las **aguafiestas**)
Don't be a spoilsport!
¡No seas aguafiestas!

spoilt ADJECTIVE
mimado *masc*
mimada *fem*
a spoilt child
un niño mimado

spoke VERB ▷ see **speak**

spoken VERB ▷ see **speak**

sponge NOUN
la **esponja** *fem*

sponge cake NOUN
el **bizcocho** *masc*

sponsor VERB
I'm doing a sponsored ten-mile walk in aid of the homeless.
Voy a caminar diez millas para conseguir donativos en beneficio de los sin techo.

DID YOU KNOW...?
In Spain it isn't usual to sponsor people to go on walks, swims and so on for charity.

spoon NOUN
la **cuchara** *fem*
I haven't got a spoon.
No tengo cuchara.

sport NOUN
el **deporte** *masc*
What's your favourite sport?
¿Cuál es tu deporte favorito?
Football is my favourite sport.
El fútbol es mi deporte favorito.
What sports do you play?
¿Qué deportes practicas?

sports bag NOUN
la **bolsa de deportes** *fem*

sports car NOUN
el **coche deportivo** *masc*

spot

> **spot** can be a noun or a verb.

A NOUN
1 el **lunar**
masc (*dot*)
a red dress
with white spots
un vestido rojo
con lunares
blancos
2 el **grano**
masc
(*pimple*)
He's covered
in spots.
Está lleno de granos.
B VERB
to spot
encontrar (*find*)
Can you spot the odd one out?
¿Puedes encontrar el que no es como
los demás?

spring NOUN
la **primavera** *fem*
It's the first day of spring.
Es el primer día de la primavera.

> **in spring**
> en primavera

springtime NOUN
la **primavera** *fem*

> **in springtime**
> en primavera

spy NOUN
el/la **espía** *masc/fem*

square NOUN
1 el **cuadrado** *masc* (*shape*)
a square and a triangle
un cuadrado y un triángulo
2 la **plaza** *fem* (*in town*)
There's a statue in the middle of
the square.
Hay una estatua en mitad de la plaza.

squash NOUN
1 (*drink*)
orange squash
la naranjada
2 el **squash** *masc* (*game*)
I play squash.
Juego al squash.

LANGUAGE TIP
In Spanish, you need to include **al** or **a**
la before the names of sports or games
when talking about playing them.

---

squirrel NOUN
la **ardilla** *fem*

stable NOUN
la **cuadra** *fem*

stack NOUN
la **pila** *fem*
a stack of
books
una pila
de libros

stadium NOUN
el **estadio** masc

staff NOUN
1 el **personal** masc (personnel)
2 el **profesorado** masc (of school)

staffroom NOUN
la **sala de profesores** fem

staircase NOUN
la **escalera** fem

stairs PL NOUN
la **escalera** fem
Go down the stairs.
Baja la escalera.
Go up the stairs.
Sube la escalera.

stamp NOUN
el **sello** masc
a Spanish stamp
un sello español
My hobby is stamp collecting.
Mi afición es coleccionar sellos.

stamp album NOUN
el **álbum de sellos** masc (PL los **álbumes de sellos**)

stamp collection NOUN
la **colección de sellos** fem (PL las **colecciones de sellos**)

stand VERB
Stand in a line.
Poneos en fila.
Stand over there, Antonio.
Quédate ahí de pie, Antonio.
I'm standing by the door.
Estoy de pie junto a la puerta.

stand for VERB
ser la abreviatura de
'LOL' stands for 'Laughing out loud'.
"LOL" es la abreviatura de "Laughing out loud".

stand up VERB
ponerse de pie
Stand up, Christine!
¡Ponte de pie, Christine!

stapler NOUN
la **grapadora** fem

star NOUN
la **estrella** fem
the moon and the stars
la luna y las estrellas
He's a TV star.
Es una estrella de la TV.

LANGUAGE TIP
Did you notice that you can use **una estrella** even when referring to a man?

---

start

start can be a verb or a noun.

A VERB
to start
1 **empezar** (begin)
What time does it start?
¿A qué hora empieza?
It starts with a P.
Empieza por P.

LANGUAGE TIP
When **start** is followed by another verb it is translated by **empezar a**.

You can start writing now.
Podéis empezar a escribir ahora.

Let's start.
Empecemos.
Start now, children.
¡Niños, empezad ahora!

2 **crear** (set up)
We want to start a football team.
Queremos crear un equipo de fútbol.
B NOUN
el **principio** masc (beginning)
at the start of the film
al principio de la película
at the start of December
a primeros de diciembre
Shall we make a start?
¿Empezamos ya?

starter NOUN
el **entrante** *masc* (*dish*)

starve VERB
I'm starving!
¡Tengo mucha hambre!

station NOUN
la **estación** *fem* (PL las **estaciones**)
Where's the station?
¿Dónde está la estación?

statue NOUN
la **estatua** *fem*

stay

> **stay** can be a verb or a noun.

A VERB
to stay
quedarse
Stay here, Owen!
¡Quédate aquí, Owen!
We stayed in London for three days.
Nos quedamos tres días en Londres.
We're going to stay with friends.
Vamos a quedarnos a dormir con unos amigos.
Why don't you stay the night?
¿Por qué no os quedáis a dormir esta noche?

B NOUN
la **estancia** *fem*
my stay in England
mi estancia en Inglaterra

stay in VERB
quedarse en casa
I'm staying in tonight.
Esta noche me quedo en casa.

steak NOUN
el **filete** *masc*
I'd like steak and chips.
Quiero un filete con patatas.

steal VERB
1 **quitar** (*take*)
Who's stolen my pencil case?
¿Quién me ha quitado el estuche?
2 **robar** (*thief*)
Our car's been stolen.
Nos han robado el coche.

step NOUN
1 el **paso** *masc* (*movement*)
a step backwards
un paso atrás
Take a step forward, boys.
Dad un paso hacia adelante, chicos.
2 el **escalón** *masc* (PL los **escalones**)
Mind the step.
Cuidado con el escalón.

stepbrother NOUN
el **hermanastro** *masc*
his stepbrother
su hermanastro

stepfather NOUN
el **padrastro** *masc*
my stepfather
mi padrastro

stepmother NOUN
la **madrastra** *fem*
my stepmother
mi madrastra

stepsister NOUN
la **hermanastra** *fem*
my stepsister
mi hermanastra

stew NOUN
el **estofado** *masc*

stick VERB
pegar
Stick the stamps on the envelope.
Pega los sellos en el sobre.

stick out VERB
Don't stick out your tongue!
¡No saques la lengua!

sticker NOUN
la **pegatina** *fem*

a
b
c
d
e
f
g
h
i
j
k
l
m
n
o
p
q
r
s
t
u
v
w
x
y
z

still

> **still** can be an adverb or an adjective.

A ADVERB
todavía
You've still got two cards.
Todavía tienes dos cartas.
I'm still hungry.
Todavía tengo hambre.

B ADJECTIVE
Keep still, Ben!
¡No te muevas, Ben!
Sit still, Jermaine!
¡Siéntate ahí quieto, Jermaine!

LANGUAGE TIP
Change **quieto** to **quieta** if you're talking to a girl.

---

stitch NOUN
el **punto** masc
I've got five stitches.
Me han dado cinco puntos.

stomach NOUN
el **estómago** masc

stomachache NOUN
I've got stomachache.
Me duele el estómago.

stone NOUN
la **piedra** fem
The boys are throwing stones.
Los niños están tirando piedras.
a stone wall
un muro de piedra
I weigh five stone.
Peso unos treinta y dos kilos.

DID YOU KNOW...?
In Spain, weight is given in kilos. A **stone** is about 6.3 kilos.

---

stool NOUN
la **banqueta** fem

stop

> **stop** can be a verb or a noun.

A VERB
to stop
parar
Stop, that's enough!
¡Para, ya basta!
Stop talking, children.
Parad de hablar, niños.
My dad wants to stop smoking.
Mi padre quiere dejar de fumar.

> **Stop it!**
> ¡Ya basta!

B NOUN
la **parada** fem
a bus stop
una parada de autobús

storey NOUN
la **planta** fem
a three-storey building
un edificio de tres plantas

storm NOUN
la **tormenta** fem

stormy ADJECTIVE
stormy weather
tiempo tormentoso

story NOUN
1 la **historia** fem (spoken)
I'm going to tell you a story.
Os voy a contar una historia.
2 el **cuento** masc (written)

stove NOUN
la **cocina** fem

straight

> **straight** can be an adjective or an adverb.

A ADJECTIVE
1 **recto** masc
recta fem
a straight line
una línea recta
2 **lacio** masc
lacia fem (hair)
I've got straight hair.
Tengo el pelo lacio.

B ADVERB
straight away
en seguida
straight on
todo recto

Go straight on.
Sigue recto.

strange ADJECTIVE
extraño *masc*
extraña *fem*
That's strange!
¡Eso es extraño!
a strange dream
un sueño extraño

stranger NOUN
el **desconocido** *masc*
la **desconocida** *fem*
Don't talk to strangers.
No hables con desconocidos.
I'm a stranger here.
Soy de fuera.

LANGUAGE TIP
Be careful! The translation of **stranger**
is not **extranjero**.

strap NOUN
1 el **tirante** *masc* (*of bra, dress*)
2 la **correa** *fem* (*of watch, camera,*
suitcase)
I need a new strap for my watch.
Necesito una correa nueva para mi
reloj.

straw NOUN
1 la **paja** *fem* (*material*)
2 la **pajita** *fem* (*for drinking*)

strawberry NOUN
la **fresa** *fem*
strawberry jam
mermelada de fresa
a strawberry ice cream
un helado de fresa

stream

stream can be a noun or a verb.

A NOUN
el **arroyo** *masc*
B VERB
1 **emitir en continuo** (*recording,*
video)
2 **emitir en directo**
The concert will be streamed live.
Emitirán el concierto en directo por
internet.

street NOUN
la **calle** *fem*
in the street
en la calle

stretch VERB
1 **estirarse**
The dog woke up and stretched.
El perro se despertó y se estiró.
2 **estirar** (*arms, legs*)
Stretch your arms!
¡Estirad los brazos!
Shall we go out and stretch our
legs?
¿Salimos a estirar las piernas?

LANGUAGE TIP
In Spanish you usually use an article
like **el**, **la** or **los**, **las** with parts of the
body.

strict ADJECTIVE
estricto *masc*
estricta *fem*

strike NOUN
la **huelga** *fem*
They are on strike.
Están en huelga.

string NOUN
la **cuerda** *fem*
a piece of string
una cuerda

stripe NOUN
la **raya** *fem*

stripy ADJECTIVE
de rayas
a stripy shirt
una camisa de rayas

strong ADJECTIVE
fuerte *masc/fem*
She's very strong.
Es muy fuerte.

student NOUN
el/la **estudiante** *masc/fem*
I'm a student.
Soy estudiante.

LANGUAGE TIP
In Spanish, you do not use an article with people's jobs.

---

study VERB
estudiar
My sister's studying for her exams.
Mi hermana está estudiando para sus exámenes.

stuff NOUN
las **cosas** *fem pl*
Have you got all your stuff?
¿Tienes todas tus cosas?

stuffy ADJECTIVE
It's stuffy in here.
Hay un ambiente muy cargado aquí.

stupid ADJECTIVE
estúpido *masc*
estúpida *fem*
a stupid joke
un chiste estúpido

subject NOUN
la **asignatura** *fem*
What's your favourite subject?
¿Cuál es tu asignatura favorita?

subtitles PL NOUN
los **subtítulos** *masc pl*
a Spanish film with English subtitles
una película española con subtítulos en inglés

subtract VERB
restar
Subtract three from five.
Réstale tres a cinco.

suburb NOUN
el **barrio de las afueras** *masc*
a suburb of London
un barrio de las afueras de Londres
They live in the suburbs.
Viven en las afueras.

success NOUN
el **éxito** *masc*
The party was a great success.
La fiesta fue un gran éxito.

LANGUAGE TIP
Be careful! The translation of **success** is not **suceso**.

---

such ADVERB
tan
such nice people
gente tan simpática
such a long journey
un viaje tan largo
We've got such a lot of work.
Tenemos tantísimo trabajo.
such as
como
towns such as Alicante and Valencia
ciudades como Alicante y Valencia

sudden ADJECTIVE
repentino *masc*
repentina *fem*
a sudden change
un cambio repentino

suddenly ADVERB
de repente

suede NOUN
el **ante** *masc*
a suede jacket
una chaqueta de ante

sugar NOUN
el **azúcar** *masc*
Do you take sugar?
¿Tomas azúcar?
More sugar?
¿Más azúcar?

suggestion NOUN
la **sugerencia** *fem*
Have you got any suggestions?
¿Tienes alguna sugerencia?

suit

suit can be a noun or a verb.

A NOUN
1 el **traje** *masc* (*man's*)
2 el **traje de chaqueta** *masc* (*woman's*)
B VERB
to suit
sentar bien a
Pink doesn't suit me.
El rosa no me sienta bien.

suitcase NOUN
la **maleta** *fem*

sum NOUN
1 la **suma** *fem*
The sum of 3 and 5 is 8.
La suma de 3 y 5 es 8.
2 I like doing sums.
Me gusta sumar, restar, multiplicar
y dividir.
She's good at sums.
Se le da bien el cálculo.

summer NOUN
el **verano** *masc*
It's very hot in summer.
Hace mucho calor en verano.
**We're going to Greece this
summer.**
Vamos a ir a Grecia este verano.

in summer
en verano
this summer
este verano
last summer
el verano pasado

summer holidays PL NOUN
las **vacaciones de verano** *fem pl*
in the summer holidays
en las vacaciones de verano

summertime NOUN
el **verano** *masc*

in summertime
en verano

sun NOUN
el **sol** *masc*
in the sun
al sol

sunbathe VERB
tomar el sol
I like sunbathing.
Me gusta tomar el sol.

sunburnt ADJECTIVE
to get sunburnt
quemarse con el sol
I got sunburnt.
Me quemé con el sol.

Sunday NOUN
el **domingo** *masc*
It's Sunday today.
Hoy es domingo.

on Sunday
el domingo

Spanish

English

A
B
C
D
E
F
G
H
I
J
K
L
M
N
O
P
Q
R
S
T
U
V
W
X
Y
Z

568

on Sundays
los domingos
every Sunday
cada domingo
last Sunday
el domingo pasado
next Sunday
el domingo que viene

LANGUAGE TIP
Days are not spelled with a capital
letter in Spanish.

Sunday school NOUN
la **catequesis** *fem*

sunflower NOUN
el **girasol** *masc*

sung VERB ▷ *see* **sing**

sunglasses PL NOUN
las **gafas de sol** *fem pl*
a pair of sunglasses
unas gafas de sol

sunny ADJECTIVE
It's a sunny day.
Hace un día de sol.

It's sunny.
Hace sol.

sunshine NOUN
el **sol** *masc*
lots of sunshine
mucho sol

super ADJECTIVE
estupendo *masc*
estupenda *fem*

supermarket NOUN
el **supermercado** *masc*
**We do our shopping at the
supermarket.**
Hacemos la compra en el supermercado.

supper NOUN
la **cena** *fem*

supply teacher NOUN
el **profesor sustituto** *masc*
la **profesora sustituta** *fem*
She's a supply teacher.
Es profesora sustituta.

LANGUAGE TIP
In Spanish, you do not use an article
with people's jobs.

support VERB
ser de
I support Real Madrid.
Soy del Real Madrid.
What team do you support?
¿De qué equipo eres?

supporter NOUN
el **aficionado** *masc*
la **aficionada** *fem*
a Liverpool supporter
un aficionado del Liverpool

suppose VERB
suponer
I suppose he's right.
Supongo que tiene razón.
**You're not supposed to do that,
Belle.**
No deberías hacer eso, Belle.

sure ADJECTIVE
seguro *masc*
segura *fem*

Are you sure, Helen?
¿Estás segura, Helen?

I'm not sure.
No estoy seguro.

surf

surf can be a noun or a verb.

A NOUN
las **olas** *fem pl* (*in sea*)
B VERB
to surf
1 **hacer surf**
I like to go surfing at the weekends.
Los fines de semana me gusta hacer surf.
2 **to surf the Net**
navegar por internet

surface NOUN
la **superficie** *fem*

surfboard NOUN
la **tabla de surf** *fem*

surfing NOUN
el **surf** *masc*
I go surfing.
Hago surf.

surname NOUN
el **apellido** *masc*
What's your surname?
¿Cuál es tu apellido?

surprise NOUN
la **sorpresa** *fem*
What a surprise!
¡Vaya sorpresa!

survey NOUN
la **encuesta** *fem*
We're doing a survey on pets.
Estamos haciendo una encuesta sobre las mascotas.

suspend VERB
expulsar temporalmente
He's been suspended.
Lo han expulsado temporalmente.

swallow VERB
tragar

swam VERB ▷ *see* **swim**

swan NOUN
el **cisne** *masc*

swap VERB
cambiar
Do you want to swap?
¿Quieres que cambiemos?
I'll swap you my stamps for your stickers.
Te cambiaré mis sellos por tus pegatinas.
Let's swap places.
Vamos a cambiarnos de sitio.

sweat

sweat can be a verb or a noun.

A VERB
to sweat
sudar
B NOUN
el **sudor** *masc*

sweater NOUN
el **jersey** *masc* (PL los **jerseys**)
a white sweater
un jersey blanco

sweatshirt NOUN
la **sudadera** *fem*
a green sweatshirt
una sudadera verde

sweet

sweet can be a noun or an adjective.

A NOUN
1 el **caramelo** *masc* (*toffee, mint etc*)
a bag of sweets
una bolsa de caramelos
2 el **postre** *masc* (*pudding*)
Sweets: ice cream or chocolate mousse
Postres: helado o mousse de chocolate
B ADJECTIVE
1 **dulce** *masc/fem* (*sugary*)
It's too sweet.
Está demasiado dulce.

2 encantador *masc*
encantadora *fem* (*delightful*)
Isn't she sweet?
¿Verdad que es encantadora?

sweetcorn NOUN
el **maíz dulce** *masc*

swim

> **swim** can be a verb or a noun.

A VERB
to swim
nadar
Can you swim?
¿Sabes nadar?
I can swim.
Sé nadar.
I can't swim.
No sé nadar.
B NOUN
I want to go for a swim.
Quiero ir a nadar.

swimmer NOUN
el **nadador** *masc*
la **nadadora** *fem*
She's a good swimmer.
Es una buena nadadora.

swimming NOUN
la **natación** *fem*
Do you like swimming?
¿Te gusta la natación?
I go swimming on Wednesdays.
Voy a nadar los miércoles.

swimming costume NOUN
el **traje de baño** *masc*

swimming pool NOUN
la **piscina** *fem*

swimming trunks PL NOUN
el **bañador** *masc*
I've got new swimming trunks.
Tengo un bañador nuevo.

swimsuit NOUN
el **traje de baño** *masc*

swing NOUN
el **columpio** *masc*

switch

> **switch** can be a noun or a verb.

A NOUN
el **interruptor** *masc*
Where's the switch?
¿Dónde está el interruptor?
B VERB
to switch
cambiar de
Switch partners!
¡Cambiad de pareja!

switch off VERB
apagar
Switch off the computer, Kiran.
Apaga el ordenador, Kiran.

switch on VERB
encender
Switch on the light, Max.
Enciende la luz, Max.

swop VERB
cambiar
Do you want to swop?
¿Quieres que cambiemos?
Let's swop places.
Vamos a cambiar de sitio.

sword NOUN
la **espada** *fem*

swum VERB ▷ *see* **swim**

symbol NOUN
el **símbolo** *masc*

sympathetic ADJECTIVE
comprensivo *masc*
comprensiva *fem*

> **LANGUAGE TIP**
> Be careful! The translation of
> **sympathetic** is not **simpático**.

system NOUN
el **sistema** *masc*

> **LANGUAGE TIP**
> Even though it ends in **-a**, **el sistema**
> is a masculine noun.

T t

table NOUN
1 la **mesa** *fem* (*piece of furniture*)
   It's on the table.
   Está en la mesa.
2 la **tabla** *fem* (*chart*)
   the three times table
   la tabla del tres

tablecloth NOUN
   el **mantel** *masc*

tablespoon NOUN
   la **cuchara grande** *fem*

tablet NOUN
   la **tableta** *fem*
   Can I download this app on my tablet?
   ¿Puedo bajarme esta aplicación a mi tableta?

table tennis NOUN
   el **tenis de mesa** *masc*
   I can play table tennis.
   Sé jugar al tenis de mesa.

LANGUAGE TIP
In Spanish, you need to include **al** or **a la** before the names of sports or games when talking about playing them.

---

tail NOUN
1 el **rabo** *masc* (*of dog*)
   The dog wagged its tail.
   El perro movía el rabo.

LANGUAGE TIP
In Spanish you usually use an article like **el**, **la** or **los**, **las** with parts of the body.

---

2 la **cola** *fem* (*of horse, bird, fish*)

   Heads or tails?
   ¿Cara o cruz?

take VERB
1 **coger**
   Take a card, Erika.
   Coge una carta, Erika.
   Who has taken my ruler?
   ¿Quién ha cogido mi regla?
   Take the first turning on the right.
   Coge el primer desvío a la derecha.
   Let's take the bus.
   Vamos a coger el autobús.

LANGUAGE TIP
Don't use **coger** in Latin America as it's considered rude in some places. Use verbs like **tomar** and **agarrar** instead.

---

2 **tomar** (*food, medicine*)
   I don't take sugar.
   No tomo azúcar.
3 **llevar** (*take along*)
   Mum's going to take me to the fair.
   Mi madre me va a llevar a la feria.
   Don't forget to take your camera.
   No te olvides de llevarte la cámara.
4 **durar** (*last*)
   How long does the journey take?
   ¿Cuánto dura el viaje?
   It takes about an hour.
   Se tarda más o menos una hora.

take away VERB
   Thirty take away nine is twenty-one.
   Treinta menos nueve son veintiuno.

a
b
c
d
e
f
g
h
i
j
k
l
m
n
o
p
q
r
s
t
u
v
w
x
y
z

Spanish

English

A
B
C
D
E
F
G
H
I
J
K
L
M
N
O
P
Q
R
S
T
U
V
W
X
Y
Z

take back VERB
   devolver
      I'm going to take this book back to the library.
      Voy a devolver este libro a la biblioteca.

take down VERB
   quitar
      Take the posters down.
      Quita los pósters.

take off VERB
   quitarse (*clothes*)
      Take your coat off.
      Quítate el abrigo.

LANGUAGE TIP
In Spanish you usually use an article like **el**, **la** or **los**, **las** with clothes you are wearing.

---

take out VERB
   sacar
      Can you take the key out of the lock?
      ¿Puedes sacar la llave de la cerradura?
      I take the dog out at about six o'clock.
      Saco al perro a pasear sobre las seis.

taken VERB ▷ *see* **take**

takeoff NOUN
   el **despegue** *masc*

tale NOUN
   el **cuento** *masc*

talk

> **talk** can be a verb or a noun.

A VERB
   to talk
   hablar
      You talk too much.
      Hablas demasiado.
      Today we're going to talk about Spain.
      Hoy vamos a hablar de España.
B NOUN
      Let's have a talk about it.
      Vamos a hablar de eso.

talkative ADJECTIVE
   hablador *masc*
   habladora *fem*

tall ADJECTIVE
   alto *masc*
   alta *fem*
      Ian is tall.
      Ian es alto.
      My sister is taller than me.
      Mi hermana es más alta que yo.
      Mark is the tallest in the class.
      Mark es el más alto de la clase.
      a very tall building
      un edificio muy alto

> **How tall are you?**
> ¿Cuánto mides?
> **I'm one metre thirty tall.**
> Mido un metro treinta.

tan NOUN
   el **bronceado** *masc*
      She's got an amazing tan.
      Tiene un bronceado increíble.

tangerine NOUN
   la **mandarina** *fem*

tap NOUN
   el **grifo** *masc*
      Turn on the tap.
      Abre el grifo.
      the hot tap
      el grifo del agua caliente

tap-dancing NOUN
   el **claqué** *masc*

target NOUN
   la **diana** *fem*

tart NOUN
   la **tarta** *fem*

a jam tart
una tarta de mermelada

tartan ADJECTIVE
**de cuadros
escoceses**
a tartan scarf
una bufanda de
cuadros escoceses

taste

> **taste** can be a noun or a verb.

A NOUN
el **sabor** *masc*
It's got a strange taste.
Tiene un sabor extraño.
Would you like a taste?
¿Quieres probarlo?
B VERB
to taste
1 **probar** (*try*)
Would you like to taste it?
¿Quieres probarlo?
2 **It tastes nice.**
Tiene buen sabor.
It tastes of fish.
Sabe a pescado.

tasty ADJECTIVE
rico *masc*
rica *fem*

tattoo NOUN
el **tatuaje** *masc*

taught VERB ▷ *see* **teach**

taxi NOUN
el **taxi** *masc*
by taxi
en taxi

taxi driver NOUN
el/la **taxista** *masc/fem*

LANGUAGE TIP
In Spanish, you do not use an article
with people's jobs.

---

tea NOUN
1 el **té** *masc*

a cup of tea
una taza de té
tea with milk
té con leche
Would you like some tea?
¿Quieres un té?
2 la **cena** *fem* (*evening meal*)
What's for tea?
¿Qué hay de cena?
to have tea
cenar
We're having tea.
Estamos cenando.

tea bag NOUN
la **bolsita de té** *fem*

teach VERB
enseñar
**Mrs Morrison teaches us
English.**
Mrs Morrison nos enseña inglés.
**My cousin is teaching me to play
the guitar.**
Mi primo me está enseñando a tocar
la guitarra.

teacher NOUN
1 el **maestro** *masc*
la **maestra** *fem* (*in primary school*)
Mr Price is our teacher.
Mr Price es nuestro maestro.
2 el **profesor** *masc*
la **profesora** *fem* (*in secondary school*)
a maths teacher
un profesor de matemáticas
She's a teacher.
Es profesora.

LANGUAGE TIP
In Spanish, you do not use an article
with people's jobs.

---

team NOUN
el **equipo** *masc*
a football team
un equipo de fútbol
She's in my team.
Está en mi equipo.

Spanish

English

A
B
C
D
E
F
G
H
I
J
K
L
M
N
O
P
Q
R
S
T
U
V
W
X
Y
Z

We're going to divide the class into two teams.
Vamos a dividir la clase en dos equipos.

tear

> **tear** can be a noun or a verb.

A NOUN
la **lágrima** *fem*

B VERB
to tear
romper
Be careful or you'll tear the page.
Ten cuidado que vas a romper la página.

teaspoon NOUN
la **cucharilla** *fem*

teatime NOUN
la **hora de cenar** *fem (supper time)*
at teatime
a la hora de cenar

tea towel NOUN
el **paño de cocina** *masc*

technology NOUN
la **tecnología** *fem*

LANGUAGE TIP
Have you noticed that there isn't an **h** in **tecnología**?

---

teddy bear NOUN
el **osito de peluche** *masc*

teenager NOUN
el/la **adolescente** *masc/fem*

teens PL NOUN
He's in his teens.
Es un adolescente.
She's in her teens.
Es una adolescente.

tee-shirt NOUN
la **camiseta** *fem*

teeth PL NOUN
los **dientes** *masc pl*
I clean my teeth three times a day.
Me lavo los dientes tres veces al día.

LANGUAGE TIP
In Spanish you usually use an article like **el**, **la** or **los**, **las** with parts of the body.

---

telephone NOUN
el **teléfono** *masc*

telephone call NOUN
la **llamada telefónica** *fem*

telephone number NOUN
el **número de teléfono** *masc*
What's your telephone number?
¿Cuál es tu número de teléfono?

television NOUN
la **televisión** *fem*
on television
en la televisión
What's on television?
¿Qué hay en la televisión?
I haven't got a television in my room.
No tengo televisión en mi habitación.

television programme NOUN
el **programa de televisión** *masc*

LANGUAGE TIP
Even though it ends in **-a**, **el programa** is a masculine noun.

---

tell VERB
1 **decir** *(say)*
Tell me why, Janice.
Dime por qué, Janice.
I'm going to tell my mum.
Se lo voy a decir a mi madre.
2 **contar** *(recount)*
I'm going to tell you a story.
Te voy a contar una historia.
I'll tell you about myself.
Te contaré cosas sobre mí.

tell off VERB
regañar
She tells me off if I'm late.
Me regaña si llego tarde.

telly NOUN
la **tele** *fem*

I watch telly a lot.
Veo mucho la tele.
on telly
en la tele

temperature NOUN

1 la **temperatura** *fem* (*in centigrade etc*)

2 la **fiebre** *fem* (*fever*)
I've got a temperature.
Tengo fiebre.

ten NUMBER
diez

ten euros
diez euros
It's ten to three.
Son las tres menos diez.
It's ten past two.
Son las dos y diez.

I'm ten.
Tengo diez años.

LANGUAGE TIP
In English you can say **I'm ten** or **I'm ten years old**. In Spanish you can only say **tengo diez años**. Have you noticed that in Spanish you need to use the verb **tener** to talk about somebody's age?

tennis NOUN
el **tenis** *masc*
I play tennis.
Juego al tenis.

LANGUAGE TIP
In Spanish, you need to include **al** or **a la** before the names of sports or games when talking about playing them.

tennis ball NOUN
la **pelota de tenis** *fem*

tennis court NOUN
la **pista de tenis** *fem*

tennis player NOUN
el **jugador de tenis** *masc*
la **jugadora de tenis** *fem*

tennis racket NOUN
la **raqueta de tenis** *fem*

tenpin bowling NOUN
los **bolos** *masc pl*
Do you want to go tenpin bowling?
¿Quieres ir a jugar a los bolos?

LANGUAGE TIP
In Spanish, you need to include **a los** before **bolos** when using it with the verb **jugar**.

tent NOUN
la **tienda de campaña** *fem*

tenth NUMBER
décimo *masc*
décima *fem*
on the tenth floor
en el décimo piso
My birthday's the tenth of April.
Mi cumpleaños es el diez de abril.
It's the tenth of July today.
Hoy es diez de julio.

on the tenth of August
el diez de agosto

LANGUAGE TIP
Use the same set of numbers that you use for counting (**uno**, **dos**, **tres** and so on) when giving Spanish dates.

term NOUN
  el **trimestre** *masc*
    It will soon be the end of term.
    Pronto será el final del trimestre.

terraced house NOUN
  la **casa adosada** *fem*

terrible ADJECTIVE
  terrible *masc/fem*
    My English is terrible.
    Mi inglés es terrible.

terrified ADJECTIVE
  aterrorizado *masc*
  aterrorizada *fem*
    I was terrified!
    ¡Estaba aterrorizado!

test NOUN
  la **prueba** *fem*
    I've got a test tomorrow.
    Tengo una prueba mañana.

text

  text can be a noun or a verb.

  A NOUN
  1 el **texto** *masc* (*in book*)
  2 el **mensaje de texto** *masc* (*from mobile*)
  B VERB
    to text
    enviar un mensaje a
    I'll text you when I get there.
    Te envío un mensaje cuando llegue.

textbook NOUN
  el **libro de texto** *masc*
    an English textbook
    un libro de texto de inglés

text message NOUN
  el **mensaje de texto** *masc*

than CONJUNCTION
  que
    She's taller than me.
    Es más alta que yo.

Are you older than him?
¿Eres mayor que él?

thanks EXCLAMATION
  gracias
    No thanks.
    No, gracias.
    Thanks for helping me.
    Gracias por ayudarme.

thank you EXCLAMATION
  gracias

    Thank you very much.
    Muchas gracias.

that

  that can be a pronoun, adjective or conjunction.

  A PRONOUN
  1 **ese** *masc*
    esa *fem*
    eso *neuter*
    That's my brother.
    Ese es mi hermano.
    That's my friend Bella.
    Esa es mi amiga Bella.

  LANGUAGE TIP
  Use the neuter form **eso** when **that** refers to something vague, something not very specific or to an object you don't recognize.

    That's right! Well done.
    ¡Eso es! Bien hecho.

  LANGUAGE TIP
  Instead of **ese**, **esa** and **eso**, use **aquel**, **aquella** and **aquello** to talk about something or someone that's quite far away.

    That's my French teacher over there.
    Aquel es mi profesor de francés.

    What's that?
    ¿Qué es eso?
    Who's that? — It's Stephen.
    ¿Quién es ese? — Es Stephen.

Who's that? — It's Sarah.
¿Quién es esa? — Es Sarah.
I know that.
Lo sé.

LANGUAGE TIP
Traditionally, the pronouns **ese**, **esa**, **aquel** and **aquella** were written with an accent to distinguish them from the unaccented adjective forms. Nowadays, you don't have to give the accents unless the sentence would be confusing otherwise.

2 que (*relative*)
the man that lives here
el hombre que vive aquí
the girl that I saw
la chica que vi

LANGUAGE TIP
We sometimes leave out **that** in English sentences like these. Don't ever leave out the **que** in Spanish.

B ADJECTIVE
ese *masc*
esa *fem*
that dog
ese perro
that woman
esa mujer
This man? — No, that one.
¿Este hombre? — No, ese.
This chair? — No, that one.
¿Esta silla? — No, esa.

LANGUAGE TIP
Instead of **ese** and **esa**, use **aquel** and **aquella** to talk about something or someone that's quite far away.

Look at that car over there!
¡Mira aquel coche!
C CONJUNCTION
que
I think that it's raining.
Creo que está lloviendo.

LANGUAGE TIP
We sometimes leave out **that** in English sentences like this one. Don't ever leave out the **que** in Spanish.

I think that Henry is ill.
Creo que Henry está enfermo.

the ARTICLE
el *masc*
la *fem*
los *masc pl*
las *fem pl*

LANGUAGE TIP
Use **el** with a masculine singular noun and **la** with a feminine singular noun. Use **los** with a masculine plural noun and **las** with a feminine plural noun.

the boy
el chico
the girl
la chica
the children
los niños
the oranges
las naranjas

LANGUAGE TIP
a combines with **el** to form **al** while **de** combines with **el** to form **del**.

We're going to the theatre.
Vamos al teatro.
a photo of the dog
una foto del perro

theatre NOUN
el **teatro** *masc*

a
b
c
d
e
f
g
h
i
j
k
l
m
n
o
p
q
r
s
t
u
v
w
x
y
z

577

A
B
C
D
E
F
G
H
I
J
K
L
M
N
O
P
Q
R
S
T
U
V
W
X
Y
Z

their ADJECTIVE
su *masc/fem* (PL **sus**)

> **LANGUAGE TIP**
> Remember to use **su** before a singular noun and **sus** before a plural one.

their house
su casa
their parents
sus padres

> **LANGUAGE TIP**
> In Spanish you usually use an article like **el**, **la** or **los**, **las** with clothes or parts of the body.

They took off their coats.
Se quitaron los abrigos.
They are washing their hands.
Se están lavando las manos.

theirs PRONOUN
el **suyo** *masc*
la **suya** *fem*

> **LANGUAGE TIP**
> Remember that the choice of **el suyo**, **la suya**, **los suyos** or **las suyas** depends entirely on the thing or things referred to.

That isn't the Smiths' car. Theirs is red.
Aquél no es el coche de los Smith. El suyo es rojo.
Those aren't the twins' books. Theirs are here.
Aquéllos no son los libros de los gemelos. Los suyos están aquí.

> **LANGUAGE TIP**
> After **ser** you can usually just use **suyo**, **suya**, **suyos** or **suyas** to agree with the noun referred to.

Is this theirs?
¿Es suyo esto?
This house is theirs.
Esta casa es suya.

These cases are theirs.
Estas maletas son suyas.
Whose is this? — It's theirs.
¿De quién es esto? — Es suyo.

> **LANGUAGE TIP**
> Because **suyo** can also mean **his**, **hers** and **yours**, you can avoid confusion by using **de ellos/de ellas** instead.

Whose is this? — It's theirs.
¿De quién es esto? — Es de ellos.

a friend of theirs
un amigo suyo

them PRONOUN
1 **los** *masc*
las *fem pl* (*direct object*)
Where are the horses? I can't see them.
¿Dónde están los caballos? No los veo.
There are some more biscuits in the cupboard. Do you want them?
Hay más galletas en el armario. ¿Las quieres?
I like these socks. I think I'll buy them.
Me gustan estos calcetines. Creo que me voy a comprarlos.
2 **les** (*indirect object*)

> **LANGUAGE TIP**
> Use **les** when **them** means **to them** or **for them**.

Can you give them a message?
¿Les puedes dar un mensaje?
I'm going to buy them a present.
Les voy a comprar un regalo.

> **LANGUAGE TIP**
> Change **les** to **se** when combining it with a direct object pronoun like **lo**.

I'll tell them.
Se lo diré.

LANGUAGE TIP
Because **se** can mean **to him**, **to her** and **to you** as well as **to them**, you can add **a ellos/a ellas** (to them) after the verb for clarity.

I'm going to give it to them.
Voy a dárselo a ellos.

3 ellos *masc pl*
ellas *fem pl (after preposition)*
It's not for you, it's for them.
No es para ti, es para ellos.
Molly and Victoria are here, and René's with them.
Molly y Victoria están aquí, y René está con ellas.

LANGUAGE TIP
Use **ellos** and **ellas** in comparisons.

I'm older than them.
Soy mayor que ellos.

LANGUAGE TIP
Use **ellos** and **ellas** after the verb **ser**.

It must be them.
Deben de ser ellos.
It's them.
Son ellos.

theme park NOUN
el **parque temático** *masc*

themselves PRONOUN
1 se *(reflexive use)*
They have hurt themselves.
Se han hecho daño.
They're enjoying themselves.
Se están divirtiendo.

2 sí mismos *masc pl*
sí mismas *fem pl (after preposition)*
They talked about themselves.
Hablaron de sí mismos.
3 ellos mismos *masc pl*
ellas mismas *fem pl (for emphasis)*
They did it themselves.
Lo hicieron ellos mismos.
The girls did it all by themselves.
Las chicas lo hicieron todo ellas mismas.

then CONJUNCTION
luego
I get dressed. Then I have breakfast.
Me visto. Luego desayuno.

there ADVERB
1 ahí *(not far away)*
Put it there, on the table.
Ponlo ahí, en la mesa.
up there
ahí arriba
down there
ahí abajo
2 allí *(further away)*
I'm going there on Friday.
El viernes voy allí.
3 there is ...
hay ...
There's a new boy in the class.
Hay un chico nuevo en la clase.
there are ...
hay ...
There are ten chairs in the room.
Hay diez sillas en la habitación.
How many biscuits are there?
¿Cuántas galletas hay?
There are lots.
Hay muchas.
There aren't many.
No hay muchas.

over there
por ahí
There he is!
¡Ahí está!
There they are!
¡Ahí están!

a b c d e f g h i j k l m n o p q r s t u v w x y z

579

A
B
C
D
E
F
G
H
I
J
K
L
M
N
O
P
Q
R
S
T
U
V
W
X
Y
Z

580

There is ...
Hay ...
There are ...
Hay ...

these

A ADJECTIVE
estos *masc pl*
estas *fem pl*
these shoes
estos zapatos
these tables
estas mesas
Which books do you need? —
These ones.
¿Qué libros necesitas? — Estos.

B PRONOUN
estos *masc pl*
estas *fem pl*
If you need felt-tips, I've got these.
Si necesitas rotuladores, tengo estos.
Of course we've got apples. Look at these!
Claro que tenemos manzanas. ¡Mira éstas!

LANGUAGE TIP
Traditionally, the pronouns **éstos** and **éstas** were written with an accent to distinguish them from the unaccented adjective forms shown in the previous category. Nowadays, you don't have to give the accents unless the sentence would be confusing otherwise.

they PRONOUN
ellos *masc pl*
ellas *fem pl*
We went to the cinema, but they didn't.
Nosotros fuimos al cine, pero ellos no.
I spoke to my sisters and they agree with me.
Hablé con mis hermanas y ellas están de acuerdo conmigo.

LANGUAGE TIP
they isn't usually translated unless it's emphatic.

Where are your friends? — They're over there.
¿Dónde están tus amigos? — Están allí.

they'd
(= **they had**) ▷ *see* **have**
(= **they would**) ▷ *see* **would**

they'll (= **they will**) ▷ *see* **will**

they're (= **they are**) ▷ *see* **be**

they've (= **they have**) ▷ *see* **have**

thick ADJECTIVE
grueso *masc*
gruesa *fem*
a thick slice
una rebanada gruesa

thief NOUN
el **ladrón** *masc*
(PL los **ladrones**)
la **ladrona** *fem*

thin ADJECTIVE
1 **delgado** *masc*
delgada *fem* (*person*)
I'm quite thin.
Soy bastante delgado.
2 **fino** *masc*
fina *fem* (*slice, book*)
a thin slice
una rebanada fina

thing NOUN
la **cosa** *fem*
I've got lots of things to do.
Tengo muchas cosas que hacer.
my things
mis cosas

think VERB
1 **pensar**
What do you think?
¿Qué piensas?

Spanish

English

Think carefully, Harry.
Piénsalo bien, Harry.
I'll think about it.
Lo pensaré.
2 **creer** (*believe*)
I think he's here.
Creo que está aquí.

LANGUAGE TIP
Although you can say both 'I think he's here' and 'I think that he's here' in English, in Spanish you cannot leave out the **que** and have to say **creo que está aquí.**

I think so.
Creo que sí.
I don't think so.
Creo que no.

third NUMBER
tercero *masc*
tercera *fem*
It's the third time.
Es la tercera vez.
I came third.
Llegué el tercero.

LANGUAGE TIP
Shorten **tercero** to **tercer** before a masculine singular noun.

the third prize
el tercer premio
My birthday's the third of September.
Mi cumpleaños es el tres de septiembre.
It's the third of December today.
Hoy es tres de diciembre.

on the third of March
el tres de marzo

LANGUAGE TIP
Use the same set of numbers that you use for counting (**uno**, **dos**, **tres** and so on) when giving Spanish dates.

thirsty ADJECTIVE
to be thirsty
tener sed
Are you thirsty?
¿Tienes sed?
I'm not thirsty.
No tengo sed.

I'm thirsty.
Tengo sed.

thirteen NUMBER
trece
thirteen euros
trece euros

I'm thirteen.
Tengo trece años.

LANGUAGE TIP
In English you can say **I'm thirteen** or **I'm thirteen years old**. In Spanish you can only say **tengo trece años**. Have you noticed that in Spanish you need to use the verb **tener** to talk about somebody's age?

thirteenth NUMBER
trece
on the thirteenth floor
en la planta trece
We break up on the thirteenth of December.
Empezamos las vacaciones el trece de diciembre.
Today's the thirteenth of May.
Hoy es trece de mayo.

on the thirteenth of August
el trece de agosto

LANGUAGE TIP
Use the same set of numbers that you use for counting (**uno**, **dos**, **tres** and so on) when giving Spanish dates.

a
b
c
d
e
f
g
h
i
j
k
l
m
n
o
p
q
r
s
t
u
v
w
x
y
z

thirtieth NUMBER
treinta
> **My birthday's the thirtieth of March.**
> Mi cumpleaños es el treinta de marzo.
> **Today's the thirtieth of July.**
> Hoy es treinta de julio.

> **on the thirtieth of August**
> el treinta de agosto

LANGUAGE TIP
Use the same set of numbers that you use for counting (**uno**, **dos**, **tres** and so on) when giving Spanish dates.

thirty NUMBER
treinta
> **thirty euros**
> treinta euros
> **My aunt is thirty.**
> Mi tía tiene treinta años.

LANGUAGE TIP
In English you can say **she's thirty** or **she's thirty years old**. In Spanish you can only say **tiene treinta años**. Have you noticed that in Spanish you need to use the verb **tener** to talk about somebody's age?

this

> **this** can be an adjective or a pronoun.

A ADJECTIVE
este *masc*
esta *fem*
> **this book**
> este libro
> **this man**
> este hombre
> **this time**
> esta vez
> **Which book do you want? — This one.**
> ¿Qué libro quieres? — Este.
> **That card? — No, this one.**
> ¿Esa tarjeta? — No, esta.

B PRONOUN
este *masc*
esta *fem*
esto *neuter*
> **This is my room.**
> Este es mi cuarto.
> **This is my class.**
> Esta es mi clase.

LANGUAGE TIP
Use the neuter form **esto** when **this** refers to something vague, something not very specific or to an object you don't recognize.

> **Look at this.**
> Mira esto.

> **this morning**
> esta mañana
> **this year**
> este año
> **this afternoon**
> esta tarde
> **What's this?**
> ¿Qué es esto?

LANGUAGE TIP
Traditionally, the pronouns **éste** and **ésta** were written with an accent to distinguish them from the unaccented adjective forms shown in the previous category. Nowadays, you don't have to give the accents unless the sentence would be confusing otherwise.

those
A ADJECTIVE
esos *masc pl*
esas *fem pl*
> **those shoes**
> esos zapatos
> **those chairs**
> esas sillas

LANGUAGE TIP
Instead of **esos** and **esas**, use **aquellos** and **aquellas** if you're talking about people or things that are quite far away.

Look at those boys over there!
¡Mira a aquellos chicos!
Which books do you need?
— Those ones.
¿Qué libros necesitas? — Esos.
B PRONOUN
esos masc pl
esas fem pl
Those aren't my boots.
Esas no son mis botas.

LANGUAGE TIP
Instead of **esos** and **esas**, use
aquellos and **aquellas** to talk about
people or things that are quite far
away.

**Those are my classmates over
there.**
Aquellos son mis compañeros de clase.

LANGUAGE TIP
Traditionally, the pronouns **esos**,
esas, **aquellos** and **aquellas** were
written with an accent to distinguish
them from the unaccented adjective
forms shown in the previous category.
Nowadays, you don't have to give the
accents unless the sentence would
otherwise be confusing.

thought VERB ▷ see **think**

thousand NOUN
a thousand
mil
a thousand euros
mil euros
two thousand pounds
dos mil libras
thousands of people
miles de personas

three NUMBER
tres
three euros
tres euros

She's three.
Tiene tres años.

LANGUAGE TIP
In English you can say **she's three** or
she's three years old. In Spanish
you can only say **tiene tres años**.
Have you noticed that in Spanish you
need to use the verb **tener** to talk
about somebody's age?

throat NOUN
la **garganta** fem
I've got a sore throat.
Me duele la garganta.

through PREPOSITION
por
**Our cat always comes in through
the window.**
Nuestro gato siempre entra por la
ventana.
I know her through my sister.
La conozco por mi hermana.

throw VERB
tirar
Throw me the ball.
Tírame la pelota.

throw away VERB
tirar
**Don't throw it
away!**
¡No lo tires!

thumb NOUN
el **pulgar** masc
**He sucks his
thumb.**
Se chupa el pulgar.

LANGUAGE TIP
In Spanish you usually use an article
like **el**, **la** or **los**, **las** with parts of the
body.

thunder NOUN
los **truenos** masc pl
There was thunder and lightning.
Hubo rayos y truenos.

thunderstorm NOUN
la **tormenta** fem

a b c d e f g h i j k l m n o p q r s t u v w x y z

583

A
B
C
D
E
F
G
H
I
J
K
L
M
N
O
P
Q
R
S
T
U
V
W
X
Y
Z

Thursday NOUN
el **jueves** masc
It's Thursday today.
Hoy es jueves.

> **on Thursday**
> el jueves
> **on Thursdays**
> los jueves
> **every Thursday**
> cada jueves
> **last Thursday**
> el jueves pasado
> **next Thursday**
> el jueves que viene

LANGUAGE TIP
Days are not spelled with a capital
letter in Spanish.

---

tick

> **tick** can be a noun or a verb.

A NOUN
la **señal** fem
Put a tick or a cross.
Pon una señal o una cruz.
B VERB
to tick
señalar
Tick the right box.
Señala la casilla correcta.

ticket NOUN
  1 la **entrada** fem (for concert, cinema, museum)
    a cinema ticket
    una entrada para el cine
  2 el **billete** masc (for bus, train, plane)
    a bus ticket
    un billete de autobús

ticket office NOUN
la **taquilla** fem

tidy

> **tidy** can be an adjective or a verb.

A ADJECTIVE
ordenado masc
ordenada fem
My room is tidy.
Mi cuarto está ordenado.
It's tidier now.
Ahora está más ordenado.
B VERB
to tidy
ordenar
You must tidy your room.
Tienes que ordenar tu cuarto.

tidy up VERB
Don't forget to tidy up afterwards, children.
No olvidéis ordenarlo todo después, niños.

tie

> **tie** can be a noun or a verb.

A NOUN
  1 la **corbata** fem (for neck)
  2 el **empate** masc (in match)
    It's a tie.
    Es un empate.
B VERB
to tie
atar
Let's tie the balloons to the door!
¡Vamos a atar los globos a la puerta!
Tie your laces.
Átate los cordones.

tiger NOUN
el **tigre** masc

tight ADJECTIVE
  1 **estrecho** masc
    estrecha fem (too small)
    This dress is a bit tight.
    Este vestido es un poco estrecho.
  2 **ceñido** masc
    ceñida fem (close-fitting)

a tight skirt
una falda ceñida

tights PL NOUN
las **medias** *fem pl*
I'm wearing black tights.
Llevo medias negras.
a pair of tights
unas medias

till

till can be a noun or a preposition.

A NOUN
la **caja** *fem*
at the till
en la caja
B PREPOSITION
hasta
He's staying till Monday.
Se queda hasta el lunes.
from nine till five
de nueve a cinco

time NOUN
1 la **hora** *fem* (*on clock*)
What time is it?
¿Qué hora es?
It's time to go.
Es hora de irse.
What time...?
¿A qué hora...?
What time do you get up?
¿A qué hora te levantas?
What time does the train arrive?
¿A qué hora llega el tren?
2 el **tiempo** *masc* (*amount of time*)
I'm sorry, I haven't got time.
Lo siento, no tengo tiempo.
3 la **vez** *fem*
fem pl las **veces** (*occasion*)
three times
tres veces
this time
esta vez
next time
la próxima vez
the first time
la primera vez

two at a time
dos a la vez
Two times two is four.
Dos por dos son cuatro.

What time is it?
¿Qué hora es?
It's lunch time.
Es la hora de comer.
How many times?
¿Cuántas veces?
Have a good time, Amanda!
¡Que lo pases bien, Amanda!

timetable NOUN
el **horario** *masc*

tin NOUN
la **lata** *fem*
a tin of soup
una lata de sopa

tin opener NOUN
el **abrelatas** *masc*
masc pl los **abrelatas**

tinsel NOUN
el **espumillón** *masc*

tiny ADJECTIVE
minúsculo *masc*
minúscula *fem*

tip NOUN
1 la **propina** *fem* (*for waiter, taxi driver*)
It's a tip for the waiter.
Es una propina para el camarero.
2 el **consejo** *masc* (*piece of advice*)

tiptoe NOUN
on tiptoe
de puntillas
He's standing on tiptoe.
Está de puntillas.

tired ADJECTIVE
cansado *masc*
cansada *fem*
I'm tired.
Estoy cansado.

tiring ADJECTIVE
cansado *masc*
cansada *fem*
> **Doing so much running is tiring.**
> Es cansado correr tanto.

tissue NOUN
el **Kleenex**® *masc*
> **Have you got a tissue?**
> ¿Tienes un Kleenex?

title NOUN
el **título** *masc*

to PREPOSITION
1 a
> **We're going to London.**
> Vamos a Londres.

LANGUAGE TIP
a combines with **el** to form **al**.

> **Can I go to the toilet?**
> ¿Puedo ir al servicio?
> **I go to school with my friend.**
> Voy al colegio con mi amigo.
> **I'm going round to Mary's.**
> Voy a casa de Mary.
> **Give it to Jane!**
> ¡Dáselo a Jane!

to my house
a mi casa
to the supermarket
al supermercado

2 de (*for*)
> **the train to London**
> el tren de Londres
> **the plane to Madrid**
> el avión de Madrid
3 hasta (*up to*)
> **Count to ten, everyone.**
> Contad todos hasta diez.
> **from nine o'clock to half past three**
> desde las nueve hasta las tres y media
4 para (*in order to*)
> **I'm doing it to help you.**
> Lo hago para ayudarte.

LANGUAGE TIP
Don't forget that **to** is often just part of the infinitive form of the verb.

---

to eat
comer
to work
trabajar
I want to buy a new camera.
Quiero comprar una cámara nueva.

toad NOUN
el **sapo** *masc*

toast NOUN
las **tostadas** *fem pl*
> **Would you like some toast?**
> ¿Quieres tostadas?
> **a piece of toast**
> una tostada

toaster NOUN
la **tostadora** *fem*

toastie NOUN
el **sándwich caliente** *masc*

today ADVERB
hoy
> **What's the date today?**
> ¿Hoy qué día es?
> **It's Monday today.**
> Hoy es lunes.

toe NOUN
el **dedo del pie** *masc*

LANGUAGE TIP
On its own **dedo** means 'finger'. So the Spanish **dedo del pie** literally means 'foot finger'!

---

toffee NOUN
el **caramelo** *masc*

together ADVERB
juntos *masc pl*
juntas *fem pl*

LANGUAGE TIP
The Spanish word **juntos** is an adjective so must agree with the noun.

**Mary and Rana are going
to go there together.**
Mary y Rana van a ir allí juntas.

toilet NOUN
1 el **servicio** masc (in school, café etc)
   Can I go to the toilet?
   ¿Puedo ir al servicio?
2 el **baño** masc (in private house)

toilet paper NOUN
el **papel higiénico** masc

told VERB ▷ see **tell**

tomato NOUN
el **tomate**
masc
   **a kilo of
   tomatoes**
   un kilo de
   tomates
   tomato soup
   sopa de tomate

tomorrow ADVERB
mañana
   **Let's go swimming
   tomorrow.**
   Vamos a nadar mañana.

   tomorrow morning
   mañana por la mañana
   tomorrow afternoon
   mañana por la tarde
   tomorrow night
   mañana por la noche
   the day after tomorrow
   pasado mañana
   See you tomorrow.
   Hasta mañana.

tongue NOUN
la **lengua** fem

tonight ADVERB
esta noche
   Are you going out tonight?
   ¿Vas a salir esta noche?

tonsillitis NOUN
la **amigdalitis** fem

too ADVERB
1 **también** (as well)
   My sister is coming too.
   Mi hermana también viene.

   Me too.
   Yo también.

2 **demasiado** (very)
   The water's too hot.
   El agua está demasiado caliente.
   You're too late.
   Llegas demasiado tarde.
   Daniel, you talk too much.
   Daniel, hablas demasiado.
   It costs too much.
   Cuesta demasiado.

   LANGUAGE TIP
   When **too much** and **too many** are
   used to describe nouns, remember to
   make them agree.

   too much noise
   demasiado ruido
   too much water
   demasiada agua
   too many mistakes
   demasiadas faltas

tooth NOUN
el **diente** masc

toothache NOUN
   I've got toothache.
   Me duelen las muelas.

toothbrush NOUN
el **cepillo de
dientes** masc

toothpaste NOUN
la **pasta de
dientes** fem

top

   top can be a noun or an adjective.

A NOUN
1 el **top** masc (T-shirt, sweater, etc)
   a black skirt and a white top
   una falda negra y un top blanco

587

2 la **parte de arriba** *fem* (*highest part*)
at the top of the page
en la parte de arriba de la página
on top of
encima de
It's on top of the fridge.
Está encima de la nevera.
3 la **cima** *fem* (*of mountain*)
the top of Snowdon
la cima de Snowdon
4 el **tapón** *masc* (PL los **tapones**)
(*of bottle*)
B ADJECTIVE
He always gets top marks in English.
Siempre saca las mejores notas en inglés.
the top floor
el piso de arriba

torch NOUN
la **linterna** *fem*

tortoise NOUN
la **tortuga** *fem*

total NOUN
el **total** *masc*

touch VERB
tocar
Don't touch that!
¡No toques eso!

touchscreen NOUN
la **pantalla táctil** *fem*

tour NOUN
la **visita** *fem*
a tour of the museum
una visita al museo

tourism NOUN
el **turismo** *masc*

tourist NOUN
el/la **turista** *masc/fem*
There are lots of tourists.
Hay muchos turistas.

tourist information office NOUN
la **oficina de turismo** *fem*

towards PREPOSITION
hacia
Come towards me.
Ven hacia mí.

towel NOUN
la **toalla** *fem*

tower NOUN
la **torre** *fem*
a tower block
una torre de pisos

town NOUN
la **ciudad** *fem*
It's a beautiful town.
Es una ciudad muy bonita.
the town centre
el centro de la ciudad
I'm going into town.
Voy al centro.

toy NOUN
el **juguete** *masc*

toy shop NOUN
la **juguetería** *fem*

tracksuit NOUN
el **chándal** *masc* (PL los **chándals**)

tractor NOUN
el **tractor** *masc*

tradition NOUN
la **tradición** *fem* (PL las **tradiciones**)

traffic NOUN
el **tráfico** *masc*
There's a lot of traffic.
Hay mucho tráfico.

traffic lights PL NOUN
el **semáforo** *masc*
Turn right at the traffic lights.
Gira a la derecha en el semáforo.

train NOUN
  el **tren** *masc*
    by train
    en tren
    We're going by train.
    Vamos en tren.

trainers PL NOUN
  las **zapatillas de deporte** *fem pl*
    a pair of trainers
    unas zapatillas de deporte

training NOUN
  el **entrenamiento** *masc*

tram NOUN
  el **tranvía** *masc*

> **LANGUAGE TIP**
> Even though it ends in **-a**, **el tranvía** is a masculine noun.

trampoline NOUN
  la **cama elástica** *fem*

translate VERB
  traducir
    I can translate the menu into English.
    Puedo traducir la carta al inglés.

translation NOUN
  la **traducción** *fem* (PL las **traducciones**)

trap NOUN
  la **trampa** *fem*

travel agent's NOUN
  la **agencia de viajes** *fem*

travelling NOUN
  I love travelling.
  Me encanta viajar.

tray NOUN
  la **bandeja** *fem*

treasure NOUN
  el **tesoro** *masc*

tree NOUN
  el **árbol** *masc*

triangle NOUN
  el **triángulo** *masc*

trick NOUN
  el **truco** *masc*
    I can do magic tricks.
    Sé hacer trucos de magia.

trip NOUN
  el **viaje** *masc*
    We're going on a trip to London.
    Vamos a hacer un viaje a Londres.

> **Have a good trip!**
> ¡Buen viaje!

trolley NOUN
  el **carrito** *masc*

trouble NOUN
  el **problema** *masc*
    The trouble is, it's too expensive.
    El problema es que es demasiado caro.
    Alfie is always getting into trouble.
    Alfie siempre se está metiendo en problemas.

> **LANGUAGE TIP**
> Even though it ends in **-a**, **el problema** is a masculine noun.

trousers PL NOUN
  los **pantalones** *masc pl*
    I'm wearing black trousers.
    Llevo unos pantalones negros.
    He's changing his trousers.
    Se está cambiando de pantalones.

truck NOUN
  el **camión** *masc* (PL los **camiones**)

true ADJECTIVE
    That's true.
    Eso es verdad.
    That's not true.
    Eso no es verdad.

> **True or false?**
> ¿Verdadero o falso?

trumpet NOUN
  la **trompeta** *fem*

Spanish · **English**

She plays the trumpet.
Toca la trompeta.

trunks PL NOUN
el **bañador** *masc*
I've got new trunks.
Tengo un bañador nuevo.

truth NOUN
la **verdad** *fem*
Tell me the truth.
Dime la verdad.

try

> **try** can be a verb or a noun.

A VERB
to try
1 **intentar** (*attempt*)
Try to remember.
Intenta acordarte.
I'm going to try.
Voy a intentarlo.
You're not trying, Richard.
No te estás esforzando, Richard.
2 **probar** (*taste*)
Would you like to try some?
¿Quieres probar un poco?
B NOUN
el **intento** *masc*
his third try
su tercer intento

Good try!
¡No ha estado mal!
Can I have a try?
¿Puedo intentarlo yo?

try on VERB
probarse
Can I try it on?
¿Puedo probármelo?

T-shirt NOUN
la **camiseta** *fem*
Put on your T-shirt.
Ponte la camiseta.

LANGUAGE TIP
In Spanish you usually use an article
like **el**, **la** or **los**, **las** with clothes you
are wearing.

tube NOUN
el **tubo** *masc*
the Tube
el metro

Tuesday NOUN
el **martes** *masc*
It's Tuesday today.
Hoy es martes.

on Tuesday
el martes
on Tuesdays
los martes
every Tuesday
cada martes
last Tuesday
el martes pasado
next Tuesday
el martes que viene

LANGUAGE TIP
Days are not spelled with a capital
letter in Spanish.

tummy NOUN
la **barriga** *fem*

tummy ache NOUN
I've got tummy ache.
Me duele la barriga.

tuna NOUN
el **atún** *masc*
a tuna salad
una ensalada de atún

tune NOUN
la **melodía** *fem*
I know the tune.
Conozco la melodía.

tunnel NOUN
el **túnel** *masc*

turkey NOUN
el **pavo** *masc*

turn

> **turn** can be a noun or a verb.

A NOUN
el **turno** *masc*
You miss a turn.
Pierdes un turno.

Whose turn is it?
¿A quién le toca?
It's my turn!
¡Me toca!

B VERB
to turn
girar
Turn right at the lights.
Gira a la derecha en el semáforo.

turn off VERB
1 **apagar** (*switch off*)
Could you turn off the light?
¿Puedes apagar la luz?
2 **cerrar** (*tap*)
Turn off the tap, please.
Cierra el grifo, por favor.

turn on VERB
1 **encender** (*switch on*)
Could you turn on the light?
¿Puedes encender la luz?
2 **abrir** (*tap*)
Turn on the tap, please.
Abre el grifo, por favor.

turn over VERB
dar la vuelta a
Turn over the cards, everyone.
Dadle todos la vuelta a las cartas.

turn round VERB
darse la vuelta
Turn round, children!
¡Daos la vuelta, niños!

turtle NOUN
la **tortuga de mar** *fem*

TV NOUN
la **tele** *fem*
on TV
en la tele

tweet

> **tweet** can be a verb or a noun.

A NOUN
el **tuit** *masc* (PL **tuits**)
B VERB
to tweet
tuitear

twelfth NUMBER
doce
on the twelfth floor
en la planta doce
We break up on the twelfth of April.
Empezamos las vacaciones el doce de abril.
Today's the twelfth of June.
Hoy es doce de junio.

on the twelfth of August
el doce de agosto

LANGUAGE TIP
Use the same set of numbers that you use for counting (**uno**, **dos**, **tres** and so on) when giving Spanish dates.

twelve NUMBER
doce
twelve euros
doce euros
I have lunch at twelve o'clock.
Como a las doce.

Spanish
English
a
b
c
d
e
f
g
h
i
j
k
l
m
n
o
p
q
r
s
t
u
v
w
x
y
z
591

A
B
C
D
E
F
G
H
I
J
K
L
M
N
O
P
Q
R
S
T
U
V
W
X
Y
Z

It is twelve thirty.
Son las doce y media.

twelve o'clock
las doce
I'm twelve.
Tengo doce años.

LANGUAGE TIP
In English you can say **I'm twelve** or **I'm twelve years old**. In Spanish you can only say **tengo doce años**. Have you noticed that in Spanish you need to use the verb **tener** to talk about somebody's age?

twentieth NUMBER
veinte
   the twentieth floor
   el piso veinte
   My birthday's the twentieth of October.
   Mi cumpleaños es el veinte de octubre.
   Today's the twentieth of April.
   Hoy es veinte de abril.

   on the twentieth of May
   el veinte de mayo

LANGUAGE TIP
Use the same set of numbers that you use for counting (**uno**, **dos**, **tres** and so on) when giving Spanish dates.

twenty NUMBER
veinte
   twenty euros
   veinte euros
   It's twenty to three.
   Son las tres menos veinte.
   It's twenty past eleven.
   Son las once y veinte.

   He's twenty.
   Tiene veinte años.

LANGUAGE TIP
In English you can say **he's twenty** or **he's twenty years old**. In Spanish you can only say **tiene veinte años**. Have you noticed that in Spanish you need to use the verb **tener** to talk about somebody's age?

twice ADVERB
dos veces

twin NOUN

LANGUAGE TIP
In Spanish you usually use different words for identical and non-identical twins

1 el **mellizo** masc
   la **melliza** fem (not identical)
   They're twins.
   Son mellizos.
   her twin sister
   su hermana melliza
2 el **gemelo** masc
   la **gemela** fem (identical twin)
   They're identical twins.
   Son gemelos.
   my twin sister
   mi hermana gemela

twinned ADJECTIVE
hermanado masc
hermanada fem
   Veracruz is twinned with Valencia.
   Veracruz está hermanada con Valencia.

twin room NOUN
　la **habitación con dos camas** *fem*
　　(PL las **habitaciones con dos**
　　camas)

Twitter® NOUN
　Twitter®

two NUMBER
　dos

　　two euros
　　dos euros
　　It's two o'clock.
　　Son las dos.
　　Get into twos.
　　Poneos en grupos de dos.

　　She's two.
　　Tiene dos años.

LANGUAGE TIP
In English you can say **she's two** or
she's two years old. In Spanish you
can only say **tiene dos años**. Have
you noticed that in Spanish you need
to use the verb **tener** to talk about
somebody's age?

type NOUN
　el **tipo** *masc*
　　What type of
　　camera have
　　you got?
　　¿Qué tipo de
　　cámara tienes?

tyre NOUN
　el **neumático** *masc*

Spanish

English

a
b
c
d
e
f
g
h
i
j
k
l
m
n
o
p
q
r
s
t
u
v
w
x
y
z

593

Spanish

English

A
B
C
D
E
F
G
H
I
J
K
L
M
N
O
P
Q
R
S
T
U
V
W
X
Y
Z

Uu

UFO NOUN
(= **unidentified flying object**)
el **OVNI** *masc*

ugly ADJECTIVE
feo *masc*
fea *fem*

UK NOUN
(= **United Kingdom**)
el **Reino Unido** *masc*
in the UK
en el Reino Unido
to the UK
al Reino Unido
I live in the UK.
Vivo en el Reino Unido.

Ulster NOUN
el **Ulster** *masc*

umbrella NOUN
1 el **paraguas** *masc* (PL los **paraguas**)
(for rain)
2 la **sombrilla** *fem* (*sun umbrella*)

umpire NOUN
el **árbitro** *masc*
la **árbitra** *fem*

unbelievable ADJECTIVE
increíble *masc/fem*
That's unbelievable!
¡Eso es increíble!

uncle NOUN
el **tío** *masc*
my uncle
mi tío
my uncles and aunts
mis tíos

uncomfortable ADJECTIVE
incómodo *masc*
incómoda *fem*
The seats are very uncomfortable.
Los asientos son muy incómodos.

under PREPOSITION
1 **debajo de**

LANGUAGE TIP
When something is positioned under
something, use **debajo de**.

The cat's under the table.
El gato está debajo de la mesa.
under there
ahí debajo
2 **por debajo de**

LANGUAGE TIP
After verbs which express movement
(like 'go' and 'run') use **por debajo
de**.

**The tunnel goes under the
river.**
El túnel pasa por debajo del río.
3 **menos de** (*less than*)
It costs under twenty pounds.
Cuesta menos de veinte libras.
children under ten
niños de menos de diez años

underground

underground can be a noun,
adjective or adverb.

A NOUN
el **metro** *masc*

by underground
en metro
the London underground
el metro de Londres

B ADJECTIVE
subterráneo *masc*
subterránea *fem*
an underground car park
un parking subterráneo

C ADVERB
bajo tierra
Moles live underground.
Los topos viven bajo tierra.

underneath

underneath can be a preposition or an adverb.

A PREPOSITION
1 debajo de

LANGUAGE TIP
When something is positioned underneath something, use **debajo de**.

The key's underneath the mat.
La llave está debajo del felpudo.

2 por debajo de

LANGUAGE TIP
After verbs which express movement (like 'go' and 'run') use **por debajo de**.

The footpath goes underneath the bridge.
El sendero pasa por debajo del puente.

B ADVERB
debajo
Look underneath, Rachel!
¡Mira debajo, Rachel!

understand VERB
entender
I don't understand this word.
No entiendo esta palabra.
Do you understand, Luis?
¿Lo entiendes, Luis?

I don't understand.
No lo entiendo.
Do you understand?
¿Lo entiendes?

understood VERB ▷ *see* **understand**

underwear NOUN
la **ropa interior** *fem*

undone ADJECTIVE
desatado *masc*
desatada *fem*
Your laces are undone.
Llevas los cordones desatados.

LANGUAGE TIP
In Spanish you usually use an article like **el**, **la** or **los**, **las** with clothes you are wearing.

undressed ADJECTIVE
to get undressed
desnudarse
I'm getting undressed.
Me estoy desnudando.

unemployed ADJECTIVE
parado *masc*
parada *fem*
He's unemployed.
Está parado.

unfair ADJECTIVE
injusto *masc*
injusta *fem*
That's unfair!
¡Eso es injusto!

unfashionable ADJECTIVE
pasado de moda *masc*
pasada de moda *fem*

unfold VERB
desplegar
Unfold the map.
Despliega el mapa.

unforgettable ADJECTIVE
inolvidable *masc/fem*

unfortunately ADVERB
lamentablemente

Spanish
English
a b c d e f g h i j k l m n o p q r s t u v w x y z

A
B
C
D
E
F
G
H
I
J
K
L
M
N
O
P
Q
R
S
T
U
V
W
X
Y
Z

Unfortunately it's too late.
Lamentablemente es demasiado tarde.
Unfortunately not.
Lamentablemente no.

unhappy ADJECTIVE
  to be unhappy
  no estar contento
  She's unhappy at school.
  No está contenta en el colegio.
  You look unhappy.
  Pareces triste.

uniform NOUN
  el **uniforme** *masc*
  We wear school uniform.
  Llevamos uniforme al colegio.

DID YOU KNOW...?
Uniforms aren't worn in most Spanish state schools but they are in most Spanish private schools.

Union Jack NOUN
  la **bandera del Reino Unido** *fem*

United Kingdom NOUN
  el **Reino Unido** *masc*
  to the United Kingdom
  al Reino Unido
  in the United Kingdom
  en el Reino Unido

United States NOUN
  los **Estados Unidos** *masc pl*
  in the United States
  en Estados Unidos
  to the United States
  a Estados Unidos

universe NOUN
  el **universo** *masc*

university NOUN
  la **universidad** *fem*
  She's at university.
  Está en la universidad.

Do you want to go to university?
¿Quieres ir a la universidad?
Lancaster University
la universidad de Lancaster

unless CONJUNCTION
  a menos que
  Don't do it unless your mum tells you to.
  No lo hagas a menos que tu madre te lo diga.

LANGUAGE TIP
a menos que is followed by a form of the verb called the subjunctive. Alternatively, you can often use **si no** (**if not**) and an ordinary form of the verb instead.

  I'll have that biscuit, unless you want it.
  Yo cogeré esa galleta, si no la quieres tú.

unlikely ADJECTIVE
  poco probable *masc/fem*
  It's possible, but unlikely.
  Es posible, pero poco probable.

unlucky ADJECTIVE
  to be unlucky
  tener mala suerte/traer mala suerte

LANGUAGE TIP
to be unlucky has two translations depending on whether it means 'to have bad luck' or 'to bring bad luck'. Look at the examples.

  I'm always unlucky.
  Siempre tengo mala suerte.
  It's unlucky to walk under a ladder.
  Trae mala suerte pasar por debajo de una escalera.
  Thirteen is an unlucky number.
  El trece trae mala suerte.

unpack VERB
  deshacer las maletas
  Have you unpacked?
  ¿Has deshecho las maletas?

I'm going to unpack my suitcase.
Voy a deshacer la maleta.

unpleasant ADJECTIVE
desagradable *masc/fem*

unpopular ADJECTIVE
poco popular *masc/fem*

unpredictable ADJECTIVE
impredecible *masc/fem*
The weather is unpredictable.
El tiempo es impredecible.

unreliable ADJECTIVE
poco fiable *masc/fem*
Our car is unreliable.
Nuestro coche es poco fiable.

unsuitable ADJECTIVE
inadecuado *masc*
inadecuada *fem*

untidy ADJECTIVE
desordenado *masc*
desordenada *fem*
My bedroom's always untidy.
Mi habitación siempre está
desordenada.
My writing is untidy.
Tengo mala letra.

until PREPOSITION
hasta
He's here until tomorrow.
Está aquí hasta mañana.
The supermarket is open until ten.
El supermercado está abierto hasta las
diez.
not until tomorrow
hasta mañana no
When will it be ready? — Not until
next week.
¿Cuándo estará listo? — Hasta la
semana que viene no.
from ... until
de ... a
from nine until five
de nueve a cinco
from the tenth until the
fourteenth of May
del diez al catorce de mayo

unusual ADJECTIVE
poco común *masc/fem* (PL **poco
comunes**)
It's an unusual name.
Es un nombre poco común.

up

up can be an adverb, adjective or
preposition.

A ADVERB
1 **hacia arriba** (*upwards*)
She looked up.
Miró hacia arriba.
2 **arriba** (*at a higher level*)
He's up on the roof.
Está arriba en el tejado.
It's up there.
Está allí arriba.
I'll come up later.
Subo más tarde.

up there
allí arriba
up here
aquí arriba

3 **up to**
hasta
Let's count up to fifty.
Vamos a contar hasta cincuenta.
up to now
hasta ahora
It's up to you.
Lo que tú quieras.
4 **What's up with her?**
¿Qué le pasa?
B ADJECTIVE
I'm always up before eight.
Siempre me levanto antes de las ocho.
He's not up yet.
Todavía no se ha levantado.
C PREPOSITION
We could walk up the road to the
bus stop.
Podríamos subir por la carretera hasta
la parada del autobús.
The post office is up the road.
Correos está más arriba.

The cat is up the tree.
El gato está subido al árbol.

upload VERB
subir

upper ADJECTIVE
superior *masc/fem*
on the upper floor
en el piso superior

upset

> upset can be an adjective or a verb.

A ADJECTIVE
1 **disgustado** *masc*
disgustada *fem*
She's still a bit upset.
Todavía está un poco disgustada.
2 **I've got an upset stomach.**
Tengo mal el estómago.
B VERB
to upset
dar un mal rato a
I don't want to upset my granny.
No quiero dar un mal rato a mi abuela.

upside down ADVERB
al revés
That painting is upside down.
Ese cuadro está al revés.

upstairs ADVERB
arriba
Where's your coat? — It's upstairs.
¿Dónde está tu abrigo? — Está arriba.

up-to-date ADJECTIVE
moderno *masc*
moderna *fem*

upwards ADVERB
hacia arriba

urgent ADJECTIVE
urgente *masc/fem*
Is it urgent?
¿Es urgente?

US NOUN
(= **United States**)
los **EE. UU.** *masc pl*
in the US
en EE. UU.
to the US
a EE. UU.
from the US
desde EE. UU.

LANGUAGE TIP
As **EE. UU.** stands for **Estados Unidos**, why are there two Es and two Us? It's to show that the abbreviation refers to something plural. Compare **JJ. OO.** for **Juegos Olímpicos** (**Olympic Games**).

---

us PRONOUN
1 **nos** (*direct and indirect object*)
He hates us.
Nos odia.
Tell us the story.
Cuéntanos la historia.
to us
nos
She's going to write to us.
Va a escribirnos.
2 **nosotros** *masc pl*
nosotras *fem pl*

LANGUAGE TIP
Use **nosotros** and **nosotras** after prepositions.

Come with us.
Ven con nosotros.

LANGUAGE TIP
Use **nosotros** and **nosotras** in comparisons.

He's older than us.
Es mayor que nosotros.

LANGUAGE TIP
Use **nosotros** and **nosotras** after the verb **ser**.

It's us.
Somos nosotros.

USA NOUN
(= **United States of America**)
los **EE. UU.** *masc pl*
in the USA
en EE. UU.
to the USA
a EE. UU.
from the USA
desde EE. UU.

LANGUAGE TIP
As **EE. UU.** stands for **Estados Unidos**, why are there two Es and two Us? It's to show that the abbreviation refers to something plural. Compare **JJ. OO.** for **Juegos Olímpicos** (**Olympic Games**).

USB stick NOUN
la **memoria USB** *fem*

use

use can be a verb or a noun.

A VERB
to use
usar (*employ*)
Can we use a dictionary in the exam?
¿Podemos usar un diccionario en el examen?
Somebody is using the computer.
Alguien está usando el ordenador.
Can I use your phone?
¿Puedo llamar por tu teléfono?
Can I use the toilet?
¿Puedo ir al baño?

B NOUN
It's no use.
Es inútil.

use up VERB
gastar
We've used up all the paint.
Hemos gastado toda la pintura.

used ADJECTIVE
I'm used to getting up early.
Estoy acostumbrado a levantarme temprano.

I'm used to it.
Estoy acostumbrado.
I'm not used to it.
No estoy acostumbrado.

useful ADJECTIVE
útil *masc/fem*

useless ADJECTIVE
to be useless
no servir para nada
This map is useless.
Este mapa no sirve para nada.

username NOUN
el **nombre de usuario** *masc*
What's your username?
¿Cuál es su nombre de usuario?

usual ADJECTIVE
habitual *masc/fem*
my usual seat
mi asiento habitual
She's late, as usual.
Llega tarde, como siempre.

as usual
como siempre

usually ADVERB
normalmente
I usually wear trousers.
Normalmente llevo pantalones.

utility room NOUN
el **lavadero** *masc*

vacancy NOUN
(*in hotel*)
'Vacancies'
"Quedan plazas"
'No vacancies'
"Completo"

vacuum cleaner NOUN
la **aspiradora** *fem*

Valentine card NOUN
la **tarjeta del día de los enamorados** *fem*

Valentine's Day NOUN
el **día de los enamorados** *masc*

valley NOUN
el **valle** *masc*

valuable ADJECTIVE
de valor
a valuable picture
un cuadro de valor

van NOUN
la **camioneta** *fem*

vandal NOUN
el **vándalo** *masc*
la **vándala** *fem*

vandalism NOUN
el **vandalismo** *masc*

vanilla NOUN
la **vainilla** *fem*
a vanilla ice cream
un helado de vainilla

vape VERB
vapear
My older sister has started to vape.
Mi hemana mayor ha empezado a vapear.

varied ADJECTIVE
variado *masc*
variada *fem*

variety NOUN
la **variedad** *fem*

various ADJECTIVE
varios *masc pl*
varias *fem pl*
There are various possibilities.
Existen varias posibilidades.

vase NOUN
el **jarrón** *masc* (PL los **jarrones**)

vegan

vegan can be an adjective or a noun.

A ADJECTIVE
vegano *masc*
vegana *fem*
vegan food
comida vegana
B NOUN
el **vegano** *masc*
la **vegana** *fem*
I'm a vegan.
Soy vegano.

vegetable NOUN
la **verdura** *fem*
vegetable soup
sopa de verduras
Would you like some vegetables?
¿Queréis verduras?

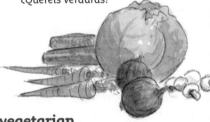

vegetarian

vegetarian can be an adjective or a noun.

A ADJECTIVE
vegetariano *masc*
vegetariana *fem*

vegetarian lasagne
lasaña vegetariana

B NOUN
el **vegetariano** *masc*
la **vegetariana** *fem*
I'm a vegetarian.
Soy vegetariano.

verb NOUN
el **verbo** *masc*

very ADVERB
muy
very tall
muy alto
not very interesting
no muy interesante
It's very hot.
Hace mucho calor.
I love you very much.
Te quiero mucho.

very soon
muy pronto
very much
mucho
I'm very sorry.
Lo siento mucho.

vest NOUN
la **camiseta** *fem*

vet NOUN
el **veterinario** *masc*
la **veterinaria** *fem*
She's a vet.
Es veterinaria.

LANGUAGE TIP
In Spanish, you do not use an article
with people's jobs.

vicar NOUN
el **pastor** *masc*
la **pastora** *fem* (de iglesia)

video

video can be a noun or a verb.

A NOUN
el **vídeo** *masc*

We're going to watch a video.
Vamos a ver un vídeo.

B VERB
to video
grabar en vídeo
We're going to video the concert.
Vamos a grabar el concierto en vídeo.

video game NOUN
el **videojuego** *masc*
I like playing video games.
Me gusta jugar con videojuegos.

view NOUN
la **vista** *fem*
There's an amazing view.
Hay una vista increíble.

village NOUN
el **pueblo** *masc*
in the village
en el pueblo

vinegar NOUN
el **vinagre** *masc*

vineyard NOUN
el **viñedo** *masc*

violent ADJECTIVE
violento *masc*
violenta *fem*

violin NOUN
el **violín** *masc*
I play the violin.
Toco el violín.

viral ADJECTIVE
  viral *masc/fem*
    to go viral
    hacerse viral

virus NOUN
  el **virus** *masc* (PL los **virus**)

visit

> **visit** can be a noun or a verb.

A NOUN
  la **visita** *fem*
  a visit to Edinburgh castle
  una visita al castillo de Edimburgo
B VERB
  to visit
  visitar
  We're going to visit the castle.
  Vamos a visitar el castillo.
  I'm going to visit some friends.
  Voy a visitar a unos amigos.

LANGUAGE TIP
Don't forget the personal **a** in examples like this one.

visitor NOUN
  1 el/la **visitante** *masc/fem*
  The museum had 900 visitors.
  El museo recibió a 900 visitantes.

  2 el **invitado** *masc*
  la **invitada** *fem*
  Today we've got a Spanish visitor.
  Hoy tenemos un invitado español.

vlog NOUN
  el **videoblog** *masc* (PL los **videoblogs**)

vocabulary NOUN
  el **vocabulario** *masc*

voice NOUN
  la **voz** *fem* (PL las **voces**)

volleyball NOUN
  el **voleibol** *masc*
  We play volleyball sometimes.
  A veces jugamos al voleibol.

LANGUAGE TIP
In Spanish, you need to include **al** or **a la** before the names of sports or games when talking about playing them.

volunteer NOUN
  el **voluntario** *masc*
  la **voluntaria** *fem*

vowel NOUN
  la **vocal** *fem*

Ww

waist NOUN
la **cintura** *fem*

waistcoat NOUN
el **chaleco** *masc*

wait VERB
esperar
> **Wait, Alison, it's not your turn.**
> Espera, Alison, que no es tu turno.

> **Wait for me!**
> ¡Espérame!
> **Wait a minute!**
> ¡Espera un momento!

waiter NOUN
el **camarero** *masc*

waiting room NOUN
la **sala de espera** *fem*

waitress NOUN
la **camarera** *fem*

wake up VERB
despertarse
> **Wake up, Peter!**
> ¡Despiértate, Peter!

Wales NOUN
Gales *masc*
> **Swansea is in Wales.**
> Swansea está en Gales.
> **Bronwen is from Wales.**
> Bronwen es de Gales.
> **the Prince of Wales**
> el Príncipe de Gales

walk

> **walk** can be a verb or a noun.

A VERB
to walk
andar
> **He walks fast.**
> Anda rápido.
> **I walked ten kilometres.**
> Anduve diez kilómetros.
> **Are you walking or going by bus?**
> ¿Vas andando o en autobús?

B NOUN
el **paseo** *masc*
> **Would you like to go for a walk?**
> ¿Quieres ir a dar un paseo?
> **It's a five-minute walk to the town centre.**
> Se tarda cinco minutos andando hasta el centro.

walking NOUN
> **My parents like walking.**
> A mis padres les gusta caminar.

wall NOUN
1 la **pared** *fem* (*inside building*)
> **There are posters on the wall.**
> Hay pósters en la pared.
2 el **muro** *masc* (*outer wall, garden wall*)
> **Tony is sitting on the wall.**
> Tony está sentado en el muro.

wallet NOUN
la **cartera** *fem*

walnut NOUN
la **nuez** *fem*
(PL las **nueces**)

want VERB
querer
> **Do you want a piece of cake?**
> ¿Quieres un trozo de tarta?
> **I don't want to play.**
> No quiero jugar.

What do you want to do tomorrow?
¿Qué quieres hacer mañana?

What do you want, Kala?
¿Qué quieres, Kala?
What do you want, boys?
¿Que queréis, niños?

war NOUN
la **guerra** *fem*

wardrobe NOUN
el **armario** *masc*

warm ADJECTIVE
1 caliente *masc/fem* (*bath, water, hands*)

It's warm.
Hace calor.
I'm warm.
Tengo calor.

2 cálido *masc*
cálida *fem* (*weather*)
3 warm clothes
ropa de abrigo

was VERB ▷ *see* **be**

wash VERB
1 lavar (*thing*)
He washes his car every Sunday.
Lava el coche todos los domingos.
2 lavarse (*get washed*)
At eight I get up, wash and get dressed.
A las ocho me levanto, me lavo y me visto.

I'm going to wash my hands.
Me voy a lavar las manos.
I want to wash my hair.
Quiero lavarme la cabeza.

Wash your hands!
¡Lávate las manos!

LANGUAGE TIP
In Spanish you usually use an article like **el**, **la** or **los**, **las** with parts of the body.

washbasin NOUN
el **lavabo** *masc*

washing machine NOUN
la **lavadora** *fem*

washing-up NOUN
to do the washing-up
fregar los platos
Who's going to do the washing-up?
¿Quién va a fregar los platos?
I often do the washing-up.
Muchas veces friego los platos.

wasn't (= was not) ▷ *see* **be**

wasp NOUN
la **avispa** *fem*

waste NOUN
It's a waste of time.
Es una pérdida de tiempo.

watch

watch can be a noun or a verb.

A NOUN
el **reloj** *masc*

I haven't got a watch.
No tengo reloj.

LANGUAGE TIP
Did you know that **un reloj** is also **a clock**?

B VERB
to watch
1 mirar (*look at*)
Watch what I do.
Mira lo que hago.

Watch me, Mum!
¡Mírame, mamá!

2 ver (*television, programme, match*)
He watches television every day.
Ve la televisión todos los días.

watch out VERB
tener cuidado
You need to watch out.
Tienes que tener cuidado.

Watch out!
¡Cuidado!

water NOUN
el **agua** *fem*

LANGUAGE TIP
Even though it's a feminine noun,
remember that you use **el** and **un** with
agua.

The water was very cold.
El agua estaba muy fría.
a glass of water
un vaso de agua

LANGUAGE TIP
Be careful! The translation of **water** is
not **wáter**.

wave

wave can be a noun or a verb.

A NOUN
la **ola** *fem*
There are big waves sometimes.
A veces hay olas grandes.
B VERB
to wave
1 saludar con la mano (*in greeting*)
They're waving at us.
Nos están saludando con la mano.

2 to wave goodbye
decir adiós con la mano
Let's wave goodbye.
Vamos a decir adiós con la mano.

wavy ADJECTIVE
wavy hair
pelo ondulado

way NOUN
1 el **camino** *masc* (*to place*)
I don't know the way.
No sé el camino.
Ask the way.
Pregunta el camino.
**Can you tell me the way to the
station?**
¿Me puedes decir cómo se llega a la
estación?

It's a long way.
Está lejos.
Which way is it?
¿Por dónde está?
It's this way.
Es por aquí.

2 la **forma** *fem* (*manner*)
**What's the best way to learn
Spanish?**
¿Cuál es la mejor forma de aprender
español?

LANGUAGE TIP
As **la manera** and **el modo** mean
the same as **la forma**, you could
alternatively say **la mejor manera** or
el mejor modo to mean **the best
way**.

**He looked at me in a strange
way.**
Me miró de forma extraña.
Do it this way, Katy.
Hazlo así, Katy.
by the way
a propósito
No way!
¡Ni hablar!

Spanish · English

a b c d e f g h i j k l m n o p q r s t u v **w** x y z

605

A
B
C
D
E
F
G
H
I
J
K
L
M
N
O
P
Q
R
S
T
U
V
W
X
Y
Z

way in NOUN
la **entrada** fem

way out NOUN
la **salida** fem
Where's the way out?
¿Dónde está la salida?

we PRONOUN
nosotros masc pl
nosotras fem pl
Shall we do it?
¿Lo hacemos nosotros?

LANGUAGE TIP
we isn't usually translated unless it's emphatic.

We do sport in the afternoon.
Hacemos deporte por la tarde.

wear VERB
llevar
He's wearing a hat.
Lleva un sombrero.
I wear glasses.
Llevo gafas.
What's she wearing?
¿Qué lleva puesto?

weather NOUN
el **tiempo** masc
The weather isn't very nice.
No hace muy buen tiempo.

What's the weather like?
¿Qué tiempo hace?
The weather's nice.
Hace buen tiempo.

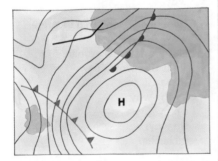

weather forecast NOUN
el **pronóstico del tiempo** masc

Web NOUN
the Web
internet
Look on the Web.
Mira en internet.

website NOUN
el **sitio web** masc

we'd
(= **we would**) ▷ see **would**
(= **we had**) ▷ see **have**

wedding NOUN
la **boda** fem
It's my cousin's wedding today.
Hoy es la boda de mi prima.

wedding anniversary NOUN
el **aniversario de boda** masc

Wednesday NOUN
el **miércoles** masc
It's Wednesday today.
Hoy es miércoles.

on Wednesday
el miércoles
on Wednesdays
los miércoles
every Wednesday
cada miércoles
last Wednesday
el miércoles pasado
next Wednesday
el miércoles que viene

LANGUAGE TIP
Days are not spelled with a capital letter in Spanish.

---

week NOUN
la **semana** fem
two weeks
dos semanas

this week
esta semana
last week
la semana pasada
every week
cada semana
next week
la semana que viene
in a week's time
dentro de una semana

weekday NOUN
on weekdays
los días entre semana

weekend NOUN
el **fin de semana** masc
What are you doing at the weekend?
¿Qué vas a hacer el fin de semana?
The shops are closed at weekends.
Las tiendas cierran los fines de semana.

at weekends
los fines de semana
last weekend
el fin de semana pasado
next weekend
el fin de semana que viene

welcome ADJECTIVE
Welcome!
¡Bienvenido!

LANGUAGE TIP
Remember to change **¡bienvenido!** to **¡bienvenida!** if you're welcoming a girl or woman. Similarly, change it to **¡bienvenidos!** if you're welcoming a mixed group or a group of men.

Welcome to Scotland!
¡Bienvenido a Escocia!

Thank you! — You're welcome!
¡Gracias! — ¡De nada!

well

well can be an adverb or an adjective.

A ADVERB
bien
The team is playing well.
El equipo está jugando bien.
as well
también
We're going to London as well as Manchester.
Vamos a Londres y también a Manchester.

B ADJECTIVE
to be well
estar bien

LANGUAGE TIP
bien never changes its ending no matter who or what it describes.

He isn't well.
No está bien.
I'm not very well at the moment.
No estoy muy bien en este momento.
How are you? — I'm very well, thank you.
¿Cómo estás? — Estoy muy bien, gracias.

Well done!
¡Bien hecho!
Get well soon!
¡Que te mejores pronto!

LANGUAGE TIP
Have you noticed the upside-down exclamation mark at the start of Spanish exclamations?

we'll (= we will) ▷ see **will**

well-behaved ADJECTIVE
well-behaved children
niños que se portan bien
He's very well-behaved.
Se porta muy bien.

wellies PL NOUN
las **botas de agua** fem pl

wellington boots PL NOUN
las **botas de agua** *fem pl*

well-known ADJECTIVE
conocido *masc*
conocida *fem*
a well-known film star
un conocido artista de cine

Welsh

> **Welsh** can be an adjective or a noun.

A ADJECTIVE
galés *masc* (PL **galeses**)
galesa *fem*
a Welsh town
una ciudad galesa
Welsh people
los galeses

He's Welsh.
Es galés.
She's Welsh.
Es galesa.

B NOUN
el **galés** *masc* (*language*)
the Welsh
los galeses

LANGUAGE TIP
galés is not spelled with a capital
letter in Spanish.

Welshman NOUN
el **galés** *masc* (PL los **galeses**)

LANGUAGE TIP
galés is not spelled with a capital
letter in Spanish.

Welshwoman NOUN
la **galesa** *fem*

LANGUAGE TIP
galesa is not spelled with a capital
letter in Spanish.

---

went VERB ▷ *see* **go**

were VERB ▷ *see* **be**

we're (= we are) ▷ *see* **be**

weren't (= were not) ▷ *see* **be**

west

> **west** can be an adjective or a noun.

A ADJECTIVE
oeste

LANGUAGE TIP
oeste never changes its ending no
matter what it describes. Did you know
that adjectives that behave like this are
called 'invariable adjectives'?

---

the west coast
la costa oeste
B NOUN
el **oeste** *masc*
in the west
en el oeste

western NOUN
la **película del oeste** *fem*
I like westerns.
Me gustan las películas del oeste.

wet ADJECTIVE
mojado *masc*
mojada *fem*
wet clothes
ropa mojada
I'm wet.
Estoy mojado.

Spanish
English

A B C D E F G H I J K L M N O P Q R S T U V W X Y Z

It's wet today.
Hoy está lloviendo.

what

> **what** can be a pronoun or an adjective.

A PRONOUN

1 qué
What are you doing, boys?
¿Qué estáis haciendo, chicos?
What's the matter?
¿Qué pasa?
What's this?
¿Qué es esto?

LANGUAGE TIP
Use **¿qué es...?** in 'what is...?' questions when asking for an explanation or definition.

Ask her what they are.
Pregúntale qué son.

2 cuál (PL **cuáles**)
What's the capital of Spain?
¿Cuál es la capital de España?

LANGUAGE TIP
You usually use **¿cuál es...?** in 'what is...?' questions when asking for specific information rather than an explanation or definition.

---

3 lo que

LANGUAGE TIP
Use **lo que** when **what** is not a question word. Because **que** is not a question word here, it does not have an accent.

I saw what happened.
Vi lo que pasó.

What?
¿Qué?
What is it?
¿Qué es?
What do you want?
¿Qué quieres?

What's the weather like?
¿Qué tiempo hace?
What's your name?
¿Cómo te llamas?
What's your phone number?
¿Cuál es tu número de teléfono?

B ADJECTIVE
qué

LANGUAGE TIP
qué never changes its ending.

What letter does it start with?
¿Por qué letra empieza?
What colour is it?
¿De qué color es?
What a pretty house!
¡Qué casa más bonita!
What delicious cherries!
¡Qué cerezas tan ricas!

What time is it?
¿Qué hora es?
What day is it today?
¿Qué día es hoy?

LANGUAGE TIP
Don't forget the written accent on question words like **qué** and **cuál** nor the upside-down question mark at the start of questions.

---

wheel NOUN
la **rueda** fem

wheelchair NOUN
la **silla de ruedas** fem

A
B
C
D
E
F
G
H
I
J
K
L
M
N
O
P
Q
R
S
T
U
V
W
X
Y
Z

when ADVERB

1 cuándo (*in questions*)
When's your birthday?
¿Cuándo es tu cumpleaños?

LANGUAGE TIP
Don't forget the written accent on question words like **¿cuándo...?** nor the upside-down question mark at the start of questions.

2 cuando (*in other sentences*)
When it rains, we stay in the house.
Cuando llueve nos quedamos en la casa.

where ADVERB, CONJUNCTION

1 dónde (*in questions*)
Where's Emma today?
¿Dónde está hoy Emma?
Where are you going?
¿A dónde vas?

Where do you live?
¿Dónde vives?

LANGUAGE TIP
Don't forget the written accent on question words like **¿dónde...?** nor the upside-down question mark at the start of questions.

2 donde (*in other sentences*)
the house where I live
la casa donde vivo

whether CONJUNCTION
si
I don't know whether to go or not.
No sé si ir o no.

which

which can be an adjective or a pronoun.

A ADJECTIVE
qué

LANGUAGE TIP
qué never changes its ending.

Which flavour do you want?
¿Qué sabor quieres?
Which number is it?
¿Qué número es?
Which one would you like?
¿Cuál quieres?
Which ones would you like?
¿Cuáles quieres?

LANGUAGE TIP
Don't forget the written accent on question words like **¿qué...?** and **¿cuál...?** nor the upside-down question mark at the start of questions.

B PRONOUN
1 cuál (PL **cuáles**) (*in questions*)
Which would you like?
¿Cuál quieres?
Which is your car?
¿Cuál es tu coche?
Which are your suitcases?
¿Cuáles son tus maletas?
Which do you prefer, rugby or football?
¿Qué te gusta más, el rugby o el fútbol?
2 que (*relative*)
the car which we sold
el coche que vendimos

LANGUAGE TIP
After a preposition **que** becomes **el que**, **la que**, **los que** or **las que** to agree with the noun referred to.

the film which I was telling you about
la película de la que te hablaba

while

> **while** can be a conjunction or a noun.

A CONJUNCTION
mientras
While you're here, we can do some sightseeing.
Mientras estás aquí podemos hacer un poco de turismo.
You hold the torch while I look inside.
Aguanta la linterna mientras yo miro dentro.

B NOUN
a while
un rato
a while ago
hace un rato
after a while
después de un rato

whipped cream NOUN
la **nata montada** *fem*

whiskers PL NOUN
los **bigotes** *masc pl*

white

> **white** can be an adjective or a noun.

A ADJECTIVE
blanco *masc*
blanca *fem*
He's wearing white trousers.
Lleva pantalones blancos.
My shirt is white.
Mi camisa es blanca.
He's got white hair.
Tiene el pelo blanco.

LANGUAGE TIP
Colour adjectives come after the noun in Spanish.

B NOUN
el **blanco** *masc*

The bride is wearing white.
La novia va vestida de blanco.

whiteboard NOUN
la **pizarra blanca** *fem*
an interactive whiteboard
una pizarra interactiva

white coffee NOUN
el **café con leche** *masc*

DID YOU KNOW...?
el café con leche is made with hot milk. If you'd like a short, strong white coffee, ask for **un cortado** instead.

Whitsun NOUN
Pentecostés *masc*

who PRONOUN

1 quién (PL **quiénes**) (*in questions*)
Who wants to start?
¿Quién quiere empezar?
Who's that?
¿Quién es ese?
Who are they?
¿Quiénes son?

LANGUAGE TIP
Don't forget the written accent on question words like **¿quién...?** nor the upside-down question mark at the start of questions.

---

2 que (*relative*)
the girl who lives there
la chica que vive allí

whole ADJECTIVE
todo *masc*
toda *fem*
the whole class
toda la clase
the whole afternoon
toda la tarde
the whole world
el mundo entero

whose PRONOUN, ADJECTIVE
de quién (*in questions*)
Whose pencil case is this?
¿De quién es este estuche?

a b c d e f g h i j k l m n o p q r s t u v w x y z

Whose turn is it?
¿De quién es el turno?

Whose is this?
¿De quién es esto?

why ADVERB
por qué
   Why are you crying?
   ¿Por qué lloras?
   Why not?
   ¿Por qué no?
   Why don't you eat meat?
   — Because I don't like it.
   ¿Por qué no comes carne? — Porque no
   me gusta.

LANGUAGE TIP
The Spanish translations for **why** and
because are very similar. When it is
used to ask a question, **¿por qué?** is
two separate words and has an accent
on the **qué**.

   That's why I can't go.
   Por eso no puedo ir.

wide ADJECTIVE
ancho *masc*
ancha *fem*
   a wide road
   una calle ancha

widow NOUN
  la **viuda** *fem*

widower NOUN
  el **viudo** *masc*

wife NOUN
  la **mujer** *fem*
   She's his wife.
   Es su mujer.

LANGUAGE TIP
Did you know that **la mujer** is also the
Spanish for **woman**?

Wi-Fi NOUN
  el **wifi** *masc*

wild ADJECTIVE
salvaje *masc/fem*

a wild animal
un animal salvaje

will VERB
  1 (*forming future*)
   It will soon be my birthday.
   Pronto será mi cumpleaños.
   We'll get there quite late.
   Llegaremos bastante tarde.
   It won't rain.
   No lloverá.
  2 (*in requests and offers*)
   Will you help me?
   ¿Me ayudas?
   I'll make the coffee.
   Yo hago el café.

win VERB
ganar
   Who is winning?
   ¿Quién va ganando?
   I've won!
   ¡He ganado!

wind NOUN
  el **viento** *masc*
   There is a lot of wind.
   Hace mucho viento.

window NOUN
  1 la **ventana** *fem*
   Look out of the window, boys.
   Mirad por la ventana, chicos.
   a shop window
   un escaparate
  2 el **cristal** *masc* (*pane*)
   He's broken the window.
   Ha roto el cristal.

windy ADJECTIVE
   a windy day
   un día
   de viento

It's windy.
Hace viento.

wine NOUN
el **vino** masc
a bottle of wine
una botella de vino
a glass of wine
una copa de vino
white wine
vino blanco
red wine
vino tinto

winner NOUN
el **ganador** masc
la **ganadora** fem

winning ADJECTIVE
the winning team
el equipo ganador

winter NOUN
el **invierno** masc
last winter
el invierno pasado

in winter
en invierno

winter sports PL NOUN
los **deportes de invierno** masc pl

wish

wish can be a noun or a verb.

A NOUN
el **deseo** masc
Make a wish!
¡Pide un deseo!
With best wishes, Lily
Un abrazo, Lily

Best wishes
Un abrazo

B VERB
to wish
desear
He wished her a happy birthday.
Le deseó feliz cumpleaños.
I wish I could go with you!
¡Ojalá pudiera ir contigo!

LANGUAGE TIP
Ojalá is followed by a form of the verb
called the subjunctive.

witch NOUN
la **bruja** fem

with PREPOSITION
1 **con**
Tea with milk?
¿Té con leche?
We're going to stay with friends.
Nos vamos a quedar con unos amigos.
I live with my dad.
Vivo con mi padre.

LANGUAGE TIP
Remember that **with me** translates as
conmigo.

Come with me.
Ven conmigo.
It begins with 'b'.
Empieza por "b".
2 **de** (in descriptions)
a woman with blue eyes
una mujer de ojos azules

without PREPOSITION
sin
I drink coffee without sugar.
Bebo el café sin azúcar.
without speaking
sin hablar

LANGUAGE TIP
Just use **sin** on its own to translate
without a.

without a coat
sin abrigo

A
B
C
D
E
F
G
H
I
J
K
L
M
N
O
P
Q
R
S
T
U
V
W
X
Y
Z

witness NOUN
el/la **testigo** *masc/fem*

LANGUAGE TIP
Did you notice that the feminine form
la testigo still ends in **-o**?

---

wives PL NOUN
las **mujeres** *fem pl*

wolf NOUN
el **lobo** *masc*

woman NOUN
la **mujer** *fem*
 three women and two men
 tres mujeres y dos hombres

won VERB ▷ *see* **win**

wonder VERB
preguntarse
 I wonder where Caroline is.
 Me pregunto dónde está Caroline.

wonderful ADJECTIVE
maravilloso *masc*
maravillosa *fem*

won't (= will not) ▷ *see* **will**

wood NOUN
 1 la **madera** *fem* (*substance*)
 It's made of wood.
 Es de madera.
 2 el **bosque** *masc* (*place*)
 We went for a walk in the wood.
 Fuimos a pasear por el bosque.

wool NOUN
la **lana** *fem*
 It's made of wool.
 Es de lana.

word NOUN
la **palabra** *fem*
 I've forgotten the word.
 Se me ha olvidado la palabra.
 What's the word for 'shop' in Spanish?
 ¿Cómo se dice "shop" en español?
 We're going to learn the words of a song.
 Vamos a aprendernos la letra de una canción.

work

---

work can be a verb or a noun.

A VERB
to work
 1 **trabajar** (*person*)
 She works in a shop.
 Trabaja en una tienda.
 2 **funcionar** (*machine, plan*)
 The heating isn't working.
 La calefacción no funciona.
B NOUN
el **trabajo** *masc*
 He's at work at the moment.
 Está en el trabajo en estos momentos.
 I've got a lot of work to do.
 Tengo mucho trabajo que hacer.
 to go to work
 ir a trabajar
 He goes to work at eight o'clock.
 Va a trabajar a las ocho.

---

 at work
 en el trabajo

---

worker NOUN
el **trabajador** *masc*
la **trabajadora** *fem*
 She's a good worker.
 Es una buena trabajadora.

worksheet NOUN
la **hoja de ejercicios** *fem*

world NOUN
el **mundo** *masc*
 the whole world
 el mundo entero

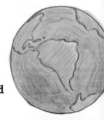

He's the world champion.
Es el campeón del mundo.

worried ADJECTIVE
preocupado *masc*
preocupada *fem*
> **She's very worried.**
> Está muy preocupada.

worry VERB
preocuparse
> **He worries too much.**
> Se preocupa demasiado.

worse ADJECTIVE, ADVERB
peor *masc/fem*
> **The weather is worse in Scotland.**
> El tiempo está peor en Escocia.
> **I'm feeling worse.**
> Me siento peor.

worst ADJECTIVE, ADVERB, NOUN
peor *masc/fem*
> **I always get the worst mark.**
> Siempre saco la peor nota.
> **Darren behaves worst.**
> Darren es el que peor se porta.
> **She's the worst in the class.**
> Es la peor de la clase.
> **Chemistry is my worst subject.**
> La química es lo que peor se me da.

worth ADJECTIVE
> **It's worth a lot of money.**
> Vale mucho dinero.

LANGUAGE TIP
In Spanish, **valer mucho** has two meanings. It can mean **to be worth a lot** or **to cost a lot**.

> **It's worth it.**
> Vale la pena.

would VERB
1 (*in offers, requests*)

LANGUAGE TIP
Use the verb **querer** to ask what someone would like or to say what you would like.

What would you like, dear?
¿Qué quieres, cielo?
My friend would like a sandwich.
Mi amigo quiere un bocadillo.
Would you like to play with me?
¿Quieres jugar conmigo?
I'd like a hot chocolate, please.
Quiero una taza de chocolate, por favor.

2 (*in polite orders*)

LANGUAGE TIP
Use the verb **poder** to ask someone to do something.

Would you close the door, please?
¿Puedes cerrar la puerta, por favor?

wrapping paper NOUN
el **papel de envolver** *masc*

write VERB
escribir
> **She's writing a story.**
> Está escribiendo un cuento.
> **I'm going to write to my friend.**
> Voy a escribir a mi amigo.
> **Write your names.**
> Escribid vuestro nombre.
> **Write to me soon, Amandeep.**
> Escríbeme pronto, Amandeep.

Write soon!
¡Escribe pronto!

LANGUAGE TIP
Have you noticed the upside-down exclamation mark at the start of Spanish exclamations?

Spanish

English

A
B
C
D
E
F
G
H
I
J
K
L
M
N
O
P
Q
R
S
T
U
V
W
X
Y
Z

write down VERB
apuntar
   I'll write down the address.
   Apuntaré la dirección.
   Can you write it down for me, please?
   ¿Me lo puedes apuntar, por favor?

writer NOUN
el **escritor** masc
la **escritora** fem
   He's a writer.
   Es escritor.

LANGUAGE TIP
In Spanish, you do not use an article with people's jobs.

---

writing NOUN
la **letra** fem
   I can't read your writing.
   No entiendo tu letra.

written VERB ▷ see **write**

wrong

> **wrong** can be an adjective or an adverb.

A ADJECTIVE
1 incorrecto masc
   incorrecta fem (answer, information)
   This answer is wrong.
   Esta respuesta es incorrecta.
   That's the wrong answer.
   Esa no es la respuesta correcta.

I got three questions wrong.
Me equivoqué en tres preguntas.
2 equivocado masc
   equivocada fem (person)
   You're wrong!
   ¡Estás equivocado!
   You're looking at the wrong page.
   Estás mirando en la página equivocada.
B ADVERB
   mal
   You're saying it wrong.
   Lo estás diciendo mal.
   Have I spelled it wrong?
   ¿Lo he escrito mal?

What's wrong?
¿Qué pasa?
What's wrong with you?
¿Qué te pasa?

wrote VERB ▷ see **write**

Xx

Xmas NOUN
la **Navidad** *fem*

X-ray

> **X-ray** can be a verb or a noun.

A VERB
to X-ray
hacer una radiografía de
They're going to X-ray my leg.
Me van a hacer una radiografía de la
pierna.
They X-rayed my arm.
Me hicieron una radiografía del brazo.

LANGUAGE TIP
In Spanish you usually use an article
like **el**, **la** or **los**, **las** with parts of the
body.

B NOUN
la **radiografía** *fem*
I'm going to have an X-ray.
Me voy a hacer una radiografía.

xylophone NOUN
el **xilófono** *masc*

Yy

yacht NOUN
1 el **yate** *masc* (*luxury motorboat*)
2 el **barco de vela** *masc* (*sailing boat*)

yard NOUN
el **patio** *masc*
in the yard
en el patio

yawn VERB
bostezar

year NOUN
1 el **año** *masc*
a hundred years
cien años
an eight-year-old child
un niño de ocho años

this year
este año
last year
el año pasado
next year
el año que viene
I'm ten years old.
Tengo diez años.

2 el **curso** *masc* (*school year*)
What year are you in?
¿En qué curso estás?
I'm in Year Six.
Estoy en sexto.
She's in Year Five.
Está en quinto.

DID YOU KNOW...?
In Spain, children start primary school at six and go on to secondary school at twelve. Compulsory education ends at sixteen but they can stay on at school till they're eighteen to do their **Bachillerato**.

---

yellow

> **yellow** can be an adjective or a noun.

A ADJECTIVE
amarillo *masc*
amarilla *fem*
I'm wearing yellow shorts.
Llevo unos pantalones cortos amarillos.

LANGUAGE TIP
Colour adjectives come after the noun in Spanish.

B NOUN
el **amarillo** *masc*
Yellow is my favourite colour.
El amarillo es mi color favorito.

yes ADVERB
sí

Do you like it? — Yes.
¿Te gusta? — Sí.

Orange juice? — Yes, please.
¿Zumo de naranja? — Sí, por favor.
Answer yes or no.
Responde sí o no.

yesterday ADVERB
ayer

When? — Yesterday.
¿Cuándo? — Ayer.
I was absent yesterday.
Ayer no vine.

yesterday morning
ayer por la mañana
yesterday afternoon
ayer por la tarde
yesterday evening
ayer por la noche

LANGUAGE TIP
Translate **yesterday evening** by **ayer por la tarde** instead if you're talking about a time when it was still light.

---

yet ADVERB
1 todavía (*in negatives*)
I haven't finished yet.
Todavía no he terminado.
2 ya (*in questions*)
Have you finished yet, children?
¿Habéis terminado ya, niños?

Not yet.
Todavía no.

yoga NOUN
el **yoga** *masc*

yoghurt NOUN
el **yogur** *masc*

you

LANGUAGE TIP
There are different Spanish words for **you** depending on whether it refers to one person or more than one person and how formal you are with them. The translation also depends on

Spanish

English

A
B
C
D
E
F
G
H
I
J
K
L
M
N
O
P
Q
R
S
T
U
V
W
X
Y
Z

whether **you** is a subject (see senses 1–4) or an object (see mainly senses 5–8). The notes that follow each translation will help you find the word you need. PRONOUN

1 tú *masc/fem*

LANGUAGE TIP
Use **tú** to refer to just one friend, family member or person your own age when **you** is the subject of the verb.

You've got a cat but I haven't.
Tú tienes un gato pero yo no.

LANGUAGE TIP
But remember that **you** isn't usually translated unless it's emphatic.

You've got a new computer, haven't you?
Tienes un ordenador nuevo, ¿verdad?

LANGUAGE TIP
Also use **tú** in comparisons.

She's younger than you.
Es más joven que tú.

LANGUAGE TIP
Use **ti** instead after a preposition like **para** or **de**.

It's for you, James.
Es para ti, James.
I'll go with you.
Iré contigo.

for you
para ti
with you
contigo

2 vosotros *masc pl*
vosotras *fem pl*

LANGUAGE TIP
Use **vosotros** and **vosotras** to refer to two or more friends, family members or people your own age when **you** is the subject of the verb.

You've got time but I haven't.
Vosotros tenéis tiempo pero yo no.

LANGUAGE TIP
But remember that **you** isn't usually translated unless it's emphatic.

You've got a new car, haven't you?
Tenéis un coche nuevo, ¿verdad?

LANGUAGE TIP
Use **vosotros/vosotras** in comparisons.

They are younger than you two.
Son más jóvenes que vosotros dos.

LANGUAGE TIP
Also use **vosotros/vosotras** after a preposition like **para** or **de**.

It's for you, girls.
Es para vosotras, niñas.

3 usted *masc/fem*

LANGUAGE TIP
Use **usted** to refer to just one person that you treat with respect, for example your teacher or an older person, when **you** is the subject of the verb.

You have a lot of books but I haven't.
Usted tiene muchos libros pero yo no.

LANGUAGE TIP
But remember that, like the other subject pronouns, **usted** is often omitted.

Have you got any more paints, Miss?
¿Tiene más pinturas, señorita?

LANGUAGE TIP
Use **usted** in comparisons.

She isn't as nice as you.
No es tan simpática como usted.

LANGUAGE TIP
Also use **usted** after a preposition like **para** or **de**.

Spanish

English

a b c d e f g h i j k l m n o p q r s t u v w x y z

A
B
C
D
E
F
G
H
I
J
K
L
M
N
O
P
Q
R
S
T
U
V
W
X
Y
Z

It's for you, Mr Smith.
Es para usted, señor Smith.

4 ustedes *masc pl & fem pl*

LANGUAGE TIP
Use **ustedes** to refer to two or more people that you treat with respect, for example your teachers or older people, when **you** is the subject of the verb.

You have a lot of books but we haven't.
Ustedes tienen muchos libros pero nosotros no.

LANGUAGE TIP
But remember that, like the other subject pronouns, **ustedes** is often omitted.

You've got a huge garden, haven't you?
Tienen un jardín enorme, ¿verdad?

LANGUAGE TIP
Use **ustedes** in comparisons.

They aren't as nice as you.
No son tan simpáticos como ustedes.

LANGUAGE TIP
Use **ustedes** after a preposition like **para** or **de**.

They are for you, Mr and Mrs Smith.
Son para ustedes, señor y señora Smith.

5 te *masc/fem*

LANGUAGE TIP
Use **te** instead of **tú** to refer to just one friend, family member or person your own age when **you** is the object of the verb.

I love you.
Te quiero.
I'll give it to you.
Te lo daré.

6 os *masc pl & fem pl*

LANGUAGE TIP
Use **os** instead of **vosotros/vosotras** to refer to two or more friends, family members or people your own age when **you** is the object of the verb.

I know you, Tracy and Abbie.
Os conozco, Tracy y Abbie.
I'll give it to you, boys.
Os lo daré, chicos.

7 lo *masc*
la *fem*

LANGUAGE TIP
Use **lo** and **la** to refer to just one person that you treat with respect, for example your teacher or an older person, when **you** is the object of the verb. **lo** and **la** are the direct object pronouns that correspond to **usted**.

I can see you, sir.
Lo veo, señor.
I can see you, Miss.
La veo, señorita.

LANGUAGE TIP
Use **le** instead (for both masculine and feminine) when **you** means 'to you' or 'for you' and is the indirect object of the verb.

I'll give you my exercise book.
Le daré mi cuaderno.
I'll write to you.
Le escribiré.

LANGUAGE TIP
Change **le** to **se** when combining it with a direct object pronoun like **lo**, **la**, **los** or **las**.

I'll give it to you.
Se lo daré.
8 **los** *masc pl*
las *fem pl*

LANGUAGE TIP
Use **los** and **los** to refer to two or more people that you treat with respect, for example your teachers or older people, when **you** is the object of the verb. **los** and **las** are the direct object pronouns that correspond to **ustedes**.

May I help you?
¿Los puedo ayudar?

LANGUAGE TIP
Use **les** instead (for both masculine plural and feminine plural) when **you** means 'to you' or 'for you' and is the indirect object of the verb.

I'll give you the keys.
Les daré las llaves.
I'll write to you.
Les escribiré.

LANGUAGE TIP
Change **les** to **se** when combining it with a direct object pronoun like **lo**, **la**, **los** or **las**.

I'll give them to you.
Se las daré.

you'd
(= **you would**) ▷ see **would**
(= **you had**) ▷ see **have**

you'll (= **you will**) ▷ see **will**

young ADJECTIVE
joven *masc/fem* (PL **jóvenes**)
You're too young.
Eres demasiado joven.
They're younger than me.
Son más jóvenes que yo.
She's the youngest in the class.
Es la más joven de la clase.
my youngest brother
mi hermano menor

Holly's the youngest.
Holly es la menor.

your ADJECTIVE
1 **tu** *masc/fem* (PL **tus**) (*to someone you call 'tú'*)

LANGUAGE TIP
Remember to use **tu** before a singular noun and **tus** before a plural one.

Is that your brother?
¿Es ese tu hermano?
your friend Helen
tu amiga Helen
your parents
tus padres
Wash your hands, Laura.
Lávate las manos, Laura.

LANGUAGE TIP
Remember that **tú** with an accent means 'you' while **tu** without an accent means 'your'.

2 **vuestro** *masc*
vuestra *fem* (*to people you call 'vosotros'*)

LANGUAGE TIP
Remember to make **vuestro** agree with the noun that follows it.

Is that your car?
¿Es ese vuestro coche?
Is this your house?
¿Es esta vuestra casa?
Write your names.
Escribid vuestros nombres.
Put on your coats, children.
Poneos los abrigos, niños.

Spanish

English

a
b
c
d
e
f
g
h
i
j
k
l
m
n
o
p
q
r
s
t
u
v
w
x
y
z

621

3 su *masc/fem* (PL **sus**) (*to people you call 'usted' and 'ustedes'*)

LANGUAGE TIP
Remember to use **su** before a singular noun and **sus** before a plural one.

---

your house
su casa
When's your birthday, Miss?
¿Cuándo es su cumpleaños, señorita?
Here are your books, Miss.
Aquí tiene sus libros, señorita.

you're (= you are) ▷ *see* **be**

yours PRONOUN
1 el **tuyo** *masc*
la **tuya** *fem* (*to someone you call 'tú'*)

LANGUAGE TIP
Remember that the choice of **el tuyo**, **la tuya**, **los tuyos** or **las tuyas** depends entirely on the thing or things referred to.

That isn't your coat. Yours is here.
Aquél no es tu abrigo. El tuyo está aquí.
Those aren't your boots. Yours are here.
Aquéllas no son tus botas. Las tuyas están aquí.

LANGUAGE TIP
After **ser** you can usually just use **tuyo**, **tuya**, **tuyos** or **tuyas** to agree with the noun referred to.

Is this yours, Marco?
¿Esto es tuyo, Marco?
Whose is this? — It's yours.
¿De quién es esto? — Es tuyo.
a friend of yours
un amigo tuyo
2 el **vuestro** *masc*
la **vuestra** *fem* (*to people you call 'vosotros'*)

LANGUAGE TIP
Remember that the choice of **el vuestro, la vuestra, los vuestros** or

las vuestras depends entirely on the thing or things referred to.

That isn't your car. Yours is here.
Aquél no es vuestro coche. El vuestro está aquí.
Those aren't your exercise books. Yours are here.
Aquéllos no son vuestros cuadernos. Los vuestros están aquí.

LANGUAGE TIP
After **ser** you can usually just use **vuestro, vuestra, vuestros** or **vuestras** to agree with the noun referred to.

These sweets are yours.
Estos caramelos son vuestros.
a friend of yours
un amigo vuestro
3 el **suyo** *masc*
la **suya** *fem* (*to people you call 'usted' and 'ustedes'*)

LANGUAGE TIP
Remember that the choice of **el suyo**, **la suya**, **los suyos** or **las suyas** depends entirely on the thing or things referred to.

That isn't your coat. Yours is here.
Aquél no es su abrigo. El suyo está aquí.
Those aren't your boots. Yours are here.
Aquéllas no son sus botas. Las suyas están aquí.

LANGUAGE TIP
After **ser** you can usually just use **suyo, suya, suyos** or **suyas** to agree with the noun referred to.

Is this yours, sir?
¿Esto es suyo, señor?
These tickets are yours.
Estas entradas son suyas.
Whose is this? — It's yours.
¿De quién es esto? — Es suyo.

a friend of yours
un amigo suyo
Yours sincerely
Le saluda atentamente

LANGUAGE TIP
Use **Le saluda atentamente** when writing to one person. Use **Les saluda atentamente** when writing to more than one person.

yourself PRONOUN
 1 **te** (*to someone you call 'tú'*)
 Are you enjoying yourself?
 ¿Te estás divirtiendo?

LANGUAGE TIP
Use **ti** instead after a preposition.

Tell me about yourself!
¡Háblame de ti!

LANGUAGE TIP
Use **tú mismo** and **tú misma** in emphatic uses.

Do it yourself!
¡Hazlo tú mismo!
 2 **se** (*to someone you call 'usted'*)
 Are you enjoying yourself?
 ¿Se está divirtiendo?

LANGUAGE TIP
Use **usted** instead after a preposition.

Tell me about yourself!
¡Hábleme de usted!

LANGUAGE TIP
Use **usted mismo** and **usted misma** in emphatic uses.

Help yourself, Mrs Day!
¡Sírvase usted misma, señora Day!

yourselves PRONOUN
 1 **os** (*to people you call 'vosotros'*)

Did you enjoy yourselves?
¿Os divertisteis?

LANGUAGE TIP
Use **vosotros/vosotras** instead after a preposition.

Tell me about yourselves!
¡Habladme de vosotros!

LANGUAGE TIP
Use **vosotros mismos** and **vosotras mismas** in emphatic uses.

Do it yourselves!
¡Hacedlo vosotros mismos!
 2 **se** (*to people you call 'ustedes'*)
 Are you enjoying yourselves?
 ¿Se están divirtiendo?

LANGUAGE TIP
Use **ustedes** instead after a preposition.

Tell me about yourselves!
¡Háblenme de ustedes!

LANGUAGE TIP
Use **ustedes mismos** and **ustedes mismas** in emphatic uses.

Help yourselves!
¡Sírvanse ustedes mismos!

youth club NOUN
 el **club juvenil** *masc*

youth hostel NOUN
 el **albergue juvenil** *masc*
 We're going to stay at a youth hostel.
 Nos vamos a alojar en un albergue juvenil.

you've (= you have) ▷ *see* **have**

yummy ADJECTIVE
 buenísimo *masc*
 buenísima *fem*

Z z

zebra NOUN
la **cebra** *fem*

zebra crossing NOUN
el **paso de peatones** *masc*

zero NOUN
el **cero** *masc*

zip NOUN
la **cremallera** *fem*

zoo NOUN
el **zoo** *masc*
We went to the zoo on Saturday.
Fuimos al zoo el sábado.